P9-DNY-943

PRINCIPLES OF CASH FLOW VALUATION

An Integrated Market-Based Approach

PRINCIPLES OF CASH FLOW VALUATION

An Integrated Market-Based Approach

Joseph Tham

Visiting Assistant Professor
Duke Center for International Development (DCID)
Sanford Institute of Public Policy
Duke University
Durham, North Carolina

Ignacio Vélez-Pareja

Dean
School of Industrial Engineering
Politécnico Grancolombiano
Bogotá, Colombia

ELSEVIER
ACADEMIC
PRESS

AMSTERDAM • BOSTON • HEIDELBERG • LONDON • NEW YORK • OXFORD
PARIS • SAN DIEGO • SAN FRANCISCO • SINGAPORE • SYDNEY • TOKYO

Elsevier Academic Press
200 Wheeler Road, Sixth Floor, Burlington, MA 01803, USA
84 Theobald's Road, London WC1X 8RR, UK

This book is printed on acid-free paper. ∞

Library of Congress Cataloging-in-Publication Data
Application submitted

British Library Cataloguing in Publication Data
A catalogue record for this book is available from the British Library

ISBN: 0-12-686040-8

For all information on all Academic Press publications
visit our Web site at www.academicpress.com

Printed in the United States of America
03 04 05 06 07 08 9 8 7 6 5 4 3 2 1

I dedicate this book to Professor Benedict Freedman, an extraordinary teacher at Occidental College.

Joseph Tham

I dedicate this book to my beloved Vilma, who, like an angel, gives me silent support from a distance.

Ignacio Vélez-Pareja

The Analyst's Prayer

Give me the intellect to seek the knowable; give me peace of mind to accept the unknowable.

Give me the strength to reject the investments with negative NPV and the wisdom to select the projects with positive NPV.

Most importantly, give me the inspiration (preferably the correct risk-adjusted cost of capital) to know the difference between a good investment and a bad investment.

CONTENTS

ix

6 The Derivation of Cash Flows

7 Using the WACC in Theory and Practice

8 Estimating the WACC for Non-Traded Firms

9 Beyond the Planning Period: Calculating the Terminal Value

10 Theory for Cost of Capital Revisited

Appendix A

Appendix B

11 How Are Cash Flows Valued in the Real World

Appendix A

Appendix B

PREFACE

Mathematics (*Valuation?*) may be defined as the subject in which we never know what we are talking about, nor whether what we are saying is true.

Bertrand Russell (1872 to 1970)

Our main objective is to present clearly and rigorously the general principles for finite cash flow valuation, with a balanced mix of theoretical ideas and practical illustrations. Roughly speaking, to value a finite stream of cash flows, we must complete two activities. First, we must estimate the expected annual cash flows, and second, we must determine the appropriate risk-adjusted discount rate(s) for the cash flow.

Principles of Cash Flow Valuation: An Integrated Market-Based Approach provides a comprehensive and practical market-based framework for the valuation of **finite** cash flows that are derived from a set of integrated financial statements, namely, the income statement, the balance sheet, and the cash budget (which has been specially adapted for valuation purposes). In addition to the standard cash flows, such as the free cash flow (FCF) and the cash flow to equity (CFE), the book discusses the novel capital cash flow (CCF) approach to valuation. With the CCF approach, the tax shield from debt financing is added directly to the FCF, and there is no need to adjust the weighted average cost of capital (WACC).

Detailed numerical examples illustrate the construction of the pro-forma financial statements, step by step. A separate chapter is devoted to the calculations on the terminal value.

To meet the needs of readers with different backgrounds in finance, we present the theory on the cost of capital in a progressive spiral fashion, from the simple and intuitive to the complex, with numerous numerical examples to facilitate understanding and learning.

Assuming perfect capitals, we derive the appropriate expressions for the WACC, as applied to the FCF and CCF, and carefully explain the subtleties that underlie the different formulations of the WACC in relationship to the risk of the tax shield. In particular, we show how to solve the "circularity" problem in the estimation of the WACC with market values. In addition, with the appropriate assumptions, we show that the results from the discount cash flow (DCF) methods are fully consistent with the Residual Income Model (RIM) and the Economic Value Added (EVA©) approach.[1]

We discuss the valuation of both traded and non-traded firms, and using a real-life detailed case study, we illustrate and calculate the discrepancies that arise in the valuation of cash flows, depending on the assumptions that are made in the formulation of the WACC.

To appeal to a wide audience, the level of the mathematics has been kept to a minimum. It would be helpful if the reader has taken some accounting courses, but prior knowledge of accounting principles is not necessary for reading the book. We use and explain the basic accounting knowledge that are needed for the purposes of the book. The book will be of interest to a wide range of readers, from students of applied finance to practitioners and experts who would like to gain a deeper appreciation for the theory on the cost of capital in the context of finite cash flow valuation.

OVERALL FEATURE:

The book presents an integrated approach to finite cash flow valuation that combines the financial statements with the theory on the cost of capital. The following details some key features of the book.

Simplifying reality

It is hardly a profound truism to state that reality is complex. We recognize that reality is complex, and consequently, we have to model the key features of reality by making relevant simplifying assumptions. We progress from the simple to the complex. The level of complexity depends on the availability of information and the purpose of the analysis.

Active reading and learning

The readers are encouraged to read and learn actively by reconstructing the financial statements for themselves on a spreadsheet. Wherever possible, we have provided sufficient detail for the readers to do so. If there are obscurities or ambiguities in the explanations given in the text and readers

---

[1]The reconciliation of the DCF methods with the RIM and EVA approaches is a good check on the results of the valuation exercise.

encounter difficulties in replicating the tables in the text, they are encouraged to e-mail the authors for assistance and clarification. We shall respond as promptly as we can. (See p. xxiii for contact information.)

Finite stream of cash flows and perpetuities

Intentionally and for reasons of practicality, whenever possible, we avoid the use of cash flows in perpetuities and present examples with finite periods. Admittedly, the use of cash flows in perpetuities greatly simplifies the exposition on the cost of capital; however, the loss in flexibility is too high a price to pay for the simplicity. In general, for the forecast or planning period, we use finite streams of cash flows. In the estimation of the (present) value in the terminal period, based on the cash flows that occur beyond the planning period, we use perpetuities.

Duration of the analysis and calculation of the terminal value

With sufficient information, we can use spreadsheets to construct financial statements of reasonable lengths such as ten to fifteen years. The longer the period of analysis, the greater is the uncertainty in the expected values of the key parameters in the model. Typically, it may be more common for the forecast period to be five to eight years. For greatest flexibility, we specify a finite stream of cash flows for the forecast period and use perpetuities only for the calculation of the terminal value at the end of the forecast period. If the forecast period is short (e.g., five years), then the contribution of the terminal value to the overall value may be substantial and the proper calculation of the terminal value may be of high importance.

The following section is a brief description of the organization and content of the book. In valuation, one of the key concepts is the cost of capital. Since it is neither possible nor advisable to present the theory on the cost of capital in one chapter, we discuss the cost of capital over several chapters with increasing degrees of complexity. In Chapters One and Two, we introduce the basic ideas related to cost of capital. In Chapter Seven we apply the ideas on cost of capital to the specific numerical example from Chapter Five, and in Chapter Ten, we revisit the theory on the cost of capital at a more advanced level.

ORGANIZATION OF THE BOOK

- Chapter One provides a clear and succinct qualitative overview on the theory of the cost of capital in the context of finite cash flow valuation.

- Chapter Two is a review of discounting and presents some numerical examples on cost of capital.
- Chapter Three is a review of some basic ideas in accounting and financial statements.
- Chapters Four and Five present detailed numerical illustrations on the construction of an integrated set of financial statements for cash flow valuation without terminal value. The estimation of the terminal value is presented in Chapter Nine.
- Chapter Six shows the derivations of various discounted cash flow methods: FCF, CFE, and CCF.
- Chapters Seven and Ten provide detailed presentations on different formulations for the WACC applied to the FCF and CCF.
- Chapter Eight discusses the cost of capital for non-traded firms and presents methods for valuing them.
- Chapter Nine discusses the estimation of the terminal value. The appendix to Chapter Nine demonstrates the equivalence between the DCF methods, and RIM and EVA$^{©}$.
- Chapter Eleven shows how to apply the integrated approach and the theory on the cost of capital to a real-life case study.

CONTENT OF THE BOOK

Chapter One

Chapter One begins with a brief discussion on market-based valuation, the motivation for investment, and the time value of money. We discuss the relevance of perfect capital markets and the absence of arbitrage for valuation, and we examine the estimation of the cost of capital and valuation of cash flows in perfect capital markets.[2] We define the different types of cash flows and the cost of capital in the Modigliani and Miller (M & M) world, with and without taxes, where roughly speaking, the M & M world is a world with perfect capital markets.[3]

In particular, we present the standard FCF, the cash flow to debt (CFD), CFE, and the alternative CCF. There is a technical definition for "free cash flow," and later in Chapter Six, we define and discuss the annual FCF more precisely.[4] After discussing the theory of valuation in M & M

---

[2]Clearly, the analysis with perfect capital markets is unrealistic. It is a point of departure for beginning the valuation exercise and provides a tractable framework for thinking about the relevant issues.

[3]The M & M world is named in honor of Modigliani and Miller, who made the fundamental and original contributions to cost of capital and valuation.

[4]For the curious reader, the free cash flow (FCF) is the sum of the cash flow to equity (CFE) and the cash flow to debt (CFD), less the tax shield (TS). In symbols, FCF = CFE + CFD − TS.

worlds with and without taxes, we present different valuation methods with the corresponding formulations for the cost of capital. We believe that an early introduction to the cost of capital provides the proper motivation and framework for studying the concepts in the later chapters.

Chapter Two

Chapter Two reviews the time value of money, inflation, and ideas related to discounting. Also, we provide an introduction to the cost of capital with finite cash flows. Formulas for cost of capital with cash flows in perpetuity are easier to understand than finite cash flows, and typically, the formulas that are derived from cash flows in perpetuity are applied to finite cash flows.[5] Since the emphasis in this book is on finite cash flows, for consistent results, we present numerical examples with finite cash flows.

Moreover, it is very likely that the reader is familiar with and has been exposed to the cost of capital as applied to cash flows in perpetuity. In the appendix to Chapter Two, for completeness and reference, we present detailed numerical examples with cash flows in perpetuity with and without growth.[6] This Appendix is for those readers who wish to read an elementary exposition on cost of capital with cash flows in perpetuity, which may facilitate the transition to cost of capital applied to finite cash flows.

Chapter Three

Chapter Three presents a basic review of financial statements and accounting concepts. To be specific, it discusses the balance sheet, the income statement, the cash flow statement according to Generally Accepted Accounting Principles (GAAP), and the annual cash budget statement. For most readers, this chapter should be a review and serve as a reference chapter for the ideas that are discussed in subsequent chapters.

Chapters Four and Five

Chapters Four and Five present detailed numerical examples to illustrate the construction of financial statements, namely the income statement (IS), the

---

[5]The reader can confirm that when the formulas for cash flows in perpetuity are applied to finite cash flows, the results are inconsistent.

[6]We stress that the results and formulas with cash flows in perpetuity may be misleading if they are applied to finite cash flows. We remind the reader that we derive finite cash flows from financial statements; we do not derive cash flows in perpetuity from financial statements.

balance sheet (BS), and the cash flow statement (CFS) for the planning or forecast period, which we assume is five years. We present the cash flow statement according to GAAP. It is important to note that we construct the financial statements in nominal terms and the costs of capital are also in nominal terms.

Both Chapters Four and Five are self-contained. To provide the reader with a strong understanding of the basic determinants of the financial statements and the cash flows that are derived from the financial statements, in our models, we use disaggregated variables such as the prices and quantities of the inputs and outputs rather than aggregated line items such as earnings before interest and taxes (EBIT) or net income (NI). Once the reader understands these models that are based on the disaggregated parameters, she may wish to simplify and model more aggregated line items. With the disaggregated models, it is feasible and convenient to conduct sensitivity analysis on the desired outcomes of the model with respect to changes in the key parameters.

To meet the needs of readers with diverse backgrounds, we present two chapters with different levels of difficulty. Chapter Five extends the simple example in Chapter Four by introducing additional assumptions and complexities into the model. The reader with a strong background should proceed directly to Chapter Five. Other readers may wish to begin with Chapter Four and then proceed to Chapter Five. Chapter Four proceeds at a slower pace and provides explanations in greater detail to ensure that all readers can follow the material.

We link the construction of the IS and the BS with the cash budget (CB) statement. Typically the CB is a monthly statement that is an important tool for cash management. Here, we employ an annual CB statement and integrate it with the IS and the BS. For ease in exposition, the CB statement is referred to as a financial statement, even though according to GAAP the CB statement is not a financial statement. We emphasize that we present a valuation framework that integrates all of the four statements: the income statement, the balance, the cash flow statement and the cash budget statement.

Chapter Six

In the first part of Chapter Six, using a new and simple approach, we derive the FCF statement from the CB statement. For the moment, the terminal value is not included in the calculation of the FCF. The second part of Chapter Six describes the typical derivation of the FCF from the income statement with the indirect method.

Rather than specifying the FCF directly without reference to the financial statements, we propose to derive the FCF statement from the CB statement, which in turn is linked to the IS and BS. This is a distinctive feature of the integrated approach that we present. We prefer this approach because the CB is closest to the idea of free cash flow. In fact, the CB records all the cash movements of a firm or a project. With this integrated approach, all four financial statements—IS, BS, CB, and FCF statements—are linked, and we can easily check for internal consistency.[7]

With this approach, we "see" most of the items that are considered as part of the FCF and the probability of mistakes in the construction of the FCF is reduced. The only items that are not included explicitly in the CB are the tax adjustment or tax savings, the opportunity costs and the terminal value in the case of a going concern. We postpone the discussion on the calculation of the terminal value to Chapter Nine.

By using the annual CB to derive the FCF statement, we do not disregard the CB, which is a very useful managerial tool for cash management. We expect the reader will find this approach more intuitive and easier to follow than the typical derivation with the indirect method from the earnings before EBIT or NI in the income statement. The reader may decide for herself after she has compared all the different approaches. With the availability of appropriate software, the cash budget can be calculated on a weekly or monthly basis.

Chapter Seven

Chapter Seven focuses on the practical issues that are related to the estimation of the cost of capital and applies the ideas on the cost of the capital to the cash flows that have been derived from the financial statements that were constructed for the complex example in Chapter Five. There is an inherent circularity in the valuation process. To estimate the WACC, we require the market values of debt and equity; to estimate the market values of debt and equity, we must know the WACC. We show how to use the spreadsheet to solve the circularity problem.[8]

Chapter Eight

Chapter Eight is about various methods for estimating the cost of capital for non-traded firms.

---

[7]Moreover, by using all the financial statements, the integrated approach bridges and (hopefully) narrows the gap between the "accounting" frame of mind and the "valuation" frame of mind.

[8]In using the CCF approach and assuming that the value of discount rate for the tax shield is equal to the return to unlevered equity, there is no circularity.

Chapter Nine

Chapter Nine examines the estimation of the terminal value and value the FCF for the complex example in Chapter Five. In addition, we show that the results with DCF methods, RIM, and EVA© are fully consistent.

Chapter Ten

Using finite streams of cash flows, Chapter Ten revisits the theory on the cost of capital and examines some of the underlying assumptions in more detail and depth.

Chapter Eleven

Chapter Eleven applies the ideas on the cost of capital to a real case study and show the discrepancies that arise from the different assumptions with respect to the estimation of the cost of capital.

We hope the ideas in the book are useful in your studies, work, and professional life and you enjoy reading the book as much as we have enjoyed writing it. Our papers on valuation are available on the Social Science Research Network (SSRN) at papers.ssrn.com. Also, see Ignacio's website at http://www.poligran.edu.co/decisiones.

We must mention that the writing of the book across continents (Joe in Ho Chi Minh City, New York City, and Boston, and Ignacio in Bogotá) would have been impossible without the Internet, which permitted the innumerable e-mails and the long, heated discussions with instant messaging. We welcome critical feedback and constructive comments and have tried our best to eliminate errors and typos. However, we are almost certain that there are errors and mistakes that are just waiting to be discovered and would appreciate notification of them.

ACKNOWLEDGMENTS AND SPECIAL THANKS

We thank Nicholas Wonder, Andreas Loeffler, Paul Fieten, Shikhar Ranjan, Gordon Sick, and Pablo Fernandez for very helpful correspondence and assistance on topics related to cash flow valuation and cost of capital.

Also, Joe wishes to thank all the participants and members of the Teaching Team in Project Appraisal at the Fulbright Economics Teaching Program (FETP) in Ho Chi Minh City, Vietnam, who had to suffer through the initial drafts of my unintelligible notes on cost of capital. In particular, I would like to thank Lora Sabin, Cao Hao Thi, Le Thi Thanh Loan and Ngo

Kim Phuong for their comments and feedback, which forced me to clarify my own thinking and improve the notes. Le Thi Thanh Loan's careful reading helped us to eliminate many errors.

Joe also wishes to thank the many groups of participants, colleagues, tutors, and lecturers in the Program on Investment Appraisal and Management (PIAM) at the Harvard Institute for International Development (HIID).

For their support in various ways, Joe thanks G.P. Shukla, Graham Glenday, Mano Ranjan, Alberto Barreix, Baher El-Hifnawi, Rags Narain, Migara Jayawardena, Savvakis Savvides, Ranjay Gulati, Farid Bassiri, Hien, Little Trang, Jim Kass, Asad Jumabhoy, and Feryal Jumabhoy.

Joe thanks Jonathan Haughton for having confidence in him and giving him his first break. Special thanks must go to Baher (a.k.a. the chief) for unknowingly (and inadvertently) provoking me along an intellectual path that has led to the writing of the book.

Ignacio wishes to thank Julio Sarmiento at Universidad Javeriana, Bogotá, Colombia, for his interest in reading and commenting on drafts and using them in teaching. Special thanks to Ramiro de la Vega and Guillermo Rossi, private financial consultants for reading drafts and collaborating in the writing of Chapter Eleven.

Also, Ignacio thanks all his undergraduate and graduate students at Politécnico Grancolombiano and Universidad Javeriana at Bogotá, Colombia, and ICESI, Cali, Colombia, who suffered the initial versions of many chapters, all written in a foreign language.

At Academic Press, Scott Bentley, Karen Maloney, and Jane Mac-Donald have been most supportive and encouraging. In addition, Dennis McGonagle, Mamata Reddy, Julio Esperas, and Jaya Nilamani and her team at Integra-India have taken every effort to produce the best book.

Special and deep-felt thanks to Jennifer Mulik, Kate Laurence, Nancy Scott, and David Trzcinski for assisting in the construction of the index during the crunch time. Also, Joe wishes to thank everyone at the Center for International Health and Development (CIHD) at the Boston University School of Public Health (BUSPH) for their understanding, tolerance and moral support.

Finally, we would like to give our deepest thanks to the anonymous reviewers who were generous in their constructive comments, which greatly improved the chapters in the book. We have tried to follow most of their recommendations and accept responsibility for all remaining errors. The final test of the relevance of the book is the approval of the reader. Again, we look forward to critical suggestions for improvement and constructive feedback from readers. Please contact Joe at ThamJx@yahoo.com or Ignacio at ivelez98@yahoo.com to provide feedback.

ABOUT THE AUTHORS

 **Joseph Tham** is visiting assistant professor at the Duke Center for International Development (DCID), Terry Sanford Institute of Public Policy at Duke University and a research associate at the Center for International Health and Development (CIHD) at Boston University School of Public Health (BUSPH). He is an applied economist with interests in the financial, economic, and risk analysis of social sector projects.

From 1996 to 2001, he was a lecturer at the Fulbright Economics Teaching Program (FETP) in Ho Chi Minh City, Vietnam, an education program managed by Harvard University. He also served as a project associate at the Center for Business and Government (CBG), John F. Kennedy School of Government at Harvard University (2000–2001). For several years, he was a lecturer in the Program on Investment Appraisal and Management (PIAM) at the Harvard Institute for International Development (HIID) and spent a year in Indonesia, analyzing educational finance for the Asian Development Bank. He holds a bachelor's degree in mathematics from Occidental College and a doctorate in education from Harvard University.

Ignacio Vélez-Pareja is Dean of the School of Industrial Engineering at Politecnico Grancolombiano in Bogotá, Colombia. His interests have been in the areas of Investment Decision Analysis and Operations Research. Recently, he has worked mainly in the financial arena. Half of his professional life has been spent in private industry and the other half in academia at the most important universities in Colombia.

He has served in different functional areas for private firms, including top management positions and as head of Industrial Engineering at Universidad de los Andes and Business Administration at Universidad Javeriana in Bogotá, Colombia. He holds a master's degree in industrial engineering from the University of Missouri at Columbia and has published in international and local journals. He is the author of two books, *Decisiones de inversión: enfocado a la valoración de empresas* and *Decisiones empresariales bajo riesgo e incertidumbre*, and has published more than 50 articles on management, finance, scientific research, education, and labor issues and music in local and international peer-reviewed academic publications such as *Cuadernos de Administración, Interfaces, Latin American Business Review, Monografías Facultad de Administración (Universidad de los Andes) and Academia, Revista Latinoamericana de Administración, CLADEA*. His academic writings can be found at http://www.poligran.edu.co/decisiones.

1

BASIC CONCEPTS IN
MARKET-BASED CASH
FLOW VALUATION

Science is built of facts, as a house is built of stones; but an accumulation of facts is no more a science than a heap of stones is a house.

—*Henri Poincaré* (1854 to 1912)

Everything that can be said can be said clearly.

—*Ludwig Wittgenstein* (1889 to 1951)

1.1 INTRODUCTION

In this chapter, we present an informal introduction to the basic concepts and ideas in market-based cash flow valuation. The simplified exposition will provide sufficient background knowledge to understand the context of the materials that are presented in subsequent chapters. Later, in the appropriate chapters, we return to these ideas in valuation and explain them with detailed numerical examples. The reader will feel comfortable because she has already been exposed to the ideas informally in this chapter.

For some readers, the concepts and ideas in this chapter will be a review. For other readers who find the explanations and discussions to be too terse, we assure them that the topics will be explored in greater detail and more formally in subsequent chapters. Most readers will be familiar with the standard after-tax Weighted Average Cost of Capital (WACC) that is applied to the Free Cash Flow (FCF). However, for many readers the WACC applied to the Capital Cash Flow (CCF), a term that Ruback (2002) has coined and popularized, will be new. Later we explain the CCF in greater detail. Now we are simply surveying the main ideas in the domain of cash flow valuation. We are providing an informal sketch of the territory that we will be covering and hope that all readers will find this introductory overview useful.

I.I.I Finite Streams of Cash Flows

In all the chapters, in constructing the nominal financial statements and calculating the costs of capital, we use finite streams of cash flows, except in the calculation of the terminal value (TV) at the end of the forecast (or planning) period, where out of necessity we use cash flows in perpetuity to account for the cash flows that occur in the years beyond the forecast period. On grounds of simplicity, it is most common to illustrate the ideas on the WACC with cash flows in perpetuity, and in some instances we do the same. In some cases, the cash flows in perpetuity might be a reasonable approximation to the finite cash flows. However, it is important to recognize that the formulas for the cost of capital that are derived from cash flows in perpetuity do not necessarily apply to cash flows that are constructed from financial statements with a finite time period. It is an obvious but often forgotten fact that we do not derive cash flows in perpetuity from the typical financial statements.

With a finite stream of cash flows, in the presence of taxes, the specification of the risk of the tax shield (TS) over time is more complex and, among other factors, depends on the assumption about the debt financing policy over the life of the cash flow. We briefly mention this issue here to alert the reader to the complexities that can arise with a finite stream of cash flows. For example, on grounds of simplicity, it is common to assume that the firm maintains a constant leverage over time. This means that in each period the firm must adjust its debt financing policy to achieve the target leverage. With finite cash flows, if we assume constant leverage over time, we must ensure that we properly model the constant leverage over time.

I.I.2 Content and Organization of the Chapters

Roughly speaking, the valuation procedure for cash flows can be defined simply as follows: estimate the expected annual cash flows, use a suitable asset pricing model, and estimate and apply the appropriate annual costs of capital to find the present value (PV) of the cash flow stream with respect to a given point in time. The ideas in this book are simply a detailed elaboration of this procedure.

In this chapter, we present the following key ideas. First, we review the different types of cash flows: the FCF, the capital cash flow (CCF), the cash flow to debt (CFD), and the cash flow to equity (CFE). Second, we briefly discuss the assumptions that underlie cash flow valuation in perfect capital markets. For perspective, we present some data on the relative sizes of the traded and non-traded markets in the U.S. and Colombia.

Third, we discuss the cost of capital with and without taxes in a world with perfect capital markets. Fourth, we briefly review the Capital Asset Pricing Model (CAPM), which is the most well-known approach for estimating the cost of capital.

I.2 MARKET-BASED PROCEDURE FOR VALUATION

Valuation is a forward-looking exercise and the need to value a stream of annual FCF can arise in many different circumstances. The basic principles for valuing an uncertain stream of FCF remain the same and it does not matter whether it is a project or a company that generates the stream of FCF. In theory, the standard and traditional procedure for valuing a finite stream of cash flows, as stated earlier is straightforward, although in recent years the use of risk-neutral valuation has become more popular. The modern risk-neutral approach with risk-neutral probabilities has arisen in conjunction with real option pricing theory. However, from a practical point of view, the use of risk-neutral probabilities is not easy.

There are two main kinds of cash flows and for each cash flow there is a corresponding cost of capital. One is the traditional FCF that does not take into account the tax savings from debt financing. The CCF is the second alternative, which incorporates the tax savings directly by adding the TS to the FCF.

For the moment, do not be concerned about the difference between the two types of cash flows. Later, we explain the differences between these two cash flows in greater detail. The motivation for the CCF will be clearer after discussion of the debt financing policy and the estimation of the value of the tax savings from the interest deduction with debt financing.

I.2.I Integrated Valuation Framework with Complete Financial Statements

In this book we present an integrated valuation framework that is based on three financial statements: the income statement (IS), the balance sheet (BS), and the cash budget (CB) statement. The integration of the annual CB statement with the IS and the BS offers a new and simple way to link the line items in the three statements. In Chapter Three, we discuss the three financial statements and explain the construction of the preliminary tables that are required for the financial statements.

In this book we propose a novel approach to derive the FCF statement from the CB statement. Technically speaking, the CB statement is not a financial statement in the context of Generally Accepted Accounting Principles (GAAP). The CB statement is a cash management tool that determines the liquidity of a firm on a monthly, weekly, or daily basis. For ease in exposition, we call the CB statement a financial statement. We have adapted the annual CB statement for the purposes of valuation to provide an integrated framework.

We briefly outline the advantages of the integrated valuation framework with the CB statement. First, the integration of the financial statements provides an immediate consistency check on the construction of the financial statements. Second, the CB is an appropriate instrument for monitoring and managing the liquidity of the firm over the life of the cash flow, and for specifying alternative financing schemes. Third, it is easy to derive the relevant cash flows from the CB statement.

We construct all the financial statements in nominal terms and we discount the annual cash flows with nominal discount rates. Simply put, the nominal financial statements are the most familiar and consistent with reality. It is a common mistake to assume that the nominal price approach and the real price approach give the same answers. Some simple examples will demonstrate the difference between the nominal and the real approaches to valuation.

For example, consider the estimation of tax liabilities with respect to depreciation allowance, which is invariant under the nominal and real approaches. If the financial statements are in real terms and there is inflation, the tax liabilities will be understated because the invariant depreciation charges have a relatively higher weight and the earnings before taxes (EBT) is lower in real terms compared to nominal terms. Clearly, the FCF derived from financial statements constructed with the real approach will differ from the FCF derived from financial statements constructed with the nominal approach.

Also, the payments for loans are made in nominal terms rather than real terms. For further details on the distinction between nominal and real values and prices, see Chapter Two. It is important to recognize that the nominal and real price approaches for valuation give different results. The correct approach is the nominal price approach. For greater details on the nominal and real price approaches, see Velez and Tham (2002).

1.3 STEPS IN CASH FLOW VALUATION

The Discounted Cash Flow (DCF) method for firm valuation is based on the capacity of the firm (or project) to generate wealth or value in the future. This market-based procedure for valuation is both easy and difficult. It is easy because we use the basic concepts from the time value of money. And it is difficult, because it is necessary to forecast the annual cash flows and we need a model to estimate and calculate the annual discount rates. In addition, to arrive at the annual cash flows, we need an appropriate model to forecast the financial statements.

In practice, the implementation of the valuation exercise is an acquired art that involves judicious decisions on the specifications of assumptions and the interpretation and meaning of the results. We assume in the examples that there are no non-conventional cash flows. A conventional cash flow has a negative (positive) cash flow (an investment or a loan) followed by a series of positive (negative) cash flows, which are considered returns (payments). A non-conventional cash flow might have more than one negative (positive) cash flow alternating with positive (negative) cash flows. A non-conventional cash flow might arise when there are clean-up costs in the terminal period such as the clean up of an oil well or an open-air mine, or huge reinvestments in the middle of the project life.[1]

We list the following deceptively simple series of steps for valuing a finite stream of cash flows.

1. Based on the financial statements that we mentioned earlier, we estimate the expected cash flows for each year of the project and the TV at the end of the forecast period.
2. Next, we estimate and specify the risk profile of the cash flow stream. In many cases, this is difficult to do because the firm might not be traded and reliable historical data might not be available. If there are comparable firms that are traded, we assume that the risk profile of the cash flow stream for the investment opportunity under consideration is similar to the risk profiles of the cash flows for the comparable firms.
3. Based on the historical data from the set of comparable firms, we determine the annual risk-adjusted discount rate (RADR) with an asset-pricing model, such as the CAPM. The risk-adjusted discount rate takes into account the correlation of the cash flow stream with the cash flow stream of a market portfolio. In subsequent chapters, we provide more details on how to estimate the cost of capital with the CAPM.
4. Finally, we discount the annual cash flows to year 0 (the reference year) and sum the discounted values to obtain the PV of the stream of cash flows.

1.3.1 Why Invest?

The manager or investment officer in a firm faces the investment decision. From an investment point of view, why would the investment officer purchase a tangible asset, such as a piece of machinery or equipment, which generates a potentially perpetual stream of future benefits for the stakeholders of the firm? We assume that the person is reasonably well informed, though not infallible. All things considered, presumably the person invests because she believes that the value of the stream of uncertain future benefits is greater than or equal to the amount that she currently has to pay for the asset, namely the machinery. The decision is made with respect to the amount of information that is available at a point in time. However, there is always the

---

[1]With a non-conventional cash flow, it might not be possible to calculate a rate of return or there might be multiple rates of return.

possibility that with the passage of time, new information arrives and based on the new information, the investor revises the assessment of the value of the expected stream of future benefits.

On the down side, the expected benefits might not materialize. For example, the technology in the machine could become obsolete or changes in economic conditions could reduce the value of the future stream of benefits. Alternatively, on the up side, the machine might turn out to be a huge success and generate more than the expected stream of future benefits.

In this book, we adopt the perspective of a financial analyst or an investment officer in a firm. The investment decision faced by an investment officer is similar to the decision that individual investors face. As investors, when we purchase shares in a company, we believe that the value of the uncertain stream of future benefits (in the form of dividend payments and capital gains) is higher than or equal to the current price for the shares. Taking into account the historical data on the performance of the company and other publicly available relevant information, investors have to make frequent decisions about buying and selling the shares that they own. If the investor has access to private information (or information that is not publicly available), the investor might arrive at a different investment decision. Conceptually, the publicly available information might convey no useful information at all to the investor because the information has already been incorporated into the market values. The investment decision to buy or sell is based on expectations about the future performance of the company.

I.3.2 The Role of Information and Expectations

In reality, there is no perfect flow of information, and there might be wide variation in the information possessed by different investors and the expectations that they hold. Furthermore, the available information is neutral unless properly interpreted and only becomes relevant when investors use the information for the purposes of investment decisions. Different investors can have varying abilities in properly processing and interpreting the *same* information. More importantly, based on the information, they might form different expectations about the value of the uncertain stream of future benefits.

In some cases, as with the early Internet-based companies with no record of financial performance, the supposedly rational investors were willing to pay (seemingly) high prices for the shares on the expectation that they would reap high financial rewards. The valuation of the uncertain future streams of cash flows is fraught with difficulties. As the subsequent collapse of many of the Internet-based companies has shown and confirmed, such bubbles of expectations are fragile and easily punctured with devastating results for investors.

The amount that we are currently willing to pay for a future stream of cash flows is known as the PV of the cash flow stream. Next, we discuss this most important topic.

1.4 PRESENT VALUE

When we make an investment, we give up opportunities for current consumption in exchange for consumption opportunities in the future. To induce the investor to make this tradeoff, the investment opportunity must provide the expectation that the value of the future stream of expected cash flows, in PV terms, is greater than the current investment cost. In other words, because the stream of cash flows occurs at different points in time in the future, they are incomparable. And with respect to a selected reference point in time, we must use a discount rate to calculate the value that is equivalent in monetary terms to the future stream of cash flows.

In Chapter Two we discuss the mechanics of discounting in detail. With the process of "discounting," we use appropriate nominal discount rates to find the PV of the stream of finite cash flows with respect to a given point in time. The discount rates take into account the risk of the stream of finite cash flows. Thus, with discounting, we are able to compare the (present) value of the uncertain stream of future benefits with the current investment cost. For the moment, we postpone further comments on nominal risk-adjusted discount rates. We simply assume that they are available for use in the discounting and valuation exercise.

Let K_0 be the current cost of the investment opportunity in year 0 and with respect to year 0, let V^{FCF}_0 be the (present) value of the stream of annual FCF. With respect to year 0 (the reference point in time), if the (present) value of the stream of cash flows V^{FCF}_0 is higher than K_0, the cost of the investment opportunity, then it seems reasonable to accept and undertake the investment opportunity. Otherwise, we should reject the investment opportunity. If the V^{FCF}_0 is higher than K_0, we say that the net present value (NPV) of the investment opportunity is positive. For the moment, this simplistic characterization of the investment decision is sufficient.

1.4.1 Perfect Capital Markets and Arbitrage Opportunities

To make sense of the complex world, we resort to simplifying assumptions in the financial models that we construct. The reasonableness of the assumptions and the robustness of the conclusions from the models depend on the extent to which we believe that the assumptions capture the key features of reality. There is an inherent tension between completeness and parsimony. On the one hand, we wish to model reality as completely as possible. The pressure towards completeness might make the model unmanageable, complex, and possibly misleading. On the other hand, we would like to make the model as simple as possible, taking into account all relevant factors.

We begin by assuming a world with perfect capital markets. Roughly speaking, in perfect capital markets, there is perfect flow of information and no transaction cost or friction of any kind. Clearly such an assumption makes a mockery of reality. Nevertheless, it is a useful starting point. An understanding of cash flow valuation and the cost of capital in a perfect world will facilitate the application of the ideas to an imperfect world. Admittedly, the discrepancies between the perfect world and the real world are huge and numerous, especially in developing and transitional economies. However, in some cases it might be reasonable to hope that the perfect world is an acceptable approximation to the real world.

I.4.2 Valuation in an Imperfect but Real World

In practice, there is not a clear dichotomy between perfect and imperfect markets. Capital markets exist along a continuum with varying degrees of perfection. Even if the markets are not perfect, market-based valuation is possible if the assets are frequently and actively traded in a competitive setting.

There are severe difficulties in the estimation of the cost of capital if the perfect world is an unacceptable approximation to the real world. How do we adjust the cost of capital to take account of the deviations of the real world from the assumptions of the model in a perfect world? In developing countries and transitional economies, how do we estimate the cost of capital with unreliable and perhaps non-existent data? In emerging markets, how do we value a firm that is not traded or for which there are no comparable traded firms? It is difficult, to say the least. We might have to rely on ad-hoc and considered judgments of analysts and experts, based on their extensive experiences. Later, we provide some data on the prevalence of small- and medium-sized firms in the U.S. and Colombia. We hope that the insights and results from the analysis in a perfect world will guide us in making robust and reasonable calculations in an imperfect world.

I.4.3 Perfect Capital Markets

What is the definition of a world with perfect capital markets? As stated previously, in a world with competitive capital markets, there is perfect flow of information and no friction of any kind. For identical traded products, the competitive pressures lead to the absence of arbitrage opportunities and the establishment of the law of one price. The absence of arbitrage means that you cannot make risk-free profits by trading.

With competitive markets, transient deviations from the law of one price might exist. However, the competitive pressures will dissipate the arbitrage opportunities. In the context of valuation, this means that investment opportunities with identical payoff structures and identical risk characteristics must have the same market price. If not, there would be opportunities for arbitrage. In simple terms, in a competitive environment with frictionless flow of information, free lunches are only available infrequently. The free lunches exist only fleetingly and are quickly gobbled up by the market participants, who are constantly on the watch for free lunches.

1.4.4 Replicating Portfolio Strategy

Because the law of one price implies that in a competitive market the price of investment opportunities with identical payoff and risk structures have the same price, we can value a new investment opportunity by constructing a portfolio of existing investment opportunities that replicate the payoff structure and risk of the new investment opportunity. Roughly speaking, we find a set of similar and comparable investment opportunities that are traded, and use the characteristics of the comparable investments to value the investment opportunity that is under consideration.

The derivation of the cost of capital in a Modigliani & Miller (M & M) world is based on the idea of the replicating portfolio strategy.[2] Without well-functioning capital markets and flow of relevant information, it can be difficult to use the replicating portfolio strategy because the data on comparable investment opportunities might not be available or simply might not exist.

1.4.5 Traded Firms in the U.S. Stock Market

Next, we present some data on traded firms in the U.S. stock market. The stock market in the U.S. qualifies as a nearly perfect market for traded firms. As of December 2002, the number of traded firms in the stock exchanges is as in Table 1.1:

TABLE 1.1   Number of Firms Listed in the U.S. Stock Exchanges

Stock exchange	Number of firms listed
NYSE	2,800
NASDAQ	3,910
AMEX	800
Total	7,510

To compare the number of traded firms, relative to nontraded firms, we show the number of firms, categorized by the number of employees. Although the totals are from different years, the two tables give a rough idea of the proportion of traded firms versus non-traded firms.[3] In the U.S. context,

---

[2]For further details on the application of the replicating portfolio strategy, consult a standard textbook in corporate finance.

[3]The number of firms listed in the stock exchanges is 0.13392% of the total firms and 0.2565% of the firms with more than four employees in 1999 and 44.86% of the firms with more than 500 employees.

a large firm is defined as a firm with 500 or more employees. We can see that the number of firms in the U.S. is more than 5.607 million, and of those firms more than 98% have fewer than 100 employees and 99.7% have fewer than 500 employees.

TABLE I.2   Employer Firms by Size Classes, 1999

Employment size of firm	Firms	Participation
Total	5,607,743	100.0%
0*	709,074	12.6%
1–4	2,680,087	47.8%
5–9	1,012,954	18.1%
10–14	399,908	7.1%
15–19	205,785	3.7%
20–24	126,755	2.3%
25–29	84,622	1.5%
30–34	61,165	1.1%
35–39	45,651	0.8%
40–44	35,340	0.6%
45–49	28,189	0.5%
50–54	22,621	0.4%
55–59	18,258	0.3%
60–64	15,445	0.3%
65–69	13,383	0.2%
70–74	11,320	0.2%
75–79	9,869	0.2%
80–84	8,620	0.2%
85–89	7,683	0.1%
90–94	6,751	0.1%
95–99	6,176	0.1%
100–499	81,347	1.5%
500–999	8,235	0.1%
1,000–1,499	2,756	0.0%
1,500–2,499	2,236	0.0%
2,500+	3,513	0.1%
<20	5,007,808	89.3%
<50	5,389,530	96.1%
<100	5,509,656	98.3%
<500	5,591,003	99.7%

*Employment is measured in March, thus some firms (start-ups after March, closures before March, and seasonal firms) will have zero employment and some annual payroll.
Source: Office of Advocacy, U.S. Small Business Administration, based on data provided by the U.S. Department of Commerce, Bureau of Census, Statistics of U.S. Businesses.

I.4.6 Traded Firms in an Emerging Market

For comparison, we provide some information on traded firms in Colombia. The profile in other emerging economies might be similar to the profile in Colombia.

TABLE I.3   Micro Enterprises by Industry Year 2000[4]

Colombia	Total micro enterprises	%
Commerce	557,759	57.7
Services	288,771	29.9
Industry	120,785	12.5
Total	967,315	100.0

This survey includes formal and informal micro enterprises. The formal enterprises in Colombia are shown in the following table.

TABLE I.4   Total Number of Formal Firms Listed in Confecamaras 2001[5]

Size	No. of firms	Weight
No data about assets	46,550	8.74%
Micro enterprises	432,269	81.19%
Small	39,963	7.51%
Medium	7,786	1.46%
Large	5,845	1.10%
Total	532,413	100.00%

Of the firms listed, 13,631 are classified as medium- and large-sized. On the other hand, the number of firms listed in the Colombian stock exchange is 137, and of these fewer than 30 stocks trade regularly. For more details on the behavior of the stocks that are traded in the stock exchange in Colombia, see Velez-Pareja (2000).

There are approximately 1.1 million firms, including those from the informal sector. The listed firms are 0.0125% of the total firms, and the frequently traded firms are 0.0027% of the total firms. If we only consider firms of more than four employees (small-, medium-, and large-sized firms) we have 0.1033% for listed firms and 0.0226% for frequently traded firms. If we only consider the 13,631 large- and medium-sized firms, the number listed in the

---

[4]National Department of Statistics. National Survey of Commercial, Service and Industrial Micro Enterprises. http://www.dane.gov.co.

[5]Confecamaras is the national association of chambers of commerce. http://www.confecamaras.org.co/. There is no agreement on the criteria to classify firms by size. Some use the level of assets, others the level of employment. And in defining these criteria there is no agreement on the limits for each category.

stock exchange is 1.01% for the listed and 0.22% for the frequently traded. The listed firms are 2.34% of the large firms and the most traded firms are 0.51%.

In summary, the small- and medium-sized firms (SME) are a substantial percentage of the number of firms in the U.S. economy and in emerging markets.

1.5 THE STANDARD AFTER-TAX WEIGHTED AVERAGE COST OF CAPITAL

In the valuation of a finite stream of nominal cash flows, one of the most important parameters is the opportunity cost of capital, also known as the WACC. Roughly speaking, the WACC is a weighted average of the costs for the different sources of financing. More specifically, the cost of capital is a weighted average of the nominal risk-adjusted cost of debt and the nominal risk-adjusted cost of equity, where the weights are the market values of debt and equity as percentages of the levered (market) value. The formula for the WACC makes intuitive sense. Unless otherwise noted, it is always assumed that in the context of discussions on the cost of capital, value refers to market value rather than book value. In some cases, market values might be unavailable and instead we might reluctantly use book values from the BS. One must remember that the book values might be poor approximations to the true market values, and the use of book values might be misleading.

For now, we simply present the well-known formula for the after-tax WACC that is applied to the FCF. The formula for the after-tax WACC applied to the FCF incorporates many implicit and restrictive assumptions. Later we discuss in greater detail the assumptions that underlie the formula and suggest ways for estimating the WACC.[6]

$$\text{After-tax WACC} = \frac{d(1-T)D}{V^L} + \frac{eE^L}{V^L} \tag{1.1}$$

In this equation, d is the market-based cost of debt, e is the market-based return to (levered) equity, T is the tax rate, D/V^L is the market value of debt D as a percent of the total levered (market) value V^L, and E^L/V^L is the market value of equity E^L as a percent of the total levered (market) value V^L.

We simply note that in the after-tax WACC that is applied to the FCF, the tax benefits of the interest deduction from debt financing are taken into account by lowering the WACC with the term $(1-T)$ applied to the cost of debt d. To apply this formulation of the WACC, we need to know the return to levered equity e for a given level of leverage, and it might be difficult to estimate the return

---

[6]For now, we have not put time subscripts for the parameters in equation 1.1. For cash flows in perpetuity, the subscripts are not required. However, for finite cash flows we need subscripts because the cost of debt d, the return to levered equity e, the debt percentage D/V^L, and the equity percentage E/V^L could vary each year.

to levered equity. In addition, it is common to assume that the discount rate for the TS is the cost of debt and the leverage over time is constant. The constant leverage assumption requires the firm to follow a specific debt financing policy.

The WACC is one of the most difficult parameters to estimate. Later, in Chapter Eight, we discuss some of the contentious issues that are involved in the empirical estimation of the cost of capital and provide some practical guidance. After this brief discussion on the WACC, we present the various kinds of cash flows.

1.6 TYPES OF CASH FLOWS

There are several types of cash flows: FCF, CFD, and CFE. Also, with debt financing we have a stream of TSs generated from the interest deductions with debt financing. For the moment, we defer the discussion on the CCF.

1.6.1 What Is Free Cash Flow?

Basically, FCF is a measure of the after-tax operational funds produced by a firm or project, without taking into account the source of debt and equity financing, that are available for distribution to the stakeholder. The FCF statement measures the expected operating benefits and costs (including opportunity costs) of the project or firm. It is important to stress that the FCF must be available for distribution to the stakeholders, namely the debt holders and the equity holders. In the ideal case, all of the FCF is distributed to the stakeholders in the firm. However, in practice, for various reasons the firm might have some excess cash that is invested in short-term marketable securities.

We return to this issue when we construct the financial statements. There might be a difference between the ideal FCF, without retention of excess cash, and the actual FCF, in which a firm invests the excess cash in short-term marketable securities at a market rate of interest that is lower than the cost of capital for the firm. The ideal FCF without retention of excess cash is (roughly) equivalent to the actual FCF with retention of excess cash under the assumption that the excess cash is invested at the cost of capital rather than the rate of interest on short-term securities. The full implication of this statement may become clearer after the detailed discussion of the various kinds of cash flows in Chapter Six. Strictly speaking, the change in the short-term marketable securities is not part of the operating cash flow (OCF).

For a going concern, we add the TV (or continuing value) to the FCF at the end of the forecast (or planning) period in year N. If it is not a going concern, then we add the liquidation value (or salvage value) to the FCF in year N. Alternatively, if the firm will be sold to another investor, then we calculate the market value of the continuing firm at that point in time. In

Chapter Six, we discuss some of the subtleties involved in the derivation of the FCF from the financial statements.

1.6.2 What Is Cash Flow to Debt?

The CFD is the portion of the FCF that accrues to the current or future debt holder. Typically, we assume that the debt is risk-free or close to risk-free even though there might be a probability of default. In this way, we do not have to distinguish between the expected return on the debt and the promised return on the debt. The debt holder is the senior claimant on the FCF. If the FCF is insufficient to pay the debt holder, the debt holder has priority on the receipt of the available FCF and the equity holder might receive nothing.[7] Most likely, if the FCF is insufficient to pay the debt holder, the terms of the debt will be renegotiated.

The CFD is constructed from the perspective of the debt holder. For the moment, we assume a simple profile for the CFD, where the debt holder provides funds at the beginning and receives payments in subsequent years. In practice, the actual profile of the CFD might be more complex with the retirement of old loans and the acquisition of new loans. In addition, with a specified debt financing policy, the CFD depends on the target leverage over the life of the FCF. With respect to the debt holder, the initial disbursement of funds is a cash outflow and the subsequent payments are cash inflows. From the perspective of the firm, the initial disbursement of funds from the debt holder is a cash inflow and the subsequent payments are cash outflows. In many cases, the firm has a target debt–equity ratio over the life of the cash flow and the CFD is constructed to reflect the debt financing policy.

1.6.3 What Is Cash Flow to Equity?

The CFE is the portion of the FCF that accrues to the equity holder after the debt holder has been paid. If there is debt financing and TSs are realized, the equity holder also receives the stream of future TSs. The equity holder is the residual claimant.

As stated previously, the equity holder might receive nothing if the FCF is insufficient to pay the claims of the debt holder.[8] To construct the CFE, we must specify the loan schedule over the life of the cash flow stream and subtract the CFD from the FCF to obtain the CFE.

---

[7]In some cases, tax liabilities might exist and, depending on the tax law, the payment of the tax liabilities might take precedence over payments to the debt holder.

[8]In the language of option pricing, the value of the levered equity is a call option on the FCF that is generated by the company.

The CFE is constructed from the perspective of the equity holder. In the simplest case, for a going concern, the equity holder provides the initial equity contribution in the beginning and receives dividend payments in subsequent years plus a share of the TV at the end of the forecast (or planning) period. With respect to the equity holder, the initial equity contribution is a cash outflow and the subsequent dividend payments and share of the TV are cash inflows. From the perspective of the firm, the initial equity contribution is a cash inflow and the subsequent dividend payments and share of the TV are cash outflows. The profile CFE might be more complex if during the life of the firm the equity holder makes additional equity contributions or repurchases equity.

1.7 WEIGHTED AVERAGE COST OF CAPITAL IN AN M & M WORLD

Next, we present (informally) the first proposition of M & M. We examine the relevance or irrelevance of capital structure in determining the value of a firm, in worlds without and with taxes. By understanding the value relationships between debt, equity and the effect of taxes, we derive the appropriate formula for the WACC that is applied to the annual FCF. The detailed algebra on the cost of capital with respect to cash flows in perpetuity is presented in the appendix to Chapter Two.

1.7.1 Weighted Average Cost of Capital in an M & M World Without Taxes

An M & M world is a world with perfect capital markets. In a world with perfect capital markets, there are no opportunities for arbitrage. In other words, the law of one price holds and there are no financial investment opportunities with positive NPVs. In practice, investment opportunities with positive NPVs exist because the world is imperfect. Usually, we assume (heroically) that the M & M world is a reasonable description of the real world.

1.7.2 An Unlevered Company Versus a Levered Company

To examine the impact of financing on value, we compare a company with all-equity financing and a company with both equity and debt financing. A company with all-equity financing is known as an unlevered firm, where the required nominal (risk-adjusted) annual rate of return is ρ. This is the minimum rate of return that the investor expects to receive by investing in the unlevered firm.

A company with both equity and debt financing is known as a levered firm. In a levered firm, the debt holder has priority claim on the annual

FCF in perpetuity and the equity holder is the residual claimant. This means that the equity holder bears a higher risk on her investment. In the following discussion, for ease in the exposition, we use cash flows in perpetuity. The key ideas remain unchanged and are relevant to finite streams of cash flows.

1.7.3 The No-Arbitrage Argument

The basic idea of the no-arbitrage argument is that in a perfect world with no taxes, the firm value does not depend on how the stakeholders, the stockholders (equity) and creditors (banks and bondholders), finance the firm. The reader should examine this idea in an intuitive manner and she will find it reasonable.[9] M & M proposed that with perfect market conditions the capital structure does not affect the value of the firm because the equity holder can borrow and lend and thus replicate the degree of leverage in the levered firm. They proved this assertion with what is known as a no-arbitrage argument.

The rough argument goes like this. Assume two identical firms. Identical means that the two have the same operational flows, with identical risk characteristics. The difference is that one firm has debt and the other does not. If the firms sell in the stock market at different prices, the market sees the same future cash flows (they are identical firms) but the investors can buy the two firms at different prices. Hence, they will buy the cheaper stock. But everybody will do that and the price of the lower one will increase. How much? The price will increase until the lower price increases up to the higher one. In equilibrium, the values for the levered and unlevered firms are the same. In a world without taxes, this means that capital structure (or debt financing) does not matter for determining the value of the firm, and the values of the unlevered and levered firms are equal. Hence, the debt financing is irrelevant. For a more rigorous discussion on the no-arbitrage proof in an M & M world, consult a standard textbook in corporate finance.

In symbols, V^L, the market value of the levered firm, is equal to V^{Un}, the market value of the unlevered firm.

$$V^L = V^{Un} \qquad (1.2)$$

And in turn, the market value of the levered firm is equal to the sum of the market value of the (levered) equity E^L and the market value of the debt D.

$$V^L = E^L + D \qquad (1.3)$$

---

[9]Franco Modigliani and Merton Miller (M & M) were awarded the Nobel Prize in Economics in 1985 and 1990, respectively, for their work in financial economics.

1.7.4 Slicing the Cake

A simple way of thinking about the irrelevance of debt financing in the absence of taxes is as follows. Let us represent the (present) value of the unlevered firm, which is the value of the stream of annual FCF, with a cake. If there is no debt financing, the entire cake belongs to the equity holder. If there is debt financing, the cake has to be shared between the debt holder and the (levered) equity holder. With debt financing, the size of the cake is not increased. Debt financing simply means that we slice the cake with a non-sticking, friction-less Teflon knife to share between the debt holder and the equity holder. With perfect capital markets, we do not lose any cake in the process of cutting and dividing the cake between the debt holder and the equity holder.

1.7.5 Debt and Equity Financing

With all-equity financing, the entire cake belongs to the equity holder. The unlevered value is equal to the annual FCF in perpetuity (without growth), discounted by the return to unlevered equity ρ. For cash flows in perpetuity without growth, the PV of the cash flow stream is simple. It is equal to the annual cash flow in perpetuity divided by the discount rate.[10] For the moment, we do not wish to discuss the additional complexities that arise with the valuation of cash flows with positive growth.

$$V^{Un} = \frac{FCF}{\rho} \qquad (1.4)$$

Suppose the FCF belongs to one debt holder and one equity holder. The FCF will be distributed between the debt holder and the equity holder. Because the FCF is shared, we give the sliced FCF a new name and call it CCF. To avoid confusion, we make the important distinction between the sliced FCF, which is the CCF, and the original undivided FCF.

The CCF (sliced FCF) is equal to the sum of the CFD and the CFE.

$$CCF = CFD + CFE \qquad (1.5)$$

And because we assume (unrealistically) that no cake is lost in the slicing process, the undivided FCF must be equal to the CCF.

$$FCF = CCF \qquad (1.6)$$

---

[10]In the appendix to Chapter Two, we present the algebraic details for cash flows in perpetuity without and with growth.

Combining equations 1.4 and 1.5, we obtain that the FCF is equal to the sum of the CFD and the CFE.

$$FCF = CFD + CFE \qquad (1.7)$$

Some readers are perplexed by the ambiguity in the meaning of the FCF. We say that the FCF is the unlevered cash flow and yet it includes the CFD because the FCF is defined as the sum of the CFD and the CFE. How can the FCF be unlevered if it includes the CFD? The distinction between the levered CCF (sliced) and the unlevered FCF (undivided) should clear up this ambiguity. The key point is the equality of the FCF and the CCF, which *is* defined in terms of the CFD. Recall that the CCF is equal to the sum of the CFD and the CFE. In this specific case without taxes, the CCF is identical with the FCF.

For the unlevered and levered values, there are associated cash flows. The FCF is associated with V^{Un}, and the CCF is associated with V^L. Similarly, the CFD is associated with the market value of debt D and the CFE is associated with the market value of levered equity E^L. The same relationships that hold for the values in equations 1.2 and 1.3 also hold for the cash flows in equations 1.6 and 1.7.

The size of the slice of cake that is distributed to the debt holder (the value of the debt) is equal to the CFD in perpetuity, discounted by the cost of debt d.

$$D = \frac{CFD}{d} \qquad (1.8)$$

With cash flows in perpetuity without growth, the interest payment on the debt is equal to the CFD, which in turn is equal to the value of debt times the cost of debt. There is no repayment of the loan principal.

The size of the slice of cake that is distributed to the equity holder (the value of the levered) is equal to the CFE in perpetuity, discounted by the return to levered equity e.

$$E^L = \frac{CFE}{e} \qquad (1.9)$$

From before, we know that the levered value is equal to the sum of the debt and the (levered) equity. In other words, the original cake is equal to the sliced cake, which in turn is equal to the sum of the two sliced pieces that are distributed to the debt holder and the equity holder.

In summary, in an M & M world, the levered value is equal to the unlevered value. In essence, the powerful insight of M & M can be stated as follows: the size (value) of the sliced cake is equal to the (size) value of the undivided cake.

1.7.6 Formula for the WACC Without Taxes

Let the WACC, a rate at which the CCF in perpetuity is discounted to obtain the value of the levered firm, be $WACC^{CCF}$. Then the levered value V^L is equal to the CCF in perpetuity, discounted by $WACC^{CCF}$.

$$V^L = \frac{CCF}{WACC^{CCF}} \qquad (1.10)$$

As mentioned earlier, in an M & M world without taxes the WACC is a weighted average of the cost of debt and the cost of equity, where the weights are the market value of debt and the market value of equity, as a proportion of the total levered value.

$$WACC^{CCF} = \frac{dD}{V^L} + \frac{eE^L}{V^L} \qquad (1.11)$$

A perceptive reader might note that the initial discussion of the WACC in equation 1.1 is applied to the FCF, and in equation 1.10 the WACC is applied to the CCF. The discrepancy does not affect anything because in the simple world without taxes, the CCF is identical to the FCF. We discuss the complications that arise with taxes later in the chapter.

1.7.7 Equality of the Unlevered and Levered Returns

In an M & M world without taxes, the WACC applied to the CCF, which is the sum of the CFD and the CFE, is a weighted average of the cost of debt and the return to levered equity. Because the annual FCF is equal to the annual CCF and the levered value is equal to the unlevered value, it must follow that the value of the WACC that is applied to the CCF is equal to the ρ that is applied to the FCF.

$$\frac{FCF}{\rho} = \frac{CCF}{WACC^{CCF}} \qquad (1.12)$$

Algebraically, in the denominators of both sides of equation 1.12, the return to unlevered equity ρ and the WACC that is applied to the CCF are equal because the cash flows in the numerators of both sides are equal in the special case without taxes.

1.8 WACC IN AN M & M WORLD WITH TAXES

Now we introduce taxes into the analysis. We hope that the discussion without taxes facilitates the understanding of the world with taxes.

As mentioned earlier, the traditional formulation of the after-tax WACC applied to the FCF accounts for the value of the TSs by lowering the cost of capital with the factor $(1 - T)$ applied to the cost of debt.

$$\text{After-tax WACC} = \frac{d(1 - T)D}{V^L} + \frac{eE^L}{V^L} \qquad (1.13)$$

This formulation of the after-tax WACC is popular because there is no need to construct the loan schedule.[11] We simply construct the FCF, specify a constant leverage for the life of the FCF, and take the benefits of debt financing into account by lowering the WACC. Some analysts use equation 1.13 even when they know that the firm does not intend to follow a debt financing policy that requires constant leverage.

Taxes are the major market imperfections. When corporate taxes exist (and there are no personal taxes), M & M proposed that the total value of the firm does change if the capital structure changes. When the firm deducts any expense, the tax liabilities are reduced. In particular, this is true for interest payments.

Another equivalent and general way to think of the TS is as follows: The TS is the difference between the taxes paid by the unlevered firm and the levered firm. In subsequent chapters, we discuss the TS in greater detail and give numerical examples.

Again, using the no-arbitrage argument that was mentioned earlier, M & M show that the value of the levered firm increases by the PV of the tax savings or TS.

$$V^L = V^{Un} + V^{TS} \qquad (1.14)$$

The correct formula for the (present) value of the TS depends on assumptions about the cash stream, the debt financing policy, and the risk of the debt. For the moment, we do not specify the value of ψ (psi), which is the appropriate discount rate to calculate the (present) value of the TS. For TS in perpetuity, the (present) value of the V^{TS} is equal to the TS in perpetuity discounted by ψ.

$$V^{TS} = \frac{TS}{\psi} \qquad (1.15)$$

The TS is equal to the tax rate T times the annual interest payment. As stated previously, the interest payment is equal to the cost of debt d times the value of the debt D. The interest payment is also equal to the CFD.

$$\text{Interest payment} = dD \qquad (1.16)$$

---

[11]However, in our integrated valuation framework we must construct the loan schedule because we construct all the financial statements.

Thus, the expression for the TS is as follows:

$$TS = TdD \tag{1.17}$$

Here, for simplicity, we have not used the general formulation of the TS in terms of the difference between the taxes paid by the unlevered and the levered firms.

The market value of the levered firm is also equal to the sum of the market value of (levered) equity and the market value of debt. Thus, we have

$$V^L = E^L + D \tag{1.18}$$

Combining equations 1.14 and 1.18, we obtain

$$V^L = V^{Un} + V^{TS} = E^L + D \tag{1.19}$$

1.8.1 The Expanding Cake

Again, for ease in exposition, we use the cake analogy. Previously, in an M & M world without taxes, the debt financing did not affect the size of the cake. The debt financing was simply equivalent to dividing the cake between the debt holder and the equity holder, with no loss in cake from the cutting process. However, in an M & M world with taxes, even though no cake is lost in the cutting process, the cake actually expands!

The increase in the size of the cake is the (present) value of the stream of TSs that are generated from the interest deduction with debt financing. The extent to which the cake increases depends on the interest payments, which are based on the amount of debt and the cost of debt, and the discount rates that are used in discounting the TSs.

The unlevered cake is simply the (present) value of the annual FCF, using the return to unlevered equity ρ. The levered cake is equal to the unlevered cake plus the (present) value of the TS that is generated by the interest deduction with debt financing.

1.8.2 Why Firms do not have 100% Debt?

Assuming that the manager of the firm would like to have the largest possible cake, the increase in the size of the cake with debt financing would suggest that the firm would have 100% debt. However, when a firm has debt there exists some contingent or hidden costs associated with the possibility that the firm could become bankrupt. These expected costs could reduce the value of the firm. The existence of these costs deters the firm from taking leverage up to 100%. The question of optimal capital structure is complex. In our models, we simply take the capital structure as given and do not assert the optimality of the capital structure that we assume or specify.

1.9 THE FUNDAMENTAL FREE CASH FLOW RELATIONSHIP

With debt financing, the cash flow that is available for distribution increases by the amount of the TS. Previously, without debt financing, only the annual FCF was available for distribution to the stakeholder, namely the all-equity stakeholder. With debt financing, the cash flow that is available for distribution to the stakeholders, namely the debt holder and the equity holder, is greater than before. Thus, the total cash flow that is available for distribution must be equal to the sum of the CFE and the CFD. The annual cash flow that is available for distribution to the stakeholders is equal to the sum of the annual FCF and the annual TS, which in turn is equal to the sum of the CFE and the CFD.

$$FCF + TS = CFE + CFD \qquad (1.20)$$

From before, we know that the CCF is equal to the sum of the CFE and the CFD.

$$CCF = CFE + CFD \qquad (1.21)$$

Combining equations 1.20 and 1.21, we obtain that the sum of the FCF and the TS is equal to the sum of the CFD and the CFE.

$$FCF + TS = CCF \qquad (1.22)$$

Rewriting equation 1.20, we obtain

$$FCF = CFD + CFE - TS \qquad (1.23)$$

We call equation 1.23 the fundamental FCF relationship and it will be used repeatedly in subsequent chapters.

1.10 THE MAIN VALUATION METHODS AND FORMULAS FOR COST OF CAPITAL

Now, after examining M & M worlds without and with taxes, we are in a position to examine the main valuation methods and the corresponding formulas for the cost of capital. For the practitioner, making sense of the bewildering number of theories on the cost of capital must be a truly challenging and daunting task. In a perfect world without taxes, the cost of a capital formula for a finite stream of FCFs, with debt and equity financing, is elegant, relatively simple, and eminently sensible. In a perfect world with taxes, complications abound.

From all the available formulations, what criteria should we use to select the best expression for the cost of capital for a finite stream of cash flows? Fundamentally, the cost of capital is a question about properly accounting for the tax benefits (if any) from the interest deduction with debt financing. In other words, what are the appropriate risk-adjusted discount rates for the TS? We will attempt to provide a rough description of the different possibilities for formulating the cost of capital.

1.10.1 The Tax Shield

One of the key issues is the appropriate discount rate for the TS. With cash flows in perpetuity and risk-free debt, it is common to assume that the discount rate for the TS is the risk-free rate. With cash flows in perpetuity and risk-free debt, the PV of the TS is equal to the tax rate T times the debt D.

In practice, for a finite stream of cash flows, it is reasonable to assume that the correct discount rate for the TS is ρ, the return to unlevered equity, and the choice of ρ is appropriate whether the percentage of debt is constant or varying over the life of the project. The issue of the appropriate discount rate for the TS is complex and will be discussed in greater detail in subsequent chapters. With respect to the cost of capital, there are two main options. We can apply the WACC to the FCF or the CCF. In addition, there is another approach, the APV, which is less common.

1.10.2 After-Tax WACC Applied to the FCF

The popular reigning champion is the after-tax WACC based on the FCF. See equation 1.1. As mentioned earlier, the value of the TS is taken into account by lowering the cost of debt d with the coefficient $(1 - T)$. However, under certain circumstances, lowering the cost of debt with the coefficient $(1 - T)$ might not be the correct way to account for the value of the TSs because the effects of debt financing are complex.

If the debt is risk-free, the cost of the debt is equal to the risk-free rate r_f. In practice, for simplicity in modeling, it is convenient to assume that the debt is risk-free, even though it is clearly unrealistic. If we do not assume that the debt is risk-free, the correct specification of the discount rate for the TS becomes more complex. With the after-tax WACC applied to the FCF, it is assumed that the leverage is constant for the life of the FCF, there are no losses carried forward (LCF), and the TSs are fully realized in the years in which the interest expenses occur. The assumption about constant leverage is particularly strong. Furthermore, in using this formulation of the WACC for the FCF, the assumption about the discount rate for the TS must be clearly stated because it affects the formula for the calculation of the return to levered equity e.

1.10.3 Alternative Expression for the WACC Applied to the FCF

With annual FCF in perpetuity and assuming that ρ rather than d is the correct discount rate for the TS, there is an alternative, less well-known formulation of the WACC that is more general and less used. We call this formulation the adjusted WACC.

$$\text{Adjusted WACC} = \rho - \frac{\text{TS}}{\text{V}^\text{L}} \tag{1.24}$$

$$= \rho - \frac{\text{TdD}}{\text{V}^\text{L}} \tag{1.25}$$

where TS is the amount of the tax shield, and is equal to the tax rate times the interest expense, ρ is the return to unlevered equity and also the discount rate for the TS, and V^L is the levered value.

This alternative expression is equivalent to the traditional after-tax weighted average formula and has certain advantages in calculation, as we shall see later. In particular, this formulation of the WACC can deal with the issue of LCF, which cannot be accommodated in the traditional after-tax formulation of the WACC.

Let θ be the debt as a percent of the levered value. Then we can rewrite equation 1.25 as follows:

$$w = \rho - \text{Td}\theta \tag{1.26}$$

1.10.4 WACC with the CCF Method

The new challenger to the traditional after-tax WACC is the WACC based on the CCF. The CCF is equal to the sum of the CFE and the CFD.

$$\text{CCF} = \text{CFE} + \text{CFD} \tag{1.27}$$

The WACC with the CCF assumes that the return to unlevered equity is the correct discount rate for the TSs in *all* periods because the future TSs are uncertain. Thus, the value of the WACC applied to the CCF is the return to unlevered equity ρ. A detailed discussion on the appropriate value of ψ is given in Chapter Seven.

Because the value of the TS is taken into account directly, there is no need to adjust the WACC. Rather than lowering the WACC, which is a cumbersome and laborious procedure, we simply construct the CCF by adding the TSs to the FCF and discount the CCF directly. Equivalently, to obtain the CCF, we simply add the CFD and the CFE.

I.10.5 Losses Carried Forward

As explained in detail in Chapter Seven, the WACC that is applied to the CCF can easily deal with LCF. We do not have to assume that the TSs are *always* realized in the year in which the interest expense occurs, and the TSs are added to the FCFs only in the years in which the TSs are *actually* realized.

I.10.6 The FCF WACC Versus the CCF WACC

Using the criteria of simplicity, flexibility, and correctness, we assess the strengths and weaknesses of the two main formulas for the WACC: the traditional WACC applied to the FCF and the WACC applied to the CCF.

The traditional after-tax formula was developed with cash flows in perpetuity. With finite streams of cash flows, we have to use the Miles and Ezzel (1980) formulation for the risk-profile of the TSs. The details for the M & E WACC are given in Chapter Ten. Unfortunately, the M & E formulation of the WACC only applies to risk-free debt, with constant leverage and risk-free TSs. Most importantly, it would be quite difficult to adjust the M & E WACC for variable leverage and LCF.

The WACC applied to the CCF is simple. For most practical purposes, it is reasonable to assume that the amounts of the TSs to be realized in future years are uncertain. With the risk-adjusted discount rates for the TSs equal to the return to unlevered equity ρ, there is no adjustment factor of $(1 - T)$ for the cost of debt, and the WACC is always equal to ρ. Briefly, there is circularity with the WACC applied to the FCF. To find the weights for the use of the WACC, we need the levered value; in turn, the levered value depends on the WACC.

The WACC applied to the CCF is flexible enough to handle variable leverage and LCF. Technically speaking, the WACC applied to the CCF is equal to the return to unlevered equity ρ only under the assumption that ρ is the correct discount rate for the TS in all periods. If the debt is risky or the TS is risky (because the TS cannot be realized in the period in which the tax savings occurs) the risk profile of the TS is more complex and the formulation of the WACC applied to the CCF can be complicated. In summary, the WACC applied to the CCF is simple, flexible, and for practical purposes, almost correct.

I.11 THE CASH FLOW TO EQUITY APPROACH

The CFE is another approach. The value of the (levered) equity can be estimated directly by discounting the CFE with the appropriate risk-adjusted returns to levered equity. The CFE is obtained directly from the CB statement and consists of the dividend payments, new equity investments, and equity repurchase. It is not common to use the CFE approach because we have to calculate the annual returns to levered (equity) if the leverage is variable.

In practice, the CFE approach is difficult to apply. Typically, the analyst assumes that there is constant leverage over the life of the cash flow stream and the return to unlevered equity is constant. With these assumptions, the return to levered equity is constant and the analyst applies the traditional after-tax WACC to the FCF without worrying about the loan schedule and the CFE.

However, because we construct a complete set of financial statements in our integrated valuation framework, we construct the loan schedule, based on the specific debt financing policy and verify that the results are consistent with the CFE approach.

The formula for the return to levered equity e depends on whether the cash flow is finite or in perpetuity, without and with growth. Among other factors, with a finite stream of cash flows, the return to levered equity is also a function of ψ, the discount rate for the TS. The general formula for the return to levered equity with finite cash flows is derived in Chapter Seven.

In some cases, it might be important to examine the profile of the CFE, especially if there are large variations in the leverage over the life of the cash flow stream. In addition, the estimation of the value of levered equity can uncover errors in modeling and is a good litmus test of the overall consistency of the calculations.

1.12 ESTIMATING THE COST OF CAPITAL

Up to this point we have simply presented the theory on the cost of capital and we have not discussed how to estimate the cost of capital for levered and unlevered firms. Now we briefly review and describe (qualitatively) the CAPM, which is one of the most common, well-known and popular methods for estimating the cost of capital. It is reasonable to assume that there is a positive relationship between the required rate of return and risk. The CAPM is one theory that specifies the relationship between required rate of return and risk.

We assume that the reader is familiar with the basic ideas related to the CAPM. We do not assess the strengths and weaknesses of the CAPM relative to other competing theories, and we assume that the CAPM is a reasonable framework for thinking about and estimating the cost of capital, even though the assumptions that underlie the CAPM are quite stringent, and in many cases might be violated in reality. In many transitional and developing countries, the appropriate data for estimating (reliably) the parameters for the CAPM simply do not exist.

First, we present the CAPM and then we briefly discuss the meaning and interpretation of the CAPM. Let r_f be the risk-free rate and let r_m be the rate of return on the market portfolio. Let E(r) be the expected return on a portfolio or asset and let $E(r_m)$ be the expected return on the market portfolio.

$$E(r) = r_f + \beta[E(r_m) - r_f] \qquad (1.28)$$

According to the CAPM, there is a linear relationship between E(r) the expected return on a portfolio or asset and the term $[E(r_m) - r_f]$, which measures the difference between the expected return on the market portfolio $E(r_m)$ and the risk-free rate r_f. The strength of the relationship is measured with the coefficient β, which is known as the "beta for the portfolio." Mathematically, the beta is equal to the covariance between the market portfolio and the return of the cash flow (or firm) divided by the variance of the market return.

$$\beta = \frac{\text{Cov}(r_m, \ r)}{\text{Var}(r_m)} \qquad (1.29)$$

The CAPM is elegant and simple. However, in practice, there are many data and econometric hurdles to overcome in estimating reliable betas.

Consider the expected return on an asset for different values of beta. If the value of β is zero, the second term in equation 1.28 is zero, and the expected return on the asset is equal to the risk-free rate r_f; if the value of β is one, the expected return on the asset is equal to the expected return on the market portfolio. In other words, if the value of β is one, the risk of the asset is equal to the risk of the market portfolio.

Based on the value of β, we can compare the risk of the asset relative to the risk of the market portfolio. If the value of β is greater than one, the risk of the asset is greater than the risk of the market portfolio, and if the value of β is less than one (and greater than zero), the risk of the asset is less than the risk of the market portfolio.

We can think of a levered firm as a portfolio that consists of the value of the debt and the value of the (levered) equity. Thus, along the lines of the WACC, it would be reasonable to assert that the beta for the portfolio is a weighted average of the betas for the debt and equity, where the weights are the market values of the debt and levered equity. Let β_A be the beta for the portfolio, let β_D be the beta for the debt, and let β_E be the beta for the levered equity. The relationship among the three betas is shown next.

$$\beta_A = \frac{\beta_D D}{V^L} + \frac{\beta_E E^L}{V^L} \qquad (1.30)$$

If we know two of the three betas we can calculate the third beta. Professional consulting companies provide estimates for the betas of all kinds of companies.

1.13 ADJUSTED PRESENT VALUE APPROACH

Next, we present the APV approach, which is another valuation method. The APV approach is a general alternative approach for valuing the impact of debt financing. It can be difficult to take account of all the effects of debt financing by simply lowering the traditional after-tax WACC. The APV approach estimates the effects of debt financing separately. The APV approach does not require the calculation of the WACC. With an appropriate discount rate for the effects of the tax savings from debt financing, the APV approach simply adds the (present) value of the tax savings to the unlevered value.

1.14 VARIOUS FORMULATIONS FOR THE COST OF CAPITAL

For clarity, we briefly review and summarize the various formulations that we have presented for the cost of capital and valuation. The most common and standard approach is to apply the WACC to the FCF. Because the FCF does not include the TS, we lower the WACC to account for the tax benefits from the interest deductions with the debt financing.

An alternative approach is to apply the WACC to the CCF. Because the CCF includes the TS, we do not need to lower the WACC. Moreover, unlike the WACC applied to the FCF, the WACC applied to the CCF is applicable to cases with and without LCF.

Another less common approach is to discount the CFE with the return to levered equity e.

An alternative method is the APV approach. If certain conditions are satisfied, all four approaches give the same results. In subsequent chapters, we discuss the relative merits of these approaches in greater detail.

1.15 SUMMARY AND CONCLUDING REMARKS

In this chapter, we provided an informal introduction to some key ideas in market-based valuation. We introduced the WACC, which is one of the key parameters in any valuation exercise. We discussed the conditions for perfect capital markets and the importance of the no-arbitrage assumption for valuation. In the context of an M & M world, without and with taxes, we discussed the different types of finite cash flows and the corresponding discount rates for the cash flows. The types of cash flows are the FCF, the CCF, the CFD, the CFE, and the TSs.

One of the key assumptions in the determination of the WACC is the appropriate discount rate for the TS. With a finite stream of cash flows, the issues surrounding the appropriate discount rate for the TS are complex and we shall explore this issue further in subsequent chapters.

In summary, there are three main points that we would like to emphasize. First, in valuation, we should construct nominal financial statements with finite streams of cash flows because cash flows in perpetuity are not flexible for practical use. Second, with finite streams of cash flows, the WACC applied to the CCF is the most appropriate. Third, we integrate the standard financial statements such as the IS and the BS with the annual CB statement, and derive the FCF statement from the CB statement.

Armed with this overview of the basic ideas in the market-based valuation of cash flows, we are ready to begin an examination of the principles of cash flow valuation and the construction of financial statements. We have tried to present a balanced mix of theory and practical ideas, and hope that the principles that we present in the book are useful and relevant to practitioners in the field. The verdict of the practitioner is the ultimate test.

Again, we urge the reader to be active and reconstruct the tables and models on a spreadsheet program in a computer as she reads. With a dash of diligence and some patience, the interested reader should be successful in learning the principles of cash flow valuation.

We wish you happy reading and learning. Be successful and enjoy!

KEY CONCEPTS AND IDEAS

Adjusted present value (APV) approach
After-tax Weighted Average Cost of
  Capital (WACC)
All-equity financing
Arbitrage opportunities
Balance sheet (BS)
Beta of the asset
Capital Asset Pricing Model (CAPM)
Capital Cash Flow (CCF)
Cash budget (CB) statement
Cash flow in perpetuity
Cash flow to debt (CFD)
Cash flow to equity (CFE)
Comparable Investment
  Opportunity (CIO)
Constant price approach
Discounted Cash Flow (DCF)
Emerging markets
Expectations
Expected market return
Finite cash flow
Forecast period
Free Cash Flow (FCF)
Income statement (IS)

Integrated valuation framework
Interest deductions
Law of one price
Levered company
Losses carried forward (LCF)
Market value of debt
Market value of equity
Market-based cash flow valuation
Modigliani and Miller (M & M) world
No-arbitrage argument
Nominal financial statements
Nominal price approach
Non-traded firm
Opportunity cost of capital
Perfect capital markets
Perfect information
Planning period
Present value (PV)
Real price approach
Replicating portfolio strategy
Required rate of return
Residual claimant
Return to levered equity
Return to unlevered equity

Risk-adjusted discounted rate (RADR)   Terminal value (TV)
Risk-free rate   Traded firm
Stream of finite cash flows   Unlevered company
Tax savings   WACC applied to the CCF
Tax shield (TS)   WACC applied to the FCF

2

TIME VALUE OF MONEY AND INTRODUCTION TO COST OF CAPITAL

How little you know about the age you live in if you think that honey is sweeter than cash in hand.

—*Ovid* (~4BC to AD 18)

A perfect capital market should be defined as one in which the M & M theory holds. (From Ezra Solomon in Brealey & Myers, *Principles of Corporate Finance*, 6th edition, p. 488.)

2.1 INTRODUCTION

In Chapter One, we presented an informal introduction to the basic concepts and ideas in market-based cash flow valuation. There we examined the different types of cash flows and the different expressions for the cost of capital in perfect markets without and with taxes.

In this chapter, there are two main sections. In the first part of the chapter, we briefly introduce real interest rates, nominal interest rates, real prices, nominal prices, compounding, discounting, and the risk premium. Because we construct all the financial statements in nominal terms, we explicitly specify the expected inflation rate and the real increases (if any) in the prices. Thus, it is extremely important to understand the differences between nominal prices, constant prices, real prices, nominal interest rates, and real interest rates. We recognize that it is difficult to estimate the expected inflation rates. However, the difficulty in estimation does not mean that it is appropriate to assume that the expected inflation rates are zero. It is better to acknowledge explicitly that the expected inflation rates will not be zero and examine the extent to which the assumption about the profile of the expected inflation rate affects the outcomes of the valuation exercise.

Some analysts do not directly model the expected inflation rates and construct the Free Cash Flow (FCF) as if the expected inflation rates are zero over the life of the cash flows.[1] However, if the FCFs are derived from financial statements that are not constructed in nominal terms, there is the potential for a misleading valuation of the cash flow profile. Incorrect results can occur if the FCF is derived from financial statements that do not properly model the expected inflation rates over the life of the FCF.

Because it is also difficult to estimate the real increases in the prices of inputs and outputs, for convenience, many analysts also assume that the real increases are zero over the life of the cash flow. Again, it is better to acknowledge explicitly that the real increases in the prices will not be zero and examine the extent to which the assumptions about the profiles of the real increases in prices affect the outcomes of the valuation exercise.

In the second part, we use numerical examples to illustrate some basic ideas on cost of capital with finite cash flows. We show that the formulas that are derived from cash flows in perpetuity give inconsistent results when applied to finite cash flows and we present an alternative approach with consistent results.

Typically, we value the relevant cash flows after we have derived the cash flows from the appropriate financial statements and it might seem premature to present the cost of capital here. However, having presented the discounting process in the earlier part of the chapter, we believe that it is appropriate to apply the same ideas in the context of the cost of capital to illustrate and strengthen the idea of discounting.

We believe that it is important to capture the reader's interest by providing an early introduction to valuation with finite cash flows, and then revisit the theory on the cost of capital again in Chapters Seven and Ten with a more detailed discussion of the underlying issues. With a taste of what is to come, we hope that the reader will read the subsequent chapters with greater motivation and enthusiasm.

In Appendix A to this chapter, as a reference and review for the reader, we present the detailed derivation of the expressions for the cost of capital for cash flows in perpetuity without and with growth. We assume that most readers are familiar with the expressions for the cost of capital for cash flows in perpetuity. In Appendix B, we present some results that are based on the CAPM applied to cash flows in perpetuity.

---

[1]Nominal prices explicitly take into account the expected inflation rates and the real increases (if any) in the prices over the life of the project. We obtain the real prices by deflating the nominal prices with the expected inflation index. If the expected inflation rates and the real increases are zero, the prices are constant with respect to a given year. The real prices and constant prices are equivalent only if the real increases are zero.

The first section of this chapter is organized as follows. First, we explain the distinction and relationship between the real rate of return and the nominal rate of return. This is also known as the Fisher relationship. Second, we explain the difference between real and nominal prices. Third, we present some numerical examples. Fourth, we explain the time value of money (TVM), the compounding process, and the discounting process.

The material in this chapter is elementary and is intended as a refresher for most readers.

SECTION I

2.I.I The Expected Inflation Rate

Nominal prices are the actual prices that we pay to purchase goods and services when we visit the grocery store, the car dealer, or the computer shop. Nominal prices are also known as current prices. To measure the relative changes in the prices of goods over time, the appropriate government agency constructs the consumer price index (CPI), which is based on a basket of goods that reflect the consumption of the typical consumer. The expected inflation rate is the percentage change in the CPI. For further details on the construction of the CPI, consult a textbook on economics.

From a valuation point of view, we are interested in real prices rather than nominal prices. We obtain the real prices from the nominal prices by removing the impact of inflation from the nominal prices. However, from a practical point of view, using real prices is difficult because we never observe real prices. Many practitioners have difficulty in dealing with real prices and prefer to use nominal prices. We wish to stress the relation- ship between nominal and real prices because we believe that an understanding of this relationship will prevent potential mistakes in cash flow valuation.

The expected inflation rate is a function of many factors and it is difficult to forecast the future inflation rate. However, because the expected inflation rates over the life of the stream of cash flows affects the present values (PVs) of the cash flows, we must model the expected inflation rates and analyze the extent to which changes in the expected inflation rates will adversely affect the PVs of the stream of cash flows.

Government agencies and other institutions regularly provide forecasts for the expected inflation rates and we use their estimates in the construction of the financial statements and the cash flows over the forecast period. We do not discuss the determination or estimation of the expected inflation rates over the life of the cash flow profile. We assume that it is possible to obtain reliable information on the expected inflation rates over the life of the cash flow profile from the appropriate government institution or agency. Alternatively, we assume that the historical information on the inflation rates is available, and based on the historical data we can specify a profile for the expected inflation rates over the life of the cash flow.

2.1.2 Relationship Between the Real Rate of Return and the Nominal Rate of Return

Next, we explain the relationship between the real rate of return and the nominal rate of return. It is best to explain the difference between the real rate of return and the nominal rate of return with a concrete single period numerical example.[2] After we understand the relationship between the real rate of return and the nominal rate of return, we examine the relationship between the real price and the nominal price.

Today, farmer John buys 10 pigs and plans to sell them at the end of year 1. He expects that by the end of year 1, the pigs will reproduce and there will be 12 pigs. Let N_0 be the number of pigs at the beginning of year 1 and N_1 be the number of pigs at the end of year 1. Let r be the real growth rate for the number of pigs. Then the real rate of return is the difference between the number of pigs in year 1 and the number of pigs in year 0, divided by the number of pigs in year 0.

$$\text{Real Rate of Return } r = \frac{[N_1 - N_0]}{N_0} \tag{2.1}$$

Substituting the appropriate values for the numbers of pigs, we obtain that the real growth rate is 20%.

$$r = \frac{12 - 10}{10} = 20.00\%$$

We can rewrite the number of pigs in year 1 as the product of the number of pigs in year 0 times one plus the real growth rate in the number of pigs.

$$N_1 = N_0(1 + r) = 10(1 + 20\%) = 12.00$$

Let P_0 be the current market price for a pig. If the price for one pig is $100, the initial value of the investment K_0 is $1,000.

---

[2]We wish to thank an anonymous reviewer for suggesting this approach to explain the difference between nominal and real prices.

Initial Value of Investment $K_0 = N_0 P_0$
$$= 10 \times 100 = 1,000.00$$

Let g be the percent increase in the price of the pig, where g is 10%. Then at the end of year 1, the price of a pig P_1 is $110.

$$P_1 = P_0(1 + g) = 100(1 + 10\%) = 110.00$$

At the end of year 1, what is the final value of the investment K_1? The final value of the investment is equal to the number of pigs at the end of year 1 times the price of a pig at the end of year 1.

$$\text{Final Value of Investment } K_1 = N_1 P_1 \qquad (2.2)$$

Substituting the appropriate values for the parameters, we obtain that at the end of year 1, when the farmer sells the 12 pigs, he receives $1,320.

$$K_1 = 12 \times 110 = 1,320.00$$

The value of the investment increases from $1,000 at the end of year 0 to $1,320 at the end of year 1. The nominal rate of return i on the initial investment is 32%.

$$\text{Nominal rate of return } i = \frac{K_1 - K_0}{K_0}$$

$$= \frac{1,320 - 1,000}{1,000} = 32\%$$

Alternatively, the final value of the investment K_1 is equal to the initial value K_0 times one plus the nominal rate of return i.

$$K_1 = K_0(1 + i) \qquad (2.3)$$

We can write the final value of the investment in terms of the real growth rate of the pigs and the increase in the price. As shown in equation 2.2, at the end of year 1, the final value of the investment is equal to the number of pigs times the new price.

We can write the expression for the final investment as follows:

$$
\begin{aligned}
K_1 &= N_1 P_1 \\
&= [N_0(1+r)][P_0(1+g)] \\
&= K_0(1+r)(1+g)
\end{aligned}
\tag{2.4}
$$

The number of pigs at the end of year 1 N_1 is equal to the number of pigs at the end of year 0 times one plus the real growth rate of the pigs. Also, the price at the end of year 1 P_1 is equal to the price at the end of year 0 times the increase in the price. With these substitutions, we see that the value of the investment in year 1 is equal to the product of the initial value of the investment, one plus the real growth rate and one plus the expected inflation rate.

We rewrite equation 2.4 as follows:

$$
\frac{K_1}{K_0} = (1+r)(1+g)
\tag{2.5}
$$

The left-hand side (LHS) of equation 2.5 is equal to one plus the nominal return. Thus, we obtain the relationship between the nominal rate of return on the investment i in terms of the real return r and the increase in the price of a pig g, which is the expected inflation rate.

Equation 2.6 is also known as the Fisher relationship between the real rate of return, the expected inflation rate, and the nominal rate of return.

$$
(1+i) = (1+r)(1+g)
\tag{2.6}
$$

If we know two of the parameters, we can solve for the third parameter. Solving for the nominal rate of return, we obtain

$$
i = (1+r)(1+g) - 1
\tag{2.7}
$$

If we know the real rate of return and the expected inflation rate, we can calculate the nominal rate of return. Equation 2.7 can be rewritten as follows:

$$
i = r + g + rg
\tag{2.8}
$$

If the real rate of return and the expected inflation rate are small, the product of these two terms will be small and can be ignored. Often, the expected inflation rate is defined (approximately) as the sum of the real interest rate and the expected inflation rate.

$$
i \cong r + g
\tag{2.9}
$$

However, with the availability of spreadsheets for modeling, the approximation is unnecessary.

Solving for the real rate of return, we obtain

$$r = \frac{(1+i)}{(1+g)} - 1 \qquad (2.10)$$

If we know the nominal rate of return and the expected inflation rate, we can calculate the real rate of return.

For example, suppose the nominal interest rate is 10% and the expected inflation rate is 4%. We divide one plus the nominal interest rate by one plus the expected inflation rate, and subtract one. The real interest rate is 5.77%.

$$r = \frac{1+i}{1+g} - 1 = \frac{1+10\%}{1+4\%} - 100\% = 5.77\%$$

In practice, we know the nominal interest rate and we do not observe the real interest rate. Typically, on grounds of simplicity, we assume that the real interest rate r remains constant over the life of the cash flow and the nominal interest rate i incorporates the expected inflation rate g. Thus, using the Fisher relationship, we deduce the real interest rate from the expected inflation rate and the nominal interest rate. The nominal interest rate of 10% is based on the expected inflation rate of 4%. If the expected inflation rate changes and the real interest rate remains constant, the nominal interest rate changes to take account of the expected inflation rate.

Thus, for the given nominal interest rate and expected inflation rate, we derive the real interest rate and then reformulate the nominal interest rate in terms of the real interest rate, which we assume to be constant, and the expected inflation rate, which can change over time.[3] For example, suppose over the life of the cash flow, the real interest rate is 5.77% and the expected inflation rate is 6% rather than 4%. Then the nominal interest rate takes into account the higher expected inflation rate and increase from 10% to 12.12%.

$$i = (1+r)(1+g) - 1$$
$$= (1 + 5.77\%)(1 + 6\%) - 100\% = 12.12\%$$

---

[3]If we model the nominal interest rate and the expected inflation rate, the (derived) real interest rate need not be constant.

Alternatively, if the expected inflation rate is 2%, the nominal interest rate decreases from 10% to 7.89%.

$$i = (1 + r)(1 + g) - 1$$
$$= (1 + 5.77\%)(1 + 2\%) - 100\% = 7.89\%$$

2.1.3 Expression for the Cost of Capital

The Fisher relationship also applies to the nominal cost of capital ρ, which is the return to unlevered equity. Typically, we assume that the real cost of capital ρ^R is constant. If it is expected that the real cost of capital will change, the real change in the cost of capital should be incorporated explicitly in the valuation.

Based on the expected inflation rate and the nominal cost of capital, we calculate the real cost of capital. Then we re-express the nominal cost of capital in terms of the real cost of capital and the expected inflation rate.

$$\rho = (1 + \rho^R)(1 + g) - 1 \qquad (2.11)$$

Equation 2.11 is a general expression for the nominal cost of capital ρ in terms of the expected inflation rate and the real cost of capital. Assume that the real cost of capital is 5.77% and the expected inflation rate is 3%. Then the nominal cost of capital is 8.94%.

$$\rho = (1 + \rho^R)(1 + g) - 1$$
$$= (1 + 5.77\%)(1 + 3\%) - 100\% = 8.94\%$$

2.2 NOMINAL PRICES, CONSTANT PRICES, AND REAL PRICES

The relationship that holds between the real interest rate and the nominal interest rate also holds between the real price and the nominal price. Let P_0 be the price of a good at the end of year 0 and let P_1 be the price of a good at the end of year 1.

Let g be the expected inflation rate and let π be the expected real increase in the price. Then we can write the following expression for the price in year 1 in terms of the other parameters. The price in year 1 is equal to the product of the price in year 0, one plus the expected real percent increase and one plus the expected inflation rate.

$$P_1 = P_0(1 + \pi)(1 + g) \qquad (2.12)$$

The real price in year 1 is equal to the nominal price in year 1 divided by one plus the expected inflation rate. When we divide the nominal price by one plus the expected inflation rate, we deflate the nominal price to obtain the real price.

$$\text{Real price in year } 1 = \frac{P_1}{1 + g} \tag{2.13}$$

In turn, the real price in year 1 is simply the price in year 0 times one plus the expected real increase in the price.

$$\text{Real price in year } 1 = P_0(1 + \pi) \tag{2.14}$$

2.2.1 Expected Real Increase Is 2% and Expected Inflation Rate Is 3%

We present a simple numerical example to illustrate the combined impact of a real increase in the price and a positive expected inflation rate. For example, suppose the current unit price of a good is $200, the expected inflation rate over the year is 3%, and the expected real increase in the price of the good is 2%. Then at the end of year 1, the nominal price of the good is $210.12.

$$P_1 = P_0(1 + \pi)(1 + g)$$

$$= 200(1 + 2\%)(1 + 3\%) = 210.12$$

The expected percent increase in the price of the good is 5.06%.

$$\frac{P_1 - P_0}{P_0} = (1 + \pi)(1 + g) - 1$$

$$= (1 + 2\%)(1 + 3\%) - 100\% = 5.06\%$$

As discussed earlier, the increase in the price of the good is greater than the simple addition of the real increase in the price of the good and the expected inflation rate. The discrepancy of 0.06% is due to the third term in equation 2.8, which is the product of the real increase and the expected inflation rate.

At the end of year 1, the expected real price of the good is $204.

$$\frac{P_1}{1 + g} = P_0(1 + \pi) = 200(1 + 2\%) = 204.00$$

2.2.2 Expected Real Increase Is 2% and Expected Inflation Rate Is 0%

To ensure that the reader is fully comfortable with the manipulation of real and nominal prices, we present three other possibilities for the real increase and the expected inflation. Suppose the expected real increase in the price of the good is 2% and the expected inflation rate is 0%. Then at the end of year 1, the nominal price of the good is $204.

$$P_1 = P_0(1 + \pi)(1 + g)$$
$$= 200(1 + 2\%)(1 + 0\%) = 204.00$$

Because the expected inflation rate is 0% at the end of year 1, the expected real price of the good is the same as the nominal price.

2.2.3 Expected Real Increase Is 0% and Expected Inflation Rate Is 3%

Suppose the expected real increase in the price of the good is 0% and the expected inflation rate is 3%. Then at the end of year 1, the nominal price of the good is $206.

$$P_1 = P_0(1 + \pi)(1 + g)$$
$$= 200(1 + 0\%)(1 + 3\%) = 206.00$$

Because the expected real increase in the price of the good is 0% at the end of year 1, the real price of the good is the same as the price of the good in year 0.

2.2.4 Real Increase Is 0% and Expected Inflation Rate Is 0%

Suppose the expected real increase in the price of the good is 0% and the expected inflation rate is 0%. Then at the end of year 1, the nominal price of the good is $200, which is the same as the real price of the good.

$$P_1 = P_0(1 + \pi)(1 + g)$$
$$= 200(1 + 0\%)(1 + 0\%) = 200.00$$

We summarize the results for the four cases in the following table. The nominal price in year 1 can take on four possible values, depending on the assumptions that we make about the expected real increase in price and the expected inflation rate.

TABLE 2.1   Nominal Prices under Different Scenarios

Expected real increase in price in year 1	Expected inflation rate in year 1	Nominal price in year 1
2%	3%	210.12
2%	0%	204.00
0%	3%	206.00
0%	0%	200.00

In the construction of the preliminary tables that are required for the financial statements, the analyst must be explicit about the assumptions that underlie the specification of the nominal prices. Without clarity about the expected real price increases and the expected inflation rates, there is the potential for confusion in the valuation exercise.

2.2.5 The Use of Nominal Prices Versus Real Prices

Now we are ready to describe the different ways in which to construct the financial statements: nominal prices, real prices, or constant prices. In this book, we use the nominal prices approach. However, it is important to know the differences between the nominal prices approach and the other two approaches. Often, it is asserted that all three methods give the same answer. The three methods are equivalent only under stringent conditions. In general, the three methods do not give the same answers and the nominal price approach, which explicitly specifies the expected inflation rate, is the correct way to construct the financial statements and derive the relevant cash flows.

In the nominal price approach, we explicitly specify the expected real increase and the expected inflation rate. In the real prices approach, we only specify the expected real increase and do not specify the expected inflation rate. In the constant prices approach, we assume that the real price increase is zero and do not specify the expected inflation rate. Thus, the constant prices approach is a special case of the real prices approach.

2.2.6 Multi-Period Example with Nominal and Real Prices

Next, we present a three-period example on nominal and real prices. Let P_i be the price in year i. Let π_i be the expected growth rate in year i and let g_i be the expected inflation rate in year i. The nominal prices in years 1–3 are shown next.

$$P_1 = P_0(1 + \pi_1)(1 + g_1) \tag{2.15}$$

$$P_2 = P_1(1 + \pi_2)(1 + g_2) \tag{2.16}$$

$$P_3 = P_2(1 + \pi_3)(1 + g_3) \tag{2.17}$$

With the appropriate substitutions, we can rewrite the prices in years 1–3 in terms of the price in year 0 — the annual expected inflation rates and the annual expected real increases in price.

$$P_1 = P_0(1 + \pi_1)(1 + g_1) \tag{2.18}$$

$$P_2 = P_0(1 + \pi_1)(1 + \pi_2)(1 + g_1)(1 + g_2) \tag{2.19}$$

$$P_2 = P_0(1 + \pi_1)(1 + \pi_2)(1 + \pi_3)(1 + g_1)(1 + g_2)(1 + g_3) \tag{2.20}$$

Define the following products, which are the indices for the expected real increases in price and the expected inflation rates.

$$\Pi(1 + \pi_i) = (1 + \pi_1) \ldots (1 + \pi_i) \tag{2.21}$$

$$\Pi(1 + g_i) = (1 + g_1) \ldots (1 + g_i) \tag{2.22}$$

Then we can write the price in year i P_i as the product of the price in year 0, the ith element of the index for the real increase in price and ith element of the index for the expected inflation rate.

$$P_i = P_0\Pi(1 + \pi_i)\Pi(1 + g_i) \tag{2.23}$$

To calculate the annual real prices, we divide the annual nominal prices by the corresponding element of the expected inflation index.

If the expected real increase in price and the expected inflation rate are constant, we can rewrite equation 2.23 as follows:

$$P_i = P_0(1 + \pi)^i(1 + g)^i \tag{2.24}$$

Next, we present a simple numerical illustration. Let the price in year 0 be 200. In year 1 the expected inflation rate is 3%, in year 2 the expected inflation rate is 4%, and in year 3, the expected inflation rate is 3%.

TABLE 2.2   Nominal Prices

Year	0	1	2	3
Expected inflation rates		3%	4%	3%
Expected real increases		2%	1%	1%
Inflation index	1.0000	1.0300	1.0712	1.1033
Real price index	1.0000	1.0200	1.0302	1.0405
Nominal price		210.12	220.71	229.60
Real price		204.00	206.04	208.10

In year 1 the expected real increase in the price is 2%, in year 2 the expected real increase in the price is 1%, and in year 3 the expected real increase in the price is 1%. Based on the expected inflation rates and the expected increases in price, we construct the two indices. In any year i, the nominal price is the product of the price in year 0, the ith element of the index for inflation, and the ith element of the index for the price increase.[4]

For example, in year 2 the value of the inflation index is 1.071 and the value of the real price increase index is 1.0302.

Element of inflation index in year $2 = (1 + 3\%)(1 + 4\%) = 1.0712$

Element of real price increase index in year $2 = (1 + 2\%)(1 + 1\%) = 1.0302$

Thus, the nominal price in year 2 is \$220.71

Nominal price in year $2 = 200 \times 1.0712 \times 1.0302 = 220.71$

The nominal price increases from \$210.12 in year 1 to \$220.71 in year 2, and \$229.60 in year 3. In real terms, the price increases from \$204 in year 1 to \$206.04 in year 2, and \$208.10 in year 3.

2.3 RISK PREMIUM WITH THE CAPITAL ASSET PRICING MODEL

In the previous section, we did not specify the risk of the interest rate. In this section, using the CAPM that we briefly reviewed in Chapter One, we explicitly introduce the idea of risk in the interest rate. Let i be the interest

---

[4]In any year i, the real price is equal to the price in year 0 times the ith element of the index for the price increase. Equivalently, the annual real prices can be obtained by deflating the nominal prices with the inflation index. We never observe the real prices. However, from a valuation point of view, it is important to know whether the prices are increasing in real terms or not.

rate on a loan or the cost of debt. Then using the CAPM, the expected return on the debt is equal to the risk-free rate plus the risk premium. The risk premium is equal to the beta for the debt times the difference between the expected return on the market portfolio and the risk-free rate.

$$E(i) = r_f + \beta_D[E(R_m) - r_f] \qquad (2.25)$$

where $E(i)$ is the expected (nominal) return on the debt, β_D is the beta for the debt, $E(R_m)$ is the expected return on the market portfolio, and r_f is the nominal risk-free rate.

For example, assume the expected inflation rate g is 3%. Based on the expected inflation rate, the expected return on the market portfolio is 12%, the nominal risk-free rate r_f is 5%, and the beta for the debt is 0.80. Let r be the real interest rate. Then using the Fisher relationship, we calculate that the real interest rate is 1.94%.

$$r = \frac{1+i}{1+g} - 1 = \frac{1+5\%}{1+3\%} - 1 = 1.94\%$$

Substituting the appropriate values for the parameters, the expected nominal return on the debt is 10.60%. For simplicity, for the expected return on the debt, we write i instead of $E(i)$.

$$i = r_f + \beta_D[E(R_m) - r_f]$$
$$= 5\% + 0.80(12\% - 5\%) = 10.60\%$$

The risk premium on the debt is 5.60%.

$$\text{Risk premium} = \beta_D[E(R_m) - r_f]$$
$$= 0.80(12\% - 5\%) = 5.60\%$$

The nominal rate of return on the debt of 10.60% is based on the expected inflation rate of 3%.

Using the Fisher relationship, we calculate the real cost of debt and express the nominal cost of debt in terms of the real cost of debt and the expected inflation rate. Let i_r be the real cost of debt. Then the real cost of debt is 7.38%.

$$i_r = \frac{1+i}{1+g} - 1 = \frac{1+10.60\%}{1+3\%} - 100\% = 7.38\%$$

Based on the real cost of debt, we can rewrite the expression for the nominal cost of debt in terms of the expected inflation rate.

$$i = (1 + i_r)(1 + g) - 1$$
$$= (1 + 7.38\%)(1 + g) - 100\%$$

If the expected inflation rate increases from 3% to 5%, the nominal cost of debt increases from 10.60% to 12.75%.

$$i = (1 + i_r)(1 + g) - 1$$
$$= (1 + 7.38\%)(1 + 5\%) - 100\% = 12.75\%$$

2.4 CALCULATING PV WITH A FINITE STREAM OF CASH FLOWS

Next, we begin our discussion on the TVM with the simplest single period case. When we give up current consumption in exchange for consumption at a future point in time, we expect to receive more at the future point in time than the current consumption that we forego. For example, if an individual has a choice between $100 today and $100 in one year's time, it is reasonable to expect that most people would prefer to have the $100 today rather than wait one year for it. However, we can offer the individual an amount X that is higher than $100 so that the individual would be indifferent about receiving X a year from now and $100 today. Thus, the amount X a year from now is equivalent to $100 today. The required rate of return for the specified period measures how much more we expect.

2.4.1 Future Value with the Nominal Risk-free Rate: Single Period Case

Suppose we agree to give up $100 worth of current consumption to obtain $114 worth of future consumption. To be concrete, we deposit or invest the $100 in a reputable financial institution that guarantees to return us $114 at the end of the year. This implies that the required nominal rate of return is 14% per year. In other words, to give up one unit of current consumption, we expect to receive 14% more consumption at the end of the year. The amount of $114 in one year's time is equivalent to $100 today.

For the moment, we assume that the $114 can be received with full certainty. Because there is no uncertainty about the amount that will be received in a year from now, the required rate of return is the risk-free rate r_f, which is equal to 14%. We write the following relationship.

Future value = Current value times$(1 + r_f) = 100(1 + 14\%) = 114.00$

In general, if we invest K dollars for a year and the annual rate of return is r_f, at the end of the year, the value of the investment is equal to the sum of the original investment of K dollars and the required return on the investment, where the return (in dollar terms) on the investment is equal to the original investment times the required rate of return. Let K_i be the value of the investment at the end of year i.

Future value of original investment = Original value of investment

$$+ \text{required return}$$
$$\text{on investment} \qquad (2.26)$$

In symbols:

$$K_1 = K_0 + r_f K_0 \qquad (2.27)$$

Rearranging equation 2.27, we obtain that at the end of year 1, K_1 the future value of the original investment is equal to the original investment K_0 times one plus the required rate of return r_f.

$$K_1 = K_0(1 + r_f) \qquad (2.28)$$

In other words, the value of the original investment K_0 has increased by the required rate of return.

We can extend the example to two periods. Suppose we invest K dollars for two years (without withdrawing any of the money in the intermediate period) and the annual required rates of return for both years are equal to r_f. Using the previous argument, at the end of year 2, K_2 the future value of the investment made at the end of year 1 is equal to the value of the investment in year 1 times one plus the rate of return r_f.

$$K_2 = K_1(1 + r_f) \qquad (2.29)$$

Substituting equation 2.28 into equation 2.29, we obtain that at the end of year 2, the value of the original investment is equal to the value of the original investment times the sum of one plus the rate of return, raised to the second power.

$$K_2 = K_0(1 + r_f)^2 \qquad (2.30)$$

And in general, if we were to invest K_0 for n years, at the end of the nth year, the value of the original investment would be given by the following expression:

$$K_n = K_0(1 + r_f)^n \qquad (2.31)$$

2.4.2 Time Value of Money

The key point is that the value of a fixed amount of money increases with the passage of time. We are compounding forward the value of the original investment with the required rate of return; in other words, the value of the original investment increases each year by the required rate of return. This is also known as the TVM.

Because cash flows, which occur at different points in time, are different in value, we cannot simply add up the elements of a finite stream of cash flows. They are incomparable and we would be adding apples and oranges. As mentioned earlier, the amount of $114 in one year's time is equivalent to $100 today. To solve this addition problem and make all the cash flows comparable (with respect to a single point in time), we must convert all the cash flows that occur at different points in time to a single point in time by discounting with respect to a common point of reference. With the process of discounting, we convert the cash flows that occur at different points in time to a common reference point and after this conversion we can add up the discounted values. The common point of reference can be any year. For example, it could be year 0, year 3, or year 7. However, the key idea is that all of the cash flows must be discounted to (or compounded to) the common point of reference.

2.4.3 Variable Rates of Return

Previously, for simplicity, we assumed that the rate of return was constant for all the years. Suppose the rate of return in year t is i_t. To be specific, assume that the required rate of return for year 1 is 14% and the required rate of return for year 2 is 15%. If we invest K dollars in year 0 (with no withdrawal of funds in the intermediate period), what would be the future value of the original investment at the end of two years? To find the future value of the original investment, we compound forward by the rate of return for year 1 and then compound forward again by the rate of return for year 2.

$$K_2 = K_0(1 + i_1)(1 + i_2) \qquad (2.32)$$

We can easily extend the compounding idea to n years.

2.4.4 The Discounting Process

Previously, we began with an investment amount and calculated the value of the original investment at future points in time. We can reverse the procedure and ask the following question. For a given amount to be received in a year from now, how much do we have to invest today? Equation 2.28 shows the relationship between K_1 the future value of the original investment and the original investment K_0. Solving for K_0, we obtain that the value of the original investment that is required at the end of year 0 is equal to the future value divided by (or discounted by) one plus the required rate of return i_1.

$$K_0 = \frac{K_1}{(1 + i_1)} \qquad (2.33)$$

The discounting process is the reverse of the previous compounding process. In other words, if a year from now we wish to receive \$114 and the required rate of return is 14%, we must invest \$100 today.

Similarly, suppose we specify a value K_2 that we would like to receive in two years from now. How much would we have to invest today to receive K_2 in two years from now? The answer is the PV of the K_2. For example, suppose in two years we would like to receive \$300 and the annual required rates of return are 14%. Substituting these values into equation 2.32, we obtain

$$300 = K_0(1 + 14\%)^2$$

Solving for K_0, we calculate that we must invest \$230.84 today if we would like to receive \$300 in two years from now.

$$K_0 = \frac{K_2}{(1 + i)^2} = \frac{300}{(1 + 14\%)^2} = 230.84$$

To summarize, at the end of year 0, using a discount rate of 14%, the PV of \$300 (in year 2) is \$230.84.

2.4.5 Variable Discount Rates

If we have variable discount rates over two years, we simply solve for K_0 in equation 2.32.

$$K_0 = \frac{K_2}{[(1 + i_1)(1 + i_2)]} \qquad (2.34)$$

At the end of year 0, using discount rates i_1 and i_2, the PV of K_2 is K_0. The discounting process can be extended easily to multiple periods.

2.4.6 Single and Multi-period Cash Flows

Next we apply the discounting process to find the PV of a finite stream of cash flows. Let CF_1 represent the certain cash flow that occurs at the end of year 1. At the end of year 0, the current or PV of CF_1, the future value that occurs in year 1, is equal to the future value CF_1 divided by one plus the interest rate.

$$V^{CF_1}{}_0 = \frac{CF_1}{1+i} \tag{2.35}$$

In general, with respect to year n, $V^{CF_i}{}_0$ is the PV of a cash flow that occurs in year i. It is important to state clearly the year i in which the cash flow occurs and the reference year n for the discounting.

We extend this example to a stream of cash flow over two periods. Let CF_1 be the certain cash flow in year 1 and let CF_2 be the certain cash flow in year 2. We assume that the risk-free rate of 14% is constant for the two years. Let $V^{CF}{}_0$ be the PV of the cash flows with respect to year 0. At the end of year 0, what is the PV of the stream of cash flows over two years? To find the answer, we have to discount the cash flows in both years to year 0 and add them up.

$$V^{CF}{}_0 = V^{CF_1}{}_0 + V^{CF_2}{}_0 \tag{2.36}$$

We already know how to discount the cash flow that occurs in year 1 to year 0. That is the first term in equation 2.36.

How about the second term? How do we discount the cash flow that occurs in year 2 to year 0? First, we discount the cash flow in year 2 to year 1.

$$V^{CF_2}{}_1 = \frac{CF_2}{1+i} \tag{2.37}$$

Second, we discount the PV in year 1 to year 0.

$$V^{CF_2}{}_0 = \frac{V^{CF_2}{}_1}{1+i} \tag{2.38}$$

Substituting equation 2.37 into equation 2.38, we obtain the PV of the cash flow in year 2 with respect to year 0.

$$V^{CF_2}{}_0 = \frac{CF_2}{(1+i)^2} \tag{2.39}$$

We substitute equations 2.35 and 2.39 into equation 2.36 and obtain

$$V^{CF_2}{}_0 = \frac{CF_1}{(1+i)} + \frac{CF_2}{(1+i)^2} \qquad (2.40)$$

The idea is extended easily to multiple periods. For example, the expression for the PV of a finite stream of cash flows over three periods is shown next.

$$V^{CF}{}_0 = V^{CF_1}{}_0 + V^{CF_2}{}_0 + V^{CF_3}{}_0$$
$$= \frac{CF_1}{1+i} + \frac{CF_2}{(1+i)^2} + \frac{CF_3}{(1+i)^3} \qquad (2.41)$$

Again, the basic idea is simple. We discount the cash flow that occurs in each year back to year 0, which is the reference year, and then add them up to obtain the PV in year 0. For the discounting process, we reiterate that it is important to specify clearly the reference year n.

2.4.7 Assessing an Investment Opportunity with the PV Concept

Next, we use the PV concept to assess an investment opportunity. Consider an investment opportunity that generates expected nominal cash flows of $300 in year 1 and $400 in year 2. How much should an investor pay for the right to this stream of expected cash flows?

Discount rates are always quoted in nominal terms and the financial statements are constructed in nominal terms. Thus, we must discount the nominal cash flows with the nominal discount rates. The nominal discount rates implicitly incorporate the adjustment for the expected inflation rate and the risk premium. For an investment, the investor should have in mind a required real risk-adjusted discount rate and for valuation purposes calculates a nominal risk-adjusted discount rate by taking into account the expected inflation rate. In this book, we assume that the investor has a nominal required rate of return that is based on the expected inflation rate. Based on the nominal required rate of return and the expected inflation rate, we derive a real required rate of return. In the analysis, we model the nominal required rate of return as a function of the real rate of return and the expected inflation rate.

However, the actual practice of investors is more complex. Informal evidence suggests that individuals and investors are more comfortable in thinking in terms of nominal rates of return rather than real rates of return. In other words, the investors can do all the calculations in nominal terms rather than real terms because they are more familiar with nominal rates of return. Moreover, the investor can take account of a whole host of factors in addition to the required rate of return. Nevertheless, for the sake of simplicity, we conduct the analysis as if the investor requires a constant required rate of return in real terms, and the nominal required rate of return takes into account the expected inflation rate.

Taking into account the risk of the cash flows, we assume that the required real rate of return is 8%. The required rate of return of 8% is the opportunity cost of capital. If we did not invest the money in this particular investment opportunity, we could invest the money in a comparable investment opportunity and obtain a real return of 8%.

The expected inflation rate for year 1 is 3% and the expected inflation rate for year 2 is 4%. Let the risk-free rate in year 1 be 5%. Then the real rate of interest in year 1 is 1.94%.

$$r = \frac{1+i}{1+g} - 1 = \frac{1+5\%}{1+3\%} - 1 = 1.94\%$$

If we assume that the real rate of interest remains constant, the risk-free rate in year 2 is 6.02%.

$$r_f = (1+r)(1+g) - 1$$
$$= (1+1.94\%)(1+4\%) - 100\% = 6.02\%$$

In year 1, the required nominal rate of return is 11.24%, and in year 2 the required nominal rate of return is 12.32%.

$$i_1 = (1+r)(1+g_1) - 1$$
$$= (1+8\%)(1+3\%) - 100\% = 11.24\%$$
$$i_2 = (1+r)(1+g_2)$$
$$= (1+8\%)(1+4\%) - 100\% = 12.32\%$$

For completeness, we calculate the risk premiums for the two years and note that the risk premiums are different in the two years. The risk premium in year 1 is 6.24% and the risk premium in year 2 is 6.30%.

Risk premium in year $1 = i_1 - r_{f1} = 11.24\% - 5\% = 6.24\%$
Risk premium in year $2 = i_2 - r_{f2} = 12.32\% - 6.02\% = 6.30\%$

Based on the nominal returns for the two years, we construct the cumulative discount factors. To find the PV of the finite stream of cash flows, we divide the annual expected cash flows by the corresponding cumulative discount factor.

$$V^{CF}_0 = V^{CF_1}_0 + V^{CF_2}_0$$

$$= \frac{CF_1}{1 + i_1} + \frac{CF_2}{(1 + i_1)(1 + i_2)}$$

$$= \frac{300}{1 + 11.24\%} + \frac{400}{(1 + 11.24\%)(1 + 12.32\%)}$$

$$= 269.69 + 320.14 = 589.83$$

We summarize the information in the following table.

TABLE 2.3   Nominal Discount Factors for an Investment Opportunity

Year	0	1	2	3
Expected inflation rate		3%	4%	
Required real return, risk-adjusted		8%	8%	
Required nominal return		11.24%	12.32%	
Nominal discount factors		1.1124	1.1232	
Cumulative discount factors	1.000	1.1124	1.2494	

Based on the cash flows and the expected inflation rates, the PV of the finite stream of cash flows is $589.83.

TABLE 2.4   Present Value of an Investment Opportunity

Year	0	1	2	3
Nominal Cash Flow (NCF)		300.00	400.00	
Discounted Cash Flow (DCF)		269.69	320.14	
PV	589.83			

Let K_0 be the amount of money that is required at the end of year 0 to purchase the right to the finite stream of cash flows. If the value of K_0 were less than $589.83, it would seem sensible to invest the money K_0. If the value of K_0 were more than $589.83, it would not make sense to invest the money. More formally, we calculate the net present value (NPV) as follows:

$$NPV^{CF}_0 = -K_0 + V^{CF_1}_0 + V^{CF_2}_0 \tag{2.42}$$

If the NPV is positive, the investment should be undertaken, and if the NPV is negative, the investment should be rejected. The discount rates for year 1 and 2 are also known as the opportunity costs of capital. They measure the annual returns that we could obtain in alternative investment opportunities. In other words, we should only invest in the current investment opportunity if the returns from the current opportunity are more than an alternative investment opportunity.

SECTION 2

2.5 VALUATION WITH A FINITE STREAM OF CASH FLOWS

In this section, building on the ideas in the previous sections, we present some numerical examples on the application of cost of capital with multi-period cash flows. We strongly encourage the reader to replicate the results of the numerical examples on a spreadsheet program. We realize that we have not presented formally the theory on the cost of capital and the numerical illustrations on the cost of capital can be difficult to follow. However, we believe that the early presentation of the numerical illustrations on the cost of capital before the presentation of the theory in Chapter Seven will make the theory easier to follow.

It is common to apply the formulas that are derived from cash flows in perpetuity to finite cash flows. However, as mentioned earlier, it is not appropriate to use the formulas that are only correct for cash flows in perpetuity. For completeness and easy reference, in the appendix to this chapter, we present detailed numerical examples on cost of capital with cash flows in perpetuity without and with growth.

With debt financing, we must specify two key issues. First, we must specify the assumption about the leverage over the life of the project, and second, we must specify the assumption about the appropriate discount rate for the tax shield (TS), which is the tax savings from the interest deduction with debt financing.

It is common to specify that the leverage is constant for the life of the FCF. In other words, it is assumed that the debt financing is rebalanced to maintain a constant leverage over the life of the FCF. In addition, it is common to assume that the return to unlevered equity is constant. With this assumption and constant leverage, the return to levered equity is constant with respect to the specified leverage and the after-tax Weighted Average Cost of Capital (WACC) that is applied to the FCF which is also constant. Alternatively, we could specify different values for the annual leverage. With variable leverage, the return to levered equity changes as a function of the leverage, and correspondingly, the after-tax WACC adjusts.

In some cases, the loan schedule can be specified and the annual leverage values that are required for calculating the WACC are derived from the annual values of the debt in the loan schedule. We present this case in Chapter Seven.

Here we present two cases for the assumption about the correct discount rate for the TS. First, we assume that the correct discount rate for the TS is the cost of debt d, and the leverage is constant. We apply the formulas that are derived for cash flows in perpetuity to the finite cash flows, and show that at the end of year 0, there is a discrepancy in the PV of the TS obtained with the WACC and the PV of the TS obtained directly.

Second, to properly account for the risk of the TS, we propose to discount the TS with ρ, the return to unlevered equity, rather than d, the cost of debt. For simplicity, we assume constant leverage. In this case, at the end of year 0, there is no discrepancy and the PV of the TS obtained with the WACC matches the PV of the TS obtained directly. In addition, we present a general approach with variable leverage.

2.5.1 Unlevered Values

From years 1 to 5, consider the following FCF that has been derived from an integrated set of financial statements.[5] Recall that the FCF is the operating cash flow (OCF) generated by the firm or project that is available for distribution to the stakeholders, namely the debt holder and the equity holder.

TABLE 2.5 Free Cash Flow (in Nominal Terms)

Year	0	1	2	3	4	5
FCF		5,896	9,956	11,280	14,057	90,000
PV of FCF @ 15.36%	71,929	77,081	78,965	79,814	78,017	

The FCF increases steadily from $5,896 in year 1 to $14,057 in year 4. The value of the FCF in year 5 is much higher because it includes the terminal value (TV). The TV takes account of the cash flows that occur in the years beyond the forecast period. For the moment, we say no more about the TV, which will be discussed in detail in Chapter Nine.

For now we assume all-equity financing with all the cash flow available for distribution, which means that the equity holder receives the full FCF. In addition, we assume that the required (real) return to unlevered equity ρ^R is 12% and constant for the life of the FCF.[6] With an expected inflation rate of

---

[5]We assume that the FCF is always net of tax, unless stated otherwise.

[6]This is a huge assumption. In Chapter Eight, we will discuss in further detail some of the estimation issues. For now, we pull this number out of thin air.

3% per year for the five years, the required nominal return to unlevered equity ρ is 15.36%.

$$\rho = (1 + \rho^R)(1 + g) - 1$$
$$= (1 + 12\%)(1 + 3\%) - 100\% = 15.36\%$$

At the end of year 0, using a discount rate of 15.36%, the PV of the cash flows from years 1 to 5 is $71,929. Let V^{Un}_n represent the PV (with respect to year n) of the FCF, discounted with ρ, the return to unlevered equity. We also call V^{Un}_n the unlevered value with respect to year n. We can calculate the PV of the FCF with respect to any point in time. For example, with respect to the end of year 1, the PV of the FCF from years 2 to 5 is $77,081 and with respect to the end of year 4, the PV of the FCF in year 5 is $78,017.

2.5.2 Debt Financing with Constant Leverage

If we know the required return to unlevered equity, with no debt financing, valuing the FCF is simple. Using the return to unlevered equity, we discount the FCF and find the value with respect to a given point in time. After we introduce debt in the presence of taxes, complications arise. Some of the relevant issues concerning cash flows in perpetuity were discussed in Chapter One. We briefly review the main points with respect to finite cash flows.

First, with debt financing, the FCF is divided between the debt holder and the equity holder. The debt holder receives the cash flow to debt (CFD) and the equity holder receives the CFE. The profile of the CFD over time depends on the debt financing policy. For example, the leverage (or the amount of debt) can be constant or variable.

Second, we need to specify the risk of the debt. With risky debt, the analysis becomes complicated. We conduct the analysis as if the debt is risk-free even though we do not use the risk-free rate r_f for the cost of debt d.[7] We assume that the (real) cost of the (risky) debt d^R is 6% and the nominal cost of debt d incorporates fully the expected inflation rate. With an expected inflation rate of 3% per year for the five years, the nominal cost of debt d is 9.18%.

$$d = (1 + d^R)(1 + g) - 1$$
$$= (1 + 6\%)(1 + 3\%) - 100\% = 9.18\%$$

---

[7] In the calculation of the WACC, we should use the expected return on the debt and not the promised return. Again, for simplicity, we assume that the expected return on the debt is equal to the promised return.

Third, in the presence of the tax rate T equal to 35%, there is the tax advantage from the interest deduction with debt financing. We assume that the risk of the TS is the same as the risk of the debt and therefore the discount rate for the TS is the same as the cost of debt d. Technically, the risk of the TS depends on the earnings before interest and taxes (EBIT). We would like to assume that the TS is risk-free, and therefore the discount rate for the TS should be the risk-free rate. The TS will be risk-free only if it is realized in the year in which the interest expense occurs and there are no losses carried forward (LCF).[8]

However, we also know that the cost of debt is not the risk-free rate and if we set the discount rate for the TS equal to the cost of debt, we are assuming that the TS is not risk-free. Because we do not want to use a discount rate for the TS that is different from the cost of debt, we specify that the discount rate for the TS is equal to the cost of debt, and inconsistently assume that the TS is also risk-free.[9]

Fourth, with debt financing, the discount rate (or WACC) for the FCF is a weighted average of the cost of debt d and the return to levered equity e, where the weights are the market values of debt and (levered) equity as percentages of the total levered values, and the WACC is lowered by the coefficient $(1 - T)$ applied to the cost of debt. Following is the familiar expression for the WACC applied to the FCF.

$$\text{WACC} = d(1 - T)\frac{D}{V^L} + e\frac{E^L}{V^L} \qquad (2.43)$$

This formulation for the WACC assumes that there is no LCF and the TSs are realized in the years in which the interest expenses occur.

Fifth, we must specify a value for the (real) return to levered equity e^R as a function of the debt–equity ratio. From the analysis with cash flow in perpetuity, we have the following expression for the return to levered equity e. The expression for the return to levered equity in equation 2.44 is correct for cash flows in perpetuity but it is inappropriate for finite cash flows.

$$e = \rho + (\rho - r_f)(1 - T)\frac{D}{E^L} \qquad (2.44)$$

For simplicity, to maintain a constant value for the return to levered equity, we assume that the leverage is constant for the life of the FCF and

---

[8]Technically, the sum of the EBIT and other income (OI) must be greater than the interest expense in any given year.

[9]In the context of the M & E formulation for the WACC, the discount rate for the TS might not be equal to the cost of the debt, even if the debt is risk-free.

equal to 30% of the annual levered value. Substituting the appropriate numerical values, we obtain that the annual return to (levered) equity e is 17.082%.

$$e = \rho + (\rho - r_f)(1 - T)\frac{D}{E^L}$$
$$= \frac{15.36\% + (1 - 35\%)(15.36\% - 9.18\%)30\%}{70\%}$$
$$= 17.082\%$$

We now summarize the main assumptions

$g = 3\%$ (constant for the life of the FCF)
$T = 35\%$ (constant for the life of the FCF)
$\%D = 30\%$ (constant for the life of the FCF)
$\rho = 15.36\%$ (constant for the life of the FCF)
$d = r_f = 9.18\%$ (constant for the life of the FCF)
$e = 17.082\%$ (with leverage equal to 40%).

Substituting the appropriate values into the formula for the WACC, we obtain that the WACC applied to the FCF is 13.748%.

$$WACC = d(1 - T)\frac{D}{V^L} + e\frac{E}{V^L}$$
$$= 9.18\%(1 - 35\%)30\% + 17.082\% \times 70\%$$
$$= 13.748\%$$

Using the WACC to discount the FCF, we obtain the annual levered values.

TABLE 2.6   Free Cash Flow (in Nominal Terms) with $\psi = d$

	Year	0	1	2	3	4	5
FCF			5,896	9,956	11,280	14,057	90,000
PV of FCF @ 13.748%		76,205	80,785	81,935	81,918	79,123	

At the end of year 0, using a discount rate of 13.75%, the PV of the cash flows from year 1 to 5 is $76,205. Let V^L_n represent the PV (with respect to year n) of the FCF, discounted with the WACC. We also call V^L_n the levered value with respect to year n. We can calculate the PV of the FCF with respect to any point in time. For example, with respect to the end of year 1, the levered value (the PV of the FCF from years 2 to 5) is $80,785, and with respect to the end of year 4, the levered value is $79,123.

2.5.3 Present Value of Tax Shield

At the end of year 0, the unlevered value V^{Un} is \$71,929, and using the WACC of 13.748%, the levered value V^L is \$76,205. The PV of the TS is the difference between the levered and the unlevered values and is equal to \$4,276.

$$V^{TS}_0 = V^L_0 - V^{Un}_0 = 76,205 - 71,929$$
$$= 4,276.00$$

To check whether the PVs of the TS obtained by using the WACC of 13.748% are correct, we calculate the PVs of the TS directly and compare the two results. Based on the annual levered values and constant leverage θ of 30%, we calculate the annual debt values.

For example, for year 0, the value of the debt is \$22,861.5 and the TS in year 1 is \$734.5.

$$D_0 = \theta V_0 = 30\% \times 76,204.9 = 22,861.47$$
$$TS_0 = TdD_0 = 35\% \times 9.18\% \times \$19,383.5 = 734.50$$

Based on the annual values of the debt, the TSs for all the years are shown next.

TABLE 2.7   The Present Value of the Tax Shields with $\psi = d$

	Year	0	1	2	3	4	5
Levered values		76,204.90	80,785.00	81,934.60	81,918.30	79,122.80	
Value of debt		22,861.50	24,235.50	24,580.40	24,575.50	23,736.80	
TS			734.50	778.70	789.80	789.60	762.70
PV of TS		2,980.20					

Using the cost of debt d to discount the TS, at the end of year 0 the PV of the TS is \$2,980.2, which is much lower than the value of \$4,276 that was obtained earlier.

2.5.4 The Corrected Return to Levered Equity and the WACC

In the previous calculation, we obtained contradictory results for the PV of the TS because we used the wrong formula for the return to levered equity, which we had derived for the cash flows in perpetuity. To obtain consistent results with finite cash flows, we must use the following formula for the return to levered equity.

$$e = \rho + (\rho - r_f)\frac{D}{E^L} \tag{2.45}$$

Note that the factor $(1 - T)$ is not present in the formula for the return to levered equity. In Chapter Seven, we provide justification for the assumption and derive the correct formula for the return to levered equity. Here we simply demonstrate that the formula gives the correct results. First, we assume that the correct discount rate for the TS is the return to unlevered equity ρ rather than the cost of debt d. In other words, we are assuming that the risk of the TS is the same as the risk of the FCF rather than the risk of the debt that generates the TS. Second, with this assumption about the discount rate for the TS, the correct formula for the return to levered equity is as shown in equation 2.45.

Substituting the appropriate numerical values, we obtain that the annual return to (levered) equity e is 18.009%, which is higher than the previous value of 17.082%.

$$e = \rho + (\rho - r_f)\frac{D}{E^L}$$
$$= 15.36\% + (15.36\% - 9.18\%)\frac{30\%}{70\%}$$
$$= 18.009\%$$

Substituting the appropriate values into the formula for the WACC, we obtain that the WACC applied to the FCF is 14.396%.

$$WACC = d(1 - T)\frac{D}{V^L} + e\frac{E}{V^L}$$
$$= 30\% \times 9.18\% \times (1 - 35\%) + 70\% \times 18.009\%$$
$$= 14.396\%$$

Using the new WACC to discount the FCF, we obtain the annual levered values.

TABLE 2.8   Free Cash Flow (in Nominal Terms) with $\psi = \rho$

	Year	0	1	2	3	4	5
FCF			5,896	9,956	11,280	14,057	90,000
PV of FCF @ 14.396%		74,444	79,266	80,721	81,061	78,674	

At the end of year 0, the unlevered value V^{Un}_0 is $71,929, and using the new WACC of 14.396%, the levered value V^L_0 is $74,444. The PV of the TS is the difference between the levered and the unlevered values and is equal to $2,515.

$$V^{TS}_0 = V^L_0 - V^{Un}_0 = 74,444 - 71,929$$
$$= 2,515.00$$

To check whether the PVs of the TS obtained by using the new WACC of 14.396% are correct, we calculate the PVs of the TS directly and compare the two results.

Based on the levered values with the new WACC, the TS for all the years are shown next.

TABLE 2.9   The Present Value of the Tax Shields with $\psi = \rho$

Year	0	1	2	3	4	5
Levered values	74,444.50	79,265.60	80,720.70	81,061.30	78,674.00	
Value of debt	22,333.30	23,779.70	24,216.20	24,318.40	23,602.20	
TS		717.60	764.00	778.10	781.40	758.30
PV of TS	2,5150.00					

And as expected, using the return to unlevered equity ρ to discount the TS at the end of year 0, the PV of the TS is $2,515, which matches the earlier value that was obtained with the WACC.

This simple numerical example illustrates the following key points. First, the well-known formulas for cash flows in perpetuity do not apply to finite cash flows. Second, the formula for the return to levered equity depends on the discount rate for the TS. Third, the formula for the return to levered equity that is used in the calculation of the WACC must be consistent with the assumption that is made about the discount rate for the TS.

2.5.5 Alternative Formulation for the WACC with Circularity

Next, we present another formulation of the WACC, which is more flexible because it can accommodate LCF. With this WACC, the adjustment for the TS in the WACC is only made for the year in which the TS is realized. In the previous analysis, we assumed that the leverage was constant for the life of the cash flow. However, in practice, the leverage might be variable. We assume that in year 1, the leverage is 30% and thereafter, each year, the leverage increases by 2 percentage points. We caution the reader that it might be difficult to model a specified leverage profile over the life of the cash flow with market values if the model is sufficiently complex.

TABLE 2.10   Variable Leverage

Year	0	1	2	3	4	5
Annual leverage		30%	32%	34%	36%	38%

Retaining the assumption that the appropriate discount rate for the TS ψ is the return to unlevered equity ρ, the formulation of the WACC is as follows:

$$\text{WACC} = w = \rho - \frac{\text{TS}}{\text{V}^{\text{L}}} \qquad (2.46)$$

With this formulation, there is the potential for circularity. Technically speaking, if the FCF is given and the annual leverages are known in advance, there is no circularity in the use of the WACC applied to the FCF. However, if we derive the FCF from a set of integrated financial statements, then there is circularity. To illustrate the implementation of the circularity with the WACC applied to the FCF, we assume that we have derived the FCF from a set of integrated financial statements. We will briefly explain a general procedure for setting up the circularity in the spreadsheet.[10] This procedure can be useful in other contexts. Here we are simply alerting the reader to the issue of circularity. For more technical details on the circularity issue, see Vélez-Pareja and Tham (2000).

First enter some trial values for the WACC. For example, we have entered the trial value of 14% for the annual WACCs. In the last step, after entering the formulas for all the other cells, we enter the formulas for the WACCs, which introduces the circularity.[11] Second, enter the formulas to calculate the levered values, which are incorrect because the correct formulas for the WACCs have not been entered. We obtain the correct levered values after we enter the formulas for the WACCs in the final step.

To use equation 2.46, we must estimate the TS as a percentage of the levered value. To calculate the TS, we need to calculate the annual values for the debt and the interest expense. In any year, the value of the debt is equal to the leverage times the levered value. The annual TS is equal to the annual interest expense (based on the debt at the beginning of the year) times the tax rate. Next, calculate the TS and calculate the TS as a percent of the levered values (at the beginning of the year). Finally, enter the formula in equation 2.46 into the cells for the WACCs.

---

[10]In Vélez-Pareja and Tham (2000), we explain how to handle the circularity in an Excel spreadsheet. Under Options in the Tool menu, select Options, select Calculate, and check the Iteration box.

[11]Rather than using the NPV formula in Excel to calculate the PV, we suggest the following alternative method for calculating the PV. This alternative method is particularly useful with variable WACCs. Start with the PV at the end of year 4, which is equal to the sum of the FCF in year 5 and the PV in year 5, discounted one period by the WACC in year 5. In this instance, the PV in year 5 is zero (a blank cell). Copy this formula to year 0 to obtain the correct formulas for the annual PVs. See Vélez-Pareja and Tham (2000), for an example.

TABLE 2.11a WACC with Circularity, with Trial Values for the WACC

	Year	0	1	2	3	4	5
FCF			5,896	9,956	11,280	14,057	90,000
WACC			14%	14%	14%	14%	14%
Levered values		75,512	80,188	81,459	81,583	78,947	
Debt		22,654	25,660	27,696	29,370	30,000	
TS			727.90	824.50	889.90	943.70	963.90
TS (% of Levered values)			0.964%	1.028%	1.092%	1.157%	1.221%

If the correct steps have been followed, the reader should obtain the following results.

TABLE 2.11b Weighted Average Cost of Capital with Circularity

	Year	0	1	2	3	4	5
FCF			5,896	9,956	11,280	14,057	90,000
WACC			14.40%	14.33%	14.27%	14.20%	14.14%
Levered values		74,748	79,613	81,067	81,353	78,851	
Debt		22,424	25,476	27,563	29,287	29,963	
TS			720.50	818.50	885.60	941.00	962.70
TS (% of Levered values)			0.964%	1.028%	1.092%	1.157%	1.221%

With increasing leverage, the WACC decreases from 14.40% in year 1 to 14.14% in year 5. In year 3, the leverage is 34% and the value of the debt at the beginning of year 3 is $27,563.

$$\text{Debt} = \text{Leverage times Levered value}$$
$$= 34\% \times 81,067 = 27,563$$

Based on the value of the debt at the beginning of year 3, the TS in year 3 is $885.6.

$$\text{TS} = \text{Tax rate times Interest expense}$$
$$= 35\% \times 9.18\% \times 27,563 = 885.60$$

The TS in year 3 as a percent of the levered value at the beginning of the year is 1.092% and the WACC for year 3 is 14.27%.

$$\text{WACC} = w = \rho - \frac{TS}{V^L} = 15.36\% - 1.092\% = 14.27\%$$

2.5.6 After-tax WACC Applied to the FCF

We also show how we can use the after-tax WACC applied to the FCF with variable leverage. We use the values for the debt shown in Table 2.11b. Again, we enter the trial value of 14% for the annual WACCs. Using the trial values for the WACC, we calculate the annual levered values.

TABLE 2.12a   WACC with Circularity, with Trial Values for the WACC

Year	0	1	2	3	4	5
FCF		5,896	9,956	11,280	14,057	90,000
WACC		14.00%	14.00%	14.00%	14.00%	14.00%
Levered values	75,512	80,188	81,459	81,583	78,947	
Return to levered equity		17.97%	18.24%	18.52%	18.82%	19.14%

Next, we enter the formula for the return to levered equity, and lastly, we enter the formula for the WACCs, which induces the circularity. The correct values are shown in Table 2.12b.

TABLE 2.12b   Weighted Average Cost of Capital with Circularity

Year	0	1	2	3	4	5
FCF		5,896	9,956	11,280	14,057	90,000
WACC		14.40%	14.33%	14.27%	14.20%	14.14%
Levered values	74,748	79,613	81,067	81,353	78,851	
Return to levered equity		18.01%	18.27%	18.54%	18.84%	19.15%

We verify that the return to levered equity in year 3 is 18.54% and the WACC in year 3 is 14.27%.

$$e = \rho + (\rho - r_f)\frac{D}{E^L}$$
$$= 15.36\% + \frac{(15.36\% - 9.18\%)34\%}{66\%}$$
$$= 18.54\%$$

$$WACC = d(1-T)\frac{D}{V^L} + e\frac{E}{V^L}$$
$$= 34\% \times 9.18\%(1-35\%) + 66\% \times 18.54\%$$
$$= 14.27\%$$

As expected, with increasing leverage the return to levered equity increases from 18.01% in year 1 to 19.15% in year 5. Also, the levered values in Table 2.12b match the levered values in Table 2.11b.

2.6 SUMMARY AND CONCLUDING REMARKS

In this chapter, we presented the time value of money with discounting and compounding and examined the relationships between nominal prices, real prices, nominal interest rates, and real interest rates. Also, we discussed risk-free discount rates and risk-adjusted discount rates. To avoid potential confusion and mistakes in cash flow valuation, it is extremely important to be clear about the distinction between real and nominal prices.

Next, using finite cash flows, we calculated the weighted average cost of capital and showed that the formulas that are derived from cash flows in perpetuity are inappropriate for finite cash flows. We presented detailed numerical examples for the standard WACC applied to the FCF and the adjusted WACC applied to the FCF.

KEY CONCEPTS AND IDEAS

Adjusted WACC

After-tax WACC

Capital Cash Flow (CCF)

Cash flows in perpetuity

Cash flow to debt (CFD)

Cash flow to equity (CFE)

Circularity

Compounding process

Constant leverage

Constant price

Consumer Price Index (CPI)

Debt–equity ratio

Debt holder

Discounting process

Equity holder

Expected inflation rate

Finite cash flows

Fisher equation

Free Cash Flow (FCF)

Leverage

Levered value

Modigliani and Miller (M & M)

Nominal interest rate

Nominal price

Present value (PV)

Real interest rate

Real price

Return to levered equity

Return to unlevered equity

Risk premium

Risk-adjusted discount rates

Risk-free discount rates

Tax savings (TS) or Tax shield (TS)

Tax rate

Time value of money (TVM)

Variable leverage

Weighted Average Cost of Capital (WACC)

APPENDIX A

A2.I CALCULATING THE PV WITH CASH FLOW IN PERPETUITY (WITHOUT GROWTH)

In this appendix, we present the formulas for the cost of capital for cash flows in perpetuity, without and with growth. We assume that most readers are familiar with the formulas for the cost of capital in the context of cash flows in perpetuity and this appendix will simply be a review to refresh ideas. Some readers might not be familiar with the algebra, and for the benefit of those readers we have presented the detailed derivations for the return to levered equity and the various formulations of the WACC. The algebra for cash flows in perpetuity is relatively simple. An understanding of the algebra gives the readers a better appreciation for the theory on the cost of capital.

First we begin without taxes and then we introduce taxes. Let CF_i be the cash flow that occurs in year i and let r be the appropriate nominal (risk-adjusted) discount rate. The formula for calculating the PV of the annual cash flow in perpetuity (without growth) is simple. The PV of the perpetuity is the annual cash flow divided by the risk-adjusted discount rate r.

$$V^{CF}_0 = \frac{CF_i}{r} \qquad (A2.1)$$

Next, we illustrate the use of perpetuities with some examples related to the cost of capital.

A2.I.I WACC in an M & M World Without Taxes

As mentioned in Chapter One, in an M & M world without taxes, the debt financing does not change the value of the annual FCF. With debt financing, the annual FCF is shared between the debt holder and the equity holder. Next, we list and review the key relationships for the cash flows and the PVs of the cash flows. First, the FCF is equal to the sum of the CFE and the CFD.

$$FCF = CFE + CFD \qquad (A2.2)$$

Without taxes, the unlevered value is equal to the levered value.

$$V^{Un} = V^{L} \tag{A2.3}$$

In turn, the levered value is equal to the sum of the value of the (levered) equity and the value of the debt.

$$V^{L} = E^{L} + D \tag{A2.4}$$

Combining equations A2.3 and A2.4, we obtain that the unlevered value is equal to the sum of the value of the (levered) equity and the value of the debt.

$$V^{Un} = E^{L} + D \tag{A2.5}$$

A2.1.2 Unlevered Value

In an M & M world without taxes, consider an unlevered (all-equity) company that generates a stream of annual FCF in perpetuity without growth. Let the required annual return to the (unlevered) equity holder be ρ. This is the nominal risk-adjusted discount rate. Unless specified otherwise, all returns are assumed to be nominal risk-adjusted returns.

With a FCF in perpetuity, it is easy to calculate the value of the unlevered company.[12] The PV of the FCF in perpetuity without growth is equal to the annual FCF divided by the return ρ.

$$V^{Un} = \frac{FCF}{\rho} \tag{A2.6}$$

For example, if the annual FCF in perpetuity is $120 and the return to unlevered equity is 10%, the PV of the FCF is $1,200.

$$V^{Un} = \frac{FCF}{\rho} = \frac{120}{10\%} = 1,200.00$$

In other words, the market value of the unlevered company is $1,200.

---

[12]To generate the FCF in perpetuity, typically we assume that the annual reinvestment is equal to the annual depreciation. With this assumption, the annual net income (NI) is equal to the FCF.

A2.I.3 Value of the Cash Flow to Debt

Suppose the company is partially financed with risk-free debt. Clearly, it is unrealistic to assume that the debt is risk-free. For simplicity, it is common to assume that the debt is risk-free even though it might not be actually risk-free.[13] Because we have assumed that the debt is risk-free, the cost of the debt d is equal to the nominal risk-free rate r_f, which is assumed to be 6%.

Assume that the debt holder receives 25% of the FCF and the equity holder receives the remaining 75% of the FCF. Then the annual cash flow to the debt holder in perpetuity is $30.

$$CFD = 25\% \times FCF = 25\% \times 120 = 30.00$$

At the end of year 0, the PV of the CFD in perpetuity is equal to the CFD divided by the cost of debt d. The annual CFD is the interest payments on the loan and there is no principal repayment.

$$D = \frac{CFD}{d} \qquad (A2.7)$$

The PV of the debt is $500.00.[14]

$$D = \frac{CFD}{d} = \frac{30}{6\%} = 500.00$$

A2.I.4 Value of the Cash Flow to Equity

We know that the CFE is 75% of the FCF. In other words, the annual CFE is $90 in perpetuity.

$$CFE = 75\% \times FCF = 75\% \times 120 = 90.00$$

What is the value of the levered equity? Let the nominal return to (levered) equity be e. The PV of the annual CFE in perpetuity is equal to the annual CFE divided by the return to levered equity e.

$$E^L = \frac{CFE}{e} \qquad (A2.8)$$

---

[13]If the debt is risk-free, the promised return on the debt is equal to the expected return on the debt.

[14]25% of the FCF does not mean that the debt holder receives 25% of the value of the FCF.

We do not know the return to levered equity e but we do know the annual CFE and the value of the levered equity. The value of the (levered) equity is equal to $700, which is the difference between the levered value and the value of the debt.

$$E^L = V^{Un} - D = 1{,}200 - 500 = 700.00$$

Based on the value of the (levered) equity, we can calculate the return to (levered) equity by rewriting equation A2.8.

Solving for e, we obtain that the (nominal) return to levered equity is 12.857%.

$$e = \frac{CFE}{E^L} = \frac{90}{700} = 12.857\%$$

A2.1.5 Formula for the Return to Levered Equity e

Using simple algebra, we derive the formula for the return to levered equity e. We know that the sum of the FCF is equal to the sum of the CFE and the CFD.

$$FCF = CFE + CFD \qquad (A2.9)$$

Substituting equation A2.6 on the LHS of equation A2.9, and substituting equations A2.7 and A2.8 on the right hand-side (RHS) of equation A2.9, we obtain

$$\rho V^{Un} = eE^L + dD \qquad (A2.10)$$

Rearranging equation A2.10, we obtain

$$eE^L = \rho V^{Un} - dD \qquad (A2.11)$$

Substituting the expression for the unlevered value on the RHS and rearranging, we obtain

$$eE^L = \rho(E^L + D) - dD \qquad (A2.12)$$

$$= \rho E^L + (\rho - d)D \qquad (A2.13)$$

Solving for e, we obtain

$$e = \rho + (\rho - d)\frac{D}{E^L} \tag{A2.14}$$

The values of ρ and d are constant. The return to levered equity e is a positive linear function of the debt–equity ratio. The higher the debt–equity ratio, the higher is the return to levered equity e.

Substituting the appropriate values for the parameters, we use the formula to verify that the return to levered equity is 12.857%.

$$e = \rho + (\rho - d)\frac{D}{E^L}$$
$$= 10\% + (10\% - 6\%)\frac{500}{700}$$
$$= 12.857\%$$

A2.1.6 Deriving the Weighted Average Cost of Capital Without Taxes

Next, we derive the formula for the WACC in an M & M world without taxes. We know that in an M & M world without taxes, the levered value is equal to the sum of the CFE and the CFD divided by the WACC w.

$$V^L = \frac{CFE + CFD}{w} \tag{A2.15}$$

Rewriting equation A2.15, we obtain

$$wV^L = CFE + CFD \tag{A2.16}$$

On the RHS of equation A2.16, we substitute equations A2.7 and A2.8.

$$wV^L = eE^L + dD \tag{A2.17}$$

Solving for the WACC, we obtain

$$w = \frac{D}{V^L}d + \frac{E}{V^L}e \tag{A2.18}$$

Let %D be the market value of debt as a percent of the levered market value and let %E be the market value of the levered equity as a percent of the levered market value.

$$w = \%Dd + \%Ee \tag{A2.19}$$

As expected, the WACC is a weighted average of the cost of the two sources of financing, where the weights are the market values of the debt and equity as percentages of the levered market value.

A2.l.7 Numerical Example

In an M & M world without taxes, the WACC is equal to the return to unlevered equity ρ. We can easily see this by comparing equations A2.6 and A2.15. Next, we verify that the WACC is equal to the return to unlevered equity ρ.

The debt as a percent of the total levered value is 41.667% and the equity as a percent of the total levered value is 58.333%.

$$\%D = \frac{D}{V^L} = \frac{500}{1,200} = 41.667\%$$

$$\%E = \frac{EL}{V^L} = \frac{700}{1,200} = 58.333\%$$

$$w = \%Dd + \%Ee$$

$$= 41.667\% \times 6\% + 58.333\% \times 12.857\%$$

$$= 2.500\% + 7.500\% = 10.000\%$$

The WACC is 10%, which is the same value as the return to unlevered equity ρ.

A2.2 WACC IN AN M & M WORLD WITH TAXES

Next we discuss the WACC in an M & M world with taxes. The familiarity with the M & M world without taxes will facilitate the analysis with taxes. As introduced informally in Chapter One, consider an M & M world with only corporate taxes. In the presence of taxes, there is a stream of annual TSs in perpetuity that is generated by the annual interest deductions with debt financing. Next, we list and review the key relationships for the cash flows and the PVs of the cash flows.

The total cash flow that is available for distribution between the debt holder and the equity holder is known as the CCF and is equal to the sum of the CFE and the CFD.

$$CCF = CFE + CFD \qquad (A2.20)$$

The CCF is also equal to the sum of the FCF and the TS.

$$CCF = FCF + TS \qquad (A2.21)$$

Combining equations A2.20 and A2.21, we obtain that the sum of the FCF and the TS is equal to the sum of the CFE and the CFD.

$$FCF + TS = CFE + CFD \qquad (A2.22)$$

In an M & M world with taxes, the levered value is equal to the sum of the unlevered value and the PV of the TS.

$$V^L = V^{Un} + V^{TS} \qquad (A2.23)$$

And in turn, the levered value is equal to the sum of the value of the (levered) equity and the value of the debt.

$$V^L = E^L + D \qquad (A2.24)$$

Combining equations A2.23 and A2.24, we obtain that the sum of the unlevered value and the PV of the TS is equal to the sum of the value of the (levered) equity and the value of the debt.

$$V^{Un} + V^{TS} = E^L + D \qquad (A2.25)$$

A2.2.1 Annual Tax Shield

The annual TS is equal to the tax rate T times the annual interest payment, where the interest payment is equal to the CFD. See equation A2.7. Because the debt is risk-free, the cost of debt d is equal to the risk-free rate r_f.

$$
\begin{aligned}
TS &= T \text{ times Interest payment} \\
&= T \times CFD \\
&= TdD = Tr_fD \qquad (A2.26)
\end{aligned}
$$

Let the tax rate T be 40%. The annual TS in perpetuity is \$12.00.

$$
\begin{aligned}
TS &= Tr_fD \\
&= 40\% \times 6\% \times 500 = 12.00
\end{aligned}
$$

A2.2.2 Capital Cash Flow

The annual CCF is equal to the sum of the annual FCF and the annual TS. The annual CCF in perpetuity is \$132.00.

$$CCF = FCF + TS$$
$$= 120 + 12.00 = 132.00$$

A2.2.3 Present Value of the Annual Tax Shield

The PV of the annual TS in perpetuity is equal to the annual TS divided by ψ, the appropriate discount rate for the TS.

$$V^{TS} = \frac{TdD}{\psi} \qquad\qquad (A2.27)$$

In each period, we assume with full certainty that the annual EBIT is sufficient for the annual TS to be realized in perpetuity. The stream of TS that is generated from the annual interest deduction with debt financing is risk-free because the annual TS is known with full certainty.[15] Because the TS is risk-free, the appropriate discount rate for the TS ψ is equal to the risk-free rate r_f. The contribution of the TS to the levered value is \$170.

$$V^{TS} = \frac{TdD}{\psi} = \frac{Tr_f D}{r_f}$$
$$= T \times D = 40\% \times 500 = 200.00$$

A2.2.4 The Levered Value V^L in the Presence of Corporate Tax

In the presence of corporate tax, the value of the levered firm V^L is equal to the sum of the value of the unlevered firm V^{Un} and the PV of the TS V^{TS}.

$$V^L = V^{Un} + V^{TS}$$
$$= V^{Un} + TD = 1,200 + 200 = 1,400.00$$

With debt financing, the levered value is \$1,400.

[15]In general, the appropriate discount rate for the TS is a complex issue that we will discuss later. Alternatively, with a finite stream of cash flows, we could have assumed that the appropriate discount rate for the TS ψ is equal to the return to unlevered equity ρ.

A2.3.1 Value of Levered Equity

The value of the levered equity is equal to the levered value less the value of the debt, which is \$900.

$$E^L = V^{Un} + V^{TS} - D$$
$$= 1{,}200 + 200 - 500 = 900.00$$

A2.3.2 Cash Flow to Equity

The annual CFE in perpetuity is equal to the annual CCF less the annual CFD.

$$CFE = CCF - CFD$$
$$= FCF + TS - CFD$$
$$= 120 + 12.00 - 30 = 102.00$$

A2.3.3 Return to Levered Equity with Taxes

Because we know the value of the (levered) equity and the annual CFE in perpetuity, we can calculate the return to (levered) equity. The annual return to levered equity e is 11.517%.

$$e = \frac{CFE}{E^L} = \frac{102.00}{900} = 11.333\%$$

A2.3.4 Formula for the Return to Levered Equity

Using simple algebra, in the presence of taxes, we derive the expression for the return to levered equity e. We know that

$$FCF + TS = CFD + CFE \qquad (A2.28)$$

Substituting the values in place of the cash flows, we obtain

$$\rho V^L + \psi V^{TS} = dD + eE^L \qquad (A2.29)$$

Rearranging equation A2.29, we obtain

$$eE^L = \rho V^L + \psi V^{TS} - dD \qquad (A2.30)$$

We make no assumption regarding the appropriate discount rate for the TS. Substitute the expression for the levered value on the RHS of equation A2.30 and simplify.

$$eE^L = \rho(E^L + D - V^{TS}) + \psi V^{TS} - dD$$

$$= \rho E^L + (\rho - d)D - (\rho - \psi)V^{TS} \qquad (A2.31)$$

Solving for the return to levered equity e, we obtain

$$e = \rho + (\rho - r_f)\frac{D}{E^L} - (\rho - \psi)\frac{V^{TS}}{E^L}e \qquad (A2.32)$$

Substitute the expression for the PV of the TS on the RHS.

$$e = \rho + (\rho - r_f)\frac{D}{E^L} - (\rho - \psi)\frac{\frac{TdD}{\psi}}{E^L} \qquad (A2.33)$$

When we specify the value of ψ, we can simplify equation A2.33.

For the FCF in perpetuity, we assume that the value of ψ and the cost of debt d are equal to the risk-free rate r_f, and obtain the well-known equation for the return to levered equity with the multiplicative coefficient $(1 - T)$.

$$e = \rho + (\rho - r_f)\frac{D}{E^L} - (\rho - \psi)\frac{\frac{T r_f D}{r_f}}{E^L}$$

$$= \rho + (\rho - r_f)(1 - T)\frac{D}{E^L} \qquad (A2.34)$$

Substituting the appropriate numerical values, we obtain that the annual return to (levered) equity is 11.333%.

$$e = \rho + (\rho - r_f)(1 - T)\frac{D}{E^L}$$

$$= 10\% + (10\% - 6\%)(1 - 40\%)\frac{500}{900} = 11.333\%$$

The return to levered equity e is a positive linear function of the debt–equity ratio. The higher the debt–equity ratio, the higher is the return to levered equity e.

A2.4.1 Traditional After-Tax WACC with the FCF

The traditional after-tax WACC, applied to the FCF, is shown in the following equation.

$$w = d(1 - T)\frac{D}{V^L} + e\frac{E}{V^L} \tag{A2.35}$$

The traditional after-tax WACC is a weighted average of the cost of debt d and the return to (levered) equity e where the weights are the market values of debt and (levered) equity as percentages of the total market (levered) value.

The contribution of the TS to the levered value is taken into account by lowering the WACC with the coefficient $(1 - T)$ for the cost of debt d.

We derive the traditional after-tax WACC as follows. We know that the levered value is equal to the FCF divided by the WACC.

$$V^L = \frac{FCF}{w} \tag{A2.36}$$

Rearranging equation A2.36, we obtain

$$wV^L = FCF \tag{A2.37}$$

Substituting the expression for the FCF on the RHS of equation A2.37, we obtain

$$wV^L = CFE + CFD - TS \tag{A2.38}$$

For each of the terms on the RHS of equation A2.38, we substitute the appropriate value formulas, and solve for the WACC.

$$wV^L = eE^L + dD - \psi V^{TS} \tag{A2.39}$$

Solving for the WACC, we obtain

$$w = d\frac{D}{V^L} + e\frac{E}{V^L} - \psi\frac{V^{TS}}{V^L} \tag{A2.40}$$

In this case, the value of ψ and the cost of the debt are equal to the risk-free rate r_f. Therefore, the term ψV^{TS} is equal to the tax rate T times the value of the debt D times the cost of the debt, in this case r_f.

$$w = d\frac{D}{V^L} + e\frac{E}{V^L} - \psi\frac{V^{TS}}{V^L}$$

$$= r_f(1-T)\frac{D}{V^L} + e\frac{E}{V^L} \qquad (A2.41)$$

Next we calculate the value of the traditional after-tax WACC by substituting the appropriate numerical values. The debt as a percent of the total levered value is 41.667% and the equity as a percent of the total levered value is 58.333%. The after-tax WACC is 8.571%.

$$w = r_f(1-T)\frac{D}{V^L} + e\frac{E}{V^L}$$

$$= 6\%(1-40\%)\frac{500}{1,400} + 11.333\%\frac{900}{1,400}$$

$$= 35.714\% \times 6\% \times (1-40\%) + 64.286\% \times 11.333\%$$

$$= 1.286\% + 7.286\% = 8.571\%$$

A2.4.2 Alternative Expression for the WACC with the FCF

We also show an alternative expression for the WACC with the FCF. We know that

$$FCF = wV^L \qquad (A2.42a)$$

and

$$FCF = \rho V^{Un} \qquad (A2.42b)$$

Combining equations A2.42a and b, we obtain

$$wV^L = \rho V^{Un} \qquad (A2.43)$$

$$= \rho(V^L - V^{TS}) \qquad (A2.44)$$

$$= \rho\left[V^L - \frac{TS}{\psi}\right] \qquad (A2.45)$$

Here we assume that the discount rate for the TS ψ is equal to the cost of debt d. Then we can rewrite equation A2.45 as follows:

$$w = \rho\left(1 - \frac{TD}{V^L}\right) \tag{A2.46}$$

Substituting the relevant numerical values, we obtain that the WACC is 8.571% and it matches the value that was obtained previously.

$$w = 10\%\left(1 - \frac{40\% \times 500}{1,400}\right) = 8.571\% $$

A2.4.3 Weighted Average Cost of Capital with the Capital Cash Flow

We define an alternative WACC that is applied to the CCF. The levered value is equal to the sum of the FCF and the TS divided by the WACC.

$$V^L = \frac{CCF}{w} \tag{A2.47}$$

We know that

$$CCF = CFD + CFE \tag{A2.48}$$

Substituting the values in place of the cash flows, we obtain

$$wV^L = dD + eE^L \tag{A2.49}$$

$$w = d\frac{D}{V^L} + e\frac{E}{V^L} \tag{A2.50}$$

Substituting the numerical values, we obtain that the WACC applied to the CCF is 9.4286%.

$$
\begin{aligned}
w &= \%Dd + \%Ee \\
&= 35.7143\% \times 6\% + 64.2857\% \times 11.333\% \\
&= 2.1429\% + 7.285\% = 9.4286\%
\end{aligned}
$$

We verify that the WACC of 9.4286% applied to the CCF gives the correct levered value.

$$V^L = \frac{CCF}{w} = \frac{132.00}{9.4286\%} = 1{,}400.0$$

A2.4.4 Another WACC Formulation with the CCF

We know that

$$CCF = FCF + TS \tag{A2.51}$$

Substituting the values in place of the cash flows, we obtain

$$wV^L = \rho V^{Un} + \psi V^{TS} \tag{A2.52}$$

Substitute the expression for the unlevered value into equation A2.75.

$$wV^L = \rho(V^L - V^{TS}) + \psi V^{TS} \tag{A2.53}$$

Simplifying and rearranging, we obtain

$$wV^L = \rho V^L + (\psi - \rho)V^{TS} \tag{A2.54}$$

Solve for the WACC.

$$w = \rho + (\psi - \rho)\frac{V^{TS}}{V^L} \tag{A2.55}$$

The formula for the WACC is a function of ψ the discount rate for the TS. If the discount rate for the TS is equal to the return to unlevered equity ρ, the next term on the RHS of equation A2.55 is zero and the WACC is simply equal to the unlevered return ρ.

Here we have assumed that the value of ψ is equal to the cost of debt d.

$$w = \rho + (d - \rho)\frac{V^{TS}}{V^L} \tag{A2.56}$$

Substituting the numerical values, we verify that the value of the WACC with the alternative formulation matches the previous value.

$$w = \rho + (d - \rho)\frac{V^{TS}}{V^L}$$

$$= 10\% + (6\% - 10\%)\frac{200}{1,400} = 9.4286\%$$

In the following two tables, we summarize the previous formulas for the WACC applied to the FCF and CCF.

TABLE A2.1   Matrix for the WACC Applied to the FCF

	Risk of the TS	WACC formula	Return to levered equity
Weighted average	$\psi = d = r_f$	$d(1-T)\frac{D}{V^L} + e\frac{E}{V^L}$	$\rho + (\rho - d)(1-T)\frac{D}{E^L}$
Weighted average	$\psi = \rho$	$d(1-T)\frac{D}{V^L} + e\frac{E}{V^L}$	$\rho + (\rho - d)\frac{D}{E^L}$
Adjusted value	$\psi = d = r_f$	$\rho\left(1 - \frac{TD}{V^L}\right)$	$\rho + (\rho - d)(1-T)\frac{D}{E^L}$
Adjusted value	$\psi = \rho$	$\rho - \frac{TdD}{V^L}$	$\rho + (\rho - d)\frac{D}{E^L}$

TABLE A2.2   Matrix for the WACC Applied to the CCF

	Risk of the TS	WACC formula	Return to levered equity
Weighted average	$\psi = d = r_f$	$d\frac{D}{V^L} + e\frac{E}{V^L}$	$\rho + (\rho - d)(1-T)\frac{D}{E^L}$
Weighted average	$\psi = \rho$	$d\frac{D}{V^L} + e\frac{E}{V^L}$	$\rho + (\rho - d)\frac{D}{E^L}$
Adjusted value	$\psi = d = r_f$	$\rho + (d - \rho)\frac{V^{TS}}{V^L}$	$\rho + (\rho - d)(1-T)\frac{D}{E^L}$
Adjusted value	$\psi = \rho$	ρ	$\rho + (\rho - d)\frac{D}{E^L}$

A2.5   FREE CASH FLOW IN PERPETUITY WITH GROWTH

In the previous section, we assumed that the growth rate g for the FCF was zero. In the following section, we derive the appropriate formulas for FCF with non-zero growth and illustrate the ideas with a simple numerical example.

Let the annual FCF in perpetuity grow at the rate of g. We know that the FCF is equal to the sum of the CFE and the CFD less the TS. For simplicity, we assume that all of the components of the FCF also increase at the growth rate g.

$$FCF = CFE + CFD - TS \qquad (A2.57)$$

To sustain the growth rate g, a fraction h of the FCF will be reinvested in perpetuity. Moreover, the unlevered value should be a positive function of the growth rate g. Here, for simplicity, we have not modeled the FCF as a function of the growth rate g.

In terms of value, we know that the sum of the unlevered value and the PV of the TS is equal to the sum of the levered equity and the value of the debt.

$$V^{Un} + V^{TS} = E^{L} + D \qquad (A2.58)$$

A2.5.I Unlevered Value

Because the annual FCF is growing in perpetuity at the rate g, the PV of the FCF V^{Un} is equal to the FCF divided by ρ minus the growth rate g, where ρ is the required rate of return for unlevered equity.

$$V^{Un} = \frac{FCF}{\rho - g} \qquad (A2.59)$$

Rearranging equation A2.59, we obtain

$$V^{Un}(\rho - g) = FCF \qquad (A2.60)$$

For example, if the annual FCF in perpetuity is \$100, the return to unlevered equity is 12%, the growth rate is 2%, and the PV of the FCF is \$1,000.

$$V^{Un} = \frac{FCF}{\rho - g} = \frac{100}{12\% - 2\%} = 1,000.00$$

A2.5.2 Value of the Debt

Assume that the debt is risk-free. Because the CFD is growing in perpetuity at the rate g, the PV of the CFD D is equal to the CFD divided by d minus the growth rate g.

$$D = \frac{CFD}{d - g} \qquad (A2.61)$$

Rearranging equation A2.61, we obtain

$$D(d - g) = CFD \qquad (A2.62)$$

For example, if the annual CFD in perpetuity is $24 and the cost of the debt is 8%, the PV of the CFD is $400.

$$D = \frac{CFD}{d - g} = \frac{24}{8\% - 2\%} = 400.00$$

A2.5.3 The Annual Tax Shield

The annual interest payment is equal to the cost of debt times the value of debt.

$$\text{Annual interest payment} = dD$$
$$= 8\% \times 400 = 32.00$$

The annual TS is equal to the tax rate times the annual interest payment. Assume that the tax rate T is 30%.

$$TS = TdD = 30\% \times 32 = 9.60$$

A2.5.3.1 Present value of the tax shield

Because the annual TS is growing at the rate g, the PV of the TS V^{TS} is equal to the TS divided by ψ minus the growth rate g, where the appropriate discount rate for the TS is ψ, which depends on the risk of the TS profile.

$$V^{TS} = \frac{TS}{\psi - g} \qquad (A2.63)$$

Rearranging equation A2.63, we obtain

$$V^{TS}(\psi - g) = TS \qquad (A2.64)$$

Here we assume that ψ is equal to the cost of debt d. Substituting the appropriate values for the parameters in equation A2.64, we obtain that the PV of the TS is $160.

$$V^{TS} = \frac{TS}{\psi - g} = \frac{9.60}{8\% - 2\%} = 9.60$$

A2.6 CASH FLOW TO EQUITY

We know that

$$CFE = FCF + TS - CFD \qquad (A2.65)$$

Substituting the appropriate values for the parameters in equation A2.65, we obtain that the annual CFE in perpetuity is \$85.60.

$$CFE = 100 + 9.60 - 24 = 85.60$$

A2.6.I Value of Levered Equity

Because the annual CFE is growing in perpetuity at the rate g, the PV of the CFE E^L is equal to the CFE divided by e minus the growth rate g, where e is the required rate of return for levered equity.

$$E^L = \frac{CFE}{e - g} \qquad (A2.66)$$

Rearranging equation A2.66, we obtain

$$E^L(e - g) = CFE \qquad (A2.67)$$

From before, we know that

$$E^L = V^{Un} + V^{TS} - D \qquad (A2.68)$$

Substituting the appropriate values for the parameters in equation A2.68, we obtain that the value of the levered equity is \$760.

$$E^L = V^{Un} + V^{TS} - D$$

$$= 1,000 + 160 - 400 = 760.00$$

A2.6.2 Return to Levered Equity

Solving for the return to levered equity in equation A2.66, we obtain

$$e = \frac{CFE}{E^L} + g \qquad (A2.69)$$

Substituting the appropriate values for the parameters, we obtain that the return to levered equity is as follows:

$$e = \frac{\text{CFE}}{\text{E}^L} + g = \frac{85.60}{760} + 2\% = 13.263\%$$

We can also calculate the return to levered equity directly with the following formula.

$$e = \rho + (\rho - d)\frac{D}{E^L} - (\rho - \psi)\frac{V^{TS}}{E^L} \qquad (A2.70)$$

We assume that the value of ψ is equal to the cost of debt d. Simplifying equation A2.70, we obtain

$$e = \rho + (\rho - d)\frac{(D - V^{TS})}{E^L} \qquad (A2.71)$$

Substituting the appropriate values for the parameters, we verify the previous answer.

$$e = \rho + (\rho - d)\frac{(D - V^{TS})}{E^L}$$

$$= 12\% + (12\% - 8\%)\frac{(400 - 160)}{760} = 13.263\%$$

If the growth rate is high, it is possible for the PV of the TS to exceed the value of D, and the return to levered equity will be lower than the return to unlevered equity. We can find the condition under which the value of the debt is greater than the PV of the TS.

$$D - V^{TS} = \frac{\text{CFD}}{d - g} - \frac{\text{TDd}}{d - g} > 0$$

$$\text{CFD} - \text{TDd} > 0$$

$$D(d - g) - \text{TDd} > 0$$

$$d(1 - T) > g \qquad (A2.72)$$

If the cost of debt times one minus the tax rate is greater than the growth rate, the value of the debt is higher than the PV of the TS.

APPENDIX B

B2.1 USING THE CAPM TO FIND THE COST OF CAPITAL

Next we show how we can use the CAPM to derive a relationship between the levered and the unlevered betas.

We use the CAPM to find the values for the cost of debt d and the return to levered equity e.

$$d = r_f + \beta_D[E(r_m) - r_f] \tag{B2.1}$$

$$e = r_f + \beta_E[E(r_m) - r_f] \tag{B2.2}$$

Even though we cannot estimate the unlevered beta β_ρ directly, we express the return to unlevered equity in the framework of the CAPM.

$$\rho = r_f + \beta_\rho[E(r_m) - r_f] \tag{B2.3}$$

If we subtract equation B2.1 from equation B2.3, we obtain

$$\rho - d = (\beta_\rho - \beta_D)[E(r_m) - r_f] \tag{B2.4}$$

From equation A2.32, the expression for the return to levered equity is as follows:

$$e = \rho + (\rho - d)\frac{D}{E^L} - (\rho - \psi)\frac{V^{TS}}{E^L} \tag{B2.5}$$

B2.1.1 Discount Rate for the Tax Shield Is the Cost of Debt d

If we assume that the discount rate for the TS is equal to the cost of debt d, we rewrite the expression for the return to levered equity, which is a positive function of the debt–equity ratio. To determine the relationship between the return to levered equity and the debt–equity ratio, we must estimate the return to unlevered equity ρ.

$$e = \rho + (\rho - d)(1 - T)\frac{D}{E^L} \tag{B2.6}$$

Substituting equations B2.3 and B2.4 into equation B2.6, we obtain

$$e = r_f + \beta_\rho[E(r_m) - r_f] + (\beta_\rho - \beta_D)[E(r_m) - r_f](1 - T)\frac{D}{E^L}$$

$$= r_f + \left[\beta_\rho + (\beta_\rho - \beta_D)(1 - T)\frac{D}{E^L}\right][E(r_m) - r_f] \tag{B2.7}$$

Comparing equations B2.2 and B2.7, we can write down the relationship between the beta for levered equity β_E and the unlevered beta β_ρ.

$$\beta_E = \beta_\rho + (\beta_\rho - \beta_D)(1 - T)\frac{D}{E^L}$$

$$= \beta_\rho\left[1 + (1 - T)\frac{D}{E^L}\right] - \beta_D(1 - T)\frac{D}{E^L} \tag{B2.8}$$

Solving for the unlevered beta, we obtain

$$\beta_\rho = \frac{\beta_E + \beta_D(1 - T)\dfrac{D}{E^L}}{1 + (1 - T)\dfrac{D}{E^L}} \tag{B2.9}$$

If the debt is risk-free, β_D is zero and we can simplify equation B2.9 as follows:

$$\beta_\rho = \frac{\beta_E}{1 + (1 - T)\frac{D}{E^L}} \tag{B2.10}$$

Using the levered beta, we can determine the value of the unlevered beta. Substituting the value of the unlevered beta into equation B2.3, we obtain the return to unlevered equity. With the known value for the return to unlevered equity, we can estimate the return to levered equity as a function of the debt–equity ratio.

B2.2 DISCOUNT RATE FOR THE TAX SHIELD IS THE RETURN TO UNLEVERED EQUITY ρ

If we assume that the discount rate for the TS is equal to the return to unlevered equity ρ, we rewrite the expression for the return to levered equity.

$$e = \rho + (\rho - d)\frac{D}{E^L} \tag{B2.11}$$

Substituting equations B2.3 and B2.4 into equation B2.11, we obtain

$$
\begin{aligned}
e &= r_f + \beta_\rho[E(r_m) - r_f] + (\beta_\rho - \beta_D)[E(r_m) - r_f]\frac{D}{E^L} \\
&= r_f + \left[\beta_\rho + (\beta_\rho - \beta_D)\frac{D}{E^L}\right][E(r_m) - r_f]
\end{aligned}
\tag{B2.12}
$$

$$
\begin{aligned}
\beta_E &= \beta_\rho + (\beta_\rho - \beta_D)\frac{D}{E^L} \\
&= \beta_\rho\left[1 + \frac{D}{E^L}\right] - \beta_D\frac{D}{E^L}
\end{aligned}
\tag{B2.13}
$$

Solving for the unlevered beta, we obtain

$$\beta_\rho = \frac{\beta_E + \beta_D\frac{D}{E^L}}{1 + \frac{D}{E^L}} \tag{B2.14}$$

If the debt is risk-free, β_D is zero and we can simplify equation B2.14 as follows:

$$\beta_\rho = \frac{\beta_E}{1 + \frac{D}{E^L}} \tag{B2.15}$$

BASIC REVIEW OF FINANCIAL STATEMENTS AND ACCOUNTING CONCEPTS

> Why did we show the book balance sheet? Only so you could draw a big X through it. Do so now.
>
> —*Brealey & Myers in* Principles of Corporate Finance, *Seventh Edition, p. 525.*

3.1 FINANCIAL STATEMENTS AND ACCOUNTING CONCEPTS

In this introductory chapter, we present some basic principles for constructing the pro-forma financial statements, namely the income statement (IS), the BS, and the cash flow statement (CFS) according to Generally Accepted Accounting Principles (GAAP), which are required for the valuation framework that we propose.[1] In addition, we also discuss the construction of the CB statement. This chapter is a review of the common financial statements and basic accounting concepts that are used in the subsequent chapters. Some previous familiarity with financial statements and accounting concepts would be helpful but it is not necessary. On purpose, we have been selective in the treatment of the basic accounting topics. We have kept the coverage and explanations on the accounting concepts to the minimum level that is required for following the ideas on valuation in the subsequent chapters. The content of this chapter should be

---

[1] As the quotation from Brealey and Myers (2000) illustrates, everybody does not agree on the usefulness of the BS for valuation. We believe that the BS can be an important component of an integrated valuation framework.

familiar to most readers.[2] This chapter also serves as a reference chapter for the basic accounting concepts that are used in the other chapters. To minimize the overall repetition, in this chapter we have not provided numerical illustrations for the ideas that are discussed in this chapter. In subsequent chapters, we present detailed numerical examples for the construction of the financial statements that use the accounting ideas and principles from this chapter. Some readers might find it helpful to read this chapter in conjunction with the numerical examples in the other chapters. In Chapter Four, using a simple numerical example, we illustrate the basic ideas for constructing the financial statements over a planning (or forecast) period of five years. In Chapter Five, we make the simple example more complex by introducing additional assumptions into the model.

For cash flow valuation, we favor an integrated approach that links the nominal financial statements in a consistent manner, and relies on the strengths and perspectives of the different financial statements to inform and improve the valuation exercise. The integration of the financial statements facilitates the sensitivity analysis that we could conduct on the key parameters of the model and provides an internally consistent validity check on the construction of the financial statements.

This chapter is organized as follows. In Section 1, we briefly describe three common financial statements: the BS, the IS, and the CFS. In addition, we describe the CB statement, which we have adapted for our purposes. As discussed earlier in Chapter One, in the context of GAAP the CB is not a financial statement. However, the CB statement is a useful and important tool for monitoring the liquidity of the firm and deriving the appropriate cash flows for valuation.

In Section 2, we present some of the preliminary tables and calculations that we complete prior to the construction of the three financial statements. We illustrate the ideas with simple numerical examples. In particular, we discuss the calculations that are related to the depreciation schedule, the loan schedule, inventories, the cost of goods sold (COGS) schedule and the adjustments for credit sales and purchases. In appendix A, we show how to derive the CB with the BS and the IS.

SECTION I

3.I.I Pro-Forma Financial Statements

In the context of GAAP, the most common financial statements are the BS, the IS, and the CFS. Besides these three financial statements, there is the Stockholders' Equity Statement, which reports the changes in the stockholders'

---

[2]Readers who have no prior knowledge of accounting and wish to have more detailed explanations or discussions of accounting concepts are encouraged to consult relevant accounting textbooks. If additional accounting concepts are required in subsequent chapters, we will explain them at that time.

equity for the relevant period and includes the dividends paid, equity repurchases, and new equity investment.

The BS reports the financial position of the firm at the end of the accounting period. The IS reports the results of the operation for the period, such as the earnings, taxes, and the net income (NI). The CFS reports the cash inflows and outflows that occur during the period.

The CB statement is important in its own right and is closely related to the CFS that is based on GAAP. However, there are differences between the CB statement and the CFS according to GAAP. We discuss these differences later in the chapter. For the purpose of cash valuation, we strongly believe that the formulation of the CB statement that we present is more useful than the cash flow according to GAAP. And most importantly, as we show later, it is easy to derive the required Free Cash Flow (FCF) from the CB statement that we construct.

3.1.2 Integrated Framework

To value the cash flow stream of a firm or a project, we propose to construct four inter-related financial statements: the BS, the IS, the CFS, and the annual CB statement. These four financial statements form the basic building blocks for the valuation exercise. For instance, the tax liabilities are calculated in the IS, and listed in the CB statement and the BS. The surplus funds that are available for reinvestment in marketable securities are calculated in the CB statement, and the interest income that is generated from the reinvestment of the surplus funds is listed in the CB and the IS for tax purposes. The cumulative cash balance at the end of the year in the CB statement is listed in the BS. Also, we derive the CFS from the line items in the IS and BS.

Next, we present a brief discussion on the BS, the IS, the CFS, and the CB statement.[3]

3.2 BALANCE SHEET

The BS measures the amount of wealth that is owned by the stockholders in the company. For a sample BS and a link to a website with additional information, see Appendix B. The main identity is the following: the (book) value of the equity is equal to the value of the assets minus the value of the liabilities.

$$(Book)Value\ of\ equity = Assets - Liabilities \qquad (3.1)$$

---

[3]For additional details on financial statements, the reader should consult a textbook in financial accounting and financial statements. For example, see Penman (2000).

To maintain the identity, a transaction on one side of the identity 3.1 must be offset by a transaction on the other side of the identity, or on the same side with the opposite sign. For example, a change in the value of the assets must be offset by a change in the value of equity. Or a change in the value of the assets must be offset by an appropriate change in the value of the liabilities.

3.2.1 Assets

The value of the assets is a measure of the capacity of the firm to generate future benefits (or cash flows). The assets of an enterprise consist of its properties in all categories. It includes both what the enterprise owns and what is owed to it. For instance, accounts receivable (AR), short-term investments, inventories, vehicles, machinery, buildings, and land are assets. Here we have only mentioned tangible assets. In a BS, you can find both tangible and intangible assets, such as goodwill. For a discussion on the valuation of intangible assets, see a textbook in accounting.

Typically in the BS, the assets are listed at book or historical values and these values might differ from the current market values for the assets. For valuation purposes, the market value is the most crucial concept. In many cases, especially in developing and transitional economies, appropriate market values for assets might be unavailable, and out of necessity book values might be used. In many countries, the book values of the assets are adjusted for inflation. However, from a valuation point of view, the analyst must recognize that the book values of the assets, even if adjusted for inflation, can be misleading and might not correctly represent the capacity of the asset to generate future cash flows.

3.2.2 Current Assets

Depending on the ease with which we convert the assets into cash, we classify assets into two types: current assets and fixed assets. Compared to the fixed assets, the current assets are more easily convertible into cash. In other words, the liquidity of the current assets is higher than the liquidity of the fixed assets. The most common examples of current assets are cash or cash equivalents, marketable securities, AR, inventories, and prepaid expenses.

Cash or cash equivalent are the monies that we have in the bank or in the safe. They are completely liquid. AR is the money that customers owe to the firm, and is based on credit sales. Based on past experiences, we can estimate the percentage of AR that might not be collected from the customers. To be conservative, we make provisions for bad debts and list it in parentheses next to AR.

Marketable securities are the temporary investments that the firm makes with the surplus cash on hand.

Inventories are the raw materials, partly finished and finished goods, which the company keeps in stock. Inventories are relevant for manufacturing and trading companies.

Prepaid expenses are expenditures that the firm has already paid for, such as insurance or advertising. These expenses are not liquid in the sense that they cannot be converted into cash. However, it means that less cash has to be spent in the future on those expenditures.

The expression for current assets is as follows:

$$\text{Current assets} = \text{Cash} + \text{Marketable securities} + \text{AR}$$
$$+ \text{Inventories} + \text{Prepaid expenses} \qquad (3.2)$$

3.2.3 Liabilities

Liabilities consist of what the firm owes to third parties. Accounts payable (AP), bonds, and loans from a bank are examples of liabilities. The liabilities of the firm show where the funds were obtained to acquire the assets. The debt holders are paid with interest and the principal repayments on the loan.

3.2.4 Current Liabilities

The current liabilities consist of what the firm owes to its suppliers and creditors and are ranked according to the priority for payment. The most common current liabilities are AP, accrued expenses, and the current part of long-term debt.

Accounts payable is the money that the firm owes to suppliers and creditors. The firm might also owe taxes to the tax authorities. Accrued expenses are expenses that the firm has incurred but have not come due. A short-term payable note is the amount that a firm owes to a bank or other financial institutions that is to be repaid within the next year.

The expression for current liabilities is as follows:

$$\text{Current liabilities} = \text{AP} + \text{Accrued expenses} + \text{Tax payable}$$
$$+ \text{Short-term notes payable}$$
$$+ \text{Current part of long-term debt} \qquad (3.3)$$

3.3 WORKING CAPITAL

Working capital is defined as the difference between the current assets and the current liabilities. An increase in working capital means that additional resources are required for operating the business; conversely, a decrease in working capital means that resources are released and are no longer required for operating the business.

$$\text{Working capital} = \text{Current assets} - \text{Current liabilities} \qquad (3.4)$$

In addition, we also define working capital, exclusive of cash or cash equivalents. Later, we use working capital, exclusive of cash or cash equivalents, in the derivation of the cash flow from operating activities for the CFS according to GAAP.

3.4 (BOOK) VALUE OF EQUITY

The equity in a firm is the contribution of the owners to the firm. It consists of the net effect of the following items: investment of stockholders in the company, the withdrawal of dividends from the company, and the repurchase of equity. In the event that the company is liquidated, the stockholders will receive the residual after all the liabilities are paid. Common or preferred stocks are examples of equity from stockholders. The equity is a residual item, and the equity holder is paid only after all other parties have been paid.[4]

When we mention equity in the context of this chapter and the BS, we refer to the book value of equity as listed in the BS. For valuation purposes, the market value of equity is the relevant concept. In subsequent chapters, we return to the distinction between the book value of equity versus the market value of equity, which depends on the profile of the cash flow that accrues to the equity holder.

3.5 INCOME STATEMENT

The main purpose of the IS is to measure the NI earned by the company or project in a given period. Roughly speaking, the NI is equal to the revenues from the output of the project minus the cost of producing the output and taxes.[5]

The IS is constructed on an accrual basis and on the assignment of costs principle. Accrual basis means that revenues (e.g., AR) and costs (e.g., AP) are registered when the transaction for the income or expense occurs, and not when the revenue is actually received or the expense actually paid. For valuation purposes, we record the revenue when it is actually received and

[4]In the language of option pricing theory, the value of the equity is equivalent to a call option on the cash flows of the firm.

[5]If there are interest deductions with debt financing, the tax liabilities are lower, compared to no debt financing.

the expense when it is actually paid. Thus, in the CFS and the CB statement, we adjust the revenues and expenses that are listed in the IS.

The assignment of costs principle means that costs that are incurred in the past are assigned to and spread over future periods. For example, the depreciation allowance is spread over many years. It is important to recognize that the depreciation allowance is not a cash outflow. The depreciation allowance is simply an accounting mechanism for allocating the capital expenditures over time. However, the profile of the depreciation allowance over the life of the cash flow has an indirect effect on the cash flow through its impact on the calculation of the tax liabilities.

3.5.1 Line Items in the Income Statement

In this section, we present the definitions of the key line items in the IS. For a sample of an IS, see Appendix B.

3.5.2 Gross Profit

The gross profit is equal to the sales revenues minus the COGS. The sales revenues are equal to the quantity sold times the unit price.

$$\text{Gross profit} = \text{Sales revenues} - \text{COGS} \qquad (3.5)$$

Later, we explain the calculations for the COGS in greater detail.

3.5.3 Earnings Before Interest and Taxes (EBIT)

The EBIT or operating profits are equal to the gross profits minus the selling and administrative expenses, inclusive of the depreciation allowance.

$$\text{EBIT (Operating profits)} = \text{Gross profit}$$
$$- \text{Selling and Administrative expenses} \qquad (3.6)$$

3.5.4 Earnings Before Taxes (EBT)

The EBT are equal to the EBIT plus other incomes (OIs) minus other expenses. Usually the OI is interest income and the other expense is interest expense.

$$\text{EBT} = \text{EBIT} + \text{Interest income} - \text{Interest expense} \qquad (3.7)$$

The interest expenses arise if there is debt financing and the other interest income is derived from the reinvestment of surplus funds in marketable securities[6] The deduction of the interest expense from the EBT provides a tax savings, if the sum of the EBIT and OI is sufficient for the tax savings to be realized in the year in which the interest expense occurs.[7]

3.5.5 Taxes

The taxes are equal to the product of the tax rate and the EBT.

$$\text{Taxes} = \text{Tax rate times EBT} \tag{3.8}$$

In general, taxes are only paid if the EBT is positive. In the case of losses, the losses can be carried forward and offset by future positive earnings. The benefits of losses carried forward (LCF) depend on the tax laws. Some countries require firms to pay taxes even if the EBT is negative. In Colombia, for instance, they say: "you are in the business to earn money. Even if you don't, then you pay on the basis of the equity." It is called presumptive rent. The tax authorities multiply the value of equity by some factor and they calculate the tax liability on that amount.

3.5.6 Net Income (NI)

The NI is equal to the EBT minus the taxes.

$$\text{NI} = \text{EBT} - \text{Taxes} \tag{3.9}$$

3.5.7 Dividends

From the NI and the payout ratio for dividends, we calculate the dividends.

$$\text{Dividends declared in year n} = \text{NI in year n times the Payout ratio} \tag{3.10}$$

We assume that the payout ratio for dividends is provided. In modeling, it is common to assume that all of the dividends are paid out in the year in which they are declared. In practice, the dividends are paid *after* the NI is

---

[6]The IS has an explicit charge for the cost of debt (if there is debt financing) but does not have an explicit charge for the equity that is contributed by the equity holder.

[7]From a valuation point of view, we should recognize the tax shields (TSs) only if the TSs are actually realized. With the possibility of LCF, the TSs might not be realized in the years in which the interest expenses occur.

declared. Thus, the company might start the fiscal year by paying some dividends from the previous year. It might be the case that only a part of the dividends that are declared in year n are actually paid in year n.

3.5.8 Retained and Accumulated Retained Earnings

In the simplest atypical case, we assume that all the dividends are paid in the year in which the dividends are declared. The retained earnings in year n are equal to the NI in year n minus the dividends in year n.

$$\text{Retained earnings in year n} = \text{NI in year n}$$
$$- \text{Dividends paid in year n} \quad (3.11)$$

The cumulative earnings in year n are equal to the retained earnings in year n plus the cumulative earnings in the previous year n − 1.

$$\text{Cumulative earnings in year n} = \text{Retained earnings in year n}$$
$$+ \text{Cumulative earnings in year n} - 1 \ (3.12)$$

For example, suppose α percent of the dividends that are declared in year n are actually paid in the next year. Then the dividends that are paid in year n are equal to α times the dividends declared in year n plus $(1 - \alpha)$ times the dividends declared in the previous year n − 1.

$$\text{Dividends paid in year n} = \alpha \times \text{Dividends declared in year n} + (1 - \alpha)$$
$$\times \text{Dividends declared in year n} - 1 \quad (3.13)$$

If all the dividends are not paid in the year that they are declared, the retained earnings in year n is as follows:

$$\text{Retained earnings in year n} = \text{NI in year n} - \text{Dividends paid in year n}$$
$$= \text{NI in year n} - \alpha \times \text{Dividends declared in}$$
$$\text{year n} + (1 - \alpha) \times \text{Dividends declared}$$
$$\text{in year n} - 1 \quad (3.14)$$

If the value of alpha is zero—that is all the dividends declared in year n are paid in the next year n + 1—the retained earnings in year n is equal to the NI in year n minus the dividends declared in the previous year n − 1.

$$\text{Retained earnings in year n} = \text{NI in year n} - \text{Dividends paid in year n}$$
$$= \text{NI in year n} - \text{Dividends declared}$$
$$\text{in year n} - 1 \quad (3.15)$$

If the value of α is one, the retained earnings in year n is simply equal to the NI in year n less the dividends declared (and paid) in year n.

3.6 CASH FLOW STATEMENT (CFS) ACCORDING TO GAAP

According to GAAP, the CFS is divided into three sections that correspond to three distinct activities: operating, investing, and financing activities.

1. Cash flow from operating activities.
2. Cash flow from investing activities.
3. Cash flow from financing activities.

The cash flows for the operating activities are calculated from the IS. The cash flows for the investing activities are based on the assets in the BS and the cash flows for the financing activities are based on the liabilities and stockholders' equity in the BS. The sum of the cash flows for the three activities is equal to the change in the cash or cash equivalents. We call this the change in the cash required for operations (CRO).[8]

3.6.1 Cash Flow from Operating Activities

For valuation, the operating cash flow (OCF) is the most useful. The OCF records the actual cash inflows and outflows from the normal operations of the firm. The OCF is different from the operational profits in the IS because of credit sales and purchases. For example, profits might be increased by sales for which payment has not yet been received and profits might be decreased by purchases for which payment has not been made.

The indirect method is the most popular approach for constructing the "cash flow from operating activities" section of the CFS according to GAAP. We begin with the NI from the IS. To obtain the OCF, we add the depreciation and related items, and subtract the change in the non-cash working capital. The series of adjustments to obtain the OCF from the NI is shown next.

Net income

Plus depreciation, amortization and provisions, such as bad debt provisions

Minus change in non-cash working capital (inventories, AR and AP)

$= $ Net OCF $\hspace{5cm}$ (3.16)

---

[8]An increase in the CRO means that additional cash is required for running the business, and a decrease in the CRO means that less cash is required for running the business.

To obtain the NI, the depreciation allowance is subtracted from the revenues. Because the depreciation allowance is not a cash outflow, we add it back to the NI. As mentioned earlier, an increase in the non-cash working capital means that additional resources are required for operating the business. Thus, an increase in the non-cash working capital represents a cash outflow that should be subtracted from the NI. Conversely, a decrease in the non-cash working capital represents a cash inflow that should be added to the NI.

3.6.2 Cash Flow from Investing Activities

To obtain the cash flow from investing activities, we make the following series of adjustments. We subtract investments in fixed assets and marketable securities and add the sale (recovery) of assets and the marketable securities. The series of adjustments to obtain the "net cash flow from investing activities" is shown next.

> Minus investment in fixed assets
> Minus investment in marketable securities
> Plus sale of marketable securities
> Plus sale of assets = Net cash flow from investing activies   (3.17)

The investment in fixed assets and marketable securities represent cash outflows and the sale (recovery) of assets, and marketable securities represent cash inflows.

3.6.3 Cash Flow from Financing Activities

To obtain the cash flow from financing activities, we make the following series of adjustments. We add the new equity and new debt and subtract principal repayments on the debt and dividend payments. The series of adjustments to obtain the "net cash flow from financing activities" is shown next.

Plus new equity
Plus new debt
Minus principal repayments on the debt
Minus dividend payments = Net cash flow from financing activities   (3.18)

Putting together all three components of the cash flow statement according to GAAP, we obtain the change in the CRO.

Net OCF
Plus net cash flow from investing activities
Plus net cash flow from financing activities = Change in the annual CRO   (3.19)

3.7 CASH BUDGET STATEMENT

Next we discuss the construction of the CB statement. As mentioned earlier, our presentation and formulation of the CB statement is similar to the cash flow statement according to GAAP, but there are differences. The CB records the actual cash inflows and outflows for the project or the company. The CB statement is one of the most important, if not the most important, tools for controlling and monitoring the liquidity of a project or company. For each period, the CB statement measures the liquidity. The time frame for the CB depends on the needs of the firm.[9] For our purposes, to be consistent with the other financial statements, we construct the annual CB statement rather than a monthly or weekly statement.

Typical items that are included in the CB statement are shown in Table 3.1. In the CB statement, all the expected cash inflows and outflows are recorded when they are actually expected to occur. Roughly speaking, the annual net cash balance (NCB) (before taking into account the debt and equity financing) is equal to the difference between the annual cash inflows and the annual cash outflows.

TABLE 3.1 Typical Items in the Cash Budget Statement

Inflows	Outflows
AR recovery	AP payments
Loans received	Salaries and fringe benefits
Equity invested	Interest charges
Sale of assets	Principal payments
Interest on marketable securities	Rent
Sales of marketable securities	Overhead expenses
Advance payments from customers	Promotion and advertising
Repayments of cash lent to third parties	Asset acquisition
	Social Security payments
	Earnings distributed or dividends paid
	Taxes
	Investment in marketable securities
	Repurchase of stock
	Loans lent to third parties

The CB statement is the perspective of the treasurer of the firm or the project. If there is a shortfall in cash, the treasurer arranges for additional debt or equity financing. If there are surplus funds, the treasurer makes decisions about how to use them.

---

[9]One of the authors, while working as treasurer of a firm in financial stress, designed a CB for five working days, three Fridays (weekends) and eleven months. That CB kept updating automatically and the estimations always covered a period of one year.

In the valuation of cash flow streams for a firm, it is important to analyze the liquidity position of the firm over the life of the cash flow or project. With a careful examination of the CB statement, the firm can evaluate different financing alternatives.

3.7.1 Annual Cash Budget Statement

There is no standard format for the construction of the CB statement. We present an approach for the construction of the CB statement that separates the line items for operations from the line items for financing and discretionary transactions. We reiterate that the structure of the CB statement is similar to the CFS that is constructed according to GAAP. However, there are differences that we will comment on.

We divide the CB statement into four sections.

1. NCB before financing and reinvestment.
2. NCB after debt financing.
3. NCB after equity financing.
4. NCB after reinvestment of surplus funds in marketable securities.

Unlike the CFS according to GAAP, we have an extra section because we distinguish the debt and equity financing. Here we introduce the debt financing before equity financing. However, depending on the circumstances, the ordering of the debt and equity financing could be reversed.

3.7.2 Net Cash Balance Before Financing and Reinvestment

In the first section of the CB statement, on the inflow side of the CB statement, we list the annual cash receipts, and on the outflow side we list the annual cash expenditures. Unlike the first section of the CFS according to GAAP, we do not start with the NI.

The NCB before financing and reinvestment is equal to the annual cash receipts minus the annual cash expenditures. The expression for the NCB before financing and reinvestment is shown next.

$$
\text{NCB before financing and reinvestment} = + \text{Annual cash receipts}
$$

$$
- \text{Annual cash expenditures,}
$$

$$
\text{including taxes and}
$$

$$
\text{investments} \qquad (3.20)
$$

This NCB before financing and reinvestment can be thought of as the OCF without any effects of financing. However, technically this is not true because the NCB includes the tax savings from the interest deduction with debt financing. In other words, the tax liabilities that are calculated in the IS and listed in the CB statement take into account the interest deduction, if any, from the debt financing.[10]

3.7.3 Net Cash Balance After Debt Financing

In the second section of the CB statement, we introduce debt financing. The NCB after debt financing is equal to the NCB before financing and reinvestment plus new bank loans minus the total payments for debt (principal plus interest). With respect to the firm, the new banks' loans are cash inflows and the total payments for debt (principal and interest) are cash outflows.[11] The expression for the NCB after debt financing is shown next.

NCB after debt financing = + NCB before financing and reinvestment

$$+ \text{New bank loans}$$

$$- \text{Total payments for debt}$$

$$\text{(principal plus interest)} \qquad (3.21)$$

Unlike the financing CF in the CFS according to GAAP, which excludes the interest payments on the debt financing, the NCB after debt financing includes *all* the cash flows to the debt holders. In the CFS according to GAAP, the interest payments are listed as part of the cash flow from the operating activities and they are not listed as part of the cash flow from the financing activities.

3.7.4 Net Cash Balance After Equity Financing

In the third section of the CB statement, we introduce equity financing. The NCB after equity financing is equal to the NCB after debt financing plus new equity investment minus the sum of the dividend payments and equity repurchase. With respect to the firm, the new equity investment is added to the NCB after debt financing because it is a cash inflow, and the dividends

---

[10]To obtain a pure unlevered OCF, which does not have any effect on debt financing, we subtract the tax savings from the NCB.

[11]From the perspective of the debt holder, the new bank loans represent cash outflows and the total repayments represent cash inflows.

and equity repurchase are subtracted from the NCB after debt financing because they are cash outflows.[12] The expression for the NCB after equity financing is shown next.

NCB after equity financing $= +$ NCB after debt financing

$$+ \text{ New equity investment} - \text{Dividend payments}$$
$$- \text{ Equity repurchase} \qquad\qquad (3.22)$$

In the CB statement, the dividend payments are listed in the year that they are actually paid rather than in the year that they are declared and calculated in the IS.

The NCB after equity financing includes *all* the cash flows to the equity holders.

3.7.5 Reinvestment of Surplus Funds

In the fourth section of the CB statement, we account for the reinvestment of the surplus funds in marketable securities. There are many ways to model the reinvestment of surplus funds. We present several issues that need to be taken into account in the modeling and construction of the CB statement. First, we check whether the NCB after equity financing is sufficient to meet the CRO. If the NCB is not sufficient, additional debt or equity financing might be necessary.

Second, we need to check whether there is any bank borrowing. It might not make sense to reinvest surplus funds at a reinvestment rate that is lower than the borrowing rate and borrow at the same time.

At this stage, to discuss the various ways to model multiple conditions in the formulation of the reinvestment of surplus funds would unnecessarily complicate the exposition. For simplicity, we impose only two conditions. First, in each year we check whether new bank loans are required. Second, we check that the surplus funds meet the CRO.

We strongly encourage you to read this section on the CB statement in conjunction with the detailed numerical examples in Chapters Four and Five. Otherwise, the expressions for calculating the various line items in the CB statement will appear abstract.

The expression for the reinvestment of surplus funds is as follows. The surplus funds that are available for reinvestment in year n is equal to the sum of the NCB (after debt and equity financing) in year n minus the CRO for year n plus the sale (recovery) of the marketable securities in the previous

---

[12]From the perspective of the equity holder, the equity investments are cash outflows and the dividends are cash inflows.

year n − 1, inclusive of the interest income, and the cumulative cash balance in the previous year n − 1.

> Reinvestment of surplus funds in year n =
>
> + NCB (after debt and equity financing) in year n
>
> − CRO for year n
>
> + Sale (recovery) of marketable securities in year n − 1
>
> + Interest income on short-term investment in year n − 1
>
> + Cumulative cash balance in year n − 1   (3.23)

We take account of the annual CRO in this section of the CB statement by subtracting the CRO from the NCB after debt and equity financing because it is not available for reinvestment in marketable securities. We add the sale (recovery) of the marketable securities in the previous year n − 1 and the concomitant interest income because they are available for reinvestment in the current year n.

Also, the cumulative cash balance from the previous year is available for investment in short-term marketable securities and is added to the NCB.

Also, we should check that we have sufficient funds for the CRO. In other words, the sum of the following four items should be positive.

> Reinvestment of surplus funds in year n =
>
> + NCB (after debt and equity financing) in year n
>
> + Sale (recovery) of marketable securities in year n − 1
>
> + Interest income on short-term investment in year n − 1
>
> + Cumulative cash balance in year n − 1   (3.24)

If not, the reinvestment of surplus funds is zero.

3.7.6 Final Net Cash Balance After Reinvestment

In year n, the final NCB after reinvestment of surplus funds is equal to the NCB (after debt and equity financing) in year n minus the reinvestment of surplus funds in year n plus the recovery of the short-term investment in the previous year n − 1, inclusive of the interest income.

> Final NCB after reinvestment in year n =
>
> + NCB (after debt and equity financing) in year n
>
> − Reinvestment of surplus funds in year n
>
> + Sale (recovery) of marketable securities in year n − 1
>
> + Interest on marketable securities in year n − 1   (3.25)

The NCB after reinvestment shows the net result of the previous decisions regarding debt and equity financing, CRO, and the investment of surplus funds in marketable securities. In practice, the value of the NCB after reinvestment can be positive or negative. How do we interpret the meaning of the value of the NCB after reinvestment? If in any year n the value of the NCB is positive, extra funds were required by the firm and the extra funds were financed with the surplus funds. Alternatively, if in any year n the value of the NCB is negative, extra funds were released by the firm and the extra funds were invested in marketable securities.

3.7.7 Cumulative Cash Balance

At the end of the year, we obtain the cumulative cash balance, which is entered as cash in the BS. In year n, the cumulative cash balance is equal to the final NCB after reinvestment in year n plus the cumulative cash balance in the previous year $n - 1$. As a check, the cumulative cash balance is equal to the annual CRO.

3.8 DIFFERENCES BETWEEN THE CFS ACCORDING TO GAAP AND THE CB STATEMENT

Now we briefly discuss and compare the differences between the sections of the CFS according to GAAP and the corresponding sections of the CB statement. From a valuation point of view, the sections of the CB statement that we propose are more useful.

First, we show that the relationship between the NCB in the first section of the CB statement and the OCF according to GAAP is as follows:

$$\text{NCB} - \text{Interest payments} + \text{Interest income}$$
$$+ \text{New investments in fixed assets} = \text{OCF from GAAP} \quad (3.26)$$

The NCB before debt and equity financing in the CB statement does not include the interest deductions and the interest income from the reinvestment of surplus cash in marketable securities. In the CB statement, the interest payments are listed in the section on debt financing and the interest income is listed in the fourth section, which deals with the reinvestment of surplus funds in marketable securities. The tax impacts of the interest income and interest expense are taken into account in the "NCB before debt and equity financing" through the tax liabilities derived from the IS. In addition, in this part of the CB statement we list all cash expenditures, including reinvestments in new assets.

The OCF, according to GAAP, includes the charge for debt financing and the interest income from the reinvestment of surplus funds in marketable securities because it is derived from the NI in the IS.[13]

According to GAAP, the second section on the cash flow from investment activities lists the investments in new assets together with the investment of surplus funds in marketable securities. Because we list the new investments in fixed assets in the CB as outflows, we must add them back in equation 3.26 to obtain the OCF according to GAAP. In the CB statement, we separate the investment in fixed assets from the reinvestment of surplus funds in marketable securities.

In the CB statement, in the fourth section, we list the investment of surplus funds in marketable securities after we have taken account of debt and equity financing.

3.9 INTEGRATION OF THE FINANCIAL STATEMENTS

It might be useful to briefly provide examples of the ways in which the financial statements are linked and integrated. The detailed illustrations are provided in Chapters Four and Five. The tax liabilities are calculated in the IS and listed in the CB statement. The tax liabilities depend on the interest deductions from debt financing and the interest income from the reinvestment of surplus funds in marketable securities. In addition, AR and AP listed in the BS are derived from the line items in the CB statement.

The plan for debt financing can be based on the availability of excess funds calculated in the CB statement. Thus, the calculation of the debt financing in the CB statement determines the interest deductions that are listed in the IS. Also, we calculate the interest income in the CB statement. Thus, we see that there is an iterative process between the IS and the CB statement.

In the IS, we also calculate the dividend payments and the cumulative retained earnings. The cumulative retained earnings are listed in the BS. Furthermore, the cumulative cash balance in the CB statement corresponds to the cash that is listed in the BS.

Thus, all three financial statements are linked. The integration of the financial statements provides an important and useful check on the consistency of the modeling.

---

[13]Interestingly, the OCF according to GAAP does not include the charge for equity financing.

SECTION 2

3.10 PRELIMINARY TABLES

In this section, we present the calculations for three preliminary tables that are completed prior to the construction of the financial statements: the depreciation allowance schedule, the loan schedule, and the COGS schedule. We explain the relationship between the quantities sold, inventories, and purchases. In addition, we present the adjustments for credit sales and purchases.

3.10.1 Depreciation Schedule

To calculate the annual depreciation allowance, we construct the depreciation schedule, which depends on the relevant tax rules and regulations. For convenience, we assume straight-line depreciation. The annual ending values of the fixed assets are shown in the depreciation schedule, and these values are entered in the BS.

In any year n, the ending value of the fixed asset is equal to the beginning value minus the depreciation allowance for the year. Suppose that at the end of year 0, the value of the fixed asset is $4,000 and the life of the fixed asset is five years.

TABLE 3.2   Depreciation Schedule

Year	0	1	2	3
Beginning value		4,000.00	3,200.00	2,400.00
Annual depreciation		800.00	800.00	800.00
Accumulated depreciation		800.00	1,600.00	2,400.00
Net fixed assets	4,000.00	3,200.00	2,400.00	1,600.00

The annual depreciation allowance is $4,000.

$$\text{Annual depreciation allowance} = \frac{4,000}{5} = 800.00$$

At the end of year 3, as listed in the depreciation schedule, the book value of the fixed asset is $1,600. However, if the asset were to be sold in year 3, the actual market value of the fixed asset in year 3 might be different from the book value that is listed in the depreciation schedule, and the market value would be listed as a cash inflow.

3.10.2 Loan Schedule

Next, we explain the construction of a simple loan schedule, which depends on the debt financing policy.[14] There are several possibilities. First, we could specify equal total payments (sum of principal and interest), based on one interest rate. Second, we could specify equal principal repayments. This format is common in many developing countries.[15]

First, we illustrate a loan schedule with equal principal repayments. At the end of year 0, assume that the amount of the loan is $3,000 and the term of the loan is three years. The annual principal repayment is $1,000.

$$\text{Annual principal payment} = \frac{3,000}{3} = 1,000.00$$

We assume that the expected inflation rate over the three years is constant at 3%. Based on a real interest rate of 5%, the nominal interest rate on the loan is 8.15%.[16]

The completed loan schedule is shown in Table 3.3.

For year 1, the interest charges are $244.50 and the total payments are $1,244.50.

Interest charges = 3,000 × 8.15% = 244.50
Total payment = 1,000 + 244.5 = 1,244.50

The total loan repayment in any year n is equal to the principal repayment plus the interest charges for the year. Over time, as we pay off the loan principal, the interest expense declines.

TABLE 3.3   Loan Schedule with Equal Principal Repayment

Year	0	1	2	3
Beginning balance (BB)		3,000.00	2,000.00	1,000.00
Interest charges		244.50	163.00	81.50
Principal payment		1,000.00	1,000.00	1,000.00
Total payment		1,244.50	1,163.00	1,081.50
Ending balance	3,000.00	2,000.00	1,000.00	0.00

[14]In practice, there might be several loans from different sources in different currencies and at different interest rates and maturities.

[15]Third, we could rebalance the debt each year to maintain a particular leverage profile over time. We do not discuss the third alternative here.

[16]With equal principal repayment, we can specify variable interest rates over the life of the loan. With constant equal payments, we can also specify variable interest rates. However, we would need to use Goal Seek in Excel to calculate the loan schedule.

At the end of year n, the ending balance is equal to the BB minus the principal repayment. In year 1, the ending balance is \$2,000.

Ending balance = BB minus the principal payment
$$= 3{,}000 - 1{,}000 = 2{,}000.00$$

As expected, the ending balance in year 3 is zero because we repay the full loan.

Next, we illustrate the same loan schedule with equal total payments (principal plus interest).

TABLE 3.4   Loan Schedule with Equal Total Payments

Year	0	1	2	3
BB		3,000.00	2,077.20	1,079.30
Interest charges		244.50	169.30	88.00
Principal payment		922.80	998.00	1,079.30
Total payment		1,167.30	1,167.30	1,167.30
Ending balance	3,000.00	2,077.20	1,079.30	0.00

In this case, the annual total payment on the loan, principal plus interest, is constant at \$1,167.30. Unlike the previous example, with equal total payments the principal repayment increases over time.[17] The calculation of the annual total payments is based on a fixed interest rate.[18]

In these examples, on grounds of simplicity, we have not distinguished the effective annual interest rate from the interest rate that is actually used for the calculation of the interest payments. For example, if the interest payments are made every six months, the interest payments are based on a rate that is lower than the effective annual interest rate. The interest rate for the interest payments, compounded twice, is equal to the effective annual interest rate.

3.10.3 Quantity Sold, Inventories, and Purchases

Here we define the relationship between the quantity sold, the inventories, and the purchases. In any year n, the inventory is a percentage of the quantity sold. Also, in any year n, the number of units purchased is equal to the quantity sold in year n plus the final inventory of the previous year n − 1 minus the initial inventory for the current year n. The initial inventory in year n is equal to the final inventory of the previous year n − 1.

Quantity sold = Initial inventory + Purchases − Final inventory   (3.27)

[17]Because the total annual payment is fixed, the interest charges decrease because the BB decrease. Thus, the principal payments must increase.

[18]To calculate the annual total payment, we use the PMT function in the Excel spreadsheet.

Rearranging equation 3.27, we obtain that the purchases are equal to the quantity sold plus the final inventory minus the initial inventory.

$$\text{Purchases} = \text{Quantity sold} + \text{Final inventory} - \text{Initial inventory} \quad (3.28)$$

3.10.4 Cost of Goods Sold (COGS)

Next, we discuss the calculation of the COGS. In the IS, for the purpose of finding the NI, we calculate the value of the COGS. In any year n, the COGS is equal to the value of the purchases plus the value of the initial inventory minus the value of the final inventory. The quantities of initial and final inventories and purchases are multiplied by their respective purchase prices. Thus, the value of the initial inventory in year n will be based on the purchase price in the previous year $n-1$ because the initial inventory in year n was purchased in the previous year $n-1$.

$$\text{COGS in year n} = \text{Purchases in year n} + \text{Final inventory in year n}$$
$$- \text{Initial inventory in year n} \quad (3.29)$$

3.10.5 Adjustments for Credit Sales and Purchases

Next, we present the adjustments for credit sales and purchases.

3.10.6 Accounts Receivable (AR)

Cash receipts from sales are divided in two types: sales on cash and sales on credit. In any year n, the cash receipts are equal to the sales revenues in year n times the percentage of sales received in the same year plus sales revenues from the previous year times the percentage of sales not received in the previous year. Let α be AR, as a percentage of the annual sales in year n.

$$\text{Cash receipts from sales revenues in year n} = (1 - \alpha) \times \text{Revenues in year n}$$
$$+ \alpha \times \text{Revenues in the}$$
$$\text{previous year } n - 1 \quad (3.30)$$

Rewriting equation 3.30, we obtain

$$\text{Cash receipts from sales revenues in year n} = \text{Revenues in year n}$$
$$- \text{AR in year n}$$
$$+ \text{AR in year } n - 1 \quad (3.31)$$

Define the change in AR as follows:

$$\text{Change in AR} = \text{AR in year n} - \text{AR in year n} - 1 \qquad (3.32)$$

Substituting equation 3.32 into equation 3.31, we obtain that the cash receipts in year n are equal to the revenues in year n minus the change in AR.

$$\text{Cash receipts from sales revenues in year n} = \text{Revenues in year n}$$
$$- \text{Change in AR} \qquad (3.33)$$

From a cash flow point of view, an increase in AR represents a cash outflow because we are selling more on credit; a decrease in AR represents a cash inflow because our customers are making payments.

3.10.7 Accounts Payable (AP)

Cash payments for purchase, salaries, and other expenses are divided into two categories: payments in cash and payments on credit. In any year n, the cash expenditures are equal to the purchases times the percentage of payments made in the same year plus purchases from the previous year times the percentage of payments not made in the previous year. Let β be AP, as a percentage of the annual purchases in year n.

$$\text{Cash expenditures from purchases in year n} = (1 - \beta) \times \text{Purchases in year n}$$
$$+ \beta \times \text{Purchases in the}$$
$$\text{previous year n} - 1 \quad (3.34)$$

Rewriting equation 3.34, we obtain

$$\text{Cash expenditures from purchases in year n} = \text{Purchases in year n}$$
$$- \text{AP in year n}$$
$$+ \text{AP in year n} - 1 \quad (3.35)$$

Define the change in AP as follows:

$$\text{Change in AP} = \text{AP in year n} - \text{AP in year n} - 1 \qquad (3.36)$$

Substituting equation 3.36 into equation 3.35, we obtain that the cash expenditures in year n is equal to the purchases in year n minus the change in AP.

$$\text{Cash expenditures from purchases in year n} = \text{Purchases in year n}$$
$$- \text{Change in AP} \qquad (3.37)$$

From a cash flow point of view, an increase in AP represents a cash inflow because we are buying more on credit; a decrease in AP represents a cash outflow because we are making payments for our purchases.

3.11 SUMMARY AND CONCLUDING REMARKS

In this chapter, we have presented four financial statements and the basic accounting concepts that are required for understanding the construction of the financial statements in the subsequent chapters. In particular, we stressed the integration of the IS, the BS, and the CB statement.

For most readers, all the material in this chapter should be familiar. If readers require additional explanations and discussions, they should consult textbooks in accounting.

KEY CONCEPTS AND IDEAS

Accounts payable (AP)
Accounts receivable (AR)
Assets
Balance sheet (BS)
Book (historical) value
Cash budget (CB) statement
Cash flow from financing activities
Cash flow from investing activities
Cash flow from operating activities
Cash flow statement (CFS) according
   to GAAP
Cash Required for Operations (CRO)
Change in accounts payable
Change in accounts receivable
Cost of Goods Sold (COGS)
Cumulative retained earnings
Current assets
Current liabilities
Depreciation schedule
Dividends
Earnings before interest and taxes (EBIT)
Earnings before taxes (EBT)
Financial statement
Generally Accepted Accounting
   Principles (GAAP)

Gross profit
Income statement (IS)
Intangible assets
Interest expense
Interest income
Inventories
Liabilities
Loan schedule
Market value
Marketable securities
Net income (NI)
Operating cash flow (OCF)
Operating profits
Payout ratio
Principal repayment
Purchases
Quantity sold
Retained earnings
Revenues
Stockholders' Equity Statement
Tangible assets
Working capital
Working capital (exclusive of cash)

APPENDIX A

In this appendix, using financial statements that will be constructed in Chapter Five, we show how to derive the CB given only the two most popular statements: the IS and the BS.

The basis of the derivation is what we call the stock balance equation. We illustrate this idea with the example from Chapter Five.

Recall that the BS is a report that shows the stock of the items listed in the balance, such as cash, AR, inventory, AP, debt, and equity. We can imagine that the BS shows the level of the different reservoirs where the stocks of the various items are kept. The IS shows the dynamic part or the movements of those stocks. It tells us the amount or flow of goods expressed in dollars (product, services, raw material, labor, and so on) that flows into or out of the reservoirs.

Then we can express the idea of the stock balance equation as follows:

$$\text{Level of the reservoir}_n = \text{Level of the reservoir}_{n-1}$$
$$+ \text{New flow into the reservoir}_n$$
$$- \text{Flow out of the reservoir}_n \qquad (A3.1)$$

For instance, if we wish to know the level of AR we would write the following equation:

$$\text{Level of AR}_n = \text{Level of AR}_{n-1} + \text{New flow into AR}_n$$
$$- \text{Flow out of AR}_n \qquad (A3.2)$$

where AR_n is the level of AR at period n. What are the new flows into AR_n and the flows out of AR_n? In this particular case we have to think about the economic activity that increases or decreases the level of AR. Accounts receivable increases when there is invoicing of the product or a service the firm offers to its customers. Accounts receivable decreases when customers pay the outstanding invoices. Then equation A3.2 can be written as follows:

$$\text{Level of AR}_n = \text{Level of AR}_{n-1} + \text{Sales revenues}_n$$
$$- \text{Collection of AR}_n \qquad (A3.3)$$

From equation A3.3, we solve for collection of AR_n and we know the inflows we have from AR, as follows:

$$\text{Collection of } AR_n = \text{Level of } AR_{n-1} + \text{Sales revenues}_n$$
$$- \text{Level of } AR_n \qquad (A3.4)$$

In a similar fashion we can derive the AP payments:

$$\text{Level of } AP_n = \text{Level of } AP_{n-1} + \text{Expenses}_n - \text{Payment of } AP_n \qquad (A3.5)$$

Solving for Payment of AP_n we have the following:

$$\text{Payment of } AP_n = \text{Level of } AP_{n-1} + \text{Expenses}_n - \text{Level of } AP_n \qquad (A3.6)$$

In the case of estimating the amount purchased, we know from the chapter that there exists a relationship between purchases, COGS, and inventories:

$$COGS_n = \text{Initial inventory}_{n-1} + \text{Purchases}_n - \text{Final inventory}_n \qquad (A3.7)$$

$$\text{Purchases} = COGS_n - \text{Initial inventory}_{n-1} + \text{Final inventory}_n \qquad (A3.8)$$

We can derive the purchase of assets or the payment of debt in a similar fashion. The same can be said about the excess of cash reinvested. For instance, the purchase of fixed assets can be estimated using the same stock balance equation.

$$\text{Net fixed assets}_n = \text{Net fixed assets}_{n-1} - \text{Depreciation}_n$$
$$+ \text{Purchase of new assets}_n \qquad (A3.9)$$

Solving for the purchase of new assets, we have the following:

$$\text{Purchase of new assets}_n = \text{Net fixed assets}_n - \text{Net fixed assets}_{n-1}$$
$$+ \text{Depreciation}_n \qquad (A3.10)$$

First we examine the financial statements.

Using equations A3.4 and A3.6 we can estimate the collection of AR and payment of AP for each year.

For instance, collection of AR for year 2 is $54,087.60.

$$\text{Collection of } AR_n = \text{Level of } AR_{n-1} + \text{Sales revenues}_n - \text{Level of } AR_n$$

$$\text{Collection of } AR_2 = 2{,}595.60 + 54{,}202.10 - 2{,}710.10 = 54{,}087.60$$

TABLE A3.1   Income Statement

	Year 0	Year 1	Year 2	Year 3	Year 4	Year 5
Sales		51,912.00	54,202.10	57,153.60	60,265.80	63,547.40
COGS		20,708.60	24,099.70	24,996.20	25,772.20	26,577.80
Gross profit		31,203.40	30,102.40	32,157.40	34,493.60	36,969.70
Selling and administrative expenses		9,441.90	9,841.50	10,308.70	10,798.50	11,325.30
Depreciation		10,000.00	10,000.00	10,000.00	10,000.00	11,345.40
EBIT		11,761.50	10,260.90	11,848.80	13,695.10	14,299.00
Interest income on marketable securities		0.00	747.40	1,230.20	1,825.90	0.00
Other expenses (interest expenses)		1,933.50	1,546.80	1,160.10	773.40	926.20
EBT		9,828.00	9,461.50	11,918.80	14,747.60	13,372.80
Taxes		3,439.80	3,311.50	4,171.60	5,161.70	4,680.50
NI		6,388.20	6,149.90	7,747.30	9,585.90	8,692.30
Dividends		4,471.70	4,305.00	5,423.10	6,710.20	6,084.60
Retained earnings		1,916.50	1,845.00	2,324.20	2,875.80	2,607.70
Accumulated retained earnings		6,388.20	8,066.40	11,508.70	15,671.60	17,653.70

TABLE A3.2   Balance Sheet

	Year 0	Year 1	Year 2	Year 3	Year 4	Year 5
Assets						
Cash	1,576.90	100.00	110.00	120.00	130.00	140.00
AR	0.00	2,595.60	2,710.10	2,857.70	3,013.30	3,177.40
Inventory	0.00	1,725.70	2,033.30	2,085.00	2,150.80	2,217.90
Investment on marketable securities	0.00	12,271.90	20,199.90	29,981.60	0.00	8,670.60
Interest accrued	0.00	0.00	0.00	0.00	0.00	0.00
Net fixed assets	40,000.00	30,000.00	20,000.00	10,000.00	45,381.60	34,036.20
Total	41,576.90	46,693.20	45,053.30	45,044.20	50,675.60	48,242.10
Liabilities and equity						
AP	0.00	2,243.40	2,440.70	2,504.80	2,583.80	2,664.50
Accrued taxes	0.00	0.00	0.00	0.00	0.00	0.00
Long-term debt	17,576.90	14,061.50	10,546.10	7,030.80	8,420.30	3,923.90
Total liabilities	17,576.90	16,305.00	12,986.90	9,535.60	11,004.10	6,588.40
Equity	24,000.00	24,000.00	24,000.00	24,000.00	24,000.00	24,000.00
Retained earnings	0.00	6,388.20	8,066.40	11,508.70	15,671.60	17,653.70
Total	41,576.90	46,693.20	45,053.30	45,044.20	50,675.60	48,242.10

Deriving the payments of AR implies we have to identify the lines that contribute to the change in the AP level. These lines (from the IS) are as follows:

1. Purchases
2. Selling and administrative expenses

Purchases are calculated using equation A3.8, as follows:

$$\text{Purchases} = \text{COGS}_n - \text{Initial inventory}_{n-1} + \text{Final inventory}_n \quad \text{(A3.11)}$$

For year 2, we have the following:

$$\text{Purchases}_2 = 24{,}099.70 - 1{,}725.70 + 2{,}033.30 = 24{,}407.30$$

Then the total items that might increase AP are as follows:

$$\text{Purchases}_2 + \text{Selling and administrative expenses}_2 = 24{,}407.30 + 9{,}841.50$$
$$= 34{,}248.90$$

Applying equation A3.6, we have

$$\text{Payment of AP}_n = \text{Level of AP}_{n-1} + \text{Expenses}_n - \text{Level of AP}_n \quad \text{(A3.12)}$$

For year 2, we have the following:

$$\text{Payment of AP}_2 = 2{,}243.40 + 34{,}248.90 - 2{,}440.70 = 34{,}051.60$$

For estimating the purchase of fixed assets we use equation A3.10, as follows:

$$\text{Purchase of new assets}_n = \text{Net fixed assets}_n$$
$$- \text{Net fixed assets}_{n-1} + \text{Depreciation}_n \quad \text{(A3.13)}$$

For year 4, we have the following:

$$\text{Purchase of new assets}_4 = \text{Net fixed assets}_4 - \text{Net fixed assets}_3$$
$$+ \text{Depreciation}_4$$

$$\text{Purchase of new assets}_4 = 45{,}381.60 - 10{,}000.00 + 10{,}000.00 = 45{,}381.60$$

Then, applying the type of formulas as we have described, we obtain the following CB statement (Table A3.3).

The reader can compare this CB statement with the one constructed in Chapter Five. She will notice that the level of aggregation obtained in this case is much less than the one constructed in Chapter Five.

TABLE A3.3   The Derived Cash Budget

	Year 0	Year 1	Year 2	Year 3	Year 4	Year 5
Cash inflows						
Total income AR		49,316.40	54,087.60	57,006.00	60,110.20	63,383.30
Total cash inflows		49,316.40	54,087.60	57,006.00	60,110.20	63,383.30
Cash outflows						
Total payments on cash		29,632.90	34,051.60	35,292.50	36,557.50	37,889.50
Purchase of fixed assets		0.00	0.00	0.00	45,381.60	0.00
Taxes		3,439.80	3,311.50	4,171.60	5,161.70	4,680.50
Total cash outflows		33,072.70	37,363.10	39,464.10	87,100.70	42,570.00
NCB		16,243.80	16,724.50	17,542.00	−26,990.50	20,813.40
Payment of loans		−3,515.40	−3,515.40	−3,515.40	1,389.50	−4,496.40
Interest charges		1,933.50	1,546.80	1,160.10	773.40	926.20
NCB after financial		10,794.90	11,662.40	12,866.50	−26,374.40	15,390.80
transactions						
Equity investment		0.00	0.00	0.00	0.00	0.00
Dividend payments		0.00	4,471.70	4,305.00	5,423.10	6,710.20
NCB after cash transactions		10,794.90	7,190.70	8,561.50	−31,797.50	8,680.60
with shareholders						
Interest income on		0.00	747.40	1,230.20	1,825.90	0.00
marketable securities						
Investment on marketable		12,271.90	7,928.00	9,781.70	−29,981.60	8,670.60
securities (netted)						
NCB after discretionary		−1,476.90	10.00	10.00	10.00	10.00
transactions paid in cash						
Accumulated cash balance	1,576.90	100.00	110.00	120.00	130.00	140.00
at end of year						

In this appendix, we present samples for the BS and the IS. They have been adapted from the website of The Coca-Cola Company and Subsidiaries. In most websites of the U.S. firms, the reader will find their annual reports where the financial statements are presented.

The Coca-Cola Company and Subsidiaries
2002 annual report
Income Statement

Year ended December 31,	2002	2001	2000
(In millions except per share data)			
Net operating revenues	$19,564	$17,545	$17,354
COGS	$7,105	$6,044	$6,204
Gross profit	$12,459	$11,501	$11,150
Selling, general, and administrative expenses	$7,001	$6,149	$6,016
Other operating charges			$1,443
Operating income	$5,458	$5,352	$3,691
Interest income	$209	$325	$345
Interest expense	$199	$289	$447
Equity income (loss)	$384	$152	($289)
OI (loss)—net	($353)	$39	$99
Gains on issuances of stock by equity investee	$0	$91	$0
Income before income taxes	$5,499	$5,670	$3,399
Income taxes	$1,523	$1,691	$1,222
NI	$3,976	$3,979	$2,177

The Coca-Cola Company and Subsidiaries
Balance sheet

December 31,	2002	2001	2000
(In millions except share data)			
Assets			
Current			
Cash and cash equivalents	$2,126	$1,866	$1,819
Marketable securities	$219	$68	$73
	$2,345	$1,934	$1,892
Trade AR, less allowances of $55 in 2002 and $59 in 2001	$2,097	$1,882	$1,757
Inventories	$1,294	$1,055	$1,066

(continues)

(continued)

Prepaid expenses and other assets	$1,616	$2,300	$1,905
Total current assets	$7,352	$7,171	$6,620
Investments and other assets			
Equity method investments			
Coca-Cola Enterprises Inc.	$972	$788	$707
Coca-Cola Hellenic Bottling Company S.A.	$872	$791	$617
Coca-Cola Amatil Limited	$492	$432	$758
Other, principally bottling companies	$2,401	$3,117	$3,164
Cost method investments, principally bottling companies	$254	$294	$519
Other assets	$2,694	$2,792	$2,364
Property, plant and equipment	$7,685	$8,214	$8,129
Land	$385	$217	$225
Buildings and improvements	$2,332	$1,812	$1,642
Machinery and equipment	$5,888	$4,881	$4,547
Containers	$396	$195	$200
	$9,001	$7,105	$6,614
Less allowances for depreciation	$3,090	$2,652	$2,446
	$5,911	$4,453	$4,168
Trademarks with indefinite lives	$1,724	$1,697	$1,917
Goodwill and other intangible assets	$1,829	$882	
Total assets	$24,501	$22,417	$20,834

The Coca-Cola Company and Subsidiaries
Balance sheet

December 31,	2002	2001	2000
(In millions except share data)			
Liabilities and share-owners' equity			
Current			
AP and accrued expenses	$3,692	$3,679	$3,905
Loans and notes payable	$2,475	$3,743	$4,795
Current maturities of long-term debt	$180	$156	$21
Accrued income taxes	$994	$851	$600
Total current liabilities	$7,341	$8,429	$9,321
Long-term debt	$2,701	$1,219	$835
Other liabilities	$2,260	$961	$1,004
Deferred income taxes	$399	$442	$358
Total liabilities	$12,701	$11,051	$11,518
Share-owners' equity			
Common stock, $.25 par value			
Authorized: 5,600,000,000 shares; issued: 3,490,818,627 shares in 2002 and 3,491,465,016 shares in 2001	$873	$873	$870
Capital surplus	$3,857	$3,520	$3,196
Reinvested earnings	$24,506	$23,443	$21,265
Accumulated other comprehensive income (loss) and unearned compensation on restricted stock	($3,047)	($2,788)	($2,722)
	$26,189	$25,048	$22,609

(continues)

(*continued*)

Less treasury stock, at cost (1,019,839,490 shares in 2002; 1,005,237,693 shares in 2001)	($14,389)	($13,682)	($13,293)
Net equity	$11,800	$11,366	$9,316
Total liabilities and share-owners' equity	$24,501	$22,417	$20,834

The Coca-Cola Company and Subsidiaries
Cash flow statement
2002 annual report

Year ended December 31, (*In millions*)	2002	2001	2000
Operating activities			
NI	$3,976	$3,979	$2,177
Depreciation and amortization	$806	$803	$773
Stock-based compensation expense	$365	$41	$43
Deferred income taxes	$40	$56	$3
Equity income or loss, net of dividends	($256)	($54)	$380
Foreign currency adjustments	($76)	($60)	$196
Gain on issuances of stock by equity investee	$0	($91)	–
(Gains) losses on sales of assets, including bottling interests	$3	($85)	($127)
Other items	$291	($17)	$76
Net change in operating assets and liabilities	($407)	($462)	($852)
Net cash provided by operating activities	$4,742	$4,110	$2,669

The Coca-Cola Company and Subsidiaries
Cash flow statement
2002 annual report

Year ended December 31,	2002	2001	2000
Investing activities			
Acquisitions and investments, principally trademarks and bottling companies	($544)	($651)	($397)
Purchases of investments and other assets	($156)	($456)	($508)
Proceeds from disposals of investments and other assets	$243	$455	$290
Purchases of property, plant, and equipment	($851)	($769)	($733)
Proceeds from disposals of property, plant, and equipment	$69	$91	$45
Other investing activities	$52	$142	$138
Net cash used in investing activities	($1,187)	($1,188)	($1,165)
Financing activities			
Issuances of debt	$1,622	$3,011	$3,671
Payments of debt	($2,378)	($3,937)	($4,256)
Issuances of stock	$107	$164	$331
Purchases of stock for treasury	($691)	($277)	($133)
Dividends	($1,987)	($1,791)	($1,685)

(*continues*)

(continued)

Net cash used in financing activities	($3,327)	($2,830)	($2,072)
Effect of exchange rate changes on cash and cash equivalents	$32	($45)	($140)
Cash and cash equivalents			
Net increase during the year	$260	$47	$208
Balance at beginning of year	$1,866	$1,819	$1,611
Balance at end of year	$2,126	$1,866	$1,819

We also present sample financial statements for hypothetical firms, which can be found at www.TheStreet.com. For further discussions and explanations, the interested reder can visit the website.

Sample Balance Sheet

Assets			
Current assets			$188,000
Cash and cash equivalents		$22,500	
AR	$55,000	$54,500	
Less: allowance for doubtful accounts	$−500		
Inventories		$35,000	
Prepaid expenses		$10,000	
Other		$66,000	
Investments			$145,000
Investment in company B		$145,000	
Property, plant & equipment			$152,000
Land		$22,000	
Buildings and improvement	$100,000	$70,000	
Less: accumulated depreciation	$−30,000		
Fixtures, furniture & equipment	$80,000	$60,000	
Less: accumulated depreciation	$−20,000		
Intangibles			$35,000
Goodwill		$35,000	
Other assets			$8,000
Total assets			$528,000
LIABILITIES & STOCKHOLDERS' EQUITY			
LIABILITIES			
Current liabilities			$93,000
Long-term liabilities			$144,000
Total liabilities			$237,000
STOCKHOLDERS' EQUITY			
Total shareholders' equity			$291,000
Paid-in capital		$190,000	
Retained earnings		$101,000	
Total liabilities & shareholders' equity			$528,000

Sample Income Statement

Revenues			$550,000
Cost of goods			
Beginning inventory		$40,000	
Net purchases		$325,000	
Cost of goods available for sale		$365,000	
Less: ending inventory		$-35,000	
COGS			$-330,000
Gross margin on sales			$220,000
Expenses			
Selling expenses		$73,000	
Sales salaries	$48,000		
Non-recurring item	$12,000		
Other	$13,000		
General & administrative expenses		$64,500	
Office salaries	$27,100		
Depreciation	$5,500		
Amortization	$3,200		
Bad debt	$4,500		
Other	$24,200		
Total operating expenses			$-137,500
Income from operations (EBIT)			$82,500
Other revenues			$21,000
Revenues		$5,200	
Dividends		$7,200	
Gains on sale of equipment		$8,600	
Other expenses			$-19,500
Interest		$9,400	
Writeoff—goodwill		$5,000	
Unusual item—loss on sale of long-term investment		$5,100	
Income before taxes and extraordinary items			$84,000
Income tax expenses			$-33,600
Income before extraordinary items			$50,400
Gain on disposal of business segment			$24,000
NI			$74,400
Other comprehensive income			$12,000
Comprehensive income			$86,400

4

CONSTRUCTING INTEGRATED PRO-FORMA FINANCIAL STATEMENTS, PART ONE

Consistency is the last refuge of the unimaginative.

—*Oscar Wilde* (1854 to 1900)

Everything should be made as simple as possible, but not simpler.

—*Albert Einstein* (1879 to 1955)

4.1 BASIC FINANCIAL STATEMENTS

In this chapter, using a simple numerical example, we illustrate the basic ideas for constructing the integrated financial statements over the forecast (or planning) period, which is assumed to be five years. For the moment we postpone the discussion of the calculation of the terminal value (TV), which is the present value (PV), with respect to the terminal period, of the cash flows that occur in the years beyond the forecast period.[1]

For flexibility, we build the model with disaggregated variables such as the expected inflation rate, the real growth rates for the input and output prices, and

[1]The selection of the length of the forecast period depends on the number of years that is required for the cash flow profile to reach a steady state. In the chapter on the terminal value we discuss this issue in further detail.

the prices and quantities for the inputs and outputs. We avoid the use of financial ratios because the fundamental determinants of the cash flows might not be transparent with the ratios. In addition, the use of the disaggregated variables facilitates relevant sensitivity analyses on the values of key parameters.

In Chapter Five, we make the simple example more complex by introducing additional assumptions into the model. We hope that the detailed exposition in this chapter eases the transition to the complex model in Chapter Five.

The appropriate degree of complexity in the modeling of the financial statements depends on the considered judgment of the analyst. Our model is generic. We hope that the basic principles that are presented here can be extended and adapted to suit the specific needs of the reader. In this chapter, we focus on the basic framework and principles for constructing the integrated set of financial statements and the preparatory tables that are linked to the financial statements. In the financial statements, and accompanying tables, we use the end of year convention. All the transactions or activities that occur during the year are listed *as if* they occur at the end of the year.

4.2 SIMPLE NUMERICAL EXAMPLE

We use a simple numerical example to illustrate the construction of the financial statements that are required for valuation. First, we construct the three typical financial statements; namely the income statement (IS), the CB, and the BS. Second, we construct the cash flow statement (CFS) according to Generally Accepted Accounting Principles (GAAP). The financial statements are linked by the accounting relationships that we have presented earlier in Chapter Three. In Chapter Six, we derive the Free Cash Flow (FCF) statement from the financial statements, and proceed to value the cash flows.

The construction of the financial statements starts from policies and targets (for example, AR policy) that are based on the history or assessment of the economic environment (for example, expected inflation rates and expected price increases). With these targets or policies we construct the financial statements. With a new firm or project, the historical data does not exist. Thus, to make the projections in the financial statements for a new firm or project, we have to find the relevant secondary information based on comparable firms or projects.

Before constructing the integrated financial statements, we build other preliminary tables that are used as inputs in the construction of the three main financial statements. In the main text, we describe the construction of all the preliminary tables and financial statements. The first table that should be constructed is the table of parameters. The table of parameters organizes all the relevant information about the company or project. We have constructed all the tables in an Excel spreadsheet program. All the subsequent tables are linked to values in the table of parameters through formulas. It is important to ensure that the cells in the subsequent tables and financial statements are properly linked to the values in the table of parameters. Thus, when a value in the table of parameters is updated or changed, all the entries and calculations in the subsequent tables are automatically updated.

4.2.1 Basic Data for the Simple Example

Consider a simple retail firm that buys and sells some product.[2] At the end of year 0, the current cost of the required assets is $40,000. The forecast period is five years and the economic life of the assets is four years. At the end of the fourth year, the firm purchases a replacement asset.

For tax purposes, we assume straight-line depreciation. The specification of the annual depreciation allowance affects the calculation of the tax liabilities. The economic depreciation of the assets is not the same as the depreciation for tax purposes, and in fact, the economic depreciation might have no relationship with the depreciation allowance for tax purposes. For convenience and simplicity, we often assume that the annual economic depreciation can be approximated by the annual depreciation allowance as calculated in the depreciation schedule.

For simplicity, in this chapter we assume (unrealistically) that the expected inflation rates over the forecast period are zero, and that there are no expected real increases in the prices of the inputs and outputs. We introduce expected real changes in the prices and the expected inflation rates in the next chapter, where we construct the financial statements in nominal terms. Constructing financial statements in nominal terms properly accounts for the positive and negative impacts of inflation on the cash flow profile and *always* gives consistent results.[3]

The basic information is listed in the following table. The expected number of units that will be sold in year 1 is $7,200 and the annual inventory is one month of sales. It is expected that the annual increase in the sale of units will be 1% for year 2, and 2% for years 3–5. The expected selling price is

---

[2]The financial statements that we construct are valid for a retail firm. The financial statements for a manufacturing concern are complex due to the different classes of inventories that they carry.

[3]To be correct, the financial statements must be constructed in nominal terms. Sometimes, the reader might see financial statements that are constructed in real prices (non-neutral inflation) or constant prices (neutral inflation). The three approaches, namely nominal prices, real prices, and constant prices will give the same results only under very restrictive conditions. If these conditions are not satisfied, the use of the other two approaches can lead to incorrect valuation of cash flows or selection of projects.

$7 per unit and the expected unit cost is $2.779 per unit. Both the selling price and the purchase prices are constant for the life of the project because the expected real changes in the price and the expected inflation rates are zero. We assume that the values for the sales unit, the sales price, and the purchase have been obtained from a market survey. In the next chapter, we discuss in greater detail the market survey.

TABLE 4.1 Basic Information

	Year 0	Year 1	Year 2	Year 3	Year 4	Year 5
Fixed assets	40,000.00					
Linear depreciation (years)	4.00					
Initial equity investment	24,000.00					
Tax rate	35.00%					
Final inventory at year 0	0.00					
Observed return to unlevered equity ρ for year 0	17.48%					
Leverage (constant) for perpetuity	30.00%					
Expected inflation rate for year 6 and beyond	0.00%					
Inflation rate		0.00%	0.00%	0.00%	0.00%	0.00%
Real annual rate of increase in selling price		0.00%	0.00%	0.00%	0.00%	0.00%
Real annual rate of increase in cost per unit		0.00%	0.00%	0.00%	0.00%	0.00%
Overhead estimated at year 0						
Real rate of increase in overhead expenses	2,184.00	0.00%	0.00%	0.00%	0.00%	0.00%
Payroll of selling and administrative force						
Real rate of increase in payroll	2,400.00	0.00%	0.00%	0.00%	0.00%	0.00%
Real rate of increase in price of fixed assets		0.00%	0.00%	0.00%	0.00%	0.00%
Sales commissions		6.00%	6.00%	6.00%	6.00%	6.00%
Advertising and promotion expenses (% of sales)		3.00%	3.00%	3.00%	3.00%	3.00%
Real rate of interest		3.00%	3.00%	3.00%	3.00%	3.00%
Premium for debt risk		4.913%	4.913%	4.913%	4.913%	4.913%

4.2.2 Cash Required for Operations

We include an item called CRO to pay for expenses such as overhead, payroll, and sales commissions. In other words, the CRO is the operating cash that is required for the daily financial transactions in the firm. The CRO is necessary because some payments are made on a cash basis, while the sales income is received on the basis of credit. We assume that the CRO at the end of year 0 is based on 20% of the sum of the annual overhead, payroll, and commission expenses in year 1. The CRO for subsequent years are shown in Table 4.2. The values for the annual overhead and payroll are listed in Table 4.1 and are expected to be constant over the forecast period. The commission expenses depend on sales and are taken from calculations that are presented later in Section 4.3.5.

$$\text{CRO in year } 0 = 20\% \times (\text{overhead} + \text{payroll} + \text{sales commission})$$
$$= 20\% \times (2{,}184 + 2{,}400 + 3{,}024)$$
$$= 20\% \times 7{,}608 = 1{,}521.60$$

Shareholders in the firm invest $24,000. A bank loan finances the remaining amount that is required. In addition, a bank loan finances the purchase of the new asset in year 4. The tax rate is 35%.

4.2.3 Reinvestment of Surplus Funds

It is assumed that any surplus funds (excess cash) less the CRO are reinvested in short-term securities that earn a market rate of return, which is less than the cost of capital for the firm. The short-term interest rate is 3%. The surplus funds will cover partially the purchase of a new fixed asset at the end of year 4. The remaining amount that is required for the purchase of the new fixed asset will be financed with debt. In subsequent chapters, we discuss in greater detail the reinvestment of surplus funds and its impacts on the valuation of cash flows.

4.2.4 Terminal Value Calculation

The time frame for the construction and analysis of the financial statements is five years. It is most likely that the life of the firm extends beyond five years, and to take account of the FCF beyond year 5 we calculate the TV. The calculation of the TV merits further detailed discussion in Chapter Nine and can be an important determinant of value if the time period for the analysis is short.

For simplicity, we postpone the calculation of the TV for the firm. Because it is a going concern, the firm does not sell the existing asset. The value generating capacity of the existing assets will be taken into account in the calculation of the TV, which we discuss in Chapter Nine. If it were not a going concern, we would list the market liquidation value of the existing assets and liabilities at the end of year 5.

4.3 GOALS AND POLICIES FOR SELECTED VARIABLES

The detailed parameters for the example are shown in Tables 4.1 and 4.2. Based on the estimates for the target variables, we construct the integrated financial statements (BS, IS, and CB). The financial statements are linked together with the basic accounting equations from Chapter Three.

Many of the estimates for the construction of the financial statements are based on the goals and policies stated by the management of the firm. For instance, the recovery of AR is an example of a management goal. In addition to the basic information, the management can stipulate some general policies. These policies and goals can be thought of as internal variables. The decision maker controls the internal variables to some extent. Examples of internal variables are inventory level, and the amount of AR and AP. Some other variables, such as the expected domestic and foreign inflation rates and interest rates, are called external or exogenous variables. The impact of both types of variables on the cash flow profile can be analyzed using sensitivity or scenario analysis.

For this example, we specify some values for the inventory policy and the policies for AR and AP. The annual final inventory is one month of sales or 8.33% of the annual sales. Accounts receivable in year n is 5% of the annual sales. In the current year n, we receive the part of the sales sold on a cash basis, plus AR of the previous year $n - 1$. For simplicity, AP in year n is 10% of the annual purchases only.

TABLE 4.2   Policies and Targets

	Year 0	Year 1	Year 2	Year 3	Year 4	Year 5
Fraction of sales to be kept as final inventory		8.33%	8.33%	8.33%	8.33%	8.33%
Percentage of sales received in the same year		95.00%				
Percentage of payments made the same year as accrued suppliers		90.00%				
Percentage of net income (NI) (dividends) paid to stockholders the year after obtaining the NI Payout ratio		70.00%				
Rate of increase in sales volume		0.00%	1.00%	2.00%	2.00%	2.00%
CRO required from year 1 to 5		100.00	110.00	120.00	130.00	140.00

In year 1, the first year of operation, the increase in the sales volume is 0%. In year 2, the increase in the sales volume is 1%, and in years 3–5 the increase in the sales volume is 2%. We assume that the sales commissions are 6% of the annual sales revenues and the expenditure on advertising and promotions are 3% of the annual sales revenues. In year n, the dividends declared to the stockholders are 70% of the NI. The dividends are actually paid in the following year.

These policies and goals calculate some of the variables. For simplicity, in this example these policies and goals are held constant over time; however, in reality the policies and goals change over time. In this case, we estimate the sales in units, and from this we can calculate the final inventory and the required purchases. And with known prices and quantities, we can calculate AR. Market research and other inquiries might allow the manager to get some estimates for selected variables such as the expected units sold for year 1, administrative costs, and sales costs.

4.4 DEPRECIATION SCHEDULE

The depreciation schedule is shown in Table 4.3. For simplicity, as mentioned earlier, we have assumed straight-line depreciation.

TABLE 4.3   Depreciation Schedule

	Year 0	Year 1	Year 2	Year 3	Year 4	Year 5
Beginning net fixed assets		40,000.00	30,000.00	20,000.00	10,000.00	40,000.00
Annual depreciation		10,000.00	10,000.00	10,000.00	10,000.00	10,000.00
Cumulative depreciation		10,000.00	20,000.00	30,000.00	40,000.00	50,000.00
New assets	0.00	0.00	0.00	0.00	40,000.00	0.00
Net fixed assets	40,000.00	30,000.00	20,000.00	10,000.00	40,000.00	30,000.00

The annual depreciation allowance is $10,000.

$$\text{Annual depreciation allowance} = \frac{40,000}{4} = 10,000.00$$

At the end of any year, the value of the net fixed assets is equal to the value of the net fixed assets at the beginning of the year plus any new assets minus the annual depreciation. The annual values of the net fixed assets are listed in the BS.

At the end of year 4, the book value of the original fixed asset is zero. However, if the asset were to be sold, the *actual* market value of the fixed asset in year 4 might be positive and would be listed as a cash inflow. Because we have assumed that the expected inflation rate and the expected real increase in the price of the fixed asset are zero, the cost of the fixed asset that will be purchased in year 4 is the same as the initial cost of the fixed asset in year 0.

4.5 ESTIMATED TARGET VARIABLES

Next, we calculate the annual sales volume, the annual sales revenue, and the sales commission.

4.5.1 Annual Sales Volume

First, we estimate the number of units that will be sold each year. In each year the number of units that are sold increases by δ_n percent.

In year 1, the increase is 0% and thus the number of units sold is the same as the number that was estimated in year 0.

In year 2, the increase is 1% and the number of units sold in year 2 is 7,344.00.

$$\text{Units sold in year 2} = \text{Units sold in year 1 times } (1 + \delta_2\%)$$
$$= 7,200.00 \times (1 + 1\%) = 7,272.00$$
$$\text{Units sold in year 3} = \text{Units sold in year 2 times } (1 + \delta_3\%)$$
$$= 7,272.00 \times (1 + 2\%) = 7,417.44$$

The number of units sold for each year of the project is shown in Table 4.5.

4.5.2 Annual Sales Revenues

Based on the annual quantity sold, we can calculate the value of the sales revenue, which is equal to the quantity sold times the unit-selling price of $7. We have assumed that the selling price is constant for five years.

$$\text{Sales revenue} = \text{Quantity sold times unit selling price} \qquad (4.1)$$

For year 1, the sales revenue is $50,400.

$$\text{Sales revenue} = 7,200 \times 7 = 50,400.00$$

For year 2, the sales revenue is $50,904.

$$\text{Sales revenue} = 7,272 \times 7 = 50,904.00$$

The sales revenues for all the years are shown in Table 4.5.

4.5.3 Selling and Administrative Expenses

The selling and administrative expenses are shown in the following table. The selling and administrative expenses consist of the sum of the sales commission, the advertising and promotion expenses, the overhead, and payroll expenses.

For year 1, the sales commission is $3,024 and the selling and administrative expenses are $9,120. Previously, the sales commission of $3,024 was used in the calculation of the CRO.

$$\text{Sales commission} = 6\% \text{ times Revenues}$$
$$= 6\% \times 50,400 = 3,024.00$$
$$\text{Advertising and promotion} = 3\% \text{ times Revenues}$$
$$= 3\% \times 50,400 = 1,512.00$$
$$\text{Selling and administrative expenses} = \text{Sales commission}$$
$$+ \text{Advertising and promotion}$$
$$+ \text{Overhead} + \text{Payroll expenses}$$
$$= 3,024 + 1,512 + 2,184 + 2,400 = 9,120$$

For year 2, the sales commission is $3,054.24 and the selling and administrative expenses are $9,165.36.

$$\text{Sales commission} = 6\% \text{ times Revenues}$$
$$= 6\% \times 50,904 = 3,054.24$$
$$\text{Advertising and promotion} = 3\% \text{ times Revenues}$$
$$= 3\% \times 50,904 = 1,527.12$$
$$\text{Selling and administrative expenses} = \text{Sales commission}$$
$$+ \text{Advertising and promotion}$$
$$+ \text{Overhead} + \text{Payroll expenses}$$
$$= 3,054.24 + 1,527.12 + 2,184 + 2,400$$
$$= 9,165.36$$

TABLE 4.4 Selling and Administrative Expenses

	Year 0	Year 1	Year 2	Year 3	Year 4	Year 5
Sales commissions		3,024.00	3,054.20	3,115.30	3,177.60	3,241.20
Overhead		2,184.00	2,184.00	2,184.00	2,184.00	2,184.00
Payroll expenses		2,400.00	2,400.00	2,400.00	2,400.00	2,400.00
Advertising and promotions		1,512.00	1,527.10	1,557.70	1,588.80	1,620.60
Selling and administrative expenses		9,120.00	9,165.40	9,257.00	9,350.50	9,445.80

The sales commissions and the selling and administrative expenses for all the years are shown in Table 4.5.

TABLE 4.5   Basic Estimated Parameters

	Year 0	Year 1	Year 2	Year 3	Year 4	Year 5
Units sold	7,200.00	7,200.00	7,272.00	7,417.40	7,565.80	7,717.10
Selling price	7.00	7.00	7.00	7.00	7.00	7.00
Sales revenues		50,400.00	50,904.00	51,922.10	52,960.60	54,019.80
Overhead	2,184.00	2,184.00	2,184.00	2,184.00	2,184.00	2,184.00
Administrative payroll	2,400.00	2,400.00	2,400.00	2,400.00	2,400.00	2,400.00
Selling commissions		3,024.00	3,054.20	3,115.30	3,177.60	3,241.20
Advertising and promotions		1,512.00	1,527.10	1,557.70	1,588.80	1,620.60
CRO for year 0 (based on 20% of overhead, payroll, and commissions expenses)	1,521.60					
Short-term rate of reinvestment		3.00%	3.00%	3.00%	3.00%	3.00%
Effective cost of debt before taxes		8.061%	8.061%	8.061%	8.061%	8.061%
Rate of interest for debt compounded twice a year		7.904%	7.904%	7.904%	7.904%	7.904%
Index for price of fixed assets		1.00	1.00	1.00	1.00	1.00
Price of future fixed assets					40,000.00	0.00

Later, we discuss some of the parameters that we have listed in Table 4.5.

4.6 PRELIMINARY TABLES FOR THE SIMPLE EXAMPLE

In this section, we prepare some preliminary tables that will be useful for constructing the financial statements. First, we construct the initial CB in year 0 to determine the amount of debt financing that is required. On purpose, we provide detailed explanations and guidelines to assist those readers who are unfamiliar with the construction of the CB statement. We request the patience of the more experienced readers.

Second, based on the amount of debt financing, we construct the loan schedule. Third, we calculate the inventory, the purchases, and the COGS. Fourth, we estimate AR and AP. For a review of the accounting relationships and concepts, the reader might wish to peruse the relevant sections in Chapter Three.

4.6.1 Initial Cash Budget Statement for Year 0

In year 0, we must determine the amount of financing that is required for the total investment plus the CRO. For this purpose, we construct the CB statement for year 0, which shows the cash inflows and outflows for year 0 (see Table 4.6). The values for the line items in the CB statement for the other years will be calculated later because those calculations require iterations between the CB statement and the IS. The CB at the end of year 0 (after financing) is equal to the CRO for that year. We show the complete CB statement in year 0, where many of the line items are zero.

In year 0, the total amount that is required for the project is equal to the sum of the cost of the fixed asset and the CRO. Of the $41,521.60 that is required, we finance $24,000 with contributions from the equity holders. This means that we need a loan of $17,521. In this model, we specify the amount of equity contribution first and the remaining amount is financed with debt. For now, we do not explain the other line items in Table 4.6. Later, we discuss the CB statement for year 0 again, in more detail.

If the equity contribution is equal to the total investment required (total fixed assets plus CRO), there is no need for debt financing.[4] With this information, we can construct the loan schedule.

TABLE 4.6   Cash Budget for Year 0 to Determine the Required Financing

	Year 0
Cash inflows	
Total income AR	
Total cash inflows	0.00
Cash outflows	
Total payments to suppliers on cash	
Overhead	
Payroll expenses	
Selling commissions	
Advertising and promotions	
Purchase of fixed assets	40,000.00
Purchase of fixed assets in year 4	
Taxes	
Total cash outflows	40,000.00
Net cash balance (NCB)	−40,000.00
Bank loan 1	17,521.60
Bank loan 2	
Payment of loans	
Interest charges	
NCB after financial transactions	−22,478.40
Equity investment	24,000.00
Dividend payments	
Repurchase of stock	
NCB after cash transactions with shareholders	1,521.60
Sales of marketable securities	
Interest income on marketable securities	
Investment on marketable securities	
NCB after discretionary transactions paid in cash	1,521.60
Accumulated cash balance at end of year	1,521.60

[4]In the spreadsheet, we use an IF statement to check for the amount of debt financing that is required. If the equity contribution is sufficient, the amount of debt is zero.

4.6.2 Loan Schedule

The bank loan is paid according to the following schedule. The effective interest rate on the loan is constant at 7.9045% per annum.

The principal will be repaid in five equal annual installments. The annual principal payment is $3,504.20.

$$\text{Annual principal payment} = \frac{17,521}{5} = 3,504.20$$

TABLE 4.7   Loan Schedule I

	Year 0	Year 1	Year 2	Year 3	Year 4	Year 5
BB		17,521.60	14,017.30	10,513.00	7,008.60	3,504.30
Interest charges debt 1		1,385.00	1,108.00	831.00	554.00	277.00
Principal payment debt 1		3,504.30	3,504.30	3,504.30	3,504.30	3,504.30
Total payment debt 1		4,889.30	4,612.30	4,335.30	4,058.30	3,781.30
Ending balance	17,521.60	14,017.30	10,513.00	7,008.60	3,504.30	0.00
Interest rate		7.904%	7.904%	7.904%	7.904%	7.904%

In the presence of inflation, the loan schedule could be more complicated. The interest rates might be linked to the expected inflation rates and become floating rates, and the principal payments might be structured to depend upon the amount of cash available, and hence, become non-constant principal payments.

For year 1, the interest charges are $1,385 and the total payments are $4,889.

$$\text{Interest charges} = 17,521 \times 7.9045\% = 1,384.95$$
$$\text{Total payment} = 1,384.95 + 3,504.20 = 4,889.15$$

The total loan repayment in any year n is equal to the principal repayment plus the interest charges for the year. The cost of debt is higher than the return on short-term investment.

At the end of year n, the EB is equal to the BB less the principal repayment. In year 1, the EB is $14,017.30.

$$\text{EB} = \text{BB less the principal payment}$$
$$= 17,521.60 - 3,504.30 = 14,017.40$$

Because the loan balance declines each year, the interest charges also decline.

In year 4, we calculate how much we need to borrow to purchase the new fixed asset. The amount of the new loan depends on the availability of the surplus funds that are invested in the marketable securities at that time.

TABLE 4.8   Loan Schedule 2

	Year 0	Year 1	Year 2	Year 3	Year 4	Year 5
BB						159.20
Interest charges debt 1						12.60
Principal payment debt 1						31.80
Total payment debt 1		0.00	0.00	0.00	0.00	44.40
EB					159.20	127.40
Interest rate		7.904%	7.904%	7.904%	7.904%	7.904%

For the moment, we simply specify that the amount of the new loan in year 4 is $159.20. After we have explained the mechanics of the CB statement for year 4, we explain the calculation of the amount of the new loan in year 4.

With the completion of the loan schedules in the IS, we list the interest payments on the two loans.

4.6.3 Inventory and Purchases

In this section, we present the calculations for the number of units in the inventory and the number of units that are purchased. Based on the number of units, we calculate the values of the inventories and the purchases. We require this information for the calculation of the COGS.

4.6.4 Final Inventory in Year 1

Next, based on the estimated sales, we calculate the number of units that have to be purchased, taking into account the inventory requirements. Previously we calculated the number of sold units, which are listed in Table 4.5.

The number of units for the inventory and purchases are shown in Table 4.9.

TABLE 4.9   Inventories and Purchases (in Units)

	Year 0	Year 1	Year 2	Year 3	Year 4	Year 5
Units sold		7,200.00	7,272.00	7,417.40	7,565.80	7,717.10
Final inventory		600.00	606.00	618.10	630.50	643.10
Initial inventory		0.00	600.00	606.00	618.10	630.50
Purchases		7,800.00	7,278.00	7,429.60	7,578.20	7,729.70

Final inventory is one month of the number of units that are sold annually. Hence, the final inventory will be the number of units sold multiplied by 8.33%. In year 1, the final inventory is 600 units.

$$\text{Final inventory in year } 1 = 7{,}200 \times 8.333\% = 600.00$$

In any year n, the initial inventory is simply the quantity left over as the final inventory in the previous year. Because year 1 is the first year of operation, there is no inventory from the previous year.

In year 2, the number of units sold is 7,272 and the final inventory is 606 units.

$$\text{Final inventory in year } 2 = 7{,}272 \times 8.333\% = 606.00$$

In a similar fashion, we calculate the values for the final inventory in years 3–5, which are shown in Table 4.9.

4.6.5 Purchases (Units)

We know that in any year, the purchases are equal to the quantity sold plus the final inventory less the initial inventory.

$$\text{Purchases} = \text{Quantity sold} + \text{Final inventory}$$
$$- \text{Initial inventory} \qquad (4.2)$$

For instance, for year 1 the purchases are equal to 7,800 units.

$$\text{Purchases} = 7{,}200.00 + 600.00 - 0 = 7{,}800.00$$

For year 2, the purchases are equal to 7,278 units.

$$\text{Purchases} = 7{,}272.00 + 606 - 600 = 7{,}278.00$$

In year 2, the initial inventory of $600 is equal to the value of the final inventory in year 1. The number of units that are purchased is equal to the number of units sold plus the change in the number of units in the inventory. The number of units purchased declines from year 1 to year 2 because in year 2, unlike in year 1, we do not have to buy the initial stock of inventory. In years 2–5, the number of units purchased steadily increases.

In a similar manner, we calculate the units that are purchased in years 3–5.

4.6.6 Cost of Goods Sold

The calculations for the COGS are shown in Table 4.10. The cost per unit is $2.7785 and it is constant for the forecast period because we have assumed that the expected inflation rate and the expected real increase in the input price are zero. Also, here we assume that the purchase price is independent of the number of units purchased. In practice, with volume discounts, it is common for the purchase price to decline with increases in the number of units purchased.

TABLE 4.10   Cost of Goods Sold

	Year 0	Year 1	Year 2	Year 3	Year 4	Year 5
Initial inventory		0.00	1,667.10	1,683.80	1,717.50	1,751.80
Purchases		21,672.60	20,222.20	20,643.30	21,056.20	21,477.30
Final inventory		1,667.10	1,683.80	1,717.50	1,751.80	1,786.90
COGS		20,005.40	20,205.50	20,609.60	21,021.80	21,442.20

In Table 4.10, we obtain the values for the inventories and purchases by multiplying the quantities in Table 4.9 with the unit purchase price.
For year 1, the COGS is $20,005.40.

$$COGS = \text{Purchases} + \text{Initial inventory} - \text{Final inventory}$$
$$= 7,800 \times 2.7785 + 0 \times 2.7785 - 600 \times 2.7785$$
$$= 21,672.30 + 0.00 - 1,667.10 = 20,005.50$$

For year 2, the COGS is $20,205.50.

$$COGS = \text{Purchases} + \text{Initial inventory} - \text{Final inventory}$$
$$= 7,278 \times 2.7785 + 600 \times 2.7785 - 606 \times 2.7785$$
$$= 20,221.90 + 1,667.10 - 1,683.80 = 20,205.20$$

In a similar manner, we calculate the COGS for years 3–5.

4.6.7 Accounts Receivable and Accounts Payable

In this section, we present the calculations for AR and AP. Unlike the IS, in the CB statement, we enter the actual cash receipts and expenditures. To obtain the cash figures that we require for the CB statement, we have to adjust the sales and purchases for the credit sales and purchases.

4.6.8 Accounts Receivable

Next, we calculate the annual values for AR and the AP. Cash receipts from sales are divided in two types: sales on cash and sales on credit. Each year, AR is 55% of the annual sales revenues.

4.6.9 Accounts Payable

Each year, AP is 10% of the value of the annual purchases. The values for the annual sales and purchases, disaggregated into cash and credit, are shown in the following table.

TABLE 4.11 Annual Sales and Purchases, in Cash and on Credit

	Year 0	Year 1	Year 2	Year 3	Year 4	Year 5
Sales on cash		47,880.00	48,358.80	49,326.00	50,312.50	51,318.80
Sales on credit		2,520.00	2,545.20	2,596.10	2,648.00	2,701.00
Purchases on cash		19,505.30	18,200.00	18,579.00	18,950.50	19,329.60
Purchases on credit		2,167.30	2,022.20	2,064.30	2,105.60	2,147.70

4.6.10 Cash Receipts and Cash Expenditures

From Table 4.5, we know the value of sales and from Table 4.10 we know the value of purchases. From Table 4.2 we know the policy and goal for payments and sales collection. With this information, we construct Tables 4.11 and 4.12
    In year 1, the cash receipts are $47,880.

$$\text{Cash receipts} = 95\% \times 50,400 = 47,880$$
$$\text{AR} = (1 - 95\%) \times 50,400 = 2,520$$

In year 2, the cash receipts are $50,879.

$$\text{Cash receipts} = 95\% \times 50,904 + 2,520$$
$$= 48,358.80 + 2,520 = 50,879$$

In year 1, the cash expenditures are $19,505.

$$\text{Cash expenditures} = 90\% \times 21,672.60 = 19,505$$
$$\text{AP} = (1 - 90\%) \times 21,672.60 = 2,167$$

In year 2, the cash expenditures are $20,367.

$$\text{Cash expenditures} = 90\% \times 20,222.20 + 2,167$$
$$= 18,200 + 2,167 = 20,367$$

TABLE 4.12 Cash Receipts and Expenditures

	Year 0	Year 1	Year 2	Year 3	Year 4	Year 5
Sales on cash		47,880.00	48,358.80	49,326.00	50,312.50	51,318.80
AR		0.00	2,520.00	2,545.20	2,596.10	2,648.00
Total sales collection		47,880.00	50,878.80	51,871.20	52,908.60	53,966.80
Purchases on cash		19,505.30	18,200.00	18,579.00	18,950.50	19,329.60
AP		0.00	2,167.30	2,022.20	2,064.30	2,105.60
Total purchases payments		19,505.30	20,367.20	20,601.20	21,014.90	21,435.20

In any year n, cash receipts are equal to revenues in year n minus AR in year n plus AR in the previous year $n - 1$. Similarly, in any year n, cash expenditures are equal to purchases in year n minus AP in year n plus AP in the previous year $n - 1$.

4.7 CONSTRUCTING THE FINANCIAL STATEMENTS FOR THE SIMPLE EXAMPLE

After constructing the preliminary tables, we are ready to construct the three inter-related financial statements, namely, IS, CB statement, and BS. Previously we had completed the CB statement for year 0 in Table 4.6.

First, we complete the line items in the IS for year 1, which is the first year of operation. For the subsequent years, as we will explain shortly, we calculate iteratively from year to year, and from financial statement to financial statement.

The partially completed IS is shown in Table 4.13. We have completed all the line items in the IS for year 1. To improve the flow of the exposition, we have relegated some of the calculations to the appendices. See Appendix A for details on the numerical calculations of the line items for the IS in year 1.

In year 1, the earnings before interest and taxes (EBIT) is $11,274.60 and the NI is $6,428.20. Recall that the dividends are declared in year 1 but they are actually paid in year 2. Thus, in year 1, the cumulative retained earnings are equal to the full value of the NI.

As mentioned earlier, we iterate forwards and backwards from the IS to the CB statement. For years 2–5, we have entered the values for the line

TABLE 4.13   Income Statement

	Year 0	Year 1	Year 2	Year 3	Year 4	Year 5
Sales		50,400.00	50,904.00	51,922.10	52,960.60	54,019.80
COGS		20,005.40	20,205.50	20,609.60	21,021.80	21,442.20
Gross profit		30,394.60	30,698.50	31,312.50	31,938.80	32,577.50
Selling and administrative expenses		9,120.00	9,165.40	9,257.00	9,350.50	9,445.80
Depreciation		10,000.00	10,000.00	10,000.00	10,000.00	10,000.00
EBIT		11,274.60	11,533.20	12,055.50	12,588.30	13,131.80
Interest income on marketable securities		0.00				
Other expenses (interest expenses)		1,385.00				
Earnings before taxes (EBT)		9,889.60				
Taxes		3,461.40				
NI		6,428.20				
Dividends		4,499.80				
Retained earnings		1,928.50				
Accumulated retained earnings		6,428.20				

items up to the EBIT. To calculate the taxes in the IS, we need to know the interest income from the investment in marketable securities with the surplus funds. The value of the surplus funds that are invested in marketable securities depends on the debt and equity financing.

The interest income is calculated in the CB statement, which is discussed in the next section. After we have determined the interest income from the investment in marketable securities, we can enter it in the IS and calculate the tax liability for the year. The tax liability for the year is then entered in the CB statement.

For example, in year 2, the annual interest income is based on the reinvestment of surplus funds at the end of year 1. After we have calculated the annual interest income in the CB statement, we return to the IS and complete the remaining line items for year 2. Next, we enter the relevant information in the BS.

In Appendix A, we also present detailed explanations for the iterations between the IS and the CB statement for year 1. For simplicity, we construct the BS last, after completing the IS and the CB statement. All the financial statements are linked, and in particular, the line items in the BS are derived from the appropriate line items in the IS and the CB statement.

To illustrate the construction of the CB statement, we revisit briefly the CB statement in year 0. Recall that there are four sections in the CB statement and we explain each section step by step. The details of the construction of the CB statements for year 1 are in Appendix A.

4.7.1 Cash Budget Statement in Year 0 Revisited

See Table 4.14. In year 0, there are no cash receipts. The cash expenditure of $40,000 is for the purchase of the fixed assets. The NCB in year 0 before financing and reinvestment is $−40,000.

NCB (loss) in year 0 (before financing and reinvestment)
$$= 0.0 − 40,000 = −40,000.00$$

Before financing and reinvestment, the NCB at the end of year 0 is equal to $ − 40,000. The amount of the bank loan is $17,521.60 and the NCB in year 0 after the debt financing is $−22,479.

NCB (loss) in year 0 (after debt financing)
$$= − 40,000 + 17,521.6 = −22,478.00$$

The equity investment is $24,000 and the NCB in year 0 after the debt and equity financing is $1,521. As expected, the NCB in year 0 is equal to the CRO in year 0.

NCB (loss) in year 0 (after debt and equity financing)
$$= −22,478.40 + 24,000 = 1,521.60$$

Because there are no other transactions in year 0, the NCB after reinvestment is $1,521 and the *final* cash balance in year 0 is the same value. The final cash balance in year 0 is entered in the BS as cash. In subsequent years, as we explain later, there are additional complications.

4.7.2 Cash Budget Statement for Year 1

The CB statement for year 1 is shown in Table 4.14.

In year 1, the NCB before debt and equity financing is $15,793.40. The NCB after debt and equity financing is $10,904.1.00 and the amount of the investment in surplus funds is $12,325.70. The investment in surplus funds generates interest income that we list in the IS in year 2. There are no dividend payments in year 1. The investment of surplus funds includes the final cash balance from year 0, which is available for investment in marketable securities.

The NCB after reinvestment is $−1,421.60, which is the result of the previous financing decisions regarding equity and debt financing. The negative value suggests that the extra cash is no longer required and is being released by the firm to be invested in marketable securities.

The final cash balance at the end of year 1 is 100. This final cash balance, which is the CRO for the year, is entered in the BS.

TABLE 4.14 Cash Budget for Year 1

	Year 0	Year 1	Year 2	Year 3	Year 4	Year 5
Cash inflows						
Total income AR	0.00	47,880.00	50,878.80	51,871.20	52,908.60	53,966.80
Total cash inflows	0.00	47,880.00	50,878.80	51,871.20	52,908.60	53,966.80
Cash outflows						
Total payments to suppliers on cash	0.00	19,505.30	20,367.20	20,601.20	21,014.90	21,435.20
Overhead	0.00	2,184.00	2,184.00	2,184.00	2,184.00	2,184.00
Payroll expenses	0.00	2,400.00	2,400.00	2,400.00	2,400.00	2,400.00
Selling commissions	0.00	3,024.00	3,054.20	3,115.30	3,177.60	3,241.20
Advertising and promotions	0.00	1,512.00	1,527.10	1,557.70	1,588.80	1,620.60
Purchase of fixed assets	40,000.00					
Purchase of fixed assets year 4	0.00	0.00	0.00	0.00	40,000.00	0.00
Taxes	0.00	3,461.40	3,778.20	4,150.60	4,531.00	4,494.80
Total cash outflows	40,000.00	32,086.70	33,310.80	34,008.70	74,896.30	35,375.70
NCB	−40,000.00	15,793.40	17,568.00	17,862.50	−21,987.70	18,591.10
Bank loan 1	17,521.60					
Bank loan 2		0.00				
Payment of loans		0.00	3,504.30			
Interest charges		0.00	1,385.00			
NCB after financial transactions	−22,478.40	10,904.10				
Equity investment	24,000.00					
Dividend payments		0.00				
Repurchase of stock						
NCB after cash transactions with shareholders	1,521.60	10,904.10				
Sales of marketable securities	0.00	0.00				
Interest income on marketable securities	0.00	0.00				
Investment on marketable securities		12,325.70				
NCB after discretionary transactions paid in cash	1,521.60	−1,421.60				
Accumulated cash balance at end of year	1,521.60	100.00				

4.7.3 Income Statement for Year 2

With the calculation of the surplus funds in year 1, we can calculate the interest income for year 2. The rate of return on short-term investment is 3%. The interest income in year 2 is $369.80.

$$\text{Interest income in year } 2 = 12,325.70 \times 3\% = 369.80$$

With the interest income entered in the IS for year 2, we can calculate the taxes for year 2, and complete the IS for year 2. The completed ISs (after the EBIT line item) for years 1 and 2 are shown in the following table.

TABLE 4.15   Partial Income Statement for Year 1 and Year 2

	Year 0	Year 1	Year 2	Year 3	Year 4	Year 5
EBIT		11,274.60	11,533.20	12,055.50	12,588.30	13,131.80
Interest income on marketable securities		0.00	369.80			
Other expenses (interest expenses)		1,385.00	1,108.00			
EBT		9,889.60	10,794.90			
Taxes		3,461.40	3,778.20			
NI		6,428.20	7,016.70			
Dividends		4,499.80	4,911.70			
Retained earnings		1,928.50	2,105.00			
Accumulated retained earnings		6,428.20	8,945.20			

In year 2, the EBIT is $11,533.20, the NI is $7,016.70, and the declared dividends are $4,911.70.

4.7.4 Iterations Between the IS and the CB Statement

Up to this point, we have completed the CB statement for year 1, and the IS for years 1 and 2. The construction of the CB statements for years 3–5 is similar to the CB statement for year 2.

4.7.5 Cash Budget Statement for Year 2

We show the completed CB statement for year 2 in Table 4.16.

TABLE 4.16 Cash Budget for Year 2

	Year 0	Year 1	Year 2	Year 3	Year 4	Year 5
Cash inflows						
Total income AR	0.00	47,880.00	50,878.80	51,871.20	52,908.60	53,966.80
Total cash inflows	0.00	47,880.00	50,878.80	51,871.20	52,908.60	53,966.80
Cash outflows						
Total payments to suppliers on cash	0.00	19,505.30	20,367.20	20,601.20	21,014.90	21,435.20
Overhead	0.00	2,184.00	2,184.00	2,184.00	2,184.00	2,184.00
Payroll expenses	0.00	2,400.00	2,400.00	2,400.00	2,400.00	2,400.00
Selling commissions	0.00	3,024.00	3,054.20	3,115.30	3,177.60	3,241.20
Advertising and promotions	0.00	1,512.00	1,527.10	1,557.70	1,588.80	1,620.60
Purchase of fixed assets	40,000.00					
Purchase of fixed assets in year 4	0.00	0.00	0.00	0.00	40,000.00	0.00
Taxes	0.00	3,461.40	3,778.20	4,150.60	4,531.00	4,494.80
Total cash outflows	40,000.00	32,086.70	33,310.80	34,008.70	74,896.30	35,375.70
NCB	−40,000.00	15,793.40	17,568.00	17,862.50	−21,987.70	18,591.10
Bank loan 1	17,521.60					
Bank loan 2		0.00	0.00			
Payment of loans	0.00	3,504.30	3,504.30			
Interest charges	0.00	1,385.00	1,108.00			
NCB after financial transactions	−22,478.40	10,904.10	12,955.70			
Equity investment	24,000.00					
Dividend payments		0.00	4,499.80			
Repurchase of stock						
NCB after cash transactions with shareholders	1,521.60	10,904.10	8,456.00			
Sales of marketable securities	0.00	0.00	12,325.70			
Interest income on marketable securities	0.00	0.00	369.80			
Investment on marketable securities		12,325.70	21,141.40			
NCB after discretionary transactions paid in cash	1,521.60	−1,421.60	10.00			
Accumulated cash balance at end of year	1,521.60	100.00	110.00			

With the value of the reinvestment of surplus funds in year 2, we can calculate the interest income and enter the amount in the IS for year 3. The calculations of the line items in the CB statement for year 2 are similar to the calculations for year 1.

The completed IS for years 1–3 is shown in Table 4.17.

TABLE 4.17   Income Statement for Years 1–3

	Year 0	Year 1	Year 2	Year 3	Year 4	Year 5
EBIT		11,274.60	11,533.20	12,055.50	12,588.30	13,131.80
Interest income on marketable securities		0.00	369.80	634.20		
Other expenses (interest expenses)		1,385.00	1,108.00	831.00		
EBT		9,889.60	10,794.90	11,858.80		
Taxes		3,461.40	3,778.20	4,150.60		
NI		6,428.20	7,016.70	7,708.20		
Dividends		4,499.80	4,911.70	5,395.70		
Retained earnings		1,928.50	2,105.00	2,312.50		
Accumulated retained earnings		6,428.20	8,945.20	11,741.70		

Similar iterations apply for the construction of the IS and CB statement for years 4 and 5. For practice and improved learning and understanding, we encourage the reader to replicate and check the results for themselves.

4.7.6 Completed Income Statement for All Years

The completed IS for all the years is shown in Table 4.18. In all the years, the EBIT is positive and increases from $9,889.60 in year 1 to $12,842.20 in year 5. Also, in all the years, the NI is positive and increases from $6,428.20 in year 1 to $8,347.40 in year 5.

TABLE 4.18   Completed Income Statement for All Years

	Year 0	Year 1	Year 2	Year 3	Year 4	Year 5
Sales		50,400.00	50,904.00	51,922.10	52,960.60	54,019.80
COGS		20,005.40	20,205.50	20,609.60	21,021.80	21,442.20
Gross profit		30,394.60	30,698.50	31,312.50	31,938.80	32,577.50
Selling and administrative expenses		9,120.00	9,165.40	9,257.00	9,350.50	9,445.80
Depreciation		10,000.00	10,000.00	10,000.00	10,000.00	10,000.00
EBIT		11,274.60	11,533.20	12,055.50	12,588.30	13,131.80
Interest income on marketable securities		0.00	369.80	634.20	911.40	0.00

(continues)

TABLE 4.18 (*continued*)

	Year 0	Year 1	Year 2	Year 3	Year 4	Year 5
Other expenses (interest expenses)		1,385.00	1,108.00	831.00	554.00	289.60
EBT		9,889.60	10,794.90	11,858.80	12,945.70	12,842.20
Taxes		3,461.40	3,778.20	4,150.60	4,531.00	4,494.80
NI		6,428.20	7,016.70	7,708.20	8,414.70	8,347.40
Dividends		4,499.80	4,911.70	5,395.70	5,890.30	5,843.20
Retained earnings		1,928.50	2,105.00	2,312.50	2,524.40	2,504.20
Accumulated retained earnings		6,428.20	8,945.20	11,741.70	14,760.70	17,217.80

4.7.7 Complete Cash Budget Statement for All Years

The complete CB statement for all the years is shown in Table 4.19.

The investment in marketable securities is listed in the BS. Similarly, the last line in the CB statement is entered as cash in the BS.

4.7.8 Calculation of the New Loan in Year 4

Now that we have an understanding of how the CB statement works, we explain the calculation for the amount of the new loan in year 4. The amount that we borrow depends on the surplus funds that are invested in marketable securities. At the end of year 4, the amount of surplus funds that is invested in marketable securities is zero because the firm uses the surplus funds to finance the purchase of the replacement asset.

We explain the procedure step by step because the calculation requires iteration between several lines in the CB statement. When the correct expression is entered in the cell for the new loan in the CB statement, the numbers will correspond to the numbers given in Table 4.19.

At the end of year 4, the NCB before financing is $-21,987.70. First, we adjust for the debt and equity financing. We subtract the payments to the debt and the equity holders.

NCB after debt financing is as follows:

$$= -21,987.70 - 3,504.30 - 554 = -26,046.00$$

NCB after debt and equity financing is as follows:

$$= -26,046 - 5,395.70 = -31,441.70$$

TABLE 4.19 Complete Cash Budget Statement for all Years

	Year 0	Year 1	Year 2	Year 3	Year 4	Year 5
Cash inflows						
Total income AR	0.00	47,880.00	50,878.80	51,871.20	52,908.60	53,966.80
Total cash inflows	0.00	47,880.00	50,878.80	51,871.20	52,908.60	53,966.80
Cash outflows						
Total payments to suppliers on cash	0.00	19,505.30	20,367.20	20,601.20	21,014.90	21,435.20
Overhead	0.00	2,184.00	2,184.00	2,184.00	2,184.00	2,184.00
Payroll expenses	0.00	2,400.00	2,400.00	2,400.00	2,400.00	2,400.00
Selling commissions	0.00	3,024.00	3,054.20	3,115.30	3,177.60	3,241.20
Advertising and promotions	0.00	1,512.00	1,527.10	1,557.70	1,588.80	1,620.60
Purchase of fixed assets	40,000.00					
Purchase of fixed assets year 4	0.00	0.00	0.00	0.00	40,000.00	0.00
Taxes	0.00	3,461.40	3,778.20	4,150.60	4,531.00	4,494.80
Total cash outflows	40,000.00	32,086.70	33,310.80	34,008.70	74,896.30	35,375.70
NCB	−40,000.00	15,793.40	17,568.00	17,862.50	−21,987.70	18,591.10
Bank loan 1	17,521.60					
Bank loan 2						
Payment of loans	0.00	3,504.30	3,504.30	3,504.30	3,504.30	3,536.20
Interest charges	0.00	1,385.00	1,108.00	831.00	554.00	289.60
NCB after financial transactions	−22,478.40	10,904.10	12,955.70	13,527.20	−25,886.80	14,765.40
Equity investment	24,000.00					
Dividend payments		0.00	4,499.80	4,911.70	5,395.70	5,890.30
Repurchase of stock						
NCB after cash transactions with shareholders	1,521.60	10,904.10	8,456.00	8,615.50	−31,282.50	8,875.00
Sales of marketable securities	0.00	0.00	12,325.70	21,141.40	30,381.10	0.00
Interest income on marketable securities	0.00	0.00	369.80	634.20	911.40	0.00
Investment on marketable securities		12,325.70	21,141.40	30,381.10	0.00	8,865.00
NCB after discretionary transactions paid in cash	1,521.60	−1,421.60	10.00	10.00	10.00	10.00
Accumulated cash balance at end of year	1,521.60	100.00	110.00	120.00	130.00	140.00

The NCB after debt and equity financing is $-31,441.70$. At the end of year 3, the amount of the surplus funds in marketable securities is $30,381.10. The expression for the amount of the new loan in year 4 is as follows:

New loan in year 4 = NCB after debt and equity financing

$\quad$ + Sale of marketable securities from year 3

$\quad$ + Interest income on marketable securities

$\quad$ − Investment on marketable securities

$\quad$ − CRO for year 4

$\quad$ + Cumulative cash balance at end of year 3 $\quad$ (4.3)

First, we add the sale of marketable securities from year 3 and the interest income from the marketable securities in year 3. Next, we subtract the investment in marketable securities. Then, we subtract the CRO in year 4 and add the cumulative cash balance in year 3.

Substituting the appropriate values for the parameters in equation 4.3, we obtain that the amount of the new loan is 159.20.

$$\text{New loan in year 4} = -31,441.70 + 30,381.10 + 911.40 - 130 + 120$$
$$= -159.20$$

The negative amount indicates the value of the new loan that is required at the end of year 4 to finance the purchase of the replacement asset.

As mentioned earlier, when the expression in equation 4.3 is entered in the cell for the new loan in the CB statement in year 4, the correct numbers will appear.

4.8 DETAILED CASH BUDGET STATEMENT IN YEAR 5

Because the CB statement for year 5 is different from the previous years, we provide some additional comments.

4.8.1 NCB Before Financing and Reinvestment in Year 5

The NCB in year 5 before financing and reinvestment is $18,591.10.

$$\text{NCB in year 5 (before financing and reinvestment)}$$
$$= \text{annual cash receipts} - \text{annual cash expenditures}$$
$$= 53,966.80 - 35,375.70 = 18,591.10$$

4.8.2 Net Cash Balance After Debt Financing in Year 5

In year 5, the NCB after debt financing is $14,765.30. There are no new loans.

NCB in year 5 (after debt financing)

$=$ NCB before financing and reinvestment

$+$ New bank loans

$-$ Total payments for debt (principal plus interest)

$= 18,591.10 + 0 - 3,536.20 - 289.60$

$= 14,765.30$

4.8.3 NCB After Debt and Equity Financing in Year 5

There is no new equity contribution or repurchase. However, dividend payments from year 4 are actually paid in year 5. Thus, the net cash (loss) in year 5 (after debt and equity financing) is $8,875.10.

NCB in year 1, (after debt and equity financing)

$=$ NCB after debt financing

$+$ New equity investment

$-$ Dividend payments

$-$ Equity repurchase

$= 14,765.40 - 5,890.30$

$= 8,875.10$

4.8.4 Reinvestment of Surplus Funds in Year 5

The investment in marketable securities for year 5 is zero because all the surplus funds in year 4 financed the purchase of the replacement asset in year 4. In year 5, the reinvestment of surplus funds is $8,865, and is listed in the BS as an investment in marketable securities.

Reinvestment of surplus funds in year 5

$=$ NCB $-$ CRO for year 5 $+$ Cumulative cash balance from year 4

$= 8,875 - 140 + 130 = 8,865.00$

4.8.5 Final Net Cash Balance After Reinvestment in Year 5

In year 5, the final NCB after reinvestment of surplus funds is equal to the NCB (after debt and equity financing) in year n minus the reinvestment of surplus funds in year 5 plus the sale (recovery) of the short-term investment in the previous year 4, inclusive of the interest income.

> Final NCB after reinvestment in year 5
> $=$ NCB (after debt and equity financing) in year 5
> $-$ Reinvestment of surplus funds in year 5
> $+$ Recovery of short-term investment in year 4
> $+$ Interest on short-term investment in year 5
> $= 8{,}875 - 8{,}865 + 0 + 0 = 10.00$

4.8.6 Cumulative Cash Balance in Year 5

The cumulative cash balance in year 5 is \$140, which is equal to the CRO for year 5. This value is entered in the BS as cash.

> Cumulative cash balance after reinvestment in year 5
> $=$ NCB in year 5 $+$ Final CB from year 4
> $= 10 + 130 = 140.00$

4.8.7 Adjustments in the Cash Budget Statement

Notice that in the CB we have included the real cash movements. In fact what we do in the CB is to adjust the figures from the IS to correct the distortions generated by the accrual and cost distribution accounting practices. We are interested in the TVM, and hence it is crucial that we register the cash inflows and outflows when they occur. We can think of the CB as the record of the movement of the checkbook. Any kind of cash inflows or outflows are recorded in the CB. This financial statement monitors the liquidity of the firm. It allows the decision-maker to make financing and investing decisions. This might be the most important and useful financial statement for a firm. If you manage a firm and only are allowed to have access to one financial statement, choose the CB.

    The last line, cumulative cash balance at the end of year, shows the amount of cash left in the bank account. This amount has to be the same as the one recorded in the BS, as Cash. As this financial statement records all the cash movements, it is close to the idea of Free Cash Flow (FCF) that will be studied later in Chapter Six.

Now we proceed to complete the BS.

4.9 BALANCE SHEET

The completed BS is shown in Table 4.20.

Some of the items in the BS are linked to other items in the IS and the CB statement. For instance, the line that is called Cash in the BS is the cash balance at the end of the year after financing and reinvestment in the CB. This is exactly the cash that we keep on hand for operating the business. Retained earnings are the line of accumulated retained earnings in the IS.[5] Also, the long-term debt in the BS is the EB from Table 2.8. The dividends for year n are actually paid in the following year $n + 1$. Thus, in the BS, in year n, we list the cumulative retained earnings up to year $n - 1$.

TABLE 4.20   Complete Balance Sheet for all Years

	Year 0	Year 1	Year 2	Year 3	Year 4	Year 5
Assets						
Cash	1,521.60	100.00	110.00	120.00	130.00	140.00
AR	0.00	2,520.00	2,545.20	2,596.10	2,648.00	2,701.00
Inventory	0.00	1,667.10	1,683.80	1,717.50	1,751.80	1,786.90
Investment on marketable securities	0.00	12,325.70	21,141.40	30,381.10	0.00	8,865.00
Interest accrued	0.00	0.00	0.00	0.00	0.00	0.00
Net fixed assets	40,000.00	30,000.00	20,000.00	10,000.00	40,000.00	30,000.00
Total	41,521.60	46,612.80	45,480.40	44,814.70	44,529.80	43,492.90
Liabilities and equity						
AP (suppliers)	0.00	2,167.30	2,022.20	2,064.30	2,105.60	2,147.70
Accrued taxes	0.00	0.00	0.00	0.00	0.00	0.00
Long-term debt	17,521.60	14,017.30	10,513.00	7,008.60	3,663.60	127.40
Total liabilities	17,521.60	16,184.50	12,535.20	9,073.00	5,769.20	2,275.10
Equity	24,000.00	24,000.00	24,000.00	24,000.00	24,000.00	24,000.00
Accumulated retained earnings	0.00	6,428.20	8,945.20	11,741.70	14,760.70	17,217.80

The BS is a snapshot of the firm at any point in time. The BS records what the firm owns (the assets) and who the claimants of those assets are. The claimants are third parties: shareholders and debt holders. These

---

[5]For simplicity, it is often assumed that the dividends are always paid in the year in which they are earned. If the dividends are always paid in the year in which they are earned, we only include the cumulative retained earnings in the BS.

claimants provide the firm with the financial resources needed to operate. The reader should notice how some items in the BS appear in the other two financial statements. For instance, as it was mentioned, the Cash item coincides with the bottom line from the CB.

In the BS the basic equity or accounting equation must hold.

$$\text{Assets} = \text{Value of equity} + \text{Liabilities} \qquad (4.4)$$

4.10 CASH FLOW STATEMENT ACCORDING TO GAAP

Next we show the CFS according to GAAP. Recall that the CFS according to GAAP has three sections. For more details on the construction of the CFS according to GAAP, refer to the discussion in Chapter Three.

1. Cash flow from operating activities.
2. Cash flow from investing activities.
3. Cash flow from financing activities.

The table for the working capital is shown next.

TABLE 4.21   Working Capital

	Year 0	Year 1	Year 2	Year 3	Year 4	Year 5
Cash	1,576.90	100.00	110.00	120.00	130.00	140.00
AR	0.00	2,595.60	2,710.10	2,857.70	3,013.30	3,177.40
Inventory	0.00	1,725.70	2,033.30	2,085.00	2,150.80	2,217.90
Current assets	1,576.90	4,421.30	4,853.40	5,062.70	5,294.00	5,535.30
AP (suppliers)	0.00	2,243.40	2,440.70	2,504.80	2,583.80	2,664.50
Accrued taxes	0.00	0.00	0.00	0.00	0.00	0.00
Current liabilities	0.00	2,243.40	2,440.70	2,504.80	2,583.80	2,664.50
Operating working capital	1,576.90	2,177.90	2,412.70	2,557.90	2,710.30	2,870.80
Non-cash operating working capital	0.00	2,077.90	2,302.70	2,437.90	2,580.30	2,730.80
Change in operating working capital	1,521.60	598.30	196.90	52.50	55.00	55.90
Change in non-cash operating working capital	0.00	2,019.90	186.90	42.50	45.00	45.90

The current assets consist of the CRO, the AR, and the inventory; the current liabilities consist of the AP. The operating working capital is equal to the current assets less the current liabilities. The non-cash operating working capital excludes the CRO.

The cash flow from operating activities, derived from the NI, is shown.

The cash flow from operating activities is equal to the NI plus the depreciation less the net change in non-cash operating working capital.

TABLE 4.22   Cash Flow from Operating Activities

	Year 0	Year 1	Year 2	Year 3	Year 4	Year 5
NI		6,428.20	7,016.70	7,708.20	8,414.70	8,347.40
Depreciation		10,000.00	10,000.00	10,000.00	10,000.00	10,000.00
Net change in non-cash operating working capital		−2,019.90	−186.90	−42.50	−45.00	−45.90
Net cash provided by operations		14,408.40	16,829.80	17,665.70	18,369.70	18,301.50

The cash flow from investing activities is shown.

TABLE 4.23   Cash Flow from Investing Activities

	Year 0	Year 1	Year 2	Year 3	Year 4	Year 5
Fixed assets		0.00	0.00	0.00	−40,000.00	0.00
Marketable securities		−12,325.70	−8,815.70	−9,239.70	30,381.10	−8,865.00
Net cash used in investing activities		−12,325.70	−8,815.70	−9,239.70	−9,618.90	−8,865.00

The cash flow from investing activities consists of the investment in new fixed assets in year 4 and the reinvestment of the surplus cash in marketable securities.

The cash flow from financing activities consists of the payments to the debt and the equity holders. We calculate the payment for debt from the BS. If the debt in year i is greater than the debt in the previous year i − 1, the difference in the value of the debt is the payment to the debt holder. If the debt in year i is lower than the debt in the previous year i − 1, the difference in the value of the debt is the value of the new debt.

In year 4, the value of the new debt is \$159.20 and the payment on the debt is \$3,504.30. The net value is a payment of \$3,345.10 to the debt holder.

TABLE 4.24   Cash Flow from Financing Activities

	Year 0	Year 1	Year 2	Year 3	Year 4	Year 5
New debt		0.0	0.00	0.00	0.00	0.00
Payments of debt		−3,504.30	−3,504.30	−3,504.30	−3,345.10	−3,536.20
Issuances of stock		0.00	0.00	0.00	0.00	0.00
Purchases of stocks		0.00	0.00	0.00	0.00	0.00
Dividends		0.00	−4,499.80	−4,911.70	−5,395.70	−5,890.30
Net cash used in financing activities		−3,504.30	−8,004.10	−8,416.00	−8,740.80	−9,426.50

The sum of the cash flows from operating, investing, and financing are shown next.

TABLE 4.25   Sum of the Cash Flows from Operating, Investing, and Financing Activities

	Year 0	Year 1	Year 2	Year 3	Year 4	Year 5
Cash flow from operating activities		14,408.40	16,829.80	17,665.70	18,369.70	18,301.50
Cash flow from investing activities		−12,325.70	−8,815.70	−9,239.70	−9,618.90	−8,865.00
Cash flow from financing activities		−3,504.30	−8,004.10	−8,416.00	−8,740.80	−9,426.50
Total		−1,421.60	10.00	10.00	10.00	10.00

As expected, the sum of the cash flows from the three activities is equal to the change in the annual CRO.

4.11 SUMMARY AND CONCLUDING REMARKS

Finally, we have constructed the three estimated financial statements. The reader should observe that we have not used any plugs. Plugs are common for checking the financial statements. Usually it is the cash balance, the investment of cash surplus, or the debt. In our procedure we have deliberately eliminated the use of plugs. It is important to stress that plugs might hide errors that cannot be detected. The idea is to construct, in an integrated manner, the financial statements that have been introduced in this chapter.

KEY CONCEPT AND IDEA

Integrated financial statements

A4.1 DETAILED IS FOR YEAR 1

We present the detailed calculations for some line items in the IS in year 1.

A4.1.1 Gross Profits in Year 1

The sales revenues are taken from Table 4.5 and the COGS are taken from Table 4.10. In year 1, the gross profits are \$30,394.60.

$$\text{Gross profit} = \text{Sales revenues} - \text{COGS}$$
$$= 50,400 - 20,005.40$$
$$= 30,394.60$$

A4.1.2 Earnings before Interest and Taxes in Year 1

The selling and administrative expenses and the depreciation allowance are taken from Tables 4.4 and 4.3, respectively. In year 1, the EBIT is \$11,274.60.

$$\text{EBIT} = \text{Gross profit} - \text{Selling and administrative expenses}$$
$$- \text{Depreciation allowance}$$
$$= 30,394.60 - 9,120 - 10,000 = 11,274.60$$

A4.1.3 Earnings before Taxes in Year 1

The interest expense is taken from the loan schedule in Table 4.7. In year 1, the EBT is \$9,889.60.

$$\text{EBT} = \text{EBIT} + \text{Interest income} - \text{Interest expense}$$
$$= 11,274.60 + 0 - 1,385 = 9,889.60$$

Here the EBT is positive. However, in other cases, it might be that the EBT in year n is insufficient for the TS from the interest payment to be realized in year n. In such a case, the losses can be carried forward and must be modeled explicitly. The details of the rules regarding LCF depend on the relevant tax laws.

A4.1.4 Net Income in Year 1

The tax rate is 35% and is listed in Table 4.1. In any year, if the EBT is negative, the taxes will be zero. In year 1, the NI is $6,428.20.

$$NI = EBT - T \text{ times EBT}$$
$$= 9,889.60 - 35\% \times 9,889.60$$
$$= 9,889.60 - 3,461.40 = 6,428.20$$

Here we assume that all the taxes for year n are paid in year n.

A4.1.5 Dividends Declared in Year 1

The payout rate for dividends is 70% and is listed in Table 4.2. *Actually*, all the dividends that are declared in year 1 will be paid in year 2. In year 1, the dividends declared are $4,499.70.

$$\text{Dividends in year } 1 = 70\% \times 6,428.20 = 4,499.70$$

In any year, if the NI is negative, the dividends will be zero.

A4.1.6 Retained Earnings in Year 1

The retained earnings in year 1 are equal to the NI in year 1 less the dividends paid in year 1. However, all the dividends are paid in year 2. Thus, in year 1, the retained earnings equal the NI for year 1.

$$\text{Retained earnings in year } 1 = NI \text{ in year } 1 - \text{Dividends paid in year } 1$$
$$= 6,428.20 - 0.0 = 6,428.20$$

A4.2 DETAILED CASH BUDGET STATEMENT FOR YEAR 1

We present the detailed calculations for the CB statement for year 1.

A4.2.1 Net Cash Balance before Financing and Reinvestment

On the inflow side of the CB statement, we list the cash receipts in year 1. On the outflow side, we list the cash expenditures for year 2. The NCB in year 1 before financing and reinvestment is $15,793.30.

$$\begin{aligned}
\text{NCB in year 1 (before financing and reinvestment)} &= \text{Cash inflows} \\
&\quad - \text{Cash outflows} \\
&= 47{,}880 - 32{,}086.70 \\
&= 15{,}793.30
\end{aligned}$$

The NCB in year 1, before financing and reinvestment, includes the tax savings from the interest deductions.

A4.2.2 Net Cash Balance after Debt Financing

The NCB in year 1 after debt financing is $10,904.10. It is equal to the NCB of $15,793.30 plus any new bank loans less the total payments for debt (principal plus interest). In this case, there are no new bank loans in year 1.

$$\begin{aligned}
\text{NCB (loss) in year 1 (after debt financing)} &= \text{NCB} - \text{Payment of loan} \\
&\quad - \text{Interest charges} \\
&= 15{,}793.30 - 3{,}504.20 - 1{,}385 \\
&= 10{,}904.10
\end{aligned}$$

A4.2.3 Net Cash Balance after Equity Financing

In year 1, there are no transactions related to the equity holder, such as new equity investment, dividend payments, or equity repurchase. Thus, the NCB in year 1 (after debt and equity financing) is $10,904.10. The dividends on the NI in year 1 are not listed in year 1 because they are actually paid in year 2.

A4.2.4 Reinvestment of Surplus Funds in Year I

The CRO for year 1 is taken from Table 4.2. In this case, the reinvestment of surplus funds in year 1 is $12,325.70.

Reinvestment of surplus funds in year 1
$$= \text{NCB} - \text{CRO for year } 1$$
$$+ \text{Cumulative cash balance from year } 1$$
$$= 10,904.10 - 100 + 1,521.60 = 12,325.70$$

A4.2.5 Final Net Cash Balance after Reinvestment

In year 1, the final NCB after investment of surplus funds is $-1,421.60.$

NCB after reinvestment in year $1 = 10,904.10 - 12,325.70 = -1,421.60$

A4.2.6 Cash Balance after Reinvestment in Year 1

Cumulative cash balance in year $1 = -1,421.60 + 1,521.60 = 100$

The cumulative cash balance in year 1 is 100 and this value is entered in the BS as cash.

A4.3 DETAILED CB STATEMENT FOR YEAR 2

Having completed a detailed exposition of the construction of the CB statement for year 1, we proceed at a faster pace for year 2 and skip some of the explanations.

A4.3.1 Net Cash Balance before Financing and Reinvestment

NCB in year 2 (before financing and reinvestment) $= 50,878.80 - 33,310.80$
$$= 17,568.00$$

A4.3.2 Net Cash Balance after Debt Financing

The NCB in year 2 after debt financing is $12,955.70

NCB in year 2 (after debt financing) $= 17,568 - 3,504.20 - 1,108$
$$= 12,955.70$$

A4.3.3 Net Cash Balance after Equity Financing

The dividends in year 2, based on the NI in year 1, are paid in year 2. The dividend payments are taken from the IS. There is no new equity investment and no equity repurchase. Thus, the NCB in year 2 (after equity financing) is $8,456.

NCB after equity financing, in year $2 = 12,955.70 - 4,499.80 = 8,456$

A4.3.4 Reinvestment of Surplus Funds

The CRO for year 2 is taken from Table 4.2. The CRO for year 2 is subtracted from the surplus funds because it is unavailable for investment in marketable securities. The sale (recovery) of short-term investment in year 2 is equal to the reinvestment of surplus funds in year 1. In year 2, the amount of surplus funds that is available for investment in marketable securities is $21,141.40.

Investment of surplus funds in year 2

$= \text{NCB} + \text{Sale of marketable securities in year } 1 + \text{interest income}$

$- \text{CRO for year } 2 + \text{Final CB from year } 1$

$= 8,456 + 12,325.70 + 369.80 - 110 + 100 = 21,141.50$

The reinvestment of surplus funds in year 1 of $21,141.50 is listed in the BS as short-term investments.

With the calculation of the surplus funds in year 2, we can calculate the interest income for year 3. The interest income in year 3 is $634.20.

Interest income in year $2 = 21,141.40 \times 3\% = 634.20$

With the interest income entered in the IS for year 3, we can calculate the taxes for year 3 and complete the IS for year 3.

A4.3.5 Final Net Cash Balance after Reinvestment

In year 2, the final NCB after investment of surplus funds is $10.

Final NCB after reinvestment in year 1

$= \text{NCB} - \text{Reinvestment of funds}$

$+ \text{Sale of marketable securities}$

$+ \text{Interest income}$

$= 8,456 - 21,414.40 + 12,325.70 + 369.80$

$= 10$

A4.3.6 Cumulative Cash Balance in Year 1

Cumulative cash balance after reinvestment in year 1

$= $ NCB in year 1

$+ $ Cumulative cash balance from year 1

$= 100 + 10 = 110.00$

The cumulative cash balance in year 1 is \$110, which is equal to the CRO for year 1. This value is entered in the BS as cash.

5

CONSTRUCTING INTEGRATED PRO-FORMA FINANCIAL STATEMENTS, PART TWO

...the universe is not only queerer than we suppose but it is queerer than we can suppose.

—*J.B.S. Haldane* (1892 to 1964)

In fact, our ordinary descriptions of nature, and the idea of exact laws, rests on the assumption that it is possible to observe the phenomena without appreciably influencing them.

—*Werner Heisenberg* (1901 to 1976)

Nature herself does not even know which way the electron is going to go.

—*Richard Feynman* (1918 to 1988), The Character of Physical Law

5.1 CONSTRUCTING FINANCIAL STATEMENTS

To value a firm, it is necessary to construct the financial statements for the forecast period and estimate the appropriate cash flows from different points of view, namely the total point of view (the Free Cash Flow [FCF]) and the equity holder's point of view (the CFE). In this chapter we extend the simple example that was presented in Chapter Four by adding more complex assumptions to make the model closer to reality.[1] We assume that the reader

[1] The readers are encouraged to read actively by constructing the financial statements for themselves on a spreadsheet.

is familiar with the tables in the simple example in Chapter Four. To facilitate the reading of this chapter and provide some continuity, we repeat some of the ideas, background information, and tables from Chapter Four. As discussed earlier in Chapter Four, the relevant financial statements are: the BS, the IS, and the CB. For the sake of completeness, although not necessary to our analysis, we derive the cash flow statement (CFS) according to Generally Accepted Accounting Principles (GAAP). For valuation purposes, the BS, the IS, and the CFS are important.[2] However, in the next chapter, we show how easy it is to derive the Free Cash Flow (FCF) with the CB statement.

5.1.1 The Construction of the Financial Statements

In this chapter we present a complex example that introduces some assumptions for the construction of the financial statements that we need for valuation.

The first step in the valuation process is to construct the three typical financial statements, namely the IS, the CFS according to GAAP, and the BS. As mentioned earlier, first we construct the CB, which is not considered a financial statement. Later we derive the FCF statement from the financial statements, and proceed to value the cash flows. The financial statements are linked by the accounting relationships that we have presented earlier.

The construction of the financial statements starts from policies or targets (for example, AR policy or target) and is based on the history or assessment of the economic environment (for example, the expected inflation rate and price increases). With these targets or policies we construct the financial statements, as follows.

The first table that we construct is the table of parameters. The table of parameters organizes all the relevant information. We have constructed all the tables in Excel. All the subsequent tables are linked to the table of parameters through formulas. Before constructing the three financial statements, we construct other supplementary tables that are used in the construction of the financial statements. In the main text, we describe the construction of all the tables and statements. The complete listing of all the tables is given in Appendix B. In these tables we show the tables as seen in a spreadsheet with the columns and lines in such a way that the reader can identify the different cells that the formula is linked to. In columns C and D the reader will find the formulas as they appear in columns E and F in the spreadsheet. Usually the formula shown is the one corresponding to year 1.

---

[2] We remind the reader that only the IS, the CFS, and the BS are the three financial statements that comply with the prescriptions of GAAP rules. The CB is an adaptation of a financial tool that determines the liquidity of a firm on a monthly or weekly basis.

However, in a few cases the formula for a different year is shown. The reader will understand the need for this change. If the reader wishes to construct the model exactly as we did in the spreadsheet, she will be able to do that by following, step by step, the explanations in the body of the chapter and the appendix.[3]

Based on the estimates for the target variables, we construct the basic financial statements (BS, IS, and CB). The financial statements are linked together with the basic accounting equations. Thus, some items in the BS are derived from other line items in the IS and there are iterative linkages between line items in the IS and the CB statement.

5.1.2 A Complex Example

In this chapter we present a complex example with some assumptions for the construction of the financial statements that we need for valuation. The analyst has to make the proper judgment about the appropriate degree of realism, which depends on the availability of the relevant data and the required accuracy of the analysis. For some purposes, the illustrations might be too complicated, whereas for other purposes it might not be complicated enough.

In the numerical example of Chapter Four, we did not specify any relationship between the quantities sold, the selling price, the quantity purchased, and the purchase price. We assumed that the selling and purchase prices were constant and that the sales volume increased each year. However, in practice, there is a relationship between the quantity sold and the selling price and a relationship between the quantity purchased and the purchase price.

Consider a simple retail firm that processes bottled water and requires an investment of $40,000 at the end of year 0.[4] The economic life of the machinery is four years. At the end of year 4 a new fixed asset is purchased. For tax purposes, we assume straight-line depreciation.

Furthermore, we assume that the economic depreciation of the machinery is the same as the depreciation for tax purposes. The initial equity contribution is $24,000. The tax rate is 35%. The firm invests any cash that is in excess of the CRO in short-term securities at the market rate. It is expected that from years 2 to 5, there are annual increases in the sale of units. We assume that both the selling and the purchase prices are affected by real price increases during the explicit forecasting period.

---

[3]It will be easier for the reader if she follows the same cell references that we have used. If the reader wishes to construct it without following our cell references, she will be able to construct the model, but it will be more difficult.

[4]Usually people speak of year 0. In reality there is no year 0, but instant 0. The year before instant 0 is year −1 and the year after instant 0 is year 1. However, we will keep the notation year 0.

5.1.3 Model Assumptions

In this chapter, all the financial statements are constructed in nominal terms and we specify the expected real increases in the prices for all the outputs and inputs. To reiterate, there is a real price increase if the expected nominal annual increase in the price is higher than the expected inflation rate, and there is a real price decrease if the expected nominal annual increase in the price is lower than the expected inflation rate.

We add the following assumptions to the model in Chapter Four.

1. We model the link between the purchase price and the purchase quantity with a negative relationship. The higher the purchase quantity, the lower the purchase price.
2. We simulate a market research study to determine the potential market for the product.
3. We specify two determinants for the quantity sold. First, we use an elasticity function to take into account the negative relationship between the expected real price increase and the quantity sold. Second, we assume that the quantity sold is also affected positively by expenditures on advertising and promotion. For further details on nominal prices and inflation, review the discussion in Chapter Two. For further discussion on elasticity, see Appendix A.

The basic information for the complex example is given in the table below.

TABLE 5.1a   Basic Information

	Year 0	Year 1	Year 2	Year 3	Year 4	Year 5
Fixed assets	40,000.00					
Linear depreciation (years)	4					
Initial equity investment	24,000.00					
Tax rate	35.00%					
Final inventory at year 0	0					
Observed return to unlevered equity ρ for year 0						
Inflation rate when ρ is observed						
Leverage (constant) for perpetuity						
Expected inflation rate for year 6 and beyond						
Nominal growth rate for sales after year 5						
Inflation rate		3.00%	3.00%	3.00%	3.00%	3.00%
Real annual rate of increase in selling price		0.00%	1.00%	1.00%	1.00%	1.00%

(continues)

TABLE 5.1a *(continued)*

	Year 0	Year 1	Year 2	Year 3	Year 4	Year 5
Real annual rate of increase in cost per unit		0.50%	0.50%	0.50%	1.00%	1.00%
Overhead estimated at year 0	2,184.00					
Real rate of increase in overhead expenses		0.50%	0.50%	0.50%	0.50%	1.00%
Payroll of selling and administrative force	2,400.00					
Real rate of increase in payroll		1.50%	1.50%	1.50%	1.50%	1.50%
Real rate of increase in price of fixed assets		0.20%	0.20%	0.20%	0.20%	0.20%
Sales commissions		6.00%	6.00%	6.00%	6.00%	6.00%
Advertising and promotion expenses (% of sales)		3.00%	3.00%	3.00%	3.00%	3.00%
Real rate of interest		3.00%	3.00%	3.00%	3.00%	3.00%
Premium for debt risk		4.91%	4.91%	4.91%	4.91%	4.91%

5.1.4 Goals and Policies for Selected Variables

Let us specify some goals, targets, and policies. The annual final inventory is one month of sales or 8.33% of the annual sales. Accounts receivable in year n is 5% of the sales in year n, and AP in year n is 10% of the purchases in that year. The dividends paid to the stockholders in year n are 70% of the net profit in the previous year n − 1.

We also assume that from year 2 onwards, the marketing effort has some effect on the units sold. For this reason we have introduced the annual increases in the sales volume.

It is assumed that any cash excess (less the CRO) is reinvested in marketable securities and earns a market rate of return. This reinvestment will cover the purchase of a new fixed asset at the end of year 4. The firm does not sell the old fixed asset.

TABLE 5.1b **Policies and Targets**

	Year 0	Year 1	Year 2	Year 3	Year 4	Year 5
Fraction of sales to be kept as final inventory		8.33%	8.33%	8.33%	8.33%	8.33%
Percentage of sales received in the same year		95.00%				
Percentage of payments made the same year (as accrued suppliers)		90.00%				

(continues)

TABLE 5.lb (*continued*)

	Year 0	Year 1	Year 2	Year 3	Year 4	Year 5
Percentage of net income (NI) (dividends) paid to stockholders the year after obtaining the NI; Payout ratio		70.00%				
Rate of increase in volume		0.00%	1.00%	2.00%	2.00%	2.00%
CRO required from year 1 to 5		100.00	110.00	120.00	130.00	140.00

With these policies and goals, we calculate some of the variables. In this case, we estimate the sales (in units), and from this we calculate the final inventory and the required purchases. Based on the sales revenues and purchases, we calculate AR and AP. Market research and other inquiries might allow the manager to get some estimates for selected variables, such as administrative and sales costs. The basic figures are given below.

In this example we are considering a new variable: the expected inflation rate over the life of the cash flow. This also means that there are nominal price increases. These increases apply not only to the selling and purchasing prices, but also to some items such as overhead and payroll expenses and the purchase of the new asset in year 4.[5]

TABLE 5.lc   Costs and Price Increases

	Year 0	Year 1	Year 2	Year 3	Year 4	Year 5
Annual nominal rate of increase in selling price		3.00%	4.03%	4.03%	4.03%	4.03%
Annual nominal rate of increase in cost per unit		3.52%	3.52%	3.52%	4.03%	4.03%
Nominal rate of increase in overhead expenses		3.52%	3.52%	3.52%	3.52%	4.03%
Nominal rate of increase in payroll		4.55%	4.55%	4.55%	4.55%	4.55%
Nominal increase in price of fixed assets		3.21%	3.21%	3.21%	3.21%	3.21%

When dealing with reality we estimate the nominal rate of increase in prices, and we might be tempted to include the number right away because people are more familiar with nominal rate increases than with real rate increases. However, to make the model coherent for sensitivity analysis, we decompose and recompose those nominal increase rates.

For instance, assume that we estimate the expected nominal changes in the selling price and the expected inflation rates. Based on the expected

---

[5]A nominal price increase rate is composed of the expected real rate of increase and the expected inflation rate. Using the Fisher relationship, we have (1 + nominal increase rate) = (1 + inflation rate) (1 + real increase rate).

inflation rates, we deflate the nominal price increases to obtain the expected real increases over the life of the cash flow. In the second stage, we write the formula for the expected nominal price changes in terms of the expected real increases and the expected inflation rates. This way we guarantee that if we change the expected inflation rates, for instance, the expected nominal increases will be consistent with the expected inflation rates.

Other information regarding the price scale for purchases, market simulation, and the elasticity price–demand effect are shown in the following tables.

5.1.5 Relationship Between the Quantity Purchased and the Purchase Price

Next, we model the behavior of the purchase price by linking the quantity purchased with the purchase price to recognize economies of scale. Usually, there is a discrete table of discounts by volume. However, we use a formula that approximates a table of discounts. We recognize that when the firm purchases a larger quantity, the company receives a better (lower) price for the product. This means that the price is a negative function of the quantity purchased. The table of discounts is as follows:

TABLE 5.1d Table of Current Prices as a Function of Quantity (Q in Thousands)

From	Up to	Mean	Base price (year 0)
5.925	6.075	6.00	4.13
6.075	6.225	6.15	3.99
6.225	6.375	6.30	3.86
6.375	6.525	6.45	3.74
6.525	6.675	6.60	3.62
6.675	6.825	6.75	3.50
6.825	6.975	6.90	3.39
6.975	7.125	7.05	3.28
7.125	7.275	7.20	3.17
7.275	7.425	7.35	3.07
7.425	7.575	7.50	2.97
7.575	7.725	7.65	2.87
7.725	7.875	7.80	2.78
7.875	8.025	7.95	2.69
8.025	8.175	8.10	2.60
8.175	8.325	8.25	2.52
8.325	8.475	8.40	2.43
8.475	8.625	8.55	2.36
8.625	8.775	8.70	2.28
8.775	8.925	8.85	2.20
8.925	9.075	9.00	2.13

The estimation of the purchasing price scale is based on the previous table. The table and graph show the behavior of the purchase price versus the quantity purchased.

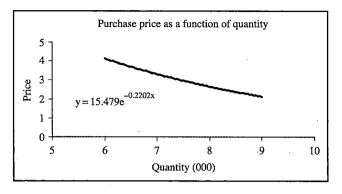

EXHIBIT 5.1 Price scale for quantity purchased.

We assume that the behavior is approximated by the following exponential equation. Note that in equation 5.1, the quantity purchased is in thousands of units.

$$\text{Base Purchase Price} = Ce^b = 15.479e^{(-0.2202 \times \text{Quantity purchased})} \qquad (5.1)$$

From the data we find the coefficients as follows:

TABLE 5.1e Inputs for Simulating the Scale of Prices for Purchases

C	15.4790
b	−0.2202

This scale is applied for all the years, and the nominal price increases are applied to the base price.

5.1.6 Simulation of Market Demand

In this model we assume that a market research study has been conducted to determine the potential market for the product. This market research study shows the sensitivity of the market demand to the output price. For illustration, we show a wide range for the output price from $3 to $11.

TABLE 5.2a   Information for the Simulation of Market Research and Elasticity Price–Demand Research

Price	Q sold
3	12,249.00
3.5	11,119.00
4	10,226.00
4.5	9,498.00
5	8,891.00
5.5	8,375.00
6	7,931.00
6.5	7,542.00
7	7,200.00
7.5	6,895.00
8	6,622.00
8.5	6,375.00
9	6,150.00
9.5	5,946.00
10	5,757.00
10.5	5,584.00
11	5,423.00

A graph of the relationship between the price and quantity sold, based on the market survey, is shown.

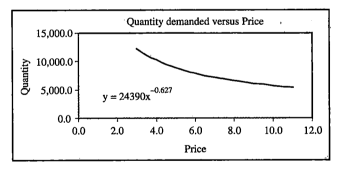

EXHIBIT 5.2   Quantity demanded in market survey.

From this data we infer the price–demand elasticity function. For convenience, we have assumed a simple functional relationship with one independent variable, namely price. For further discussion on demand functions, see Appendix A. In this case we assume that the relationship between price and quantity demanded is as follows:

$$Q = \beta_0 \times Price^{\beta} \qquad (5.2)$$

where β_0 is a constant and β is the elasticity coefficient.

TABLE 5.2b Elasticity Coefficient and Price Derived from the Market Research

Elasticity coefficient β	−0.627
Constant coefficient β_0	24,389.86
Selling price	7.00

There is a negative relationship between the real price and the quantity sold. That is, if the real price were to increase, there would be a decrease in the quantity sold. To reiterate, there is a real increase in the price if the expected nominal price increase is higher than the expected inflation rate. Again, for further discussion on real versus nominal price changes, see Appendix A.

In a going concern we study the history of prices and sales to derive the price elasticity of a given product or service. In practice we might have many products and services. Next we need to group them into homogeneous categories, find a typical product for each group, and apply the elasticity of that typical product (service) to the group. One way to identify the groups might be with the Pareto rule, which states that approximately 80% of the revenues (costs) are generated by 20% of the products.

As specified earlier, it is expected that from year 2 to year 5, there are annual increases in the sale of units. The expected selling price used in the market study is $7 per unit. Both the selling price and the purchase prices are affected by nominal price increases during the forecast period. The equation for the market demand was given previously. At the base price of $7 per unit, the quantity sold is 7,200.

$$\text{Quantity} = 24,389.86 \times (\text{Price})^{-0.627}$$
$$= 7,200 \text{ units}$$

5.2 IMPACT ON DEMAND OF CHANGES IN PRICE AND OF EXPENDITURES ON ADVERTISING AND PROMOTION

5.2.1 Annual Sales

In this example, quantities sold are affected by two factors: the change in the real price on the quantity sold and the marketing and advertising activities. The relationship between the quantity sold and real price increases is negative, and the relationship between the quantity sold and marketing efforts is positive. The total impact on quantity sold depends on the net effect of the changes in prices and the marketing efforts.

5.2.2 Impact on Demand of Change in Price

In this section we explain the meaning and interpretation of equation 5.2. We start the analysis with the simplest demand function (with only one variable), in which the (natural) logarithm of the quantity sold is a linear function of the (natural) logarithm of its own price. Later we introduce the effect of the marketing efforts:

$$Q_n = e^{\beta_0} P^{\beta_1}{}_n \tag{5.3}$$

or

$$Ln(Q_n) = \beta_0 + \beta_1 Ln(P_n) \tag{5.4}$$

where Q_n is the quantity demanded of the good in year n and P_n is the real price of the good in period n. The reader should note that the β_0 in equation 5.4 is **not** the same as the β_0 in equation 5.2. This should not cause any confusion.

For ease in the interpretation of the slope coefficient, we choose the log–log formulation. The slope coefficient β_1 is the price elasticity of demand. In particular, if the real price increases by one percent, the quantity demanded increases by β_1 percent. We use the price elasticity of demand β_1 to measure the responsiveness of the quantity demanded to changes in the price. For example, suppose $\beta_1 = -0.60$. If the price of the good increases by 1%, the quantity demanded decreases by 0.60%. For more discussion and details on demand functions, see Appendix C.

The quantity sold in year n + 1 can be written in terms of the quantity sold in the previous year n, the price elasticity of demand, and the percent change in price. See Appendix A for more details. The effect of elasticity upon demand can be expressed as follows:

$$Q_{n+1} = Q_n(1 + \beta_1 \%\Delta P) \tag{5.5}$$

The percent change in the price in equation 5.5 refers to the real change in price, where the expected real price increase is equal to the ratio of one plus the nominal price increase to one plus the expected inflation rate minus one.

$$\%\Delta P = \frac{1 + \text{nominal price rate increase}}{1 + \text{expected inflation}} - 1 \tag{5.6}$$

If the expected nominal increase in price for the good is equal to the expected inflation rate, there is no real increase in the price. Then the quantity sold in year n + 1 is equal to the quantity sold in the previous year n.

Let

$$\lambda = (1 + \beta_1 \%\Delta P) \tag{5.7}$$

We call λ an adjustment factor for the quantity demanded. The quantity demanded in period $n + 1$ is equal to the quantity demanded in the previous period n times the adjustment factor λ. Substituting equation 5.6 into equation 5.7, we obtain an expression for the adjustment factor.

Adjustment factor λ

$$\lambda = 1 + \beta_1 \left[\frac{1 + \text{nominal price rate increase}}{1 + \text{expected inflation}} - 1 \right] \qquad (5.8)$$

For year 1, the expected nominal increase in the selling price is equal to the expected inflation rate and therefore there is no real increase in the selling price. From years 2 to 5, the expected real increase in the selling price is 1% and the expected inflation rate is 3%. With the real increases in the price, we expect that the quantities sold decrease. The price elasticity of demand is -0.627. Thus, the decrease in the quantity sold in the next period is approximately 0.627%, which equals one minus the adjustment factor.

$$\text{Adjustment factor } \lambda = 1 + \beta_1 \text{ times real price increase}$$
$$= 1 - 0.627 \times 1\%$$
$$= 1 - 0.627\% = 99.373\%$$

5.2.3 Impact on Demand of Expenditures on Advertising and Promotion

In addition to the real price effect on the quantity sold, we also take into account the impact of marketing effort with a multiplicative factor. This marketing effort is a consequence of the promotions and advertising, good service, and the quality of the product. It results in an increase in the volume sold. If the effect of the marketing effort is separated from the other economic effects, such as the output price, the sales volume of one year can be expressed as a function of the volume sold in the previous year and the marketing effort effect. To be specific, the quantity sold in year $n + 1$ is equal to the product of the quantity sold in the previous year n times one plus the volume increase.

$$Q_{n+1} = Q_n(1 + \text{volume increase}) \qquad (5.9)$$

When combined with the price effect, these two act simultaneously and the combined effect is taken into account by multiplying the factors and not adding the factors. The expression for the quantity sold with both effects is shown in equation 5.10. Usually the marketing effort is positive and increases the number of units sold. The elasticity effect might be positive or negative, depending on the change in the real price.

$$Q_{n+1} = Q_n(1 + \text{volume increase})(\text{adjustment factor}) \qquad (5.10)$$

For example, in year 2, the increase in the volume from the marketing effort is 1%. However, as calculated earlier, the real increase in the price results in a 0.627% decrease in the quantity sold, and the value of the adjustment factor is 99.373%. Combining the two effects, the net effect is an increase of 0.367% in year 2.

$$Q_2 = Q_1(1 + \text{volume increase})(\text{adjustment factor}) \qquad (5.11)$$
$$= Q_0(1 + 1\%) \times 99.373\%$$
$$= Q_0(1 + 0.367\%)$$

In the next table, we summarize the discussion up to this point.

TABLE 5.3   Simulation of Price-Demand Elasticity and Market Effort

	Year 0	Year 1	Year 2	Year 3	Year 4	Year 5
Real increase in selling price		0.00%	1.00%	1.00%	1.00%	1.00%
β_1 (Real increase in selling price)		0.00000	−0.00627	−0.00627	−0.00627	−0.00627
Adjustment factor		1.00000	0.99373	0.99373	0.99373	0.99373
1+ increase in volume		1.00	1.01	1.02	1.02	1.02
Combined effect on quantity sold		1.00000	1.00367	1.01360	1.01360	1.01360

In year 2, relative to year 1, the increase in the quantity sold is 0.367%. In years 3 to 5, the increase in the quantity sold, relative to the previous year, is 1.360%.

The number of units sold for each year of the forecasting period is shown in Table 5.4. Based on the quantity sold, we calculate the value of the sales revenue, which is equal to the quantity sold times the selling price per unit.

$$\text{Sales Revenue} = (\text{Quantity sold})(\text{unit selling price}) \qquad (5.12)$$

With all the information gathered up to now, we estimate the quantity sold for years 1 to 5. Each year, the number of units sold increases by x%. In the particular case of units sold, the procedure to calculate the amount to be sold for any year is

Units sold in year n = Units sold in year n−1

$$(1 + \text{increase in volume}) \times \text{Adjustment factor} \quad (5.13)$$

For year 0, we use the formula Quantity $= 24{,}389.86(\text{Price})^{-0.627}$. In year 1, we take the demand in the previous year (year 0 in this case) and multiply it by the adjustment factor. The adjustment factor happens to be 1 in year 1 because there is no real increase in price and there is no market effort. We make similar calculations in the subsequent years. The reader will notice that the actual increases in Table 5.3 are not the ones we estimated in Table 5.1b. This happens because the quantity sold results from an increase in volume due to, say, promotions, quality, and service, which cause the demand to increase. At the same time, the increase in the nominal price above the expected inflation rate drives the demand down. In any year n, the quantity sold is as follows:

$$Q_n = Q_{n-1}(1 + \text{Increase in volume}) \times \text{Adjustment factor} \quad (5.14)$$

Usually the marketing efforts increase the demand, while the effect of elasticity might make the demand go down or up depending on the expected real increase in the price and the expected inflation rate.

5.2.4 Preliminary Tables for the Complex Example

From the basic parameters we construct the table of estimated variables.

TABLE 5.4   Basic Estimated Variables

	Year 0	Year 1	Year 2	Year 3	Year 4	Year 5
Units sold	7,200.00	7,200.00	7,226.40	7,324.70	7,424.40	7,525.40
Selling price	7.00	7.20	7.50	7.80	8.10	8.40
Sales revenues		51,912.00	54,202.10	57,153.60	60,265.80	63,547.40
Overhead	2,184.00	2,260.80	2,340.20	2,422.50	2,507.60	2,608.70
Administrative payroll	2,400.00	2,509.10	2,623.10	2,742.30	2,867.00	2,997.30
Selling commissions		3,114.70	3,252.10	3,429.20	3,615.90	3,812.80
Advertising and promotions		1,557.40	1,626.10	1,714.60	1,808.00	1,906.40
CRO for year 0 (based on 20% of overhead, payroll and commissions expenses)	1,576.90					

(continues)

TABLE 5.4   (*continued*)

	Year 0	Year 1	Year 2	Year 3	Year 4	Year 5
Short-term rate of reinvestment		6.09%	6.09%	6.09%	6.09%	6.09%
Rate of interest for debt using CAPM $d = r_f + \text{risk premium}$		11.00%	11.0%	11.0%	11.0%	11.0%
Factor for increase in price of fixed assets		1.03	1.07	1.10	1.13	1.17
Price of fixed assets at year 5					45,381.60	0.00

5.2.5 Annual Increase in the Volume of Sales

Next, we introduce the expenditure on advertising and promotion, and assume that advertising leads to increases in sales. In year 2, the sales volume increases by 1%. In years 3 to 5, the sales volume increases by 2%. With historical data, we can determine the strength of the expected relationship between the sales volume and the expenditures on advertising and promotions.

5.2.6 Annual Expenditures on Advertising and Promotion

The annual expenditures on advertising and promotion are equal to 3% of the annual sales.

5.2.7 Cash Required for Operations

In year 0, the CRO is calculated as 20% of the annual amounts of overhead, payroll, and sales commissions in year 1. Although overhead and payroll are the same as in the simple example, the sales commissions change because of the change in the nominal price in year 1. In year 1, the CRO is $100. Thereafter, it increases by $10 per year.

5.2.8 Expected Domestic Inflation Rate

We assume the expected domestic inflation rate is constant at 3% for the five years.

5.2.9 Annual Sales Volume

The number of units sold in year 1 is 7,200.

$$\text{Units sold in year 2} = \text{Units sold in year 1 times } (1 + x\%)$$
$$\text{times Adjustment factor}$$
$$= 7,200.0 \times (1 + 1\%) \times 0.99373 = 7,226.40$$

In the same manner, we calculate the units sold for the other years.

5.2.10 Annual Sales Revenue

Based on the annual quantity sold, in any year n, we calculate the value of the sales revenue, which is equal to the quantity sold times the unit selling price.

$$\text{Sales revenue} = (\text{Quantity sold})(\text{unit selling price}) \qquad (5.15)$$

For year 1, the sales revenue is $51,912.00.

$$\text{Sales revenue} = 7,200 \times 7.20 = 51,912.00$$

In the same manner, we calculate the units sold for the other years.

5.3 REAL RATE OF INTEREST, THE RISK-PREMIUM FOR DEBT, AND THE REINVESTMENT RETURN: INTEREST RATES ESTIMATION

One way to calculate interest rates is to estimate the expected inflation rate and combine it with the real rate of interest and a market-based risk premium. A real rate of interest is a rate valid in an economy with no inflation and a risk free investment. There are countries with near zero inflation. The interest rate paid by treasury bonds in those countries might be a good estimate of the real rate of interest. One way to calculate the real rate of interest in the presence of inflation is to deflate the risk free rate in an economy by the inflation rate. For details refer to Chapter Two.

In practice, when we find the nominal interest rate (either the cost of debt or the reinvestment rate of return), we might be tempted to include the number right away. However, as mentioned earlier, we decompose and recompose those rates. For instance, assume we know the actual rate of interest for the cost of debt. We decompose it into the expected inflation rate, the real rate, and the risk premium. Then, using these components, we formulate the interest rate in the model using equation 5.16. This way we guarantee that if we change the inflation rate, for instance, the nominal cost of debt will be consistent with the inflation rate.

Here we assume that the cost of debt fully accounts for the expected inflation rate. In some cases, the cost of debt can be fixed and is not a function of the expected inflation rate. Thus, if the actual inflation is higher than the expected inflation rate, the company gains on the debt financing. If the actual inflation rate is lower than the expected inflation rate, the company loses on the debt financing.

We have included a real rate of interest and a risk premium π to recognize a margin for the debt holder. The nominal cost of debt, using the CAPM, is calculated as follows:[6]

$$i = \text{Risk free rate} + \text{risk premium}$$
$$= (1 + r)(1 + g^{Inf}) - 1 + \pi \tag{5.16}$$

where r is the real rate of interest, g^{Inf} is the inflation rate, and π is the risk premium.

The reinvestment interest rates have been calculated by taking into account the expected inflation rate, the real rate of interest, and the Fisher relationship. Any excess cash is used to buy marketable securities at the end of the year. Because we assume that the marketable securities are bought at the end of the year, the interest is calculated with the interest rate estimated for the following year.

We assume that the real rate of interest is 3% and the risk-premium for debt is 4.91%. With these parameters, the cost of debt is 11.00%.

$$i = (1 + r)(1 + g^{Inf}) - 1 + \pi$$
$$= (1 + 3\%)(1 + 3\%) - 1 + 4.91\% = 11.00\%$$

5.4 DEPRECIATION SCHEDULE

The depreciation schedule is shown in the next table.

TABLE 5.5   Depreciation Schedule

	Year 0	Year 1	Year 2	Year 3	Year 4	Year 5
Beginning net fixed assets		40,000.00	30,000.00	20,000.00	10,000.00	45,381.60
Annual depreciation		10,000.00	10,000.00	10,000.00	10,000.00	11,345.40
Cumulated depreciation		10,000.00	20,000.00	30,000.00	40,000.00	51,345.40
New assets	0.00	0.00	0.00	0.00	45,381.60	0.00
Net fixed assets	40,000.00	30,000.00	20,000.00	10,000.00	45,381.60	34,036.20

[6]Alternatively, we could use the Fisher relationship to calculate the risk premium; however, we prefer to be consistent with the CAPM. The Fisher relationship indicates that the nominal rate of interest is made up of the real rate, the inflation rate, and a risk premium. These components are multiplicative and not additive.

For tax purposes, we have assumed straight-line depreciation for four years and assume that in year 4 we buy additional fixed assets. In Table 5.5 a new asset is included at year 4. The value of the new asset is taken from Table 5.4 and is equal to the price in year 0 times the value of the expected inflation index for year 4.

5.5 INITIAL CASH BUDGET FOR YEAR 0

In this example we need to know from the beginning if the initial equity investment is enough for the sum of the total investment and the CRO we plan to have at the beginning. For this purpose we construct the CB for year 0, which shows the inflows and outflows for that year.[7]

TABLE 5.6 Cash Budget for Year 0 to Determine Extra Funds

Cash inflows	
Total income AR	0.00
Total cash inflows	0.00
Cash outflows	
Total payments of AP	0.00
Overhead	0.00
Payroll expenses	0.00
Selling commissions	0.00
Advertising and promotions	0.00
Purchase of fixed assets	40,000.00
Purchase of fixed assets in year 5	0.00
Taxes	0.00
Total cash outflows	40,000.00
Net cash increase (decrease)	−40,000.00
Bank loan 1	17,576.90
Bank loan 2	
Payment of loans	0.00
Interest charges	0.00
NCB after cash returns to debt holders	−22,424.00
Equity investment	24,000.00
Dividend payments	
Repurchase of stock	
NCB after cash returns to shareholders	1,576.90
Sales of marketable securities	0.00
Interest income on marketable securities	0.00
Investment on marketable securities	
NCB after discretionary transactions paid in cash	1,576.90
Accumulated cash balance at end of year	1,576.90

[7]For a going concern this initial CB is not necessary. We know the value of the cash from the balance in the bank.

The total amount required for starting the firm is equal to the sum of the cost of the fixed asset and the CRO. Of the $41,576.90 that is required, we finance $24,000 with contributions from equity holders. This means that we need a loan of $17,576.90 for the remaining amount.

5.6 LOAN SCHEDULE

The bank loan is paid according to the following schedule. We assume that the loan principal is repaid in equal annual amounts. Some readers may prefer a loan schedule with constant total payment. However, when we have indexed interest rates, the existing functions in a spreadsheet for calculating a uniform payment will not work. They work for a constant interest rate. The solution to this issue is to use the goal seek facility in Excel.

The total loan repayment in any year n is equal to the principal repayment plus the interest charges for the year. At the end of year n, the ending balance (EB) is equal to the BB plus the interest charges less the loan repayment (principal plus interest). Because the loan balances decline each year, the interest charges also decline.

We have two loans, an initial one at the end of year 0 and another one to finance the purchase of the additional fixed assets at the end of year 4. The two loan schedules are shown in the following tables.

TABLE 5.7a   Loan Schedule I

	Year 0	Year 1	Year 2	Year 3	Year 4	Year 5
BB		17,576.90	14,061.50	10,546.10	7,030.80	3,515.40
Interest charges debt 1		1,933.50	1,546.80	1,160.10	773.40	386.70
Principal payment debt 1		3,515.40	3,515.40	3,515.40	3,515.40	3,515.40
Total payment debt 1		5,448.80	5,062.20	4,675.50	4,288.80	3,902.10
EB	17,576.90	14,061.50	10,546.10	7,030.80	3,515.40	0.00
Interest rate		11.00%	11.00%	11.00%	11.00%	11.00%

The second loan schedule is based on the CB. We do not know in advance the amount of this loan in year 4 and we need to construct the CB for year 4.

TABLE 5.7b   Loan Schedule 2

	Year 0	Year 1	Year 2	Year 3	Year 4	Year 5
BB						4,904.90
Interest charges debt 2						539.50
Principal payment debt 2						981.00
Total payment debt 2		0.00	0.00	0.00	0.00	1,520.50
EB					4,904.90	3,923.90
Interest rate		11.00%	11.00%	11.00%	11.00%	11.00%

The value of the new debt in year 4, which is $4,904.90, is calculated from the CB as follows:

- NCB + Payment of loans + Interest charges
- Equity investment + Dividend payments
- + Repurchase of stock − Sales of marketable securities
- Interest income on marketable securities
- Accumulated cash balance at end of year
- + CRO for year 4 = New debt at year 4 = $4,904.90

The purpose of this calculation is to determine the size of the deficit in a given year. The negative items reduce the deficit and the positive items increase the deficit. The deficit increases with the outflows indicated: Payment of loans, Interest charges, Dividend payments, Repurchase of stock and the CRO. The items that decrease the deficit are those that represent outflows. In this case, we have as inflows the NCB, Equity investment, Sales of marketable securities, Interest income on marketable securities, and the cash we carry over from the previous year (accumulated cash balance at end of year).

5.7 INVENTORY AND QUANTITY PURCHASED

Next, based on estimated sales, we calculate the number of units that have to be purchased, taking into account the inventory requirements. The values for the inventory and purchases are shown in the next table.

In any year n, the number of units purchased is equal to the quantity sold in year n plus the final inventory of the previous year $n - 1$ minus the initial inventory for the current year n. The initial inventory in year n is equal to the final inventory of the previous year $n - 1$. Purchases in units in Table 5.8 are calculated from the basic relationship from Chapter Four.

$$\text{Purchases}_n = \text{Quantity sold}_n + \text{Final inventory}_n$$
$$- \text{Final inventory}_{n-1} \qquad (5.17)$$

For instance, for year 1

$$\text{Purchases} = 7,200 - 0 + 600 = 7,800.00$$

Based on the units sold and the required inventory, we calculate the annual quantities that have to be purchased. The annual quantities purchased are shown in the following table. Now we can calculate the numbers for the inventories and purchases.

TABLE 5.8   Inventories and Purchases

	Year 0	Year 1	Year 2	Year 3	Year 4	Year 5
Units sold		7,200.00	7,226.40	7,324.70	7,424.40	7,525.40
Final inventory		600.00	602.20	610.40	618.70	627.10
Initial inventory		0.00	600.00	602.20	610.40	618.70
Purchases		7,800.00	7,228.60	7,332.90	7,432.70	7,533.80

Units sold is taken from Table 5.4. Final inventory in Table 5.8 is found by applying the policy to maintain one month as final inventory. Hence, the final inventory is the units sold multiplied by 8.33%. In any year, the initial inventory is simply the quantity left as final inventory in the previous year.

The purchases decrease from 7,800 units in year 1 to 7,228.60 in year 2. Thereafter, the purchases increase steadily from 7,228.60 units in year 2 to 7,533.80 units in year 5. Because the units purchased declines from year 1 to year 2, the unit purchase price increases because we have specified a negative relationship between the price and the quantity purchased. This is simply a one-time effect for a start-up business.

5.8 RELATIONSHIP BETWEEN THE QUANTITY PURCHASED AND THE PURCHASE PRICE

We have modeled the behavior of the purchasing price by linking the quantities purchased and prices to recognize the scale economies in purchases.

This scale is kept constant along the years and the nominal price increases are applied to the base price.

Consider the following example. Suppose in year 0 the purchases are 6,000 units. The firm can buy the purchases at a unit price of $4.13. If there is an increase in the nominal price in year 1 of 10%, in year 1 the firm buys the same 6,000 units at $4.54.

Purchase price in year 1 = (Base price in year 0)(increase in price)

$$= 4.13 \times (1 + 10\%)$$
$$= 4.54 \tag{5.18}$$

And if the nominal price increase in year 2 is again 10%, the firm buys the 6,000 units at $4.99.

Returning to our numerical example, in year 1 the initial quantity purchased, according to inventory policy and market research, is 7,800. The estimated quantity to be sold is 7,200 units and the inventory is 600 units. If we look at Table 5.1d, where the simulation of prices as a function of quantity is shown, the price is $2.78. However, in year 21 there is an increase in price of 3.52% (see Table 5.1c). Thus, the unit price in year 1 is $2.88.

$$\text{Unit cost in year } 1 = \text{Base price in year 0 times increase in price}$$
$$= 2.78 \times (1 + 3.5\%)$$
$$= 2.88$$

Using the quantities purchased for each year, we estimate the base unit cost with the formula in exhibit 5.1 and the actual purchase price, which takes into account the cumulative nominal increases in the price.

TABLE 5.9 Nominal Cost per Unit

	Year 0	Year 1	Year 2	Year 3	Year 4	Year 5
Cumulative increase in basic cost per unit		1.035	1.072	1.109	1.154	1.200
Cost per unit without considering price increase (from formula in exhibit 1)		2.78	3.15	3.08	3.01	2.95
Actual cost per unit (applying the cumulative factor for increase in price)		2.88	3.38	3.42	3.48	3.54

As previously mentioned, the scale for discounts is constant for all the years. But the prices for each quantity changes as the quantities purchased change every year. If there are no nominal price increases, the scale and prices are the prices found in Table 5.1d. But the nominal unit price for the purchases might change every year (despite no increase in price) because the quantities purchased change. When there are price increases, the actual price to be paid changes as a function of the quantity purchased and price increases.

An increase in the quantity purchased lowers the price. If there is a big increase in the quantity purchased, the decrease in the price could more than offset the nominal increase in the price, leading to an overall decrease in purchase price.

For illustration, we show the calculations of the unit cost for year 2. In year 2, the quantity purchased is 7,228.60 units. Based on this value, the base cost per unit is $3.20. In years 1 and 2, the increase in the unit cost is 3.52%.

$$\text{Base unit cost} = 15.479e^{(-0.2202\times\text{Quantity purchased})}$$
$$= 15.479e^{-(0.2202\times7,228.6)} = 3.15$$
$$\text{Actual unit cost} = (\text{Base unit cost})(\text{Cumulative Increase in price})$$
$$= 3.15 \times 1.072\%$$
$$= 3.38$$

For years 3 to 5, we follow a similar series of steps. Next, we calculate the annual quantities sold and the annual revenues. Based on the quantities sold, we calculate the required inventories and the quantities purchased. With the values of the quantities purchased, we examine the relationship between the quantity purchased and the unit cost.

5.9 COST OF GOODS SOLD

In the IS, for tax purposes, we have to calculate the value of the COGS. The COGS is calculated by taking into account the relationship developed in Chapter Three, in units:

$$\text{Quantity sold (Q)} = \text{II} + \text{P} - \text{FI} \qquad (5.19)$$

where II is initial inventory, P is purchases, and FI is final inventory.
 And in dollars,

$$\text{COGS} = \$\ \text{II} + \$\ \text{P} - \$\ \text{FI} \qquad (5.20)$$

 In any year n, the COGS is equal to the value of the purchases plus the value of the initial inventory minus the value of the final inventory. The quantities in inventory and purchases are multiplied by their respective purchase prices. The following tables show COGS.

TABLE 5.10   Determination of Cost of Goods Sold

	Year 0	Year 1	Year 2	Year 3	Year 4	Year 5
Initial inventory		0.00	1,725.70	2,033.30	2,085.00	2,150.80
Purchases		22,434.40	24,407.30	25,047.90	25,837.90	26,644.90
Final inventory		1,725.70	2,033.30	2,085.00	2,150.80	2,217.90
COGS		20,708.60	24,099.70	24,996.20	25,772.20	26,577.80

5.10 SELLING AND ADMINISTRATIVE EXPENSES

Based on the annual sales revenues, we calculate the annual sales commissions and the expenditures on advertising and promotions. The sales commission is 6% of the annual sales revenues and the expenditures on advertising and promotions are 3% of the annual sales revenues.

The table for the selling and administrative expenses is shown next.

TABLE 5.11   Determination of Selling and Administrative Expenses

	Year 0	Year 1	Year 2	Year 3	Year 4	Year 5
Selling commissions		3,114.70	3,252.10	3,429.20	3,615.90	3,812.80
Overhead		2,260.80	2,340.20	2,422.50	2,507.60	2,608.70
Administrative payroll		2,509.10	2,623.10	2,742.30	2,867.00	2,997.30
Advertising and promotions		1,557.40	1,626.10	1,714.60	1,808.00	1,906.40
Total selling and administrative expenses		9,441.90	9,841.50	10,308.70	10,798.50	11,325.30

5.11 RECEIVABLES AND PAYABLES

Next, we calculate the annual values for the receivables, payables, and cash balances.

Cash receipts from sales are divided into two categories: sales on cash and sales on credit. Sales on cash are the sales for the year multiplied by the percent defined in Table 5.1b. Sales on credit are defined as sales for the year multiplied by one minus the percent defined in the same table.

As explained in Chapter Three, in any year n, the cash receipts are equal to the sales revenues in year n times the percentage of sales received in the same year plus the sales revenues from the previous year times the percentage of sales not received in the previous year.

Cash payments for purchase and overhead expenses are divided into two categories: payments on cash and credit. Payments in cash are the purchases for the year multiplied by the percent defined in Table 5.1b. Payments on credit are defined as purchases and overhead for the year multiplied by one minus the percent defined in the same table.

In any year n, the cash expenditures are equal to the purchases times the percentage of payments made in the same year plus the purchases from the previous year times the percentage of payments not made in the previous year.

From Table 5.4, we know the amount of sales and from Table 5.10 we know the amount of purchases. From Table 5.1b we know the policy and goal for payments and sales collection. With this information, Table 5.12 and Table 5.13 are constructed. The reader should verify the total collection and total payments to suppliers in Table 5.13.

The calculation of the sales and purchases, on cash and credit, are shown in the following table.

TABLE 5.12   Sales and Purchases, on Cash and Credit

	Year 0	Year 1	Year 2	Year 3	Year 4	Year 5
Sales on cash		49,316.40	51,492.00	54,295.90	57,252.50	60,370.10
Sales on credit		2,595.60	2,710.10	2,857.70	3,013.30	3,177.40
Purchases on cash		20,190.90	21,966.60	22,543.10	23,254.10	23,980.40
Purchases on credit		2,243.40	2,440.70	2,504.80	2,583.80	2,664.50

This table is calculated from sales or purchases multiplied by the percent stipulated as AR and AP policies. AR and AP are shown in the next table.

TABLE 5.13   Accounts Receivable and Accounts Payable

	Year 0	Year 1	Year 2	Year 3	Year 4	Year 5
Sales on cash		49,316.40	51,492.00	54,295.90	57,252.50	60,370.10
AR recovery		0.00	2,595.60	2,710.10	2,857.70	3,013.30
Total sales collection		49,316.40	54,087.60	57,006.00	60,110.20	63,383.30
Purchases on cash		20,190.90	21,966.60	22,543.10	23,254.10	23,980.40
AP purchases		0.00	2,243.40	2,440.70	2,504.80	2,583.80
Total purchases payments		20,190.90	24,210.00	24,983.80	25,758.90	26,564.20

Table 5.12 is calculated from sales or expenses on cash by applying the respective percent from Table 5.1b to the respective total values to obtain AR and AP.

Total sales collection and total purchases payments are the sum of cash sales (or cash purchases) plus sales (purchases) on credit.

5.12 THE LOGIC OF THE MODEL

Because we have covered a lot of new material, we summarize the working of the model up to this point. Let us see how the model works for year 1.

5.12.1 Year 1

1. Based on the results from the market research, for year 0, we specify an initial unit price of $7. In addition, we specify the nominal price increase and the expected inflation rate for year 1. If the expected nominal price increase for year 1 is different from the expected inflation

rate, there is an expected real change in the price and the quantity sold changes. In the example the expected nominal price increase and the expected inflation rate are the same. For that reason, in year 1, the quantity sold does not change and is equal to 7,200 units.

2. With the quantity at year 0, we calculate the final inventory, which is 8.33% of the sales and equal to 600 units.

3. With the final inventory we define the purchase quantity, which is equal to the sales plus the change in inventory.

4. The purchase quantity defines the unit cost. We specified the negative relationship between the purchase quantity and the nominal unit cost in greater detail.

5. As can be seen, the purchasing price (and the gross margin!) is a function of the inventory policy as it should be, even if finance text-books do not say that! And of course, the inventory is a function of the quantity sold, which in turn depends on the selling price used in the simulation of the market survey.

The inventory policy affects the gross margin (the unit cost) because it depends on the amount to be purchased. If we have more stock, we have to buy more and if we buy more quantity, we get a lower price.

5.12.2 Year 2

For year 2, there are a few differences.

1. The quantity sold in year 1 is 7,200 units.

2. Again, we specify an increase in the nominal output price for year 2.

3. The expected increase in the nominal price could be equal to or different from the expected inflation rate. If the expected increase in the nominal price is different from the expected inflation rate, the annual quantity sold will be affected.

4. We forecast an increase in units for year 2. The increase in units might be caused by marketing and promotional strategies, quality, and service.

5. Now we have two determinants for the quantity sold. First, the estimated volume increase pushes the quantity sold upwards. And second, the nominal price increase through the price elasticity pushes demand upwards or downwards, depending on its relation to the expected inflation rate. The quantity sold for year 2 is 7,441.1 units, as was calculated.

6. With the quantity sold in year 2, we calculate the final inventory for year 2. With the final inventory we define the purchase quantity. The purchase quantity defines the unit cost.

5.13 CONSTRUCTING FINANCIAL STATEMENTS FOR THE COMPLEX EXAMPLE

Here we show a detailed procedure to construct the financial statements.

5.13.1 Income Statement (IS)

The IS for year 1 is shown in the following table.

TABLE 5.14 Pro-Forma Income Statement Year 1

	Year 0	Year 1	Year 2	Year 3	Year 4	Year 5
Sales		51,912.00	54,202.10	57,153.60	60,265.80	63,547.40
COGS		20,708.60	24,099.70	24,996.20	25,772.20	26,577.80
Gross profit		31,203.40	30,102.40	32,157.40	34,493.60	36,969.70
Selling and administrative expenses		9,441.90	9,841.50	10,308.70	10,798.50	11,325.30
Depreciation		10,000.00	10,000.00	10,000.00	10,000.00	11,345.40
Earnings before interest and taxes (EBIT)		11,761.50	10,260.90	11,848.80	·13,695.10	14,299.00
Interest income on marketable securities		0.00				
Other expenses (interest expenses)		1,933.50				
Earnings before taxes (EBT)		9,828.00				
Taxes		3,439.80				
NI		6,388.20				
Dividends		4,471.70				
Retained earnings		1,916.50				
Accumulated retained earnings		6,388.20				

In year 1, the NI is $6,388.20. To calculate the taxes for year 2, we must estimate the interest income for year 2, which in turn depends on the amount of surplus funds at the end of year 1 that is invested in marketable securities. For the calculation of the surplus funds, we construct the CB statement.

5.13.2 Cash Budget (CB) Statement

The complete CB statement is shown in the following table.

TABLE 5.15   The Complete Pro-Forma Cash Budget Statement

	Year 0	Year 1	Year 2	Year 3	Year 4	Year 5
Cash inflows						
Total income AR	0.00	49,316.40	54,087.60	57,006.00	60,110.20	63,383.30
Total cash inflows	0.00	49,316.40	54,087.60	57,006.00	60,110.20	63,383.30
Cash outflows						
Total payments for AP	0.00	20,190.90	24,210.00	24,983.80	25,758.90	26,564.20
Overhead	0.00	2,260.80	2,340.20	2,422.50	2,507.60	2,608.70
Payroll expenses	0.00	2,509.10	2,623.10	2,742.30	2,867.00	2,997.30
Selling commissions	0.00	3,114.70	3,252.10	3,429.20	3,615.90	3,812.80
Advertising and promotions	0.00	1,557.40	1,626.10	1,714.60	1,808.00	1,906.40
Purchase of fixed assets	40,000.00					
Purchase of fixed assets in year 5	0.00	0.00	0.00	0.00	45,381.60	0.00
Taxes	0.00	3,439.80	3,311.50	4,171.60	5,161.70	4,680.50
Total cash outflows	40,000.00	33,072.70	37,363.10	39,464.10	87,100.70	42,570.00
Net cash increase (decrease)	−40,000.00	16,243.80	16,724.50	17,542.00	−26,990.50	20,813.40
Bank loan 1	17,576.90					
Bank loan 2		0.00	0.00	0.00	4,904.90	0.00
Payment of loans	0.00	3,515.40	3,515.40	3,515.40	3,515.40	4,496.00
Interest charges	0.00	1,933.50	1,546.80	1,160.10	773.40	926.20
NCB after financial transactions	−22,423.10	10,794.90	11,662.40	12,866.50	−26,374.40	15,390.80
Equity investment	24,000.00					
Dividend payments		0.00	4,471.70	4,305.00	5,423.10	6,710.20
Repurchase of stock						
NCB after cash transactions with shareholders	1,576.90	10,794.90	7,190.70	8,561.50	−31,797.50	8,680.60
Sales of marketable securities	0.00	0.00	12,271.90	20,199.90	29,981.60	0.00
Interest income on marketable securities	0.00	0.00	747.40	1,230.20	1,825.90	0.00
Investment on marketable securities		12,271.90	20,199.90	29,981.60	0.00	8,670.60
NCB after discretionary transactions paid in cash	1,576.90	−1,476.90	10.00	10.00	10.00	10.00
Accumulated cash balance at end of year	1,576.90	100.00	110.00	120.00	130.00	140.00

In year 1, the value of the surplus funds is $12,271.90, and based on this amount the interest income is $747.40. By iterating between the CB statement and the IS, we complete both statements.

The complete IS is shown next.

TABLE 5.16   The Complete Pro-Forma Income Statement

	Year 0	Year 1	Year 2	Year 3	Year 4	Year 5
Sales		51,912.00	54,202.10	57,153.60	60,265.80	63,547.40
COGS		20,708.60	24,099.70	24,996.20	25,772.20	26,577.80
Gross profit		31,203.40	30,102.40	32,157.40	34,493.60	36,969.70
Selling and administrative expenses		9,441.90	9,841.50	10,308.70	10,798.50	11,325.30
Depreciation		10,000.00	10,000.00	10,000.00	10,000.00	11,345.40
EBIT		11,761.50	10,260.90	11,848.80	13,695.10	14,299.00
Interest income on marketable securities		0.00	747.40	1,230.20	1,825.90	0.00
Other expenses (interest expenses)		1,933.50	1,546.80	1,160.10	773.40	926.20
EBT		9,828.00	9,461.50	11,918.80	14,747.60	13,372.80
Taxes		3,439.80	3,311.50	4,171.60	5,161.70	4,680.50
NI		6,388.20	6,149.90	7,747.30	9,585.90	8,692.30
Dividends		4,471.70	4,305.00	5,423.10	6,710.20	6,084.60
Retained earnings		1,916.50	1,845.00	2,324.20	2,875.80	2,607.70
Accumulated retained earnings		6,388.20	8,066.40	11,508.70	15,671.60	17,653.70

For review, we briefly describe the iterations between the CB and the IS for year 2 and year 3 and the links that the line items in the CB statement and IS have with the BS. In year 2, the net cash increase (decrease) before financing is $16,724.50. Taking into account the debt financing, the NCB in year 2 is $11,662.40. After taking into account the dividend payments, the NCB is $7,190.70.

In year 3, the investment of surplus funds in year 2 is $20,199.90, and is listed in the BS as short-term investments.

Investment of surplus funds in year 2 =

+ NCB (after dividends) in year 2

− CRO for year 2

+ Sales of marketable securities in year 1

+ Interest income on marketable securities in year 1

+ Final cash balance in year 1

= 7,190.80 − 110 + 12,271.90 + 747.4 + 100

= 20,199.90

The interest income of $747.40 from the investment of the surplus funds in year 1 is listed in the IS for year 2.

The final cash balance at the end of year after reinvestment (of surplus funds) in the CB statement is listed as cash in the BS and matches the annual values for the CRO.

On the other hand, the new debt, $4,903.10, is calculated in the CB as follows:

- NCB + Payment of loans + Interest charges
- Equity investment + Dividend payments
+ Repurchase of stock - Sales of marketable securities
- Interest income on marketable securities
+ Investment on marketable securities
- Accumulated cash balance at end of year
+ CRO for year 4 = New debt at year 4

As explained earlier in Section 5.5 on the loan schedule, the purpose of this calculation is to determine the size of the deficit we have at a given year. The reader should verify the value of the new debt in year 4 by entering the appropriate formula in the cell.

5.13.3 Balance Sheet

Based on the CB statement and the IS, we construct the BS. The complete BS is shown.

TABLE 5.17 Pro-Forma Balance Sheet

	Year 0	Year 1	Year 2	Year 3	Year 4	Year 5
Assets						
Cash	1,576.90	100.00	110.00	120.00	130.00	140.00
AR	0.00	2,595.60	2,710.10	2,857.70	3,013.30	3,177.40
Inventory	0.00	1,725.70	2,033.30	2,085.00	2,150.80	2,217.90
Investment on marketable securities	0.00	12,271.90	20,199.90	29,981.60	0.00	8,670.60
Interest accrued	0.00	0.00	0.00	0.00	0.00	0.00
Net fixed assets	40,000.00	30,000.00	20,000.00	10,000.00	45,381.60	34,036.20
Total	41,576.90	46,693.20	45,053.30	45,044.20	50,675.60	48,242.10
Liabilities and equity						
AP		0.00	2,243.40	2,440.70	2,504.80	2,583.80	2,664.50

(continues)

TABLE 5.17 (*continued*)

	Year 0	Year 1	Year 2	Year 3	Year 4	Year 5
Accrued taxes	0.00	0.00	0.00	0.00	0.00	0.00
Long-term debt	17,576.90	14,061.50	10,546.10	7,030.80	8,420.30	3,923.90
Total liabilities	17,576.90	16,305.00	12,986.90	9,535.60	11,004.10	6,588.40
Equity	24,000.00	24,000.00	24,000.00	24,000.00	24,000.00	24,000.00
Retained earnings	0.00	6,388.20	8,066.40	11,508.70	15,671.60	17,653.70
Total	41,576.90	46,693.20	45,053.30	45,044.20	50,675.60	48,242.10

The dividends for year n are actually paid in the following year n + 1.

5.13.4 The Cash Flow Statement (CFS) According to GAAP

Now that we have the BS we can derive the CFS according to GAAP. Although this statement is usually made as an *ex post* report, we estimate it for future years. For deriving the CFS, we need to calculate the working capital report, which is used in deriving the FCF in the next chapter. Also, we modify the working capital to calculate the CFS. As discussed in the introductory Chapter Three, we need the non-cash working capital.

TABLE 5.18   Working Capital

Working capital	Year 0	Year 1	Year 2	Year 3	Year 4	Year 5
Cash	1,576.90	100.00	110.00	120.00	130.00	140.00
AR	0.00	2,595.60	2,710.10	2,857.70	3,013.30	3,177.40
Inventory	0.00	1,725.70	2,033.30	2,085.00	2,150.80	2,217.90
Current assets	1,576.90	4,421.30	4,853.40	5,062.70	5,294.00	5,535.30
AP	0.00	2,243.40	2,440.70	2,504.80	2,583.80	2,664.50
Accrued taxes	0.00	0.00	0.00	0.00	0.00	0.00
Current liabilities	0.00	2,243.40	2,440.70	2,504.80	2,583.80	2,664.50
Operating working capital	1,576.90	2,177.90	2,412.70	2,557.90	2,710.30	2,870.80
Non-cash operating working capital	0.00	2,077.90	2,302.70	2,437.90	2,580.30	2,730.80
Operating working capital	1,576.90	2,177.90	2,412.70	2,557.90	2,710.30	2,870.80
Change in operating working capital	1,576.90	601.00	234.80	145.20	152.40	160.60
Change in non-cash operating working capital	0.00	2,077.90	224.80	135.20	142.40	150.60
Non-operating working capital						
Investment on marketable securities	0.00	12,271.90	20,199.90	29,981.60	0.00	8,670.60
Change in non-operating working capital		12,271.90	7,928.00	9,781.70	−29,981.60	8,670.60

We have calculated the operating and non-operating working capital. Both of them are needed for Chapter Six. However, for calculating the CFS according to GAAP we only need the non-cash operating working capital.

We calculate the three modules for the CFS according to GAAP. The first one is the operating activities cash flow. Here we record the items related to the IS.

TABLE 5.19   Cash Flow Statement: Net Cash Provided by Operations

	Year 1	Year 2	Year 3	Year 4	Year 5
CFS					
Operating activities					
NI	6,388.20	6,149.90	7,747.30	9,585.90	8,692.30
Depreciation	10,000.00	10,000.00	10,000.00	10,000.00	11,345.40
Net change in non-cash operating working capital	−2,077.90	−224.80	−135.20	−142.40	−150.60
Net cash provided by operations	14,310.30	15,925.10	17,612.10	19,443.60	19,887.20

Now we calculate the investing activities from the BS. This information is taken from the BS.

TABLE 5.20   Cash Flow Statement: Investing Activities

	Year 1	Year 2	Year 3	Year 4	Year 5
Investing activities					
Fixed assets	0.00	0.00	0.00	−45,381.60	0.00
Marketable securities	−12,271.90	−7,928.00	−9,781.70	29,981.60	−8,670.60
Net cash used in investing activities	−12,271.90	−7,928.00	−9,781.70	−15,400.00	−8,670.60

And finally, we calculate the financing activities. These are related to the liabilities and equity.

TABLE 5.21   Cash Flow Statement: Financing Activities

	Year 1	Year 2	Year 3	Year 4	Year 5
Financing activities					
New debt	0.00	0.00	0.00	1,389.50	0.00
Payments of debt	−3,515.40	−3,515.40	−3,515.40	0.00	−4,496.40
Issuances of stock	0.00	0.00	0.00	0.00	0.00
Purchases of stocks	0.00	0.00	0.00	0.00	0.00
Dividends	0.00	−4,471.70	−4,305.00	−5,423.10	−6,710.20
Net cash used in financing activities	−3,515.40	−7,987.10	−7,820.30	−4,033.50	−11,206.50

Combining the three modules (adding) we obtain the net increase (decrease) in cash during the year. This is shown as the final line in Table 5.22a.

TABLE 5.22a   Combining the Results for the Cash Flow Statement

Net cash provided by operations	14,310.30	15,925.10	17,612.10	19,443.60	19,887.20
Net cash used in investing activities	−12,271.90	−7,928.00	−9,781.70	−15,400.00	−8,670.60
Net cash used in financing activities	−3,515.40	−7,987.10	−7,820.30	−4,033.50	−11,206.50
Net increase (decrease) during the year	−1,476.90	10.00	10.00	10.00	10.00

To this line we add the balance at the beginning of the year (EB of previous year) to get the cash balance at the end of year. This line has to be identical to the cash in hand that appears in the BS as an asset.

TABLE 5.22b   Cash Flow Statement: Cash and Cash Equivalents

	Year 1	Year 2	Year 3	Year 4	Year 5
Net increase (decrease) during the year	−1,476.90	10.00	10.00	10.00	10.00
Balance at beginning of year	1,576.90	100.00	110.00	120.00	130.00
Balance at end of year	100.00	110.00	120.00	130.00	140.00

With this financial statement we can analyze where the funds came from and in which activities the funds were spent or directed.

As we said in Chapter Three, there is a relationship between the CB and the CFS. The relationship between the NCB and the operating cash flow (OCF) from the CFS according to GAAP is as follows:

$$\text{NCB} - \text{Interest expenses} + \text{Interest income}$$
$$+ \text{Investment in fixed assets} = \text{OCF from GAAP} \qquad (5.21)$$

Thus, the OCF according to GAAP includes the charge for debt financing and the interest income from the reinvestment of surplus funds in marketable securities.

This is illustrated in the example.

TABLE 5.23   Cash Flow Statement and Cash Budget Statement

	Year 1	Year 2	Year 3	Year 4	Year 5
NCB	16,243.80	16,724.50	17,542.00	−26,990.50	20,813.40
Plus investment in assets				45,381.60	
Minus interest charges	−1,933.50	−1,546.80	−1,160.10	−773.40	−926.20
Plus interest income	0.00	747.40	1,230.20	1,825.90	0.00
OCF from GAAP	14,310.30	15,925.10	17,612.10	19,443.60	19,887.20
Net cash provided by operations	14,310.30	15,925.10	17,612.10	19,443.60	19,887.20

5.14 SUMMARY AND CONCLUDING REMARKS

In this chapter, we constructed the financial statements for a complex example, using the basic ideas on accounting presented in Chapter Three. In addition to the typical GAAP prescribed financial statements, we presented a non-GAAP regulated financial statement: the CB statement.

We have shown the links between the different financial statements. In particular we have shown the link between the CB and the CFS. The reader can observe that the CB provides much more information than the CFS does. This will be particularly useful when we construct the FCF statement in Chapter Six.

Again, we stress that we did not use any balancing accounts to reconcile any difference (this is common in textbooks and practitioners) in the construction of the financial statements. We do use plugs in the sense of closing accounts that combine some other items to close the financial statements. With these financial statements, we can derive the FCF in the next chapter.

KEY CONCEPTS AND IDEAS

Adjustment factor
Cash Flow Statement (CFS)
Discount in purchase price
Elasticity Coefficient
Generally Accepted Accounting Principles (GAAP)
Market effort
Price elasticity of demand

APPENDIX A

A5.1 A BRIEF INTRODUCTION TO PRICE-DEMAND ELASTICITY

The demand for a good can be represented in terms of a demand function. There are many determinants of demand and it is not possible to generalize and give a complete list of all the factors that determine price–demand elasticity. For example, the demand for a good might depend on its own price, the price of its substitutes or complements, the income of consumers, and the taste of consumers. At any given point in time, combinations of the different factors can affect the demand for a good. From an analytic point of view, it is important to understand the impact of each specific factor. We would like to know the impact on demand if there is a change in one factor, holding constant the values of all the other variables. Here we assume that these variables act under *ceteris paribus* conditions. To be specific, we like to analyze the responsiveness of demand to a change in the value of one factor, with no changes in the values of the other factors.

   This is a procedural mechanism to explain the effect of one variable. The reader should be aware that it is a construct for pedagogical purposes.

A5.1.1 Own Price

One of the key determinants of demand is the real price of the good. For the moment, we assume that there is no inflation. We would expect that there is a negative relationship between the quantity demanded and the real price. In other words, if the real price increases, there would be a decrease in the quantity demanded. And conversely, if the real price decreases, there would be an increase in the quantity demanded. If a change in the price leads to a big change in the quantity demanded, we say that the demand is elastic or responsive. On the other hand, if a change in the price leads to a small change in the quantity demanded, we say that the demand is inelastic or unresponsive. Later we will be more specific about the measurement of responsiveness.

A5.1.2 Income

Clearly the income of consumers is an important determinant of demand. The relationship between a change in income and the quantity demanded depends on the nature of the good. In some cases (luxury goods), the relationship might be positive, whereas for other goods the relationship might be negative. As an example we could mention the table salt, or candies.

A5.1.3 Substitutability

If there exist several substitutes for the good, demand will be affected by an increase in price. The greater the number of substitute goods, the greater the effect of an increase in price on the demand. If there were a close substitute for the good, we would expect that an increase in the price of the good would lead the consumers to shift their demand to the substitute good.

A5.1.4 Kind of Goods

Luxury goods are highly affected by a price increase, while non-luxury goods (necessary goods) are less affected by a price increase. An increase in the price of tap water or potatoes affects the demand less than the increase in the price of air tickets or a Ferrari or a Jaguar car.

A5.1.5 Habits and Time

Elasticity price demand for goods that have been accepted by the market for a long time (based on long time series data) will be low. Moreover, when analyzing the behavior of the price–demand elasticity for some goods, provisions should be taken to consider the dampening effect of the habit change because habits are not easy to change.

A5.1.6 Taste

The taste of the consumer is a general term that we use to cover all the other non-specific determinants of demand. Sometimes demand can change for no apparent reason and we say that the change in demand is due to a change in consumer taste. Sometimes, the change in taste can be motivated by new findings in medical research, fashion, or simply a change in the weather.

A5.1.7 Determinants of Quantity Sold

From a practical point of view, it might not be feasible to construct a demand function with more than two or three variables. Also, it is important to remember that it is not possible to capture all the factors in a simple model. The first difficulty is the availability of relevant data. Second, even if the data were available, the complexity of the demand function might not make it user friendly. Usually the data is unavailable or might be unreliable. In such cases, the use of the demand function provides a qualitative analysis of the impact of changes in key variables on the demand for the good.

Clearly, a change in the real price of the good affects the quantity sold. To be specific, there is a negative relationship between the real price and the quantity sold. In addition to the impact of changes in the real price on the quantity sold, marketing and advertising activities also lead to an increase in sales. The relationship between marketing efforts and the quantity sold is positive. The overall impact on the quantity sold depends on the net effect of the changes in prices and the marketing efforts. If the price increases, the quantity sold decreases. However, the quantity sold can increase if the increase in sales from the marketing efforts is higher than the decrease in sales from the increase in price.

First, we consider the simplest demand function with one function. We assume that the quantity demanded is a function only of its own real price:

$$Q_n = f(P_n) \qquad\qquad (A5.1)$$

where Q_n is the quantity demanded of the good in period n and P_n is the real price of the good in period n.

There are many ways to specify the functional form for the demand equation. The simplest way is to assume a linear relationship, which we can justify by saying that a linear approximation is reasonable because the changes in prices and quantities are small.

$$Q_n = \alpha_0 + \alpha_1 P_n \qquad\qquad (A5.2)$$

What is the meaning of the equation in equation A5.2? The equation shows a linear relationship between the quantity demanded and the real price of the good. In particular, if the real price of the good increases by one unit, the quantity demanded of the good increases by the value of the slope coefficient α_1. For the moment, we assume that there is no inflation. Because the relationship between the quantity demanded and the real price is negative, we would expect that the sign of the coefficient α_1 is negative. The negative relationship makes sense because we would expect that the consumer would purchase fewer units if the price increased and vice versa.

Another way to specify the demand equation is in terms of an exponential or a log–log relationship.

$$Q_t = e^{\beta_0} P_t^{\beta_1} \tag{A5.3}$$

or

$$Ln(Q_n) = \beta_0 + \beta_1 Ln(P_n) \tag{A5.4}$$

What is the meaning of the equation in equations A5.3 and A5.4? In A5.4, the equation shows a linear relationship between the (natural) logarithm of the quantity demanded and the (natural) logarithm of the real price of the good. The log–log specification is popular because the slope coefficient β_1 has a convenient interpretation. The slope coefficient β_1 is the price elasticity of demand. In particular, if the price increases by one percent, the quantity demanded decreases by β_1 percent. In symbols,

$$\text{Price elasticity of demand} = \beta_1 = \frac{\Delta Q/Q}{\Delta P/P} = \frac{\%\Delta Q}{\%\Delta P} \tag{A5.5}$$

where $\%\Delta Q$ is the percentage change in the quantity demanded and $\%\Delta P$ is the percentage change in the real price.

Solving for the change in quantity in equation A5.5, we obtain the change in quantity demanded in terms of the price elasticity of demand, the quantity demanded in year n, the price in year n, and the real change in the price.

$$\%\Delta Q = \%\Delta P \beta_1 \tag{A5.6}$$

This means that the change in demand is the price elasticity of demand (β_1) times the (real) percent change in price ($\%\Delta P$). Using regression methods and time series data, we can calculate the value of β_1. In this case, we use β_1 as the elasticity coefficient. This is the coefficient of the price in the log–log equation. When we use the log–log equation, we linearize the exponential function and we can use linear regression methods to find out the value of β_1, the price elasticity of demand.

We use the price elasticity of demand β_1 to measure the responsiveness of the quantity demanded to changes in the price. For example, suppose $\beta_1 = -0.60$. If the price of the good increases by 1%, the quantity demanded will decrease by 0.60%. Strictly speaking, the value of β_1 should be negative because the relationship between the quantity demanded and the price is negative. However, we usually refer to the absolute value of the price elasticity of demand.

If the (absolute) value of β_1 is 1, we say that the good is unit elastic. Conventionally, we say that the demand is elastic if the (absolute) value of β_1 is greater than 1. This means that if the price were to increase by 1%, the quantity demanded would change by *more* than 1%. On the other hand, we say that the demand is inelastic if the (absolute) value of β_1 is less than 1. It means that if the price were to change by 1%, the quantity demanded would change by *less* than 1%.

As a summary, there are three classes of goods:

1. Goods with elastic demand.
2. Goods with unitary price–demand elasticity.
3. Goods with inelastic demand.

Class 1 is a category of goods whose demand changes in a larger proportion relative to the change in the price. Class 2 includes goods whose demand changes in exactly the same proportion in which the price changes. And Class 3 includes goods whose demand changes in a proportion less than the change in price. These changes are associated with the β, if the absolute value of β is greater than 1 (Class 1), equal to 1 (Class 2), and less than 1 (class 3).

A5.1.8 An Expression for the Quantity Demanded

The percent change in demand, $\%\Delta Q$, is used to adjust the demand. If quantity before adjustment is Q, the adjustment is $Q\%\Delta Q$, or

$$\text{Change in demand in units} = \Delta Q = Q\%\Delta Q = Q\%\Delta P\beta_1 \qquad (A5.7)$$

$$\text{Let } \Delta Q = Q_{n+1} - Q_n \qquad (A5.8)$$

Combining and rearranging equations A5.7 and A5.8, we obtain an expression for the quantity demanded. The adjusted quantity is as follows:

$$Q_{n+1} = Q_n + Q_n\%\Delta Q = Q_n(1 + \beta_1\%\Delta P) \qquad (A5.9)$$

Let

$$\lambda = (1 + \beta_1\%\Delta P) \qquad (A5.10)$$

We call λ an adjustment factor for the quantity demanded. We see that the quantity demanded in period n + 1 is equal to the quantity demanded in period n times the adjustment factor. If the adjustment factor is greater than 1, the quantity demanded in period n + 1 will increase, and if the adjustment factor is less than 1, the quantity demanded in period n + 1 will decrease. The size of the adjustment factor depends on the price elasticity of demand and the percent change in price.

In the equations A5.9 and A5.10, the adjustment factor takes into account the price demand elasticity of the good. This adjustment factor $(1 + \beta_1 \% \Delta P)$ adjusts the demand by multiplying the demand with the factor. For instance, if we have the demand in period n, it has to be adjusted with the adjustment factor for the same period.

$$Q_{n \text{ adjusted}} = Q_{n \text{ unadjusted}} \times \text{Adjustment Factor} \qquad (A5.11)$$

$$\text{Adjustment factor} = 1 + \text{price-demand elasticity}$$
$$= 1 + \beta_1 (\text{real increase in price}) \qquad (A5.12)$$

and

$$Q_{n \text{ adjusted}} = Q_{n \text{ unadjusted}} \times (1 + \beta_1 \times (\text{real increase in price})) \qquad (A5.13)$$

Use of this β_1 in a linear equation allows us to measure the effect of the increase in price on the demand. This adjustment factor multiplies a given demand and includes the effect of the price increase in the demand. When β_1 is equal to -1, and there is a real increase in price, the demand is reduced by the same percentage as the increase in price. If the absolute value of β_1 is greater than 1, the demand is affected by more than the percentage of the real price increase, and if the absolute value of β is less than 1, the demand is affected by less than the real increase in price. Then if we set β_1 equal to 0, we say that the good is completely inelastic. This means that the price could increase and the demand will not be affected.

Next, we present a summary of the behavior of the demand given a nominal increase in price and a negative elasticity. There are three basic cases:

1. Nominal price increase greater than the expected inflation rate.
2. Nominal price increase equal to the expected inflation rate.
3. Nominal price increase less than the expected inflation rate.

Assuming that the rest of the economy is affected by the inflation rate in terms of price increases, we can say that Case 1 will show a decrease in demand. Case 2 leaves demand unchanged, and Case 3 increases demand.

APPENDIX B

B5.I A DETAILED SPREADSHEET EXAMPLE

In this appendix you will find the tables as seen in Excel. In columns C and D you will find the formulation in the line and columns E and F as a guide for constructing the model in Excel. In some exceptional cases in columns C and D you will find the formulation in columns F and G and even column J. We will indicate when this does not apply.

The reader should be aware that the configuration of Excel might vary and the separator in the formulas (such as the IF function) is not a comma (,), but a semicolon (;). Also, the language used in the Excel configuration might change the formulation.

Remember, if the reader wants to simplify the replication of the model, he/she should use exactly the same cell positions.

TABLE B5.1a   Basic Information

	B	C	D	E	F	G	H	I	J
2									
3	Table 5.1a. Basic information			Year 0	Year 1	Year 2	Year 3	Year 4	Year 5
4	Fixed assets			40,000.0					
5	Linear depreciation (years)			4.0					
6	Initial equity investment			24,000.0					
7	Tax rate			35.0%					
8	Final inventory at year 0			0.0					
9									
10									
11									
12									
13									
14									
15	Inflation rate				3.0%	3.0%	3.0%	3.0%	3.0%
16	Real annual rate of increase in selling price				0.0%	1.0%	1.0%	1.0%	1.0%
17	Real annual rate of increase in cost per unit				0.5%	0.5%	0.5%	1.0%	1.0%
18	Overhead estimated at year 0			2,184.0					
19	Real rate of increase in overhead expenses				0.5%	0.5%	0.5%	0.5%	1.0%
20	Payroll of selling and administrative force			2,400.0					
21	Real rate of increase in payroll				1.5%	1.5%	1.5%	1.5%	1.5%
22	Real rate of increase in price of fixed assets				0.2%	0.2%	0.2%	0.2%	0.2%
23	Sales commissions				6.0%	6.0%	6.0%	6.0%	6.0%
24	Advertising and promotion expenses (% of sales)				3.0%	3.0%	3.0%	3.0%	3.0%
25	Real rate of interest				3.0%	3.0%	3.0%	3.0%	3.0%
26	Premium for debt risk				4.91%	4.91%	4.91%	4.91%	4.91%

TABLE B5.1b Policies and Targets

	B	C	D	E	F	G	H	I	J
				Year 0	Year 1	Year 2	Year 3	Year 4	Year 5
30					8.3%	8.3%	8.3%	8.3%	8.3%
31	Fraction of sales to be kept as final inventory								
	(1/12 = 8.3333333%)								
32	Percentage of sales received in the same year				95.0%				
33	Percentage of payments made the same year as accrued suppliers)				90.0%				
34	Percentage of NI (dividends) paid to stockholders the year				70.0%				
	after obtaining the NI. Payout ratio								
35	Rate of increase in volume				0.0%	1.0%	2.0%	2.0%	2.0%
36	Minimum NCB required from year 1 to 5				100.0	110.0	120.0	130.0	140.0

TABLE B5.1c Costs and Price Increases

	B	C	D	E	F	G	H	I	J
				Year 0	Year 1	Year 2	Year 3	Year 4	Year 5
38									
39	Annual nominal rate of increase in selling price		$=(1+F\$15)*(1+F16)-1$		3.0%	4.0%	4.0%	4.0%	4.0%
40	Annual nominal rate of increase in cost per unit		$=(1+F\$15)*(1+F17)-1$		3.5%	3.5%	3.5%	4.0%	4.0%
41	Nominal rate of increase in overhead expenses		$=(1+F\$15)*(1+F19)-1$		3.5%	3.5%	3.5%	3.5%	4.0%
42	Nominal rate of increase in payroll		$=(1+F\$15)*(1+F21)-1$		4.5%	4.5%	4.5%	4.5%	4.5%
43	Nominal increase in price of fixed assets		$=(1+F\$15)*(1+F22)-1$		3.2%	3.2%	3.2%	3.2%	3.2%

TABLE B5.ld   Table of Prices as a Function of Quantity (Q in thousands)

	B	C	D	E	F	G	H
45				From	Up to	Mean	Base price (year 0)
46				5.925	6.075	6.00	4.13
47				6.075	6.225	6.15	3.99
48				6.225	6.375	6.30	3.86
49				6.375	6.525	6.45	3.74
50				6.525	6.675	6.60	3.62
51				6.675	6.825	6.75	3.39
52				6.825	6.975	6.90	3.50
53				6.975	7.125	7.05	3.28
54				7.125	7.275	7.20	3.17
55				7.275	7.425	7.35	3.07
56				7.425	7.575	7.50	2.97
57				7.575	7.725	7.65	2.87
58				7.725	7.875	7.80	2.78
59				7.875	8.025	7.95	2.69
60				8.025	8.175	8.10	2.60
61				8.175	8.325	8.25	2.52
62				8.325	8.475	8.40	2.43
63				8.475	8.625	8.55	2.36
64				8.625	8.775	8.70	2.28
65				8.775	8.925	8.85	2.20
66				8.925	9.075	9.00	2.13

TABLE B5.le   Equation and Inputs for Simulating the Scale of Prices for Purchases

	B	C	D	E
70	C			15.479
71	b		$Ce^{(b^*\text{Quantity purchased})} = 15.45^*\text{EXP}$	−0.2202
72	Formula		$(-0.22^*\text{Quantity purchased})$	

TABLE B5.2a   Information for the Simulation of Market Research and Elasticity Price–Demand Research

	B	C	D
75			
76		Price	Q sold
77		3.0	12,249.0
78		3.5	11,119.0
79		4.0	10,226.0
80		4.5	9,498.0
81		5.0	8,891.0
82		5.5	8,375.0
83		6.0	7,931.0
84		6.5	7,542.0
85		7.0	7,200.0
86		7.5	6,895.0
87		8.0	6,622.0
88		8.5	6,375.0
89		9.0	6,150.0
90		9.5	5,946.0
91		10.0	5,757.0
92		10.5	5,584.0
93		11.0	5,423.0

TABLE B5.2b   Elasticity Coefficient and Price Derived from Market Research

	B	C	D	E
97	Elasticity coefficient b			−0.627
98	Constant coefficient b0			24,389.860
99	Selling price			7.000

TABLE B5.3 Simulation of Elasticity Price–Demand and Market Effort

	B	C	Year 0	Year 1	Year 2	Year 3	Year 4	Year 5
104	Real selling price increase							
105		$= (1 + \text{F39})/(1 + \text{F15}) - 1$		0.00%	1.00%	1.00%	1.00%	1.00%
106	Elasticity $= -0.63*$(Real increase in selling price)	$= +\$E\$97*\text{F105}$		0.00000	−0.00627	−0.00627	−0.00627	−0.00627
107	Adjustment factor (1 + elasticity)	$= 1 + \text{F106}$		1.00000	0.99373	0.99373	0.99373	0.99373
108	(1 + increase in volume)	$= +(1 + \text{F35})$		1.00	1.01	1.02	1.02	1.02
109	1 + Net increase in demand taking into account market effort and elasticity = (1 + increase in volume)*(1 + elasticity).	$= \text{F107}*\text{F108}$		1.00000	1.00367	1.01360	1.01360	1.01360

TABLE B5.4 Basic Estimated Variables

	B	C	D	E	F	G	H	I	J
111		Year 0		Year 0	Year 1	Year 2	Year 3	Year 4	Year 5
112	Units sold	= E98*E99^E97	= E112*F109	7,200.0	7,200.0	7,226.4	7,324.7	7,424.4	7,525.4
113	Selling price	= E99	= E113*(1 + F39)	7.0	7.2	7.5	7.8	8.1	8.4
114	Sales revenues		= +F113*F112		51,912.0	54,202.1	57,153.6	60,265.8	63,547.4
115	Overhead	= E18	= E115*(1 + F41)	2,184.0	2,260.8	2,340.2	2,422.5	2,507.6	2,608.7
116	Administrative payroll	= E20	= E116*(1 + F42)	2,400.0	2,509.1	2,623.1	2,742.3	2,867.0	2,997.3
117	Selling commissions		= F114*F23		3,114.7	3,252.1	3,429.2	3,615.9	3,812.8
118	Advertising and promotions		= F114*F24		1,557.4	1,626.1	1,714.6	1,808.0	1,906.4
119	Minimum NCB required for year 0 (based on 20% of overhead, payroll, and commissions expenses)	= +(F115 + F116 + F117)*0.2		1,576.9					
120	Short-term rate of reinvestment		= ((1 + F15)*(1 + F25) − 1)		6.09%	6.09%	6.09%	6.09%	6.09%
121									
122	Rate of interest for debt using CAPM $d = r_f +$ risk premium		= F120 + F26		11.0%	11.0%	11.0%	11.0%	11.0%
123	Factor for increase in price of fixed assets	= (1 + F43) (Year 1)	= F123*(1 + G43)(Year2)		1.03	1.07	1.10	1.13	1.17
124	Price of future fixed assets when acquired	= E4*I123						45,381.60	0.0

TABLE B5.5 Depreciation Schedule

	B	C	D	E	F	G	H	I	J
				Year 0	Year 1	Year 2	Year 3	Year 4	Year 5
126									
127	Depreciation schedule								
128	Beginning net fixed assets	= +E132			40,000.0	30,000.0	20,000.0	10,000.0	45,381.6
129	Annual depreciation	= ($E$132 + E131)/$E$5 (Year 1)	= (+I131)/$E$5 (Year 5)		10,000.0	10,000.0	10,000.0	10,000.0	11,345.4
130	Cumulated depreciation	= +F129 + E130			10,000.0	20,000.0	30,000.0	40,000.0	51,345.4
131	New assets	= E124		0.0	0.0	0.0	0.0	45,381.6	0.0
132	Net fixed assets	= +E4 + E131	= +F128 − F129 + F131	40,000.0	30,000.0	20,000.0	10,000.0	45,381.6	34,036.2

TABLE B5.6 Cash Budget for Year 0 to Determine Extra Funds

	B	C	D	E
135	Cash inflows			
136	Total income AR			
137	Total cash inflows	$= SUM(E135:E136)$		0.0
138	Cash outflows			
139	Total payments for AP			
140	Overhead			
141	Payroll expenses			
142	Selling commissions			
143	Advertising and promotions			
144	Purchase of fixed assets	$= +E4$		40,000.0
145	Purchase of fixed assets in year 4			
146	Taxes			
147	Total cash outflows	$= SUM(E144:E146)$		40,000.0
148	NCB	$= E137 - E147$		$-40,000.0$
149				
150	Bank loan 1	$= IF(E148 + E155 - E119 <= 0,$ $-(E148 + E155) + E119,0)$		17,576.9
151	Bank loan 2			
152	Payment of loans			
153	Interest charges			
154	NCB after financial transactions	$= SUM(E148:E153)$		$-22,423.1$
155	Equity investment	$= E6$		24,000.0
156	Dividend payments			
157	Repurchase of stock			
158	NCB after cash transactions with shareholders	$= SUM(E154:E157)$		1,576.9
159				
160	Sales of marketable securities			
161	Interest income on marketable securities			
162	Investment on marketable securities	$= -IF(E158 > E119,E158 - E119,0)$		0.0
163	NCB after discretionary transactions paid in cash	$= SUM(E158:E162)$		1,576.9
164	Accumulated cash balance at end of year	$= E163$		1,576.9

TABLE B5.7a   Loan Schedule I

	B	C	D	E	F	G	H	I	J
167				Year 0	Year 1	Year 2	Year 3	Year 4	Year 5
168	BB		= E172		17,576.9	14,061.5	10,546.1	7,030.8	3,515.4
169	Interest charges debt 1		= F173*F168		1,933.5	1,546.8	1,160.1	773.4	386.7
170	Principal payment debt 1		= +($E172)/5		3,515.4	3,515.4	3,515.4	3,515.4	3,515.4
171	Total payment debt 1		= F169 + F170		5,448.8	5,062.2	4,675.5	4,288.8	3,902.1
172	EB	= E150	= F168 – F170	17,576.9	14,061.5	10,546.1	7,030.8	3,515.4	0.0
173	Interest rate		= +F122		11.0%	11.0%	11.0%	11.0%	11.0%

TABLE B5.7b   Loan Schedule 2

B	C	D	E	F	G	H	I	J
			Year 0	Year 1	Year 2	Year 3	Year 4	Year 5
175								
176	BB	= I172 (Year 5)						4,904.9
177	Interest charges debt 2	= J181*I176 (Year 5)						539.5
178	Principal payment debt 2	= +($I180)/5(Year5)						981.0
179	Total payment debt 2	= I177 + I178 (Year 5)		0.0				1,520.5
180	EB	= I261 (Year 4) = J176 – J178 (Year 5)			0.0	0.0	4,904.9	3,923.9
181	Interest rate	= F173		11.0%	11.0%	11.0%	11.0%	11.0%

TABLE B5.8 Inventories and Purchases

	B	C	D	E	F	G	H	I	J
183				Year 0	Year 1	Year 2	Year 3	Year 4	Year 5
184	Units sold	= F112 (Year 1)			7,200.0	7,226.4	7,324.7	7,424.4	7,525.4
185	Final inventory in units	= F184*F31 (Year 1)			600.0	602.2	610.4	618.7	627.1
186	Initial inventory in units	= E8 (Year 1)	= F185 (Year 2)		0.0	600.0	602.2	610.4	618.7
187	Purchases in units	= F184 + F185 − F186 (Year 1)			7,800.0	7,228.6	7,332.9	7,432.7	7,533.8

TABLE B5.9   Cost per Unit

	B	C	D	E	F	G	H	I	J
		Year 0		Year 0	Year 1	Year 2	Year 3	Year 4	Year 5
190									
191	Cumulative increase in basic cost per unit	= (1 + F40) (Year 1)	= (1 + G40)*F191 (Year 2)		1.035	1.072	1.109	1.154	1.200
192	Cost per unit without considering price increase	= $E$70*EXP($E$71*F187/1000) (Year 1)			2.78	3.2	3.1	3.0	2.9
193	Actual cost per unit	= F192*F191	= G192*G191		2.9	3.4	3.4	3.5	3.5

TABLE B5.I0 · Determination of Cost of Goods Sold

B	C		D	E	F	G	H	I	J
195				Year 0	Year 1	Year 2	Year 3	Year 4	Year 5
196 Initial inventory	= +F186*F193 (Year 1)	= +F198 (Year 2)			0.0	1,725.7	2,033.3	2,085.0	2,150.8
197 Purchases	= +F187*F193 (Year 1)	= +G187*G193 (Year 2)			22,434.4	24,407.3	25,047.9	25,837.9	26,644.9
198 Final inventory	= +F185*F193 (Year 1)	= +G185*G193 (Year 2)			1,725.7	2,033.3	2,085.0	2,150.8	2,217.9
199 COGS	= +F196 + F197 − F198 (Year 1)	= +G196 + G197 − G198 (Year 2)			20,708.6	24,099.7	24,996.2	25,772.2	26,577.8

TABLE B5.II Determination of Selling and Administrative Expenses

	B	C	D	E	F	G	H	I	J
				Year 0	Year 1	Year 2	Year 3	Year 4	Year 5
201									
202	Selling commissions	= +F117			3,114.7	3,252.1	3,429.2	3,615.9	3,812.8
203	Overhead	= +F115			2,260.8	2,340.2	2,422.5	2,507.6	2,608.7
204	Payroll expenses	= +F116			2,509.1	2,623.1	2,742.3	2,867.0	2,997.3
205									
206	Advertising and promotions	= +F118			1,557.4	1,626.1	1,714.6	1,808.0	1,906.4
207	Selling and administrative expenses	= SUM(F202:F206)			9,441.9	9,841.5	10,308.7	10,798.5	11,325.3

TABLE B5.12 Sales and Purchases, on Cash and Credit

	B	C	D	E	F	G	H	I	J
				Year 0	Year 1	Year 2	Year 3	Year 4	Year 5
209									
210	Sales on cash		= +F114*$F$32		49,316.4	51,492.0	54,295.9	57,252.5	60,370.1
211	Sales on credit		= F114 − F210		2,595.6	2,710.1	2,857.7	3,013.3	3,177.4
212	Purchases on cash		= +F197*$F$33		20,190.9	21,966.6	22,543.1	23,254.1	23,980.4
213	Purchases on credit		= F197 − F212		2,243.4	2,440.7	2,504.8	2,583.8	2,664.5

TABLE B5.13 Accounts Receivable and Accounts Payable

	B	C	D	E	F	G	H	I	J
				Year 0	Year 1	Year 2	Year 3	Year 4	Year 5
216	Table 5.8b: Total sales collection and payments								
217	Sales on cash	= +F210			49,316.4	51,492.0	54,295.9	57,252.5	60,370.1
218	AR recovery	= E211			0.0	2,595.6	2,710.1	2,857.7	3,013.3
219	Total sales collection	= +F218 + F217			49,316.4	54,087.6	57,006.0	60,110.2	63,383.3
220	Purchases on cash	= +F212			20,190.9	21,966.6	22,543.1	23,254.1	23,980.4
221	AP purchases	= E213			0.0	2,243.4	2,440.7	2,504.8	2,583.8
222	Total purchases payments	= +F221 + F220			20,190.9	24,210.0	24,983.8	25,758.9	26,564.2

TABLE B5.I4 The Complete Pro-Forma Income Statement

	B	C	D	E	F	G	H	I	J
				Year 0	Year 1	Year 2	Year 3	Year 4	Year 5
224									
225	Sales	= +F114			51,912.0	−54,202.1	57,153.6	60,265.8	63,547.4
226									
227	COGS	= +F199			20,708.6	24,099.7	24,996.2	25,772.2	26,577.8
228									
229	Gross profit	= F225 − F227			31,203.4	30,102.4	32,157.4	34,493.6	36,969.7
230									
231	Selling and administrative expenses	= +F207			9,441.9	9,841.5	10,308.7	10,798.5	11,325.3
232	Depreciation	= F129			10,000.0	10,000.0	10,000.0	10,000.0	11,345.4
233	EBIT	= F229 − F231 − F232			11,761.5	10,260.9	11,848.8	13,695.1	14,299.0
234	Interest income on marketable securities	= +F271			0.0	747.4	1,230.2	1,825.9	0.0
235	Other expenses (interest expenses)	= +F169 + F177			1,933.5	1,546.8	1,160.1	773.4	926.2
236	EBT	= F233 + F234 − F235			9,828.0	9,461.5	11,918.8	14,747.6	13,372.8
237	Taxes	= IF(F236 < 0,0,F236*$E$7)			3,439.8	3,311.5	4,171.6	5,161.7	4,680.5
238	NI	= F236 − F237			6,388.2	6,149.9	7,747.3	9,585.9	8,692.3
239	Dividends	= IF(F238*$F$34 < 0,0,F238*$F$34)			4,471.7	4,305.0	5,423.1	6,710.2	6,084.6
240	Retained earnings	= F238 − F239			1,916.5	1,845.0	2,324.2	2,875.8	2,607.7
241	Accumulated retained earnings	= E241 + F238 − E239			6,388.2	8,066.4	11,508.7	15,671.6	17,653.7

TABLE B5.I5   The Complete Pro-Forma Cash Budget Statement

	B	C	D	E	F	G	H	I	J
243									
244				Year 0	Year 1	Year 2	Year 3	Year 4	Year 5
245	Cash inflows								
246	Total income AR	= +E219			49,316.4	54,087.6	57,006.0	60,110.2	63,383.3
247	Total cash inflows	= E246		0.0	49,316.4	54,087.6	57,006.0	60,110.2	63,383.3
248	Cash outflows								
249	Total payments for AP	= +E222		0.0	20,190.9	24,210.0	24,983.8	25,758.9	26,564.2
250	Overhead	= E203		0.0	2,260.8	2,340.2	2,422.5	2,507.6	2,608.7
251	Payroll expenses	= E204		0.0	2,509.1	2,623.1	2,742.3	2,867.0	2,997.3
252	Selling commissions	= E202		0.0	3,114.7	3,252.1	3,429.2	3,615.9	3,812.8
253	Advertising and promotions	= E206		0.0	1,557.4	1,626.1	1,714.6	1,808.0	1,906.4
254	Purchase of fixed assets	= +E4		40,000.0					
255	Purchase of fixed assets year 4	= +E124		0.0	0.0	0.0	0.0	45,381.6	0.0
256	Taxes	= +E237	= +F237	0.0	3,440.6	3,312.2	4,172.1	5,162.0	4,680.9
257	Total cash outflows	= SUM(E249:E256)		40,000.0	33,073.5	37,363.8	39,464.6	87,101.1	42,570.4
258	NCB	= E247 – E257		–40,000.0	16,243.0	16,723.9	17,541.4	–26,990.9	20,812.9
259									
260	Bank loan 1	= +E150		17,576.9					
261	Bank loan 2	= IF(– (E274 + F258 – F263 – F264 – F267 + F270 +F271 – F36 + F266 –F268) > 0, –(E274 + F258 –F263 – F264 – F267 + F270 +F271 – F36 + F266 – F268), 0) (Year 1)	= IF(– (F274 + G258 – G263 –G264 – G267 + G270 + G271 –G36 + G266 – G268) > 0, –(F274 + G258 – G263 – G264 –G267 + G270 + G271 –G36 + G266 – G268),0) (Year 2)	0.0				4,904.9	0.0

No.	Item	Formula						
262	Payment of loans	= E170 + E178	0.0	3,515.4	3,515.4	3,515.4	3,515.4	4,496.4
263	Interest charges	= +E169 + E177	0.0	1,933.5	1,546.8	1,160.1	773.4	926.2
264	NCB after financial transactions	= E258 + E261 + E260 − E263 − E264	−22,423.1	10,794.9	11,662.4	12,866.5	−26,374.4	15,390.8
265								
266	Equity investment	= E6	24,000.0					
267	Dividend payments	= +E239 (Year 1)		0.0	4,471.7	4,305.0	5,423.1	6,710.2
268	Repurchase of stock							
269	NCB after cash transactions with shareholders	= E265 − E267 + E266 − E268	1,576.9	10,794.9	7,190.7	8,561.5	−31,797.5	8,680.6
270	Sales of marketable securities	= D272	0.0	0.0	12,271.9	20,199.9	29,981.6	0.0
271	Interest income on marketable securities	= E120*E270	0.0	0.0	747.4	1,230.2	1,825.9	0.0
272	Investment on marketable securities	= (IF((F269 + F270 + F271 +E274) > F36, F269 + F270 +F271 + E274 − F36,0)) (Year 1)		12,271.9	20,199.9	29,981.6	0.0	8,670.6
273	NCB after discretionary transactions paid in cash	= E269 − E272 + E270 + E271; = F269 − F272 + F270 + F271	1,576.9	−1,476.9	10.0	10.0	0.0	10.0
274	Accumulated cash balance at end of year	= E273	1,576.9	100.0	110.0	120.0	130.0	140.0

TABLE B5.16 Pro-Forma Balance Sheet

	B	C	D	E	F	G	H	I	J
		Year 0		Year 0	Year 1	Year 2	Year 3	Year 4	Year 5
277									
278	Assets								
279									
280	Cash	= E274		1,576.9	100.0	110.0	120.0	130.0	140.0
281	AR	= E211		0.0	2,595.6	2,710.1	2,857.7	3,013.3	3,177.4
282	Inventory	= +E198		0.0	1,725.7	2,033.3	2,085.0	2,150.8	2,217.9
283	Investment on marketable securities	= SUM($E$272:E272) − SUM($E$270:E270)		0.0	12,271.9	20,199.9	29,981.6	0.0	8,670.6
284	Interest accrued	= +E234 − E271		0.0	0.0	0.0	0.0	0.0	0.0
285	Net fixed assets	= +E132		40,000.0	30,000.0	20,000.0	10,000.0	45,381.6	34,036.2
286	Total	= SUMA(E280:E285)		41,576.9	46,693.2	45,053.3	45,044.2	50,675.6	48,242.1
287									
288	Liabilities and equity								
289									
290	AP	= E213		0.0	2,243.4	2,440.7	2,504.8	2,583.8	2,664.5
291	Accrued taxes	= SUM($E$237:E237) − SUM($E$256:E256)		0.0	0.0	0.0	0.0	0.0	0.0
292	Long-term debt	= SUM($E$260:E261) − SUM($E$263:E263)		17,576.9	14,061.5	10,546.1	7,030.8	8,420.3	3,923.9
293	Total liabilities	= SUM(E290:E292)		17,576.9	16,305.0	12,986.9	9,535.6	11,004.1	6,588.4
294	Equity	= +E6	= +E294	24,000.0	24,000.0	24,000.0	24,000.0	24,000.0	24,000.0
295	Retained earnings	= E241	= F241	0.0	6,388.2	8,066.4	11,508.7	15,671.6	17,653.7
296									
297	Total	= SUM(E290:E296) − E293		41,576.9	46,693.2	45,053.3	45,044.2	50,675.6	48,242.1

TABLE B5.17   Working Capital

	B	C	D	E	F	G	H	I	J
				Year 0	Year 1	Year 2	Year 3	Year 4	Year 5
301				Year 0	Year 1	Year 2	Year 3	Year 4	Year 5
302	Cash	= E280		1,576.9	100.0	110.0	120.0	130.0	140.0
303	AR	= E281		0.0	2,595.6	2,710.1	2,857.7	3,013.3	3,177.4
304	Inventory	= E282		0.0	1,725.7	2,033.3	2,085.0	2,150.8	2,217.9
305	Current assets	= SUM(E302:E304)		1,576.9	4,421.3	4,853.4	5,062.7	5,294.0	5,535.3
306	AP	= E290		0.0	2,243.4	2,440.7	2,504.8	2,583.8	2,664.5
307	Accrued taxes	= E291		0.0	0.0	0.0	0.0	0.0	0.0
308	Current liabilities	= SUM(E306:E307)		0.0	2,243.4	2,440.7	2,504.8	2,583.8	2,664.5
309	Operating working capital	= E305 − E308	= F305 − F308	1,576.9	2,177.9	2,412.7	2,557.9	2,710.3	2,870.8
310	Non-cash operating working capital	= E305 − E302 − E308	= F305 − F302 − F308	0.0	2,077.9	2,302.7	2,437.9	2,580.3	2,730.8
311				Year 0	Year 1	Year 2	Year 3	Year 4	Year 5
312	Operating working capital	= E305 − E308	= F305 − F308	1,576.9	2,177.9	2,412.7	2,557.9	2,710.3	2,870.8
313	Change in operating working capital	= E309	= F309 − E309	1,576.9	601.0	234.8	145.2	152.4	160.6
314	Change in non-cash operating working capital	= E310	= F310 − E310	0.0	2,077.9	224.8	135.2	142.4	150.6
315	Non-operating working capital								
316	Investment on marketable securities	= E283	= F283	0.0	12,271.9	20,199.9	29,981.6	0.0	8,670.6
317	Change in non-operating working capital		= F316 − E316		12,271.9	7,928.0	9,781.7	−29,981.6	8,670.6

TABLE B5.18 Cash Flow Statement: Net Cash Provided by Operations

	B	C	D	E	F	G	H	I	J
					Year 1	Year 2	Year 3	Year 4	Year 5
320									
321	NI		= F238		6,388.2	6,149.9	7,747.3	9,585.9	8,692.3
322	Depreciation		= F232		10,000.0	10,000.0	10,000.0	10,000.0	11,345.4
323	Net change in non-cash operating working capital		= −F314		−2,077.9	−224.8	−135.2	−142.4	−150.6
324	Net cash provided by operations		= SUM(F321:F323)		14,310.3	15,925.1	17,612.1	19,443.6	19,887.2

TABLE B5.19 Cash Flow Statement: Investing Activities

	B	C	D	E	F	G	H	I	J
					Year 1	Year 2	Year 3	Year 4	Year 5
326	Investing activities								
327	Fixed assets		= −F131		0.0	0.0	0.0	−45,381.6	0.0
328	Marketable securities		= −(F283 − E283)		−12,271.9	−7,928.0	−9,781.7	29,981.6	−8,670.6
329	Net cash used in investing activities		= SUM(F327:F328)		−12,271.9	−7,928.0	−9,781.7	−15,400.0	−8,670.6

TABLE B5.20 Cash Flow Statement: Financing Activities

	B	C	D	E	F	G	H	I	J
					Year 1	Year 2	Year 3	Year 4	Year 5
331	Financing activities				0.0	0.0	0.0	1,389.5	0.0
332	New debt	= IF(F292 – E292 < 0,0,F292 – E292)			–3,515.4	–3,515.4	–3,515.4	0.0	–4,496.4
333	Payments of debt	= IF(F292 – E292 > 0,0,F292 – E292)			0.0	0.0	0.0	0.0	0.0
334	Issuances of stock	= IF(F294 – E294 > 0,F294 – E294,0)			0.0	0.0	0.0	0.0	0.0
335	Purchases of stocks	= IF(F294 – E294 < 0,(F294 – E294),0)			0.0	–4,471.7	–4,305.0	–5,423.1	–6,710.2
336	Dividends	= –E239			0.0	–7,987.1	–7,820.3	–4,033.5	–11,206.5
337	Net cash used in financing activities				–3,515.4				

TABLE B5.21 Cash Flow Statement: Cash and Cash Equivalents

	B	C	D	E	F	G	H	I	J
					Year 1	Year 2	Year 3	Year 4	Year 5
340	Net increase (decrease) during the year		= F324 + F329 + F337		−1,476.9	10.0	10.0	10.0	10.0
341	Balance at beginning of year		= E280		1,576.9	100.0	110.0	120.0	130.0
342	Balance at end of year		= SUM(F340:F341)		100.0	110.0	120.0	130.0	140.0

TABLE B5.22 Cash Flow Statement and Cash Budget Statement

	B	C	D	E	F	G	H	I	J
347	NCB	= F258			16,243.8	16,724.5	17,542.0	−26,990.5	20,813.4
348	plus Investment in assets							45,381.6	
349	minus Interest charges	= −F264			−1,933.5	−1,546.8	−1,160.1	−773.4	−926.2
350	plus Interest income	= F271			0.0	747.4	1,230.2	1,825.9	0.0
351	OCF from GAAP	= SUM(F347:F350)			14,310.3	15,925.1	17,612.1	19,443.6	19,887.2
352	Net cash provided by operations	= F324			14,310.3	15,925.1	17,612.1	19,443.6	19,887.2

TABLE B5.23 Net Cash Balance = Operating Cash Flow − Interest = Interest Deductions

	B	C	D	E	F	G	H	I	J
354	OCF from GAAP		= F351		14,310.3	15,925.1	17,612.1	19,443.6	19,887.2
355	Minus investment in assets							−45,381.6	
356	Plus interest charges		= −F349		1,933.5	1,546.8	1,160.1	773.4	926.2
357	Minus interest income		= −F350		0.0	−747.4	−1,230.2	−1,825.9	0.0
358	NCB		= SUM(F354:F357)		16,243.8	16,724.5	17,542.0	−26,990.5	20,813.4

6

THE DERIVATION OF CASH FLOWS

Profit is an opinion. Cash is a fact.

—*Anonymous*

SECTION I

6.I DERIVATION OF FREE CASH FLOWS

In the previous chapter, we illustrated the construction of three financial statements for a hypothetical start-up firm: the income statement (IS), balance sheet (BS), and cash flow statement (CFS), according to Generally Accepted Accounting Principles (GAAP). In addition, we constructed the CB statement. We presented an integrated framework for the IS, the CB statement, and the BS with inter-related items from each of the financial statements. It is important to reiterate and stress that we derive the finite cash flows from the financial statements that are not based on ratios.

In this chapter, using two different approaches, we derive the Free Cash Flow (FCF) statement, exclusive of the terminal value (TV), which is relevant for valuation. Later, in Chapter Nine, we include the TV. First, we show a new method for deriving the appropriate cash flows from the CB statement. We hope that most readers agree that it is an easy method. Because the CB is not a common statement, some readers might not be familiar with it and would prefer to derive the excess cash that is invested in marketable securities without constructing the CB statement.

In Appendix A, using the IS and the BS, we show the standard procedure for deriving the excess cash that is invested in marketable securities without constructing the CB statement.

229

Second, using the standard approach, we derive the cash flows from line items in the IS. We can derive the cash flows from the earnings before interest and taxes (EBIT) or the net income (NI). In the main text of this chapter, we show the derivation of the FCF from the EBIT, and in Appendix B we show the derivation of the FCF and CCF from the NI.

In the next chapter, we discuss the estimation of the cost of capital with ·finite cash flows. In Chapter Eight, we discuss the estimation of the WACC for non-traded firms. And in Chapter Nine, we present the calculation of the TV.

The chapter is organized as follows. In Section 1, we briefly review the fundamental cash flow relationship and discuss the differences between the cash flow relationships in the CB statement versus the Free Cash Flow (FCF). In addition, we discuss the definition of the operating cash flow (OCF) and its relationship to the excess cash that is retained in the firm, the inflation adjustments for financial statements, and the treatment of tax savings.

In Section 2, we derive the FCF from the CB statement. And in Section 3, we derive the FCF from the EBIT in the IS.

6.2 THE FUNDAMENTAL FREE CASH FLOW RELATIONSHIP

First, we briefly review the fundamental FCF relationship and discuss the difference between the cash flow relationship in the CB statement and the FCF statement.

In an M & M world without taxes, the FCF is equal to the sum of the CFE and the cash flow to debt (CFD).

$$FCF = CFE + CFD \qquad (6.1)$$

The sum of the CFE and the CFD is also equal to the CCF, which is the cash flow that is distributed to the stakeholders in the firm, namely the equity holder and the debt holder. For more details on the CCF, see Ruback (2000).

$$CCF = CFE + CFD \qquad (6.2)$$

In the standard formulation with cash flows in perpetuity, the theoretical framework assumes that the FCF is the OCF generated by the firm and that there is no excess cash invested in marketable securities. In other words, all the OCF is distributed to the stakeholders in the firm and no excess cash is retained in the firm. With perfect capital markets, whenever the firm requires financing for new investments, the firm is always able to borrow money in the capital markets to finance new projects and there is no need to retain excess cash. However, in practice, it is common for firms to retain excess cash that is not required for operations and invest it in marketable securities. In our example, we assume that the excess cash is retained and invested in marketable securities to finance the purchase of a new fixed asset in year 4.

In an M & M world with taxes, the sum of the FCF and the tax shield (TS) is equal to the sum of the CFE and the CFD.

$$FCF + TS = CFE + CFD \qquad (6.3)$$

From the CB statement, it is easy to obtain the CFE and CFD. Only the TS is not explicitly listed in the CB statement. The estimation of the TS can be complicated. In general terms, the TS is equal to the difference in the taxes paid by the unlevered and levered firm. Later, we discuss the estimation of the TS in more detail.

Rewriting equation 6.3, we obtain the following fundamental cash flow relationship with the FCF as a function of three components.

$$FCF = CFE + CFD - TS \qquad (6.4)$$

6.2.1 Cash Budget Statement Versus Free Cash Flow

Next, we briefly discuss the difference between the construction of the cash flows in the CB statement and the FCF statement. The CB statement records the actual cash inflows and the actual cash outflows. As mentioned earlier in Chapter One, the FCF is a measure of the after-tax operating funds produced by a firm or project without taking into account the source of the debt and equity financing. Later, we discuss in more detail the meaning of "operating funds" and its relationship to excess cash that is retained in the firm.

The FCF statement records the resources that the firm requires and the benefits that it generates. The key difference between the CB statement and the FCF statement is that the FCF must take into account the opportunity cost of the resources. As a consequence, some items that are included in the FCF statement might not be actual cash inflows or outflows. Another key difference is also the fact that in the CB we list all the transactions of cash flow that the firm has, inflows and outflows, and in the FCF we do not include all the transactions.[1]

For example, the opportunity costs of resources are included in the FCF statement, but they are not recorded in the CB statement. For instance, when a firm uses an existing facility, the current commercial value of the

---

[1]This means that any definition of FCF should include the value of the investment even if it is not listed in any financial statement. A typical example would be the equity investment in kind.

facility is listed as an opportunity cost in the outflow side of the FCF statement. Even if there is no disbursement of cash to purchase the facility (because it is already there), the current market value of the facility (and not the historical cost of the facility) has to be taken into account from the point of view of the FCF statement because the facility is required for the project. If the facility were not there, the firm would have to purchase the facility at the current market price and not at the historical price. Consequently, the facility has to be considered as part of the FCF valued at the current market price.

Similarly, at the end of the forecast period for the cash flow, we have to list the TV of the firm or the in-use values (if any) of the existing assets. For the moment, we postpone the discussion of the calculations for the TV.

6.2.2 Operating Cash Flow

In the previous discussion on the fundamental cash flow relationship, we assumed that no excess cash was retained in the firm. However, many firms keep excess cash that is over and above the CRO. This is an example of the discrepancy between the assumptions of the theoretical model with cash flows in perpetuity and the use of finite cash flows in practice. The excess cash is retained in the firm and is not distributed to the equity holder. Usually the excess cash is invested in short-term marketable securities at the market interest rate, which may be lower than the appropriate cost of capital for the firm, and generates taxable interest income. Many authors and practitioners assume unrealistically that the excess cash is invested at the cost of capital.

For the moment, we do not discuss the various reasons why it might be rational for the firm to retain excess cash. For example, the buildup of the excess cash might be used to purchase a new fixed asset in the future. Or it might provide the firm with greater flexibility in terms of future investment opportunities. But how should we treat the excess cash that is retained in the firm and invested in marketable securities?

Strictly speaking, the investment in marketable securities is not directly related to the operations of the firm and thus should not be included as part of the operating cash flow (OCF) generated by the firm. Because the excess cash earns a rate of return that is less than the cost of capital, the retention of the excess cash leads to a loss in value. When using the OCF and disregarding the actual return of the reinvestment of the excess cash, it is assumed that the excess cash is invested implicitly at the same discount rate. This automatic or implicit reinvestment overestimates the value of the firm for two reasons: one is that the reinvestment is done at a higher rate than the actual and two that those virtual returns are not taxed. From a theoretical and conceptual point of view, it would seem strange for a firm to retain excess cash.[2]

However, the fact remains that the excess cash is not distributed to the equity holder and earns an *actual* return that is less than the cost of capital. At the same time, the firm would only retain the excess cash if the value of the greater flexibility in investment opportunities provided by the excess cash is more than the loss that the excess cash (invested in marketable securities) incurs by providing an explicit rate of return that is lower than the cost of capital.

To account for the excess cash that is invested in marketable securities, we define the following (approximate) relationship between the total FCF and the operating FCF. The change in the total FCF is equal to the sum of the operating FCF and the change in excess cash that is invested in marketable securities.

$$\text{Total FCF} = \text{Operating FCF} + \text{Change in excess cash invested in marketable securities} \qquad (6.5)^3$$

The operating FCF must be free from any effect of the retention of excess cash in the firm. In particular, we must adjust the operating FCF for any taxes paid on interest income from the marketable securities. Later, we discuss these points more fully.

The definition of the operating FCF in equation 6.5 is different from the "cash flow from operating activities" as defined in the CFS according to GAAP. On the differences between the CFS according to GAAP and the different sections of the CB statement, see the previous discussion in Chapter Three.

In an M & M world with cash flows in perpetuity, the excess cash is zero and thus there is no distinction between the total FCF and the operating FCF. In practice, the retention of the excess cash leads to a loss in value because the actual rate of return earned on the marketable securities is less than the cost of capital for the firm. We can calculate the effect of the excess cash on the value of the firm by comparing the present value (PV) of the total FCF with and without retention of excess cash. This will be done in an appendix of Chapter Seven after we have calculated the levered value with the total FCF.

From a valuation point of view, the total cash flow is more important than the OCF because the excess cash has been retained in the firm. However, it is also useful to estimate the OCF so that we can calculate the impact of the retention of the excess cash on the PV of the total cash flow.

---

[2]We stress the fact that using the OCF we overestimate the value. The implicit reinvestment of excess cash generates an implicit return that is not taxed because it doesn't go through the IS. And on top of that it is not real. Recall that net income is an opinion but cash is a fact. The funds remain in the firm and are not received by the shareholders. It is an illusion to assume that the funds are distributed to the shareholders when in fact the excess cash is in the firm.

[3]Technically, equation 6.5 is not fully correct because we have subtracted the tax on the interest income (from the excess cash invested in marketable securities) from the operational FCF.

For the moment, we alert the reader to the fact that we can define the OCF with respect to the FCF or the CCF. For convenience, we prefer to discuss the total CCF and the operating CCF rather than the total FCF and the operating FCF. In a subsequent section, we present a detailed derivation of the operating CCF from the CB statement. And then we define the relationship between the operating CCF and the operating FCF.

6.2.3 Inflation Adjustments for Financial Statements

In countries where adjustments for inflation are applied to the financial statements, the only change in the FCF is the one related to taxes paid after adjustments for inflation in the financial statements and possibly the dividends paid. We say possibly because we could define the payout ratio with or without adjustments for inflation in such a manner that the dividends are the same in absolute value.[4] Thus, it is necessary to include only the change in the taxes paid due to the adjustments for inflation because adjustments for inflation do not create wealth or value.[5] Also, the accounting adjustment of prices for some items such as fixed assets and inventories narrows the gap between book values and market values. The reader has to distinguish between the adjustments of the financial statements for inflation and the impacts of inflation on the value of a firm or a project.

6.2.4 Treatment of Tax Savings

In estimating the tax savings from the interest deduction with debt financing, we must check when the tax savings occur. We assume that the taxes are paid in the year in which they accrue. There are several cases.

> **Case 1:** The sum of the EBIT and other income (OI) is greater than the interest expense for the year.
> If the sum of the EBIT and the OI is greater than the interest expense for the current year and taxes are paid the same year, the tax savings are realized in the current year, and the tax savings are equal to the tax rate times the interest expense. This is the simplest case.
> **Case 2:** The sum of the EBIT and OI is zero or less.
> If the sum of the EBIT and OI is zero or less than zero, there are no tax savings in the current year. Also, see the comments on case 3.

---

[4]In Colombia, the payout ratio is applied only to the non-adjusted net income because the inflation profits cannot be distributed.

[5]However, in some cases, the inflation adjustments might affect the value through its impact on the tax savings.

Case 3: The sum of the EBIT and OI is positive but less than the interest expense for the year.

The tax savings depend on the tax laws regarding losses carried forward (LCF). If we cannot carry the losses forward, the tax savings for the year are simply equal to the sum of the EBIT and the OI times the tax rate. Because the interest expense is greater than the sum of the EBIT and the OI, the full value of the interest expense is not realized in the current year.

If we can carry the losses forward, the tax savings can be realized in subsequent years. The full extent of the benefits from LCF depends on the relevant tax laws and regulations. The LCF that earn tax savings from the debt point of view are those related to the amount of loss associated to the interest payments.

SECTION 2

6.3 DERIVING THE FCF FROM THE CB STATEMENT

In this section, we derive the total FCF, exclusive of the TV, from the CB statement. Deriving the FCF from the CB statement is simple because we can literally read the numbers off the CB statement.

For convenience and easy reference, we list the two financial statements for the complex example of Chapter Five, the IS, the BS, and the CB statement.

TABLE 6.1 Pro-Forma Balance Sheet

	Year 0	Year 1	Year 2	Year 3	Year 4	Year 5
Assets						
Cash	1,576.90	100.00	110.00	120.00	130.00	140.00
AR	0.00	2,595.60	2,710.10	2,857.70	3,013.30	3,177.40
Inventory	0.00	1,725.70	2,033.30	2,085.00	2,150.80	2,217.90
Investment on marketable securities	0.00	12,271.90	20,199.90	29,981.60	0.00	8,670.60
Interest accrued	0.00	0.00	0.00	0.00	0.00	0.00
Net fixed assets	40,000.00	30,000.00	20,000.00	10,000.00	45,381.60	34,036.20
Total	41,576.90	46,693.20	45,053.30	45,044.20	50,675.60	48,242.10
Liabilities and equity						
AP	0.00	2,243.40	2,440.70	2,504.80	2,583.80	2,664.50
Accrued taxes	0.00	0.00	0.00	0.00	0.00	0.00
Long-term debt	17,576.90	14,061.50	10,546.10	7,030.80	8,420.30	3,923.90
Total liabilities	17,576.90	16,305.00	12,986.90	9,535.60	11,004.10	6,588.40
Equity	24,000.00	24,000.00	24,000.00	24,000.00	24,000.00	24,000.00
Retained earnings	0.00	6,388.20	8,066.40	11,508.70	15,671.60	17,653.70
Total	41,576.90	46,693.20	45,053.30	45,044.20	50,675.60	48,242.10

TABLE 6.2 The Pro-Forma Income Statement

	Year 0	Year 1	Year 2	Year 3	Year 4	Year 5
Sales		51,912.00	54,202.10	57,153.60	60,265.80	63,547.40
COGS		20,708.60	24,099.70	24,996.20	25,772.20	26,577.80
Gross profit		31,203.40	30,102.40	32,157.40	34,493.60	36,969.70
Selling and administrative expenses		9,441.90	9,841.50	10,308.70	10,798.50	11,325.30
Depreciation		10,000.00	10,000.00	10,000.00	10,000.00	11,345.40
EBIT		11,761.50	10,260.90	11,848.80	13,695.10	14,299.00
Interest income on marketable securities		0.00	747.40	1,230.20	1,825.90	0.00
Other expenses (interest expenses)		1,933.50	1,546.80	1,160.10	773.40	926.20
Earnings before taxes (EBT)		9,828.00	9,461.50	11,918.80	14,747.60	13,372.80
Taxes		3,439.80	3,311.50	4,171.60	5,161.70	4,680.50
NI		6,388.20	6,149.90	7,747.30	9,585.90	8,692.30
Dividends		4,471.70	4,305.00	5,423.10	6,710.20	6,084.60
Retained earnings		1,916.50	1,845.00	2,324.20	2,875.80	2,607.70
Accumulated retained earnings		6,388.20	8,066.40	11,508.70	15,671.60	17,653.70

TABLE 6.3 The Pro-Forma Cash Budget Statement

Cash inflows						
Total income AR	0.00	49,316.40	54,087.60	57,006.00	60,110.20	63,383.30
Total cash inflows	0.00	49,316.40	54,087.60	57,006.00	60,110.20	63,383.30
Cash outflows						
Total payments for AP	0.00	20,190.90	24,210.00	24,983.80	25,758.90	26,564.20
Overhead	0.00	2,260.80	2,340.20	2,422.50	2,507.60	2,608.70
Payroll expenses	0.00	2,509.10	2,623.10	2,742.30	2,867.00	2,997.30
Selling commissions	0.00	3,114.70	3,252.10	3,429.20	3,615.90	3,812.80
Advertising and promotions	0.00	1,557.40	1,626.10	1,714.60	1,808.00	1,906.40
Purchase of fixed assets	40,000.00					
Purchase of fixed assets year 5	0.00	0.00	0.00	0.00	45,381.60	0.00
Taxes	0.00	3,440.60	3,312.20	4,172.10	5,162.00	4,680.90
Total cash outflows	40,000.00	33,073.50	37,363.80	39,464.60	87,101.10	42,570.40
Net cash increase (decrease)	−40,000.00	16,243.80	16,724.50	17,542.00	−26,990.50	20,813.40
Bank loan 1	17,576.90					
Bank loan 2		0.00	0.00	0.00	4,904.90	0.00
Payment of loans	0.00	3,515.40	3,515.40	3,515.40	3,515.40	4,496.40
Interest charges	0.00	1,933.50	1,546.80	1,160.10	773.40	926.20
Net cash balance (NCB) after cash returns to debt holders	−22,423.10	10,794.90	11,662.40	12,866.50	−26,374.40	15,390.80
Equity investment	24,000.00					

(continues)

TABLE 6.3 (*continued*)

Dividend payments		0.00	4,471.70	4,305.00	5,423.10	6,710.20
Repurchase of stock						
NCB after cash returns to shareholders	1,576.90	10,794.90	7,190.70	8,561.50	−31,797.50	8,680.60
Sales of marketable securities	0.00	0.00	12,271.90	20,199.90	29,981.60	0.00
Interest income on marketable securities	0.00	0.00	747.40	1,230.20	1,825.90	0.00
Investment on marketable securities		12,271.90	20,199.90	29,981.60	0.00	8,670.60
NCB after discretionary transactions paid in cash	1,576.90	−1,476.90	10.00	10.00	10.00	10.00
Accumulated cash balance at end of year	1,576.90	100.00	110.00	120.00	130.00	140.00

We know that the FCF is equal to the sum of the CFE and the CFD minus the TS.

$$FCF = CFE + CFD - TS \qquad (6.6)$$

The CFE and the CFD consist of sets of line items in the CB statement. The only component of the FCF that is not explicitly in the CB statement is the tax savings. Next, we discuss each of the components of the FCF.

6.3.1 Cash Flow to Equity

From the point of view of the equity holder, the relevant cash flow items from the CB statement are the equity contributions, and the dividends or equity repurchase. In the complex example, there is no equity repurchase during the forecast period and we can simply read the CFE, exclusive of the TV, off the CB statement. For the moment, we do not discuss the ending cash balance in the terminal period, which we examine in the chapter on the TV.

TABLE 6.4 Cash Flow to Equity in the Complex Case

	Year 0	Year 1	Year 2	Year 3	Year 4	Year 5
Minus investment from stockholders	−24,000.00	0.00	0.00	0.00	0.00	0.00
Plus dividends paid	0.00	0.00	4,471.70	4,305.00	5,423.10	6,710.20
Plus equity repurchase	0.00	0.00	0.00	0.00	0.00	0.00
CFE	−24,000.00	0.00	4,471.70	4,305.00	5,423.10	6,710.20

This approach for calculating the CFE (using only dividends, equity repurchase, and equity investment) is fully consistent with the CAPM in the sense that the beta in the CAPM model is estimated from the dividends paid and not on the basis of a full distribution of available funds. This implies that the FCF calculated from the CFD, CFE, and TS as proposed is consistent with the CAPM.

6.3.2 Cash Flow to Debt

We can simply read the information for the CFD directly from the CB statement, which in turn is linked to the data from the loan schedule. We construct the CFD from the point of view of the debt holder. The CFD consists of the *actual* cash flows to and from the debt holder. In year 0, when the debt holder provides the funds to the firm, the loan is a cash outflow. Similarly, in year 4, when the firm takes out a new loan to purchase the fixed asset, the loan is an outflow to the debt holder. In years 1 to 5, the payments for the loan principal and interest charges are inflows to the debt holder.

TABLE 6.5   Cash Flow to Debt

	Year 0	Year 1	Year 2	Year 3	Year 4	Year 5
Bank loans inflows	−17,576.90	0.00	0.00	0.00	−4,904.90	0.00
Payment of loans	0.00	3,515.40	3,515.40	3,515.40	3,515.40	4,496.40
Interest charges	0.00	1,933.50	1,546.80	1,160.10	773.40	926.20
CFD	−17,576.90	5,448.80	5,062.20	4,675.50	−616.10	5,422.60

In this example we have assumed that the new debt is contracted in year 4 to cover the deficit that arose from the purchase of a new fixed asset in year 4. Only part of the new loan in year 4 is repaid in year 5 and this partial payment is shown in the CB statement. The outstanding balance on the loan is repaid in perpetuity in the years beyond the forecast period. Thus, if we calculate the PV of the CFD in years 1 to 5, we find that the PV is less than the original loan amount. To be complete, the PV of the payments to the debt holder after the forecast period has to be included in the CFD. The PV of the CFD in perpetuity in the years beyond the forecast period is equal to the amount of outstanding debt in year 5. We discuss the repayment of the second loan again in the chapter on the estimation of the TV.

6.3.3 Tax Shield

Of the three components of the FCF, the TS is the only component that cannot be read off the CB statement. In estimating the TS, first we have to check when the taxes are paid. In some cases, there might be accrued taxes. Second, we have to ensure that the sum of the EBIT and the OI is sufficient for the TS to be realized in the year that the interest payment occurs.

To check whether the taxes are paid in the current year or the next year, we examine the BS. In the BS, a liability for accrued taxes would indicate that the taxes have not been paid in the current year and hence the tax savings are not earned in the current year.

In the complex example of Chapter Five, the taxes are paid in the current year and we verify that the sum of the EBIT and the OI is sufficient for the tax savings to be realized in the current year. Thus, in this case, the annual tax savings are equal to the annual interest expenses times the tax rate.

$$\text{Tax savings} = \text{Annual interest expense times Tax rate} \qquad (6.7)$$

The tax savings are shown in the following table.

TABLE 6.6a Tax Savings.

	Year 1	Year 2	Year 3	Year 4	Year 5
Interest expense	1,933.50	1,546.80	1,160.10	773.40	926.20
Tax rate (in%)	35.00	35.00	35.00	35.00	35.00
Tax savings	676.70	541.40	406.00	270.70	324.20

Remember that the tax savings are correctly calculated as the annual interest expenses times the tax rate only when the EBIT plus OI is greater than the interest charge.

To guarantee that we obtain the correct tax savings, we have to use the following expression, which holds when all the taxes are paid in the same year that they are incurred.

$$\text{Tax savings TS} = \text{Taxes on (EBIT} + \text{OI)} - \text{Taxes accrued for the period} \qquad (6.8)$$

To understand this expression we present a simple example. Assume a tax rate of 40%. The EBITs for both the unlevered and levered firms are $100. The interest charges are $150, which is more than the EBIT.

TABLE 6.6b Tax Savings Calculations

	Levered	Unlevered
EBIT	100	100
Interest charges	150	0
EBT	−50	100
Tax	0	40
Net profit	−50	60

The taxes paid by the unlevered firm are $40 and the taxes paid by the levered firm are $0. In this case, the tax savings is $40. This means that we only earn the tax savings on the EBIT that was offset by the interest charges. If we apply equation 6.8 to the levered firm we have

$$\text{Tax savings TS} = 40\% \times 100 - 0 = 40$$

When we have an EBIT that is less than the interest charges, not all the tax savings are earned in the year that the interest payment is made. Depending on the provisions for LCF, the tax savings might be realized in future years.

If we use equation 6.7 and calculate the tax savings as the annual interest expenses times the tax rate we would overestimate that tax savings. In that case we would wrongly calculate the TS as follows.

$$\text{Tax savings} = 40\% \times 150 = 60$$

Using the usual definition, the TS would be overstated by $20.

Alternatively, assume that the EBIT is $200, which is more than the interest charges.

TABLE 6.6c Tax Savings Calculations

	Levered	Unlevered
EBIT	200	200
Interest charges	150	0
EBT	50	200
Tax	20	80
Net profit	30	60

The difference in taxes is now $60, which is equal to the $80 paid by the unlevered firm less the $20 paid by the levered firm. And again, applying equation 6.8, we obtain the correct value for the tax savings.

$$\text{Tax savings} = 40\% \times 200 - 20 = 60$$

Next, we apply equation 6.8 to the complex example.

TABLE 6.6d Tax Savings, General Formulation

Tax savings	Year 1	Year 2	Year 3	Year 4	Year 5
Plus tax on EBIT	4,116.50	3,591.30	4,147.10	4,793.30	5,004.70
Plus tax on OI	0.00	261.60	430.60	639.10	0.00
Minus tax of levered	−3,439.80	−3,311.50	−4,171.60	−5,161.70	−4,680.50
TS	676.70	541.40	406.00	270.70	324.20

In our complex example the results are the same as the ones we obtained in Table 6.6a.

6.3.4 Deferred Taxes

In case the taxes are not paid in the current year, the calculation of the tax savings has to be made with the values of the items of the previous year. If a fraction of the taxes are paid in the current year and the remaining taxes are paid the following year, we have to determine the fraction that is paid in the current year (say a%) and the remaining $(1 - a\%)$ in the following year. With this fraction we calculate the respective tax savings.

As an illustration, for the complex example, suppose that 60% of the taxes in year n are paid in that year and 40% of the taxes are paid in the following year, then in the presence of deferred taxes, the annual tax savings would be as follows:

TABLE 6.6e   Calculation of Deferred Taxes

	Year 0	Year 1	Year 2	Year 3	Year 4	Year 5
Interest expenses		1,842.10	1,473.70	1,105.30	736.90	620.20
Tax rate (in%)		35.00	35.00	35.00	35.00	35.00
Tax savings		644.70	515.80	386.80	257.90	217.10
Tax savings TS for tax paid current year		386.80	309.50	232.10	154.70	130.20
Tax savings TS for tax paid next year	0.00	257.90	206.30	154.70	103.20	86.80
Total tax savings		644.70	515.80	386.80	257.90	217.10
Total tax savings for every year		386.80	567.40	438.40	309.50	233.40

In year 1, the tax savings are 60% of the TSs for year 1. In year 1, the tax savings are 60% of the TSs for year 2 and 40% of the TSs for year 1.

6.3.5 Total Free Cash Flow

We have shown the calculations of the three components of the total FCF. To obtain the total FCF, exclusive of the TV, we simply apply the fundamental FCF relationship. We add the CFE and the CFD and subtract the TS, which was calculated in Table 6.6d.

TABLE 6.7   Total Free Cash Flow Complex Case

	Year 0	Year 1	Year 2	Year 3	Year 4	Year 5
CFD	−17,576.90	5,448.80	5,062.20	4,675.50	−616.10	5,422.60
CFE	−24,000.00	0.00	4,471.70	4,305.00	5,423.10	6,710.20
TS	0.00	676.70	541.40	406.00	270.70	324.20
FCF = CFD + CFE − TS	−41,576.90	4,772.10	8,992.50	8,574.40	4,536.20	11,808.60

We remind the reader that in the calculation of the FCF, we have not taken into account the calculation of the TV.

6.3.6 Capital Cash Flow

To obtain the CCF, we simply add the CFE and the CFD, which can be obtained from the CB statement.

TABLE 6.8   Deriving Total CCF from CFD and CFE

	Year 0	Year 1	Year 2	Year 3	Year 4	Year 5
CFD	−17,576.90	5,448.80	5,062.20	4,675.50	−616.10	5,422.60
CFE	−24,000.00	0.00	4,471.70	4,305.00	5,423.10	6,710.20
Total CCF = CFD + CFE	−41,576.90	5,448.80	9,533.90	8,980.40	4,806.90	12,132.70

Again, we remind the reader that in the calculation of the CCF we have not taken into account the calculation of the TV.

6.4 TOTAL CCF VERSUS OPERATING CCF

Previously, in equation 6.5, we stated the relationship between the total FCF and the operating FCF. As we have seen, it is much easier to derive the CCF from the CB statement because both of the components, the CFE and the CFD, can be read directly off the CB statement. Thus, we begin by deriving the total CCF and then the operating CCF from the CB statement. Then, for completeness, we present the relationship between the operating CCF and the operating FCF.

We provide the correct formulation for the operating CCF by stating a general relationship between the line items in the CB statement and the CCF. From a conceptual point of view, the operating CCF must not include any effect of the excess cash that is invested in marketable securities. Thus, as shown in the following section, we adjust for the interest income from the excess cash that is invested in marketable securities.

6.4.1 Total Capital Cash Flow

We state a general relationship between the various sections of the CB statement and the final line item in the CB statement, which is the change in the CRO. In particular, we derive an expression for the total CCF in terms of the line items in the CB statement. We show the relationship between the annual NCB before debt and equity financing and the annual change in the CRO.

In year n, we begin with the line item in the first section of the CB statement, namely the NCB before debt and equity financing. Next, we subtract the CFD and the CFE. We add the interest income that we earn on the value of the marketable securities at the beginning of year n. Then we subtract the investment in marketable securities in year n and add the recovery of the marketable securities from the previous year n − 1.

NCB (before debt and equity financing) in year n

− CFD in year n − CFE in year n + Interest income in year n

− Investment in marketable securities in year n

+ Sale (recovery) of marketable securities in year n

= Change in CRO in year n   (6.9)

All the line items in equation 6.9 can be read from the CB statement. In the CB statement, as discussed earlier, the CFD and the CFE consist of all the line items that are relevant to the debt and equity holders, respectively.

Next, to facilitate the algebraic manipulation, we define the change in the value of the marketable securities. Because the recovery of marketable securities in year n is equal to the value of the investment of marketable securities in year n − 1, we can define the change in the value of the market securities in year n as follows:

Change in marketable securities = Investment in market securities

in year n minus investment in

market securities in year n − 1   (6.10)

For algebraic simplicity, equation 6.10 combines two line items in the CB statement.

Then in terms of the change in the value of the marketable securities, we rewrite equation 6.9 as follows. Recall that the CCF is simply the sum of the CFD and CFE.

NCB (before debt and equity financing) in year n

− CCF in year n + Interest income in year n

− Change in investment in marketable securities in year n

= Change in CRO in year n   (6.11)

Solving for the CCF in equation 6.11, we obtain the following relationship for the total CCF. In any year n, the CCF equals the NCB (before debt and equity financing) less the change in the CRO plus the interest income, and less the change in the investment in marketable securities.

Total CCF in year n = NCB (before debt and equity financing) in year n

− Change in CRO in year n

+ Interest income in year n

− Change in investment in marketable

securities in year n   (6.12)

In equation 6.12, the NCB (before debt and equity financing) takes account of the taxes that are paid on the interest income from the excess cash that has been invested in marketable securities. To be specific, the tax on interest income from the excess cash has been subtracted from the NCB (before debt and equity financing).

To derive the operating CCF, we wish to separate the effect of the interest income (from the excess cash that is invested in marketable securities) from the NCB. Thus, using an algebraic trick, we adjust equation 6.12 by adding back the taxes on the interest income to the NCB and at the same time subtracting the taxes on the interest income. With this adjustment we are able to identify the operating CCF and the non-operating CCF.

Total CCF in year n = {NCB (before debt and equity financing) in year n

+ Tax on interest income from marketable securities

− Change in CRO in year n}

+ {Interest income in year n

− Tax on interest income from marketable securities

− Change in investment in marketable

securities in year n}   (6.13)

6.4.2 Operating Capital Cash Flow

Next we derive the operating CCF from the revised expression for the total CCF in equation 6.13. As shown in equation 6.14, the operating CCf in year n consists of the first three line items on the RHS of equation 6.13. To remove the effect of the excess cash, we added back the tax on the interest income to the NCB.

Operating CCF in year n = NCB (before debt and equity financing) in year n

$$+ \text{Tax on interest income from marketable}$$

$$\text{securities} - \text{Change in CRO in year n} \qquad (6.14)$$

Recall that the NCB (before debt and equity financing) is net of tax. In other words, in the NCB we subtracted the tax on interest income. To remove the effect of the tax on the interest income from the marketable securities, we undo the effect by adding back the tax on interest income.

6.4.3 Non-operating Capital Cash Flow

We name the set of three remaining line items on the RHS of equation 6.13 as the non-operating CCF.

Non-operating CCF in year n = Interest income in year n

$$- \text{Tax on interest}$$

$$\text{income from marketable securities}$$

$$- \text{Change in investment in}$$

$$\text{marketable securities in year n} \qquad (6.15)$$

The first two terms in equation 6.15 is equivalent to the interest income, net of tax. Thus, the non-operating CCF consists of the (negative) change in investment in marketable securities and the net-of-tax interest income.

With a little algebraic manipulation, we have clearly defined the total CCF as the sum of the operating CCF and the non-operating CCF, where the expression for the operating CCF is given in equation 6.14, and the expression for the non-operating CCF is given in equation 6.15.

$$\text{Total CCF} = \text{Operating CCF} + \text{Non-operating CCF} \qquad (6.16)$$

The operating CCF and the non-operating CCF for the complex example are shown in Table 6.9.

TABLE 6.9   Operating and Non-Operating Capital Cash Flow

	Year 0	Year 1	Year 2	Year 3	Year 4	Year 5
NCB	−40,000.00	16,243.80	16,724.50	17,542.00	−26,990.50	20,813.40
Plus tax on interest received		0.00	261.60	430.60	639.10	0.00
Minus investment in CRO	−1,576.90	−100.00	−110.00	−120.00	−130.00	−140.00
Plus return of CRO	0.00	0.00	0.00	0.00	0.00	0.00
Plus recovery of CRO		1,576.90	100.00	110.00	120.00	130.00
Operating CCF from CB	−41,576.90	17,720.70	16,976.10	17,962.50	−26,361.50	20,803.40
Sales of marketable securities	0.00	0.00	12,271.90	20,199.90	29,981.60	0.00
Interest income on marketable securities	0.00	0.00	747.40	1,230.20	1,825.90	0.00
Minus tax on interest received		0.00	−261.60	−430.60	−639.10	0.00
Investment on marketable securities	0.00	−12,271.90	−20,199.90	−29,981.60	0.00	−8,670.60
Non-operating CCF		−12,271.90	−7,442.20	−8,982.10	31,168.40	−8,670.60
Total CCF	−41,576.90	5,448.80	9,533.90	8,980.40	4,806.90	12,132.70

6.4.4 Other Relationships for Operating Cash Flows

We can define the relationships for other OCFs, such as the operating FCF or the operating CFE. As mentioned earlier, we focus on the CCF because it is the simplest and easiest.

A similar relationship holds between the total FCF, the operating FCF, and the non-operating FCF.

$$\text{Total FCF} = \text{Operating FCF} + \text{Non-operating FCF} \qquad (6.17)$$

The operating and the non-operating FCF are shown in the next table.

TABLE 6.10   Operating and Non-Operating Free Cash Flow

	Year 0	Year 1	Year 2	Year 3	Year 4	Year 5
NCB	−40,000.00	16,243.80	16,724.50	17,542.00	−26,990.50	20,813.40
Minus total tax savings for every year	0.00	−676.70	−541.40	−406.00	−270.70	−324.20
Plus tax on interest received		0.00	261.60	430.60	639.10	0.00
Minus investment in CRO	−1,576.90	−100.00	−110.00	−120.00	−130.00	−140.00

(continues)

TABLE 6.10 (*continued*)

	Year 0	Year 1	Year 2	Year 3	Year 4	Year 5
Plus return of CRO		0.00	0.00	0.00	0.00	0.00
Plus recovery of CRO	0.00	1,576.90	100.00	110.00	120.00	130.00
Operating FCF		17,044.00	16,434.80	17,556.50	−26,632.20	20,479.20
Plus sales of marketable securities	0.00	0.00	12,271.90	20,199.90	29,981.60	0.00
Plus interest income on marketable securities	0.00	0.00	747.40	1,230.20	1,825.90	0.00
Minus tax on interest received		0.00	−261.60	−430.60	−639.10	0.00
Minus investment on marketable securities	0.00	−12,271.90	−20,199.90	−29,981.60	0.00	−8,670.60
Non-operating FCF		−12,271.90	−7,442.20	−8,982.10	31,168.40	−8,670.60
Total FCF	−41,576.90	4,772.10	8,992.50	8,574.40	4,536.20	11,808.60

We know that the total CCF is equal to the sum of the total FCF and the TS.

$$\text{Total CCF} = \text{Total FCF} + \text{TS} \qquad (6.18)$$

Because the non-operating FCF and the non-operating CCF are identical, the operating CCF is equal to the sum of the operating FCF and the TS.

$$\text{Operating CCF} = \text{Operating FCF} + \text{TS} \qquad (6.19)$$

In the following table, we show the operating FCF and the TS.

TABLE 6.11   Operating Free Cash Flow and the Tax Shield

	Year 0	Year 1	Year 2	Year 3	Year 4	Year 5
Operating FCF		17,044.00	16,434.80	17,556.50	−26,632.20	20,479.20
Total tax savings for every year	0.00	676.70	541.40	406.00	270.70	324.20
Operating CCF = Operating FCF + TS	−41,576.90	17,720.70	16,976.10	17,962.50	−26,361.50	20,803.40

In turn, the operating CFE is simply the operational CCF minus the CFD.

$$\text{Operating CFE} = \text{Operating CCF} - \text{CFD} \qquad (6.20)$$

6.5 DERIVING THE FCF FROM THE CFS ACCORDING TO GAAP

Although the CB is not a financial statement according to GAAP, it has valuable information for constructing the FCF and CFE. The standard financial statements do not include the CB statement, and in some cases the external analyst might not have sufficient information to construct the CB statement. Is it possible to derive the FCF from the CFS according to GAAP?

In Chapter Three, we showed the following relationship between the OCF from the first section of the CFS according to GAAP and the NCB (before equity and debt financing) in the first section of the CB statement.

$$OCF = NCB - \text{Interest deductions} + \text{Interest income}$$
$$+ \text{New investments in fixed assets} \qquad (6.21)$$

If we have the three GAAP financial statements, prepared and aggregated, we cannot derive the FCF because the information about the payment of taxes and interest charges is not given explicitly in the CFS according to GAAP and has to be derived by examining the IS and the BS. However, if we construct the three financial statements from scratch, we know the actual occurrence of the annual interest charges and the annual tax payments. We can examine the IS and the BS to determine whether the taxes are paid in the same year that they are incurred or in the future. In addition, from the IS and the BS, we can determine the timing and amount of the interest income from the marketable securities.

If we assume that we have the disaggregated IS and BS statements and the CFS according to GAAP, we can use the following procedure to derive the total FCF from the CFS according to GAAP.

OCF from GAAP

+ Interest charges

− Total tax savings for every year

Net increase (decrease) of cash during the year

− Investment in assets

+ Sales of marketable securities

− Investment on marketable securities = Total FCF   (6.22)

The actual numbers for the complex example are shown in the following table.

TABLE 6.12   Total FCF from OCF

	Year 1	Year 2	Year 3	Year 4	Year 5
Net cash provided by operations	4,310.30	5,925.10	7,612.10	9,443.60	8,541.80
Plus interest charges	1,933.50	1,546.80	1,160.10	773.40	926.20
Minus total tax savings for every year	−676.70	−541.40	−406.00	−270.70	−324.20
Net increase (decrease) of cash during the year	11,476.90	9,990.00	9,990.00	9,990.00	11,335.40
Minus investment in assets				−45,381.60	
Plus sales of marketable securities	0.00	12,271.90	20,199.90	29,981.60	0.00
Minus investment on marketable securities	−12,271.90	−20,199.90	−29,981.60	0.00	−8,670.60
Total FCF	4,772.10	8,992.50	8,574.40	4,536.20	11,808.60

6.6 DERIVING THE FCF FROM THE EBIT IN THE IS

Next, we present the traditional derivation of the FCF from the EBIT in the IS. Both methods, the CB approach and the IS approach, give the same answers and the reader should select the approach with which they are most comfortable. However, we believe that a careful comparison of the merits of the two approaches will persuade the reader that the derivation of the various cash flows—FCF, CFE, and CCF—is easier with the CB statement than with the IS.

We calculate the FCF without the TV, which we introduce later in Chapter Nine. Also we distinguish the operating FCF and the non-operating FCF.

6.6.1 Adjustments to the Income Statement

The CB statement records the actual cash inflows and outflows as they occur. In contrast, the IS (and the BS) uses the accrual principle, and thus the line items in these financial statements do not necessarily occur at the time that they are recorded.

For example, in the IS, a typical accrual item is the sales figure. The sales figure includes sales on credit, which can be paid in subsequent periods. Similarly, the purchases might include items that we have bought on credit and will pay for in subsequent years.

To derive the CFS from the EBIT (or the NI) in the IS we must make adjustments that undo the effects of the accrual principle that is used in the construction of the IS. We have to adjust for income and expense recognition, taxes, and investments.

6.6.2 Depreciation Charges and Amortization

Clearly, depreciation charges and amortization are not cash flow items. In other words, the depreciation allowance in a particular year does not represent a cash outflow.[6] The depreciation schedule is an accounting device to allocate the capital costs over the appropriate time horizon. The construction of the depreciation schedule is based on and subject to the relevant tax laws and regulations. However, the timing and amount of the depreciation allowance has an indirect effect on cash flows. For example, the deduction of the depreciation allowance from the revenues lowers the taxes.

Because the depreciation allowance of $8,000 is subtracted from the revenues in the IS, we must add back the depreciation allowance to get the cash flow.

6.6.3 Working Capital Adjustment

As discussed in Chapter Three, the working capital is a measure of the short-term cash requirement and is defined as the difference between the current assets and the current liabilities. Typical current assets are CRO, AR, inventory, investment on marketable securities, and interest accrued. Typical current liabilities are AP and accrued taxes. If there is an increase in the working capital, additional cash is required for operating the business. Conversely, if there is a decrease in the working capital, the business is generating excess cash from its operations.

Most of the items in the working capital statement are adjustments for the income and expense recognition in the IS. Consider changes in AR, which is a current asset. If there is an increase in AR, more of the sales are on credit and we have not received payment for the sales. An increase in AR represents a cash outflow. Conversely, a decrease in AR represents a cash inflow. Similarly, an increase in the inventories represents a cash outflow and a decrease in the inventories represents a cash inflow.[7]

Next, consider changes in AP, which is a current liability. If there is an increase in AP, more of the purchases are on credit and we have not made payment for the purchases. An increase in AP represents a cash inflow. Conversely, a decrease in AP represents a cash outflow because we are paying for purchases that were bought on credit.[8]

---

[6]However, the profile of the depreciation allowance can affect the cash flow profile through its impact on the annual tax liabilities.

[7]In the CB statement, we do not consider the inventories explicitly because the annual purchases and the annual AP take into account the annual inventories.

[8]For example, AP increases from $2,339 in year 1 to $2,617 in year 2. In the calculation of the working capital, the increase in AP is subtracted from the current assets. The reduction in the working capital represents a cash inflow. With a decrease in AP, we subtract a negative number from the current assets, which results in an increase in the working capital and thus an increase in the cash outflow.

An increase in the investment in marketable securities represents additional retention of excess non-operating cash in the firm. Alternatively, it means that **less** cash is distributed to the stake-holders of the firm. A decrease in the investment in marketable securities represents a decrease in the non-operating cash in the firm.

We consider both operating working capital and non-operating working capital.

In the operating working capital, we distinguish the cash operating working capital from the non-cash operating working capital, which excludes the CRO. The non-operating working capital consists of the investment in marketable securities.

TABLE 6.13   Operating and Non-Operating Working Capital Statement and Change

	Year 0	Year 1	Year 2	Year 3	Year 4	Year 5
Cash	1,576.90	100.00	110.00	120.00	130.00	140.00
AR	0.00	2,595.60	2,710.10	2,857.70	3,013.30	3,177.40
Inventory	0.00	1,725.70	2,033.30	2,085.00	2,150.80	2,217.90
Current assets	1,576.90	4,421.30	4,853.40	5,062.70	5,294.00	5,535.30
AP	0.00	2,243.40	2,440.70	2,504.80	2,583.80	2,664.50
Accrued taxes	0.00	0.00	0.00	0.00	0.00	0.00
Current liabilities	0.00	2,243.40	2,440.70	2,504.80	2,583.80	2,664.50
Operating working capital	1,576.90	2,177.90	2,412.70	2,557.90	2,710.30	2,870.80
Non-cash operating working capital	0.00	2,077.90	2,302.70	2,437.90	2,580.30	2,730.80
Operating working capital	1,576.90	2,177.90	2,412.70	2,557.90	2,710.30	2,870.80
Change in operating working capital	1,576.90	601.00	234.80	145.20	152.40	160.60
Change in non-cash operating working capital	0.00	2,077.90	224.80	135.20	142.40	150.60
Non-operating WC						
Investment on marketable securities	0.00	12,273.40	20,201.60	29,983.40	0.00	8,671.40
Change in non-operating working capital		12,273.40	7,928.20	9,781.80	−29,983.40	8,671.40

The operating working capital increases from $1,576.90 in year 0 to $2,870.80 in year 5. In year 1, the amount of additional operating working capital that is required for the firm is $601.00, and in year 5 the amount of additional operating working capital that is required for the firm is $160.60.

6.6.4 Deriving the FCF from the EBIT

Now that we have discussed the necessary adjustments that have to be made to the line items in the IS, we are ready to derive the operating and non-operating

FCF from the EBIT. The sequence of adjustments for deriving the operating FCF from the EBIT is as follows.

First, we subtract the taxes on the EBIT because it is a cash outflow for the firm. Second, as discussed earlier, we add back the depreciation because it is not a cash flow item and subtract the change in operating working capital. We subtract any capital investments because these are cash outflows that are not taken into account in the EBIT.

EBIT

  − Tax on EBIT

  + Depreciation

  − Change in operating working capital

  + Change in deferred tax savings

  − Capital investment in assets

Operating FCF from EBIT

  − Change in non-operating working capital

Interest income on marketable securities

  − Income tax on interest

  = Total FCF from EBIT   (6.23)

For year n, add net salvage value (TV or continuing value).

To derive the total FCF from the operating FCF, we add the interest income on marketable securities and subtract the taxes that are paid on the interest income from marketable securities.

TABLE 6.14   **Deriving the Operating and Non-Operating FCF from the EBIT**

	Year 0	Year 1	Year 2	Year 3	Year 4	Year 5
EBIT	0.00	11,761.50	10,260.90	11,848.80	13,695.10	14,299.00
Minus tax on EBIT	0.00	−4,116.50	−3,591.30	−4,147.10	−4,793.30	−5,004.70
Plus depreciation	0.00	10,000.00	10,000.00	10,000.00	10,000.00	11,345.40
Minus change in operating working capital	−1,576.90	−601.00	−234.80	−145.20	−152.40	−160.60
Plus change in deferred tax savings		0.00	0.00	0.00	0.00	0.00
Minus capital investment in assets	−40,000.00	0.00	0.00	0.00	−45,381.60	0.00
Operating FCF from EBIT	−41,576.90	17,044.00	16,434.80	17,556.50	−26,632.20	20,479.20

(continues)

TABLE 6.14   (*continued*)

	Year 0	Year 1	Year 2	Year 3	Year 4	Year 5
Minus change in non-operating working capital	0.00	−12,271.90	−7,928.00	−9,781.70	29,981.60	−8,670.60
Interest income on marketable securities	0.00	0.00	747.40	1,230.20	1,825.90	0.00
Minus income tax on interest	0.00	0.00	−261.60	−430.60	−639.10	0.00
Total FCF from EBIT	−41,576.90	4,772.10	8,992.50	8,574.40	4,536.20	11,808.60

For the numerical example, the sequence of adjustments for deriving the FCF from the EBIT is shown in Table 6.14. In year 1, based on the EBIT, the tax liability is \$4,116.5 and not \$3,439.8, which is the tax liability shown in the IS.

Observe that the FCF is exactly the same as the one calculated from the CB. With this procedure we need to work with the BS and the IS, and we have to create a new financial statement, namely the change in working capital statement. With the CB we only need the CB, but we need to check if we really have to pay taxes (more precisely, if we have enough EBIT plus interest income to earn the TS).

6.7 DERIVING THE CFE FROM THE NI

The major goal in valuation is to value the equity market value. This can be done indirectly by using the FCF and deducting the debt from the total value, or directly by valuing the CFE.

The CFE can be derived from the NI. The procedure is as follows:

NI

+ Depreciation and amortization

+ Proceeds from new debt

− Interest income on marketable securities

+ Tax on interest income

− Principal payments

− Change in operating working capital

− Investment Operating CFE from NI

+ Interest income on marketable securities

−. Tax on interest income

− Change in non-operating working capital

= Total CFE from NI   (6.24)

TABLE 6.15 Deriving Operating and Non-Operating CFE from NI

CFE from NI	Year 0	Year 1	Year 2	Year 3	Year 4	Year 5
NI	0.00	6,388.20	6,149.90	7,747.30	9,585.90	8,692.30
Plus depreciation and amortization	0.00	10,000.00	10,000.00	10,000.00	10,000.00	11,345.40
Plus proceeds from new debt	17,576.90	0.00	0.00	0.00	4,904.90	0.00
Minus interest income on marketable securities		0.00	−747.40	−1,230.20	−1,825.90	0.00
Plus tax on interest income		0.00	261.60	430.60	639.10	0.00
Minus principal payments	0.00	−3,515.40	−3,515.40	−3,515.40	−3,515.40	−4,496.40
Minus change in operating working capital	−1,576.90	−601.00	−234.80	−145.20	−152.40	−160.60
Minus investment	−40,000.00	0.00	0.00	0.00	−45,381.60	0.00
Operating CFE from NI	−24,000.00	12,271.90	11,914.00	13,287.10	−25,745.30	15,380.80
Plus interest income on marketable securities		0.00	747.40	1,230.20	1,825.90	0.00
Minus tax on interest income		0.00	−261.60	−430.60	−639.10	0.00
Minus change in non-operating working capital		−12,271.90	−7,928.00	−9,781.70	29,981.60	−8,670.60
Total CFE from NI		0.00	4,471.70	4,305.00	5,423.10	6,710.20

Again, observe that we arrived at the same values that were obtained with the CB statement.

6.8 ADVANTAGES OF USING THE CASH BUDGET APPROACH

In this chapter, we derived the FCF from the CB statement. Next, we briefly review and summarize some of the advantages with the CB statement:

It is simple. The adjustments refer to real figures found in the CB, except for a virtual adjustment to the taxes paid (the TS).

It provides managerial tools. The construction of the different financial statements provides managerial tools for control and follow-up.

It allows for immediate checking for consistency. The BS and the relationship between cash flows provide a way to check that the different cash flows and pro-forma financial statements are consistent.

It is a closer to what happens in reality. In the model, different real assumptions can be introduced, such as the reinvestment of cash surpluses.

It provides a tool for sensitivity analysis and scenario analysis. The spreadsheet where these figures come from includes all the relationships between the basic variables such as prices, price increases, volume, volume increase, price–demand elasticity, AR, AP, inventory policies, and cash requirement policies.

6.9 SUMMARY AND CONCLUDING REMARKS

In this chapter, we presented a simple approach and the standard indirect method for deriving the operating and non-operating FCF, CFE, and CCF from the CB and from the IS. We also derived the operating and non-operating FCF from the CFS. We showed that there is consistency among the procedures.

KEY CONCEPTS AND IDEAS

Tax shield (TS) with LCF
Operating and non-operating cash flow
Operating and non-operating
   working capital
Cash operating working capital
   versus non-cash operating
   working capital

APPENDIX A

A6.1 CALCULATING EXCESS CASH FROM THE IS AND THE BS

The formula for calculating the excess cash without using the CB statement is shown in the following equation. If we do not have the CB available to calculate the excess cash invested in year n, we have to model the excess cash using the BS and the IS. The extra excess cash to be invested has to be calculated taking into account the sources of cash for a given year n, as follows.

The cash generation comes from the NI in year n plus depreciation charges and amortizations plus the available cash from previous market securities invested.

$$NI_n + Depreciation_n + Amortization_n$$
$$+ \text{Investment in market securities}_{n-1} \qquad (A6.1)$$

From this we have to subtract the working capital increase.

$$- [(\text{Cash on hand}_n + AR_n + Inventory_n - AP_n)$$
$$- (\text{Cash on hand}_{n-1} + AR_{n-1} + Inventory_{n-1} - AP_{n-1})] \qquad (A6.2)$$

From this result we subtract the loan principal payment (the interest charges are already subtracted in the resulting NI) and dividends. After these operations we have to subtract the investment in fixed assets.

Then, the excess cash to be invested at year n is as follows:

$$NI_n + Depreciation_n + Amortization_n$$
$$+ \text{Investment in market securities}_{n-1} - \text{Cash on hand}_n$$
$$- AR_n - Inventory_n + AP_n + \text{Cash on hand}_{n-1} + AR_{n-1}$$
$$+ Inventory_{n-1} - AP_{n-1} - \text{Investment in assets}$$
$$- \text{Loan principal payment}_n - Dividends_n$$
$$= \text{Net cash to invest} \qquad (A6.3)$$

We think this calculation is far from intuitive. However, we can manage the construction of the financial statements (BS and IS) and the construction of the FCF without the CB. We illustrate these ideas with the numbers from the complex example.

TABLE A6.1   Complex Example

	Year 1	Year 2	Year 3	Year 4	Year 5
NI_n	6,388.20	6,149.90	7,747.30	9,585.90	8,692.30
Plus depreciation$_n$	10,000.00	10,000.00	10,000.00	10,000.00	11,345.40
Plus amortization$_n$	0.00	0.00	0.00	0.00	0.00
Plus investment in market securities$_{n-1}$	0.00	12,271.90	20,199.90	29,981.60	0.00
Minus cash on hand$_n$	−100.00	−110.00	−120.00	−130.00	−140.00
Minus AR_n	−2,595.60	−2,710.10	−2,857.70	−3,013.30	−3,177.40
Minus inventory$_n$	−1,725.70	−2,033.30	−2,085.00	−2,150.80	−2,217.90
Plus AP_n	2,243.40	2,440.70	2,504.80	2,583.80	2,664.50
Plus cash on hand$_{n-1}$	1,576.90	100.00	110.00	120.00	130.00
Plus AR_{n-1}	0.00	2,595.60	2,710.10	2,857.70	3,013.30
Plus inventory$_{n-1}$	0.00	1,725.70	2,033.30	2,085.00	2,150.80
Minus AP_{n-1}	0.00	−2,243.40	−2,440.70	−2,504.80	−2,583.80
Minus investment in assets	0.00	0.00	0.00	−45,381.60	0.00
Minus loan principal payment$_n$	−3,515.40	−3,515.40	−3,515.40	1,389.50	−4,496.40
Minus dividends$_n$	0.00	−4,471.70	−4,305.00	−5,423.10	−6,710.20
= Net cash to invest	12,271.90	20,199.90	29,981.60	0.00	8,670.60
Excess cash investment in CB	12,271.90	20,199.90	29,981.60	0.00	8,670.60

APPENDIX B

In this appendix we show the derivation of the total FCF and CCF from the NI.

B6.I DERIVING THE FCF FROM NI

The sequence of adjustments for deriving the total FCF from the NI is as follows:

> NI
> + Depreciation
> − Change in operating working capital
> − Interest income on marketable securities
> + Tax on interest income
> − Capital investment in the project (assets)
> + Interest charges
> − Total tax savings for every year
> Operating FCF from NI
> − Change in non-operating working capital
> + Interest income on marketable securities
> − Tax on interest income
> = Total FCF from NI   (B6.1)

For year n, add net salvage (or market value or continuing value).

We add back the interest charges because we want to exclude the impact of debt financing in the FCF. We subtract the tax savings from the interest deduction because the tax savings are taken into account by the adjustment in the Weighted Average Cost of Capital (WACC). If we do not make this adjustment, the financing effect would be counted twice.

We also subtract the after-tax interest income from marketable securities because it is included in the NI. When calculating the total FCF, we add back the after-tax interest income, because we need to include the total actual operations that are related to the operating FCF.

For the numerical example, the sequence of adjustments for deriving the FCF from the NI is shown.

As expected, the FCFs obtained here match the FCF that was derived from the CB statement in this chapter.

TABLE B6.I   Deriving the Operating and Non-Operating FCF from the NI

	Year 0	Year 1	Year 2	Year 3	Year 4	Year 5
NI	0.00	6,388.20	6,149.90	7,747.30	9,585.90	8,692.30
Plus depreciation	0.00	10,000.00	10,000.00	10,000.00	10,000.00	11,345.40
Minus change in operating working capital	−1,576.90	−601.00	−234.80	−145.20	−152.40	−160.60
Minus interest income on marketable securities		0.00	−747.40	−1,230.20	−1,825.90	0.00
Plus tax on interest income		0.00	261.60	430.60	639.10	0.00
Minus capital investment in the project (assets)	−40,000.00	0.00	0.00	0.00	−45,381.60	0.00
Plus interest charges	0.00	1,933.50	1,546.80	1,160.10	773.40	926.20
Minus total tax savings for every year	0.00	−676.70	−541.40	−406.00	−270.70	−324.20
Operating FCF from NI	−41,576.90	17,044.00	16,434.80	17,556.50	−26,632.20	20,479.20
Minus change in non-operating working capital		−12,271.90	−7,928.00	−9,781.70	29,981.60	−8,670.60
Plus interest income on marketable securities		0.00	747.40	1,230.20	1,825.90	0.00
Minus tax on interest income		0.00	−261.60	−430.60	−639.10	0.00
Total FCF from NI		4,772.10	8,992.50	8,574.40	4,536.20	11,808.60

B6.2 DERIVING THE CCF FROM NI

The sequence of adjustments for deriving the total CCF from the NI is as follows:

NI
+ Depreciation charges
+ Interest expenses
− Interest income on marketable securities
+ Tax on interest income
− Change in operating working capital
− Capital investment in the project (in cash or in kind)
Operating CCF from NI
+ Interest income on marketable securities
− Tax on interest income
− Change in non-operating working capital
= Total operating CCF   (B6.2)

For year n, add net salvage (or market value or continuing value).

In this case we add back the interest charges because the CCF includes the effect of the debt financing. However, we do not subtract the tax savings from the interest deduction because we do not take account of the impact of debt financing in the WACC for the CCF.

As in the case of the FCF we also subtract the after-tax interest income from marketable securities because it was included in the NI. When calculating the Total CCF we add back the after-tax interest income because we need to include the total actual operations that are related to the operating CCF.

For the numerical example, the sequence of adjustments for deriving the CCF from the NI is shown.

TABLE B6.2   Deriving the Operating and Non-Operating CCF from the NI

	Year 0	Year 1	Year 2	Year 3	Year 4	Year 5
NI	0.00	6,388.20	6,149.90	7,747.30	9,585.90	8,692.30
Plus depreciation charges	0.00	10,000.00	10,000.00	10,000.00	10,000.00	11,345.40
Plus interest expenses	0.00	1,933.50	1,546.80	1,160.10	773.40	926.20
Minus interest income on marketable securities		0.00	−747.40	−1,230.20	−1,825.90	0.00
Plus tax on interest income		0.00	261.60	430.60	639.10	0.00
Minus change in operating working capital	−1,576.90	−601.00	−234.80	−145.20	−152.40	−160.60
Minus capital investment in the project (in cash or in kind)	−40,000.00	0.00	0.00	0.00	−45,381.60	0.00
Operating CCF from NI	−41,576.90	17,720.70	16,976.10	17,962.50	−26,361.50	20,803.40
Plus interest income on marketable securities		0.00	747.40	1,230.20	1,825.90	0.00
Minus tax on interest income		0.00	−261.60	−430.60	−639.10	0.00
Minus change in non-operating working capital		−12,271.90	−7,928.00	−9,781.70	29,981.60	−8,670.60
Non-operating CCF		−12,271.90	−7,442.20	−8,982.10	31,168.40	−8,670.60
Total CCF from NI		5,448.80	9,533.90	8,980.40	4,806.90	12,132.70

As expected, the CCF obtained here matches the CCF that was derived from the CB statement in this chapter.

7

USING THE WACC IN THEORY AND PRACTICE

What we have to do is to be forever curiously testing new opinions and courting new impressions.

—*Walter Pater* (1839 to 1894), 1873

SECTION I

7.1 APPROACHES TO THE COST OF CAPITAL

In this chapter, from theoretical and practical points of view, we reexamine the cost of capital for valuing a finite cash flow stream, which is based on forecasted financial statements over the life of the cash flow. We emphasize and reiterate that the theoretical results for estimating and calculating the cost of capital are valid only under stringent conditions that might not hold in practice, especially in countries with shallow, illiquid, and incomplete capital markets. For example, in many countries the data for modeling and estimating the popular and well-known CAPM is not available.[1] Nevertheless, the conceptual framework of the CAPM is useful in thinking about and estimating a reasonable value for the cost of capital. For traded firms, we use the CAPM to provide guidance on the range of possible values for the cost of capital that are consistent with the market values. For non-traded firms, we use parameters from comparable traded firms to estimate a reasonable value for the cost of capital.

[1] Even in countries with developed capital markets, it is easy to find fault with the simple CAPM. Here we do not assess the relative merits of the CAPM.

From a practical point of view, it is most important for the analyst to assess the extent and degree to which it is acceptable to assume that the theoretical models are reasonable approximations to reality. And if the theoretical assumptions do not hold, the analyst must make appropriate, judicious adjustments to the relevant parameters. As mentioned earlier in Chapter One, it might be possible to obtain values that are reasonable approximations to market values, if the assets are frequently and actively traded in a competitive setting. If the asset is not traded, we have to find a set of comparable assets that are traded, and value the non-traded asset based on the parameters of the set of comparable traded assets. In Chapter Eight, we discuss this issue in further detail.[2] Before we begin, it is helpful to review briefly what we have covered up to this point in the book. In Chapter One, in the context of perfect capital markets, we presented a qualitative discussion on cash flows and their corresponding discount rates. In Chapter Two, we presented some numerical examples on discounting finite cash flows with the weighted average cost of capital (WACC). In the appendix to Chapter Two, we presented a detailed discussion on the cost of capital applied to cash flows in perpetuity.

In Chapter Five, we constructed the nominal financial statements for a complex example and in Chapter Six we showed different ways to derive the cash flows from the financial statements. Most readers are familiar with the expressions for the cost of capital and return to levered equity that are derived from cash flows in perpetuity. We wish to reiterate that the expressions for the cost of capital and the return to levered equity that are applicable to cash flows in perpetuity are not appropriate for the finite cash flows in the forecast period. With finite cash flows there is a terminal period beyond which we assume that cash flows are in perpetuity and we take account of these cash flows in perpetuity by calculating a terminal value (TV).

Looking ahead, in the next chapter we discuss using the CAPM to estimate the cost of capital for a non-traded firm. In addition, we examine some alternative methods for estimating the cost of capital.

In Chapter Nine, we complete the construction of the free cash flow (FCF) by including the TV in the valuation exercise. In Chapter Ten, we present an advanced chapter on the cost of capital for those readers with a strong analytic background and interest in issues related to the cost of capital. In Chapter Eleven we study a complex real life case with adjustment for inflation, losses carried forward (LCF), unpaid taxes, foreign exchange debt, and presumptive income.

This chapter is organized as follows. In Section 2, we review some of the basic ideas from the previous chapters. To minimize repetition, the reader is encouraged to review Chapter One for the basic ideas that were presented on the cost of capital.

---

[2]In some cases, the discrepancies between theoretical models and reality might be huge and irreconcilable and the analysts will have to use their best judgment, taking into account the relevant available information.

In Section 3, we present three simple formulations for the cost of capital. In Section 4 we present a three-dimensional framework for classifying the different formulations for the WACC. In Section 5, we use the cash flows from the complex example of Chapter Five to illustrate the three different ways to use the cost of capital. In addition we show that the CFE approach gives consistent answers.

In Appendix A, we provide an algebraic treatment for the cost of capital and discuss some of the subtleties in the cost of capital to give the interested reader a deeper appreciation for some of the assumptions that underlie the estimation of the cost of capital. If the level of the algebra is too difficult, the reader might want to skim or skip this appendix,

In Appendix B, we discuss how we can use the CAPM to estimate the parameters for the cost of capital.

In Appendix C, we show the calculations of the levered values with the operational cash flows.

SECTION 2

7.2 REVIEW OF BASIC IDEAS

First, we briefly review the main ideas in an M & M world without and with taxes. With finite cash flows, we introduce subscripts to indicate the timing of the cash flows and the present values (PVs) of the cash flows. In addition, the appropriate discount rates for the different cash flows can vary across time. In many instances, we assume that the expected inflation rates are constant and the real discount rates are also constant over the life of the cash flow. Over time, the nominal discount rates vary due to changes in leverage, the expected inflation rates, and the real discount rates. We retain the time subscripts to stress the fact that we are dealing with finite cash flows rather than cash flows in perpetuity. In the following equations, all values are market values at the end of each period. And the leverage for year i is based on the value at the beginning of year i (or the end of year $i-1$). With finite cash flows, the profile of the leverage is more complex because the debt financing policy can vary over the life of the cash flow.

In an M & M world without taxes, with respect to the end of year i, the levered value V^L_i is equal to the unlevered value V^{Un}_i. And the levered value V^L_i is equal to the sum of the levered equity E^L_i and the debt D_i.

$$V^L_i = V^{Un}_i \qquad (7.1)$$

$$V^L_i = E^L_i + D_i \qquad (7.2)$$

Briefly, in an M & M world without taxes, equations 7.1 and 7.2 summarize the fact that debt financing does not create value.

7.2.1 Impact of Taxes

In an M & M world with taxes and no leverage costs, in any year i, the levered value increases by the PV of the tax shield (TS). To be specific, the levered value V^L_i is equal to the sum of the levered equity E^L_i and the debt D_i. In turn, the levered value V^L_i is equal to the sum of the unlevered value V^{Un}_i and V^{TS}_i, which is the PV of the TS from the interest deduction with debt financing.

$$V^L_i = E^L_i + D_i \qquad (7.3)$$

$$V^L_i = V^{Un}_i + V^{TS}_i \qquad (7.4)$$

Combining equations 7.3 and 7.4, we obtain

$$V^{Un}_i + V^{TS}_i = E^L_i + D_i \qquad (7.5)$$

As we will discuss in more detail, the PV of the TS depends on the realization of the annual TSs and the discount rate for the TS, which takes into account the risk profile of the TS over the life of the cash flow.

7.2.2 Cash Flow Relationships

For each of the equations 7.3 and 7.4, we can write the corresponding cash flow relationships. With respect to the end of year i, the CCF is equal to the sum of the CFE and the cash flow to debt (CFD). Both the CFE and CFD are easily obtained from the CB statement.

$$CCF_i = CFE_i + CFD_i \qquad (7.6)$$

Alternatively, with respect to the end of year i, the CCF is equal to the sum of the FCF and the TS.

$$CCF_i = FCF_i + TS_i \qquad (7.7)$$

Combining equations 7.6 and 7.7, we obtain

$$FCF_i + TS_i = CFE_i + CFD_i \qquad (7.8)$$

Equation 7.8 is the fundamental cash flow relationship that we had presented earlier in Chapter Six.

Typically, practitioners, analysts, and writers of finance textbooks assume that the TS in year i is equal to the tax rate times the interest payment, where the interest payment is equal to the value of the debt at the beginning of the period times the cost of debt d_i.

$$TS_i = TD_i d_i \tag{7.9}$$

In many cases, the expression for the annual TS in equation 7.9 does not hold. For example, if there are losses, then the TS is zero for that year and the tax savings may be realized in subsequent years. In general terms, it is preferable to think of the TS as the difference in the taxes paid by the unlevered and levered firms.

7.2.3 Relationships Between Values and Cash Flows

Next, we write the expressions for the values in terms of the corresponding cash flows. With respect to the end of the year $i - 1$, the unlevered value V^{Un}_{i-1} is equal to the sum of the FCF in year i and V^{Un}_i, discounted by ρ_i, the return to unlevered equity for year i, where V^{Un}_i is the PV in year i of all the FCF in the years beyond year i.

$$V^{Un}_{i-1} = (FCF_i + V^{Un}_i)/(1 + \rho_i) \tag{7.10}$$

$$E^L_{i-1} = (CFE_i + E^L_i)/(1 + e_i) \tag{7.11}$$

$$D_{i-1} = (CFD_i + D_i)/(1 + d_i) \tag{7.12}$$

$$V^{TS}_{i-1} = (TS_i + V^{TS}_i)/(1 + \psi_i) \tag{7.13}$$

With respect to the end of the year $i - 1$, the value of the levered equity E^L_{i-1} is equal to the sum of the CFE in year i and E^L_i, discounted by e_i, the return to levered equity for year i, where E^L_i is the PV in year i of all the CFE in the years beyond year i.

With respect to the end of the year $i - 1$, the value of the debt D_{i-1} is equal to the sum of the CFD in year i and D_i, discounted by d_i, the cost of debt for year i, where D_i is the PV in year i of all the CFD in the years beyond year i.

With respect to the end of the year $i - 1$, the PV of the TS V^{TS}_{i-1} is equal to the sum of the TS in year i and V^{TS}_i, discounted by ψ_i, the appropriate discount rate for the TS in year i, where V^{TS}_i is the PV in year i of all the TSs in the years beyond year i.

Equations 7.10 to 7.13 are important for understanding the derivations of the relevant expressions for the cost of capital. Starting with the cash flows in the terminal year N, we use equations 7.10 to 7.13 to iterate and discount backwards to year 0. If year i is the terminal year N, the values in year i are equal to the PV of the cash flows in perpetuity beyond N, with respect to year N.

7.2.4 Two-Period Example

For the convenience of the reader, we use a simple two-period cash flow to illustrate the use of these algebraic expressions. There are no cash flows beyond year 2.

TABLE 7.1   Values and Cash Flows

Year	0	1	2
FCF		FCF_1	FCF_2
Unlevered return		ρ_1	ρ_2
Unlevered value	V^{Un}_0	V^{Un}_1	

At the end of year 1, the unlevered value is equal to the FCF in year 2 discounted by ρ_2, the return to unlevered equity for year 2.

$$V^{Un}_1 = (FCF_2 + V^{Un}_2)/(1 + \rho_2)$$
$$= FCF_2/(1 + \rho_2) \qquad (7.14)$$

In year 2, the unlevered value V^{Un}_2 is zero because the FCF in year 2 is the terminal cash flow and there are no cash flows beyond year 2.

At the end of year 0, the unlevered value V^{Un}_0 is equal to the sum of the FCF in year 1 and V^{Un}_1, discounted by ρ_1, the return to unlevered equity for year 1, where V^{Un}_1 is the PV, with respect to year 1, of the FCF in year 2.

$$V^{Un}_0 = (FCF_1 + V^{Un}_1)/(1 + \rho_1)$$
$$= FCF_1/(1 + \rho_1) + V^{Un}_1/(1 + \rho_1) \qquad (7.15)$$

Substituting equation 7.14 into equation 7.15, we obtain

$$V^{Un}_0 = FCF_1/(1 + \rho_1) + FCF_2/[(1 + \rho_1)(1 + \rho_2)] \qquad (7.16)$$

Similar interpretations apply for the values of the levered equity, the values of debt, and the PVs of the TSs.

7.2.5 Discount Rate for the Tax Shield

The value of ψ_i depends on the risk profile of the TS. For cash flows in perpetuity, it is common to assume that the value of ψ_i is equal to the cost of debt d_i because the risk of the TS is the same as the risk of the CFD.[3]

---

[3]If the debt is risky, the TSs might not necessarily be risky. Consequently the discount rate for the TS might not be the same as the discount rate for the debt.

However, with finite cash flows, for subtle reasons to be discussed later in the advanced WACC in Chapter Ten, it is more appropriate (and convenient) to assume that the value of ψ_i is equal to ρ_i, the return to unlevered equity. This means that the risk of the TS is correlated directly with the FCF rather than the CFD.

From a practical point of view, with finite cash flows, the formulas are simpler if we assume that the value of ψ_i is equal to ρ_i. However, in principle there is no reason why the value of ψ_i should be restricted to d_i or ρ_i. Here we do not explore these other possibilities.

7.2.6 Return to Levered Equity e_i

When we assume that the value of ψ_i is equal to ρ_i, with finite cash flows, in year i the expression for the return to equity e_i is as follows:

$$e_i = \rho_i + (\rho_i - d_i)\frac{D_{i-1}}{E_{i-1}} \tag{7.17}$$

Recall that for cash flows in perpetuity, with the assumption that the value of ψ_i is equal to d_i, there is a multiplicative coefficient $(1 - T)$ for the debt–equity ratio. For the expression for the return to levered equity with the multiplicative coefficient $(1 - T)$, see the appendix to Chapter Two, which discusses cash flows in perpetuity. It is important to emphasize that when we assume that ρ_i is the appropriate discount rate for the TS, there is no multiplicative coefficient $(1 - T)$ for the debt–equity ratio on the RHS of equation 7.17. Later, in the appendix to this chapter, we present the general algebraic expression for the return to levered equity. Because the return to unlevered equity ρ_i is always higher than the cost of debt d_i, the second term on the RHS of equation 7.17 is positive. Thus, the return to levered equity e_i is higher than the return to unlevered equity ρ_i. As a residual claimant on the FCF, the risk to the levered equity holder is higher than the risk to the unlevered equity holder and correspondingly, the rate of return e_i is also higher than ρ_i.

There is a positive linear relationship between the return to levered equity and the debt–equity ratio. For each unit increase in the debt–equity ratio, the return to levered equity increases by the difference between the return to unlevered equity ρ_i and the cost of debt d_i.

Next, we present numerical and graphical illustrations of equation 7.17. We assume that the return to unlevered equity is 15% and the cost of debt is 11%.

The following table shows the relationship between D_i, the amount of debt, the debt–equity ratio, E_i, the amount of equity, and e_i, the return to levered equity. As expected, there is a positive linear relationship between the return to levered equity e and the debt–equity ratio.

TABLE 7.2   Relationship Between D_i, the Amount of Debt, the Debt–Equity Ratio, and e_i, the Return to Levered Equity for $\rho = 15\%$ and $d = 11\%$

Debt, D_i	Equity, E_i	D/E Ratio	e_i
0	1000	0.00	15.00%
100	900	0.11	15.44%
200	800	0.25	16.00%
300	700	0.43	16.71%
400	600	0.67	17.67%
500	500	1.00	19.00%
600	400	1.50	21.00%
700	300	2.33	24.33%
800	200	4.00	31.00%
900	100	9.00	51.00%

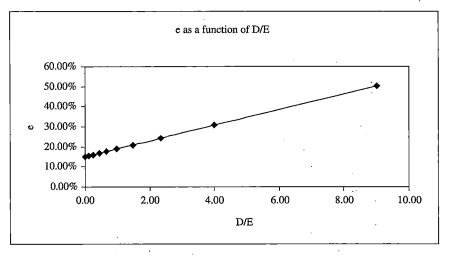

EXHIBIT 7.1   Return to levered equity e as a function of D/E.

If the amount of debt is $100, the debt–equity ratio is 0.11 and the return to levered equity is 15.44%. If the amount of debt increases from 100 to 200, the return to levered equity increases by 0.56 percentage points, from 15.44% to 16%.

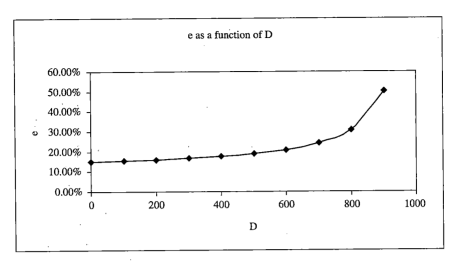

EXHIBIT 7.2 Return to levered equity e as a function of D.

The relationship between e_i, the return to levered equity, and the amount of debt D_i is non-linear. If the amount of debt increases from 500 to 600, the return to levered equity increases by 2 percentage points, from 19% to 21%.

SECTION 3

7.3 THREE SIMPLE EXPRESSIONS FOR THE COST OF CAPITAL

With regard to expressions for the cost of capital, there is an embarrassment of riches. First, we present three simple expressions for the cost of capital applied to finite cash flows and briefly examine the strengths and weaknesses of each of the expressions. As mentioned earlier, we prefer to discuss finite cash flows because the cash flows have been derived from financial statements with a finite forecast period.

The first two expressions are applied to the FCF and the third expression is applied to the CCF. The three expressions are presented in order of familiarity. The first expression is probably the most well known and commonly applied, whereas the third one is probably unfamiliar to many readers.

1. Standard after-tax WACC applied to the FCF.
2. Adjusted WACC applied to the FCF.
3. WACC applied to the CCF.

If the same consistent assumptions are satisfied, all three expressions for the cost of capital must give the same answer.

7.3.1 Standard After-Tax WACC Applied to the FCF

The first approach is the standard WACC that is applied to the FCF. We assume that the discount rate for the TS is the return to unlevered equity ρ.

$$\text{After-tax WACC} = \frac{d_i(1-T)\,D_{i-1}}{V^L_{i-1}} + \frac{e_i\,E^L_{i-1}}{V^L_{i-1}} \qquad (7.18)$$

where d_i is the market-based cost of debt, e_i is the market-based return to (levered) equity, T is the tax rate, D_{i-1}/V^L_{i-1} is the market value of the debt D_{i-1} as a percent of the total levered (market) value V^L_{i-1}, and E^L_{i-1}/V^L_{i-1} is the market value of equity E^L_{i-1} as a percent of the total levered (market) value V^L_{i-1}.

As mentioned earlier, to account for the tax benefits from the interest deduction with debt financing, we lower the WACC^{FCF} with the multiplicative coefficient $(1-T)$ applied to the cost of debt because the FCF does not include the TS. With the WACC^{FCF}, we assume that the TSs are always realized in the years that they occur and there is enough EBIT to earn the TS.

One advantage of the standard after-tax WACC^{FCF} is that we do not have to estimate the actual values for the annual TSs if we assume or know that the TSs will always be realized in the years that they occur.

As shown in equation 7.17, the expression for the return to levered equity is a function of the debt–equity ratio. Typically, we assume that the leverage and the return to unlevered equity are constant, in which case the return to levered equity is constant, and the WACC^{FCF} is easy to use. Furthermore, if there is little variability in the leverage over the life of the cash flow profile, the error in using this formulation for the WACC can be small. However, these days, with the wide availability of computing power, it is easy to model the variable leverage as a function of the debt financing policy over the life of the cash flow.

We illustrate the use of the standard after-tax WACC^{FCF} with a simple numerical example. Over the life of the FCF, we assume that the expected inflation rate is constant and the nominal cost of debt is 11%. The tax rate T is 35%. In addition, we assume that the leverage will be continually rebalanced so that it is constant at 40%. Because the leverage is expected to be constant and the return to unlevered equity is assumed to be constant, the return to levered equity is also constant. Assume that e_i the return to levered equity, derived from the CAPM at the leverage of 40% (or a debt–equity ratio of 0.667), is 28.57%.

Under these assumptions, the WACC^{FCF} is constant at 20%.

$$
\begin{aligned}
\text{After-tax WACC} &= \frac{d_i(1-T)\,D_{i-1}}{V^L_{i-1}} + \frac{e_i\,E^L_{i-1}}{V^L_{i-1}} \\
&= 11\% \times (1-35\%) \times 40\% + 28.57\% \times 60\% \\
&= 20.00\%
\end{aligned}
$$

If there is high variability in the leverage over the life of the cash flow profile and the return to levered equity is not properly modeled as a function of the changing debt–equity ratio, the WACC^{FCF} of 20% will be incorrect.

For example, if the leverage is 60% rather than 40%, and we assume that the return to levered equity remains unchanged, the **incorrect** after-tax WACC is 15.72%.

$$\text{After-tax WACC} = \frac{d_i(1-T)\,D_{i-1}}{V^L_{i-1}} + \frac{e_i\,E^L_{i-1}}{V^L_{i-1}}$$
$$= 11\% \times (1-35\%) \times 60\% + 28.57\% \times 40\%$$
$$= 15.72\%$$

To find the correct value for the after-tax WACC, the return to levered equity e_i must be consistent with the specified debt–equity ratio of 60%.

When we use the WACC^{FCF} to value a FCF that has been derived from a set of integrated financial statements, we encounter the problem of circularity. In general, if we use market values, there is circularity even if we do not obtain the FCF from integrated financial statements. To calculate the annual levered values, we need to know the annual WACCs. In turn, the annual WACCs depend on the debt and equity values as percentages of the levered values. Later, with detailed numerical examples, we show how to implement the circularity.

7.3.2 Adjusted WACC Applied to the FCF

The second formulation of the WACC^{FCF} overcomes some of the weaknesses of the standard formula for the WACC^{FCF}. We call this the "adjusted WACC applied to the FCF." Again, we assume that the discount rate for the TS is the return to unlevered equity ρ_i. In any year i, the adjusted WACC^{FCF} is equal to ρ_i less the TS in year i as a percent of the levered value at the beginning of year i (or end of year $i-1$).

$$\text{Adjusted WACC}^{\text{FCF}}_i = \rho_i - \frac{\text{TS}_i}{V^L_{i-1}} \tag{7.19}$$

And if we assume no LCF in any year i, there is enough EBIT to earn the TS, the taxes are paid in the same year, and the annual TS is equal to the interest payment times the tax rate, then we can rewrite equation 7.19 as follows:

$$\text{Adjusted WACC}^{\text{FCF}}_i = \rho_i - \frac{Td_iD_{i-1}}{V^L_{i-1}} \tag{7.20}$$

In this formulation, in any year i, we lower the WACC by subtracting the TS as a percent of the levered value from the return to unlevered equity. If we can calculate the TS, this formulation is flexible and can easily accommodate any LCF. The adjusted WACC^{FCF} makes the correction to ρ_i only by the amount of the TS that is actually realized in year i and does not necessarily assume that the TSs are always realized in the years that they occur. Also, unlike the first formula for the standard after-tax WACC^{FCF}, with the adjusted WACC^{FCF}, we do not need to calculate the return to levered equity e_i. However, we must know the value of the return to unlevered equity ρ_i, which might not be easy to obtain. If there are tax complexities such as LCF and deferred taxes, the values of the standard WACC and the adjusted WACC are different.

We illustrate the use of the adjusted WACC^{FCF} with a simple numerical example. Over the life of the FCF, we assume that the expected inflation rate is constant and the nominal cost of debt is 11%. Previously we assumed that the return to levered equity is 28.57%. The relationship between the return to levered equity and the return to unlevered equity is given by equation 7.17. The reader can verify that an unlevered return to equity of 21.54% corresponds to a levered return to equity of 28.57%. Remember that we have assumed that the appropriate discount rate for the TS ψ_i is equal to the return to unlevered equity ρ_i.

The tax rate T is 35%. In addition, we assume that the leverage will be continually rebalanced so that it is constant at 40%.

$$\text{Adjusted WACC}^{\text{FCF}}_{\ i} = \rho_i - \frac{\text{TS}_i}{V^{\text{L}}_{\ i-1}}$$
$$= 21.54\% - 35\% \times 11\% \times 40\% = 20.00\%$$

As expected in this simple illustration, with no LCF and the TSs earned in full in the years in which the TSs occur, the value of the standard after-tax WACC^{FCF} is equal to the value of the adjusted WACC^{FCF}.

If the leverage changes from 60% to 40%, the WACC changes from 20% to 19.23%. As mentioned earlier, with the adjusted WACC^{FCF} it is not necessary to recalculate the return to levered equity for the new leverage.

$$\text{Adjusted WACC}^{\text{FCF}}_{\ i} = \rho_i - \frac{\text{TS}_i}{V^{\text{L}}_{\ i-1}}$$
$$= 21.54\% - 35\% \times 11\% \times 60\% = 19.23\%$$

Earlier, when we did not recalculate the new return to levered equity based on the new leverage, the after-tax WACC^{FCF} was incorrectly calculated as 15.7%, whereas with the revised leverage of 60%, the correct value is 19.23%.

When we use the adjusted WACC^{FCF}, we encounter the problem of circularity if the leverage is not specified. To calculate the annual levered values, we need to know the annual WACC. In turn the WACC depends on the annual TSs as percentages of the levered values.

7.3.3 WACC Applied to the CCF

Unlike the first two expressions for the WACC, the third WACC is applied to the CCF rather than the FCF. We know that in any year i, the CCF is equal to the sum of the CFE and the CFD.

$$CCF_i = CFE_i + CFD_i \qquad (7.21)$$

With the assumption that in each year, the value of ψ_i is always equal to the return to unlevered equity ρ_i, the WACC applied to the CCF is the simplest and most elegant. With the $WACC^{CCF}$, there is no need to lower the WACC because the CCF already includes the TS.

$$WACC^{CCF}_i = \rho_i \qquad (7.22)$$

Thus, the value of the $WACC^{CCF}$ is 21.54%.

In any period i, even if the leverage changes, the return to levered equity e_i takes into account the new leverage, and the weighted average of the cost of debt d_i and the cost of levered equity e_i remains equal to the return to unlevered equity ρ_i.[4]

We can also express the $WACC^{CCF}$ as a weighted average of the cost of debt and the cost of levered equity, without the multiplicative coefficient $(1 - T)$.

$$WACC^{CCF}_i = \frac{d_i D_{i-1}}{V^L_{i-1}} + \frac{e_i E^L_{i-1}}{V^L_{i-1}} \qquad (7.23)$$

Also, in common with the adjusted $WACC^{FCF}$, we do not have to worry about LCF. The TSs are only taken into account in the CFE if the TSs are actually realized and we do not have to assume that the TSs are always realized.

Furthermore, to use the $WACC^{CCF}$, all we need to know is the value for the return to unlevered equity ρ_i. We do not have to calculate the return to levered equity e_i. With the $WACC^{CCF}$, there is no circularity if we know the value for the return to unlevered equity ρ_i.

SECTION 4

7.4 GENERAL FRAMEWORK

In the previous section, we presented three simple approaches for estimating the cost of capital. Now we present a general framework for classifying the WACCs that are applied to the FCF and the CCF. There are many different ways for calculating the WACC and for the beginner the plethora of possibilities can be

---

[4]The values for ψ_i and ρ_i can change over time.

confusing. For the moment, we avoid complexities. To facilitate the discussion, we classify the menagerie of WACCs along three dimensions. We hope that the structured framework assists the reader in making the correct decision with respect to the calculation of the cost of capital in practice. In Chapter Ten, we discuss additional subtleties with respect to the WACCs. First, we present a qualitative discussion on the dimensions of the framework. Second, we specify the appropriate formulas and calculations for the cells in the framework.

With a clear understanding of the assumptions, the reader can select the formula that is most convenient and suitable. Next, we list and discuss the WACCs along the three dimensions. The first dimension is the type of cash flow: FCF or CCF. The second dimension is the risk of the TS and the third dimension is the formulation of the expression for the WACC.

7.4.1 First Dimension

On the first dimension we specify the appropriate cash flow for the cost of capital: the FCF or the CCF. We briefly review the relative merits of the FCF and the CCF.

The CCF is simply the sum of the CFE and the CFD.

$$CCF_i = CFE_i + CFD_i \tag{7.24}$$

As discussed earlier, the FCF is exclusive of the TS and the CCF is inclusive of the TS.

$$CCF_i = FCF_i + TS_i \tag{7.25}$$

For the $WACC^{FCF}$, we lower the WACC to take account of the tax benefits of the interest deduction from the debt financing. This assumes that the TSs are fully realized in the year that they occur, which means no LCF.

For the $WACC^{CCF}$, there is no need to lower the WACC to take account of the TS because the CFE, as a component of the CCF, already includes the TS. Furthermore, the TSs are only taken into account in the years that the TSs are actually realized.

With no LCF, the $WACC^{FCF}$ and the $WACC^{CCF}$ give the same answer. However, if there is LCF, the $WACC^{FCF}$ overstates the levered value, relative to the $WACC^{CCF}$, because the WACC applied to the FCF assumes that the TSs are realized in the years that they occur.

7.4.2 Second Dimension

The second dimension of the matrix is the risk of the TS. The risk of the TS determines the appropriate value that we should use to discount the TS. Typically, we assume that the debt is risky. Furthermore, we also assume that the risk of the TSs is equal to the risk of the debt that is generating the TS. Thus, the appropriate discount rate for the TS ψ_i is equal to the cost of debt d_i.[5]

For completeness and without justification or demonstration, we state that the value for the discount rate applied to the TS affects the formula for the calculation of the return to levered equity e_i. Later, in Appendix A, we show that the return to levered equity is a function of the discount rate for the TS.

For reasons that we explain in Chapter Ten, the risk of the TS might not be risk-free and in fact, the TS might be correlated with the FCF. In general, the risk of the TS is complex. Here, for simplicity, we consider two possible values for ψ_i: the cost of debt d_i or the return to unlevered equity ρ_i. If the risk of the TS is the same as the risk of the debt that is generating the TS, the appropriate value of ψ_i is the cost of debt d_i. Alternatively, if the risk of the TS is the same as the risk of the FCF, the appropriate value of ψ_i is the return to unlevered equity ρ_i. If we assume that the discount rate for the TS is ρ_i, which is higher than the cost of debt d_i, the levered values are lower.

7.4.3 Third Dimension

For the FCF and CCF, there are two equivalent ways to write the formulas for the WACCs. The first way is the standard weighted average formulation. Roughly speaking, the weighted average formula for the WACC, applied to the FCF or the CCF, is a weighted average of the cost of debt d_i and the return to levered equity e_i, where the weights are the market values of the debt and equity.

The weighted average formula is easier to use if the leverage and return to unlevered equity are constant over the life of the cash flow profile. If the leverage is not constant, we must adjust the return to levered equity e_i to take proper account of the variable leverage. Again, we remind the reader that the formula for the return to levered equity e_i that is derived from cash flows in perpetuity is different from the formula for the return to levered equity e_i that is derived for finite cash flows.

We name the second way the adjusted value formulation. The adjusted value formula defines the WACC relative to the return to unlevered equity and does not require the calculation of the return to levered equity e_i.

---

[5]Technically speaking, if the debt is risky and the TSs are risk-free, it is not correct to discount the TSs with the cost of debt d, which is higher than the risk-free rate. Sometimes practitioners might not distinguish between the cost of debt and the discount rate for the TS. For simplicity, they assume that the debt is risk-free, even though it might not be risk-free, and use the risk-free rate to discount the TSs.

7.4.4 Matrix for the WACC Applied to the FCF

For completeness, we present the matrix for the WACC applied to the FCF and the relevant formulas for the cells in the matrix. Based on the risk of the TS (second dimension) and the formulation of the WACC (third dimension), there are four formulas for the WACC applied to the FCF.

The formulas in the cells of the matrix just look complex and the reader should not be intimidated. In Appendix A, we present the detailed algebra for the formula for the return to levered equity e_i.

TABLE 7.3   Matrix for the WACC Applied to the FCF

	Risk of TS	WACC formula	Return to levered equity e
Weighted average	$\psi_i = d_i$	$\dfrac{d_i(1-T)\,D_{i-1}}{V^L_{i-1}} + \dfrac{e_i E^L_{i-1}}{V^L_{i-1}}$	$e_i = \rho_i + (\rho_i - d_i)\dfrac{D_{i-1}}{E_{i-1}} - (\rho_i - d_i)\dfrac{V^{TS}_{i-1}}{E^L_{i-1}}$
Weighted average	$\psi_i = \rho_i$	$\dfrac{d_i(1-T)\,D_{i-1}}{V^L_{i-1}} + \dfrac{e_i E^L_{i-1}}{V^L_{i-1}}$	$e_i = \rho_i + (\rho_i - d_i)\dfrac{D_{i-1}}{E_{i-1}}$
Adjusted value	$\psi_i = d_i$	$\rho_i - \dfrac{TS_i}{V^L_{i-1}} - (\rho_i - d_i)\dfrac{V^{TS}_{i-1}}{V^L_i}$	$e_i = \rho_i + (\rho_i - d_i)\dfrac{D_{i-1}}{E_{i-1}} - (\rho_i - d_i)\dfrac{V^{TS}_{i-1}}{E^L_{i-1}}$
Adjusted value	$\psi_i = \rho_i$	$\rho_i - \dfrac{TS_i}{V^L_{i-1}}$	$e_i = \rho_i + (\rho_i - d_i)\dfrac{D_{i-1}}{E_{i-1}}$

7.4.5 Matrix for the WACC Applied to the CCF

Next, we present the matrix for the WACC applied to the CCF and the relevant formulas for the cells in the matrix.

TABLE 7.4   Matrix for the WACC Applied to the CCF

	Risk of TS	WACC formula	Return to levered equity e
Weighted average	$\psi_i = d_i$	$\dfrac{d_i D_{i-1}}{V^L_{i-1}} + \dfrac{e_i E^L_{i-1}}{V^L_{i-1}}$	$e_i = \rho_i + (\rho_i - d_i)\dfrac{D_{i-1}}{E_{i-1}} - (\rho_i - d_i)\dfrac{V^{TS}_{i-1}}{E^L_{i-1}}$
Weighted average	$\psi_i = \rho_i$	$\dfrac{d_i D_{i-1}}{V^L_{i-1}} + \dfrac{e_i E^L_{i-1}}{V^L_{i-1}}$	$e_i = \rho_i + (\rho_i - d_i)\dfrac{D_{i-1}}{E_{i-1}}$
Adjusted value	$\psi_i = d_i$	$\rho_i - (\rho_i - d_i)\dfrac{V^{TS}_{i-1}}{V^L_{i-1}}$	$e_i = \rho_i + (\rho_i - d_i)\dfrac{D_{i-1}}{E_{i-1}} - (\rho_i - d_i)\dfrac{V^{TS}_{i-1}}{E^L_{i-1}}$
Adjusted value	$\psi_i = \rho_i$	ρ_i	$e_i = \rho_i + (\rho_i - d_i)\dfrac{D_{i-1}}{E_{i-1}}$

7.4.6 How Do We Estimate the Cost of Capital? Practical Issues

With a clear understanding of the three simple expressions for the cost of capital, we now discuss some practical issues related to the estimation of the parameters for the cost of capital. What is the information that is required to calculate the parameters for the cost of capital? And if there is circularity, how do we model the circularity in the spreadsheet?

Remember that we assume that the discount rate for the TS is equal to the required return to unlevered equity ρ_i. In addition, we assume that we know the cost of debt d_i and the tax rate T.

Next we summarize the required information for using the three expressions to calculate the cost of capital. The selection of the formula for the cost of capital depends on two pieces of information.

TABLE 7.5   Information requirement for Calculating the Cost of Capital with the Assumption that $\psi_i = \rho_i$

	Calculate e_i?	Calculate ρ_i?	Calculate TS?	Circularity?
1. Standard WACC applied to the FCF	Yes	No	No	Yes
2. Adjusted WACC applied to the FCF	No	Yes	Yes	Yes
3. WACC applied to the CCF	No	Yes	No	No

First, we must determine whether we know the value for the return to levered equity e_i or the value for the return to unlevered equity ρ_i. Both of these parameters, the returns to unlevered and levered equities, are related to each other through the expression for the return to levered equity in equation 7.17. In Chapter Eight, we show how to use the CAPM to find the relationship between the return to unlevered and levered equity.

If we know the value for the return to unlevered equity ρ_i, we can use equation 7.17 to calculate the return to levered equity e_i.

Alternatively, if we know the value for the return to levered equity e_i, we rewrite equation 7.17 and solve for the return to unlevered equity ρ_i in terms of the return to levered equity e_i.

$$\rho_i = \frac{d_i D_{i-1}}{V^L_{i-1}} + \frac{e_i E^L_{i-1}}{V^L_{i-1}} \tag{7.26}$$

SECTION 5

7.5 NUMERICAL EXAMPLES WITH THE COMPLEX EXAMPLE

We illustrate the three expressions for the cost of capital with the cash flows for the complex example.

For calculating the WACC and levered value we have to estimate ρ_i or e_i. In this example we assume that we estimate ρ_i.[6] The point estimation of ρ is done at year 0. Then we have to deflate the ρ_i and use a real ρ_i. Assuming real ρ_i is constant, we inflate the real ρ_i with the expected inflation rate for every year.

In the complex example the nominal ρ_i is 21% and inflation at the moment of the estimation is 3%. During the forecasted period and for perpetuity, the inflation rate is constant at 3% per annum. This means that the nominal ρ_i will be 21%. We remind the reader that the cost of debt (from Chapter Five) is 11% per annum, the tax rate is constant at 35%, and we read the debt balances from the BS in Chapter Five. In this example we assume that the market values of the debt are the same as the book values of the debt.

7.5.1 Standard WACC Applied to the FCF

First, we demonstrate the standard WACC applied to the FCF. As mentioned earlier, when we use the standard WACC applied to the FCF, there is circularity. For the convenience of the reader who might be unfamiliar with circularity, we explain how to set up the circularity.

We present two tables. In Table 7.6a, we put a starting value of 20% in the cells for the WACCs. The starting value is arbitrary.[7] After we have completed the formulas for the other cells, in the last step, we enter the appropriate formulas for the WACCs, which initiate the circularity.

In the first row of Table 7.6a, we list the FCF for the complex example, inclusive of the TV from Chapter Nine where we show the calculation of the TV.[8] The FCF in terminal year 5 includes the TV, which includes the PV of the TSs in perpetuity because the FCF in year 6 has been discounted by the WACC. The annual values of the debt are taken from Table 9.8 in Chapter Nine. The value of the levered equity is equal to the difference between the levered value and the value of debt.

---

[6]The estimation of ρ_i is studied in Chapter Eight.

[7]For ease in the calculation, we select a starting value that is close to the estimated WACC. A judicious choice of the trial value can facilitate the convergence of the circularity calculation.

[8]As will be studied in Chapter Nine, the terminal value depends on the discount rate for the forecasting period because the terminal value is a function of the levered value of the firm. In this example we use the same FCF with the TV for the initial table but in reality it should change.

TABLE 7.6a Valuation with the Standard WACC Applied to the FCF (with trial values for the WACC)

	Year 0	Year 1	Year 2	Year 3	Year 4	Year 5
FCF with TV		4,772.10	8,992.50	8,574.40	4,536.20	66,916.43
Value of debt	17,576.90	14,061.50	10,546.10	7,030.80	8,420.30	
D%		39.71%	29.09%	21.51%	13.99%	15.10%
d(1 − T)		7.15%	7.15%	7.15%	7.15%	7.15%
Contribution of debt $D\%d_i(1-T)$		2.84%	2.08%	1.54%	1.00%	1.08%
E%		60.29%	70.91%	78.49%	86.01%	84.90%
$e_i = \rho_i + (\rho_i - d_i)\dfrac{D_{i-1}}{E_{i-1}}$		27.59%	25.10%	23.74%	22.63%	22.78%
Contribution of equity $e_iE\%$		16.63%	17.80%	18.63%	19.46%	19.34%
WACC		20.00%	20.00%	20.00%	20.00%	20.00%
Levered value	44,263.45	48,344.01	49,020.28	50,249.95	55,763.69	
Equity = Levered value − Debt	26,686.54	34,282.48	38,474.14	43,219.18	47,343.39	

Based on the WACCs (which are not the correct WACCs and simply values that have been selected to begin the process) and reverse discounting, we calculate the annual levered values. At the end of year 4, with a stipulated WACC of 20%, the incorrectly calculated levered value is $55,763.69.

$$V^L{}_4 = (FCF_5 + V^L{}_5)/(1 + 20\%)$$
$$= (66,916.43 + 0)/(1 + 20\%) = 55,763.69.$$

At the end of year 3, with a WACC of 20%, the levered value is $50,249.95.

$$V^L{}_3 = (FCF_4 + V^L{}_4)/(1 + 20\%)$$
$$= (4,536.20 + 55,763.69)/(1 + 20\%) = 50,249.95$$

Continuing in this backward iterative fashion, we calculate the levered values for years 2 to 0.

Based on the annual values of the debt, we calculate the annual debt–equity ratios and enter the formula for the return to levered equity. If all the steps have been performed correctly, you should obtain the values in Table 7.6a. Again, we emphasize that the calculated values in Table 7.6a are not correct.

In the final step, enter the formula for the standard WACC applied to the FCF in the cells for the WACC in the second line. Circularity occurs and the reader should obtain the correct values in Table 7.6b. The formula for the WACC is simply the weighted sum of the contribution of the cost of debt and the return to equity.

To set up the spreadsheet to handle circularities, follow these instructions:

1. Select the option Tools in the pull-down menu in Excel.
2. Select Options.
3. Select the tab Calculate.
4. In the dialog box select Iteration and click OK.

This procedure can be done before starting the work in the spreadsheet or when Excel declares the presence of circularity.

The values in Table 7.6b are the correct levered values. The leverage decreases from 39.72% in year 1 to 15.15% in year 5, and correspondingly,

TABLE 7.6b   Valuation with the Standard WACC Applied to the FCF

	Year 0	Year 1	Year 2	Year 3	Year 4	Year 5
FCF with TV		4,772.10	8,992.50	8,574.40	4,536.20	66,916.43[9]
Value of debt	17,576.90	14,061.50	10,546.10	7,030.80	8,420.30	
D%		39.72%	29.24%	21.67%	14.09%	15.15%
$d_i(1 - T)$		7.15%	7.15%	7.15%	7.15%	7.15%
Contribution of debt D%d(1 − T)		2.84%	2.09%	1.55%	1.01%	1.08%
E%		60.28%	70.76%	78.33%	85.91%	84.85%
$e_i = \rho_i + (\rho_i - d_i)\dfrac{D_{i-1}}{E_{i-1}}$		27.59%	25.13%	23.77%	22.64%	22.79%
Contribution of equity $e_iE\%$		16.63%	17.78%	18.62%	19.45%	19.33%
WACC		19.47%	19.87%	20.17%	20.46%	20.42%
Levered value	44,250.80	48,094.63	48,660.60	49,898.91	55,570.75	
Equity = Levered value − Debt	26,673.89	34,033.09	38,114.45	42,868.14	47,150.45	

the return to levered equity decreases from 27.59% in year 1 to 22.79% in year 5. The WACC^{FCF} increases from 19.47% in year 1 to 20.42% in year 5.

7.5.2 Adjusted WACC Applied to the FCF

Next, we illustrate the adjusted WACC applied to the FCF for the complex example. We enter trial values in the cells for the WACC in Table 7.7a and calculate the annual levered values. Again, we emphasize that the values in Table 7.7a are not correct.

[9]For simplicity in the exposition we have used the same FCF for year 5 although as it will be shown in Chapter Nine, the FCF in the last year depends on the terminal value and the terminal value will depend on the levered value, creating a circularity.

TABLE 7.7a Valuation with the Adjusted WACC applied to the FCF (with trial values for the WACC)

	Year 0	Year 1	Year 2	Year 3	Year 4	Year 5
FCF with TV		4,772.13	8,992.53	8,574.40	4,536.24	66,916.43
TS		676.71	541.37	406.03	270.68	324.18
ρ_i		21.00%	21.00%	21.00%	21.00%	21.00%
$\dfrac{TS_i}{V^L_{i-1}}$		1.53%	1.12%	0.83%	0.54%	0.58%
WACC		20.00%	20.00%	20.00%	20.00%	20.00%
LevVal = Levered value	44,237.24	48,312.6	48,982.5	50,204.7	55,709.3	
Equity = LevVal − Debt	26,660.3	34,251.0	38,436.4	43,173.9	47,289.1	

Next, we calculate the TS as a percentage of the levered values. If the reader has performed all the steps properly, the reader should obtain the incorrectly calculated values in Table 7.7a.

In the final step, enter the formula for the adjusted WACC applied to the FCF in the cells for the WACC. Circularity occurs and the reader should obtain the correct values in Table 7.7b. See the previous section on how to handle circularity in the spreadsheet.

TABLE 7.7b Valuation with the Adjusted WACC Applied to the FCF

	Year 0	Year 1	Year 2	Year 3	Year 4	Year 5
FCF with TV		4,772.13	8,992.53	8,574.40	4,536.24	66,916.43
TS		676.71	541.37	406.03	270.68	324.18
$\dfrac{TS_i}{V^L_{i-1}}$		1.53%	1.13%	0.83%	0.54%	0.58%
ρ_i		21.00%	21.00000%	21.00%	21.00%	21.00%
$WACC = \rho_i - \dfrac{TS_i}{V^L_{i-1}}$		19.47%	19.87%	20.17%	20.46%	20.42%
LevVal = Levered value	44,250.80	48,094.6	48,660.6	49,898.9	55,570.8	
Equity = LevVal − Debt	26,673.89	34,033.09	38,114.45	42,868.14	47,150.45	

As expected, the formula for the adjusted WACC applied to the FCF gives the same values as the formula for the standard WACC applied to the FCF.

7.5.3 WACC Applied to the CCF

The WACC applied to the CCF is the simplest and most elegant. And there is no circularity. The CCF is equal to the sum of the CFE and the CFD,

TABLE 7.8   Valuation with the WACC Applied to the CCF

	Year 0	Year 1	Year 2	Year 3	Year 4	Year 5
CFD		5,448.84	5,062.15	4,675.46	−616.15	9,346.53
CFE		0.00	4,471.74	4,304.96	5,423.08	57,894.08
CCF		5,448.84	9,533.89	8,980.42	4,806.93	67,240.61
WACC for CCF		21.00%	21.00%	21.00%	21.00%	21.00%
Levered value	44,250.80	48,094.6	48,660.6	49,898.9	55,570.8	
Equity = LevVal − Debt	26,673.89	34,033.09	38,114.45	42,868.14	47,150.45	

which can be easily obtained from the CB statement. Using reverse discounting, we calculate the annual levered values.

As expected, in Table 7.8 the answers for the levered values with all three expressions match.

7.5.4 Cash Flow to Equity Approach

For completeness, we show that the CFE approach also gives consistent results. Table 7.9a shows the results before inserting the formulas for the returns to levered equity. In this case, we have used 25% as the starting value for the return to levered equity.

TABLE 7.9a   Valuation with the CFE Approach (with trial values for the Return to Levered Equity)

	Year 0	Year 1	Year 2	Year 3	Year 4	Year 5
CFE		0.00	4,471.74	4,304.96	5,423.08	57,894.08
Return to equity		25.00%	25.00%	25.00%	25.00%	25.00%
$e_i = e_i = \rho_i + (\rho_i - d_i)\frac{D_{i-1}}{E_{i-1}}$						
Levered equity	26,258.08	32,822.60	36,556.51	41,390.67	46,315.26	
Value of debt	17,576.91	14,061.53	10,546.15	7,030.77	8,420.30	
Levered value = Equity + Debt	43,835.00	46,884.13	47,102.66	48,421.44	54,735.56	

After inserting the formula for the return to levered equity and inducing circularity, the reader should obtain the correct results in Table 7.9b. See the previous section on how to handle circularity in the spreadsheet.

TABLE 7.9b Valuation with the CFE Approach

	Year 0	Year 1	Year 2	Year 3	Year 4	Year 5
CFE		0.00	4,471.74	4,304.96	5,423.08	57,894.08
Return to equity		27.59%	25.13%	23.77%	22.64%	22.79%
$e_i = \rho_i + (\rho_i - d_i)\frac{D_{i-1}}{E_{i-1}}$						
Levered equity	26,673.89	34,033.09	38,114.45	42,868.14	47,150.45	
Value of debt	17,576.91	14,061.53	10,546.15	7,030.77	8,420.30	
Levered value =	44,250.80	48,094.63	48,660.60	49,898.91	55,570.75	
Equity + Debt						

7.6 SUMMARY AND CONCLUDING REMARKS

In this chapter, we presented a comprehensive and general framework for thinking about the cost of capital with finite cash flows. The formulas for the cost of capital can be categorized along three dimensions. In the first dimension, we have the type of cash flow. It can be either the FCF or the CCF. In the second dimension, we have to specify the discount rate for the TS. In the third dimension, we can use either the weighted average approach or the adjusted value formulation.

Next, we illustrated the cost of capital for three cases: the standard WACC applied to the FCF, the adjusted WACC applied to the FCF, and the WACC applied to the CCF.

APPENDIX A

A7.1 ALGEBRAIC APPROACH

Now, we briefly derive the general algebraic expressions for the cost of capital that is applied to finite cash flows. First, we show that in general the return to levered equity e_i is a function of ψ_i. This is the most important point. Second, we derive the general expressions for the WACCs. There are four cases: two formulations for the WACC applied to the FCF and two formulations for the WACC applied to the CCF.

First, we rewrite equations 7.10 to 7.13 as follows:

$$V^{Un}_{i-1}(1 + \rho_i) - V^{Un}_i = FCF_i \qquad (A7.1)$$

$$E^L_{i-1}(1 + e_i) - E^L_i = CFE_i \qquad (A7.2)$$

$$D_{i-1}(1 + d_i) - D_i = CFD_i \qquad (A7.3)$$

$$V^{TS}_{i-1}(1 + \psi_i) - V^{TS}_i = TS_i \qquad (A7.4)$$

We emphasize that in equation A7.4 we make no assumption about the value of ψ_i, which depends on the risk profile of the TS. Also, in general terms, the TS equals the difference in the taxes paid by the unlevered and levered firms.

A7.1.1 General Expression for the Return to Levered Equity e_i

We know that

$$FCF_i + TS_i = CFE_i + CFD_i \qquad (A7.5)$$

284

To obtain the general expression for the WACC, substitute equations A7.1 to A7.4 into equation A7.5.

$$V^{Un}_{i-1}(1 + \rho_i) - V^{Un}_i + V^{TS}_{i-1}(1 + \psi_i) - V^{TS}_i = E^L_{i-1}(1 + e_i) - E^L_i$$
$$+ D_{i-1}(1 + d_i) - D_i \quad (A7.6)$$

Simplifying, we obtain

$$V^{Un}_{i-1}\rho_i + V^{TS}_{i-1}\psi_i = E^L_{i-1}e_i + D_{i-1}d_i \quad (A7.7)$$

Substitute the expression for the unlevered value and solve for the return to levered equity.

$$E^L_{i-1}e_i = (E^L_{i-1} + D_{i-1} - V^{TS}_{i-1})\rho_i + V^{TS}_{i-1}\psi_i - D_{i-1}d_i \quad (A7.8)$$

Collecting terms and rearranging, we obtain

$$E^L_{i-1}e_i = E^L_{i-1}\rho_i + (\rho_i - d_i)D_{i-1} - (\rho_i - \psi_i)V^{TS}_{i-1} \quad (A7.9)$$

Solving for the return to levered equity, we obtain

$$e_i = \rho_i + (\rho_i - d_i)\frac{D_{i-1}}{E_{i-1}} - (\rho_i - \psi_i)\frac{V^{TS}_{i-1}}{E^L_{i-1}} \quad (A7.10)$$

The return to levered equity e_i is a positive linear function of the debt–equity ratio. In addition, it is also a linear function of the PV of the TS to equity ratio, where the direction (sign) of the relationship depends on the value of ψ_i. Many readers might not be aware that the return to levered equity depends on the value of ψ_i.

If we assume that the appropriate discount rate for the TS is equal to the return to unlevered equity ρ_i, the third term in equation A7.10 drops out and we can simplify the equation as follows:

$$e_i = \rho_i + (\rho_i - d_i)\frac{D_{i-1}}{E_{i-1}} \quad (A7.11)$$

As we had stated earlier, with finite cash flows, the expression for the levered equity is simple when we assume that the value of ψ_i is equal to ρ_i.

A7.1.2 Standard WACC Applied to the FCF

After deriving the general expression for the return to levered equity, we are ready to derive the algebraic expressions for the WACC applied to the FCF. We know that

$$FCF_i = CFD_i - TS_i + CFE_i \quad (A7.12)$$

Let $WACC^{FCF}_i$ be the standard WACC that is applied to the FCF in year i. With respect to the end of the year $i - 1$, the levered value V^L_{i-1} is equal to the sum of the FCF in year i and V^L_i, discounted by the WACC for year i, where V^L_i is the PV in year i of all the FCF in the years beyond year i.

$$V^L_{i-1} = (FCF_i + V^L_i)/(1 + WACC^{FCF}_i) \qquad (A7.13)$$

We rewrite equation A7.13 as follows:

$$V^L_{i-1}(1 + WACC^{FCF}_i) - V^L_i = FCF_i \qquad (A7.14)$$

Substitute the expression for the FCF into the RHS of equation A7.14.

$$V^L_{i-1}(1 + WACC^{FCF}_i) - V^L_i = CFD_i - TS_i - CFE_i \qquad (A7.15)$$

Substitute the expressions for the CFD and the CFE into the RHS of equation A7.15. Do not substitute the expression for the TS.

$$V^L_{i-1}(1 + WACC^{FCF}_i) - V^L_i = D_{i-1}(1 + d_i) - D_i - TS_{i-1}$$
$$+ E^L_{i-1}(1 + e_i) - E^L_i \qquad (A7.16)$$

Simplifying and rearranging, we obtain

$$V^L_{i-1}WACC^{FCF}_i = D_{i-1}d_i - TS_i + E^L_{i-1}e_i \qquad (A7.17)$$

We assume that the TSs are equal to the annual interest payment times the tax rate.

$$V^L_{i-1}WACC^{FCF}_i = D_{i-1}d_i - TD_{i-1}d_i + E^L_{i-1}e_i \qquad (A7.18)$$

Solve for the WACC.

$$WACC^{FCF}_i = \frac{d_i(1 - T)D_{i-1}}{V^L_{i-1}} + \frac{e_iE^L_{i-1}}{V^L_{i-1}} \qquad (A7.19)$$

The expression for the standard after-tax WACC in equation A7.19 is familiar to most readers. However, the reader must remember that the correct expression for the return to levered equity on the RHS of equation A7.19 depends critically on the assumption about the value of the discount rate for the TS ψ_i. The value of ψ_i affects the value of the return to levered equity e_i, which in turn affects the value of the $WACC^{FCF}_i$.

A7.1.3 Adjusted WACC Applied to the FCF

Let $\text{WACC}^{\text{Adj}}_i$ be the adjusted WACC that is applied to the FCF in year i. We follow the same steps that we outlined for the standard after-tax WACC^{FCF}.

$$V^L_{i-1}\text{WACC}^{\text{Adj}}_i = D_{i-1}d_i - TS_i + E^L_{i-1}e_i \qquad (A7.20)$$

From before, we know the following:

$$V^{Un}_{i-1}\rho_i + V^{TS}_{i-1}\psi_i = E^L_{i-1}e_i + D_{i-1}d_i \qquad (A7.21)$$

Next, we substitute the RHS of equation A7.21 into the RHS of equation A7.20.

$$V^L_{i-1}\text{WACC}^{\text{Adj}}_i = V^{Un}_{i-1}\rho_i + V^{TS}_{i-1}\psi_i - TS_i \qquad (A7.22)$$

Substitute the expression for the unlevered value in the RHS of equation A7.22.

$$V^L_{i-1}\text{WACC}^{\text{Adj}}_i = (V^L_{i-1} - V^{TS}_{i-1})\rho_i + V^{TS}_{i-1}\psi_i - TS_i \qquad (A7.23)$$

Rearrange and simplify the terms.

$$V^L_{i-1}\text{WACC}^{\text{Adj}}_i = V^L_{i-1}\rho_i - (\rho_i - \psi_i)V^{TS}_{i-1} - TS_i \qquad (A7.24)$$

Solving for the adjusted WACC, we obtain

$$\text{WACC}^{\text{Adj}}_i = \rho_i - \frac{TS_i}{V^L_{i-1}} - (\rho_i - \psi_i)\frac{V^{TS}_{i-1}}{V^L_i} \qquad (A7.25)$$

Because we have assumed that the value of ψ_i is equal to the return to unlevered equity ρ_i, the second term in equation A7.25 drops out and we can simplify the equation as follows:

$$\text{WACC}^{\text{Adj}}_i = \rho_i - \frac{TS_i}{V^L_{i-1}} \qquad (A7.26)$$

A7.1.4 Standard WACC Applied to the CCF

We know that the CCF is equal to the sum of the CFE and the CFD.

$$CCF_i = CFE_i + CFD_i \qquad (A7.27)$$

Let WACC^{CCF} be the WACC that is applied to the CCF. With respect to the end of the year $i - 1$, the levered value V^L_{i-1} is equal to the sum of the

CCF in year i and V^L_i, discounted by the WACC for year i, where V^L_i is the PV in year i of all the CCF in the years beyond year i. ·

$$V^L_{i-1} = (CCF_i + V^L_i)/(1 + WACC^{CCF}_i) \qquad (A7.28)$$

We rewrite the equation as follows:

$$V^L_{i-1}(1 + WACC^{CCF}_i) - V^L_i = CCF_i \qquad (A7.29)$$

Substitute the expression for the CCF into the RHS of equation A7.29.

$$V^L_{i-1}(1 + WACC^{CCF}_i) - V^L_i = CFD_i + CFE_i \qquad (A7.30)$$

Then substitute the expressions for the CFD and CFE into the RHS of equation A7.30.

$$V^L_{i-1}(1 + WACC^{CCF}_i) - V^L_i = D_{i-1}(1 + d_i) - D_i$$
$$+ E^L_{i-1}(1 + e_i) - E^L_i \qquad (A7.31)$$

Simplify and rearrange the terms.

$$V^L_{i-1}WACC^{CCF}_i = D_{i-1}d_i + E^L_{i-1}e_i \qquad (A7.32)$$

Solving for the WACC, we obtain

$$WACC^{CCF}_i = \frac{d_i D_{i-1}}{V^L_{i-1}} + \frac{e_i E^L_{i-1}}{V^L_{i-1}} \qquad (A7.33)$$

Compare the standard WACC applied to the FCF with the WACC applied to the CCF. In equation A7.33, the WACC applied to the CCF does not have the multiplicative coefficient $(1 - T)$ applied to the cost of debt d_i.

A7.I.5 Adjusted WACC Applied to the CCF

We know that the CCF is also equal to the sum of the FCF and the TS.

$$CCF_i = FCF_i + TS_i \qquad (A7.34)$$

Let $WACC^{Adj}_i$ be the adjusted WACC applied to the CCF. We follow the same steps that we outlined for the standard WACC applied to the CCF.

$$V^L_{i-1}WACC^{Adj}_i = V^{Un}_{i-1}\rho_i + V^{TS}_{i-1}\psi_i \qquad (A7.35)$$

Substitute the expression for the unlevered value on the RHS of equation A7.35 and rearrange.

$$V^L_{i-1}WACC^{Adj}_i = V^L_{i-1}\rho_i - (\rho_i - \psi_i)V^{TS}_{i-1} \qquad (A7.36)$$

Solving for the WACC, we obtain

$$\text{WACC}^{\text{Adj}}_i = \rho_i - (\rho_i - \psi_i) \frac{V^{\text{TS}}_{i-1}}{V^{\text{L}}_{i-1}} \qquad (\text{A7.37})$$

Because we have assumed that the value of ψ_i is equal to the return to unlevered equity ρ_i, we can simplify equation A7.37 as follows:

$$\text{WACC}^{\text{Adj}}_i = \rho_i \qquad (\text{A7.38})$$

B7.1 USING THE CAPM TO FIND THE COST OF CAPITAL

Next we discuss how we can use the CAPM to find the relationship between the levered beta and the unlevered beta.

From equation A7.10, we know that the general expression for the return to levered equity e_i is as follows:

$$e_i = \rho_i + (\rho_i - d_i)\frac{D_{i-1}}{E_{i-1}} - (\rho_i - \psi_i)\frac{V^{TS}_{i-1}}{E^L_{i-1}} \qquad (B7.1)$$

For simplicity, we assume that the return to unlevered equity ρ_i, the cost of debt d_i, and the discount rate for the TS ψ_i are constant.

$$e_i = \rho + (\rho - d)\frac{D_{i-1}}{E_{i-1}} - (\rho - \psi)\frac{V^{TS}_{i-1}}{E^L_{i-1}}1 \qquad (B7.2)$$

The return to levered equity e_i is a function of the debt–equity ratio and the ratio of the PV of the TS to the value of the levered equity. If these two ratios change over time, the return to levered equity e_i also changes.

Using the CAPM, we write the expressions for the cost of debt d_i, the return to unlevered equity ρ_I, and the return to levered equity e_i as follows:

$$d_i = r_f + \beta_D[E(r_m) - r_f] \qquad (B7.3)$$

$$\rho_i = r_f + \beta_\rho[E(r_m) - r_f] \qquad (B7.4)$$

$$e_i = r_f + \beta_E[E(r_m) - r_f] \qquad (B7.5)$$

The expression for the return to levered equity in equation B7.5 is based on a specified leverage. If we assume that the discount rate for the TS is equal to the return to unlevered equity ρ_i, we can simplify equation B7.2 as follows:

$$e_i = \rho_i + (\rho_i - d_i)\frac{D_{i-1}}{E_{i-1}} \qquad (B7.6)$$

Substituting equations B7.3 and B7.4 into equation B7.6 and simplifying, we obtain

$$e_i = r_f + \beta_\rho[E(r_m) - r_f] + (\beta_\rho - \beta_D)[E(r_m) - r_f]D_{i-1}/E^L_{i-1}$$
$$= r_f + [\beta_\rho + (\beta_\rho - \beta_D)D_{i-1}/E^L_{i-1}][E(r_m) - r_f] \qquad (B7.7)$$

If we compare equations B7.5 and B7.7, we obtain the relationship between the beta for levered equity β_E and the unlevered beta, β_ρ.

$$\beta_E = \beta_\rho + (\beta_\rho - \beta_D)\frac{D_{i-1}}{E^L_{i-1}}$$
$$= \beta_\rho\left(1 + \frac{D_{i-1}}{E^L_{i-1}}\right) - \beta_D\frac{D_{i-1}}{E^L_{i-1}} \qquad (B7.8)$$

APPENDIX C

C7.I THE CALCULATION OF LEVERED VALUES WITH OCFs

In Chapter Six we announced that we would show the difference between the levered values with total cash flows and OCFs. In that chapter we calculated the levered value using the OCFs.

C7.I.I Operating CFD, CFE, TS, FCF, and CCF

As shown in Chapter Six, the OCFs are shown in the table below.

TABLE C7.I   OCFs and non-OFCs

	Year 1	Year 2	Year 3	Year 4	Year 5
Operating FCF	17,043.98	16,434.75	17,556.50	−26,632.16	75,587.07
Operating CFE	12,271.85	11,913.97	13,287.07	−25,745.32	66,564.72
CFD	5,448.84	5,062.15	4,675.46	−616.15	9,346.53
TS	676.71	541.37	406.03	270.68	324.18
Operating FCF + TS	17,720.69	16,976.12	17,962.53	−26,361.47	75,911.25
CFD + Operating CFE	17,720.69	16,976.12	17,962.53	−26,361.47	75,911.25
Non-operating FCF	−12,271.85	−7,442.23	−8,982.11	31,168.40	0.00
Non-operating CFE	−12,271.85	−7,442.23	−8,982.11	31,168.40	0.00

C7.I.2 Standard WACC Applied to the FCF

In the first row of Table A7.1, we list the FCF for the complex example, inclusive of the TV, (this TV is different from the one calculated for total cash flows) calculated using the approach shown in Chapter Nine but using OCFs.[10] The FCF in terminal year 5 includes the TV, which includes the PV of the TSs in perpetuity because the FCF in year 6 has been discounted by the WACC. The annual values of the debt are taken from the loan schedules

[10]As will be studied in Chapter Nine, the terminal value depends on the discount rate for the forecasting period because the terminal value is a function of the levered value of the firm.

TABLE C7.2a   The Levered Value Calculated using the Operating FCF and Traditional WACC

		Year 1	Year 2	Year 3	Year 4	Year 5
FCF with TV		17,043.98	16,434.75	17,556.50	−26,632.16	66,916.43
Debt						
D%		35.15%	32.86%	30.31%	29.13%	15.15%
D(1−T)		7.15%	7.15%	7.15%	7.15%	7.15%
Contribution of debt		2.51%	2.35%	2.17%	2.08%	1.08%
Equity						
E%		64.85%	67.14%	69.69%	70.87%	84.85%
$e_i = \rho_i + (\rho_i - d_i)\frac{D_{i-1}}{E_{i-1}}$		26.42%	25.90%	25.35%	25.11%	22.79%
Contribution of equity		17.13%	17.38%	17.67%	17.80%	19.33%
WACC		19.65%	19.73%	19.83%	19.88%	20.42%
Levered value	50,005.84	42,786.38	34,795.40	24,139.90	55,570.75	
Levered equity value	32,428.93	28,724.85	24,249.25	17,109.14	47,150.45	

for the complex example. The value of the levered equity is equal to the difference between the levered value and the value of debt.

If we calculate the present value of the non-operating FCF discounted at the same rate we used to calculate the return of market reinvestment and add it to the levered value and levered equity we will have.

TABLE C7.2b   The PV of the Non-Operating FCF and the Net Levered Values

	Year 0	Year 1	Year 2	Year 3	Year 4	Year 5
PV(non-operating FCF at r_f)	−1,097.47	11,107.54	19,226.22	29,379.21	0.00	
PV(non-operating CFE at r_f)	−1,097.47	11,107.54	19,226.22	29,379.21	0.00	
Levered val Plus PV(non-oper FCF)	48,908.37	53,893.92	54,021.62	53,519.11	55,570.75	
Levered equity value Plus PV(non-oper FCF)	31,331.46	39,832.39	43,475.47	46,488.34	47,150.45	

C7.1.3 Adjusted WACC applied to the FCF

Next, we illustrate the adjusted WACC applied to the operating FCF for the complex example.

TABLE C7.3a   The Levered Value with the Operating FCF and Adjusted WACC

	Year 0	Year 1	Year 2	Year 3	Year 4	Year 5
Operating FCF with TV		17,043.98	16,434.75	17,556.50	(26,632.16)	66,916.43
Adjusted WACC		19.65%	19.73%	19.83%	19.88%	20.42%
Levered value	50,005.84	42,786.38	34,795.40	24,139.90	55,570.75	

We add the PV of the non-operating FCF at r_f.

TABLE C7.3b **The Levered Value and Equity Value Adjusted with the PV of the Non-Operating FCF**

	Year 0	Year 1	Year 2	Year 3	Year 4	Year 5
PV(non-operating FCF at r_f)	−1,097.47	11,107.54	19,226.22	29,379.21	0.00	
PV(non-operating CFE at r_f)	−1,097.47	11,107.54	19,226.22	29,379.21	0.00	
Levered val Plus PV(non-oper FCF)		48,908.37	53,893.92	54,021.62	53,519.11	55,570.75
Levered equity value Plus PV(non-oper FCF)		31,331.46	39,832.39	43,475.47	46,488.34	47,150.45

C7.1.4 WACC applied to the CCF

When using the WACC applied to the CCF there is no circularity. The CCF is equal to the sum of the CFE and the CFD, which can be obtained from the CB statement. Now we calculate the annual levered values.

TABLE C7.4a **The Levered Value with the CCF**

	Year 0	Year 1	Year 2	Year 3	Year 4	Year 5
CCF		17,720.69	16,976.12	17,962.53	−26,361.47	67,240.61
Discount rate for CCF ρ		21.00%	21.00%	21.00%	21.00%	21.00%
Levered value with CCF	50,005.84	42,786.38	34,795.40	24,139.90	55,570.75	

TABLE C7.4b **The Levered Value and Equity Value Adjusted with the PV of the Non-Operating CCF**

	Year 0	Year 1	Year 2	Year 3	Year 4	Year 5
PV(non-operating CCF at r_f)	−1,097.47	11,107.54	19,226.22	29,379.21	0.00	
PV(non-operating CCF at r_f)	−1,097.47	11,107.54	19,226.22	29,379.21	0.00	
Levered val Plus PV(non-oper CCF)		48,908.37	53,893.92	54,021.62	53,519.11	55,570.75
Levered equity value Plus PV(non-oper CCF)		31,331.46	39,832.39	43,475.47	46,488.34	47,150.45

C7.1.5 Cash Flow to Equity approach

Now we show that the CFE approach gives the same results. The table below shows the results after solving for the circularity.

TABLE C7.5a   The Levered Equity and Total Value from the Operating CFE

	Year 0	Year 1	Year 2	Year 3	Year 4	Year 5
Operating CFE		12,271.85	11,913.97	13,287.07	−25,745.32	57,894.08
$e_i = \rho_i + (\rho_i - d_i)\frac{D_{i-1}}{E_{i-1}}$		26.42%	25.90%	25.35%	25.11%	22.79%
Equity value	32,428.93	28,724.85	24,249.25	17,109.14	47,150.45	
Debt	17,576.91	14,061.53	10,546.15	7,030.77	8,420.30	
Levered value	50,005.84	42,786.38	34,795.40	24,139.90	55,570.75	

TABLE C7.5b   The Levered Value and Equity Value Adjusted with the PV of the Non-Operating CFE

	Year 0	Year 1	Year 2	Year 3	Year 4	Year 5
PV(non-operating FCF at r_f)	−1,097.47	11,107.54	19,226.22	29,379.21	0.00	
PV(non-operating CFE at r_f)	−1,097.47	11,107.54	19,226.22	29,379.21	0.00	
Levered val Plus PV(non-oper FCF)	48,908.37	53,893.92	54,021.62	53,519.11	55,570.75	
Levered equity value Plus PV(non-oper FCF)	31,331.46	39,832.39	43,475.47	46,488.34	47,150.45	

From the previous tables we can see that all the levered values match. Now we can see the differences between levered values calculated with OCFs and total cash flows.

TABLE C7.6   Comparison of the Levered Values

	Total cash flow	OCF	Difference	OCF + Non-OCF	Difference
Total levered value	44,250.80	50,005.84	13.01%	48,908.37	10.53%
Levered equity	26,673.89	32,428.93	21.58%	31,331.46	17.46%

As predicted, the levered values with OCFs and OCFs plus the PV of non-OCF are higher than those calculated with the total cash flows. The OCFs assume that all available funds are distributed. The calculation with the total cash flows assume that each year the cash excess can be reinvested at market rates that are lower than the WACC.

C7.1.6 Total and Levered Values with Different Assumptions Regarding Reinvestment

On the other hand, if we assume that the reinvestment rate is the WACC, in one case, or if we assume that there is no reinvestment and all the available cash is distributed, that is, given (virtually) to the equity holders, the results of the differences and overestimation of levered and equity values are as follows:

TABLE C7.7   Comparison Levered and Equity Values for Different Assumptions Regarding Reinvestment

	Levered Value	Difference	Equity	Difference
With WACC as reinvestment rate	46,836.54	5.84%	29,259.63	9.69%
No reinvestment and all cash excess to CFE	49,505.39	11.87%	31,928.48	19.70%
Total FCF	44,250.80	0.00%	26,673.89	0.00%

Again, as expected, the levered and equity values are much higher when calculated assuming reinvestment at WACC and/or assuming no reinvestment at all and any excess cash is assumed to be distributed (virtual distribution because those funds are retained in the firm).

8

ESTIMATING THE WACC FOR NON-TRADED FIRMS

Statistician: A man who believes figures don't lie, but admits that under analysis some of them won't stand up either.

—Evan Esar (1899 to 1995), Esar's Comic Dictionary

8.1 PRACTICAL APPROACHES TO THE COST OF CAPITAL FOR TRADED AND NON-TRADED FIRMS

In Chapter Seven, we presented the general conceptual framework for the weighted average cost of capital (WACC) in the context of perfect capital markets. One of the most common methods for determining the appropriate value for the cost of capital is the capital asset pricing model (CAPM). Despite the many conceptual and empirical shortcomings of the CAPM, it is a useful framework for thinking about the estimation of the cost of capital for traded firms. In the previous chapters, we heroically assumed that the CAPM is a suitable model for estimating and calculating the cost of capital for traded firms.

The key idea is to calculate one of the following two parameters: e, the levered cost of equity or ρ, the unlevered cost of equity. If the levered return e is known for a given period, the initial period, for instance, the unlevered return ρ can be calculated. On the contrary, if the unlevered return ρ is known, the levered return e can be calculated. Both the return to unlevered equity ρ and the return to levered equity e cannot be independent variables. In other words, at the same time, we cannot have ρ and e as inputs. For this reason several options to calculate the levered and unlevered returns with only systematic risk are presented. In general, we need ρ or e as a starting point to use the procedure described in Chapter Seven.

In this chapter, we examine some practical approaches for estimating the cost of capital for non-traded firms. By definition, the CAPM does not apply to non-traded firms. Furthermore, the stringent requirements of the CAPM might not be satisfied for many firms, both traded and non-traded, in emerging markets.

To estimate the cost of capital for a non-traded firm, we find the appropriate information for a set of traded firms that are similar in key respects to the non-traded firm and assume that the cost of capital derived from the traded firms is appropriate for the non-traded firm. For example, we select traded firms for which the size, market share, operating environment, and leverage are comparable to the non-traded firm.

The chapter is organized as follows. First, we derive the relationship between the betas for an unlevered firm and a levered firm. The difference in the betas of the unlevered and levered firms measures the impact of leverage on the risk of the return to the levered equity holder, relative to the unlevered equity holder. Second, we briefly review the use of the CAPM for estimating the cost of capital for traded firms. Third, we discuss the estimation of the cost of capital in contexts where the assumptions of the CAPM are not satisfied. In particular, we refer to non-traded firms in developed markets and firms, both traded and non-traded, in emerging markets.

8.2 FINDING THE RELATIONSHIP BETWEEN LEVERED AND UNLEVERED BETAS

In this section we present the basic derivation of the formulas that relate the beta of the unlevered firm with the beta of the levered firm. If we know the beta for an unlevered firm, we can lever it to find the beta for a levered firm; conversely, if we know the beta for a levered firm, we can unlever it to find the beta for an unlevered firm.

In Chapter Seven, for finite cash flows, we derived the following general expression for the return to levered equity e. The return to levered equity is a function of two ratios: the debt–equity ratio and the ratio of the present value (PV) of the tax shield (TS) to the value of levered equity. Because the return to levered equity is a function of the PV of the TS, it is a function of the appropriate discount rate for the TS

$$e_i = \rho_i + (\rho_i - d_i)\frac{D_{i-1}}{EL_{i-1}} - (\rho_i - \psi_i)\frac{V^{TS}_{i-1}}{EL_{i-1}} \qquad (8.1)$$

where e_i is the return to levered equity in year i,

ρ_i is the return to unlevered equity in year i,
d_i is the cost of debt in year i,
D_{i-1} is the market value of debt in the beginning of year i,
E^L_{i-1} is the market value of equity in the beginning of year i,
ψ_i is the appropriate discount rate for the tax savings in year i, and
V^{TS}_{i-1} is the value of tax savings at the beginning of year i.

Depending on whether the cash flows are finite or in perpetuity and the appropriate discount rate for the TS, we can rewrite the expression for the return to levered equity.

If we assume that the appropriate discount rate for the tax savings ψ_i is equal to the cost of debt d_i, equation 8.1 can be rewritten as follows:

$$e = \rho_i + (\rho_i - d_i)\frac{D_{i-1}}{E^L_{i-1}} - (\rho_i - d_i)\frac{V^{TS}_{i-1}}{E^L_{i-1}} \tag{8.2}$$

This expression is valid for finite cash flows or cash flows in perpetuity. Equation 8.1 can be simplified further based on whether the cash flows are finite or in perpetuity.

If the cash flows (with no growth) are in perpetuity and the discount rate for the tax shield is d_i, then V^{TS}_{i-1}, the (present) value of the tax savings, is TD_{i-1} and the expression for e_i is as follows. This is the most common formulation for the return to levered equity e. For the advanced reader, we note that in a more sophisticated analysis, the specification of the stochastic process for the cash flows in perpetuity, without and with growth, would raise additional subtle complexities.

$$\begin{aligned} e &= \rho_i + (\rho_i - d_i)\frac{D_{i-1}}{E^L_{i-1}} - (\rho_i - d_i)\frac{TD_{i-1}}{E^L_{i-1}} \\ &= \rho_i + (\rho_i - d_i)(1 - T)\frac{D_{i-1}}{E^L_{i-1}} \end{aligned} \tag{8.3}$$

Alternatively, if the cash flows are finite, the formula for the return to levered equity e is as follows. This formulation for the return to levered equity e is less well known.

$$e = \rho_i + (\rho_i - d_i)\left(\frac{D_{i-1} - V^{TS}_{i-1}}{E^L_{i-1}}\right) \tag{8.4}$$

If we assume that ψ_i, the appropriate discount rate for tax savings is ρ_i rather than the cost of debt d_i, equation 8.1 can be simplified as follows:

$$\begin{aligned} e &= \rho_i + (\rho_i - d_i)\frac{D_{i-1}}{E^L_{i-1}} - (\rho_i - \rho_i)\frac{V^{TS}_{i-1}}{E^L_{i-1}} \\ &= \rho_i + (\rho_i - d_i)\frac{D_{i-1}}{E^L_{i-1}} \end{aligned} \tag{8.5}$$

This expression is valid for both cash flows in perpetuity and finite cash flows.

Using the expression for the return to levered equity and the CAPM, we can determine the relationship between the betas for the levered and unlevered firms.

Based on the CAPM we can write the following expressions for the unlevered return, the levered return and the cost of debt.

$$\rho = r_f + \beta_{unlev}(R_m - r_f) \tag{8.6}$$

$$e = r_f + \beta_{lev}(R_m - r_f) \tag{8.7}$$

$$d = r_f + \beta_D(R_m - r_f) \tag{8.8}$$

where r_f is the risk-free rate,

R_m is the expected return on the market portfolio,
β_{unlev} is the beta for the unlevered firm,
β_{lev} is the beta for the levered firm, and
β_D is the beta for the debt.

Substituting equations 8.6 to 8.8 into equations 8.3 and 8.5, the levered β's can be written in two ways as follows:

$$\beta_{lev} = \beta_{unlev} + (\beta_{unlev} - \beta_D)(1 - T)\frac{D_{i-1}}{E^L_{i-1}} \tag{8.9}$$

and

$$\beta_{lev} = \beta_{unlev} + (\beta_{unlev} - \beta_D)\frac{D_{i-1}}{E^L_{i-1}} \tag{8.10}$$

It is important to be clear about the reasons for the different expressions for the return to levered equity in equations 8.3 and 8.5 and the corresponding expressions for the betas in equations 8.9 and 8.10. Expression 8.3 is valid only for cash flows in perpetuity and assumes that the discount rate for the TS is equal to the cost of debt. Expression 8.5 holds for both finite cash flows and cash flow in perpetuity and assumes that the discount rate for the TS is equal to the return to unlevered equity.

Typically, when we work with finite cash flows and assume that the discount rate for the TS is the cost of debt, these formulas cannot be used. For finite cash flows, we use the following expression.

$$\beta_{lev} = \beta_{unlev} + (\beta_{unlev} - \beta_D)\left(\frac{D_{i-1} - V^{TS}_{i-1}}{E^L_{i-1}}\right) \tag{8.11}$$

For cash flows in perpetuity, we use equation 8.9. Dropping the subscript $i - 1$ and the superscript L, we solve for the unlevered beta.

$$\beta_{\text{unlev}} = \frac{\beta_{\text{lev}} + \left[\beta_D \frac{D_{\text{lev}}}{E_{\text{lev}}}(1-T)\right]}{\left[1 + \frac{D_{\text{lev}}}{E_{\text{lev}}}(1-T)\right]} \tag{8.12}$$

where $\psi_i = d_i$.

If we assume that the discount rate for the tax savings is not d_i but ρ_i, we use equation 8.10 and solve for the unlevered beta.

$$\beta_{\text{unlev}} = \frac{\beta_{\text{lev}} + \left[\beta_D \frac{D_{\text{lev}}}{E_{\text{lev}}}\right]}{\left[1 + \frac{D_{\text{lev}}}{E_{\text{lev}}}\right]} \tag{8.13}$$

As mentioned earlier, we assume that the unlevered beta for the proxy (traded) firm is comparable to the unlevered beta for the nontraded firm.

$$\beta^{\text{Proxy}}{}_\rho = \beta^{\text{NonTrad}}{}_\rho \tag{8.14}$$

8.3 VALUATION FOR TRADED FIRMS

Typically the cost of capital and cost of equity are calculated on the assumption that the firm is traded. We do the same in this section. Usually we do not need to estimate the value for a traded firm because we can get it easily by opening the business section of the newspaper or visiting the appropriate web page for the traded firm.

8.3.1 Estimating the Return to Levered Equity e for a Traded Firm

We use the CAPM to calculate the WACC with three different formulations.

1. After-tax WACC applied to the FCF.
2. Adjusted WACC applied to the FCF.
3. WACC applied to the capital cash flow (CCF).

8.3.2 Using the CAPM to Find the Cost of Capital

For simplicity, in the current discussion we drop the time subscripts.

$$\text{After-tax WACC}^{\text{FCF}} = \frac{d(1-T)D}{V^L} + \frac{eE^L}{V^L} \tag{8.15}$$

We use the following equations based on the CAPM to find values for the cost of debt d and the return to levered equity e.

$$d = r_f + \beta_D(R_m - r_f) \tag{8.16}$$

$$e = r_f + \beta_{lev}(R_m - r_f) \tag{8.17}$$

After we obtain the values for the cost of debt and the return to levered equity, we calculate the after-tax WACC applied to the FCF by substituting the values into equation 8.15.

We use the following values for the parameters. Assume that the expected return on the market portfolio R_m is 18%, the risk-free rate r_f is 8%, and the beta for the debt is 0.300. Substituting the appropriate values into equation 8.16, we obtain that the cost of debt d is 11%.

$$d = r_f + \beta_D(R_m - r_f)$$
$$= 8\% + 0.300 \times [18\% - 8\%] = 11.00\%$$

Assume that the beta for the levered equity is 2.057. Substituting the appropriate values into equation 8.17, we obtain that the return to levered equity e, for a leverage of 40%, is 28.57%.

$$e = r_f + \beta_{lev}(R_m - r_f)$$
$$= 8\% + 2.057 \times [18\% - 8\%] = 28.57\%$$

Previously, in Chapter Seven, these values for the cost of debt and return to levered equity were used to calculate the after-tax WACC applied to the FCF.

8.3.3 Adjusted WACC Applied to the FCF

The formula for the adjusted WACC applied to the FCF depends on the return to unlevered equity. Here we assume that the discount rate for the TS is equal to the return to unlevered equity.

$$WACC^{FCF} = \rho - TdD/V^L \tag{8.18}$$

From a practical point of view, we do not observe the "return to unlevered equity ρ" because we simply do not observe a sufficient number of firms with zero debt financing that are comparable to the firms with a given level of leverage. Thus, we must estimate the return to unlevered equity ρ indirectly by first estimating the return to levered equity e, which in turn is based on estimating the beta for the levered firm.

Again, we assume that the discount rate for the TS is equal to the return to unlevered equity ρ. In this formulation of the WACC, we must use the unlevered beta β_ρ. However, the unlevered beta β_ρ cannot be observed. Even though we cannot estimate the unlevered beta β_ρ directly, we express the return to unlevered equity in the framework of the CAPM.

In equation 8.13 we found the relationship between the levered and unlevered β when we assumed that the discount rate for the TS is the unlevered cost of equity ρ.

$$\beta_{\text{unlev}} = \frac{\beta_{\text{lev}} + \left[\beta_D \frac{D}{E}\right]}{\left[1 + \frac{D}{E}\right]} \tag{8.19}$$

Based on the unlevered beta in equation 8.19, we use the following equation to find the return to unlevered equity ρ.

$$\rho = r_f + \beta_{\text{unlev}}(R_m - r_f) \tag{8.20}$$

For instance, there is a stock traded at the stock exchange with a beta β_{proxy} of 2.0571, a debt D_{proxy} of 80, E_{proxy} worth 120, and we desire to estimate the unlevered beta for a stock not registered in the stock exchange. The debt equity ratio is 0.667, the beta for the debt is 0.300, and the beta for the levered equity is 2.057. Substituting these values into equation 8.19, we obtain that the unlevered beta is 1.354.

$$\beta_{\text{unlev}} = \frac{\beta_{\text{lev}} + \left[\beta_D \frac{D}{E}\right]}{\left[1 + \frac{D}{E}\right]} = \frac{2.057 + 0.30 \times 0.667}{1 + 0.667} = 1.354$$

Using equation 8.20, we obtain that the return to unlevered equity is 21.54%.

$$\rho = r_f + \beta_{\text{unlev}}(R_m - r_f)$$
$$= 8\% + 1.354 \times [18\% - 8\%] = 21.54\%$$

With the value for the return to unlevered equity ρ, we can calculate the adjusted WACC applied to the FCF in equation 8.18.

8.3.4 WACC Applied to the CCF

Assuming that the discount rate for the TS is equal to the return to unlevered equity, the WACC applied to the CCF is equal to the return to unlevered equity ρ.

$$\text{WACC}^{\text{CCF}} = \rho \tag{8.21}$$

We can show that the unlevered beta is a weighted average of the levered beta and the beta for debt. Previously, from equation 8.10, we have the following expression for the beta for levered equity.

$$\beta_{lev} = \beta_{unlev} + (\beta_{unlev} - \beta_D)\frac{D_{i-1}}{E^L_{i-1}} \tag{8.22}$$

Rearranging the expression, we obtain

$$\beta_{lev} + \beta_D\frac{D_{i-1}}{E^L_{i-1}} = \beta_{unlev}\left(1 + \frac{D_{i-1}}{E^L_{i-1}}\right) \tag{8.23}$$

and

$$\frac{\beta_{lev}E^L_{i-1} + \beta_D D_{i-1}}{E^L_{i-1}} = \beta_{unlev}\left(\frac{E^L_{i-1} + D_{i-1}}{E^L_{i-1}}\right) \tag{8.24}$$

Multiply by E^L_{i-1}.

$$\beta_{lev}E^L_{i-1} + \beta_D D_{i-1} = \beta_{unlev}\left(E^L_{i-1} + D_{i-1}\right) \tag{8.25}$$

Solving for β_{unlev}, we obtain

$$\beta_{unlev} = \frac{\beta_{lev}E^L_{i-1} + \beta_D D_{i-1}}{E^L_{i-1} + D_{i-1}} \tag{8.26}$$

We substitute the value of the unlevered beta into equation 8.20 and estimate the WACC applied to the CCF.

We verify that the beta for the WACC applied to the CCF is a weighted average of the beta for debt and the beta for levered equity.

$$\beta_{unlev} = \frac{\beta_{lev}E^L_{i-1}}{V^L} + \frac{\beta_D D_{i-1}}{V^L}$$
$$= 2.057 \times 60\% + 0.300 \times 40\% = 1.354$$

And this is the same value we found using equation 8.20.
The return to unlevered equity is then 21.54%.

$$\rho = 8\% + 1.354 \times (19\% - 8\%) = 21.54\%$$

8.4 VALUATION FOR NON-TRADED FIRMS

For traded firms, we have been working with the heroic assumptions regarding the validity of the CAPM, which is the predominant model for estimating the risk associated with an asset. To review briefly, the CAPM states that in equilibrium assets should be priced such that the expected return is equal to the risk-free rate of interest plus a premium for risk. The premium for risk is equal to the beta of the asset (a measure of the sensitivity of the return of the assets in terms of the market return) multiplied by the market risk premium (market return, R_m minus risk-free rate, r_f). The CAPM is used as an *ex ante* model. This means that it calculates a point estimate for the future return. To do this we have to substitute into the model the expected values for the risk-free rate, the market return, and the beta for the asset. Usually we use the historical values for these parameters.

It is easy to predict that when we do not have sufficient publicly available financial information the CAPM fails, because in its essence the CAPM requires historical data that usually is not available for small and medium enterprises (SME) and non-traded firms. There are many authors who believe that the CAPM and other similar models do not apply even in many developed markets. What to say of emerging markets? Clearly, the heroic assumptions of the CAPM are not valid in emerging markets.

In Chapter One we presented the stock market in Colombia to illustrate the situation with regard to firms in emerging markets. The lack of information imposes restrictions on the access to equity funds. Because well-known methods, such as the CAPM, might not be valid in the context of non-traded firms (most of them SME) in emerging markets, we have to provide alternative methods to estimate the return to equity.

8.4.1 Valuing Firms, both Traded and Non-traded, in Emerging Markets

The emerging markets are important in their own right and it is necessary to assess the relevance of typical models, such as the CAPM, for non-traded firms, especially in emerging markets.

Bruner et al. (2002) mention four reasons to justify the study of non-traded firms and emerging markets. First, "there is currently no clear single 'best practice' for valuation [. . .] in emerging markets." [. . .] Even there is "substantial disagreement about fundamental issues, such as estimating the cost of capital [. . .]." Second, there are differences between emerging and developed markets regarding "accounting transparency, liquidity, corruption, volatility, governance, taxes and transaction costs." Third, the World

Bank reports that during 2000, "US$300 million flowed into some 150 countries not regarded as developed," of which more than 83% went into 30 countries "most widely followed by international investors." Fourth, those 30 emerging countries "grow at real rates two or three times higher than developed countries."

On the other hand, Bekaert and Harvey (2003) show using a survey on 16 countries,[1] that U.S. holdings have been increased 11.3 times from 5 years before liberalization of the economy[2] to 5 years after liberalization[3] of the economy, ranging from 4.9 for Philippines to 28.4 for Greece. And the U.S. share of market capitalization has doubled ranging from 0.9 times for Philippines to 17.9 times for Brazil.[4]

Usually we reject any model or approach that is not consistent with the CAPM. However, when working with an emerging market, do we think the conditions in an emerging market are consistent with the assumptions of the CAPM? What would we do with the CAPM when frequently in the emerging markets we have negative risk market premium? What can we do when the best proxy to the risk-free rate is at a level higher than the market rate for short-term deposit in any financial institution?

Another fact we have to recognize is that usually non-traded firms are not for sale and, even in the U.S., the investors in non-traded firms might not be fully diversified. Thus, what degree of consistency with the CAPM could we expect from all these firms? If we set the standard for the non-traded firms in developed markets and the firms in emerging markets so as to comply with the CAPM, all the valuation of the firms would be wrong. What we are doing in that case is to set a standard that we know in advance is not valid. As we said earlier, many people think that the CAPM is not valid even in developed markets.

We cannot close our minds and continue to think that the CAPM is the absolute truth. We know that if we do not have a better model, we have to use the CAPM. However, when dealing with emerging markets and non-traded firms, is it better to use a model we know is wrong or should we use accounting betas? Is it better that we subjectively estimate the levered

---

[1]These countries are Argentina, Brazil, Chile, Colombia, Greece, India, Indonesia, Korea, Malaysia, Mexico, Philippines, Portugal, Taiwan, Thailand, Turkey and Venezuela.

[2]Bekaert and Harvey provide a website with detailed time lines for 45 emerging markets that provided the basis for the dates in Bekaert and Harvey (2000). See http://www.duke.edu:80/~charvey/Country_risk/chronology/chronology_index.htm.

[3]"By financial liberalization, [the authors] mean allowing inward and outward foreign equity investment. In a liberalized equity market, foreign investors can, without restriction, purchase or sell domestic securities. In addition, domestic investors can purchase or sell foreign securities."

[4]The authors made the calculations for the increase in average and individual U.S. holdings and the U.S. share of market capitalization.

return e or the unlevered return ρ? Is it better to use comparables or unlevered betas?

Does it make any sense to use a model that might be good for the 7,510 traded firms, as mentioned in Chapter One, but that is probably wrong for many of the 2,210,077 firms with more than 4 employees and fewer than 1,000, and definitely wrong for the 3,389,161 firms with fewer than 5 employees in the U.S.? Many would answer this question by saying that the 7,510 firms have a value much higher than the others. That is true, but it is also true that those firms do not need methods for valuing the firm such as the discounted cash flow (DCF) method. Investors can buy a newspaper or visit the stock exchange website and immediately know the market value of the firm.

Does it make any sense to use the CAPM for investors, who we assume are diversified, when they definitely are not? Perhaps the challenge is to modify those proxy methods that presumably measure the systematic (market) risk and find ways to include the non-systematic risk in some way. Are these ways inconsistent with the CAPM? Yes, they might be. The problem is not that reality is inconsistent with the model. The problem is that the model is inconsistent with reality. This is the issue. Unfortunately, many people try to force reality to comply with the model.

These critical comments on the CAPM are not intended to disqualify the CAPM. Many have tried and the CAPM is still alive and well. Our goal is to offer alternative valuation tools for non-traded firms, or traded and non-traded firms in emerging markets.

8.4.2 Systematic Risk and Total Risk

We have to realize that most of the investors in non-traded firms might not be diversified. Some procedures for estimating the cost of capital capture total risk (systematic and non-systematic), while others capture only systematic risk. The methods that include total risk are those based on subjective assessment of risk, and those based on the analysis of historical data include only systematic risk.

In the valuation of non-traded firms, we have to define whether the risky cash flows have to be valued with total or systematic risk in the discount rate.

There is ample evidence that for non-traded firms (in particular, small enterprises) some additional premium have to be considered. To mention a couple of papers, we quote McMahon and Stanger (1995) and Heaton (1998).

McMahon and Stanger (1995) say that the financial objective function for small enterprises has to be redefined, taking into account several dimensions: Return, Risk, Liquidity, Diversification, Transferability, Flexibility, Control, and Accountability. They recognize that some returns might be pecuniary and others might be non-pecuniary. In particular, on unsystematic risk they state

"[...] there is need to comment on the nature of risk from the viewpoint of small enterprise owner-manager. Contrary to precepts of existing financial thought, there is good reason to believing both systematic and unsystematic risk are important to owner-manager of small enterprises. [...] The principal sources of unsystematic or enterprise or specific risk, which appear to require attention, and which should be made explicit in the financial objective function of a small enterprise [...]."

[...]

"In summary, the available empirical evidence on the small firm effect suggests that it exists and persists on stock exchanges around the world, and that this is so for main boards and second boards. There is some evidence which is not conclusive that the cause of small firm effect may be related to the limited availability of information on listed small enterprises, and to a lack of marketability of their shares. Hence, it is argued that ignorance and illiquidity confront investors in small enterprises with greater unique or unsystematic risk, and that they therefore expect to receive higher returns than would be predicted from the CAPM which prices only systematic risk. It is probable that the existence of transaction costs which bear more heavily on small enterprises, and which CAPM assumes away, also plays a part in accounting for the small firm effect."

On the other hand, Heaton (1995) states

"An appraiser must also consider the impact on required return of smallness itself beyond the systematic risk captured by beta. In a study on the effect of size on required return, Banz [1981] found that returns for small companies were substantially higher, even after the adjustments for beta risk had been made. In one test, Banz created portfolios with identical beta risk, and found "the average excess return from holding very small firms long and very large firms short is, on average, 1.52% per month or 19.8% on an annualized basis".

[...]

"Because of the difficulty of estimating the cost of capital of small illiquid businesses, venture capital companies which specialize in buying and selling small illiquid businesses, will often use a discount rate of 20–50% for the cost of equity capital.".

Bekaert (1995) distinguishes "[...] barriers arising from emerging market specific risks (EMSRs) that discourage foreign investment and lead to de facto segmentation.[5] EMSRs include liquidity risk, political risk,[6] economic policy risk, and perhaps currency risk."[7] Contrary to what some might think, these risks are not diversifiable. Hence, they become part of the total risk. Bekaert and Harvey (2003) note that "[...] World Bank surveys of institutional investors in developed markets found that liquidity problems were seen as major impediments to investing in emerging markets."

[5]According to Bekaert and Harvey (2003), "a segmented (integrated) country is a country that imposes taxes (no taxes) on incoming and outgoing investments."

[6]Political risk can be measured as the yield spread on dollar-denominated emerging market bonds, relative to dollar yields. The yield spread is the difference between the yield on dollar-denominated emerging market bonds and the dollar yields.

[7]Bekaert and Harvey (2003).

Moreover, Bekaert et al. (1997) find "political risk to be priced in emerging market securities."

In summary, there is evidence that non-traded firms (SME) and even traded firms in emerging markets bear some non-diversifiable risk that has to be included in the total risk measurements.

8.4.3 The Estimation of the Cost of Levered Equity with Systematic Risk

As mentioned earlier, the situation of non-traded firms or firms in emerging markets is that either the orthodox approach, such as the CAPM and other similar models, does not work or there is lack of data. Given these restrictions we have to develop approaches that allow us to solve the problem.

Many practitioners use betas or market risk premiums derived for the 500 S&P in the U.S., and then add a country risk premium. This country risk premium is usually the spread between the yield U.S. Treasury Bills and the yield of sovereign debt in U.S. dollars issued by a country. Others use comparable stocks and so on. We list and describe procedures that include those approaches.

If the firm is non-traded and we believe that the CAPM is an appropriate model for estimating the cost of capital, we must find a set of traded firms that are comparable to the non-traded firm in terms of size, leverage, and industry characteristics. For simplicity in the exposition, we assume that there is one traded firm that is comparable to the non-traded firm. We call the traded firm the proxy firm.

8.4.3.1 Using a proxy traded firm

Because we assume that ψ_i, the appropriate discount rate for tax savings, is ρ, we use equation 8.13.

$$\beta_{\text{unlev}} = \frac{\beta_{\text{lev}} + \left[\beta_D \frac{D_{\text{lev}}}{E_{\text{lev}}}\right]}{\left[1 + \frac{D_{\text{lev}}}{E_{\text{lev}}}\right]} \tag{8.27}$$

Changing the subscript from Lev to Proxy, we have

$$\beta_{\text{unlev}} = \frac{\beta_{\text{proxy}} + \left[\beta_D \frac{D_{\text{proxy}}}{E_{\text{proxy}}}\right]}{\left[1 + \frac{D_{\text{proxy}}}{E_{\text{proxy}}}\right]} = \beta^{\text{nontraded}}_{\rho} \tag{8.28}$$

where D_{proxy} is the market value of debt for the proxy firm and E_{proxy} is the market value of equity for the proxy firm.

These calculations should not be made for a single isolated proxy firm. We should identify the industry sector where the firm operates, calculate the unlevered betas for many similar firms in that business line, take a weighted (by sales or operating income) average of these unlevered betas, and lever up the beta for the non-traded firm. When doing this we have to be aware that the market value of equity has to be calculated and this creates circularity (this has been solved in Chapter Seven).

An alternative is to assume that the debt equity ratio for the non-traded firm will converge to the average of the traded firms in the same business line.

Using equation 8.10 we obtain the following expression:

$$\beta_{\text{not traded}} = \beta_{\text{unlev}} + (\beta_{\text{unlev}} - \beta_{\text{D}}) \frac{D_{\text{not traded}}}{E_{\text{not traded}}} \qquad (8.29)$$

Rearranging the previous equation we have

$$\beta_{\text{not traded}} = \beta_{\text{unlev}} \left[1 + \frac{D_{\text{not traded}}}{E_{\text{not traded}}} \right] - \left[\beta_{\text{D}} \frac{D_{\text{not traded}}}{E_{\text{not traded}}} \right] \qquad (8.30)$$

where, $\beta_{\text{non-traded}}$ is the levered beta for the stock not registered at the stock exchange, $D_{\text{not traded}}$ is the market value of debt, $E_{\text{non-traded}}$ is the equity market value for the stock not registered in the stock. In this case, we assume that ρ is the discount rate for the tax savings.

If the debt is risk-free, the β_{D} is zero, and substituting β_{unlev} from equation 8.28 into equation 8.30, we obtain the following well-known equation:

$$\beta_{\text{not traded}} = \beta_{\text{proxy}} \frac{\left[1 + \frac{D_{\text{not traded}}}{E_{\text{not traded}}} \right]}{\left[1 + \frac{D_{\text{proxy}}}{E_{\text{proxy}}} \right]} \qquad (8.31)$$

Using the following illustrative values and assuming risk-free debt ($\beta_{\text{D}} = 0$), the beta for the non-traded firm is 1.071.

$$\beta_{\text{nt}} = \beta_{\text{proxy}} \frac{\left[1 + \frac{D_{\text{not traded}}}{E_{\text{not traded}}} \right]}{\left[1 + \frac{D_{\text{proxy}}}{E_{\text{proxy}}} \right]} = 1.3 \frac{\left[1 + \frac{70}{145} \right]}{\left[1 + \frac{80}{100} \right]} = 1.3 \times \frac{1.48275862}{1.8} = 1.071$$

Recall that the equity for the non-traded firm is unknown. That value is what we are looking for. Hence, there is circularity when using this approach.

With the beta for the non-traded firm, and keeping in mind the issue of circularity, we calculate the cost of levered equity, e, as

$$e_{\text{not traded}} = r_f + \beta_{\text{not traded}} (R_m - r_f) \qquad (8.32)$$

where $e_{\text{not traded}}$ is the return to levered equity for the non-traded and $\beta_{\text{not traded}}$ is the beta for the non-traded firm.

8.4.3.2 Accounting betas

Next we discuss an approach that is based on book value. The book values are adjusted by either inflation adjustments or asset revaluation and thus, the book values are good proxies to the market values. The models developed to predict risks using accounting information are referred to as accounting risk models (ARMs). Among these models is the regression of several accounting variables of a firm: for instance, the accounting return, the quick ratio, the current ratio, and the book leverage. These models assume that the accounting information incorporates information that allows us to measure risk.

We can measure the accounting return of a firm by using the following expression:

$$e_t = \frac{D_t + E_t + ER_t - NEI_t}{E_{t-1}} - 1 \qquad (8.33)$$

where e_t is the return to equity in period t, D_t is the dividends paid in period t, E_t is the equity in period t, ER_t is equity repurchase in period t, NEI_t is the new equity investment in period t, and E_{t-1} is the equity in period $t-1$.

We present an example for a public firm and we use the accounting return measured as dividends plus equity divided by the book value of equity of the previous year.[8] We do not conduct any regression models at his time. Instead, we calculate the average of some indexes and from that we estimate the return to equity (see Tables 8.1 and 8.2).

TABLE 8.1 Financial Information for Compañía Nacional de Chocolates

Date	Book value for equity E	Dividends paid D	$e_t = ((D_t + E_t)/E_{t-1}) - 1$
Mar-95	546,700.52	$0	
Jun-95	563,745.79	$0	3.12%
Sep-95	549,097.79	$0	−2.60%
Dec-95	561,882.38	$0	2.33%
Mar-96	544,304.62	$0	−3.13%
Jun-96	566,816.16	$0	4.14%
Sep-96	567,560.62	$0	0.13%
Dec-96	608,808.37	$0	7.27%
Mar-97	719,957.35	$0	18.26%
Jun-97	846,828.94	$7,381	18.65%
Sep-97	885,689.07	$7,496	5.47%

(continues)

[8]In this particular case there was no new equity, nor equity repurchase.

TABLE 8.1 (*continued*)

Date	Book value for equity E	Dividends paid D	$e_t = ((D_t + E_t)/E_{t-1}) - 1$
Dec-97	831,811.47	$7,512	−5.23%
Mar-98	673,276.10	$7,842	−18.12%
Jun-98	676,738.46	$8,770	1.82%
Sep-98	547,263.97	$11,559	−17.42%
Dec-98	633,984.09	$6,401	17.02%
Mar-99	643,547.71	$9,614	3.02%
Jun-99	688,732.37	$10,525	8.66%
Sep-99	673,644.99	$10,481	−0.67%
Dec-99	711,111.20	$10,602	7.14%
Mar-00	698,350.90	$11,249	−0.21%
Jun-00	677,131.00	$11,721	−1.36%
Sep-00	688,043.00	$11,662	3.33%
Dec-00	701,038.17	$11,743	3.60%
Mar-01	616,113.11	$12,382	−10.35%
Jun-01	655,407.67	$167,457	33.56%
Sep-01	638,510.79	$0	−2.58%
Dec-01	639,569.92	$0	0.17%

TABLE 8.2 **Macroeconomic Information**

Date	Consumer price Index (CPI)	Inflation $i_f = (CPI_t/CPI_{t-1}) - 1$	Risk-free rate r_f	Real interest rate $i_r = ((1 + r_f)/(1 + i_f)) - 1$	Risk premium $i_\theta = e_t - R_{ft}$
Mar-95	54.21				
Jun-95	57.03	5.19%	6.97%	1.70%	−3.86%
Sep-95	58.33	2.28%	6.74%	4.36%	−9.34%
Dec-95	59.86	2.63%	6.97%	4.23%	−4.64%
Mar-96	65.17	8.87%	6.98%	−1.74%	−10.11%
Jun-96	68.27	4.75%	6.85%	2.01%	−2.71%
Sep-96	70.90	3.85%	6.53%	2.58%	−6.40%
Dec-96	72.81	2.70%	6.16%	3.36%	1.11%
Mar-97	77.51	6.46%	5.79%	−0.63%	12.47%
Jun-97	81.01	4.52%	5.47%	0.91%	13.18%
Sep-97	83.67	3.28%	5.28%	1.94%	0.19%
Dec-97	85.69	2.41%	5.36%	2.88%	−10.60%
Mar-98	92.43	7.87%	6.78%	−1.01%	−24.90%
Jun-98	97.78	5.79%	7.19%	1.32%	−5.37%
Sep-98	98.57	0.80%	7.79%	6.93%	−25.22%
Dec-98	100.00	1.45%	7.19%	5.65%	9.83%
Mar-99	104.92	4.92%	5.22%	0.28%	−2.19%
Jun-99	106.55	1.55%	4.33%	2.74%	4.32%
Sep-99	107.76	1.14%	4.55%	3.38%	−5.22%
Dec-99	109.23	1.36%	3.52%	2.13%	3.61%
Mar-00	115.12	5.39%	3.22%	−2.06%	−3.43%
Jun-00	116.85	1.50%	3.57%	2.04%	−4.93%

(*continues*)

TABLE 8.2 (*continued*)

Date	Consumer price Index (CPI)	Inflation $i_f = (CPI_t/CPI_{t-1})$ -1	Risk-free rate r_f	Real interest rate $i_r = ((1 + r_f)/(1 + i_f))$ -1	Risk premium $i_\theta = e_t - R_{ft}$
Sep-00	117.68	0.71%	3.41%	2.68%	−0.07%
Dec-00	118.79	0.94%	3.15%	2.18%	0.45%
Mar-01	124.12	4.49%	3.23%	−1.20%	−13.58%
Jun-01	126.12	1.61%	3.08%	1.45%	30.47%
Sep-01	127.06	0.75%	2.91%	2.14%	−5.48%
Dec-01	127.87	0.64%	2.82%	2.16%	−2.65%
			Average	1.94%	−2.41%

The risk premium is calculated from the CAPM formulation.

$$e = r_f + \beta(R_m - r_f) \Rightarrow$$

$$\text{Risk premium} = \beta(R_m - r_f) = e - r_f$$

For instance from Tables 8.1 and 8.2, for December 2001, the risk premium is −2.65%.

$$\text{Risk premium} = 0.17\% - 2.82\% = -2.65\%$$

The real rate of interest is calculated from the Fisher relationship using the data from Table 8.2.

$$(1 + r_f) = (1 + i_f)(1 + i_r) \Rightarrow i_r = (1 + r_f)/(1 + i_f) - 1$$
$$= 1.0282/1.0064 - 1$$
$$= 2.16\%$$

Assuming an expected inflation rate for that quarter of 1.4%, the estimated risk-free rate for Q1 2002 is 3.37% and the cost of equity is 0.96%,

$$r_{f\,2001} = ((1 + i_{f\,est.})(1 + i_{r\,avg.}) - 1) = ((1 + 1.4\%)(1.94\%) - 1)$$
$$= 3.37\%$$
$$\text{Cost of equity } e = r_{f\,2001} + i_{\theta average} = 3.37\% - 2.41\% = 0.96\%$$

As we can see, this result is inconsistent because from the data we have obtained a negative market risk premium. This is a typical situation in the Colombian market. In these cases the practitioners use the market risk premium (MRP) calculated from a developed market such as the U.S.

market for the Standards & Poor's 500 (S&P 500). The value for this estimate ranges from 6% to 7.5% per annum.

This MRP, based on the S&P 500 has to be adjusted for inflation. The adjustment for inflation implies the deflation of the market risk premium based on the S&P 500 with the inflation rate in the U.S. and inflating with the local inflation.

$$MRP_{domestic} = (1 + MRP_{S\&P\ 500})(1 + i_{fdom})/(1 + i_{fUS}) - 1 \qquad (8.34)$$

where $MRP_{domestic}$ is the market risk premium for the domestic market, $MRP_{S\&P\ 500}$ is the market risk premium based on the S&P 500 in the U.S., i_{fdom} is the domestic inflation rate and i_{fUS} is the inflation rate in the U.S.[9]

If we were to use that value for the market risk premium as 1.5% per quarter, we would need β for the firm.

In this case we can find a rough estimate for β. If we know the risk-free rate and the market return, r_f, a rough estimate for β is found by dividing the average accounting risk premium for the firm by the average risk premium for the market (see Table 8.3). In this case we have the following estimates:

TABLE 8.3   Risk-free Rate and Market Return

Date	r_f	R_m	$R_m - r_f$
Mar-95			
Jun-95	6.97%	1.98%	−5%
Sep-95	6.74%	−11.67%	−18%
Dec-95	6.97%	−0.17%	−7%
Mar-96	6.98%	3.68%	−3%
Jun-96	6.85%	9.96%	3%
Sep-96	6.53%	−11.67%	−18%
Dec-96	6.16%	−2.99%	−9%
Mar-97	5.79%	26.55%	21%
Jun-97	5.47%	10.75%	5.27%
Sep-97	5.28%	24.43%	19.15%
Dec-97	5.36%	−2.74%	−8.11%
Mar-98	6.78%	−17.65%	−24.43%
Jun-98	7.19%	−4.71%	−11.89%
Sep-98	7.79%	−23.40%	−31.19%
Dec-98	7.19%	28.89%	21.70%
Mar-99	5.22%	−17.94%	−23.16%
Jun-99	4.33%	7.99%	3.65%
Sep-99	4.55%	−5.44%	−9.99%

(continues)

[9]This adjustment is needed when we need to estimate the Ke for a domestic investor, for instance, when valuing a firm or appraising a project in domestic currency. Of course, if the analysis is made from the point of view of a U.S. investor or in U.S. dollars the adjustment is not needed.

TABLE 8.3 (*continued*)

Date	r_f	R_m	R_m-r_f
Dec-99	3.52%	7.35%	3.83%
Mar-00	3.22%	−3.93%	−7.14%
Jun-00	3.57%	−20.42%	−23.99%
Sep-00	3.41%	−1.78%	−5.19%
Dec-00	3.15%	−4.51%	−7.66%
Mar-01	3.23%	12.90%	9.67%
Jun-01	3.08%	9.43%	6.35%
Sep-01	2.91%	−6.82%	−9.73%
Dec-01	2.82%	5.15%	2.33%
		Average	−4.73%

From Tables 8.2 and 8.3, the estimate for β is $-2.41\%/(-4.73\%) = 0.5095$. Using this beta and a quarterly risk market of 1.5% adjusted by the inflation rate, and assuming a U.S. inflation rate of 0.5% per quarter and a domestic inflation per quarter of 1.4%, we have

$$Ke = 3.37\% + 0.5095((1 + 1.5\%)(1 + 1.4\%)/(1 + 0.005) - 1)$$

$$= 3.37\% + 0.5095 \times 2.870\%$$

$$= 3.37\% + 1.46\%$$

$$= 4.83\%$$

This is a quarterly return on equity. If we wish to calculate an annual Ke, we have to capitalize four times a year and we obtain 20.77%.

As an alternate procedure we can use another ARM method to estimate β for the firm based on accounting figures.

This time we regress the accounting return on the accounting market return. We use the stock exchange index as a proxy of the accounting market return and calculate $R_m - r_f$.[10] Then this result is regressed on the difference between the accounting return and the risk-free rate ($R_j - r_f$) (see Table 8.4 and Exhibit 8.1). This is known as the accounting beta.

---

[10] To be precise and theoretically correct we have to regress accounting returns for the firm on accounting returns for the market. See Bowman (1979). To simplify the example, we use the market return as a proxy to the accounting market return. However, we regressed three versions of the return on equity (ROE) for the firm on the ROE for the market using net income (NI) for the quarter and first, equity for the quarter, second the equity for the previous quarter and third, an average of equity of the quarter and equity from the previous period. In all cases beta was not significant.

TABLE 8.4 Market Risk Premium and Risk Premium for Compañía Nacional de Chocolates

Date	R_{tj}	r_f	R_m	$R_m - r_f$	$R_{tj} - r_f$
Mar-95					
Jun-95	3.12%	6.97%	1.98%	−4.99%	−3.86%
Sep-95	−2.60%	6.74%	−11.67%	−18.41%	−9.34%
Dec-95	2.33%	6.97%	−0.17%	−7.14%	−4.64%
Mar-96	−3.13%	6.98%	3.68%	−3.30%	−10.11%
Jun-96	4.14%	6.85%	9.96%	3.11%	−2.71%
Sep-96	0.13%	6.53%	−11.67%	−18.20%	−6.40%
Dec-96	7.27%	6.16%	−2.99%	−9.15%	1.11%
Mar-97	18.26%	5.79%	26.55%	20.76%	12.47%
Jun-97	18.65%	5.47%	10.75%	5.27%	13.18%
Sep-97	5.47%	5.28%	24.43%	19.15%	0.19%
Dec-97	−5.23%	5.36%	−2.74%	−8.11%	−10.60%
Mar-98	−22.49%	6.78%	−17.65%	−24.43%	−24.90%
Jun-98	1.82%	7.19%	−4.71%	−11.89%	−5.37%
Sep-98	−17.42%	7.79%	−23.40%	−31.19%	−25.22%
Dec-98	17.02%	7.19%	28.89%	21.70%	9.83%
Mar-99	−3.73%	5.22%	−17.94%	−23.16%	−2.19%
Jun-99	8.66%	4.33%	7.99%	3.65%	4.32%
Sep-99	−0.67%	4.55%	−5.44%	−9.99%	−5.22%
Dec-99	7.14%	3.52%	7.35%	3.83%	3.61%
Mar-00	−6.89%	3.22%	−3.93%	−7.14%	−3.43%
Jun-00	−1.36%	3.57%	−20.42%	−23.99%	−4.93%
Sep-00	3.33%	3.41%	−1.78%	−5.19%	−0.07%
Dec-00	3.60%	3.15%	−4.51%	−7.66%	0.45%
Mar-01	−10.35%	3.23%	12.90%	9.67%	−13.58%
Jun-01	33.56%	3.08%	9.43%	6.35%	30.47%
Sep-01	−2.58%	2.91%	−6.82%	−9.73%	−5.48%
Dec-01	0.17%	2.82%	5.15%	2.33%	−2.65%
			Average	−4.73%	−2.41%

In this case it is easy to find difficulties with the behavior of the market return and the risk premium. For example, the data in the previous table shows an unusual negative value for the market risk premium for several years: for 13 out of 22 years the market risk premium is negative.

Regressing the data we find that β is 0.5111 and R^2 is 0.4034. β is statistically significant with a probability of 0.0372% for the t statistic. This data is from a real traded firm in the Colombian stock market.[11] β estimated with the market values for that firm in June, 2001 is 0.78. The Superintendencia de Valores, Colombia calculated β on a monthly basis from March 1995 to December 2001. The data we used in this example can be observed in the next exhibit.

[11]The firm is Compañía Nacional de Chocolates and the data is at the Superintendencia de Valores website, at http://www.supervalores.gov.co/. We used the CDTs return as a proxy of the risk-free rate.

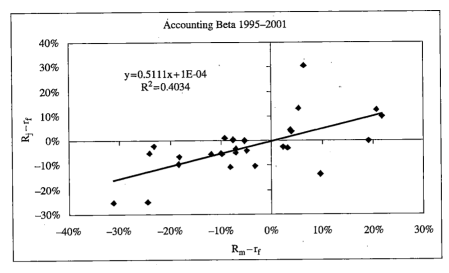

EXHIBIT 8.1 Accounting beta.

We can calculate β even if we have a negative market risk premium. The problem arises when we try to apply the CAPM. Then we have to proceed as we did previously. In this case, assuming a market risk premium of 1.5% we get

$$e = r_{f2002} + \beta(R_m - r_f)$$
$$= 3.37\% + 0.5111(1.5\%)\% = 4.14\%$$

This value for e is a cost of equity per quarter. If we prefer to use the annual value we have to compound it four times a year. In this example, the annual cost of equity is 20.80%. The estimation of e is close to the previous one.

8.4.3.3 Adjusting Betas or MRPs from Developed Markets

In this section, we examine two approaches to do the following: adjusting betas or MRPs, derived for the S&P 500 in the U.S. and adding a country

---

[12]To be precise and theoretically correct we have to regress accounting return for the firm on accounting return for the market. In this example we do not have that market information processed. Just to simplify the example, we use the market return as a proxy to the accounting market return.

[13]The data can be found at the Superintendencia de Valores website, at http://www.supervalores.gov.co/.

[14]They regress the monthly returns for the stock and the monthly return for the market based on the index of the stock market (in this case they considered two stock markets that were trading in Colombia). The lineal model they used for the regression is $Y_i = \alpha + \beta X_i + \epsilon_I$, where Y_i is the stock return, α the independent return for the stock, β is the stock's beta and ϵ, the statistical error.

risk (CR) premium. One approach is very popular and is used by most practitioners and the other one has been proposed by Lessard (1996).[15]

The most popular approach consists in using CAPM and adding a CR to the MRP and multiplying it by the beta for a similar firm in the U.S. as follows:

$$Ke = r_f + \beta_{firm\ US}[(R_m - r_f) + CR] \qquad (8.35)$$

The approach proposed by Lessard indicates that the risk for the firm should include the beta for the firm in the domestic economy, estimated as

$$\beta_{non\ traded} = \beta_{firm\ in\ U.S.} \times \beta_{country} \qquad (8.36)$$

"The country beta is [. . .] the product of two underlying dimensions: (1) the volatility of the stock market (or of the macroeconomy of the country in question) relative to that of the U.S. and (2) the correlation of these changes in value with the U.S. benchmark portfolios" (Lessard, 1996, p. 60).

Then, using CAPM the Ke for the firm would be

$$Ke = r_f + \beta_{non\ traded}(R_m - r_f) + CR \qquad (8.37)$$

In this case, as we mentioned above, we need to adjust the MRP with the U.S. inflation and the domestic inflation.

Using information from the Lessard paper we compare the two approaches to see how different they are.

Selected country (such as the sovereign bond risk premium) and betas are taken from J.P. Morgan and from International Finance Corporation, Emerging Stock Markets Fastbook, 1996, respectively,[16] cited by Lessard (1996) and are as follows (see Tables 8.5 and 8.6).

TABLE 8.5 Selected Emerging Countries Risks (1996)

Country	CR
U.S.	0.00%
Peru	4.34%
Panama	5.14%
Mexico	5.97%
Brazil	6.10%
Argentina	7.18%
Venezuela	8.11%
Ecuador	11.13%

[15]The proposal from Lessard is for offshore projects and we have adapted the proposal to find the Ke for equity.

[16]Cited by Lessard (1996).

TABLE 8.6   Selected Emerging Countries Betas (1996)

Country	Country beta
Venezuela	−0.18
Mexico	0.83
Chile	0.65
U.S.	1.00
Argentina	1.96
Brazil	2.42

TABLE 8.7   General Data for Example

Market risk premium, MRP in U.S. based on S&P 500	6.00%
Beta for comparable U.S. firm $\beta_{\text{firm U.S.}}$	1.3
Country Beta	1.26
Country risk CR	7.70%
Estimated domestic firm beta $\beta_{\text{non traded}}$	1.638
Most popular method: Risk premium $= \beta_{\text{firm U.S.}}(R_m - R_f) + CR$	17.81%
Lessard method: Risk premium $= \beta_{\text{non-traded}}(R_m - R_f) + CR$	17.53%

Assuming a risk premium of 6% as above, we can see the differences in the risk premium (ultimately in Ke, due to the addition of the risk free rate) using both approaches. Assuming we do not know the country risk or the country beta (just using the Lessard information) and hence using the average for country risk and country beta for Latin American countries, we have an estimated country risk and beta of 7.70% and 1.26 respectively (see Tables 8.7 and 8.9 and Exhibits 8.2 and 8.3). Assuming that the comparable firm in the U.S. has a beta of 1.3 we have the data given in Table 8.7.

At first sight, they are close to each other. However, we should examine what happens when we perform a sensitivity analysis. In this case we will only consider the risk premium calculated with the two methods. We have considered no inflation adjustment in this comparison. This means that the risk premium we calculate is suitable for an analysis performed from the foreign investor's point of view. If we are estimating the MRP for a country different from the U.S. we need to deflate the MRP with the U.S. inflation rate and inflate with the domestic inflation rate as we did above.

The risk premium for selected emerging countries is shown in the next tables and exhibits (see Tables 8.8 and 8.9).

TABLE 8.8 Risk Premium with the Two Methods for Selected Country Risk

Country	CR	Popular	Lessard
U.S.	0.00%	7.80%	9.83%
Peru	4.34%	13.44%	14.17%
Panama	5.14%	14.48%	14.97%
Mexico	5.97%	15.56%	15.80%
Brazil	6.10%	15.73%	15.93%
Argentina	7.18%	17.13%	17.01%
Venezuela	8.11%	18.34%	17.94%
Ecuador	11.13%	22.27%	20.96%

Table 8.8 shows that the popular method defines a risk premium below and above the Lessard method. In the next figure we can observe this behavior graphically.

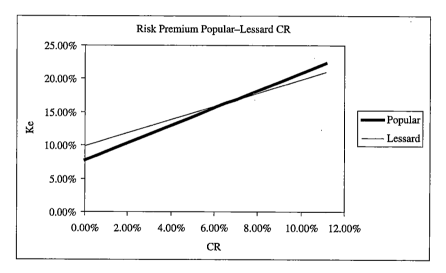

EXHIBIT 8.2 Risk premium versus country beta.

TABLE 8.9 Risk Premium with the Two Methods for Selected Country Beta

Country	Country beta	Popular	Lessard
Venezuela	−0.18	17.8%	6.3%
Mexico	0.83	17.8%	14.2%
Chile	0.65	17.8%	12.8%
U.S.	1.00	17.8%	15.5%
Argentina	1.96	17.8%	23.0%
Brazil	2.42	17.8%	26.6%

· This table shows that the popular method defines a constant risk premium and the Lessard method has a good fit to the country beta. In the next figure we can observe this behavior graphically.

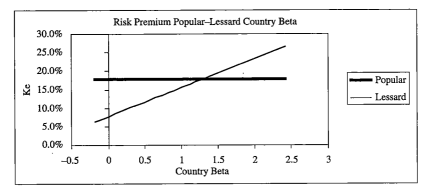

EXHIBIT 8.3 Risk premium versus country beta.

When comparing the two methods using the two variables (CR and Country beta) at the same time we find the following (see Tables 8.10 to 8.12).

TABLE 8.10 Risk Premium with the Popular Method for Selected Country Risk and Country Beta

	CR	Venezuela −0.18	Chile 0.65	México 0.83	U.S 1.00	Argentina 1.96	Brazil 2.42
U.S.	0.00%	7.8%	7.8%	7.8%	7.8%	7.8%	7.8%
Peru	4.34%	13.4%	13.4%	13.4%	13.4%	13.4%	13.4%
Panama	5.14%	14.5%	14.5%	14.5%	14.5%	14.5%	14.5%
Mexico	5.97%	15.6%	15.6%	15.6%	15.6%	15.6%	15.6%
Brazil	6.10%	15.7%	15.7%	15.7%	15.7%	15.7%	15.7%
Argentina	7.18%	17.1%	17.1%	17.1%	17.1%	17.1%	17.1%
Venezuela	8.11%	18.3%	18.3%	18.3%	18.3%	18.3%	18.3%
Ecuador	11.13%	22.3%	22.3%	22.3%	22.3%	22.3%	22.3%

Value of country beta is given in italics.

TABLE 8.11 Risk Premium with the Lessard Method for Selected Country Risk and Country Beta

	CR	Venezuela −0.18	Chile 0.65	México 0.83	U.S 1.00	Argentina 1.96	Brazil 2.42
U.S.	0.00%	−1.4%	5.1%	6.5%	7.8%	15.3%	18.9%
Peru	4.34%	2.9%	9.4%	10.8%	12.1%	19.6%	23.2%
Panama	5.14%	3.7%	10.2%	11.6%	12.9%	20.4%	24.0%
Mexico	5.97%	4.6%	11.0%	12.4%	13.8%	21.3%	24.8%

(continues)

TABLE 8.11 *(continued)*

	CR	Venezuela	Chile	México	U.S	Argentina	Brazil
Brazil	6.10%	4.7%	11.2%	12.6%	13.9%	21.4%	25.0%
Argentina	7.18%	5.8%	12.3%	13.7%	15.0%	22.5%	26.1%
Venezuela	8.11%	6.7%	13.2%	14.6%	15.9%	23.4%	27.0%
Ecuador	11.13%	9.7%	16.2%	17.6%	18.9%	26.4%	30.0%

Value of country beta is given in italics.

TABLE 8.12 Differences in Risk Premium Between Both Methods for Selected Country Risk and Country Beta

		Venezuela	Chile	Mexico	U.S	Argentina	Brazil
	CR	*−0.18*	*0.65*	*0.83*	*1.00*	*1.96*	*2.42*
U.S.	0.00%	9.2%	2.7%	1.3%	0.0%	−7.5%	−11.1%
Peru	4.34%	10.5%	4.0%	2.6%	1.3%	−6.2%	−9.8%
Panama	5.14%	10.7%	4.3%	2.9%	1.5%	−5.9%	−9.5%
Mexico	5.97%	11.0%	4.5%	3.1%	1.8%	−5.7%	−9.3%
Brazil	6.10%	11.0%	4.6%	3.2%	1.8%	−5.7%	−9.2%
Argentina	7.18%	11.4%	4.9%	3.5%	2.2%	−5.3%	−8.9%
Venezuela	8.11%	11.6%	5.2%	3.8%	2.4%	−5.1%	−8.6%
Ecuador	11.13%	12.5%	6.1%	4.7%	3.3%	−4.1%	−7.7%

Value of country beta is given in italics.

As can be seen, the differences is assessing the risk premium might be important. It ranges from −9.2% for Brazil to 11.6% for Venezuela (we do not mention the high difference for Ecuador because the country beta was not available). We prefer the Lessard method in the absence of statistical information on the country in question. Moreover, if we need to use this type of approach it is clear that it is preferable to have a method that recognizes the fact that the macro economy or the stock market of a country shows a relevant variation. In other words, it is not intuitively attractive for a method to calculate a risk premium as a constant without a link to the country beta.

There are alternate proposals such as the ones proposed by Estrada (1999) and Godfrey and Espinosa (1996). Estrada proposes to consider only the downside risk as the one that the investor tries to avoid. This simply recognizes the existence of the negative MRP. On the other hand and in the same line of thought, Godfrey and Espinosa propose to use the standard deviation of returns as the appropriate measure of risk.

If e, %D, and %E (the leverage and the proportion of equity to levered value) are known, ρ is calculated with $\rho = e\%E + d\%D$. As it is necessary to know the market values that are the result of discounting the future cash flows at WACC, there is circularity, but it is possible to solve the circularity issue with a spreadsheet, as shown in Chapter Seven.

As a final comment, if the investor is not diversified, then the levered beta should be adjusted to consider the non systematic risk. This could be done using the standard deviation of the returns of the traded firm instead of the beta of the traded firm and unlever and lever it as we do with the beta. In the case of using accounting betas we should use the standard deviation of the accounting returns instead of the accounting beta. When using the standard deviation for the traded firm there would be no need to introduce the MRP in the calculation of e because the standard deviation of the traded firm already has the MRP taken into account. We have to remember that the standard deviation measures the total risk premium for the traded firm. For instance, the expression for e would be e $= R_f +$ (Standard deviation)$_t$ $(1 + D_{nt}/E_{nt})/(1 + D_t/E_t)$, where the subscripts t and nt, stand for traded and not traded (see Levy and Sarnat, 1982; Levy, 1990).

8.4.4 Estimation of the Unlevered Return to Equity, ρ with Systematic Risk

There is another option to calculate the unlevered return ρ with the unlevered β. We can use the CAPM and unlever β using equations 8.12 and 8.13, depending on the assumption for the discount rate for tax savings.

If we assume ρ as the discount rate for the tax savings, the unlevered β is given by equation 8.13.

$$\beta_{\text{unlev}} = \frac{\beta_{\text{proxy}} + \left[\beta_D \frac{D_{\text{proxy}}}{E_{\text{proxy}}}\right]}{\left[1 + \frac{D_{\text{proxy}}}{E_{\text{proxy}}}\right]} \tag{8.38}$$

If the debt is risk-free, β_D is zero, and

$$\beta_{\text{unlev}} = \frac{\beta_{\text{proxy}}}{\left[1 + \frac{D_{\text{proxy}}}{E_{\text{proxy}}}\right]} \tag{8.39}$$

After we know this unlevered β for a number of firms similar to the non-traded firm, we can use a weighted average of them to estimate β_{unlev}, as we did previously. From this estimate we can now estimate ρ as follows:

$$\rho = r_f + \beta_{\text{unlev}}(R_m - r_f) \tag{8.40}$$

Recall that according to M & M, the unlevered return ρ is constant[17] and independent from the capital structure of the firm.

---

[17]This is true given a constant inflation. If inflation is not constant we have to estimate a real ρ and inflate it accordingly to the inflation rate of each period.

In Appendix A we present some approaches that try to make explicit the subjectivity of the investor in a systematic way.

As a final comment, if the investor is not diversified, then the levered beta should be adjusted to take into account the non-systematic risk. This could be done using the standard deviation of the returns of the traded firm instead of the beta of the traded firm and unlever it as we do with the levered beta. When using the standard deviation for the traded firm there would be no need to introduce the MRP in the calculation of ρ because the standard deviation of the traded firm already has the MRP taken into account. We have to remember that the standard deviation measures the total risk premium for the traded firm. For instance, the expression for ρ would be $\rho = r_f + (\text{Standard deviation})_t/(1 + D_t/E_t)$, where the subscript t, stands for traded (see Levy and Sarnat, 1982; Levy, 1990).

8.5 SUMMARY AND CONCLUDING REMARKS

In this chapter we presented some ideas for estimating the return to unlevered and levered equity for non-traded firms. This issue is delicate and could frustrate some readers who think finance is a well-defined discipline that provides the analyst with proven and exact answers. There are numerous problems to be solved. In reality, we use the available models, make adjustments to the existing models, and sometimes rely on the experience of a firm's manager and owner to estimate (subjectively) some of the parameters.

We have presented an approach to estimate the levered and unlevered returns e and ρ for non-traded firms with systematic risk. The details for the approaches for total risk are given in the appendix. The analyst has to judge if the investor is diversified or not. If the investor is diversified and the firm is not traded, the analyst should use those approaches that only estimate systematic risk. If the investor is not diversified, the analyst should use the total risk approach.

A8.I ESTIMATION WITH TOTAL RISK

In this appendix we present some approaches based on subjective estimation of the cost of levered and unlevered equity. The current thinking in finance makes great efforts to avoid subjectivity. Estrada (1999) for instance, notes that one of the advantages of his proposal is that it "is not based on subjective measures of risk." There is a difference between subjective and arbitrary estimation. Subjective estimation is based on experience and common sense. Arbitrary estimation has no basis in the individual making the estimate. Sometimes there is no alternative and we have to conduct a subjective assessment of the variables. In this case, we have to offer some systematic procedures to make explicit the subjectivity.

A8.I.I Estimation of the Levered Cost of Equity e with Total Risk

To calculate equity e with total risk we have several alternatives:

1. Subjectively and assisted by a methodology such as the one presented by Cotner and Fletcher (2000), as applied to the owner of the firm. With this approach the owner, given the leverage level of the firm, estimates the perceived risk. This risk premium is added to the risk-free rate and the result is an estimate for e with total risk. The methodology proposed by Cotner and Fletcher is the Analytical Hierarchy Process (AHP). Appendix B includes a summary of this paper. They consider that the investor in a non-traded firm (usually an SME) is not fully diversified. Hence, the risk premium calculated from the estimations of the owner include non-systematic risk. That is, the risk premium estimated directly from the owner is the total risk. This thinking applies to any subjective estimation made directly by the owner. This leads to a conclusion: those methods that derive the cost of equity using a method that only includes systematic risk have to be adjusted to include total risk.

2. Subjectively as 1, but direct. We ask the owner for a given value level of debt and a given cost of debt—what is the required return to equity? This might be seen as non-academic and non-scientific but sometimes there is no other option but to proceed this way. And do not be surprised if the owner does not know how to answer the question and requests the analyst to provide the answer.

3. Using a calibrator that aids the investor to define his subjective appreciation of risk. Calculate the market return, R_m, and the risk-free rate, r_f, and the market risk premium as the average of $R_m - r_f$, where R_m is the return of the market based upon the stock exchange index and r_f is the risk-free rate (say, the return of treasury bills or similar). Then, subjectively, the owner could estimate if he prefers, in terms of risk, to stay in the actual business or to buy the stock exchange index basket. If the actual business is preferred, one could say that the beta of the actual business is lower than 1, the market beta, and the risk perceived is lower than the MRP, $R_m - r_f$. This is an upper limit for the risk premium of the owner. This upper limit could be compared with zero risk premium, the risk-free rate which is the lower limit for the risk perceived by the equity owner.

If the owner prefers to buy the stock exchange index basket, we could say that the investor thinks his actual business is riskier than the market. Then, the beta should be greater than 1 and the perceived risk for the actual business should be greater than $R_m - r_f$.

In the first case, the owner could be confronted with different combinations—from 0% to 100%—of the stock exchange index basket, the risk-free investment, and the actual business. After several trials, the owner eventually will find the indifference combination of risk-free and the stock exchange index basket. The perceived risk could be calculated as the MRP ($R_m - r_f$) times the proportion of the stock exchange index basket accepted. In fact what has been found is the beta for the actual business.

In the second case one must choose the highest beta found in the stock exchange index basket. (The stock exchange or any governmental control office usually calculates these betas. In Colombia the betas for each stock are calculated by the *Superintendencia de Valores*, similar to the U.S. Securities Exchange Commission, SEC.) This beta is used to multiply the market risk premium $R_m - r_f$, and the result is an estimate of the risk premium for the riskiest stock in the index. This might be an upper limit for the risk perceived by the owner. In case this risk is lower than the perceived risk by the owner, it might be considered as the lower limit. In the case that the riskier stock is considered riskier than the actual business, the lower limit is the MRP, $R_m - r_f$. In this second case, the owner could be confronted with different combinations—from 0 to 100%—of the stock exchange index basket, the riskiest stock, and the actual business. After several trials, the owner eventually will find the indifference combination of risk-free and the stock exchange index basket. The perceived risk can be calculated as a weighted risk. That is, the MRP $(R_m - r_f)$ times the proportion of the stock exchange index basket accepted plus the risk premium for the riskiest stock in the index (its β times the market risk premium, $R_m - r_f$) times the proportion accepted for that stock.

In both cases the result might be an estimation of the risk premium for the actual business. This risk premium can be added to the risk-free rate, which might be a rough estimate of e.

If e, %D, and %E are known, ρ is calculated with $\rho = e\%E + d\%D$. As it is necessary to know the market values that are the result of discounting the future cash flows at WACC, circularity is found, but it is possible to solve it with a spreadsheet.

A8.I.2 The Estimation of the Unlevered Return to Equity, ρ with Total Risk

Another option is to calculate ρ directly. One of the following alternatives could be used:

1. According to M & M, the WACC before taxes ρ is constant[18] and independent from the capital structure of the firm. We could ask the owner for an estimate on how much she is willing to earn, assuming no debt. A hint for this value can be found by looking at how much she could earn in a risk-free security when bought in the secondary market. On top of this, a risk premium, subjectively calculated, must be included.

2. Another way to estimate ρ is to assess subjectively the risk for the firm. This risk can be used to calculate ρ, adding it to the risk-free rate. (As mentioned, Cotner and Fletcher [2000] present a methodology to calculate the risk of a firm not publicly held.) This methodology can be applied to the managers and other executives of the firm. This gives the risk premium for the firm. As this risk component is added to the risk-free rate, the result is ρ calculated in a subjective manner. A hint that helps in the process is to establish minimum or maximum levels for ρ. The minimum might be the cost of debt before taxes. The maximum might be the opportunity cost of the owners, if it can be estimated, that is, if it has been told by them. Or if, by observation, it is known by observing where they are investing (other investments made by them). In this case a question arises. When we

---

[18]Again, this is true given a constant inflation rate. If inflation is not constant we have to estimate a real ρ and inflate it according to the inflation rate of each period.

have a small firm, probably the owner and the firm are indistinguishable. It doesn't make any sense to think separately of the owner and the firm.

It has to be remembered that ρ is, according to M & M, constant and independent from the capital structure of the firm.

The ρ is named in other texts as K_A cost of the assets or the firm (for instance, Ruback, 2000), or K_u cost of unlevered equity (for instance, Fernandez, 1999a, b).

If ρ is estimated directly and we wish to estimate the WACC (or the e), we will find circularities. However, as was shown in Chapter Seven, the total value of the firm can be calculated with ρ using the capital cash flow (CCF). In this case no circularities are present and there is no need to calculate the leverage ratio for every period.

APPENDIX B

The Analytical Hierarchy Process (AHP) summary from Cotner, John S. and Harold D. Fletcher, Computing the Cost of Capital for Privately Held Firms, *American Business Review*, June 2000, pp. 27–33.

Owners and managers in a privately held firm do not usually view their firm as a diversified portfolio but as a capital project. For these firms it is more relevant to estimate the cost of capital in such a way that total risk is included in that estimation. This means that we have to estimate a total risk premium.

The analyst benefits from a method that incorporates quantifiable and non-quantifiable risk factors, and direct and indirect effects of these factors in the organization's total risk.

The authors mention different proxy methods to arrive at the estimation of e. One method is to look at similar traded firms and use that beta. Another is to use the accounting betas. The third method is to add an equity risk premium (normally three to six percentage points) to the firm's own long-term debt.

The authors propose the AHP approach. "The AHP is well suited to the task of estimating an equity risk premium, and is a workable alternative to the various proxy approaches. AHP enables both objective and subjective criteria to be incorporated into a comprehensive model of a decision problem (Saaty, 1990). Moreover, AHP lends itself to assessment by a group working together (*perhaps the Delphi method, we think*) as well as by an individual decision-maker."

The first step is to establish a range of equity risk premiums that is appropriate to the firm (see Table A8.1).

For example:

TABLE B8.1   Levels of Risk Premia (Alternatives) for AHP Model

Descriptor term for risk	Risk premium
Very low risk	6%
Low risk	9%
Medium risk	14%
High risk	21%
Very high risk	30%

The description might be similar across the firms but the size of the risk might vary. "Consequently, the range and level of risk premia must be established in the context of the firm's operations."

Decision criteria. The second step is to specify the important factors that impact the firm's risk. These are referred as decision criteria.

Decision criteria:

1. Revenue factors
   a. Level of sales
   b. Variance in sales
   c. Growth rate in sales
2. Operating factors
   a. Amount of fixed operating costs
   b. Operating leverage
3. Financial factors
   a. Interest coverage
   b. Debt capacity
   c. Composition of debt
4. Management/Ownership factors
   a. Confidence of investors in management
   b. Organizational experience
   c. Control
5. Strategic factors
   a. Suppliers
   b. Buyers
   c. New entrants
   d. Industry rivalry
   e. Substitutes

Relating criteria to alternatives. "In the third stage of the analysis, the AHP participants assess the condition of each factor (criterion) in the model, and then select the most appropriate descriptor term for a level of risk premium relative to that criterion."

Criteria weights. "The fourth step of the process determines the relative importance of each criterion to the total risk in the organization. These are the weights in the AHP model. Computing these weights is accomplished via the systematic pair wise comparison technique that is integral to the analytical hierarchy process." (In Appendix C we include a simple approach to find consistent weights for the criteria.)

As a final stage in the analytical hierarchy process, the numerical values corresponding to the descriptor terms selected for each criterion (and subcriterion) are multiplied by the weight computed for that criterion. The resulting products are then summed. That total is the "weighted average" equity risk premium for the organization being analyzed."

APPENDIX C

When assigning weights to a set of characteristics, we must check for consistency. One method is an old procedure proposed by Churchman and Ackoff (1954). We compare by pairs or groups of characteristics and check if the assigned weights are consistent with the importance we perceive in them. These comparisons indicate in numbers what is appreciated in a subjective way. The values or weights are adjusted until the numbers match the subjective preferences. If one factor is preferred over another factor, its weight reflects that. The same has to be checked with the sum of the weights of two or three factors.

An example will illustrate the idea. Assume that we have five characteristics that we want to weigh. The initial weights might be as follows:

Characteristic	Weight
M	7
A	5
C	10
P	7
B	9

The analyst should make some of the following comparisons:
If characteristic C is more important than all the other characteristics,

$$C > M + A + P + B$$

However,

$$10 < 7 + 5 + 7 + 9 = 28$$

She should reassign the weights in such a way that this condition, $C > M + A + P + B$, is valid. In this case the characteristic C should have more than 28 points, given that the others are correct. She has to evaluate all the possible combinations as follows:

Compare C with M + A + P + B	Compare M with A + P + B
Compare C with M + A + P	Compare M with P + B
Compare C with M + A	Compare M with B
Compare C with M	Compare A with P + B
Compare A with P	Compare P with B

It is the same with all the possible combinations.

9

BEYOND THE PLANNING PERIOD: CALCULATING THE TERMINAL VALUE

> Given a choice between two theories, take the one which is funnier.
>
> —*Blore's Razor*

9.1 INTRODUCTION

Typically, the expected life of the firm or project is longer than the planning (or forecast) period of five to ten years. In fact, we assume unrealistically that the firm will last forever, even though we know that some firms do file for bankruptcy. In practice, on grounds of simplicity and based on the availability of historical data, for valuation purposes we construct the financial statements for only five to ten years. However, we do not want to disregard the value of the free cash flows (FCFs) that occur beyond the planning period. At the end of year N, which is the end of the planning period, we estimate a terminal value (TV) for the FCFs that occur beyond the planning (or forecast) period and add it to the FCF that occurs in year N.

In the previous chapters, we constructed nominal financial statements for five years and stated that we would postpone discussion on the calculation of the TV. In this chapter, we examine the issues that are related to the calculation of the TV.

In appendix D, we present the reconciliation of economic value added (EVA®), residual income (RI) and the discounted cash flow (DCF) methods discussed in Chapter Seven.

333

The chapter is organized as follows. First, we briefly discuss the TV, the transfer value, and the liquidation value. Second, we present the standard approach for estimating the TV. Third, we discuss the adjustments that have to be made and examine how to estimate the key parameters in the expression for the TV. Fourth, we illustrate the calculation of the TV with the complex example from Chapter Five.

9.2   OPERATION VERSUS LIQUIDATION

With respect to the end of year 0, the estimation of the TV at the end of year N is complex. Among other variables, the TV calculation depends on assumptions about the skills of the future management team, the overall macroeconomic conditions, the cost of capital, and the growth rate of the FCFs in the years beyond the planning period. In some cases, if the planning period is short, say five years, with respect to year 0, the present value (PV) of the TV can even be higher than the PV of the FCF, exclusive of the TV. See Copeland et al. (2000) and Damodaran (1996). With a longer planning period, the relative weight of the TV in the valuation can be lessened. However, the uncertainties surrounding the other determinants of the FCF are also higher.

Here we assume that the equity holders continue to operate the business. For a going concern, the estimation of the TV is unavoidable. To reiterate, at the end of the forecast period N, we estimate the TV, which is the PV, with respect to the end of year N, of the future cash flows that occur in the years beyond the forecast period N, and add the TV to the FCF in year N.

At the end of the planning (or forecast) period, the current equity holder has several options. She could continue to operate the business, she could sell the business as a going concern, or she could liquidate the business by selling the assets. At the end of year N, the equity holder chooses the option that yields the highest value. In principle, the estimates of the TV (or continuing value) and the transfer value (to another investor) should be close to each other. In many cases, the value as a going concern is probably higher than the liquidation value (or salvage value). However, as we will discuss, because of variations in the judgments of analysts, there might be big differences among the TV, transfer value, and liquidation value.

Depending on the robustness of the assumptions and the availability of market-based information, discrepancies can exist between the three estimates.[1] The current equity holder would be willing to sell and transfer the business to another investor as a going concern if the new investor is willing to pay more than the estimated TV for the business. For

---

[1] If there are huge discrepancies between the TV, the transfer value, and the liquidation value, the analyst should attempt to identify and point out the reasons for the discrepancies.

example, an investor, with a new management team, might be willing to pay a transfer value that is more than the estimated TV for the business because they believe that they can generate higher cash flows.[2] Similarly, if the particular industry is in a slump for the foreseeable future and the salvage value is higher than the TV or the continuing value, the equity holder might simply liquidate the business and sell the assets rather than stay in business.

9.3 CALCULATING THE SALVAGE (OR LIQUIDATION) VALUE

The calculation of the salvage value in year N is made easier if there are competitive secondary markets for estimating the market values of the operating assets, which might differ from the book values of the operating assets listed in the BS.[3] For example, there is an active market for used vehicles and thus we can determine easily the salvage value of a used truck. There might be similar markets for the operating assets. The calculation of the salvage value is problematic if there are no secondary markets for the operating assets. In the absence of market-based information, the book values of the operating assets, adjusted for inflation, can be a reasonable working estimate of the market values of the operating assets and serve as a basis for negotiations.

9.4 TERMINAL VALUE VERSUS SALVAGE VALUE

In many cases, in year N, the TV might be higher than the salvage value. That is, the value of the business as a going concern might be higher than the sum of the individual market values of the operating assets. One reason for the difference between the TV and the salvage value might be attributable to the exceptional skills and experience of the existing management team. They might be able to generate higher cash flows than another management team.

Also, the business might provide proprietary products and services whose value is more than the sum of the constituent assets. In addition, among the different investors, there might be differences in the cost of

---

[2]Alternatively, the new investor might have a lower cost of capital or have different expectations about the future of the industry.

[3]The market values of the operating assets take into account the true economic depreciation from usage and technological obsolescence and are unrelated to the depreciation schedule for tax purposes.

capital, market information, and expectations. In summary, for various reasons, the TV of a firm might be higher than the liquidation value.

9.5 THE STANDARD APPROACH FOR ESTIMATING THE TV

In this section, we present the standard approach for estimating the TV and examine the relevant issues. Calculating the TV is much more difficult than what the formula suggests. Unlike the forecast period, in the years beyond the terminal year N, the use of cash flows in perpetuity is unavoidable.

Before proceeding to the formula for the TV, we emphasize two differences between the FCF in the forecast period and the FCF that we use for estimating the TV. First, as we explain in more detail in the next section, in the formula for the TV, we use the operating FCF with some particular conditions rather than the FCF that was calculated from the CB statement. The reason is because the FCF from the CB statement includes the effects of the investment of the surplus funds and cash or cash equivalents in marketable securities. Second, we make an adjustment for reinvestment, which takes account of the loss in the productivity of the fixed assets that generate the cash flows.

Typically, in the forecast period, the reinvestment in new assets does not occur every year. Instead, the reinvestment might occur every few years. For simplicity, in the years beyond the terminal year N, to account for the reinvestment to maintain the productivity of the existing assets, we assume that the reinvestment occurs every year and subtract the annual allowance for depreciation from the annual FCF in perpetuity.[4] This is reasonable because the annual allowance for depreciation is cash available to the firm that actually might be devoted to the replenishment of fixed assets.

Let FCF^{Op}_i be the operating FCF in year i. In the estimation of the TV, we use the Net Operating Profit Less Adjusted Tax (NOPLAT) as the equivalent to the FCF^{Op}_i. NOPLAT is defined as follows:

$$NOPLAT = EBIT - Tax \text{ on } EBIT \qquad (9.1)$$

We have to remember that earnings before interest and taxes (EBIT), and hence NOPLAT, has the depreciation charges subtracted, which implies the accrual of income and expense. This means that when we use NOPLAT

---

[4]Frequently, in the forecast period, analysts assume that the annual reinvestment in the operating assets is equal to the annual depreciation allowance. With this and other simplifying assumptions, the net income is approximately equal to the FCF and the formula for the TV can be stated in terms of the net income or the FCF.

as the equivalent to operating FCF, we are saying that it is a cash flow that results from an operation of the firm with the following assumptions:

1. No AR. Every sale is received in cash. No credit. This assumption is implicit in the use of NOPLAT.[5]
2. No AP. Every expense is paid as it is used. No credit. This assumption is implicit in the use of NOPLAT.
3. Total distribution of available funds to capital owners. Roughly speaking, this is equivalent to saying that any excess cash is reinvested at the weighted average cost of capital (WACC).[6]
4. No reinvestment of cash excess in market securities.
5. No cash left in hand.
6. The amount of depreciation charges is invested to keep the productive capacity at a constant level.
7. The inventory policy is kept constant. This assumption is implicit in the use of NOPLAT.
8. We earn 100% of the tax savings. That is, there is enough EBIT to earn the tax savings.
9. Because of assumption 8, we pay taxes the same year that we accrue the interest charges.
10. Because of 1, 2, 4 and 5, we liquidate any existing current assets and liabilities at year N.

Let g be the constant nominal growth rate of NOPLAT in the years beyond the terminal year N. Then NOPLAT in year N + 1 is equal to NOPLAT in year N times one plus the growth rate of NOPLAT, g.

$$NOPLAT_{N+1} = NOPLAT_N(1 + g) \qquad (9.2)$$

It might be more appropriate to define the growth in NOPLAT relative to the expected inflation rate in the years beyond the terminal year N. Let π be the real growth rate in NOPLAT and let η^{Exp} be the expected inflation rate. Then the relationship between the nominal growth rate, the expected inflation rate, and the real growth rate in NOPLAT is as follows:

$$(1 + g) = (1 + \pi)(1 + \eta^{Exp}) \qquad (9.3)$$

---

[5]The assumptions of no AP and no AR might be seen as keeping the AR and AP constant and equal to the AR and AP listed in the last explicit forecasted year. This would mean that over time, the AR and AP are decreasing in relative weight down to zero.

[6]Due to complexities in the model, this equivalence may not always hold true. As mentioned earlier, this automatic or implicit reinvestment overestimates the value of the firm because the virtual returns are not taxed.

The growth rate of NOPLAT is not the same as the growth in sales.[7]

With these qualifications about NOPLAT and g in mind, we present the formula for the TV. With respect to year N, the TV is the PV of NOPLAT in perpetuity from year $N + 1$ and onwards, discounted with the nominal WACC that takes into account the expected inflation rate η^{Exp}.

$$TV^{FCF}_N = \frac{NOPLAT_{N+1}}{WACC_{N+1} - g} \tag{9.4}$$

$$TV^{FCF}_N = \frac{NOPLAT_N(1 + g)}{WACC_{N+1} - g} \tag{9.5}$$

At this time let us assume that NOPLAT will grow at a constant rate after the firm has been consolidated and hence it is in a steady state. Even if the firm has reached its full capacity level, it is possible that NOPLAT will grow. In this steady state we can assume a growth rate that is associated with several factors, as follows:

- A real increase in the operations of the firm. For instance, the natural growth of the population might represent a growth opportunity for the firm.
- A differential in nominal price increases in inputs and outputs. If price increases of outputs are higher than the inflation rate or price increases in the inputs are lower than the inflation rate, there will be real increases in the operating income of the firm. If price increases of outputs are higher than the price increases of inputs, there will also be an increase in the firm's NOPLAT.
- Forecasted constant and systematic market efforts might induce a growth of the firm's NOPLAT.

9.5.1 Assumptions in the Model

There are many implicit assumptions in the expression for the TV in equation 9.4, in addition to what we mentioned at the beginning of this Section 9.5. We list the assumptions and later we discuss how to estimate the parameters in equation 9.4.

1. We assume that the expected inflation rate and the WACC in the years beyond year N are constant. The constant WACC implies that the capital structure (or leverage) is constant.
2. We assume that the tax rate is constant and the tax savings are earned in full and in perpetuity.
3. The growth rate for NOPLAT g is constant and takes into account increases in the volume and prices of the inputs and outputs.

---

[7]Also, the growth rate of the FCF might not be the same as the growth rate of the net income or the EBIT.

4. In the period beyond year N, we assume that the investment in new equipment and assets takes into account technological advances and improvements in productivity.
5. Unlike the years in the forecast period, in the years $N+1$ and beyond, for simplicity, we assume that all NOPLAT is distributed to the stakeholders and there is no reinvestment of surplus cash.[8] With no reinvestment of surplus cash, the PV of NOPLAT is overstated for two reasons. First, no investment of surplus cash is (approximately) equivalent to reinvestment at the WACC rather than the lower return from investment in short-term securities. Second, the taxes are undervalued because the interest income from the reinvestment is not taxed.
6. We assume that there is a direct relationship between the investment and the productivity capacity of the fixed assets to generate NOPLAT.

9.5.2 Simple Numerical Example

We illustrate the use of the formula for the TV with a simple numerical example. Assume that in year N the business is in steady state and the value of NOPLAT is $1,000.[9] In the period beyond year N, we estimate that NOPLAT will grow at the expected inflation rate of 3% because NOPLAT has reached a steady state. Assume that the WACC is 14%. Then with respect to year N, the TV is $9,364.

$$TV^{NOPLAT}{}_N = \frac{NOPLAT_N(1+g)}{WACC_{N+1} - g}$$
$$= 1{,}000(1+3\%)/(14\% - 3\%) = 9{,}364.00$$

where $TV^{NOPLAT}{}_N$ is the TV based on NOPLAT, $WACC_{N+1}$ is the constant WACC in perpetuity, and g is the growth rate of NOPLAT. We have assumed that there is no real growth in NOPLAT. We must have strong reasons to believe that NOPLAT will grow at a real rate in perpetuity. If there is real growth in NOPLAT, we need to account for the investment that generates the real growth by subtracting a fraction of NOPLAT in year N. Later we explain in greater detail the case with real growth in NOPLAT.

9.5.3 Estimating the Key Parameters

Next, we discuss in greater detail some of the issues that are related to the estimation of the key parameters.

[8]This is *as if* we are able to reinvest the surplus cash at the cost of capital (see Lorie and Savage, 1955).
[9]If the forecast period is short, the FCF might not be in a steady state and it might be necessary to model the FCF with different growth rates.

First, as mentioned earlier, we equate the operating FCF to NOPLAT.

Second, we determine the nominal growth rate for NOPLAT g, which is different from the nominal growth rate for sales. We discuss the various underlying assumptions about g and examine how we should think about the estimation of g.

Third, we estimate the amount of reinvestment as a fraction of NOPLAT if the growth rate of NOPLAT in the years beyond the terminal year N is non-zero.

Fourth, we estimate whether there is any excess return over the discount rate or the WACC, to the investments that we make in the years beyond the terminal period. For the mathematical treatment of the reinvestment in perpetuity, we assume that the expected return to the reinvestments of excess cash in the years beyond the terminal period is equal to the cost of capital.

9.5.4 Growth in the Steady State

Usually the analyst assumes that the cash flows that occur in the years beyond the terminal year are in steady state and will grow at a constant nominal rate.

A planning period of five years might be too short a period for the cash flow of the firm to reach a steady state, in which case the planning period for the pro-forma financial statements can be extended so that the analysis is consistent with a steady state. For various reasons (some of them have been mentioned), in a steady state, the nominal growth rate of the cash flow might be higher than the expected inflation rate. In other words, the cash flow is growing in real terms. However, one must be cautious in identifying and specifying a real growth rate for the cash flow in perpetuity.

The estimation of the growth rate in perpetuity is a sensitive issue. It becomes most critical as the explicit forecast period is shorter. Copeland et al. (2000) show that the proportion of the TV to the total levered value ranges from 20% to 125%, depending on the length of the forecasting period. Hence, the TV could represent a large portion of the levered value. And the TV depends highly on the size of the growth g.

In practice we must examine the behavior of the growth rate of value drivers such as sales and NOPLAT to recognize a pattern that allows us to say whether the firm has reached a steady state. If we identify such a situation, an average based on the period where the steady state is recognized, might be a good estimate for the growth of NOPLAT.

9.5.5 Estimating the Growth Rate of NOPLAT, g

It is not easy to estimate g, the nominal growth rate of NOPLAT, in the period beyond year N. As mentioned earlier, the growth rate of NOPLAT is different from the growth in sales or net income (NI).

Consider the following real-life example, (Table 9.1a) which shows that the annual nominal increases in sales are quite different from the annual nominal increases in the FCF.

TABLE 9.1a   Relationship Between Sales and Operating FCF

	Year 1	Year 2	Year 3	Year 4	Year 5	Year 6	Year 7
Sales	168,273	192,300	218,953	248,497	281,402	318,837	360,306
Operating FCF	16,632	20,430	24,407	28,940	34,017	39,986	46,684
Nominal increase in sales		14.30%	13.90%	13.50%	13.20%	13.30%	13.00%
Nominal increase in FCF		22.80%	19.50%	18.60%	17.50%	17.50%	16.80%

In the case of our complex example we have the following figures (see Table 9.1b).

TABLE 9.1b   Relationship Between Sales and Operating and Total FCF, Complex Example

	Year 1	Year 2	Year 3	Year 4	Year 5	Average
FCF	4,772.10	8,992.50	8,574.40	4,536.20	11,808.60	
Increase in FCF		88.40%	−4.60%	−47.10%	160.30%	49.30%
EBIT	11,761.50	10,260.90	11,848.80	13,695.10	14,299.00	
Increase in EBIT		−12.80%	15.50%	15.60%	4.40%	5.70%
EBIT + OI	11,761.50	11,008.20	13,078.90	15,521.00	14,299.00	
Increase in EBIT + OI		−6.40%	18.80%	18.70%	−7.90%	5.80%
Sales	51,912.00	54,202.10	57,153.60	60,265.80	63,547.40	
Increase in sales		4.40%	5.40%	5.40%	5.40%	5.20%
NOPLAT	7,645.00	6,669.60	7,701.70	8,901.80	9,294.40	
Increase in NOPLAT		−12.80%	15.50%	15.60%	4.40%	5.70%

For g, we choose the growth of NOPLAT for period N, which in our example in Table 9.1b is 4.41%. The important issue to note in the table is that NOPLAT, FCF, and sales grow at different rates. In year 5, the growth in the FCF is a whopping 160% whereas the growth in sales at 5.40% is closer to the growth rate of the NOPLAT.

When using this growth rate from sales, we must realize that the rate includes the expected inflation rate, which means that we have to calculate the real rate of growth for year 5 and then inflate it with the inflation rate for year 6 and onwards. In our case both rates are equal. For illustration, we calculate the nominal rate for year 6.

$$\text{Real } g_{\text{NOPLATyr5}} = \frac{(1 + \text{Nominal } g_{\text{NOPLATyr5}})}{(1 + \text{Inflation rate}_{\text{year 5}})} - 1$$
$$= \frac{1.044}{1.03} - 1$$
$$= 1.37\%$$

Now we inflate the real rate of growth with the inflation rate for year 6 and onwards.

$$\text{Nominal } g_{\text{NOPLAT yr 5}} = (1 + \text{Real } g_{\text{NOPLAT yr 5}})(1 + \text{Inflation rate}_{\text{yr 6}}) - 1$$
$$= 1.0137 \times 1.03 - 1$$
$$= 4.41\%$$

We must take care in estimating the growth rate of NOPLAT in perpetuity. If the estimate is too high, it might suggest that the business has not reached a steady state, and it might be appropriate to model several periods with different growth rates. Most importantly, the growth rate of NOPLAT cannot exceed the growth rate of the economy. Otherwise, over time, the firm will be larger than the economy.

9.6 TV CALCULATED FOR THE DISCOUNTED CASH FLOW METHOD USING NOPLAT AND CONSTANT LEVERAGE

When calculating the TV we must guarantee that at least the cash flows remain constant, which implies that we require some investment to maintain that condition. To do this we use NOPLAT with no growth. This implies reinvestment of the depreciation to keep the cash flows constant. Using NOPLAT also implies that there is no AR and AP. The NOPLAT has an implicit inventory policy. If we calculate the TV with these conditions we assume that there is no growth in NOPLAT. The depreciation is reinvested just to maintain the NOPLAT at its actual level. In this case, the formulation for the TV would be the following:

$$TV = \frac{NOPLAT_N}{WACC_{N+1}}$$

To sustain growth in NOPLAT beyond the terminal period, we estimate the required amount of reinvestment in the fixed assets. We assume that this reinvestment occurs every year and we deduct a portion of NOPLAT to take account of the reinvestment. Let h be the proportion of NOPLAT that is to be deducted. The amount resulting from this proportion can be identified with capital expenditures. Then the new formula for the TV, taking into account the reinvestment, is as follows:

$$TV^{NOPLAT}{}_N = \frac{NOPLAT_N(1 + g)(1 - h)}{WACC_{N+1} - g} \tag{9.6}$$

For the moment, assume that the value of h is 0.270. Later we explain the calculations for h.

For our hypothetical example we assume that θ, the debt percentage, is 30%. The amount of the debt d is equal to θ times TV_N, and the interest payment is equal to the cost of debt d times the amount of debt. Then the WACC for year $N + 1$, assuming that the discount rate for the tax savings is the unlevered cost of equity, is calculated as follows:

$$
\begin{aligned}
WACC_{N+1} &= \rho - TS_{N+1}/TV_N \\
&= \rho - Td\theta TV_N/TV_N = \rho - Td\theta \qquad (9.7) \\
&= 21\% - 35\% \times 11\% \times 30\% = 19.85\%
\end{aligned}
$$

Substituting the appropriate numbers, we obtain that the TV is $45,869.27.

$$
\begin{aligned}
TV^{NOPLAT}{}_N &= \frac{NOPLAT_N(1+g)(1-h)}{WACC_{N+1} - g} \\
&= \frac{9,294.4(1 + 4.41\%)(1 - 0.27)}{19.85\% - 4.41\%} = 45,869.27
\end{aligned}
$$

9.7 AMOUNT OF REINVESTMENT FOR GROWTH IN THE FCF

If we have growth g, we have to guarantee that this growth can be sustained by reinvesting a fraction of NOPLAT in addition to the depreciation charge. It can be shown that the fraction to be invested is

$$
h = \frac{g}{\overline{ROMVIC}} \qquad (9.8)
$$

where h is the fraction to be invested, g is the rate of growth, and $\overline{ROMVIC}$ is the average return on the Market Value of Invested Capital (MVIC).

The fraction of NOPLAT that is to be reinvested is equal to the growth rate g divided by the average Return on the Market Value of Invested Capital (ROMVIC).

The detailed derivation of the formula is given in Appendix A. There we show the derivation of the expression g/ROMVIC as the fraction to be invested to ensure growth g.

Next, we show the calculations of the ROMVIC. In the calculations we deflate the $\overline{ROMVIC}$ and inflate the real $\overline{ROMVIC}$ to take into account the inflation rate that will prevail after year $N + 1$. We deflate the $\overline{ROMVIC}$ with the average expected inflation rate and then we inflate that real $\overline{ROMVIC}$ with the inflation rate estimated for years $N + 1$ and onwards.

This is necessary to have a consistent model in relation with inflation. In turn, the ROMVIC is calculated as follows:

$$\text{ROMVIC}_t = \frac{\text{NOPLAT}_t}{\text{MVIC}_{t-1}} \qquad (9.9)$$

9.8 CALCULATING THE ROMVIC

In Table 9.2, we show the NOPLAT and the levered value to calculate the ROMVIC and the h.

TABLE 9.2   Calculating the ROMVIC and g/ROMVIC

	Year 0	Year 1	Year 2	Year 3	Year 4	Year 5	Year 6
NOPLAT		7,644.95	6,669.57	7,701.69	8,901.81	9,294.37	
Levered value	44,250.80	48,094.63	48,660.60	49,898.91	55,570.75		
ROMVIC		17.3%	13.9%	15.8%	17.8%	16.7%	
Average ROMVIC						16.31%	
Real ROMVIC						12.9197%	
ROMVIC year N + 1							16.31%
h = g/ROMVIC							0.270

Obviously the total value is a number that cannot be obtained at this stage because it involves the discount rate (WACC), and this rate depends on the cash flows calculated, including the TV. This means that there is circularity between the TV, the ROMVIC, and the WACC. At this moment we assume those values and in the next section we explain how to obtain them.

The average ROMVIC is 16.31% and we use g = 4.41%. With these values we calculate h as 0.270. In other words, to maintain a growth rate of 4.41% in perpetuity, we reinvest 27.00% of the NOPLAT in perpetuity. To be conservative, we use the average ROMVIC, which is 16.31%, rather than the ROMVIC in year 5, which is 16.73%.

$$h = \frac{g}{\text{ROMVIC}} = \frac{4.41\%}{0.1631} = 0.270$$

In this approach to calculate h, the fraction to be invested is based on that proposed by Copeland et al. (2000). See Appendix A for details.

As we do not use constant ratios to estimate financial statements, the ROMVIC is not constant. The ROMVIC is a given value in the model. However, we estimate the ROMVIC for calculating the TV as the average ROMVIC during the explicit forecast period. This average ROMVIC can be seen as a target ROMVIC in perpetuity in the same way that we estimate a target leverage to define the WACC for perpetuity. Although these values cannot be used from the beginning but only after the circularity is solved, we show the values obtained with them.

9.9 ADDITIONAL ADJUSTMENTS

We need to make an additional adjustment to the TV in year N. We are assuming that all the funds generated are distributed to the equity holder. At the end of year 5, the amount of excess cash is $8,670.60. This cash must be returned to the equity holder. The use of NOPLAT implies that in perpetuity we do not have AR and AP. Hence, we have to recover cash, AR, and market securities investments, and pay AP. And then we add the net recovery to the calculated TV (see Table 9.3).

TABLE 9.3   Recovery of Some Current Assets

	Year 0	Year 1	Year 2	Year 3	Year 4	Year 5
Cash recovery						140.00
AR recovery						2,651.10
Market securities recovery						8,670.60
AP payment						−2,223.20
Net current assets recovery						9,238.60

The cash on hand can be recovered immediately and the AR and AP are recovered and paid at year $N + 1$ (in our example at year 6). Hence, the discount rate prevailing from year 6 and onwards is $WACC^{Perpetuity}$. For this reason we discount the book value of AR and AP by $WACC^{Perpetuity}$. In the example, for AR we have an outstanding AR of 3,177.40 (see BS in Table 6.1) and when discounted at $WACC^{Perpetuity}$, 19.85%, we obtain 2,651.10 (3,177.40/1.1985). We do the same with the AP. The cash excess investment is recovered with its return at year 6, but we assume that from year 6 and onwards any reinvestment is made at $WACC^{Perpetuity}$, and when we calculate that return and discount it back at the same rate we have the outstanding value (see Table 9.3).

Then the adjusted terminal or continuing value is as follows:

$$\text{Adjusted TV} = \text{TV} + \text{Net current assets recovery}$$

$$\text{Adjusted TV} = 45,869.27 + 9,238.60 = 55,107.86 \qquad (9.10)$$

TABLE 9.4 FCF withTV and other Adjustments

	Year 1	Year 2	Year 3	Year 4	Year 5
FCF	4,772.13	8,992.53	8,574.40	4,536.24	11,808.57
Adjusted TV					55,107.86
FCF with TV	4,772.13	8,992.53	8,574.40	4,536.24	66,916.43

The FCF with the TV, including the TV and other adjustments, is shown in Table 9.4. This is the FCF that we used in Chapter Seven to calculate the total value of the firm and to estimate the values of the annual WACCs.

When dealing with the APV approach to valuation we must be careful when calculating the total FCF. The APV approach states that the FCF (unlevered) should be discounted at the unlevered cost of equity ρ, and the tax savings should be discounted at the appropriate rate. We must remember that the TV we add to the FCF in Table 9.4 is the levered TV. What does this mean? It means that in the TV we have included the tax savings value. Hence, if the discount rate for the tax savings is not the unlevered cost of equity ρ, we overestimate the total value calculated with the APV approach. If we expect to calculate the APV, we should separate the TV for the unlevered FCF from the TV of the tax savings in perpetuity. Then we have the unlevered value of the FCF plus the unlevered value of the TV added together, and the tax savings and the TV of the tax savings added together. The FCF plus the unlevered TV is discounted back to year 0 at the unlevered cost of equity ρ, and the tax savings plus the TV of tax savings is discounted back to year 0 at the appropriate discount rate for the tax shield and then we calculate the APV.

9.10 A COMMENT ON CONSTANT LEVERAGE

When we teach capital structure and the cost of capital we say that we have to use market values. When we say that the WACC is constant, it implies the continuous adjustment of the debt in order to keep a constant leverage. Obviously, to have constant and targeted leverage means that there is no circularity between the calculation of the WACC and the total value. In reality this is the appeal of the idea of a constant WACC. What has to be done to maintain that constant leverage? We can distinguish two major cases: one is the case of a firm that is traded on the stock market and the other is the case of a non-traded firm.

Assuming that the market price is correct, the manager calculates the firm's leverage from the market value of equity and the market value of debt. To simplify the illustration, let us assume that the book value of debt is a reasonable estimate of the market value of debt. In this case, assume that the market value of equity (price of stock times number of stocks) is 2,000, the old debt is 250, and the desired leverage is 30%. Then the firm has to keep the following relationship:

$$\text{Leverage } \theta = \frac{\text{Old debt} + \text{New debt}}{\text{Market value of equity} + \text{Old debt} + \text{New debt D}}$$

$$= \frac{D_{old} + D_{new}}{E + D_{old} + D_{new}}$$

Solving for D_{new} we have

$$D_{new} = \frac{\theta E + \theta D_{old} - D_{old}}{1 - \theta} = \frac{30\% \times 2,000 + 30\% \times 250 - 250}{1 - 30\%} = 607.14$$

Then the firm has to acquire new debt for a value of 607.14. If we add 607.14 to the old 250 we have a total debt of 857.14, and this amount divided by 2,857.14 is 30%. In the case of a firm not traded in the stock exchange, constant leverage is a problem because every time the firm wants to check and update the leverage, they need the market value of the firm. The solution of this problem is theoretically simple: Keep the future estimates updated and perform the firm valuation to see if the firm needs to pay or acquire more debt.

As this permanent valuation of the firm by the manager is highly improbable, we have to deal with non-constant WACCs.

As shown in Chapter Seven on the WACC, we presented methods to calculate the total value.

9.10.1 Tax Savings with Terminal Value

From Chapter Six we know that the tax savings are as follows:

TABLE 9.5 Tax Savings

	Year 1	Year 2	Year 3	Year 4	Year 5
Tax savings	676.70	541.40	406.00	270.70	324.20

In our hypothetical example the tax savings equal the tax rate times the interest paid.

9.10.2 Cash Flow to Equity with Terminal Value

Now with the FCF and the TV we can derive the new CFE. The TV is the total value of the firm at year 5. That is, the PV of the FCF from year 6 to perpetuity. This total value is divided between debt and equity. Thus, from the TV we have to subtract the value of debt at year 5 and the resulting value is the net TV for equity. In our case we have to add the reinvestment of excess cash at year 5.

From the BS we observe that there is an outstanding debt of $3,923.90. This means that the TV for the CFE has to be adjusted by the subtraction of that debt, and the cash flow to debt (CFD) has to be adjusted by the addition (payment) of the outstanding value of debt. The CFE is calculated in the next table.

TABLE 9.6   Derivation of CFE with TV

	Year 0	Year 1	Year 2	Year 3	Year 4	Year 5
CFE		0.00	4,471.74	4,304.96	5,423.08	6,710.15
TV						45,869.27
Recovery of current assets						9,238.59
Debt outstanding						−3,923.93
CFE with TV		0.00	4,471.74	4,304.96	5,423.08	57,894.08

In the previous table we added the TV to the CFE calculated in Chapter Six, subtracted from the TV of the debt balance at year 5, and added the reinvestment of excess cash recovery to arrive at the CFE with TV. Now we can calculate the CFD.

9.10.3 Cash Flow to Debt with Terminal Value

Another issue arises regarding the amount of debt. It occurs when we have debt at the end of the planning horizon. This is the typical situation in a going concern. For the valuation to be consistent, we require that the PV of the CFD be equal to the actual debt at the beginning. In our example, the beginning of the analysis is at year 0. If this is not the case, as usually it is not, we have to make some adjustments.

For our complex example we have the following CFD.

TABLE 9.7   Cash Flow to Debt

	Year 0	Year 1	Year 2	Year 3	Year 4	Year 5
Debt balance	17,576.90	14,061.50	10,546.10	7,030.80	8,420.30	3,923.90
CFD		5,448.80	5,062.20	4,675.50	−616.10	5,422.60

If we calculate the PV of the CFD we find that it is not equal to $17,576.90 because we have outstanding debt in year 5.

The PV of the debt at 11% is $15,248.25. The difference between this value and the actual debt is $2,328.66. This amount is the PV at 11% of the outstanding value of debt at year 5.

Next we create an artificial payment of the debt balance at year N. This artificial payment is the same value that we subtracted from the TV to find the TV for the CFE.

At the same time we contract a new debt to repay that balance. The net value for this transaction is zero and we have a new debt balance equal to the old one. As stated previously, this is an artificial payment to guarantee that the PV of the CFD is equal to the actual value of the debt, and to recognize that we subtracted that value from the TV to derive the CFE. We have an adjusted CFD that includes the payment of the old debt. This makes the debt balance at year N equal to 0, and the PV of the adjusted CFD will always be equal to the debt balance at the end of year 0 (see Table 9.8).

Then we calculate the total debt (θ times TV) that is required to keep the leverage constant, but as we already have the old debt at N, the actual new debt to be contracted is $\theta \times$ TV − Old debt.

TABLE 9.8 Derivation of Adjusted CFD and New Debt

	Year 0	Year 1	Year 2	Year 3	Year 4	Year 5
Debt balance	17,576.90	14,061.50	10,546.10	7,030.80	8,420.30	3,923.90
CFD		5,448.80	5,062.20	4,675.50	−616.10	5,422.60
New debt payment						3,923.90
Adjusted CFD		5,448.80	5,062.20	4,675.50	−616.10	9,346.50
PV(CFD at d)	17,576.90	14,061.50	10,546.10	7,030.80	8,420.30	

The PV of the CFD at d is exactly the value of debt at year 0.

9.10.4 Capital Cash Flow with Terminal Value

Now with the FCF and the TS we can derive the new CFE.

TABLE 9.9 Derivation of CCF with TV

	Year 0	Year 1	Year 2	Year 3	Year 4	Year 5
CFE with TV		0.00	4,471.74	4,304.96	5,423.08	57,894.08
Adjusted CFD		5,448.84	5,062.15	4,675.46	−616.15	9,346.53
CCF = CFD + CFE		5,448.84	9,533.89	8,980.42	4,806.93	67,240.61
FCF with TV		4,772.13	8,992.53	8,574.40	4,536.24	66,916.43
TS		676.70	541.40	406.00	270.70	324.20
CCF = FCF + TS		5,448.80	9,533.90	8,980.40	4,806.90	67,240.61

The TS is taken from Table 9.5 and the CFE and CFD from Tables 9.6 and 9.7. This CCF is the one we used in Chapter Seven to calculate the total value of the firm using the cost of unlevered equity as the discount rate.

9.11 CALCULATING TV WITH THE CCF AND APV APPROACHES

We can also calculate the TV with the CCF and APV approaches. See Appendix B.

9.12 SUMMARY AND CONCLUDING REMARKS

In cash flow valuation, it is impractical to construct financial statements with a long planning period. Thus, there is a need to estimate the TV, which is the PV, with respect to the terminal year N of the cash flows that occur in perpetuity in the years beyond year N. In this chapter, we have examined some of the critical issues that are related to the calculation of the TV.

APPENDIX A

A9.1 TV AND AMOUNT OF REINVESTMENT

In this appendix, we examine the case where the growth rate of NOPLAT in the years beyond the terminal year N might be higher than the growth rate of the FCF in the forecast period. Thus, we have to subtract a percentage h to account for the higher growth rate.

A9.2 RETURN ON THE MARKET VALUE OF INVESTED CAPITAL (MVIC)

Let $MVIC_i$ be the market value of the invested capital in year i, which is the total value at market prices, and let $ROMVIC_i$ be the return on the MVIC in year i. Then the ROMVIC in year $i + 1$ is defined as the ratio of NOPLAT in year $i + 1$ to the MVIC in the beginning of year $i + 1$.

$$ROMVIC_{i+1} = \frac{NOPLAT_{i+1}}{MVIC_i} \qquad (A9.1)$$

The reader should be aware that the ROMVIC is calculated using market value for the invested capital and that we use the invested capital for the previous year. Unlike other authors, we define the ROMVIC in terms of the MVIC instead of book values. The NOPLAT incorporates the allowance for depreciation to account for the annual reinvestment in the productivity of the existing assets. This is equivalent to assuming that the depreciation allowance is reinvested and guarantees that NOPLAT remains constant.

A9.3 ADDITIONAL REINVESTMENT FOR HIGHER GROWTH OF NOPLAT

Let X be the amount of reinvestment that is required for higher growth of NOPLAT. Then the incremental NOPLAT generated by investment X is equal to investment X times the ROMVIC.

$$\text{Incremental NOPLAT} = X \times \text{ROMVIC} \qquad (A9.2)$$

The ROMVIC in equation A9.2 is not related to a particular period. The equation explains the meaning and definition of ROMVIC. How do we calculate the ROMVIC during the explicit period? Equation A9.2 is intended to show the values of NOPLAT that are related to the other values of the MVIC and explain to the reader how to calculate the ROMVIC.

Also, NOPLAT in year $N + 1$ is equal to NOPLAT in year N times one plus g.

$$\text{NOPLAT}_{N+1} = \text{NOPLAT}_N(1 + g) \qquad (A9.3)$$

Solving for the growth rate g, we obtain that g is equal to the incremental NOPLAT divided by the NOPLAT in year N.

$$g = \frac{\text{NOPLAT}_{N+1} - \text{NOPLAT}_N}{\text{NOPLAT}_N}$$

$$= \frac{\text{Incremental NOPLAT}}{\text{NOPLAT}_N} \qquad (A9.4)$$

Combining equations A9.2 and A9.4, and solving for the amount of investment X, we obtain the following:

$$X = \frac{g \times \text{NOPLAT}_N}{\text{ROMVIC}} \qquad (A9.5)$$

In equation A9.5 we use the ROMVIC as defined and estimated by the analyst. It could be an expected future ROMVIC, the last ROMVIC—if we believe that the value has reached the steady state—or (as we did in the body of the paper) we could use the average ROMVIC during the explicit forecasting period or the average historical ROMVIC (in case we have the MVIC for past years).

Rearranging equation A9.5, we see that the ratio of investment amount X to NOPLAT in year N is equal to the ratio of growth rate g to the ROMVIC.

$$\frac{X}{NOPLAT_N} = \frac{g}{ROMVIC} = h \qquad (A9.6)$$

The fraction of NOPLAT in the year N that is reinvested is equal to the amount of investment X divided by NOPLAT in the year N.

Let h be the fraction of NOPLAT in the year N that is reinvested. Then NOPLAT adjusted for reinvestment is equal to NOPLAT in year N times one minus h.

$$NOPLAT \text{ adjusted for reinvestment} = NOPLAT_N(1 - h) \qquad (A9.7)$$

and the formula for the TV is as follows:

$$TV^{FCF}_N = \frac{NOPLAT_N(1 - h)(1 + g)}{WACC^{Perpetuity} - g} \qquad (A9.8)$$

Substituting equations A9.3 and A9.6 into equation A9.8, we obtain the following:

$$TV^{FCF}_N = \frac{NOPLAT_{N+1}\left(1 - \frac{g}{ROMVIC}\right)}{WACC^{Perpetuity} - g}$$

$$= \frac{NOPLAT_{N+1}\left(\frac{ROMVIC - g}{ROMVIC}\right)}{WACC^{Perpetuity} - g} \qquad (A9.9)$$

If the ROMVIC is equal to the $WACC^{Perpetuity}$, the expression for the TV can be simplified as follows:

$$TV^{FCF}_N = \frac{NOPLAT_{N+1}\left(\frac{WACC^{Perpetuity} - g}{WACC^{Perpetuity}}\right)}{WACC^{Perpetuity} - g}$$

$$TV^{FCF}_N = \frac{NOPLAT_{N+1}}{WACC^{Perpetuity}} \qquad (A9.10)$$

APPENDIX B

B9.1 INDEPENDENT CALCULATION OF THE TV LEVERED VALUE

B9.2 VALUE OF DEBT IN THE TERMINAL PERIOD N

Let the CFD in year $N + 1$ be CFD_{N+1}. We assume that the CFD in perpetuity is also growing at g% per year. This implies a growing interest payment, a growing debt, and a constant leverage from $N + 1$ and onwards. At the end of year N, the PV of the debt is equal to the cash flow to debt in the year $N + 1$ divided by the cost of debt d less the growth rate g.

$$V^{TV\_D}{}_N = \frac{CFD_{N+1}}{d - g} \qquad (B9.1)$$

Let θ be the PV of the debt in year N as a percent of the levered TV in year N, exclusive of the current cash flow in year N.

$$\theta = \frac{V^{TV\_D}{}_N}{V^{TV\_L}{}_N} \qquad (B9.2)$$

Combining the last two lines, we obtain an expression for the CFD in year $N + 1$.

$$CFD_{N+1} = (d - g)V^{TV\_D}{}_N = (d - g)\theta V^{TV\_L}{}_N \qquad (B9.3)$$

and the interest at year $N + 1$, Int_{N+1} is

$$Int_{N+1} = dV^{TV\_D}{}_N = d\theta V^{TV\_L}{}_N \qquad (B9.4)$$

To use this line, we need the levered value in year N, and to calculate the levered value we need the TV of the TS. Next we show how to derive these values.

B9.3 VALUE OF THE TAX SHIELD IN THE TERMINAL YEAR N

At the end of year N, the PV of the TS is equal to the TS in year $N+1$ divided by ρ less the growth rate g.

$$V^{TV\_TS}{}_N = \frac{TS_{N+1}}{\rho - g} = \frac{TInt_{N+1}}{\rho - g} \tag{B9.5}$$

We already know that

$$Int_{N+1} = dV^{TV\_D}{}_N = d\theta V^{TV\_L}{}_N \tag{B9.6}$$

Substituting, we obtain

$$V^{TV\_TS}{}_N = \frac{Td\theta V^{TV\_L}{}_N}{\rho - g} \tag{B9.7}$$

In this line, the value of the TS in terminal period N, exclusive of the current TS in year N, is expressed in terms of the levered value in terminal period N. Next, we find a relationship between the levered value in terminal period N and the unlevered value in year N, exclusive of the current FCF in year N.

B9.4 LEVERED VALUE IN THE TERMINAL YEAR N

We estimate the levered value in year N by finding a relationship between the levered and unlevered values. In an M & M world, the levered value in year N is equal to the sum of the unlevered value in year N (exclusive of the FCF in year N) and the PV of the TS in year N (exclusive of the TS in year N).

$$V^{TV\_L}{}_N = V^{TV\_Un}{}_N + V^{TV\_TS}{}_N \tag{B9.8}$$

Substituting, we obtain

$$V^{TV\_L}{}_N = V^{TV\_Un}{}_N + \frac{Td\theta V^{TV\_L}{}_N}{\rho - g} \tag{B9.9}$$

Reorganizing, we have

$$V^{TV\_Un}{}_N = V^{TV\_L}{}_N - \frac{Td\theta V^{TV\_L}{}_N}{\rho - g} \tag{B9.10}$$

and

$$V^{TV\_Un}{}_N = V^{TV\_L}{}_N \left(1 - \frac{Td\theta}{\rho - g}\right) \tag{B9.11}$$

Define ϕ as follows.

$$\phi = 1 - \frac{Td\theta}{\rho - g} \tag{B9.12}$$

Then, the levered value will be as follows:

$$V^{TV\_L}{}_N = \frac{V^{TV\_Un}{}_N}{\phi} \tag{B9.13}$$

but the unlevered value is:

$$V^{TV\_Un}{}_N = \frac{FCF_{N+1}}{(\rho - g)} \tag{B9.14}$$

and the levered TV is:

$$V^{TV\_L}{}_N = \frac{FCF_{N+1}}{(\rho - g)\phi} \tag{B9.15}$$

Now we can calculate the value of the tax savings with respect to the end of year N as

$$V^{TV\_TS}{}_N = V^{TV\_L}{}_N - V^{TV\_Un}{}_N \tag{B9.16}$$

With the relationship between the levered and the unlevered, we can write the expression for the PV of the TS in the terminal period, exclusive of the current TS, directly in terms of the unlevered value.

Substituting, we obtain an expression for the value of the TS in terminal period N.

$$V^{TV\_TS}{}_N = \frac{Td\theta V^{TV\_Un}{}_N}{(\rho - g)\phi} \tag{B9.17}$$

Using this expression, in one step we can calculate the value of the TS in the terminal period, exclusive of the current TS. At the end of year N, the unlevered value, exclusive of the current FCF, is known. With the specification of the debt, as a percent of the levered value at the end of year N, we can find the value of the TS.

For clarity in exposition, we show the calculations in several steps for our complex example. Assuming that θ, the debt percentage, is 30%, the fraction of NOPLAT to be invested is 0.270, and $NOPLAT_{N+1}$ is

$$NOPLAT(1 - h)(1 + g) \tag{B9.18}$$

where h is the fraction of NOPLAT to be invested in perpetuity and g is the growth rate, we have

$$9{,}294.40(1 + 4.40\%) \times (1 - 0.270) = 7{,}079.98$$

The unlevered value at year N is 42,675.86.

$$TV^{Un}_{N} = \frac{FCF_N(1+g)(1-h)}{\rho - g} = \frac{FCF_{N+1}}{\rho - g} = \frac{7,079.98}{21\% - 4.41\%} = 42,675.86$$

Next, we calculate the value of ϕ in order to estimate the terminal value.

$$\phi = 1 - \frac{Td\theta}{\rho - g} = 1 - \frac{35\% \times 11.0\% \times 30\%}{21\% - 4.41\%} = 0.93038027$$

The value of the TS in perpetuity (growing) is 3,193.41.

$$V^{TV\_TS}_{N} = \frac{Td\theta V^{TV\_Un}_{N}}{(\rho - g)\phi} = \frac{35\% \times 11.0\% \times 30\% \times 42,675.86}{(21\% - 4.41\%)0.930380269} = 3,193.41$$

Now we can construct the TS flow (see Tables B9.1 and B9.2) and the FCF (see Table B9.3). The TS flow is

TABLE B9.1   Tax Shield and Total Tax Shield

	Year 1	Year 2	Year 3	Year 4	Year 5
TS	676.71	541.37	406.03	270.68	324.18
PVTSVn					3,193.41
Total TS	676.71	541.37	406.03	270.68	3,517.59

TABLE B9.2   TV Unlevered and TV for TS

	Year 5
TV unlevered	42,675.86
PV(TS$_N$)	3,193.41
TV levered = TV unlevered + PV(TS$_N$)	45,869.27

and the FCF is

TABLE B9.3   Free Cash Flow with Terminal Value

	Year 1	Year 2	Year 3	Year 4	Year 5
FCF (no TV)	4,772.13	8,992.53	8,574.40	4,536.24	11,808.57
TV unlevered					42,675.86
PV(TS$_N$)					3,193.41
Recovery of market securities					9,238.59
FCF (with TV)	4,772.13	8,992.53	8,574.40	4,536.24	66,916.43

B9.5 TV WITH CCF AND APV

The TV can be obtained by using the CCF and the APV.

Now we can construct the TS flow and the FCF. The TS flow in Table B9.4 is

TABLE B9.4   Tax Savings

	Year 1	Year 2	Year 3	Year 4	Year 5
TS	676.70	541.40	406.00	270.70	324.20

and the FCF (see Table B9.5) is

TABLE B9.5   FCF withTV for APV Calculation

	Year 1	Year 2	Year 3	Year 4	Year 5
FCF (no TV)	4,772.13	8,992.53	8,574.40	4,536.24	11,808.57
TV unlevered					42,675.86
Total TS	676.71	541.37	406.03	270.68	3,517.59
Recovery of current assets					9,238.59

When using the APV approach, all the lines in Table B9.5 are discounted at ρ, the unlevered return to equity except the total TS, which is discounted at the appropriate discount rate and could be ρ, the unlevered return to equity.

The CCF is calculated in the Table B9.6.

TABLE B9.6 Capital Cash Flow

	Year 1	Year 2	Year 3	Year 4	Year 5
FCF (with TV)	4,772.13	8,992.53	8,574.40	4,536.24	66,916.43
TS	676.71	541.37	406.03	270.68	324.18
CCF	5,448.84	9,533.89	8,980.42	4,806.93	67,240.61

The CCF will be discounted at the unlevered cost of equity ρ. We showed these calculations in Chapter Seven.

APPENDIX C

C9.1 PURE FCF AND NON-PURE FCF

When we calculate the FCF to estimate the total value, we usually add the levered TV with equation 9.6. However, when using the APV or CCF approaches we have to be careful with this FCF, which includes the levered TV. To avoid this error we must distinguish between pure and non-pure FCFs. The FCF we present in Table 9.4 should not be used for APV or CCF purposes because it is a non-pure FCF. In which sense is it a non-pure FCF? In the sense that it includes the levered TV. The pure FCF does not include the item that is implicit in the TV and that is related to the PV of the TS in perpetuity. We will explain this idea with a simple array of flows.

Assume that we have an explicit forecasted period of five years, a TV at year 5, and that all cash flows in year 6 are in perpetuity. Also, assume that we have a growing perpetuity from year 6 and onwards as in Table C9.1.

TABLE C9.1   Cash Flow Relationships

Year	1	2	3	4	5	6
FCF	FCF1	FCF2	FCF3	FCF4	FCF5	FCF6
TS	TS1	TS2	TS3	TS4	TS5	TS6
CFE	CFE1	CFE2	CFE3	CFE4	CFE5	CFE6
CFD	CFD1	CFD2	CFD3	CFD4	CFD5	CFD6

Next we calculate the TVs associated with each item.

Value relationships

$$(\rho_6 - g)V^{TV-Un}{}_5 = FCF_6 \qquad (C9.1)$$

$$(\psi_6 - g)V^{TV-TS}{}_5 = TS_6 \qquad (C9.2)$$

$$(e_6 - g)V^{TV-E}{}_5 = CFE_6 \qquad (C9.3)$$

$$(d_6 - g)V^{TV-D}{}_5 = CFD_6 \qquad (C9.4)$$

$$FCF^T{}_6 = FCF_6 + V^{TV-Un}{}_5 \qquad (C9.5)$$

$$TS^T{}_6 = TS_6 + V^{TV-TS}{}_5 \qquad (C9.6)$$

$$CFE^T{}_6 = CFE_6 + V^{TV-E}{}_5 \qquad (C9.7)$$

$$CFD^T{}_6 = CFD_6 + V^{TV-D}{}_5 \qquad (C9.8)$$

The cash flows we calculate using these expressions are pure cash flows. Specially, the cash flow associated with the FCF. Observe that the TV we calculate for the FCF item is the unlevered TV, and in the tax savings item we calculate the TV of the tax savings. When we include the levered value of the TV in the FCF, as in Table 9.4, we are including the TV of the tax savings. In this section we propose to explicitly separate each item. The pure cash flows comply with the classical M & M formulation, as follows:

$$FCF^T{}_6 + TS^T{}_6 = CFE^T{}_6 + CFD^T{}_6 \qquad (C9.9)$$

For our complex example we have the pure FCF in Table C9.2:

TABLE C9.2   Pure Cash Flows

	Year 1	Year 2	Year 3	Year 4	Year 5
FCF	4,772.13	8,992.53	8,574.40	4,536.24	11,808.57
Unlevered TV					42,675.86
Recovery of current assets					9,238.59
Pure FCF with TV unlevered	4,772.13	8,992.53	8,574.40	4,536.24	64,723.02
TS	676.71	541.37	406.03	270.68	324.18
PV(TS$_N$)					3,193.41
Total TS	676.71	541.37	406.03	270.68	3,517.59
CCF = Pure FCF + TVun + Total TS	5,448.84	9,533.89	8,980.42	4,806.93	67,240.61
CCF = FCF + TS	5,448.84	9,533.89	8,980.42	4,806.93	67,240.61
FCF = CFD + CFE − TS	4,772.13	8,992.53	8,574.40	4,536.24	66,916.43
FCF = Pure FCF + TVun + PV(TS$_N$)	4,772.13	8,992.53	8,574.40	4,536.24	66,916.43
FCF = FCF + Levered TV	4,772.13	8,992.53	8,574.40	4,536.24	66,916.43

Now, when using the APV and CCF approach, we discount the pure FCF at the unlevered cost of equity ρ and the total tax savings at the appropriate discount rate.

The basic cash flow relationships are satisfied and the following calculations for FCFs match each other, in particular for year 5:

$$FCF = CFD + CFE - TS = 66,916.43$$
$$FCF = \text{Pure FCF} + PVTSVN = 66,916.43$$
$$FCF = FCF + \text{Levered TV} = 66,916.43$$

This FCF can be discounted at the WACC.
The same can be said regarding the CCF:

$$CCF = CFD + CFE = 67,240.61$$
$$CCF = FCF + TS = 67,240.61$$

This CCF can be discounted at the unlevered cost of equity ρ.

APPENDIX D

D9.I MATCHING THE RESIDUAL INCOME METHOD, EVA® AND DCF

In Chapter Seven, we presented several different ways to value cash flows. In the first method, we apply the standard after-tax WACC to the FCF. In the second method, we apply the adjusted WACC to the FCF, and in the third method, we apply the WACC to the CCF. In addition, we can also discount the CFE with the appropriate returns to levered equity. As shown in Chapter Seven, when properly calculated, all four methods give the same results. We refer to these four ways as the DCF methods.

In recent years, two new approaches, the residual income method (RIM) and the EVA have become popular. Supporters claim that the RIM and EVA superior to the DCF methods. It might be case that the RIM and EVA approaches are useful tools for assessing managerial performance and providing proper incentives. However, from a valuation point of view, the RIM and EVA are problematic because they use book values from the BS. From the beginning of this book, we have stressed that the valuation of cash flows must be based on market values. Does it make sense to use book values for valuation purposes? It is easy to show that under certain conditions, the results from the RIM and EVA exactly match the results from the DCF methods. Thus, it is strange to claim that the RIM and EVA methods are superior to the DCF methods when in fact they are algebraically equivalent.

This appendix is organized as follows. In Section 1, we present the basic ideas for the RIM and EVA methods. In Section 2, we show how the results of these two methods match the results of the DCF methods.

D9.2 WHAT IS VALUE ADDED?

The basic idea of the RIM is as follows. In the IS, the cost of debt financing, in the form of interest payments, is listed. However, there is no charge for the equity that is invested in the company. Thus, it seems plausible that if we were to specify an explicit charge for equity, and subtract the charge for equity from the NI, the difference would be the value added. Let NI_i be the NI in year i, and let e_i be the required return to equity in year i. Typically, proponents of RIM assume that the required return to equity is constant. The equity charge in year i is defined as the required return to equity times the book value of equity at the beginning of year i, as it is listed in the BS.

$$\text{Equity charge in year i} = \text{Book value of equity in beginning of} \\ \text{year i times e} \qquad \text{(D9.1)}$$

The RI is the difference between the NI and the equity charge.

$$\text{RI} = \text{NI less Equity charge} \qquad \text{(D9.2)}$$

Thus, proponents claim that if the RI is positive, value has been added, and if the RI is negative, value has been lost.

Alternatively (roughly speaking), we could begin with the EBIT, which does not include the interest charges for debt financing. In this case, we use the WACC, which takes into account both the cost of debt and the required return to equity. Thus, we use the WACC to estimate the charge for the total capital invested and subtract the capital charge from the EBIT. Typically, proponents of EVA assume that the WACC is constant. The capital charge in year i is defined as the WACC times the book value of the invested capital at the beginning of year i, as it is listed in the BS.

$$\text{Capital charge in year i} = \text{Total capital invested in beginning of} \\ \text{year i times WACC} \qquad \text{(D9.3)}$$

The value added is the difference between the EBIT$(1 - \text{Tax rate})$ or NOPLAT, and the capital charge.

$$\text{Value added} = \text{NOPLAT less capital charge} \qquad \text{(D9.4)}$$

Again, proponents claim that if NOPLAT is higher than the capital charge, value is created, and if NOPLAT is lower than the capital charge, value has been destroyed.

For complex numerical examples, several assumptions must be met for the results from the RIM and EVA to match the results from the DCF methods. The key assumption for the reconciliation between the RIM and EVA and the DCF methods is the following. The return to equity e (in the case of RIM) and the WACC (in the case of EVA) must be calculated based on market values of the CFE and the FCF, respectively. What appears incongruous is that we apply the return to equity and the WACC, based on market values, to the book values of equity and capital invested from the BS, to estimate the equity charge and capital charge, respectively.

D9.3 ASSUMPTIONS AND FINANCIAL STATEMENTS FOR THE COMPLEX EXAMPLE

Next, we show that, with some adjustments, the levered values obtained with the RIM and EVA exactly match the levered values obtained with the CCF method. Recall that the complex example of Chapter Five has the following features.

- AR and AP policies.
- Inventory policy.
- Reinvestment of cash excess at market rates.
- Purchase price discounts for quantities.
- Inflation, nominal prices, and price demand elasticity.
- TV.
- Debt and debt balance outstanding at final year.
- The example is consistent with M & M propositions.
- We assume a constant unlevered return to equity.
- Payout ratio.

For easy reference, we present the three financial statements again in Tables D9.1–D9.3.

TABLE D9.1   Pro-Forma Income Statement

	Year 0	Year 1	Year 2	Year 3	Year 4	Year 5
Sales		51,912.00	54,202.10	57,153.60	60,265.80	63,547.40
COGS		20,708.60	24,099.70	24,996.20	25,772.20	26,577.80
Gross profit		31,203.40	30,102.40	32,157.40	34,493.60	36,969.70
Selling and administrative expenses		9,441.90	9,841.50	10,308.70	10,798.50	11,325.30
Depreciation		10,000.00	10,000.00	10,000.00	10,000.00	11,345.40
EBIT		11,761.50	10,260.90	11,848.80	13,695.10	14,299.00
Interest income on marketable securities		0.00	747.40	1,230.20	1,825.90	0.00
Other expenses (interest expenses)		1,933.50	1,546.80	1,160.10	773.40	926.20
EBT		9,828.00	9,461.50	11,918.80	14,747.60	13,372.80
Taxes		3,439.80	3,311.50	4,171.60	5,161.70	4,680.50
NI		6,388.20	6,149.90	7,747.30	9,585.90	8,692.30
Dividends		4,471.70	4,305.00	5,423.10	6,710.20	6,084.60
Retained earnings		1,916.50	1,845.00	2,324.20	2,875.80	2,607.70
Accumulated retained earnings		6,388.20	8,066.40	11,508.70	15,671.60	17,653.70

TABLE D9.2   Balance Sheet

	Year 0	Year 1	Year 2	Year 3	Year 4	Year 5
Assets						
Cash	1,576.90	100.00	110.00	120.00	130.00	140.00
AR	0.00	2,595.60	2,710.10	2,857.70	3,013.30	3,177.40
Inventory	0.00	1,725.70	2,033.30	2,085.00	2,150.80	2,217.90
Investment on marketable securities	0.00	12,271.90	20,199.90	29,981.60	0.00	8,670.60
Interest accrued	0.00	0.00	0.00	0.00	0.00	0.00
Net fixed assets	40,000.00	30,000.00	20,000.00	10,000.00	45,381.60	34,036.20
Total	41,576.90	46,693.20	45,053.30	45,044.20	50,675.60	48,242.10
Liabilities and equity						
AP (suppliers)	0.00	2,243.40	2,440.70	2,504.80	2,583.80	2,664.50
Accrued taxes	0.00	0.00	0.00	0.00	0.00	0.00
Long-term debt	17,576.90	14,061.50	10,546.10	7,030.80	8,420.30	3,923.90
Total liabilities	17,576.90	16,305.00	12,986.90	9,535.60	11,004.10	6,588.40
Equity	24,000.00	24,000.00	24,000.00	24,000.00	24,000.00	24,000.00
Retained earnings	0.00	6,388.20	8,066.40	11,508.70	15,671.60	17,653.70
Total	41,576.90	46,693.20	45,053.30	45,044.20	50,675.60	48,242.10

TABLE D9.3   Pro-Forma Cash Budget

	Year 0	Year 1	Year 2	Year 3	Year 4	Year 5
Cash inflows						
Total income AR	0.00	49,316.40	54,087.60	57,006.00	60,110.20	63,383.30
Total cash inflows	0.00	49,316.40	54,087.60	57,006.00	60,110.20	63,383.30
Cash outflows						
Total payments to suppliers on cash	0.00	20,190.90	24,210.00	24,983.80	25,758.90	26,564.20
Overhead	0.00	2,260.80	2,340.20	2,422.50	2,507.60	2,608.70
Payroll expenses	0.00	2,509.10	2,623.10	2,742.30	2,867.00	2,997.30
Selling commissions	0.00	3,114.70	3,252.10	3,429.20	3,615.90	3,812.80
Advertising and promotions	0.00	1,557.40	1,626.10	1,714.60	1,808.00	1,906.40
Purchase of fixed assets	40,000.00					
Purchase of fixed assets year 4	0.00	0.00	0.00	0.00	45,381.60	0.00
Taxes	0.00	3,439.80	3,311.50	4,171.60	5,161.70	4,680.50
Total cash outflows	40,000.00	33,072.70	37,363.10	39,464.10	87,100.70	42,570.00
NCB	−40,000.00	16,243.80	16,724.50	17,542.00	−26,990.50	20,813.40
Bank loan 1	17,576.90					

(continues)

TABLE D9.3 *(continued)*

Bank loan 2		0.00	0.00	0.00	4,904.90	0.00
Payment of loans	0.00	3,515.40	3,515.40	3,515.40	3,515.40	4,496.40
Interest charges	0.00	1,933.50	1,546.80	1,160.10	773.40	926.20
NCB after financial transactions	−22,423.10	10,794.90	11,662.40	12,866.50	−26,374.40	15,390.80
Equity investment	24,000.00					
Dividend payments		0.00	4,471.70	4,305.00	5,423.10	6,710.20
Repurchase of stock						
NCB after cash transactions with shareholders	1,576.90	10,794.90	7,190.70	8,561.50	−31,797.50	8,680.60
Sales of marketable securities	0.00	0.00	12,271.90	20,199.90	29,981.60	0.00
Interest income on marketable securities	0.00	0.00	747.40	1,230.20	1,825.90	0.00
Investment on marketable securities		12,271.90	20,199.90	29,981.60	0.00	8,670.60
NCB after discretionary transactions paid in cash	1,576.90	−1,476.90	10.00	10.00	10.00	10.00
Accumulated cash balance at end of year	1,576.90	100.00	110.00	120.00	130.00	140.00

D9.3.I Residual Income Method for the Complex Example

Based on these financial statements, we reconcile the results of the RIM with the previous results obtained with the DCF methods. The calculations for the RI are shown in the following table. The NI is from the IS and the equity book value is from the BS. Because of the complexities in the complex example, as we will explain, we must make some adjustments to calculate the RI in year 5.

The annual returns to levered equity were calculated in Chapter Seven. In any year i, we use the return to levered equity to calculate the annual equity charge, based on the book value of equity at the beginning of the year. For example, the equity charge in year 1 is $6,621.49.

Equity charge in year 1 = Book value of equity times return to levered equity

$$= 24,000 \times 27.59\% = 6,621.49$$

Similarly, we can calculate the equity charges for the other years. In any year i, the RI equals the NI less the equity charge. The RI in year 1 is $−233.29.

$$RI \text{ in year } 1 = NI \text{ less equity charge}$$
$$= 6,388.20 - 6,621.49 = -233.29$$

In years 1, 2 and 5, the RIs are negative, and in years 3 and 4, the RIs are positive. In year 5, the RI is \$−347.18. However, we have not taken into account some of the items that are appropriate in the terminal period. For detailed discussions on the required adjustments in the terminal period, see Chapter Nine. We simply state the adjustment. We start with the TV in year 5, subtract the equity book value in year 5, add the recovery of operating items, and subtract the debt outstanding. The RI in year 5, taking into account the terminal period adjustments, is \$9,183.03 (see Tables D9.4).

TABLE D9.4   RI Calculations for the Complex Example

	Year 0	Year 1	Year 2	Year 3	Year 4	Year 5
NI		6,388.20	6,149.95	7,747.25	9,585.93	8,692.32
$e = \rho + (\rho - d)\, D/E$		27.59%	25.13%	23.77%	22.64%	22.79%
Charge for equity		6,621.49	7,637.08	7,621.21	8,039.20	9,039.50
RI		−233.29	−1,487.13	126.04	1,546.73	−347.18
TV = NOPLAT(1 + g)						45,869.27
(1 − h)/(WACC$_{\text{perpet}}$−g)						
minus Liquidating value						−41,653.72
(equity book value)						
Plus recovery of						9,238.59
operating items						
Debt outstanding						−3,923.93
RI with TV		−233.29	−1,487.13	126.04	1,546.73	9,183.03
PV (RI at e)	2,673.89	3,644.89	6,048.05	7,359.45	7,478.90	
Equity book value	24,000.00	30,388.20	32,066.41	35,508.70	39,671.55	41,653.72
Plus equity bok value	26,673.89	34,033.09	38,114.45	42,868.14	47,150.45	
Debt balance	17,576.91	14,061.53	10,546.15	7,030.77	8,420.30	17,576.91
Total value = Equity	44,250.80	48,094.63	48,660.60	49,898.91	55,570.75	
value + debt						

Next, we calculate the PV of the annual RIs, using the annual returns to levered equity. In any year i, the value of levered equity equals the sum of the book value of equity and the PV of the RI. In year 0, the levered equity value is \$26,673.89.

$$\text{Levered equity in year } 0 = \text{Book value of equity} + \text{PV of RI}$$

$$= 24,000 + 2,673.89 = 26,673.89$$

Adding the levered equity values to the values of debt, we verify that the total levered values derived from the RIM exactly match the previous levered values that were obtained from the CCF method.

D9.3.2 Economic Value Added for the Complex Example

The calculations of the EVA for the complex example are shown in the following table. The starting point for the EVA calculations is NOPLAT plus the after-tax OI. The book values of the invested capital are from the BS. Again, as in the RIM calculations, we have to make some adjustments in the terminal period. The annual WACCs were calculated in Chapter Seven. In any year i, we use the WACC to calculate the annual capital charge, based on the book value of invested capital at the beginning of the year. In year 1, the capital charge is $8,095.330.

$$\text{Capital charge in year } 1 = \text{Book value of equity times return to levered equity}$$
$$= 41,576.90 \times 19.47\% = 8,095.33$$

Similarly, we can calculate the capital charges for the other years.

In any year i, the EVA equals NOPLAT plus the after-tax OI less the capital charge.

$$\text{EVA in year } 1 = \text{NOPLAT} + \text{after-tax OI less capital charge}$$
$$= 7,644.95 - 8,095.33 = -450.38$$

In years 1, 2, 3 and 5, the EVAs are negative, and in year 4 the EVA is positive. However, in year 5 we have to make some adjustments to the EVA. As discussed earlier, we begin with the TV in year 5, subtract the book value of invested capital in year 5, and add the recovery of operating items. The EVA in year 5, taking into account the terminal period adjustments, is $9,005.84 (see Table D9.5).

TABLE D9.5   EVA Calculations for the Complex Example

	Year 0	Year 1	Year 2	Year 3	Year 4	Year 5
EBIT		11,761.47	10,260.87	11,848.75	13,695.09	14,299.03
OI		0.00	747.36	1,230.17	1,825.88	0.00
Tax on EBIT + OI		4,116.51	3,852.88	4,577.62	5,432.34	5,004.66
NOPLAT+ after-tax OI		7,644.95	7,155.35	8,501.30	10,088.63	9,294.37
Book value of invested capital	41,576.91	44,449.74	42,612.56	42,539.46	48,091.85	45,577.65
WACC		19.47%	19.87%	20.17%	20.46%	20.42%
Capital invested charge		8,095.33	8,834.10	8,593.08	8,702.53	9,818.74
EVA		−450.38	−1,678.76	−91.78	1,386.10	−524.37

(continues)

TABLE D9.5 (*continued*)

TV = NOPLAT $(1+g)(1-h)/$ $(WACC_{perpet}-g)$					45,869.27
Minus liquidating value					−45,577.65
Plus recovery of operating items					9,238.59
Total EVA = EVA + TV		−450.38	−1,678.76	−91.78	1,386.10	9,005.84
PV(Total EVA)	2,673.89	3,644.89	6,048.05	7,359.45	7,478.90	
Cap invested +PV(EVA)	44,250.80	48,094.63	48,660.60	49,898.91	55,570.75	

Next, we calculate the PV of the annual EVAs, using the annual WACCs applied to the FCF. In any year i, the levered value equals the sum of the book value of invested capital and the PV of the EVA. In year 0, the levered value is $44,250.80.

$$\text{Levered value in year } 0 = \text{Book value of invested capital}$$
$$+ \text{PV of EVA} = 41{,}576.90 + 2{,}673.89$$
$$= 44{,}250.80$$

We verify that the total levered values derived from the EVA match exactly the previous levered values that were obtained from the CCF method.

D9.4 SUMMARY AND CONCLUDING REMARKS

In this appendix, we assessed the claim that the RIM and EVA are superior to the DCF methods. In particular, using the complex example from Chapter Five, we demonstrated that the results obtained from the RIM and EVA match exactly the results from the DCF methods.

10

THEORY FOR COST
OF CAPITAL REVISITED

> In fine, nothing is said now (*on the WACC*) that has not been said before.
>
> —*Terence* (195 BC to 159 BC)

> A question that sometimes drives me hazy: am I or are the others crazy?
>
> —*Albert Einstein*

10.1 COST OF CAPITAL WITH A FINITE STREAM OF CASH FLOWS

In Chapter One, we presented an informal introduction to the basic conceptual ideas on the cost of capital. In Chapter Two, we used numerical examples with finite cash flows to illustrate the calculations for the cost of capital in an M & M world without and with taxes.[1]

In this chapter, we revisit the theory for the cost of capital applied to a finite stream of cash flows. In particular, we discuss the Miles and Ezzel (M & E) formulation for the WACC applied to finite cash flows. The M & E formulation provides justification for using the return to unlevered equity ρ to discount the TS. Compared to the previous chapters, this chapter is more

---

[1]In the appendix to Chapter Two, we presented detailed numerical examples on the cost of capital with cash flows in perpetuity. However, as mentioned earlier, for valuation purposes, cash flows in perpetuity are not flexible enough to accommodate the diverse assumptions that arise in practice.

difficult.[2] It is conceptual and theoretical, and in addition, we have to introduce new notation for finite cash flows. However, the basic ideas will be familiar from the presentations in the previous chapters. We illustrate all the concepts with two-period numerical examples, which provide a much-needed antidote for the theory. The approach presented here can be easily extended to cash flows over more than two periods.

We advise the reader to skim over the chapter to get a general sense of the material, work through the numerical examples, and then reread the theoretical part of the chapter carefully to gain a solid understanding.[3] We hope this chapter gives the reader a deeper appreciation for theory on the cost of capital as applied to finite cash flows derived from financial statements.

In an M & M world without taxes, the cost of capital calculations with a finite stream of cash flows is straightforward. And the ideas from the previous chapters carry over to a finite stream of cash flows.

In an M & M world with taxes, the policy on debt financing has important implications for the cost of capital because of the benefits of the TSs. In this chapter, we do not specify the values for the annual leverage.[4] Instead, we specify the loan schedule and calculate the values for the annual leverage from the values of the annual debt in the loan schedule. With the loan schedule, we can show the relationship between the debt financing and the variable leverage over time.

With respect to the TS, there are two key issues. First, based on the risk profile of the TS, we must determine the appropriate discount rate for the TS. Second, we must decide how to incorporate the effect of the TS in the WACC. We can lower the WACC and apply the WACC to the FCF, or alternatively, we can calculate a WACC that is applied to the CCF, which already includes the TSs. In addition, we present two different formulations for the WACC: the standard weighted average formula and an alternative adjusted formulation that is based on deviation from the return to unlevered equity.

The chapter is organized as follows. In Section 1, we briefly review the value and cash flow relationships for finite cash flows. In Section 2, we introduce a simple two-period numerical example to illustrate the ideas from Section 1. In Section 3, we introduce the multi-period WACC. In Section 4, we discuss the various options for debt financing. In Section 5, we

---

[2]The practical issues that are involved in the estimation of the different components of the cost of capital are discussed in Chapters Seven and Eight.

[3]Do not be discouraged by the algebra. The algebra is simply unavoidable and we have kept the level of the algebra to the bare minimum. We believe that the rewards from understanding the theory will be well worth the effort in struggling through the algebra.

[4]If the profile for the leverage over the life of the FCF is specified, typically the loan schedule is not constructed. However, in some cases, to determine the CFD, we have to construct the loan schedule based on the specified leverage profile.

examine the Miles and Ezzell (M & E) formulation for the WACC. In Section 6, we present the WACC with a fixed loan schedule, and in Section 7 we present the various formulation for the WACC with a fixed leverage. In Section 8, we present the algebra for the various formulations of the WACC. In Sections 9 through 15, we provide more details for the various formulations of the WACC. In Appendix A, we use a simple example to illustrate the derivation of the M & E formulation. In Appendix B, we present a detailed numerical example with constant leverage.

An understanding of the M & M world without taxes facilitates the transition to the M & M world with taxes. We begin with the M & M world without taxes. The discussion on the M & M world without taxes might seem unnecessarily complicated. However, we use the same structure to discuss the M & M world with taxes, and the familiarity with the structure from the M & M world without taxes should improve the comprehension of the subtleties involved with taxes.

10.1.1 WACC in an M & M World Without Taxes

We begin by discussing the WACC for a finite stream of expected nominal (annual) cash flows in an M & M world without taxes. All the values, such as unlevered values, levered values, values of levered equity, and debt are market values. With finite cash flows, we have to be careful about the calculations for the values at the end of the year. We do not present the detailed financial statements here. We assume that the FCF has been derived from the relevant financial statements, namely the IS, the CB statement and the BS, using the integrated framework presented in Chapters Four and Five.

10.1.2 Value Relationships

In an M & M world without taxes, in each year, the levered value is equal to the unlevered value, where V^L_i is the market levered value in year i and V^{Un}_i is the market unlevered value in year i. Consider a simple two period example.

$$V^L_0 = V^{Un}_0 \qquad (10.1)$$

$$V^L_1 = V^{Un}_1 \qquad (10.2)$$

In turn, in each year, the levered value equals the sum of the (levered) equity and the debt, where E^L_i is the value of the (levered) equity in year i and D_i is the value of the debt in year i.

$$V^L_0 = E^L_0 + D_0 \qquad (10.3)$$

$$V^L_1 = E^L_1 + D_1 \qquad (10.4)$$

We calculate the PVs of the FCF, the PVs of the CFD and the PVs of the CFE. And we verify that in each year, the WACC is equal to the weighted average of the cost of debt and the return to equity, where the weights are the market values of debt and (levered) equity as percentages of the total levered (market) values. The WACC for year i is w_i, the rate of return to levered equity in year i is e_i, and the leverage in year i is θ_i. It is important to recognize that the leverage in year i is the debt at the beginning of year i (or the end of year i − 1) as a percentage of the levered value at the beginning of year i (or the end of year i − 1).

$$w_1 = \%D_1 d_1 + \%E_1 e_1 \qquad (10.5)$$

$$w_2 = \%D_2 d_2 + \%E_2 e_2 \qquad (10.6)$$

where

$$\theta_i = \%D_i = D_{i-1}/V^L_{i-1} \qquad (10.7)$$

$$(1 - \theta_i) = \%E_i = E_{i-1}/V^L_{i-1} \qquad (10.8)$$

10.1.3 Cash Flow Relationships

Next, we present some cash flow relationships. In any year i, the FCF equals the sum of the CFE and the CFD.

$$FCF_1 = CFE_1 + CFD_1 \qquad (10.9)$$

$$FCF_2 = CFE_2 + CFD_2 \qquad (10.10)$$

10.1.4 Unlevered Value in Year 1

In year 1, the unlevered value equals the FCF in year 2 discounted by the return to unlevered equity ρ_2.

$$V^{Un}_1 = FCF_2/(1 + \rho_2) \qquad (10.11)$$

10.1.5 Unlevered Value in Year 0

In year 0, the unlevered value equals the FCF in years 1 and 2, discounted to year 0 by the returns to unlevered equity ρ_1 and ρ_2.

$$V^{Un}{}_0 = FCF_1/(1 + \rho_1) + FCF_2/[(1 + \rho_1)(1 + \rho_2)] \qquad (10.12)$$

Substituting equation 10.11 into equation 10.12, we obtain

$$V^{Un}{}_0 = (FCF_1 + V^{Un}{}_1)/(1 + \rho_1) \qquad (10.13)$$

In year 0, the unlevered value equals the discounted value of the sum of the FCF in year 1 and the unlevered value with respect to year 1, where the discount rate is the return to unlevered equity ρ_1.

10.2 NUMERICAL EXAMPLE

We use a numerical example to illustrate the ideas that we have just presented. Let FCF_i be the expected nominal FCF in year i and let ρ_i be the nominal risk-adjusted return to unlevered equity in year i. Let the FCF in year 1 be \$500 and let the FCF in year 2 be \$600.

For simplicity, assume that the expected inflation rate is constant for the life of the FCF, and the nominal risk-adjusted return to unlevered equity is constant for the two years and equal to 16%. We drop the time subscript for the return to unlevered equity. At the end of year 0, the unlevered market value $V^{Un}{}_0$ is \$876.93.

$$
\begin{aligned}
V^{Un}{}_0 &= FCF_1/(1 + \rho) + FCF_2/(1 + \rho)^2 \\
&= 500.00/(1 + 16\%) + 600.00/(1 + 16\%)^2 \\
&= 431.03 + 445.90 = 876.93
\end{aligned}
$$

In other words, based on the expected cash flows and the risk-adjusted discount rates, at the end of year 0, the fair market price for the right to the cash flow stream over two years is \$876.93.

At the end of year 1, the equity holder receives the FCF of \$500, and $V^{Un}{}_1$, the unlevered market value (of the FCF in year 2), is \$517.24.

$$
\begin{aligned}
V^{Un}{}_1 &= FCF_2/(1 + \rho) \\
&= 600.00/(1 + 16\%) = 517.24
\end{aligned}
$$

10.2.1 Unlevered Equity Schedule

Next, we construct the unlevered equity schedule, which may be new for many readers (see Table 10.1). The format of the unlevered equity schedule is the same as the structure of a loan schedule and is useful for estimating and summarizing the inter-temporal PVs of the FCF. In any year i, the EB of the equity schedule is equal to the BB plus the dividend accrued less the FCF.

$$EB_i = BB_i + \rho BB_i - FCF_i \qquad (10.14)$$

$$EB_i = (1 + \rho)BB_i - FCF_i \qquad (10.15)$$

The dividend accrued each year is based on the required rate of return to unlevered equity ρ and is equal to the BB times the return to unlevered equity ρ. Based on the outstanding market value of the equity and the required rate of return, the dividend accrued measures the required return (in dollar terms) and may differ from the actual dividends payments that are calculated in the (IS) and paid out to the equity holder.

Here we assume that the dividends accrued are equal to the dividend payments from the IS and we obtain the values for the equity repurchase from the CB statement. For this simple example, in each year, the difference between the FCF and the dividend accrued is the equity repurchase.[5] Typically, the equity holder simply receives the dividends actually paid. However, in this example, the FCF exceeds the dividends.

In year 1, the equity repurchase is $359.69 and in year 2, the equity repurchase is $517.24.

TABLE 10.1 Unlevered Equity Schedule

Year	0	1	2
BB		876.93	517.24
Dividend Accrued		140.30	82.75
FCF		500.00	600.00
EB	876.93	517.24	0.00

Equity repurchase in year 1 = FCF_1 − Dividends accrued in year 1
= 500 − 140.31 = 359.69
Equity repurchase in year 2 = FCF_2 − Dividends accrued in year 2
= 600 − 82.76 = 517.24

---

[5]With new equity contributions, the profile of the CFE might be more complex.

As expected, based on the equity schedule, at the end of year 0, the unlevered PV is \$876.93 and at the end of year 1, the unlevered PV is \$517.24.

10.2.2 Loan Schedule for the Debt Financing

We assume that the amount of the debt at the end of year 0 is \$300 and the nominal risk-adjusted cost of the debt is 10% and constant for the two years. The loan principal will be repaid with two equal principal payments. We recognize that this loan schedule is atypical. However, the loan schedule simplifies the calculations and, based on the annual outstanding balances for the loan, we estimate the annual interest payments. With this loan schedule, the amount of the loan is not fixed and the annual leverages are not constant (see Table 10.2).[6] It might be more common to specify a target for the leverage, and later, we present the construction of a loan schedule with a constant debt–equity ratio for both years.

In any year i, the EB of the loan schedule is equal to the BB plus the interest accrued less the total loan payment (Pmt).

$$EB_i = BB_i + dBB_i - Pmt_i \qquad (10.16)$$

$$EB_i = (1 + d)BB_i - Pmt_i \qquad (10.17)$$

TABLE 10.2   Loan Schedule

Year	0	1	2
BB		300.00	150.00
Interest accrued		30.00	15.00
Principal payment		150.00	150.00
Total payment		180.00	165.00
EB	300.00	150.00	0.00

At the end of year 0, the value of the debt is \$300, and at the end of year 1, the value of the debt is \$150.

The annual loan payment is equal to the principal repayment plus the accrued interest. In year 1, the CFD holder CFD_1 is \$180 and in year 2, the CFD holder CFD_2 is \$165.

$$
\begin{aligned}
D_0 &= CFD_1/(1 + d) + CFD_2/(1 + d)^2 \\
&= 180/(1 + 10\%) + 165/(1 + 10\%)^2 \\
&= 163.64 + 136.36 = 300.00
\end{aligned}
$$

[6]The amount of the loan would only be fixed in the unusual case that only annual interest payments are made and the loan is repaid with a balloon payment at the end.

Next, we write down the following algebraic relationships for the values of debt in year 0 and year 1.

10.2.3 Value of Debt in Year 1

In year 1, the value of debt equals the CFD in year 2 discounted by the cost of debt d.

$$D_1 = CFD_2/(1+d) \tag{10.18}$$

10.2.4 Value of Debt in Year 0

In year 0, the value of debt equals the CFD in years 1 and 2 discounted to year 0 by the cost of debt d.

$$D_0 = CFD_1/(1+d) + CFD_2/(1+d)^2 \tag{10.19}$$

Substituting equation 10.18 into equation 10.19, we obtain

$$D_0 = (CFD_1 + D_1)/(1+d) \tag{10.20}$$

In year 0, the debt equals the discounted value of the sum of the CFD in year 1 and the debt with respect to year 1, where the discount rate is the cost of debt d.

10.2.5 Annual Cash Flow to Equity (Levered)

The annual CFE equals the FCF less the CFD (see Table 10.3).[7] We obtain the CFD from the loan schedule in Table 10.2.

In year 1, the CFE is $320 and in year 2, the CFE is $435.

$$CFE_1 = FCF_1 - CFD_1 = 500 - 180 = 320.00$$
$$CFE_2 = FCF_2 - CFD_2 = 600 - 165 = 435.00$$

TABLE 10.3   Cash Flow to Equity (Levered)

Year	0	1	2
FCF		500.00	600.00
CFD		180.00	165.00
CFE		320.00	435.00

[7]Generally, the CFE is the profile of the dividend payments. Here we assume that any discrepancy between the CFE and the dividend payments are due to equity repurchase or additional equity contributions.

To value the CFE, we estimate the expected returns to levered equity in the two years. Because the debt–equity ratios are different in the two years, the expected returns to equity are also different because the returns to equity are functions of the debt–equity ratios.

10.2.6 Debt–Equity Ratios

The unlevered values and the values of debt are shown in Table 10.4. In any year, the value of (levered) equity equals the levered value less the value of debt. Without taxes, the levered value is equal to the unlevered value.

$$E^L_0 = V^L_0 - D_0 = 876.93 - 300 = 576.93$$
$$E^L_1 = V^L_1 - D_1 = 517.24 - 150 = 367.24$$

In year 1, the market value of the debt at the end of year 0 as a percent of the levered market value at the end of year 0 is 34.21%.

$$\%D_1 = D_0/V^L_0 = 300.00/876.93 = 34.21\%$$

In year 2, the market value of the debt at the end of year 1 as a percent of the levered market value at the end of year 1 decreases to 29% from 34.21% in year 1.

$$\%D_2 = D_1/V^L_1 = 150.00/517.24 = 29.00\%$$

TABLE 10.4   Debt–Equity Ratios

Year	0	1	2
Unlevered value	876.93	517.24	
Value of debt	300.00	150.00	
Value of (levered) equity	576.93	367.24	
Debt (% Levered value)		34.21%	29.00%
Equity (% Levered value)		65.79%	71.00%
Debt–equity ratio		0.51999	0.40845

In year 1, the debt–equity ratio is 0.52 and in year 2, the debt–equity ratio is 0.408.

10.2.7 Returns to Levered Equity in Year 1 and Year 2

Let e_1 be the return to levered equity in year 1, and let e_2 be the return to levered equity in year 2. Because the leverage changes from year 1 to year 2, the returns to (levered) equity are different for the two years. Now we do not derive the formula that we use for calculating the return to levered equity. Later in this chapter, we derive a general expression for the return to levered equity.

$$e_1 = \rho + (\rho - d)D_0/E^L{}_0$$

$$= 16\% + (16\% - 10\%) \times 0.51999 = 19.120\%$$

$$e_2 = \rho + (\rho - d)D_1/E^L{}_1$$

$$= 16\% + (16\% - 10\%) \times 0.40845 = 18.451\%$$

The return to levered equity in year 1 e_1 is 19.12% and the return to levered equity in year 2 e_2 is 18.451%. The return to levered equity decreases from 19.12% in year 1 to 18.45% in year 2 because the debt–equity ratio decreases from 0.52 in year 1 to 0.41 in year 2.

We verify that these returns to levered equity are correct by calculating the PV of the CFE in year 1 and year 0.

$$E^L{}_1 = CFE_2/(1 + e_2) = 435/(1 + 18.451\%) = 367.24$$

$$E^L{}_0 = CFE_1/(1 + e_1) + CFE_2/[(1 + e_1)(1 + e_2)]$$

$$= 320/(1 + 19.12\%) + 435/[(1 + 19.12\%)(1 + 18.451\%)]$$

$$= 268.64 + 308.29 = 576.93$$

We can write down the following algebraic relationships for the values of (levered) equity in year 0 and year 1.

10.2.8 Value of (Levered) Equity in Year 1

In year 1, the value of (levered) equity equals the CFE in year 2 discounted by the return to levered equity e_2.

$$E^L{}_1 = CFE_2/(1 + e_2) \qquad (10.21)$$

10.2.9 Value of (Levered) Equity in Year 0

In year 0, the value of (levered) equity equals the CFE in year 1 and year 2 discounted to year 0 by the returns to levered equity e_1 and e_2.

$$E^L{}_0 = CFE_1/(1 + e_1) + CFE_2/[(1 + e_1)(1 + e_2)] \qquad (10.22)$$

Substituting equation 10.21 into equation 10.22, we obtain

$$E^L{}_0 = (CFE_1 + E^L{}_1)/(1 + e_1) \qquad (10.23)$$

In year 0, the levered value is equal to the discounted value of the sum of the CFE in year 1 and the levered value with respect to year 1, where the discount rate is the return to levered equity e_1.

10.2.10 Levered Equity Schedule

For completeness, based on the returns to equity, we construct the levered equity schedule (see Table 10.5). Based on the value and cash flow relationships, the sum of the values in the loan schedule and the levered equity schedule equal the corresponding values in the unlevered equity schedule. Again, we assume that the actual dividend payments are equal to the dividends accrued. In this case, there are equity repurchases because the cash flows to the equity holder exceed the actual dividend payments.

In year 1, the equity repurchase is $359.69 and in year 2, the equity repurchase is $517.24.

Equity repurchase in year 1 = CFE_1 − Dividends accrued in year 1

$$= 320 - 110.31 = 179.69$$

Equity repurchase in year 2 = CFE_2 − Dividends accrued in year 2

$$= 435 - 67.76 = 367.24$$

TABLE 10.5   Levered Equity Schedule

Year	0	1	2
BB		576.93	367.24
Dividend accrued		110.31	67.76
CFE		320.00	435.00
EB	576.93	367.24	0.00

At the end of year 0, the levered equity value is $576.93 and at the end of year 1, the levered equity value is $367.24.

10.2.11 Calculation of the Multi-period WACC

Next, we calculate the multi-period WACCs. We know that in an M & M world without taxes, the annual WACCs are equal to the returns to unlevered equity ρ_i. Let w_1 be the WACC in year 1, and let w_2 be the WACC in year 2.

$$w_1 = \%D_1 d + \%E^L{}_1 e_1 = 34.21\% \times 10\% + 65.79\% \times 19.12\%$$
$$= 16.00\%$$
$$w_2 = \%D_2 d + \%E^L{}_2 e_2 = 29\% \times 10\% + 71\% \times 18.451\%$$
$$= 16.00\%$$

As expected, in the absence of taxes, the WACC is unchanged and equal to the return to unlevered equity ρ. To maintain the constant WACC, the decrease in the debt percentage from 34.21% in year 1 to 29% in year 2 is exactly offset by a decrease in the return to levered equity from 19.12% in year 1 to 18.451% in year 2.

10.3 LOAN SCHEDULE WITH CONSTANT LEVERAGE

In the previous section, we specified the loan schedule and based on the loan schedule, we derived the values for the annual leverage. Now we specify the leverage for each year and illustrate how to derive the corresponding loan schedule that is consistent with the target values for the leverage. We assume that θ_1 is 30% and θ_2 is 40%.

First, we calculate the annual unlevered values. Without taxes, the levered values are equal to the unlevered values. Second, based on the levered values, we calculate the annual values for debt.

At the end of year 0, the value of the debt is 30% of the levered value and is equal to $263.08, and at the end of year 1, the value of debt 40% of the levered value and is equal to $206.90. In any year, to maintain the target level of leverage, the CFD is equal to the interest accrued less the change in the value of the debt. In year 1, the CFD is $82.49 and in year 2, the CFD is $227.59 (see Table 10.6).

$$CFD_1 = dD_0 - (D_1 - D_0)$$
$$= 10\% \times 263.08 - 206.90 + 263.08 = 82.49$$
$$CFD_2 = dD_1 - (D_2 - D_1)$$
$$= 10\% \times 206.90 - 0 + 206.90 = 227.59$$

TABLE 10.6 Loan Schedule With Specified Leverage

Year	0	1	2
FCF		500.00	600.00
Unlevered values	876.93	517.24	
Leverage		30.00%	40.00%
Value of debt	263.08	206.90	
Interest accrued		26.31	20.69
Change in value of debt		−56.18	−206.90
CFD		82.49	227.59

The annual debt–equity ratios are shown in Table 10.7. Using the debt–equity ratios, we calculate the returns to levered equity.

$$e_1 = \rho + (\rho - d)D_0/E^L{}_0$$
$$= 16\% + (16\% - 10\%) \times 0.4286 = 18.57\%$$
$$e_2 = \rho + (\rho - d)D_1/E^L{}_1$$
$$= 16\% + (16\% - 10\%) \times 0.6667 = 20.00\%$$

TABLE 10.7 Debt–Equity Ratios

Year	0	1	2
Unlevered value	876.93	517.24	
Value of debt	263.08	206.90	
Value of (levered) equity	613.85	310.34	
Debt (% Levered value)		30.00%	40.00%
Equity (% Levered value)		70.00%	60.00%
Debt–equity ratio		0.4286	0.6667

The return to levered equity in year 1 e_1 is 18.57% and the return to levered equity in year 2 e_2 is 20%. The return to levered equity increases from 18.57% in year 1 to 20% in year 2 because the debt–equity ratio increases from 0.429 in year 1 to 0.667 in year 2. The reader can verify that the CFE discounted by these returns to levered equity gives the correct values for the annual values of the (levered) equity.

10.3.1 Calculation of the Multi-period WACC

Next, we calculate the multi-period WACCs. We know that in an M & M world without taxes, the annual WACCs are equal to the returns to unlevered equity ρ_i.

$$w_1 = \%D_1d + \%E_1e_1 = 30\% \times 10\% + 70\% \times 18.57\% = 16.00\%$$
$$w_2 = \%D_2d + \%E_2e_2 = 40\% \times 10\% + 60\% \times 20\% = 16.00\%$$

As expected, in the absence of taxes, the WACC is unchanged and equal to the return to unlevered equity ρ. To maintain the constant WACC, the increase in the debt percentage from 30% in year 1 to 40% in year 2 is exactly offset by an increase in the return to levered equity from 18.57% in year 1 to 20% in year 2.

10.4 POLICY ON DEBT FINANCING AND THE WACC IN THE PRESENCE OF TAXES

Next, we examine the theory of the WACC for a finite stream of cash flows in an M & M world with taxes. For ease in reading and understanding, we follow the same structure that we used in the earlier exposition of the WACC in an M & M world without taxes. To minimize repetition, we do not present the value and cash flow relationships for an M & M world with taxes because they have been discussed in previous chapters. The reader is encouraged to refer to the discussion in the previous chapters.

Very briefly, in any year i, the levered value equals the sum of the levered equity and the debt. Also, the levered value equals the sum of the unlevered value and the PV of the TS. The CCF equals the sum of the CFE and the CFD. Also, in any year i, the CCF equals the sum of the FCF and the TS. In any year i, for simplicity, we assume that the TS equals the interest payment times the tax rate. Although, technically speaking, in any year i, the TS equals the taxes paid by the unlevered firm less the taxes paid by the levered firm.

First, we discuss how the policy on debt financing affects the cost of capital. For simplicity, we assume that there are only corporate taxes and that the debt and the TSs are risk-free. In practice, the actual extent of the benefits of debt financing is an empirical matter. With the presence of personal and other taxes, the overall effect of debt financing can be reduced.

We make two major assumptions. First, we pretend that the debt is risk-free even though we do not use the risk-free rate for the cost of debt.[8]

Second, we assume that the TSs are also risk-free. With finite cash flows, the discount rate for the TSs might not be the risk-free rate even if the TSs in year n are always risk-free with respect to the previous year n−1. Technically, from the point of view of a stochastic binomial process, the tax shields are pre-visible. The uncertainty in the dollar amount of the debt through time means that the tax shields are uncertain, and thus with respect to the orginal reference point, the subsequent tax shields are not risk-free.[9]

---

[8]With this assumption, we avoid the distinction between the promised return on the debt and the expected return on the debt. From a practical point of view, the discrepancy between the promised return and the expected return might be small.

[9]Furthermore, if the debt is risky, there are complex interactions between the cost of debt d and the appropriate discount rate for the TS ψ.

10.4.1 Risk-free Tax Shields

We assume that the annual TSs are risk-free in the sense that the annual EBIT are always sufficient for the TSs to be realized in the years in which the interest deductions occur.[10] However, the issue of risk-free TSs is subtle. Later in the chapter we will elaborate further on the meaning of the risk-free TS. Roughly speaking, it is not appropriate to use the risk-free rate for the TS if the amount of the TS is unknown. For the moment, we do not consider the case where the EBIT might be insufficient for the TSs to be realized in the year in which the interest deductions occur. We assume that there are no LCF.

With a finite stream of cash flows, we have to be careful about the specification of the policy with regard to debt financing. There are two possibilities. We might have a fixed loan schedule or alternatively, at the beginning of each year, we might have to rebalance the debt to maintain a constant leverage.

10.4.2 Fixed Loan Schedule

If there is a fixed loan schedule and the annual values of the debt are known in advance, then for all the years, the annual leverage and the annual TSs are known. This assumes that over time, there are no changes in the values of the debt. Because the amounts of the annual TSs are known and the EBIT are sufficient for the TSs to be realized in the current years, ψ_i the discount rates for the TS in year i are equal to the risk-free rate r_f.[11] The discount rate for the TS in year i depends on the risk of the EBIT rather than the risk of the debt, which may or may not be risk-free. In the next section we provide further discussion on the fixed loan schedule.

10.4.3 Constant Leverage

Alternatively, we assume that the annual leverage is constant and unrealistically, the debt is continually rebalanced to achieve the target leverage. If the debt policy is to maintain a constant leverage, only the value of the debt at the beginning of any year i is known and the values of the annual debts in the

---

[10]If there is other income (OI), for the TSs to be realized, the sum of the EBIT and OI for the year must be greater than the interest expense for the year.

[11]The rate for discounting the TS in year i to the previous year i − 1 is ψ_i. The discount rate ψ_i is not the cumulative rate for discounting the TS in year i to the reference year n.

future years beyond year i are unknown. Because the value of the debt at the beginning of year i is known, the interest payments for year i are known and the TS that will be realized at the end of year i is also known.

However, with respect to year i, the interest payments for the years beyond year i are unknown. Hence, the TSs that will be realized are also unknown and it might not be appropriate to use the risk-free rate to discount the TSs in the years beyond year i. Here we do not provide a rigorous demonstration for the validity of this profile for the appropriate discount rates for the TS. In the next section we provide further explanations in the context of the discussion on the M & E formulation of the WACC for the FCF.

10.5 THE MILES AND EZZEL (M & E) WACC

Assuming that the debt and the TS are risk-free, for a finite stream of cash flows with constant leverage, Miles and Ezzel (M & E) derive the following formula for the annual WACC.

$$\text{WACC}^{\text{ME}} = (1 + \rho)\left[1 - \frac{Tr_f\theta}{1 + r_f}\right] - 1 \qquad (10.24)$$

where ρ is the annual rate of return to unlevered equity, T is the tax rate, and θ is the debt as a percent of the levered value.

All the parameters—ρ, T, d, and θ—are constant. Furthermore, Miles and Ezzell show that the expression for the WACC in equation 10.24 can be re-written in the standard after-tax formulation of the WACC. In Appendix A, we present an informal derivation of the M & E WACC.

In the M & E formulation, it is important to emphasize that the one-year ahead TSs are always risk-free. For example, with respect to any reference year n, the TSs for the next year $n + 1$ are always known and ψ_{n+1}, the discount rate for the TS in year $n + 1$, is the risk-free rate. However, with respect to year n, all the subsequent TSs in the years beyond $n + 1$ are uncertain and must be discounted with the return to unlevered equity ρ because the TSs are correlated with the FCF.[12]

Compare this result with the discount rate for the TS with the FCF in perpetuity without growth. With the cash flow in perpetuity without growth, the constant amount of debt implies that we know the annual interest payment and that we know the value of the annual TS. Also, with cash

---

[12]The M & E formulation can be modified to take account of variable leverage by specifying a different WACC for each year. However, it would be more difficult to account for LCF if in any year i, the EBIT is not sufficient for the TS to be realized in year i.

flows in perpetuity without growth, the constant amount of debt implies that the leverage is constant.[13]

With a finite stream of cash flow, the constant leverage does not imply that we know values for the annual interest payments because the value of the debt in each period is unknown and depends on the resolution of the uncertainty associated with the FCF. Thus, with respect to the original reference point, the interest payments are unknown and the discount rates for the TSs in the future periods are not the risk-free rate. Even though the TSs are always realized in the year in which they occur, there is uncertainty in the values of the TSs that are realized because they are a function of the leverage.

10.5.1 The M & E Argument in the Limit

We take the M & E argument a step further and imagine that the one-period ahead is one week, rather than one year, and the leverage is rebalanced every week. Then in the M & E formulation of the WACC, the discount rate for the TS in the first week will be the risk-free rate and the discount rates for the TSs in the subsequent weeks will be the return to unlevered equity ρ.

We take the M & E argument another step further and imagine that the one-period ahead is one day. Again, in the M & E formulation of the WACC, the discount rate for the TS in the first day will be the risk-free rate and the discount rates for the TSs in the subsequent days will be the return to unlevered equity ρ. Thus, with a finite stream of cash flow, and assuming constant leverage, it is reasonable to assume that the future TSs are uncertain and discount ALL the annual TSs with the return to unlevered equity ρ.

If the discount rate for the TS is the same as the return to unlevered equity, then it is much easier to use the WACC applied to the CCF rather than the WACC applied to the FCF.[14] The WACC applied to the CCF would simply be equal to the return to unlevered equity. The difference between the M & E WACC and the WACC applied to the CCF would be to use the risk-free rate to discount the TS for one day!

---

[13]On the issue of cash flows in perpetuity, professor Nicholas Wonder has provided the following insightful comments. It is possible to have unending cash flows where the debt level, *in expectation*, is the same in each period and nevertheless, the debt is random. When we are assessing risk, the main point is not whether the expected value of debt is flat or growing with the expected changes in equity value. Rather, it is what happens to debt when equity is unexpectedly large or small. For example, tax shields can be discounted at the risk-free rate if risk-free debt is expected to grow at the same rate as equity, so long as the actual dollar value of debt is known in advance and does not change when equity growth is more or less expected.

[14]If the annual TSs are unknown (for example, if the loan schedule is not constructed), it is still possible to derive a WACC applied to the FCF with the assumption that the discount rate for the TS is the return to unlevered equity ρ.

The WACC with the CCF assumes that the return to unlevered equity is the correct discount rate for the TSs in all periods because the future TSs are uncertain. This is not an unreasonable assumption and is almost correct.

10.5.2 Relaxation of the M & E Assumptions (Optional)

Suppose the assumptions underlying the M & E WACC do not hold. To be specific, assume the following:

1. Debt percentage is variable.
2. Debt is risky.
3. TSs are risky.

With these new assumptions, what is the correct formula for the cost of capital? If the debt is risky, and the payoff structure for the TS is identical to the payoff structure for the levered equity holder, the discount rate for the TS is equal to the return to levered equity e. Alternatively, if the debt is risk-free and the TS is risky, the discount rate for the TS might even be higher than e. For further details, see Tham & Wonder (2001a, b). Here, we simply alert the reader to the complications that can arise with the relaxations of the M & E assumptions. Further discussion on the relaxations of these assumptions is beyond the scope of this book.

10.6 WACC FOR A FINITE STREAM OF CASH FLOWS IN AN M & M WORLD WITH TAXES

From a practical point of view, what should we do? There is a menagerie of WACCs. To provide an overview of the possibilities, we list the different WACC formulations for two specifications: fixed loan schedule and fixed percentage of debt. At this moment, all the different formulations of the WACC may seem confusing. However, there is an underlying unity that will only be clear after we derive the formulas. The theory on the cost of capital applied to finite cash flows is complex and we ask for the reader's patience. The reader might wish to skip this section and return to it after reading the rest of the chapter.

10.6.1 Fixed Loan Schedule

We assume that the loan schedule is specified and the annual interest payments are known. Furthermore, in each year i, the EBIT are sufficient for the TS to be realized in the years in which the interest payments are made.

With a specified loan schedule, there are several possibilities. First, if we only pay the annual interest payments (and make a balloon payment at the end), the amount of the loan is fixed over the life of the FCF and the annual interest payments are known. However, even though the amount of the loan outstanding is fixed, the leverage is not constant. In this case, we can assume that in each year i, the appropriate discount rate for the TS ψ_i is equal to the cost of debt d_i. This loan schedule is uncommon and we do not present the formulas for this case.

Second, over the life of the loan schedule, the loan repayments include both principal repayment and interest payments. For example, we can assume that the loan is repaid in equal installments. It is possible that the interest payments are known with full certainty, in which case the discount rate for the tax shield is the risk-free rate. However, it is unlikely that we know the interest payments with full certainty. Thus, even in this case, we assume that in each year i, the appropriate discount rate for the TS ψ is equal to the return to unlevered equity ρ rather than the cost of debt d.

$$\psi_i = \rho \qquad (10.25)$$

For this case of the specified loan schedule, we propose two WACCs. For each WACC, we have two formulations, the standard and the adjusted, and the WACC can be applied to the FCF or the CCF. Furthermore, for the WACCs, we list consistent formulas for the return to levered equity.

10.6.2 Option 1: WACC Applied to Finite FCF (Fixed Amount of Debt) with $\psi = \rho$

A1.1 Standard weighted average formulation

$$w^{FCF}{}_i = \frac{d_i(1-T)D_{i-1}}{V^L{}_{i-1}} + \frac{e_i E^L{}_{i-1}}{V^L{}_{i-1}} \qquad (10.26)$$

where

$$e_i = \rho_i + (\rho_i - d_i)\frac{D_{i-1}}{E_{i-1}} \qquad (10.27)$$

A1.2 Alternative adjusted formulation in terms of the unlevered return ρ

$$w^{FCF}{}_i = \rho_i - \frac{TS_i}{V^L{}_{i-1}} \qquad (10.28)$$

10.6.3 Option 2: WACC Applied to the Finite CCF (Fixed Amount of Debt) with $\psi = \rho$

A2.1 Standard weighted average formulation

$$w^{CCF}{}_i = \frac{d_i D_{i-1}}{V^L{}_{i-1}} + \frac{e_i E^L{}_{i-1}}{V^L{}_{i-1}} \qquad (10.29)$$

where

$$e_i = \rho_i + (\rho_i - d_i)\frac{D_{i-1}}{E_{i-1}} \qquad (10.30)$$

A2.2 Alternative formulation in terms of the unlevered return ρ

$$w^{CCF}{}_i = \rho \qquad (10.31)$$

We summarize the formulas for the WACCs with a fixed loan schedule in Table 10.8.

TABLE 10.8   Menagerie of WACCs for Fixed Loan Schedule with the FCF and the CCF

Leverage	Assumption for ψ	FCF
Fixed loan schedule	Standard, $\psi = \rho$	$w^{FCF}{}_i = \dfrac{d_i(1-T)D_{i-1}}{V^L{}_{i-1}} + \dfrac{e_i E^L{}_{i-1}}{V^L{}_{i-1}}$
		$e_i = \rho_i + (\rho_i - d_i)\dfrac{D_{i-1}}{E_{i-1}}$
	Alternative, $\psi = \rho$	$w^{FCF}{}_i = \rho_i - \dfrac{TS_i}{V^L{}_{i-1}}$

		CCF
Fixed loan schedule	Standard, $\psi = \rho$	$w^{CCF}{}_i = \dfrac{d_i D_{i-1}}{V^L{}_{i-1}} + \dfrac{e_i E^L{}_{i-1}}{V^L{}_{i-1}}$
		$e_i = \rho_i + (\rho_i - d_i)\dfrac{D_{i-1}}{E_{i-1}}$
	Alternative, $\psi = \rho$	$w^{FCF}{}_i = \rho$

10.7 FIXED PERCENTAGE OF DEBT

In each year i, the debt is rebalanced to maintain the specified percentages of debt in terms of the total levered values. Also, in each year i, the EBIT are sufficient for the TSs to be realized in the year in which the interest payments are made.

With a fixed percentage of debt, there are three ways to specify the appropriate discount rates for the annual TSs: the M & E specification, the Harris and Pringle (H & P) approach, and the standard specification with formulas derived from cash flows in perpetuity. The H & P approach assumes that the proper discount rate for the tax shield is the return to unlevered equity ρ.

10.7.1 M & E Specification for the WACC Applied to the FCF

The discount rate for the one-period ahead TS is the cost of debt d and the discount rate for the subsequent TSs is the return to unlevered equity ρ.

$$\text{WACC}^{\text{ME}} = (1 + \rho) \left[1 - \frac{\text{Tr}_f \theta}{1 + r_f} \right] - 1 \qquad (10.32)$$

10.7.2 Harris & Pringle (H & P) Specification

The discount rate for the TSs in all periods is the return to unlevered equity ρ. We propose two WACCs. For each WACC, we have two formulations and the WACC can be applied to the FCF or the CCF. The formulas are identical with the formulas that were listed for the fixed loan schedule. However, from a conceptual point of view, it is important to distinguish a debt financing policy with a fixed amount of debt from a debt policy with a fixed percentage of debt.

10.7.2.1 Option 1: WACC applied to FCF (fixed percentage of debt and $\psi = \rho$)

B1.1 Standard weighted average formulation

$$w^{\text{FCF}}{}_i = \frac{d_i(1 - T)D_{i-1}}{V^L{}_{i-1}} + \frac{e_i E^L{}_{i-1}}{V^L{}_{i-1}} \qquad (10.33)$$

where

$$e_i = \rho + (\rho - d)\frac{D_{i-1}}{E_{i-1}} \qquad (10.34)$$

B1.2 Alternative formulation in terms of the unlevered return ρ

$$w^{\text{FCF}}{}_i = \rho - \frac{\text{TS}_i}{V^L{}_{i-1}} \qquad (10.35)$$

10.7.2.2 Option 2: WACC applied to the CCF (fixed percentage of debt and $\psi = \rho$)

B2.1 Standard weighted average formulation

$$w^{\text{CCF}}{}_i = \frac{d_i D_{i-1}}{V^L{}_{i-1}} + \frac{e_i E^L{}_{i-1}}{V^L{}_{i-1}} \qquad (10.36)$$

where

$$e_i = e_i = \rho + (\rho - d)\frac{D_{i-1}}{E_{i-1}}1 \qquad (10.37)$$

B2.2 Alternative formulation in terms of the unlevered return ρ

$$w^{\text{CCF}}{}_i = \rho \qquad (10.38)$$

10.7.3 Standard (inaccurate) Specification

The discount rate for the TSs in all periods is the cost of debt d. The standard (inaccurate) specification of the WACC for the FCF applies the formulas that have been derived from FCF in perpetuity to finite cash flows. Using the general expressions that we present later, it is possible for the interested reader to derive the correct formulas for the WACC with finite cash flows, using the cost of debt to discount the TSs. However, we do not present these formulas here.

10.7.3.1 Option I: WACC applied to FCF (fixed percentage of debt and $\psi = d$)

C1.1 Standard weighted average formulation

$$w^{FCF}{}_i = \frac{d_i(1-T)D_{i-1}}{V^L_{i-1}} + \frac{e_i E^L_{i-1}}{V^L_{i-1}} \tag{10.39}$$

where

$$e_i = \rho + (1 - T/(1-T))(\rho - d)\frac{D_{i-1}}{E_{i-1}} \tag{10.40}$$

C1.2 Alternative formulation in terms of the unlevered return ρ

$$w^{FCF}{}_i = \rho\left[1 - \frac{V^{TS}_{i-1}}{V^L_{i-1}}\right] \tag{10.41}$$

For easy reference, in Table 10.9, we list the formulas for all the different WACCs for a fixed percent of debt.

TABLE 10.9   Menagerie of WACCs for Fixed Percent of Debt

Leverage	Assumption for ψ	
M & E WACC	$\psi = r_f$, one period ahead $\psi = \rho$, future periods	$WACC^{ME} = (1+\rho)\left[1 - \frac{Tr_f\theta}{1+r_f}\right] - 1$
H & P	Standard, $\psi = \rho$	$W^{FCF}{}_i = \frac{d_i(1-T)D_{i-1}}{V^L_{i-1}} + \frac{e_i E^L_{i-1}}{V^L_{i-1}}$
		$e_i = \rho + (\rho - d)\frac{D_{i-1}}{E_{i-1}}$
	Alternative, $\psi = \rho$	$w^{FCF}{}_i = \rho - \frac{TS_i}{V^L_{i-1}}$
H & P	Standard, $\psi = \rho$	$W^{CCF}{}_i = \frac{d_i D_{i-1}}{V^L_{i-1}} + \frac{e_i E^L_{i-1}}{V^L_{i-1}}$
		$e_i = \rho + (\rho - d)\frac{D_{i-1}}{E_{i-1}}$
	Alternative, $\psi = \rho$	$w^{CCF}{}_i = \rho$
Standard formulation	Standard, $\psi = d$	$w^{FCF}{}_i = \frac{d_i(1-T)D_{i-1}}{V^L_{i-1}} + \frac{e_i E^L_{i-1}}{V^L_{i-1}}$
		$e_i = \rho_i + (1-T)(\rho_i - d_i)\frac{D_{i-1}}{E_{i-1}}$
	Alternative, $\psi = d$	$W^{FCF}{}_i = \rho\left[1 - \frac{V^{TS}_{i-1}}{V^L_{i-1}}\right]$

The taxonomy in the table will make more sense after the reader has read the whole chapter.

10.8 THEORY ON THE COST OF CAPITAL APPLIED TO FINITE CASH FLOWS

Up to this point, we have examined qualitatively the main issues involved with the discount rate for the TS in an M & M world with taxes. For most readers, the discussion up to this point should be sufficient for them to appreciate the complexities associated with the estimation of the WACC in the presence of taxes. Some readers might prefer a more algebraic approach.

Next, we present the general algebraic derivations for the WACC in an M & M world with taxes. We show the standard WACC applied to the CCF, the standard WACC applied to the FCF, and the alternative adjusted WACC applied to the FCF. We do not discuss all the different formulations. We use numerical examples to illustrate only the H & P formulations and build on the two-period numerical example that was presented in the previous section in an M & M world without taxes.

10.8.1 Value Relationships

In an M & M world with taxes, in each year, the levered value equals the sum of the unlevered value and the PV of the TS.

$$V^L_0 = V^{Un}_0 + V^{TS}_0 \qquad (10.42)$$

$$V^L_1 = V^{Un}_1 + V^{TS}_1 \qquad (10.43)$$

In turn, in each year, the levered value equals the sum of the value of (levered) equity and the value of debt.

$$V^L_0 = E^L_0 + D_0 \qquad (10.44)$$

$$V^L_1 = E^L_1 + D_1 \qquad (10.45)$$

Combining equations 10.42 and 10.43 with equations 10.44 and 10.45, respectively, we obtain that in each year the sum of the unlevered value and the PV of the TS equals the sum of the value of (levered) equity and the value of debt.

$$V^{Un}_0 + V^{TS}_0 = E^L_0 + D_0 \qquad (10.46)$$

$$V^{Un}_1 + V^{TS}_1 = E^L_1 + D_1 \qquad (10.47)$$

10.8.2 Cash Flow Relationships

Next, we present some cash flow relationships that will be useful for deriving the general formulations for the different WACCs. Consider the cash flows in year 2. In year 2, the CCF equals the sum of the FCF and the TS.

$$CCF_2 = FCF_2 + TS_2 \qquad (10.48)$$

Also, in year 2, the CCF equals the sum of the CFE and the CFD.

$$CCF_2 = CFE_2 + CFD_2 \qquad (10.49)$$

Combining equations 10.48 and 10.49, we obtain that in year 2, the sum of the FCF and the TS equals the sum of the CFE and the CFD.

$$FCF_2 + TS_2 = CFE_2 + CFD_2 \qquad (10.50)$$

The cash flow relationship that we specify for year 2 also holds for year 1.

$$FCF_1 + TS_1 = CFE_1 + CFD_1 \qquad (10.51)$$

10.8.3 Tax Shield in Year 1 and Year 2

For ease in the derivation and exposition of the formulas for the various WACCs, we assume that in any year i, the TS equals the tax rate T times the annual interest payment, where the interest payment equals the cost of debt d times the value of the debt at the beginning of the year. As discussed earlier, in general terms, the tax shield is the difference between the taxes paid by the unlevered and levered firms.

$$TS_2 = T \text{ times Interest payment in year 2}$$
$$= TdD_1 \qquad (10.52)$$

$$TS_1 = T \text{ times Interest payment in year 1}$$
$$= TdD_0 \qquad (10.53)$$

10.8.4 Present Value of the Tax Shield in Year 1

In year 1, the PV of the TS equals the TS in year 2 discounted by the appropriate discount rate for the TS ψ_2.

$$V^{TS}_1 = TS_2/(1 + \psi_2) = TdD_1/(1 + \psi_2) \qquad (10.54)$$

10.8.5 Present Value of the Tax Shield in Year 0

In year 0, the PV of the TS equals the TS in years 1 and 2 discounted to year 0 by the appropriate discount rates for the TS ψ_1 and ψ_2.

$$V^{TS}_0 = TS_1/(1 + \psi_1) + TS_2/[(1 + \psi_1)(1 + \psi_2)] \qquad (10.55)$$

Substituting equation 10.54 into equation 10.55, we obtain

$$V^{TS}_0 = (TS_1 + V^{TS}_1)/(1 + \psi_1) \qquad (10.56)$$

In year 0, the PV of the TS equals the discounted value of the sum of the TS in year 1 and the PV of the TS with respect to year 1, where the discount rate is ψ_1.

10.9 STANDARD WACC APPLIED TO THE CCF

First, we derive the expression for the WACC applied to the CCF because it is the simplest. In year 2, let $WACC^{CCF}_2$ be the WACC applied to the CCF. Then the levered value in year 1 equals the CCF discounted by the WACC.

$$V^L_1 = CCF_2/(1 + WACC^{CCF}_2) \qquad (10.57)$$

Rewriting the equation, we obtain that

$$V^L_1(1 + WACC^{CCF}_2) = CCF_2 \qquad (10.58)$$

Express the CCF in terms of the CFE and the CFD by substituting equation 10.49 on the RHS of equation 10.58.

$$V^L_1(1 + WACC^{CCF}_2) = CFE_2 + CFD_2 \qquad (10.59)$$

Replace the cash flow expressions with the value expressions for the CFD and the CFE by substituting equations on the RHS of equation 10.59.

$$V^L_1(1 + WACC^{CCF}_2) = E^L_1(1 + e_2) + D_1(1 + d) \qquad (10.60)$$

Simplifying and solving for the WACC, we obtain that

$$WACC^{CCF}_2 = \%D_2 d + \%E_2 e_2 \qquad (10.61)$$

where

$$\%D_2 = D_1/V^L{}_1 \tag{10.62}$$

$$\%E_2 = E^L{}_1/V^L{}_1 \tag{10.63}$$

The WACC applied to the CCF is a weighted average of the cost of debt and the cost of equity, where the weights are the market values of debt and (levered) equity as percentages of levered market value. Because we have included the TS in the CCF, there is no need to lower the WACC by multiplying the cost of debt with the coefficient $(1 - T)$.

A similar expression for the WACC applied to the CCF holds for year 1.

$$WACC^{CCF}{}_1 = \%D_1 d + \%E_1 e_1 \tag{10.64}$$

where

$$\%D_1 = D_0/V^L{}_0 \tag{10.65}$$

$$\%E_1 = E^L{}_0/V^L{}_0 \tag{10.66}$$

We know that

$$V^L{}_0(1 + WACC^{CCF}{}_1) = CCF_1 + V^L{}_1 \tag{10.67}$$

$$V^L{}_0(1 + WACC^{CCF}{}_1) = CFE_1 + CFD_1 + V^L{}_1 \tag{10.68}$$

Substituting equations 10.23 and 10.20 into equation 10.68, we obtain

$$V^L{}_0(1 + WACC^{CCF}{}_1) = E^L{}_0(1 + e_1) - E^L{}_1$$
$$+ D_0(1 + d) - D_1 + V^L{}_1 \tag{10.69}$$

Simplifying the equation and solving for the WACC in year 1, we obtain

$$WACC^{CCF}{}_1 = \%D_1 d + \%E_1 e_1 \tag{10.70}$$

10.10 STANDARD AFTER-TAX WACC APPLIED TO THE FCF

Next, we derive the expression for the standard after-tax WACC applied to the FCF. In year 2, let $WACC^{FCF}{}_2$ be the WACC applied to the FCF. Then the levered value in year 1 equals the FCF in year 2 discounted by the WACC.

$$V^L{}_1 = FCF_2/(1 + WACC^{FCF}{}_2) \tag{10.71}$$

Rewriting the equation, we obtain that

$$V^L_1(1 + WACC^{FCF}_2) = FCF_2 \qquad (10.72)$$

On the RHS of equation 10.72, replace the FCF by substituting equation 10.50.

$$V^L_1(1 + WACC^{FCF}_2) = CFE_2 + CFD_2 - TS_2 \qquad (10.73)$$

On the RHS of equation 10.73, replace the cash flow expressions with the value expressions for the CFE and the CFD.

$$V^L_1(1 + WACC^{FCF}_2) = E^L_1(1 + e_2) + D_1(1 + d) - TS_2 \qquad (10.74)$$

$$V^L_1 + V^L_1 WACC^{FCF}_2 = E^L_1 + E^L_1 e_2 + D_1 + D_1 d - TS_2 \qquad (10.75)$$

Simplifying the equation and substituting equation 10.52 for the TS on the RHS of equation 10.75, we obtain

$$V^L_1 WACC^{FCF}_2 = E^L_1 e_2 + D_1 d - TdD_1 \qquad (10.76)$$

$$V^L_1 WACC^{FCF}_2 = E^L_1 e_2 + D_1 d(1 - T) \qquad (10.77)$$

Solving for the WACC in year 2, we obtain that

$$WACC^{FCF}_2 = \%D_2 d(1 - T) + \%E_2 e_2 \qquad (10.78)$$

where

$$\%D_2 = D_1/V^L_1 \qquad (10.79)$$

$$\%E_2 = E^L_1/V^L_1 \qquad (10.80)$$

The WACC applied to the FCF is a weighted average of the cost of debt and the cost of equity, where the weights are market values of debt and (levered) equity as percentages of levered market value. The WACC is applied to the FCF, which does not include the TS. To take account of the benefits of the TS from the interest deduction with debt financing, we lower the WACC by multiplying the cost of debt with the coefficient $(1 - T)$.

We can write a similar expression for the WACC applied to the FCF in year 1.

$$WACC^{FCF}_1 = \%D_1 d(1 - T) + \%E_1 e_1 \qquad (10.81)$$

where

$$\%D_1 = D_0/V^L_0 \qquad (10.82)$$

$$\%E_1 = E^L_0/V^L_0 \qquad (10.83)$$

We know that

$$V^L_0(1 + WACC^{FCF}_1) = FCF_1 + V^L_1 \tag{10.84}$$

$$V^L_0(1 + WACC^{FCF}_1) = CFE_1 + CFD_1 - TS_1 + V^L_1 \tag{10.85}$$

Substituting the appropriate expressions into the RHS of equation 10.85, we obtain

$$V^L_0(1 + WACC^{CCF}_1) = E^L_0(1 + e_1) - E^L_1 + D_0(1 + d) - D_1$$
$$- TdD_0 + V^L_1 \tag{10.86}$$

Simplifying the equation and solving for the WACC in year 1, we obtain

$$WACC^{FCF}_1 = \%D_1 d(1 - T) + \%E_1 e_1 \tag{10.87}$$

10.11 RETURN TO (LEVERED) EQUITY

Next, we derive the general expression for the return to levered equity. In an M & M world with taxes, the formulation for the return to levered equity is more complicated than the standard expression. In particular, in addition to the debt equity ratio, the return to levered equity is a function of the discount rate for the TS and the PV of the TS as a percentage of the levered value. We derive the general expression for the return to levered equity as follows. We know that in year 2, the sum of the FCF and the TS equals the sum of the CFE and the CFD. The TS can be specified in general terms as the difference in the taxes paid by the unlevered and levered firms.

$$FCF_2 + TS_2 = CFE_2 + CFD_2 \tag{10.88}$$

For each of the cash flows in equation 10.88, substitute the formulas for the values in place of the cash flow expressions. Then we obtain

$$(1 + \rho)V^{Un}_1 + (1 + \psi_2)V^{TS}_1 = (1 + e_2)E^L_1 + (1 + d)D_1 \tag{10.89}$$

Simplifying the equation and rearranging the terms, we obtain

$$e_2 E^L_1 = \rho V^{Un}_1 - dD_1 + \psi_2 V^{TS}_1 \tag{10.90}$$

Substituting the expression for the unlevered value into the RHS of equation 10.90, we obtain

$$e_2 E^L_1 = \rho(E^L_1 + D_1 - V^{TS}_1) - dD_1 + \psi_2 V^{TS}_1 \tag{10.91}$$

Collecting terms, rearranging and solving for the return to levered equity in year 2, we obtain

$$e_2 = \rho + (\rho - d)D_1/E^L{}_1 - (\rho - \psi_2)V^{TS}{}_1/E^L{}_1 \qquad (10.92)$$

The expression for the return to levered equity depends on the discount rate for the TS. Depending on the value of ψ_2, we write different expressions for the return to levered equity e_2. Consider several cases.

10.11.1 Case 1

If the discount rate for the TS ψ equals the unlevered return to equity ρ, we obtain the following expression for the return to levered equity e.

$$e_2 = \rho + (\rho - d)D_1/E^L{}_1 \qquad (10.93)$$

The return to levered equity is a linear function of the debt–equity ratio. In the expression for the return to levered equity, the factor $(1 - T)$ does not modify the debt–equity ratio.

10.11.2 Case 2

If the debt and TS are risk-free, both the values of d and ψ are equal to the risk-free rate r_f. The expression for the return to levered equity e is as follows:[15]

$$e_2 = \rho + (\rho - r_f)D_1/E^L{}_1 - (\rho - r_f)V^{TS}{}_1/E^L{}_1 \qquad (10.94)$$

$$= \rho + (\rho - r_f)(D_1 - V^{TS}{}_1)/E^L{}_1 \qquad (10.95)$$

In the calculation of the adjusted debt–equity ratio, we subtract the value of the TS from the value of the debt in the numerator of the debt–equity ratio.

10.11.3 Case 3

The third case is unusual. However, if the discount for the TS ψ is equal to the return to levered equity e, from equation 10.91 we obtain the following expression for the return to levered equity e.

$$e_2 E^L{}_1 = \rho(E^L{}_1 + D_1 - V^{TS}{}_1) + e_2 V^{TS}{}_1 - dD_1 \qquad (10.96)$$

---

[15]By substituting the expression for the PV of the TS $V^{TS}{}_1$, it is possible to derive an expression for the return to levered equity that is similar to the well-known expression for the return to levered equity with the tax rate. Substitute equation 10.54 into equation 10.95. Factor out the debt–equity ratio and rearrange the equation to obtain the following.

$$e_2 = \rho_2 + \left(\frac{1 + r_f - Tr_f}{1 + r_f}\right)(\rho_2 - r_f)\frac{D_1}{E^L{}_1}$$

Moving the terms with e_2 to the LHS, and solving for e_2, we obtain

$$e_2(E^L{}_1 - V^{TS}{}_1) = \rho(E^L{}_1 - V^{TS}{}_1) + (\rho - d)D_1 \tag{10.97}$$

$$e_2 = \rho + (\rho - d)D_1/(E^L{}_1 - V^{TS}{}_1) \tag{10.98}$$

In the calculation of the adjusted debt–equity ratio, we subtract the value of the TS from the value of the levered equity in the denominator of the debt–equity ratio.

For all three cases that we have listed for the return to levered equity in year 2, we can write similar expressions for the return to levered equity in year 1 e_1.

10.12 ALTERNATIVE ADJUSTED WACC APPLIED TO THE FCF (OPTIONAL)

In the previous sections, we derived the WACC applied to the CCF and the WACC applied to the FCF. Now, for completeness, we derive an alternative adjusted formulation for the WACC applied to the FCF. Most readers might want to skip this section.

In year 2, let $WACC^{FCF}{}_2$ be the WACC applied to the FCF. Then the levered value in year 1 is equal to the FCF in year 2 discounted by the WACC.

$$V^L{}_1 = FCF_2/(1 + WACC^{FCF}{}_2) \tag{10.99}$$

Rewriting the equation, we obtain that

$$V^L{}_1(1 + WACC^{FCF}{}_2) = FCF_2 \tag{10.100}$$

On the RHS of equation 10.100, replace the FCF with the value expression in terms of the unlevered value by substituting equation 10.11.

$$V^L{}_1(1 + WACC^{FCF}{}_2) = (1 + \rho)V^{Un}{}_1 \tag{10.101}$$

We rewrite the unlevered value in terms of the levered value and the TS.

$$V^L{}_1(1 + WACC^{FCF}{}_2) = (1 + \rho)(V^L{}_1 - V^{TS}{}_1) \tag{10.102}$$

Simplifying the equation, we obtain

$$V^L{}_1 WACC^{FCF}{}_2 = V^L{}_1\rho - (1 + \rho)V^{TS}{}_1 \tag{10.103}$$

Solving for the WACC, we obtain

$$WACC^{FCF}{}_2 = \rho - (1 + \rho)V^{TS}{}_1/V^L{}_1 \tag{10.104}$$

Equation 10.104 is an adjusted formulation for the WACC applied to the FCF in terms of the return to unlevered equity ρ, the discount rate for the TS ψ, and the TS as a percentage of the levered value.

10.12.1 Alternative Adjusted WACC in Year 1 Applied to the FCF

We can derive a similar expression for the alternative WACC in year 1 applied to the FCF. We know that

$$V^L_0(1 + WACC^{FCF}_1) = FCF_1 + V^L_1 \qquad (10.105)$$

On the RHS of equation 10.105, replace the FCF with the value expression in terms of the unlevered value by substituting equation 10.13.

$$V^L_0(1 + WACC^{FCF}_1) = (1 + \rho)V^{Un}_0 - V^{Un}_1 + V^L_1 \qquad (10.106)$$

$$V^L_0(1 + WACC^{FCF}_1) = (1 + \rho)V^{Un}_0 + V^{TS}_1 \qquad (10.107)$$

Using equation 10.42, rewrite the expression for the unlevered value in equation 10.107 in terms of the levered value.

$$V^L_0(1 + WACC^{FCF}_1) = (1 + \rho)(V^L_0 - V^{TS}_0) + V^{TS}_1 \qquad (10.108)$$

$$V^L_0(1 + WACC^{FCF}_1) = (1 + \rho)V^L_0 - (1 + \rho)V^{TS}_0 + V^{TS}_1 \qquad (10.109)$$

Substitute equation 10.56 into equation 10.109 and rearrange.

$$V^L_0(1 + WACC^{FCF}_1) = (1 + \rho)V^L_0 - (1 + \rho)V^{TS}_0$$
$$+ (1 + \psi_1)V^{TS}_0 - TS_1 \qquad (10.110)$$

$$V^L_0(1 + WACC^{FCF}_1) = (1 + \rho)V^L_0 - (\rho - \psi_1)V^{TS}_0 - TS_1 \qquad (10.111)$$

Solving for the WACC in year 1, we obtain

$$WACC^{FCF}_1 = \rho - (\rho - \psi_1)V^{TS}_0/V^L_0 - TS_1/V^L_0 \qquad (10.112)$$

The WACC in year 1 is a function of the PV of the TS as a percent of the levered value and the TS as a percent of the levered value.

10.12.2 Assuming the Discount Rate for the Tax Shield is ρ

Substituting the expression for the value of the TS in year 1 into equation 10.104, we obtain

$$WACC^{FCF}_2 = \rho - [(1 + \rho)/(1 + \psi_2)](TS_2/V^L_1) \qquad (10.113)$$

If we assume that the appropriate discount rate for the TS is equal to the return to unlevered equity, the adjusted WACC equals the return to unlevered equity ρ less the TS as a percentage of the levered market value.

$$\text{WACC}^{\text{FCF}}{}_2 = \rho - \text{TS}_2/\text{V}^{\text{L}}{}_1 \qquad (10.114)$$

Using equation 10.112, we can write a similar expression for the alternative adjusted WACC in year 1 applied to the FCF.

$$\text{WACC}^{\text{FCF}}{}_1 = \rho - \text{TS}_1/\text{V}^{\text{L}}{}_0 \qquad (10.115)$$

10.13 ALTERNATIVE WACC APPLIED TO THE CCF (OPTIONAL)

Now, we derive an alternative expression for the WACC applied to the CCF. In year 2, let $\text{WACC}^{\text{CCF}}{}_2$ be the WACC applied to the CCF. Then the levered value in year 1 is equal to the CCF in year 2 discounted by the WACC.

$$\text{V}^{\text{L}}{}_1 = \text{CCF}_2/(1 + \text{WACC}^{\text{CCF}}{}_2) \qquad (10.116)$$

Rewriting the equation, we obtain that

$$\text{V}^{\text{L}}{}_1(1 + \text{WACC}^{\text{CCF}}{}_2) = \text{CCF}_2 \qquad (10.117)$$

Express the CCF in terms of the FCF and the TS by substituting equation 10.48 on the RHS of equation 10.117.

$$\text{V}^{\text{L}}{}_1(1 + \text{WACC}^{\text{CCF}}{}_2) = \text{FCF}_2 + \text{TS}_2 \qquad (10.118)$$

On the RHS of equation 10.118, replace the cash flow expressions with the value expressions.

$$\text{V}^{\text{L}}{}_1(1 + \text{WACC}^{\text{CCF}}{}_2) = \text{V}^{\text{Un}}{}_1(1 + \rho) + \text{V}^{\text{TS}}{}_1(1 + \psi_2) \qquad (10.119)$$

Simplifying the equation, we obtain that

$$\text{V}^{\text{L}}{}_1\text{WACC}^{\text{CCF}}{}_2 = \text{V}^{\text{Un}}{}_1\rho + \text{V}^{\text{TS}}{}_1\psi_2 \qquad (10.120)$$

On the RHS of equation 10.120, express the unlevered value in terms of the levered value and the PV of the TS.

$$\text{V}^{\text{L}}{}_1\text{WACC}^{\text{CCF}}{}_2 = (\text{V}^{\text{L}}{}_1 - \text{V}^{\text{TS}}{}_1)\rho + \text{V}^{\text{TS}}{}_1\psi_2 \qquad (10.121)$$

Rearranging the equation and solving for the WACC, we obtain that

$$\text{WACC}^{\text{CCF}}_2 = \rho + (\psi_2 - \rho)V^{\text{TS}}_1/V^{\text{L}}_1 \qquad (10.122)$$

As expected, if the discount rate for the TS is equal to the return to unlevered equity, the WACC applied to the CCF is equal to the return to unlevered equity. We can derive a similar expression for the WACC in year 1. We know that

$$V^{\text{L}}_0(1 + \text{WACC}^{\text{CCF}}_1) = \text{FCF}_1 + \text{TS}_1 + V^{\text{L}}_1 \qquad (10.123)$$

On the RHS of equation 10.123, replace the cash flow expressions with the value expressions.

$$V^{\text{L}}_0(1 + \text{WACC}^{\text{CCF}}_1) = V^{\text{Un}}_0(1 + \rho) + V^{\text{TS}}_0(1 + \psi_1) \\ - V^{\text{Un}}_1 - V^{\text{TS}}_1 + V^{\text{L}}_1 \qquad (10.124)$$

Simplify the equation and express the unlevered value in terms of the levered value.

$$V^{\text{L}}_0\text{WACC}^{\text{CCF}}_1 = \rho V^{\text{L}}_0 - \rho V^{\text{TS}}_0 + V^{\text{TS}}_0\psi_1 \qquad (10.125)$$

Solving for the WACC, we obtain that

$$\text{WACC}^{\text{CCF}}_1 = \rho + (\psi_1 - \rho)V^{\text{TS}}_0/V^{\text{L}}_0 \qquad (10.126)$$

10.14 NUMERICAL EXAMPLE

Next, we present a numerical example for the calculation of the WACC for a finite stream of cash flows in an M & M world with taxes. To calculate the PV of the TSs, we need to specify the appropriate risk-adjusted discount rates for the TSs in year 1 and year 2. Let ψ_i be the discount rate for the TS in year i. We assume that the appropriate discount rates for the TSs in year 1 and year 2 are equal to the return to unlevered equity ρ rather than the cost of debt d.

We extend the numerical example that was presented for the M & M world without taxes. We retain the same loan schedule, which determines the annual variable leverage. In Appendix B, we present an example with constant leverage. For convenience, we summarize the key information.

$$\text{FCF}_1 = 500 \qquad \text{FCF}_2 = \$600$$
$$V^{\text{Un}}_0 = \$876.93 \qquad V^{\text{Un}}_1 = \$517.24$$
$$\text{CFD}_1 = \$180 \qquad \text{CFD}_2 = \$165$$
$$D_0 = 300 \qquad D_1 = 150$$
$$\rho = 16\% \qquad T = 34\%$$
$$d = 10\% \qquad \psi_i = \rho = 16\%$$

10.14.1 Amount of the Tax Shields

First, in the presence of taxes, we calculate the TSs that are realized in year 1 and year 2.

$$TS_1 = TdD_0 = 34\% \times 10\% \times 300 = 10.200$$

$$TS_2 = TdD_1 = 34\% \times 10\% \times 150 = 5.100$$

10.14.2 Summary of the Cash Flows

In year i, the CCF equals the FCF plus the TS. The CFE equals the CCF less the CFD (see Table 10.10).

$$CCF_1 = FCF_1 + TS_1 = 500 + 10.2 = 510.20$$

$$CCF_2 = FCF_2 + TS_2 = 600 + 5.1 = 605.10$$

$$CFE_1 = CCF_1 - CFD_1 = 510.2 - 180 = 330.20$$

$$CFE_2 = CCF_2 - CFD_2 = 605.1 - 165 = 440.10$$

TABLE 10.10   CFE (Levered)

Year	0	1	2
FCF		500.00	600.00
TS		10.20	5.10
CCF		510.20	605.10
CFD		180.00	165.00
CFE		330.20	440.10

10.14.3 Present Value of the Tax Shields

At the end of year 0, the value of the TS is

$$V^{TS}_0 = TS_1/(1 + \psi) + TS_2/(1 + \psi)^2$$

$$= 10.20/(1 + 16\%) + 5.10/(1 + 16\%)^2$$

$$= 8.7931 + 3.7901 = 12.5832$$

At the end of year 1, the value of the TS is

$$V^{TS}_1 = TS_2/(1 + \psi) = 5.10/(1 + 16\%) = 4.3966$$

With the PVs of the TSs, we calculate the levered values, the percent of debt and equity, and the debt equity ratios.

10.15 ADJUSTED PRESENT VALUE (APV) APPROACH

With the APV approach, to obtain the levered value at the end of year i, we add the value of the TS to the unlevered value.

$$V^L_0 = V^{Un}_0 + V^{TS}_0$$

$$= 876.932 + 12.583 = 889.515$$

$$V^L_1 = V^{Un}_1 + V^{TS}_1$$

$$= 517.241 + 4.397 = 521.638$$

10.15.1 Percent Debt and Percent Equity in Year 1

The values for the annual leverage are based on the levered values rather than the unlevered values. In year 1, the value of the debt as a percent of the levered value is 33.726% and the value of the equity as a percent of the levered value is 66.274%. The debt–equity ratio is 0.5089.

$$\%D_1 = D_0/V^L_0 = 300.00/889.515 = 33.726\%$$
$$\%E_1 = E^L_0/V^L_0 = (889.515 - 300)/889.515 = 589.515/889.515 = 66.274\%$$
$$D_0/E^L_0 = 300.00/589.515 = 0.5089$$

10.15.2 Percent Debt and Percent Equity in Year 2

In year 2, the value of the debt as a percent of the levered value is 28.756% and the value of the equity as a percent of the levered value is 71.244%. The debt–equity ratio is 0.4036.

$$\%D_2 = D_1/V^L_1 = 150.00/521.638 = 28.756\%$$
$$\%E_2 = E^L_1/V^L_1 = (521.638 - 150)/521.638 = 371.638/521.638 = 71.244\%$$
$$D_1/E^L_1 = 150.00/371.638 = 0.4036$$

The information to calculate the debt–equity ratios is shown in Table 10.11.

TABLE 10.11   Debt–Equity Ratios

Year	0	1	2
Unlevered value	876.932	517.241	
Value of TS	12.583	4.397	
Levered value	889.515	521.638	
Value of debt	300.000	150.000	
Value of (levered) equity	589.515	371.638	
Percent debt		33.726%	28.756%
Percent equity		66.274%	71.244%
Debt–equity ratio		0.5089	0.4036

The values for the annual leverage are lower than the values that were obtained in the M & M world without taxes. Compare the values here with the values in Table 10.4.

10.15.3 Returns to Levered Equity in Year 1 and Year 2

Because the debt–equity ratio varies, the returns to levered equity in year 1 and year 2 are different. Let e_i be the return to levered equity in year i. The return to levered equity in year 1 is 19.05% and the return to levered equity in year 2 is 18.42%.

$$e_1 = \rho + (\rho - r_f)D_0/E^L{}_0$$

$$= 16\% + (16\% - 10\%)0.5089 = 19.0534\%$$

$$e_2 = \rho + (\rho - r_f)D_1/E^L{}_1$$

$$= 16\% + (16\% - 10\%)0.4036 = 18.4216\%$$

We verify that these returns to levered equity are correct by calculating the PV of the CFE in year 1 and year 0.

$$E^L{}_1 = CFE_2/(1 + e_2)$$

$$= 440.1/(1 + 18.4216\%) = 371.64$$

$$E^L{}_0 = CFE_1/(1 + e_1) + CFE_2/[(1 + e_1)(1 + e_2)]$$

$$= 330.2/(1 + 19.05\%) + 440.1/[(1 + 19.05\%)(1 + 18.423\%)]$$

$$= 277.35 + 312.16 = 589.51$$

10.15.4 WACC Applied to the CCF

Let $WACC^{CCF}_i$ be the WACC applied to the CCF in year i. As expected, the WACC in year 1 and year 2 are equal to the return to unlevered equity ρ.

$$WACC^{CCF}_1 = \%D_1d + \%E_1e$$

$$= 33.726\% \times 10\% + 66.274\% \times 19.053\%$$

$$= 3.373\% + 12.627\% = 16.00\%$$

$$WACC^{CCF}_2 = \%D_2d + \%E_2e$$

$$= 28.756\% \times 10\% + 71.244\% \times 18.422\%$$

$$= 2.876\% + 13.125\% = 16.000\%$$

Next, we verify that the CCF discounted with the WACCs are equal to the levered values in year 1 and year 2.

$$V^L_0 = CCF_1/(1 + WACC^{CCF}_1) + CCF_2/[(1 + WACC^{CCF}_1)(1 + WACC^{CCF}_2)]$$

$$= 510.20/(1 + 16\%) + 605.10/(1 + 16\%)^2$$

$$= 439.8276 + 449.6879 = 889.515$$

$$V^L_1 = CCF_2/(1 + WACC^{CCF}_2) = 605.10/(1 + 16\%) = 521.638$$

10.15.5 Standard After-Tax WACC Applied to the FCF

Let $WACC^{FCF}_i$ be the standard after-tax WACC applied to the FCF in year i. The WACC in year 1 is 14.853% and the WACC in year 2 is 15.022%.

$$WACC^{FCF}_1 = \%D_1d + \%E_1e$$

$$= 33.726\% \times 10\% \times (1 - 34\%) + 66.274\% \times 19.053\%$$

$$= 2.226\% + 12.627\% = 14.853\%$$

$$WACC^{FCF}_2 = \%D_2d + \%E_2e$$

$$= 28.756\% \times 10\% \times (1 - 34\%) + 71.244\% \times 18.422\%$$

$$= 1.898\% + 13.125\% = 15.022\%$$

Next, we verify that the FCF discounted with the WACCs are equal to the levered values in year 1 and year 2.

$$V^L_0 = FCF_1/(1 + WACC^{FCF}_1) + FCF_2/[(1 + WACC^{FCF}_1)(1 + WACC^{FCF}_2)]$$

$$= 500.00/(1 + 14.853\%) + 600.00/[(1 + 14.853\%)(1 + 15.022\%)]$$

$$= 435.3379 + 454.1776 = 889.52$$

$$V^L_1 = FCF_2/(1 + WACC^{FCF}_2) = 600.00/(1 + 15.022\%) = 521.64$$

10.15.6 Alternative WACC Applied to the FCF

For illustration, we show the calculations with the alternative formula for the WACC applied to the FCF.

$$WACC^{FCF}_1 = \rho - TS_1/V^L_0 = 16\% - 10.20/889.515 = 14.853\%$$

$$WACC^{FCF}_2 = \rho - TS_2/V^L_0 = 16\% - 5.10/521.638 = 15.022\%$$

As expected, the values obtained here match the previous values that were calculated with the standard weighted average formula.

We summarize the results of the numerical example in Table 10.12.

TABLE 10.12   Results of the Numerical Example

Year	0	1	2
Return to levered equity		19.0534%	18.4216%
WACC applied to the CCF		16.00%	16.00%
WACC applied to the FCF		14.853%	15.022%

10.16 SUMMARY AND CONCLUDING REMARKS

In this chapter, we revisited the theory for the cost of capital in M & M worlds without and with taxes in the context of finite streams of cash flows. In detail, we have shown that the estimation of the cost of capital with finite cash flows is more complex than the estimation with cash flows in perpetuity. Moreover, the formulas and results that are derived from cash flows in perpetuity are not appropriate for finite cash flows. In addition, the correct expressions for the cost of capital with finite cash flows depend critically on the assumptions regarding the risk of the debt, the debt financing policy, and the risk of the TS.

KEY CONCEPTS AND IDEAS

M & E WACC
WACC with fixed amount of debt
WACC with fixed percentage
  of debt

APPENDIX A

AI0.I DERIVATION OF THE M & E WACC

In this appendix, we present an informal derivation of the M & E WACC. In the M & E formulation of the WACC for a finite stream of FCFs, the one-year ahead discount rate for the TS is the risk-free rate r_f because the amount of the TS that will be realized at the end of the period is known. The TSs in subsequent years are discounted with the return to unlevered equity ρ_i. We assume that the return to unlevered equity is constant and the cost of debt is equal to the risk-free rate r_f. To be specific, consider a three-period finite stream of FCFs. Using backward induction, the argument presented here can be extended to N periods.

AI0.I.I Levered Value in Year 2

At the end of year 2, the expression for the unlevered value is as follows:

$$V^{Un}{}_2 = FCF_3/(1 + \rho) \qquad (A10.1)$$

At the end of year 2, the levered value is equal to the sum of the unlevered value and the TS.

$$V^L{}_2 = V^{Un}{}_2 + V^{TS}{}_2 \qquad (A10.2)$$

The amount of the TS in year 3 is equal to the tax rate T times the cost of debt d and the amount of debt at the end of year 2.

$$TS_3 = TdD_2 = Td\theta V^L{}_2 \qquad (A10.3)$$

where θ is the amount of debt as a percent of the levered value. We assume that the leverage θ is constant.

At the end of year 2, the value of the TS is

$$V^{TS}{}_2 = TS_3/(1 + \psi_3) = Tr_f \theta V^L{}_2/(1 + r_f) \qquad (A10.4)$$

where ψ_3 is the discount rate for the TS in year 3.

With respect to year 2, the TS in year 3 is one year ahead and the value of ψ_3 is equal to the risk-free rate r_f.

Substituting equation A10.1 and equation A10.4 into equation A10.2, we obtain

$$V^L{}_2 = FCF_3/(1 + \rho) + Tr_f \theta V^L{}_2/(1 + r_f) \qquad (A10.5)$$

Let

$$\phi = 1 - Tr_f \theta/(1 + r_f) \qquad (A10.6)$$

Then rewriting equation A10.5, we obtain

$$V^L{}_2 = FCF_3/[(1 + \rho)\phi] \qquad (A10.7)$$

A10.1.2 Levered Value in Year 1

At the end of year 1, the expression for the levered value is as follows:

$$V^L{}_1 = FCF_2/(1 + \rho) + FCF_3/(1 + \rho)^2 + TS_2/(1 + r_f)$$
$$+ TS_3/[(1 + r_f)(1 + \rho)] \qquad (A10.8)$$

The discount rate for the one-year ahead TS in year 2 is the risk-free rate r_f and the discount rate for the TS in year 3 is the return to unlevered equity ρ. We can rewrite the equation as follows:

$$V^L{}_1 = FCF_2/(1 + \rho) + TS_2/(1 + r_f) + V^L{}_2/(1 + \rho) \qquad (A10.9)$$

Moving the TS in year 2 to the LHS, substituting the expression for $V^L{}_2$ into equation A10.9 and simplifying, we obtain

$$V^L{}_1 = FCF_2/[(1 + \rho)\phi] + FCF_3/[(1 + \rho)^2 \phi^2] \qquad (A10.10)$$

A10.1.3 Levered Value in Year 0

At the end of year 0, the levered value is

$$V^L{}_0 = FCF_1/(1+\rho) + TS_1/(1+r_f) + V^L{}_1/(1+\rho) \qquad (A10.11)$$

Again, moving the TS in year 1 to the LHS, substituting the expression for $V^L{}_1$ and simplifying, we obtain

$$\begin{aligned} V^L{}_0 = {} & FCF_1/[(1+\rho)\phi] + FCF_2/[(1+\rho)^2\phi^2] \\ & + FCF_3/[(1+\rho)^3\phi^3] \end{aligned} \qquad (A10.12)$$

Define the M & E WACC as follows:

$$WACC^{ME} = (1+\rho)\phi - 1 \qquad (A10.13)$$

Then

$$\begin{aligned} V^L{}_0 = {} & FCF_1/(1+WACC^{ME}) + FCF_2/(1+WACC^{ME})^2 \\ & + FCF_3/(1+WACC^{ME})^3 \end{aligned} \qquad (A10.14)$$

B10.1 NUMERICAL EXAMPLE WITH CONSTANT LEVERAGE

In the text, in the previous numerical example with taxes, we specified the loan schedule. Based on the interest payments in the loan schedule, we determined the annual TSs and the PVs of the TSs. With a specified loan schedule, the leverage is variable over the two years. Here, for completeness, we illustrate the calculations of the WACC with a debt policy based on constant leverage for the two years.

At the beginning of any year i, the levered market value depends on the PV of the TS at the end of the year. The TS depends on the interest payments for the year, which in turn depends on the market value of the debt that is defined in terms of the levered value at the beginning of the year. To reiterate, we assume that the EBIT is sufficient for the TSs to be realized in the year in which the interest payments are made.

To overcome this circularity we define the levered value in year i in terms of the unlevered value in year i. With the relationships between the levered and unlevered values we are able to determine the levered values from the unlevered values and there is no need to calculate the WACCs.

B10.1.1 Leverages in Year 1 and Year 2

With the levered value in year i we can calculate the value of the debt and the TS. Let θ_i be the market value of the debt at the beginning of year i as a percentage of the levered value at the beginning of year i. We assume that the value of the debt at the end of year 0 and year 1 will be 30% of the levered market value at the end of year 0 and year 1.

$$\theta_1 = \%D_1 = D_0/V^L{}_0 = 30\%$$

$$\theta_2 = \%D_2 = D_1/V^L{}_0 = 30\%$$

Rearranging equations B10.1 and B10.2, we obtain that

$$D_0 = \theta_1 V^L_0 \tag{B10.1}$$

$$D_1 = \theta_2 V^L_1 \tag{B10.2}$$

B10.1.2 Relationship between the Levered and Unlevered Value in Year 1

The levered value in year 1 is equal to the unlevered value plus the PV of the TS that will be realized at the end of year 2.

$$V^L_1 = V^{Un}_1 + V^{TS}_1 \tag{B10.3}$$

Substituting equation 10.54 in equation B10.3, we obtain

$$V^L_1 = V^{Un}_1 + TdD_1/(1 + \psi_2) \tag{B10.4}$$

Substituting equation B10.2 in equation B10.4, we obtain

$$V^L_1 = V^{Un}_1 + Td\theta_2 V^L_1/(1 + \psi_2) \tag{B10.5}$$

Solving for the levered value, we obtain that

$$V^L_1 = (1 + \psi_2)V^{Un}_1/(1 + \psi_2 - Td\theta_2) = \xi_2 V^{Un}_1 \tag{B10.6}$$

where

$$\xi_2 = (1 + \psi_2)/(1 + \psi_2 - Td\theta_2) \tag{B10.7}$$

We can re-express equation B10.7 in terms of the FCF in year 2.

$$V^L_1 = \xi_2 FCF_2/(1 + \rho) \tag{B10.8}$$

B10.1.3 Relationship between the Levered and Unlevered Value in Year 0

The levered value in year 0 is equal to the unlevered value plus the PV of the TS.

$$V^L_0 = V^{Un}_0 + V^{TS}_0 \tag{B10.9}$$

From equation 10.56, we know that

$$V^{TS}_0 = (TS_1 + V^{TS}_1)/(1 + \psi_1) \tag{B10.10}$$

Substituting equation B10.10 into equation B10.9, we obtain

$$V^L{}_0 = V^{Un}{}_0 + (TS_1 + V^{TS}{}_1)/(1 + \psi_1) \qquad (B10.11)$$

Substituting equation 10.53 into equation B10.11, we obtain

$$V^L{}_0 = V^{Un}{}_0 + (TdD_0 + V^{TS}{}_1)/(1 + \psi_1) \qquad (B10.12)$$

Substituting equation B10.1 into equation B10.12 and rearranging, we obtain

$$V^L{}_0 = V^{Un}{}_0 + (Td\theta_1 V^L{}_0 + V^{TS}{}_1)/(1 + \psi_1) \qquad (B10.13)$$

$$V^L{}_0 - Td\theta_1 V^L{}_0/(1 + \psi_1) = V^{Un}{}_0 + V^{TS}{}_1/(1 + \psi_1) \qquad (B10.14)$$

Solving for the levered value on the LHS of equation B10.14, we obtain

$$V^L{}_0 = \xi_1 [V^{Un}{}_0 + V^{TS}{}_1/(1 + \psi_1)] \qquad (B10.15)$$

where

$$\xi_1 = (1 + \psi_1)/(1 + \psi_1 - Td\theta_1) \qquad (B10.16)$$

BI0.2 BASIC INFORMATION

For convenience, we summarize the basic information.

$$FCF_1 = 500 \qquad FCF_2 = \$600$$
$$V^{Un}{}_0 = \$876.932 \qquad V^{Un}{}_1 = \$517.2414$$
$$\rho_1 = \rho_2 = 16\% \qquad T = 34\%$$
$$d = 10\% \qquad \psi_i = \rho_i = 16\%$$

$\theta_1 = \theta_2 = 30\%$

$\xi_2 = (1 + \psi_2)/(1 + \psi_2 - Td\theta_2)$

$\quad = (1 + 16\%)/(1 + 16\% - 34\% \times 10\% \times 30\%) = 100.8871\%$

$\xi_1 = (1 + \psi_1)/(1 + \psi_1 - Td\theta_1)$

$\quad = (1 + 16\%)/(1 + 16\% - 34\% \times 10\% \times 30\%) = 100.8871\%$

B10.2.1 Levered Values in Year 0 and Year 1

The levered value in year 1 is \$521.83.

$$V^L_1 = \xi_2 V^{Un}_1$$
$$= 100.8871\% \times 517.2414 = 521.8298$$

The PV of the TS in year 1 is \$4.5884.

$$V^{TS}_1 = V^L_1 - V^{Un}_1$$
$$= 521.830 - 517.2414 = 4.5884$$

The levered value in year 0 is \$888.702.

$$V^L_0 = \xi_1 [(V^{Un}_0 + V^{TS}_1 / (1 + \psi_1)]$$
$$= 100.8871\% [876.932 + 4.589 / (1 + 16\%)]$$
$$= 888.702$$

B10.2.2 Values of Debt in Year 0 and Year 1

In year 0, the value of the debt is \$265.41 and in year 1, the value of the debt is \$156.55.

$$D_0 = \theta_1 V^L_0 = 30\% \times 888.702 = 266.61$$
$$D_1 = \theta_2 V^L_1 = 30\% \times 521.830 = 156.55$$

We summarize the results in Table B10.1.

TABLE B10.1   Summary of Results

Year	0	1	2
Unlevered values	876.932	517.2414	
Levered values	888.702	521.8299	
Value of debt	266.611	156.549	
PV of TS	11.770	4.5885	
Value of (levered) equity	622.092	365.281	

For completeness, we calculate the various WACCs and verify that they give the correct answers. First, we calculate the TSs and the CCFs.

BI0.2.3 Tax Shields in Year I and Year 2

$$TS_1 = TdD_0 = 34\% \times 10\% \times 266.61 = 9.065$$

$$TS_2 = TdD_1 = 34\% \times 10\% \times 156.55 = 5.323$$

BI0.2.4 Capital Cash Flow in Year I and Year 2

$$CCF_1 = FCF_1 + TS_1 = 500 + 9.065 = 509.065$$

$$CCF_2 = FCF_2 + TS_2 = 600 + 5.323 = 605.323$$

BI0.2.5 Return to Levered Equity

Because the leverage is constant, the returns to levered equity will be the same in both years.

$$e_i = \rho + (\rho - d)D_{i-1}/E^L_{i-1} = 16\% + (16\% - 10\%)30\%/70\%$$
$$= 18.571\%$$

The reader can verify that the CFE discounted by the return to levered equity gives the correct values for the annual levered equity.

BI0.3 WACC APPLIED TO THE CCF

As expected, the WACC applied to the CCF is equal to the return to unlevered equity.

$$WACC^{CCF}w_i = \%D_i d + \%E_i e_i$$
$$= 30\% \times 10\% + 70\% \times 18.571\% = 16.000\%$$

BI0.4 STANDARD AFTER-TAX WACC APPLIED TO THE FCF

The standard after-tax WACC applied to the FCF is

$$WACC^{FCF}_i = \%D_i d(1 - T) + \%E_i e_i$$
$$= 30\% \times 10\%(1 - 34\%) + 70\% \times 18.571\%$$
$$= 14.980\%$$

We verify that the FCF discounted with the WACCs are equal to the levered values in year 1 and year 2.

$$V^L{}_0 = FCF_1/(1 + WACC^{FCF}) + FCF_2/(1 + WACC^{FCF})^2$$
$$= 500.00/(1 + 14.98\%) + 600.00/(1 + 14.98\%)^2$$
$$= 434.8582 + 453.8440 = 888.70$$
$$V^L{}_1 = FCF_2/(1 + WACC^{FCF}) = 600.00/(1 + 14.98\%) = 521.83$$

BI0.5 ALTERNATIVE ADJUSTED WACC FOR THE FCF

For illustration, we show the calculations with the alternative formula for the WACC applied to the FCF.

$$WACC^{FCF}{}_1 = \rho - TS_1/V^L{}_0 = 16\% - 9.065/888.702 = 14.980\%$$
$$WACC^{FCF}{}_2 = \rho - TS_2/V^L{}_1 = 16\% - 5.323/521.8299 = 14.980\%$$

HOW ARE CASH FLOWS
VALUED IN THE REAL WORLD

(This chapter has been written in collaboration with
Ramiro de la Vega and Guillermo Rossi.)

Any intelligent fool can make things bigger and more
complex ... It takes a touch of genius ... and a lot of
courage to move in the opposite direction.

—*Albert Einstein*

11.1 INTRODUCTION

In the previous chapters, we presented the principles of cash flow valuation
within an integrated theoretical framework that is based on the typical
financial statements. We stressed the use of market values in the
valuation of cash flows and examined the subtleties behind the calculation
of the cost of capital under ideal conditions. The natural question arises.
How are these ideas used in practice by practitioners? How are cash flows
valued in the real world.

In this chapter we show how we can apply the ideas to a project for a
telecommunications firm in Colombia. In particular, we compare the valuations that are based on market values with the valuations that are based on
book values. This case study is much more complicated than the example
that was presented in Chapter Five, and has many additional assumptions
and conditions.

In Appendix A, we present the transcripts of interviews with two financial
practitioners from multinational firms with operations in Japan and the

Philippines.[1] The practitioners comment on how the cost of capital is estimated in practice. In Appendix B, we present the background information and financial statements for the case.

The main objectives of this chapter are as follows:

1. First, we illustrate a detailed valuation model.
2. Second, we show the CB statement.
3. Third, we show how bad practices in the estimation of the WACC can generate errors greater than ±5%. As a rule of thumb, a discrepancy of 5% is acceptable. However, higher discrepancies might not be tolerable and with the availability of computing facilities, the higher discrepancies are unnecessary and avoidable.
4. Fourth, we discuss in more detail the items that have to be included in the correct calculation of the tax savings.
5. Fifth, and this is related to the previous point, we discuss subtleties that might be found in a real case, at least in the context of developing countries, taking into account issues such as inflation adjustments (IA), losses due to fluctuations in foreign exchange, and presumptive income (PI) taxation.

From the basic financial statements of the telecommunications firm (the IS, the BS and the CB) we derive the different cash flows: the FCF, the CFE, the CFD, and the cash flow of tax savings. We show the calculation of levered value using different approaches and conditions, including five market-based approaches and three based on book values. The first four market-based methods should be familiar from discussions in the previous chapters. The fifth market-based method is a slight variation. In the previous chapters, we have not discussed valuation based on book values. Thus, here is an opportunity to assess the degree to which market-based approaches deviate from the values obtained with book values.

1. Using market value valuations (the WACC is calculated based on market values).
    1.1 Using a version of the WACC that we call the adjusted WACC, and define as $\rho - TS/(\text{levered value})$. (Case 1)
    1.2 Using the PV of the CFE, discounting it with the cost of levered equity e, and adding the value of debt. In this case we use market values to determine leverage and the cost of debt as the proportion of interest divided by debt from the previous period. (Case 2)

---

[1] Guillermo Rossi worked as Vice President of Finance for IMPSA (an Argentinean multinational). He is currently a private consultant for the same firm. Ramiro de la Vega, a private financial consultant from Colombia, contributed the financial statements and served as a sounding board for the case study.

    1.3 Using the CCF and discounting it with the unlevered cost of equity ρ. (Case 3)

    1.4 Using the traditional approach of discounting the FCF with the traditional WACC expression, and using market values to determine leverage and the cost of debt as the proportion of interest divided by debt from the previous period. (WACC = e%E + d (1 − T)%D where %D is the leverage, %E is the proportion of equity, d is the cost of debt, and T is the tax rate.) (Case 4)

    1.5 Using the traditional approach of discounting the FCF with the traditional WACC expression and using market values to determine leverage. The cost of debt d is the internal rate of return (IRR) of the CFD (WACC = e%E + d(1 − T)%D where %D is the leverage, %E is the proportion of equity, d is the cost of debt, and T is the tax rate.) (Case 5)

2. Calculating the levered value using book values to calculate the levered value.

    2.1. Using a constant cost of debt equal to the IRR of the CFD. (Case 6)

    2.2. Using the cost of debt for each period as in case 4. (Case 7)

    2.3. Using a constant WACC (for this case we show a sensitivity table for different WACC values.) (Case 8)

First, we briefly present and discuss the adjustments of the financial statements for inflation and the adjustments for gains and losses in the exchange rate. We also present the concept of PI and losses carried forward (LCF) and how to incorporate them into the calculation of the cost of capital. All this is necessary because the case study is located in a country where these conditions hold for the project.

For the case we present basic information, such as the parameters used for the estimation. Besides that we present some context and further information about the project. The complementary information can be found in the appendix.

II.I.I Inflation Adjustments to Financial Statements

In some countries the tax law requires that firms apply the so-called System for Integral Adjustments for Inflation. Since 1992, Colombia has applied this rule.

II.I.2 Monetary and Non-monetary Assets

In this context we distinguish between monetary and non-monetary assets or rights. A monetary asset or right is not affected by changes in the general level of prices or, in other words, by changes in the value of money. The purchasing power of those assets will change with fluctuations in the money's value. A non-monetary asset, on the contrary, is an asset or right whose face value is unchanged even with a reduction in the money's value. Typical examples of monetary assets are cash in hand and AR. Typical non-monetary assets are fixed assets such as land and buildings.

II.I.3 Adjustments to the Non-monetary Assets

Adjustments in the inflation system alter all the non-monetary assets by using an index (in Colombia it is known as PAAG) that reflects the inflation rate. Some non-monetary assets are excluded from this adjustment: inventories and the purchase of goods or inventory. There are other exceptions to this rule.

The value of the adjustment to the non-monetary assets is listed as a greater value of the assets. At the same time, a taxable profit is also listed.

This means that the depreciation, depletion, and amortization are calculated based on the adjusted value of the asset. The accumulated depreciation and amortization are also adjustable.

II.I.4 Adjustments to Equity

Equity is adjusted when it has a positive value. This adjustment is listed as a loss in the IS. The value of the adjustment is also listed in the BS as a higher value for equity. Although from the accounting point of view it increases equity, it is only an accounting operation and is not part of the CFE.

The adjustment to equity implies a cost for holding equity instead of debt. In a non-inflationary situation, the cost of equity is not deductible. However, when equity is adjusted and that adjustment is tax deductible, the nominal tax rate changes, which affects the after-tax cost of debt, as follows:

Assume a new investment ΔI that can be financed by equity or by debt as shown in Table 11.1.

TABLE II.I   Financing a New Investment

	Investment financing	
RHS of BS	**Debt**	**Equity**
Equity	E	$E + D = E + \Delta I$
Debt	$D = \Delta I$	–

The deductible items regarding the financing are as follows (see Table 11.2).

TABLE II.2   The Cost of Investment Financing

RHS of BS	Cost of investment financing	
	Debt	Equity
Cost of equity adjustment	$i_f \times E$	$i_f(E + \Delta I) = i_f(E + D)$
Interest on debt	$dD = d\Delta I$	–

where i_f is the inflation rate.
Total tax savings for each alternative are shown in Table 11.3.

TABLE II.3   Tax Savings for each Alternative

	Investment financing	
	Debt	Equity
Cost of debt before taxes	d	
Tax savings for debt	$Td\Delta I = TdD$	
Tax savings for equity adjustment	Ti_fE	$Ti_f(E + D)$
Total tax savings	$TdD + Ti_fE$	$Ti_f(E + D)$

The net tax savings for debt is the difference between financing the new investment with debt or with equity:

$$\text{Net tax savings} = TdD + Ti_fE - Ti_f(E + D) = TdD - Ti_fD \qquad (11.1)$$

The net tax savings for financing the investment with debt is as follows:

$$TS = TD(d - i_f) \qquad (11.2)$$

Hence, the cost of debt after taxes is given below.

$$d' = d - T(d - i_f) \qquad (11.3)$$

$$d' = d\left[1 - T\left(1 - \frac{i_f}{d}\right)\right] \qquad (11.4)$$

The meaning of the second term inside the parenthesis is that the effective tax rate is reduced by the proportion of the inflation rate to the cost of debt d. The effective tax rate when we have adjustments for inflation is as follows:

$$T' = T\left(1 - \frac{i_f}{d}\right) \qquad (11.5)$$

If we have a cost of debt of 11%, a tax rate T of 40%, and the inflation rate is 3%, the after-tax cost of debt is as follows:

WHEN adjustments for inflation are made

$$d' = 11\%\left[1 - 40\%\left(1 - \frac{3\%}{11\%}\right)\right] = 7.8\%$$

WHEN adjustments for inflation are NOT made
$$\text{After-tax cost of debt} = 11\%(1 - 40\%) = 6.6\%$$

The after-tax cost of debt is higher than (not lower) than the after-tax cost of debt with no adjustment.

II.I.5 Monetary Assets

Monetary assets are not adjusted by inflation. When there is inflation, the monetary assets lose their purchasing power or value.

II.I.6 Gains and Losses in the Exchange Rate

Some assets such as foreign exchange, securities, deposits, and similar assets in foreign exchange have to be expressed in local currency at the exchange rate of the date of the financial statement. The difference between the adjusted value and the book value is listed as a profit or loss in the exchange rate for tax purposes (see Vélez-Pareja, 2003b).

The non-monetary liabilities such as debt in foreign exchange are adjusted with the exchange rate at the time of the financial statements. The adjustment is a greater value of the liability, and the value of the adjustment is listed as an expense in the IS. This expense is known as a loss in foreign exchange.

More precisely, when devaluation of the domestic currency occurs and a firm has debt in foreign currency, an exchange loss occurs when valuing the balance of debt and the principal payment in the domestic currency. The interest charges include the extra cost of the devaluation (a loss in exchange), and are directly included in the IS as a cost. The exchange loss generated by the debt balance and the principal payment is tax deductible. Given that it is an extra cost associated with the debt, we consider that this extra cost earns a tax shield (TS) or tax savings.

The exchange loss for every item is calculated as the difference between the price of the foreign currency in the current year and the price in the previous year, multiplied by the amount in foreign currency. In the case of a debt in foreign currency we have to adjust two items that are not listed in the

IS: the debt balance and the principal payment. These two adjustments generate two losses in exchange. One is related to the principal payment and the other is related to the debt balance. The amount of the adjustment is listed in the IS as an extra financial cost. The adjustment is listed in the BS as an additional value to the debt balance.

II.I.7 Presumptive Income Taxation

The PI taxation is common in developing economies. This kind of tax is applied when a government considers that there might not be transparency in the filing of income tax returns by the taxpayer. For this reason, governments estimate or presume some minimum level of income on which taxes should be levied.

There are several ways to implement this type of tax. Some of them are as follows:

1. Standard assessments that assign lump-sum taxes to taxpayers according to the occupation or business activity.
2. Estimated assessments that assign to each taxpayer a level of income estimated by indicators or proxies of wealth specific to a given profession or economic activity. These key indicators can range from location of property to numbers of skilled employees to seating capacity.
3. Value of land is used to tax businesses and persons in the agricultural industry. This method assesses income based on the potential output of land or crop yield, and on soil quality and productivity ratings.
4. Factors such as net wealth and the value of assets enable income estimation through net worth comparisons at the beginning and end of each year. This approach usually is accompanied by adjustments to financial statements for inflation. Presumptions based on net wealth often encourage taxpayers to increase liabilities.
5. Taxes on visible signs of wealth ensure that wealthy citizens pay an appropriate amount of tax. The taxes apply only to individuals and usually include main and secondary residences, the number of domestic servants, cars, yachts, private planes, and racehorses.
6. Some schemes specify a tax burden or minimum tax irrespective of the taxpayer's level of income or economic activity. Others levy the tax as a relatively low percentage of turnover or assets.

In Colombia presumptive income taxation works on the basis of a percent of equity book value, after IAs. If EBT are lower than the value calculated as a percentage of the book value of equity, taxes are calculated on the PI.

Although it might be irrelevant in terms of levered total and equity value calculations, for the sake of completeness, we consider four basic cases for the effect of PI on the calculation of tax savings.

1. $EBIT < 0, TS = 0$ (11.6)

2. $EBIT < Int, TS = (EBIT - PI)T$ (11.7)

3. $EBIT = Int, TS = Int \times T - PI \times T$
   $= T(Int - PI) = T \times (EBIT - PI)$ (11.8)

4. $EBIT > Int, TS = T \times Int$ (11.9)

where TS = tax savings, Int = interest charges, $EBIT$ = earnings before interest and taxes, PI = presumptive income, T = tax rate. When we indicate EBIT the reader should think not only in terms of EBIT but in terms of any OI or accounting transaction that increases the basis against which the TS can be offset. The same consideration is valid when we mention interest. In that cases, we should include (as will be seen below) not only interest charges generate TS, but also we have to include IAs, LCF, and losses in foreign exchange.

We illustrate this idea with a simple example (see Table 11.4).

TABLE 11.4 Calculation of TS with PI

EBIT	100	100	100	100
Interest charges	150	100	80	
EBT	−50	0	20	100
PI	5	5	5	5
T = 40%	2	2	8	40
TS	38	38	32	0

We can check that the TS is the difference in taxes paid. The Excel formulation might be as follows:

$$= IF(EBIT < 0, 0, IF (EBIT <= Int, (EBIT - PI)^*T, Int^*T)) \quad (11.10)$$

The reader can verify this formulation.

If we include LCF or loss amortization, we should modify the previous Excel formulation to the following:

$$= IF(EBIT < 0, 0, IF (EBIT <= Int + LCF,$$
$$(EBIT - PI)^*T, (Int + LCF)^*T)) \quad (11.11)$$

In the following simple example we illustrate this idea (see Table 11.5):

TABLE 11.5   Calculation of TS with LCF and PI

EBIT	100	100	100	100
Interest charges	150	100	80	
EBT	−50	0	20	100
LCF			5	
EBT after LCF	−50	0	15	100
PI	5	5	5	5
T = 40%	2	2	6	40
TS	38	38	34	0

We can verify that the difference in taxes is exactly the amount calculated with the formula.

11.2 CASE STUDY: TIMANCO S. A. E. S. P. EMPRESA DE TELECOMUNICACIONES

This project entails the setup of a firm to provide telephone service at Neiva an intermediate city in Colombia, South America. This project will install 16,500 phone lines and 22,480 pairs of telephone lines in the distribution network to satisfy a part of the total demand. The feasibility study was based on detailed demand and market research and commercial quotes from specialized suppliers.[2]

The project was estimated for a 32-year period. The initial investment was made from 2000 to 2002. Hence, we consider the project as an ongoing concern and we value it at the end of 2003. The financial statements for 2003 have been considered as historical financial statements. In the appendix we present the relevant data and financial statements.

In Appendix A, we focus on a detailed estimation of demand, cost, and price. This estimation considers the demand as a function of the population's income level. It is a good demonstration of how today's technological tools can overcome shortcuts employed by people who continue to operate as if they were living in an age without inexpensive computing tools.

---

[2]In this section we have made some simplifications to make the presentation easier. These simplifications refer to the exact and detailed determination of the basis for calculating the TS and the calculation of the unlevered cost of equity. We have kept the assumptions and procedures to determine the unlevered cost of equity that the consultant used in the report. The details for this purpose can be found in Velez-Pareja and Tham, *Timanco S.A.: Unpaid Taxes, Losses Carried Forward, Foreign Debt, Presumptive Income and Adjustment for Inflation. The Treatment with DCF and EVA©*, downloadable from Social Science Research Network, 2003.

In this case we cannot use the traditional formulation for the WACC because, as we can see in the CB, taxes are not paid in the same year as they are accrued. Taxes are paid in advance. This means that the TSs are not earned in the same year that they are accrued. As discussed in Chapter Six, we have to apportion the accrued or theoretical TS according to the payment of taxes. As seen in past chapters, we have to use alternate formulations or approaches for the WACC calculation. In this case study, we use the adjusted WACC applied to the FCF, the CCF, and the calculation of the PV of the CFE to calculate the levered value.

Also, we need to recognize different sources of TSs. In this case study we have interest payments, a loss in the exchange rate of a foreign exchange debt, equity IAs, LCF and, indirectly, PI.

In the following tables (Table 11.6) we analyze the basis for the TS calculation. The TS is used to calculate the FCF. After the calculation of the TS, we derive the CFD and the CFE by referencing the CB. We obtain the CFD from the financing cash flow section and the CFE from the equity cash flow section of the CB.

The CFD and CFE are shown in the following tables (Table 11.6), after the TS has been calculated.

The percent of tax paid in year i is the tax paid in year i divided by the total tax accrued. Decimals will hide this explanation, but it can be seen clearly in years 2007–2008 (see Table 11.6).

As mentioned above, there are several sources of TSs associated with the financing activity of the firm. One is the interest payments that are calculated as the tax rate times the domestic interest rate times the value of debt at the beginning of the year plus the foreign interest rate times the value of debt at the beginning of the year converted to domestic currency. These amounts are listed in the IS.

On the other hand, there are two other sources of tax savings when there is foreign exchange debt and when IAs are made to the financial statements. One is the loss in exchange rate because of debt that is listed in the IS and the other is the equity IA. The sum of these items provides the basis for the TS calculation.

However, as pointed out in Chapters Six and Seven, the earnings of the TS depend on the EBIT plus OI that might increase the amount against which the interest (and other items) can be offset. For that reason we calculate the EBIT plus OI plus IA profit plus PI plus OI for non-deductible items. From Chapter Six we know that the tax savings will depend on the magnitude of the sum. If the sum is less than the basis for the tax savings calculation, the TS will not be totally earned. Then, to calculate the TS we use the expression (11.11) in a spreadsheet. This is what we call the accrued TS.

TABLE 11.6 Calculation of the Basis for Tax Shield and Yearly Tax Shield for Years 2003 to 2019 (Units in Billion Pesos)

Basis for the TS	2003	2004	2005	2006	2007	2008	2009	2010	2011	2012	2013	2014	2015	2016	2017	2018	2019
Interest payments from the IS and CB	0.00	1.10	1.70	1.70	1.50	1.20	0.90	0.50	0.10	0.00	0.00	0.00	0.00	0.00	0.00	0.00	0.00
IA for equity	0.50	0.20	0.10	0.00	0.10	0.20	0.30	0.50	0.60	0.80	1.00	1.20	1.50	1.80	2.10	2.40	2.80
Prior years deductible losses (LCF)	0.00	0.00	0.00	2.80	2.10	0.00	0.00	0.00	0.00	0.00	0.00	0.00	0.00	0.00	0.00	0.00	0.00
Loss in exchange from the IS	0.30	0.50	0.40	0.30	0.10	0.00	0.00	0.00	0.00	0.00	0.00	0.00	0.00	0.00	0.00	0.00	0.00
Total basis for TS	0.80	1.90	2.30	4.90	3.80	1.50	1.30	1.00	0.80	0.80	1.00	1.20	1.50	1.80	2.10	2.40	2.80
EBIT	-4.40	-2.50	0.40	3.70	7.70	10.40	11.80	13.60	15.40	17.20	19.10	21.20	23.40	25.70	27.80	29.80	32.00
OI	0.00	0.00	0.20	0.60	0.80	1.10	1.40	1.60	2.00	2.60	3.40	4.20	5.10	6.10	7.00	7.90	8.80
IA profit	0.10	0.90	0.70	0.40	0.30	0.10	0.00	-0.20	-0.40	-0.60	-0.80	-1.10	-1.40	-1.70	-1.90	-2.20	-2.50
Total non-deductible items	0.00	0.00	0.00	-2.70	-2.10	0.00	0.00	0.10	0.10	0.10	0.10	0.10	0.10	0.10	0.10	0.10	0.10
EBIT + OI + IA + non-deductible items	-4.30	-1.70	1.40	2.10	6.80	11.60	13.30	15.00	17.00	19.20	21.70	24.30	27.20	30.30	33.00	35.60	38.50
PI	0.00	0.30	0.30	0.30	0.30	0.50	0.70	1.00	1.30	1.60	2.00	2.40	2.90	3.40	4.00	4.60	5.30
Nominal tax rate (in %)	35.00	35.00	35.00	35.00	35.00	35.00	35.00	35.00	35.00	35.00	35.00	35.00	35.00	35.00	35.00	35.00	35.00
TS = Tax rate × Total basis for TS	0.30	0.70	0.80	1.70	1.30	0.50	0.40	0.40	0.30	0.30	0.30	0.40	0.50	0.60	0.70	0.80	1.00
TS	0.00	0.00	0.40	0.60	1.30	0.50	0.40	0.40	0.30	0.30	0.30	0.40	0.50	0.60	0.70	0.80	1.00
Tax accrued	0.00	0.10	0.10	0.10	1.80	3.60	4.30	5.10	5.90	6.70	7.60	8.50	9.50	10.60	11.60	12.40	13.50
Tax paid year n	0.00	0.00	0.00	0.10	0.10	0.70	2.00	3.00	3.50	4.10	4.70	5.40	6.00	6.80	7.50	8.30	9.00
Tax paid year n + 1	0.00	0.00	0.10	0.10	0.00	1.70	2.90	2.30	2.10	2.40	2.60	2.90	3.10	3.50	3.80	4.00	4.10
% Tax year n paid year n	0.00	0.00	30.20	71.10	4.40	19.80	47.20	58.80	59.70	61.00	62.30	63.10	63.50	63.80	65.20	66.70	66.80
% Tax year n paid year n + 1	0.00	0.00	100.00	69.80	28.90	95.60	80.20	52.80	41.20	40.30	39.00	37.70	36.90	36.50	36.20	34.80	33.30
TS earned year n	0.00	0.00	0.10	0.40	0.10	0.10	0.20	0.20	0.20	0.20	0.20	0.30	0.30	0.40	0.50	0.60	0.70
TS earned year n + 1	0.00	0.00	0.00	0.30	0.20	1.30	0.40	0.20	0.10	0.10	0.10	0.10	0.20	0.20	0.20	0.30	0.30
Total TS earned in year n	0.00	0.00	0.10	0.70	0.20	1.40	0.60	0.40	0.30	0.30	0.30	0.40	0.50	0.60	0.70	0.80	0.90

TABLE 11.6 Calculation of the Basis for Tax Shield and Yearly Tax Shield (continued) for Years 2020 to 2032 (Units in Billion Pesos)

Basis for the TS	2020	2021	2022	2023	2024	2025	2026	2027	2028	2029	2030	2031	2032
Interest payments from the IS and CB	0.00	0.00	0.00	0.00	0.00	0.00	0.00	0.00	0.00	0.00	0.00	0.00	0.00
IA for equity	3.20	3.70	4.20	4.70	5.30	5.90	6.50	7.20	7.90	8.60	9.40	10.20	11.00
Prior years deductible losses (LCF)	0.00	0.00	0.00	0.00	0.00	0.00	0.00	0.00	0.00	0.00	0.00	0.00	0.00
Loss in exchange from the IS	0.00	0.00	0.00	0.00	0.00	0.00	0.00	0.00	0.00	0.00	0.00	0.00	0.00
Total basis for TS	3.20	3.70	4.20	4.70	5.30	5.90	6.50	7.20	7.90	8.60	9.40	10.20	11.00
EBIT	34.60	37.50	39.30	40.20	41.10	42.10	43.20	44.30	45.50	46.80	48.20	49.60	51.00
OI	9.90	11.20	12.60	14.00	15.60	17.30	19.10	21.00	23.00	25.10	27.40	29.80	32.30
IA profit	−2.80	−3.20	−3.60	−4.00	−4.50	−5.10	−5.70	−6.30	−6.90	−7.60	−8.30	−9.10	−9.90
Total non-deductible items	0.10	0.10	0.10	0.10	0.10	0.20	0.20	0.20	0.20	0.20	0.20	0.20	0.20
EBIT + OI + IA + non-deductible items	41.90	45.70	48.50	50.30	52.30	54.40	56.70	59.20	61.80	64.50	67.40	70.40	73.60
PI	6.10	6.90	7.80	8.80	9.80	10.80	11.90	13.00	14.30	15.50	16.90	18.30	19.80
Nominal tax rate (in %)	35.00	35.00	35.00	35.00	35.00	35.00	35.00	35.00	35.00	35.00	35.00	35.00	35.00
TS = Tax rate × Total basis for TS	1.10	1.30	1.50	1.70	1.90	2.10	2.30	2.50	2.80	3.00	3.30	3.60	3.90
TS	1.10	1.30	1.50	1.70	1.90	2.10	2.30	2.50	2.80	3.00	3.30	3.60	3.90
Tax accrued	14.70	16.00	17.00	17.60	18.30	19.00	19.90	20.70	21.60	22.60	23.60	24.70	25.80
Tax paid year n	9.70	10.50	11.50	12.40	13.00	13.50	14.00	14.60	15.20	15.90	16.60	17.30	18.10
Tax paid year n + 1	4.50	4.90	5.40	5.50	5.20	5.30	5.60	5.90	6.10	6.40	6.70	7.00	7.30
% Tax year n paid year n	66.40	66.00	67.70	70.20	70.90	70.70	70.50	70.40	70.40	70.30	70.30	70.20	70.20
% Tax year n paid year n + 1	33.20	33.60	34.00	32.30	29.80	29.10	29.30	29.50	29.60	29.60	29.70	29.70	29.80
TS earned year n	0.80	0.90	1.00	1.20	1.30	1.50	1.60	1.80	1.90	2.10	2.30	2.50	2.70
TS earned year n + 1	0.30	0.40	0.40	0.50	0.50	0.50	0.60	0.70	0.70	0.80	0.90	1.00	1.10
Total TS earned in year n	1.10	1.20	1.40	1.60	1.80	2.00	2.20	2.40	2.70	2.90	3.20	3.50	3.80

As the TS are earned as a reduction of the tax paid, we assume that the TSs are earned when taxes are paid. As we can see from the CB and the BS, the taxes are not paid in the same year that they are accrued. Taxes are paid in advance in the year that they are accrued and the remaining tax is paid in the next year. This means that we have to estimate which proportion of each tax accrued is paid in the same year and which is paid in the following year. This is shown in the previous table, which examines the Tax accrued, the Tax paid year n, the Tax paid year n + 1, the % Tax year n paid year n, and the % Tax year n paid year n + 1. The last two percentages indicate how much of the TS is earned in each year. This can be seen for year 2005. The tax for 2005 is paid 30.2% in 2005 and 69.8% in 2006. Hence, the TS for 2005 (0.4) is earned 30.2% (0.1) in 2005 and 69.8% (0.3) in 2006. For year 2006 the tax is paid 71.1% in 2006 and 28.9% in 2007. Hence, the TS of 2005 (0.6) earned 71.1% (0.4) in 2006 and 28.9% (0.2) in 2007. Then the TS for 2006 is 0.7 (0.4 + 0.3).

The CFD and CFE can be read from the CB, as explained above.

With the CFD, the CFE, and the TS we can derive the FCF and the CCF as indicated in the Table 11.7.

As discussed in previous chapters, we have to estimate the unlevered cost of equity. To do this we estimate the unlevered beta and the market risk premium (in this case the U.S. risk premium), as mentioned in Chapter Eight. We also estimate the risk-free rate in the U.S., the local country risk, and the domestic inflation rate. With these data we make the following estimates using the Fisher relationship and the capital asset pricing model (CAPM) (see Table 11.8):

Using the Fisher relationship, we have the following:

Domestic risk-free rate

$$R_{fdom} = (1 + \text{U.S. risk-free rate})(1 + \text{Domestic inflation rate}) - 1 \quad (11.12)$$

Using the CAPM we have

$$\rho = R_{fdom} + \beta_{unl}(R_m - r_f) + CR \quad (11.13)$$

where ρ is the cost of unlevered equity, β_{unl} is the unlevered β for the firm (see Chapter Eight for estimation of unlevered β), r_f is the U.S. risk-free rate, R_{fdom} is the domestic risk-free rate, and CR is the country risk.

Numerical estimates are shown in the following tables.

With this information we can now solve the circularity and calculate the adjusted WACC and the levered value. The circularity solution was presented in Chapter Seven. To value correctly the firm and at the same time to calculate the adjusted WACC we need to derive the TV. The procedure to derive the TV is presented in Chapter Nine.

TABLE II.7 CFD, CFE, and TS: Derivation of the CCF and FCF for Years 2003 to 2019 (Units in Billion Pesos)

	2003	2004	2005	2006	2007	2008	2009	2010	2011	2012	2013	2014	2015	2016	2017	2018	2019
CFD	−11.70	−5.50	2.30	3.90	5.00	5.00	5.00	5.00	1.70	0.00	0.00	0.00	0.00	0.00	0.00	0.00	0.00
CFE	−9.00	0.00	0.00	0.00	0.00	1.50	3.30	4.00	4.80	5.70	6.60	7.50	8.50	9.50	10.70	11.70	12.70
TS	0.00	0.00	0.10	0.70	0.20	1.40	0.60	0.40	0.30	0.30	0.30	0.40	0.50	0.60	0.70	0.80	0.90
FCF = CFD + CFE − TS	−20.70	−5.50	2.20	3.20	4.70	5.20	7.70	8.60	6.20	5.40	6.20	7.10	8.00	8.90	10.00	10.90	11.70
CCF = CFD + CFE	−20.70	−5.50	2.30	3.90	5.00	6.50	8.30	9.10	6.50	5.70	6.60	7.50	8.50	9.50	10.70	11.70	12.70

TABLE 11.7   CFD, CFE, and TS: Derivation of the CCF and FCF (continued) for Years 2020 to 2032 (Units in Billion Pesos)

	2020	2021	2022	2023	2024	2025	2026	2027	2028	2029	2030	2031	2032
CFD	0.00	0.00	0.00	0.00	0.00	0.00	0.00	0.00	0.00	0.00	0.00	0.00	0.00
CFE	13.70	15.00	16.40	17.60	18.40	19.30	20.20	21.30	22.40	23.50	24.80	26.10	27.40
TS	1.10	1.20	1.40	1.60	1.80	2.00	2.20	2.40	2.70	2.90	3.20	3.50	3.80
FCF = CFD + CFE − TS	12.70	13.80	15.00	15.90	16.60	17.30	18.00	18.80	19.70	20.60	21.60	22.60	23.70
CCF = CFD + CFE	13.70	15.00	16.40	17.60	18.40	19.30	20.20	21.30	22.40	23.50	24.80	26.10	27.40

TABLE 11.8 Basic Information for Estimation of the Unlevered Cost of Equity ρ for Years 2003 to 2019

Proxy data	2003 (in %)	2004 (in %)	2005 (in %)	2006 (in %)	2007 (in %)	2008 (in %)	2009 (in %)	2010 (in %)	2011 (in %)	2012 (in %)	2013 (in %)	2014 (in %)	2015 (in %)	2016 (in %)	2017 (in %)	2018 (in %)	2019 (in %)
Unlevered beta$_{unl}$	34.00	34.00	34.00	34.00	34.00	34.00	34.00	34.00	34.00	34.00	34.00	34.00	34.00	34.00	34.00	34.00	34.00
Premium risk $(R_m - r_f)$	5.20	5.20	5.20	5.20	5.20	5.20	5.20	5.20	5.20	5.20	5.20	5.20	5.20	5.20	5.20	5.20	5.20
Country risk premium	9.80	9.80	9.80	9.80	9.80	9.80	9.80	9.80	9.80	9.80	9.80	9.80	9.80	9.80	9.80	9.80	9.80
r_f = Risk-free rate U.S.	5.00	5.00	5.00	5.00	5.00	5.00	5.00	5.00	5.00	5.00	5.00	5.00	5.00	5.00	5.00	5.00	5.00
Domestic inflation rate	6.00	5.00	4.00	3.50	3.00	3.00	3.00	3.00	3.00	3.00	3.00	3.00	3.00	3.00	3.00	3.00	3.00
$r_{f\,dom} = (1 + r_f)$ $(1 + infl) - 1$	11.30	10.20	9.20	8.60	8.10	8.10	8.10	8.10	8.10	8.10	8.10	8.10	8.10	8.10	8.10	8.10	8.10
$\rho = r_{f\,dom} + beta_{unl}$ $(R_m - r_f) + CR$	22.80	21.70	20.70	20.10	19.60	19.60	19.60	19.60	19.60	19.60	19.60	19.60	19.60	19.60	19.60	19.60	19.60

TABLE II.8 Basic Information for Estimation of the Unlevered Cost of Equity ρ (continued) for Years 2020 to 2032

Proxy data	2020 (in %)	2021 (in %)	2022 (in %)	2023 (in %)	2024 (in %)	2025 (in %)	2026 (in %)	2027 (in %)	2028 (in %)	2029 (in %)	2030 (in %)	2031 (in %)	2032 (in %)
Unlevered beta$_{unl}$	34.00	34.00	34.00	34.00	34.00	34.00	34.00	34.00	34.00	34.00	34.00	34.00	34.00
Premium risk $(R_m - r_f)$	5.20	5.20	5.20	5.20	5.20	5.20	5.20	5.20	5.20	5.20	5.20	5.20	5.20
Country risk premium	9.80	9.80	9.80	9.80	9.80	9.80	9.80	9.80	9.80	9.80	9.80	9.80	9.80
r_f = Risk-free rate U.S.	5.00	5.00	5.00	5.00	5.00	5.00	5.00	5.00	5.00	5.00	5.00	5.00	5.00
Domestic inflation rate	3.00	3.00	3.00	3.00	3.00	3.00	3.00	3.00	3.00	3.00	3.00	3.00	3.00
$r_{f\,dom} = (1 + r_f)(1 + infl) - 1$	8.10	8.10	8.10	8.10	8.10	8.10	8.10	8.10	8.10	8.10	8.10	8.10	8.10
$\rho = r_{f\,dom} + beta_{unl}\,(R_m - r_f) + CR$	19.60	19.60	19.60	19.60	19.60	19.60	19.60	19.60	19.60	19.60	19.60	19.60	19.60

The adjusted WACC (from Chapter Seven) is

$$\text{Adjusted WACC} = \rho - \text{TS}/(\text{Levered value}) \qquad (11.14)$$

where TS is the tax savings actually earned in the year.

For the TV calculation we need to estimate the WACC in perpetuity (Chapter Nine). This firm does not have debt from year 12 and onwards, hence the prevailing WACC in perpetuity should be the unlevered cost of equity ρ. In this case we assume that the inflation rate in perpetuity is the same as the rate prevailing over the last 25 years of the estimation period. This means that the unlevered cost of equity in perpetuity could be the same as the cost estimated for the last 25 years. Observe in the Table 11.8 how the unlevered cost of equity is affected by the domestic inflation rate.

From the same chapter we recall the idea of ROMVIC, which is defined as NOPLAT divided by the MVIC. This implies that the TV depends on the levered value and vice versa. This is another source of circularity.

We also have to adjust the TV with the recovery of AR and AP, and with the cash in hand and outstanding investment in securities. These adjustments give rise to the adjusted TV (see Tables 11.9a and 11.9b).

In Table 11.9b we calculate the levered value using the FCF and the adjusted WACC.

Now we calculate the levered value from the PV(CFE) plus debt (see Table 11.10). In this case we also encounter circularity. We do not show the details regarding the solution of circularity.

As expected, the levered value is identical to the value calculated with the FCF and the adjusted WACC. Next we check the calculation with the CCF (see Table 11.11).

As expected, the levered value is identical to the value calculated with the FCF, the adjusted WACC, and the PV(CFE).

In the next case, Table 11.12, as the factor $(1 - T)$ implies that the full TS is earned each year, we use the TS calculated on the accrued base for calculating the TS. This implies a different FCF. On the other hand, the cost of debt after taxes has to be adjusted to $d' = d[1 - T(1 - i/d)]$ taking into account the IA. With this warning we calculate the levered value using the FCF and the traditional WACC formulation (see Table 11.12)

$$\text{WACC} = d\%D(1 - T) + e\%E. \qquad (11.15)$$

In Table 11.13 we calculate the levered value with the traditional WACC, non-constant WACC, with market value for WACC calculation and cost of debt d = Interest paid/debt.

TABLE II.9a Case I: Adjusted WACC and FCF, Non-constant WACC, Market Value for WACC Calculation, and Cost of Debt d = Interest Paid/Debt for Years 2003 to 2019 (Units in Billion Pesos)

	2003	2004	2005	2006	2007	2008	2009	2010	2011	2012	2013	2014	2015	2016	2017	2018	2019
EBIT	−4.40	−2.50	0.40	3.70	7.70	10.40	11.80	13.60	15.40	17.20	19.10	21.20	23.40	25.70	27.80	29.80	32.00
NOPLAT	−2.90	−1.70	0.20	2.40	5.00	6.70	7.70	8.80	10.00	11.20	12.40	13.80	15.20	16.70	18.10	19.30	20.80
Growth NOPLAT (in %)				898.90	106.40	33.90	14.50	14.80	13.00	11.90	11.20	10.70	10.40	10.10	8.20	6.90	7.50
Expected g																	
WACC in perpetuity = ρ																	
Nonbearing interest liabilities	0.00	0.70	0.10	0.10	1.80	3.00	2.30	2.20	2.40	2.70	2.90	3.20	3.50	3.90	4.10	4.20	4.60
Cap invested = Market value − nonbearing interest liabilities	25.80	36.20	42.10	46.80	49.30	51.70	54.70	57.00	61.80	68.50	75.70	83.40	91.60	100.40	110.00	120.60	132.10
ROMVIC		−0.10	0.00	0.10	0.10	0.10	0.10	0.20	0.20	0.20	0.20	0.20	0.20	0.20	0.20	0.20	0.20
h = g/ROMVIC																	
Levered TV																	
Recovery of excess cash invested																	
Recovery of cash in hand																	
Payment of AP (discounted one year)																	
Recovery of AR (discounted one year)																	
Adjusted TV																	

TABLE 11.9a Case I: Adjusted WACC and FCF, Non-constant WACC, Market Value for WACC Calculation, and Cost of Debt d = Interest Paid/Debt (continued) for Years 2020 to 2032 (Units in Billion Pesos)

	2020	2021	2022	2023	2024	2025	2026	2027	2028	2029	2030	2031	2032	2033
EBIT	34.60	37.50	39.30	40.20	41.10	42.10	43.20	44.30	45.50	46.80	48.20	49.60	51.00	
NOPLAT	22.50	24.40	25.60	26.10	26.70	27.30	28.10	28.80	29.60	30.40	31.30	32.20	33.20	
Growth NOPLAT(in %)	8.00	8.40	5.00	2.10	2.30	2.40	2.60	2.70	2.80	2.80	2.90	2.90	2.90	
Expected g														2.90
WACC in perpetuity = ρ														19.60
Non bearing interest liabilities	5.00	5.50	5.50	5.20	5.30	5.60	5.90	6.10	6.40	6.70	7.00	7.30	7.70	
Cap invested = Market value – nonbearing interest liabilities	144.70	158.50	174.30	192.30	212.70	235.90	262.80	294.00	330.20	372.50	421.80	479.60	–7.70	
ROMVIC	0.20	0.20	0.20	0.10	0.10	0.10	0.10	0.10	0.10	0.10	0.10	0.10	0.10	
h = g/ROMVIC														
Levered TV													164.00	
Recovery of excess cash invested													390.30	
Recovery of cash in hand													0.80	
Payment of AP (discounted one year)													–6.40	
Recovery of AR (discounted one year)													6.40	
Adjusted TV													555.10	

TABLE 11.9b   Calculation of Weighted Average Cost of Capital and Levered Value for Years 2003 to 2019 (Units in Billion Pesos)

	2003	2004	2005	2006	2007	2008	2009	2010	2011	2012	2013	2014	2015	2016	2017	2018	2019
FCF	−20.70	−5.50	2.10	2.90	4.70	5.90	7.70	8.60	6.20	5.40	6.20	7.10	8.00	8.90	10.00	10.9	11.7
TV																	
Total FCF + TV	−20.70	−5.50	2.10	2.90	4.70	5.90	7.70	8.60	6.20	5.40	6.20	7.10	8.00	8.90	10.00	10.9	11.7
WACC = ρ − TS/ (Levered value)		21.70	20.20	17.90	19.10	18.30	18.50	18.80	19.10	19.20	19.20	19.10	19.10	19.00	19.00	18.9	18.9
Levered value	25.80	36.90	42.30	46.90	51.10	54.60	57.00	59.20	64.30	71.20	78.60	86.60	95.10	104.30	114.10	124.8	136.6

TABLE 11.9b Calculation of Weighted Average Cost of Capital and Levered Value (continued) for Years 2020 to 2032 (Units in Billion Pesos)

	2020	2021	2022	2023	2024	2025	2026	2027	2028	2029	2030	2031	2032	2033
FCF	12.70	13.80	15.00	15.90	16.60	17.30	18.00	18.80	19.70	20.60	21.60	22.60	23.70	
													555.10	
Total FCF + TV	12.70	13.80	15.00	15.90	16.60	17.30	18.00	18.80	19.70	20.60	21.60	22.60	578.70	
WACC = $\rho - TS/$ (Levered value) (in %)	18.80	18.80	18.80	18.70	18.70	18.70	18.70	18.70	18.70	18.80	18.80	18.80	18.80	
Levered value	149.70	164.10	179.80	197.60	218.00	241.50	268.70	300.10	336.70	379.20	428.80	486.90		

TABLE II.10   Case 2: Present Value (Cash Flow to Equity), Non-constant Cost of Equity e, Market Value for e Calculation, and Cost of Debt d = Interest paid/debt for Years 2003 to 2019 (Units in Billion Pesos)

	2003	2004	2005	2006	2007	2008	2009	2010	2011	2012	2013	2014	2015	2016	2017	2018	2019
CFE	−9.00	0.00	0.00	0.00	0.00	1.50	3.30	4.00	4.80	5.70	6.60	7.50	8.50	9.50	10.70	11.70	12.70
TV for equity																	
Total CFE + TV	−9.00	0.00	0.00	0.00	0.00	1.50	3.30	4.00	4.80	5.70	6.60	7.50	8.50	9.50	10.70	11.70	12.70
Debt value	12.00	19.10	19.00	17.20	13.80	10.10	6.00	1.50	0.00	0.00	0.00	0.00	0.00	0.00	0.00	0.00	0.00
d = Interest paid/debt (in %)	17.50	13.80	11.40	10.90	9.40	9.40	9.30	9.30	9.20	9.40	9.40	9.40	9.40	9.40	9.40	9.40	9.40
$e = \rho + (\rho - d)D/E$ (in %)		28.60	30.60	27.70	25.60	23.40	22.00	20.80	19.90	19.60	19.60	19.60	19.60	19.60	19.60	19.60	19.60
PV(CFE)	13.90	17.80	23.30	29.70	37.30	44.50	51.00	57.60	64.30	71.20	78.60	86.60	95.10	104.30	114.10	124.80	136.60
Levered value = PV(CFE) + debt	25.80	36.90	42.30	46.90	51.10	54.60	57.00	59.20	64.30	71.20	78.60	86.60	95.10	104.30	114.10	124.80	136.60

TABLE 11.10 Case 2: Present Value (Cash Flow to Equity) (continued), Non-constant Cost of Equity e, Market Value for e Calculation, and Cost of Debt d = Interest paid/debt for Years 2020 to 2032 (Units in Billion Pesos)

	2020	2021	2022	2023	2024	2025	2026	2027	2028	2029	2030	2031	2032
CFE	13.70	15.00	16.40	17.60	18.40	19.30	20.20	21.30	22.40	23.50	24.80	26.10	27.40
TV for equity													555.10
Total CFE + TV	13.70	15.00	16.40	17.60	18.40	19.30	20.20	21.30	22.40	23.50	24.80	26.10	582.50
Debt value	0.00	0.00	0.00	0.00	0.00	0.00	0.00	0.00	0.00	0.00	0.00	0.00	0.00
d = Interest paid/debt (in %)	9.40	9.40	9.40	9.40	9.40	9.40	9.40	9.40	9.40	9.40	9.40	9.40	9.40
$e = \rho + (\rho - d)D/E$ (in %)	19.60	19.60	19.60	19.60	19.60	19.60	19.60	19.60	19.60	19.60	19.60	19.60	19.60
PV(CFE)	149.70	164.10	179.80	197.60	218.00	241.50	268.70	300.10	336.70	379.20	428.80	486.90	0.00
Levered value = PV(CFE) + debt	149.70	164.10	179.80	197.60	218.00	241.50	268.70	300.10	336.70	379.20	428.80	486.90	0.00

TABLE 11.11 Case 3: Present Value (Capital Cash Flow), Discount Rate Cost of Unlevered Equity ρ for Years 2003 to 2019 (Units in Billion Pesos)

	2003	2004	2005	2006	2007	2008	2009	2010	2011	2012	2013	2014	2015	2016	2017	2018	2019
CCF		−5.50	2.30	3.90	5.00	6.50	8.30	9.10	6.50	5.70	6.60	7.50	8.50	9.50	10.70	11.70	12.70
TV																	
Total CCF + TV		−5.50	2.30	3.90	5.00	6.50	8.30	9.10	6.50	5.70	6.60	7.50	8.50	9.50	10.70	11.70	12.70
PV(CCF)	25.80	36.90	42.30	46.90	51.10	54.60	57.00	59.20	64.30	71.20	78.60	86.60	95.10	104.30	·114.10	124.80	136.60

TABLE II.II Case 3: Present Value (Capital Cash Flow) (continued), Discount Rate: Cost of Unlevered Equity ρ for Years 2020 to 2032 (Units in Billion Pesos)

	2020	2021	2022	2023	2024	2025	2026	2027	2028	2029	2030	2031	2032
CCF	13.70	15.00	16.40	17.60	18.40	19.30	20.20	21.30	22.40	23.50	24.80	26.10	27.40
TV													555.10
Total CCF + TV	13.70	15.00	16.40	17.60	18.40	19.30	20.20	21.30	22.40	23.50	24.80	26.10	582.50
PV(CCF)	149.70	164.10	179.80	197.60	218.00	241.50	268.70	300.10	336.70	379.20	428.80	486.90	

TABLE II.12 Case 4: Traditional WACC, Non-constant WACC, Market Value for WACC Calculation, and Cost of Debt d = Interest/debt for Years 2003 to 2019 (Units in Billion Pesos)

	2003	2004	2005	2006	2007	2008	2009	2010	2011	2012	2013	2014	2015	2016	2017	2018	2019
EBIT	−4.40	−2.50	0.40	3.70	7.70	10.40	11.80	13.60	15.40	17.20	19.10	21.20	23.40	25.70	27.80	29.80	32.00
NOPLAT	−2.90	−1.70	0.20	2.40	5.00	6.70	7.70	8.80	10.00	11.20	12.40	13.80	15.20	16.70	18.10	19.30	20.80
Growth NOPLAT (in %)	0.00	0.00	0.00	898.90	106.40	33.90	14.50	14.80	13.00	11.90	11.20	10.70	10.40	10.10	8.20	6.90	7.50
Expected g																	
WACC in perpetuity = ρ (in %)	0.00	0.00	0.00	0.00	0.00	0.00	0.00	0.00	0.00	0.00	0.00	0.00	0.00	0.00	0.00	0.00	0.00
Nonbearing interest liabilities	0.00	0.70	0.10	0.10	1.80	3.00	2.30	2.20	2.40	2.70	2.90	3.20	3.50	3.90	4.10	4.20	4.60
Cap invested = Market value – nonbearing interest liabilities	23.00	33.10	38.70	43.90	46.80	48.90	51.60	53.50	57.90	64.10	70.80	77.90	85.50	93.80	102.80	112.80	123.70
ROMVIC (in %)		−7.20	0.70	6.30	11.40	14.40	15.80	17.10	18.70	19.30	19.40	19.40	19.50	19.50	19.30	18.80	18.50
h = g/ROMVIC																	
Levered TV																	
Recovery of excess cash invested																	
Recovery of cash in hand																	
Payment of AP (discounted one year)																	
Recovery of AR (discounted one year)																	
Adjusted TV																	

TABLE II.12 Case 4: Traditional WACC, Non-constant WACC, Market Value for WACC Calculation, and Cost of Debt

d = Interest/debt. (continued) for Years 2020 to 2032 (Units in Billion Pesos)

	2020	2021	2022	2023	2024	2025	2026	2027	2028	2029	2030	2031	2032	2033
EBIT	34.60	37.50	39.30	40.20	41.10	42.10	43.20	44.30	45.50	46.80	48.20	49.60	51.00	
NOPLAT	22.50	24.40	25.60	26.10	26.70	27.30	28.10	28.80	29.60	30.40	31.30	32.20	33.20	
Growth NOPLAT (in %)	8.00	8.40	5.00	2.10	2.30	2.40	2.60	2.70	2.80	2.80	2.90	2.90	2.90	
Expected g														2.90
WACC in perpetuity = ρ														19.60
Nonbearing interest liabilities	5.00	5.50	5.50	5.20	5.30	5.60	5.90	6.10	6.40	6.70	7.00	7.30		
Cap invested = Market value – nonbearing interest liabilities	135.90	149.30	164.80	182.50	202.80	226.10	253.40	285.30	322.60	366.30	417.70	478.30		
ROMVIC (in %)	18.20	17.90	17.10	15.80	14.60	13.50	12.40	11.40	10.40	9.40	8.50	7.70	6.90	
H = g/ROMVIC													0.18	
Levered TV													166.30	
Recovery of excess cash invested													390.30	
Recovery of cash in hand													0.80	
Payment of AP (discounted one year)													−6.40	
Recovery of AR (discounted one year)													6.40	
Adjusted TV													557.30	

TABLE II.I3 Case 4: Traditional WACC, Non-constant WACC, Market Value for WACC Calculation, and Cost of Debt d = Interest paid/Debt; Calculation of WACC and Levered Value for Years 2003 to 2019 (Units in Billion Pesos)

	2003	2004	2005	2006	2007	2008	2009	2010	2011	2012	2013	2014	2015	2016	2017	2018	2019
CFD	−11.70	−5.50	2.30	3.90	5.00	5.00	5.00	5.00	1.70	0.00	0.00	0.00	0.00	0.00	0.00	0.00	0.00
CFE	−9.00	0.00	0.00	0.00	0.00	1.50	3.30	4.00	4.80	5.70	6.60	7.50	8.50	9.50	10.70	11.70	12.70
TS (accrued)	0.30	0.70	0.80	1.70	1.30	0.50	0.40	0.40	0.30	0.30	0.30	0.40	0.50	0.60	0.70	0.80	1.00
FCF	−21.00	−6.10	1.50	2.20	3.60	6.00	7.90	8.70	6.20	5.40	6.20	7.10	7.90	8.90	9.90	10.90	11.70
FCF with TV	−21.00	−6.10	1.50	2.20	3.60	6.00	7.90	8.70	6.20	5.40	6.20	7.10	7.90	8.90	9.90	10.90	11.70
D		51.90	56.40	48.90	39.00	28.40	19.50	11.20	2.80	0.00	0.00	0.00	0.00	0.00	0.00	0.00	0.00
d = Interest paid/debt (in %)		13.80	11.40	10.90	9.40	9.40	9.30	9.30	9.20	9.40	9.40	9.40	9.40	9.40	9.40	9.40	9.40
$d' = d[1 - T(1 - i/d)]$ (in %)		10.70	8.80	8.30	7.10	7.10	7.10	7.10	7.00	7.20	7.20	7.20	7.20	7.20	7.20	7.20	7.20
Contribution to WACC (in %)		5.60	5.00	4.10	2.80	2.00	1.40	0.80	0.20	0.00	0.00	0.00	0.00	0.00	0.00	0.00	0.00
E		48.10	43.60	51.10	61.00	71.60	80.50	88.80	97.20	100.00	100.00	100.00	100.00	100.00	100.00	100.00	100.00
$e = \rho + (\rho - d)D/E$ (in %)		30.30	32.60	29.00	26.20	23.70	22.10	20.90	19.90	19.60	19.60	19.60	19.60	19.60	19.60	19.60	19.60
Contribution to WACC (in %)		14.60	14.20	14.80	16.00	17.00	17.80	18.60	19.40	19.60	19.60	19.60	19.60	19.60	19.60	19.60	19.60
WACC (in %)		20.10	19.20	18.90	18.80	19.00	19.20	19.40	19.60	19.60	19.60	19.60	19.60	19.60	19.60	19.60	19.60
Levered value	23.10	33.80	38.80	44.00	48.60	51.90	53.90	55.70	60.40	66.80	73.70	81.10	89.10	97.70	106.90	117.00	128.30

TABLE 11.13 Case 4: Traditional WACC, Non-constant WACC, Market Value for WACC Calculation and Cost of Debt
d = Interest paid/Debt; Calculation of WACC and Levered Value (continued) for Years 2020–2033 (Units in Billion Pesos)

	2020	2021	2022	2023	2024	2025	2026	2027	2028	2029	2030	2031	2032	2033
CFD	0.00	0.00	0.00	0.00	0.00	0.00	0.00	0.00	0.00	0.00	0.00	0.00	0.00	
CFE	13.70	15.00	16.40	17.60	18.40	19.30	20.20	21.30	22.40	23.50	24.80	26.10	27.40	
TS (accrued)	1.10	1.30	1.50	1.70	1.90	2.10	2.30	2.50	2.80	3.00	3.30	3.60	3.90	
FCF	12.60	13.70	14.90	15.90	16.50	17.20	17.90	18.70	19.60	20.50	21.50	22.50	23.60	
FCF with TV	12.60	13.70	14.90	15.90	16.50	17.20	17.90	18.70	19.60	20.50	21.50	22.50	580.90	
D%	0.00	0.00	0.00	0.00	0.00	0.00	0.00	0.00	0.00	0.00	0.00	0.00	0.00	
d = Interest paid/debt (in %)	9.40	9.40	9.40	9.40	9.40	9.40	9.40	9.40	9.40	9.40	9.40	9.40	9.40	
d' = d[1 − T(1 − i/d)] (in %)	7.20	7.20	7.20	7.20	7.20	7.20	7.20	7.20	7.20	7.20	7.20	7.20	7.20	
Contribution to WACC (in %)	0.00	0.00	0.00	0.00	0.00	0.00	0.00	0.00	0.00	0.00	0.00	0.00	0.00	
E%	100.00	100.00	100.00	100.00	100.00	100.00	100.00	100.00	100.00	100.00	100.00	100.00	100.00	
e = ρ + (ρ − d)D/E (in %)	19.60	19.60	19.60	19.60	19.60	19.60	19.60	19.60	19.60	19.60	19.60	19.60	19.60	
Contribution to WACC (in %)	19.60	19.60	19.60	19.60	19.60	19.60	19.60	19.60	19.60	19.60	19.60	19.60	19.60	
WACC (in %)	19.60	19.60	19.60	19.60	19.60	19.60	19.60	19.60	19.60	19.60	19.60	19.60	19.60	
Levered value	140.90	154.80	170.20	187.80	208.10	231.70	259.30	291.40	329.00	373.00	424.70	485.60	0.00	

We cannot expect that the levered value with the standard after-tax WACC matches the values obtained from the other methods for the simple reason that when using this traditional WACC formulation, we assume (see Chapter Seven) that the total tax savings are earned in the same year that the taxes are accrued, which means that the taxes are paid totally in the same year. This is not the case, as mentioned above, and hence the levered value is not the same. The difference with the other calculations is -10.70%.

The next case (Table 11.14) considers the cost of debt d as constant and equal to the IRR of the CFD. We do not show here the calculation of the TV (based on the new market value), but show directly the result of the calculation of the levered value.

As expected, the levered value is different. In this case the difference is -13.1%.

It is usual to consider the cost of debt as the IRR of the CFD and hence, constant during the estimating period. In our case that IRR is 11.2%, but we adjust the cost in the same manner as before to take into account the IA. Another usual practice is to calculate the TV as (see Table 11.15).

$$TV = \frac{FCF(1+g)}{WACC - g} \qquad (11.16)$$

As in the last example, we omit the detailed calculation of the TV and show only the new FCF with that TV.

With this approach the difference is -3.70%.

II.3 VALUATION METHODS BASED ON BOOK VALUES

Another case uses book values to estimate the WACC and use the correct cost of debt. In this case the cost of debt is estimated as above, with the yearly proportion of interest divided by the debt at the beginning of the year. In this case we proceed to show the TV calculations (depending on the levered value) and then we illustrate the calculation of the levered value. We omit the details of TV calculation (the TV depends on the levered market value). We simply present the FCF and the levered value and WACC calculation (see Table 11.16).

As expected, the levered value is different. In this case the difference is -6.10%. It is usual to consider the cost of debt as the IRR of the CFD and hence, the cost of debt is constant during the estimating period. In our case the IRR is 11.2%, but we adjust the cost in the same manner as before to take into account the IA. Using the same FCF as before, the results are as follows.

Typically we consider the WACC as a constant value. We now construct a sensitivity table where we show the levered value for different values of the WACC. For comparison purposes we have selected some values such as the

TABLE II.14 Case 5: Traditional WACC, Non-constant WACC, Market Value for WACC Calculation, and Cost of Debt d = IRR of CFD for Years 2003–2019 (Units in Billion Pesos)

	2003	2004	2005	2006	2007	2008	2009	2010	2011	2012	2013	2014	2015	2016	2017	2018	2019
FCF with TV	−21.00	−6.10	1.50	2.20	3.60	6.00	7.90	8.70	6.20	5.40	6.20	7.10	7.90	8.90	9.90	10.90	11.70
D%		53.30	57.10	49.00	39.00	28.30	19.50	11.20	2.80	0.00	0.00	0.00	0.00	0.00	0.00	0.00	0.00
IRR of CFD (in %)		11.20	11.20	11.20	11.20	11.20	11.20	11.20	11.20	11.20	11.20	11.20	11.20	11.20	11.20	11.20	11.20
$d' = d[1-T]$		9.00	8.70	8.50	8.30	8.30	8.30	8.30	8.30	8.30	8.30	8.30	8.30	8.30	8.30	8.30	8.30
$(1 - i/d)]$ (in %) Contribution to WACC (in %)		4.80	5.00	4.20	3.20	2.40	1.60	0.90	0.20	0.00	0.00	0.00	0.00	0.00	0.00	0.00	0.00
E%		46.70	42.90	51.00	61.00	71.70	80.50	88.80	97.20	100.00	100.00	100.00	100.00	100.00	100.00	100.00	100.00
$e = \rho + (\rho - d)D/E$ (in %)		36.00	35.70	29.80	25.90	23.00	21.70	20.70	19.90	19.60	19.60	19.60	19.60	19.60	19.60	19.60	19.60
Contribution to WACC (in %)		16.80	15.30	15.20	15.80	16.50	17.40	18.40	19.30	19.60	19.60	19.60	19.60	19.60	19.60	19.60	19.60
WACC (in %)		21.60	20.30	19.40	19.00	18.80	19.10	19.30	19.50	19.60	19.60	19.60	19.60	19.60	19.60	19.60	19.60
Levered value	22.40	33.40	38.70	44.00	48.80	51.90	54.00	55.70	60.40	66.80	73.70	81.10	89.10	97.70	106.90	117.00	128.30

TABLE II.14 Case 5: Traditional WACC, Non-constant WACC; Market Value for WACC Calculation, and Cost of Debt d = IRR of CFD (continued) for Years 2020 to 2032 (Units in Billion Pesos)

	2020	2021	2022	2023	2024	2025	2026	2027	2028	2029	2030	2031	2032
FCF with TV	12.60	13.70	14.90	15.90	16.50	17.20	17.90	18.70	19.60	20.50	21.50	22.50	604.40
D%	0.00	0.00	0.00	0.00	0.00	0.00	0.00	0.00	0.00	0.00	0.00	0.00	0.00
d = IRR of CFD (in %)	11.20	11.20	11.20	11.20	11.20	11.20	11.20	11.20	11.20	11.20	11.20	11.20	11.20
d' = d[1 − T(1 − i/d)] (in %)	8.30	8.30	8.30	8.30	8.30	8.30	8.30	8.30	8.30	8.30	8.30	8.30	8.30
Contribution to WACC (in %)	0.00	0.00	0.00	0.00	0.00	0.00	0.00	0.00	0.00	0.00	0.00	0.00	0.00
E%	100.00	100.00	100.00	100.00	100.00	100.00	100.00	100.00	100.00	100.00	100.00	100.00	100.00
E = $\rho + (\rho - d)D/E$ (in %)	19.60	19.60	19.60	19.60	19.60	19.60	19.60	19.60	19.60	19.60	19.60	19.60	19.60
Contribution to WACC (in %)	19.60	19.60	19.60	19.60	19.60	19.60	19.60	19.60	19.60	19.60	19.60	19.60	19.60
WACC (in %)	19.60	19.60	19.60	19.60	19.60	19.60	19.60	19.60	19.60	19.60	19.60	19.60	19.60
Levered value	140.90	154.80	170.20	187.80	208.10	231.70	259.30	291.40	329.00	373.00	424.70	485.60	

TABLE II.15 Case 6: Traditional WACC, non-constant WACC, Book Value for WACC Calculation, and Cost of Debt d = IRR of CFD for Years 2003 to 2019 (Units in Billion Pesos)

	2003	2004	2005	2006	2007	2008	2009	2010	2011	2012	2013	2014	2015	2016	2017	2018	2019
FCF with TV	−21.00	−6.10	1.50	2.20	3.60	6.00	7.90	8.70	6.20	5.40	6.20	7.10	7.90	8.90	9.90	10.90	11.70
D%		90.80	94.80	82.40	55.90	36.70	21.60	5.30	0.00	0.00	0.00	0.00	0.00	0.00	0.00	0.00	0.00
d = IRR of CFD (in %)		11.20	11.20	11.20	11.20	11.20	11.20	11.20	11.20	11.20	11.20	11.20	11.20	11.20	11.20	11.20	11.20
$d' = d[1 - T$ $(1 - i/d)]$ (in %)		7.30	7.30	7.30	7.30	7.30	7.30	7.30	7.30	7.30	7.30	7.30	7.30	7.30	7.30	7.30	7.30
Contribution to WACC (in %)		6.60	6.90	6.00	4.10	2.70	1.60	0.40	0.00	0.00	0.00	0.00	0.00	0.00	0.00	0.00	0.00
E%		9.20	5.20	17.60	44.10	63.30	78.40	94.70	100.00	100.00	100.00	100.00	100.00	100.00	100.00	100.00	100.00
$e = \rho + (\rho - d)$ D/E (in %)		125.20	193.20	62.10	30.30	24.50	22.00	20.10	19.60	19.60	19.60	19.60	19.60	19.60	19.60	19.60	19.60
Contribution to WACC (in %)		11.60	10.10	10.90	13.40	15.50	17.20	19.00	19.60	19.60	19.60	19.60	19.60	19.60	19.60	19.60	19.60
WACC (in %)		18.20	17.00	16.90	17.40	18.20	18.80	19.40	19.60	19.60	19.60	19.60	19.60	19.60	19.60	19.60	19.60
Levered value	24.90	35.50	40.10	44.70	48.80	51.70	53.60	55.30	59.90	66.20	73.00	80.30	88.10	96.50	105.50	115.30	126.30

TABLE II.15 Case 6: Traditional WACC, Non-constant WACC, Book Value for WACC Calculation, and Cost of Debt d = IRR of CFD (continued) for Years 2020 to 2032 (Units in Billion Pesos)

	2020	2021	2022	2023	2024	2025	2026	2027	2028	2029	2030	2031	2032
FCF with TV	12.60	13.70	14.90	15.90	16.50	17.20	17.90	18.70	19.60	20.50	21.50	22.50	560.10
D%	0.00	0.00	0.00	0.00	0.00	0.00	0.00	0.00	0.00	0.00	0.00	0.00	0.00
d = IRR of CFD (in %)	11.20	11.20	11.20	11.20	11.20	11.20	11.20	11.20	11.20	11.20	11.20	11.20	11.20
d' = d[1 – T(1 – i/d)] (in %)	7.30	7.30	7.30	7.30	7.30	7.30	7.30	7.30	7.30	7.30	7.30	7.30	7.30
Contribution to WACC (in %)	0.00	0.00	0.00	0.00	0.00	0.00	0.00	0.00	0.00	0.00	0.00	0.00	0.00
E%	100.00	100.00	100.00	100.00	100.00	100.00	100.00	100.00	100.00	100.00	100.00	100.00	100.00
e = $\rho + (\rho - d)D/E$ (in %)	19.60	19.60	19.60	19.60	19.60	19.60	19.60	19.60	19.60	19.60	19.60	19.60	19.60
Contribution to WACC (in %)	19.60	19.60	19.60	19.60	19.60	19.60	19.60	19.60	19.60	19.60	19.60	19.60	19.60
WACC (in %)	19.60	19.60	19.60	19.60	19.60	19.60	19.60	19.60	19.60	19.60	19.60	19.60	19.60
Levered value	138.50	151.90	166.80	183.60	203.10	225.80	252.20	282.90	318.80	360.90	410.20	468.20	

TABLE 11.16 Case 7: Traditional WACC, Non-constant WACC, Book Value for WACC Calculation, and Cost of Debt d = Interest paid/Debt for Years 2003 to 2019 (Units in Billion Pesos)

	2003	2004	2005	2006	2007	2008	2009	2010	2011	2012	2013	2014	2015	2016	2017	2018	2019
FCF with TV	−21.00	−6.10	1.50	2.20	3.60	6.00	7.90	8.70	6.20	5.40	6.20	7.10	7.90	8.90	9.90	10.90	11.70
D%		90.80	94.80	82.40	55.90	36.70	21.60	5.30	0.00	0.00	0.00	0.00	0.00	0.00	0.00	0.00	0.00
d = Interest paid/debt (in %)		17.50	13.80	11.40	10.90	9.40	9.40	9.30	9.30	9.20	9.40	9.40	9.40	9.40	9.40	9.40	9.40
$d' = d[1 - T (1 - i/d)]$ (in %)		13.10	10.40	8.70	8.10	7.10	7.10	7.10	7.10	7.00	7.20	7.20	7.20	7.20	7.20	7.20	7.20
Contribution to WACC (in %)		11.90	9.80	7.10	4.50	2.60	1.50	0.40	0.00	0.00	0.00	0.00	0.00	0.00	0.00	0.00	0.00
E%		9.20	5.20	17.60	44.10	63.30	78.40	94.70	100.00	100.00	100.00	100.00	100.00	100.00	100.00	100.00	100.00
$e = \rho + (\rho - d)$ D/E (in %)		63.10	145.90	61.00	30.70	25.60	22.50	20.20	19.60	19.60	19.60	19.60	19.60	19.60	19.60	19.60	19.60
Contribution to WACC (in %)		5.80	7.60	10.70	13.50	16.20	17.60	19.10	19.60	19.60	19.60	19.60	19.60	19.60	19.60	19.60	19.60
WACC (in %)		17.70	17.40	17.90	18.10	18.80	19.10	19.50	19.60	19.60	19.60	19.60	19.60	19.60	19.60	19.60	19.60
Levered value	24.20	34.70	39.20	44.10	48.40	51.50	53.50	55.30	59.90	66.20	73.00	80.30	88.10	96.50	105.50	115.30	126.30

TABLE 11.16 Case 7: Traditional WACC, Non-constant WACC, Book Value for WACC Calculation, and Cost of Debt d = Interest paid/Debt (continued) for Years 2020 to 2032 (Units in Billion Pesos)

	2020	2021	2022	2023	2024	2025	2026	2027	2028	2029	2030	2031	2032
FCF with TV	12.60	13.70	14.90	15.90	16.50	17.20	17.90	18.70	19.60	20.50	21.50	22.50	560.10
D%	0.00	0.00	0.00	0.00	0.00	0.00	0.00	0.00	0.00	0.00	0.00	0.00	0.00
d = Interest paid/debt (in %)	9.40	9.40	9.40	9.40	9.40	9.40	9.40	9.40	9.40	9.40	9.40	9.40	9.40
$d' = d[1 - T(1 - i/d)]$ (in %)	7.20	7.20	7.20	7.20	7.20	7.20	7.20	7.20	7.20	7.20	7.20	7.20	7.20
Contribution to WACC (in %)	0.00	0.00	0.00	0.00	0.00	0.00	0.00	0.00	0.00	0.00	0.00	0.00	0.00
E%	100.00	100.00	100.00	100.00	100.00	100.00	100.00	100.00	100.00	100.00	100.00	100.00	100.00
$e = \rho + (\rho - d)D/E$ (in %)	19.60	19.60	19.60	19.60	19.60	19.60	19.60	19.60	19.60	19.60	19.60	19.60	19.60
Contribution to WACC (in %)	19.60	19.60	19.60	19.60	19.60	19.60	19.60	19.60	19.60	19.60	19.60	19.60	19.60
WACC (in %)	19.60	19.60	19.60	19.60	19.60	19.60	19.60	19.60	19.60	19.60	19.60	19.60	19.60
Levered value	138.50	151.90	166.80	183.60	203.10	225.80	252.20	282.90	318.80	360.90	410.20	468.20	

average WACC in some of the above cases. For this situation we use the TV based on the same popular formula (See Table 11.17):

$$TV = \frac{FCF(1 + g)}{WACC - g} \qquad (11.17)$$

TABLE 11.17   Case 8: Levered Value and Levered Equity Calculated with Constant WACC

Constant WACC	Total levered value	Difference with correct value	Equity levered Value	Difference with correct value
10.0%	107.90	317.80%	95.90	591.90%
11.0%	87.20	237.70%	75.20	442.70%
12.0%	71.60	177.20%	59.60	330.10%
13.0%	59.60	130.60%	47.60	243.30%
14.0%	50.10	94.10%	38.20	175.30%
15.0%	42.60	65.00%	30.70	121.10%
16.0%	36.60	41.60%	24.60	77.50%
17.0%	31.60	22.50%	19.70	41.90%
18.0%	27.60	6.70%	15.60	12.50%
19.0%	24.20	−6.40%	12.20	−11.90%
20.0%	21.30	−17.40%	9.40	−32.50%
21.0%	18.90	−26.80%	6.90	−49.90%
22.0%	16.80	−34.80%	4.90	−64.80%
23.0%	15.10	−41.70%	3.10	−77.60%
24.0%	13.50	−47.70%	1.60	−88.80%

To understand this table we must take into account some selected values for the WACC:

1. WAAC for year 1, book values, case 7, 17.70%
2. Average WACC, case 1, market values, 18.90%
3. Average WACC, book values, case 7, 19.30%

In this table we call attention to how the sensitivity increases for lower values compared with higher values for the constant WACC. The TV was calculated with the simple equation mentioned above and using the same constant WACC listed in the first column.

As a summary, we show in the next table the different values and the different approaches with the error in relation to the correct total levered market value.

Ultimately, what is of interest in valuing a firm is the levered market value of equity. This is calculated by subtracting the debt from the total levered value or by discounting the CFE at the appropriate discount rate. We calculate the levered equity value and show the differences. The relative differences increase dramatically (see Table 11.18).

TABLE II.18 Summary of Total Levered and Equity Calculation and Differences

Case No.	Approach	Constant WACC	Value for WACC	Cost of debt	Levered value (in billion pesos)	Difference	Equity = Lev. Val. – Debt (in billion pesos)	Difference
1	Adjusted WACC and FCF	No	Market	d = Interest paid/debt	25.80		13.90	
2	CCF	No	Market	d = Interest paid/debt	25.80	0.00%	13.90	0.00%
3	PV(CFE)	No	Market	d = Interest paid/debt	25.80	0.00%	13.90	0.00%
4	Traditional WACC	No	Market	d = Interest paid/debt	23.10	−10.70%	11.10	−20.00%
5	Traditional WACC	No	Market	d = IRR of CFD	22.40	−13.10%	10.50	−24.50%
6	Traditional WACC	No	Book	d = IRR of CFD	24.90	−3.70%	12.90	−6.80%
7	Traditional WACC	No	Book	d = Interest paid/debt	24.20	−6.10%	12.30	−11.40%
8	Traditional WACC (18.00%)	Yes	Book	d = IRR of CFD	27.60	6.70%	15.60	12.50%
9	Traditional WACC (19.00%)	Yes	Book	d = IRR of CFD	24.20	−6.40%	12.20	−11.90%
10	Traditional WACC (20.00%)	Yes	Book	d = IRR of CFD	21.30	−17.40%	9.40	−32.50%
11	Traditional WACC (21.00%)	Yes	Book	d = IRR of CFD	19.30	−25.10%	7.40	−46.70%

11.4 CONCLUDING REMARKS

In this chapter we have introduced briefly the basic concepts for IA, its effect on the effective tax rate, and the after-tax cost of debt. Also, we have presented the basic concepts for calculating the loss in exchange rate when we have debt in foreign currency.

In this case we performed a sensitivity analysis where different approaches calculated the value of the firm, including the typical approach of using constant discount rates to valuate a FCF.

The results are interesting. The differences between the results from the first three methods and the others range from −25.10% to 6.70%. The traditional constant WACC approach at 21%, with book value and the cost of debt equal to the IRR of the CFD is below the baseline comparison by 25.10%, whereas the traditional constant WACC approach at 18%, with book value and the cost of debt equal to the IRR of the CFD is above the baseline comparion by 6.70%. In the case of the levered value of equity, these differences range from −46.70% to 12.50%, respectively.

We can refine our analysis and consider only four cases. All of the cases use the traditional WACC approach (two cases using market value and two using book value, Cases 4 to 7). The difference lies in the use of the cost of debt as the proportion of interest paid to debt and the IRR of the CFD. These four cases show differences ranging from −3.70% (Case 6) to −13.10% (Case 5). The differences among the levered equity values range from −6.80% to −24.50%. In any case, most errors (an exception made for Case 6, total levered value) are greater than the standard accepted ±5.00%.

The key lesson to learn from this chapter is that not using the correct market value approach could lead to significant differences in levered values for total firm and equity.

APPENDIX A

AII.I THE PRACTITIONER'S POINT OF VIEW

Recently we were discussing how people use and obtain the discount rate to appraise investment projects and to value firms. We were skeptical that practitioners would take into account market values or any value at all. We decided to contact people in the field. We have transcribed some excerpts from the statements of two financial officers. One of the officers is from Latin America, where he works with a multinational firm that is a partner of an important U.S. firm, which is developing an infrastructure project in the Philippines. The other officer is from a European firm that has worldwide operations. The European financial officer is posted in Japan.

The European executive reported the following:

1. Cost of equity e is fixed, based on risk-free interest (Government bonds) + some adjustment to reflect risk (based on our impression of the risk).
2. Interest rate on debt d is the interest rate on debt we can obtain for a specific project in a specific country.

WACC is then calculated as

$$d(1 - T)\%D + \%Ee \qquad (A11.1)$$

where D% and E% are the (book value) portions of financing done with debt and equity, and T is the company tax rate in the country where the project is to take place. (I think at least this last point is rather questionable).

The executive from the Philippines had the following to say:

"With respect to WACC, it is difficult in practice to follow what finance textbooks suggest, mainly because the variables for its determination are of such a level of uncertainty that in the end it doesn't add anything more than just a rule of thumb discount rate following good judgment and experience. In the case of one of the components of WACC, the cost of equity, in our case we invest all over the world, mainly in developing countries with very small or inefficient capital markets; therefore, to determine the cost of equity following dubious Betas and Market Premiums doesn't really provide a better base than pure judgment. You may say, why not benchmark a country with an efficient market and adjust the cost of equity using some type of country risk measure? Well, the problem here is that you have to use a firm or industry similar to the one you are investing in, and even if you find it, this doesn't really mean that the risks of that industry or firm in another country are the same, or that the correlation of that given industry versus the market is the same in both countries. Local factors are important. For example, the energy industry (where we mostly invest) is so dependent on local regulations, local competition, local infrastructure, local energy sources, etc., that it's a long shot to try to benchmark the risks on one market with those of another. This is why in most of the cases, in my experience, firms do not pay much attention to WACC.

For academic purposes WACC and CAPM are great, but for practical purposes you run into the problems I mentioned before. I know firms (for example our partner in the Philippines project) that take their cost of debt and add a country risk premium, when the investment is in a country different from the one where they source their debt; this is the most sophistication I have seen being put in practice. The country risk is determined by some type of investment committee that supposedly has some knowledge and experience of the factors that determine relevant risk matters in the country. This is used as the cost of equity in order to discount the CFE. In my opinion, the use of wise judgment is more appropriate than the extrapolation of CAPM along different countries. The other reason why WACC is normally not used is because we are more focused on the analysis of the equity component, and not so much on the project cash flows. This is because we fine tune as much as possible the debt component in the financial models, which can represent reality much better than averaging the cost of equity with the cost of debt. In any case, I think that more effort should be devoted to the determination of the risk of the investment, since WACC and CAPM have the problems mentioned above. I am working nowadays in a method that relies on probabilistic tools to determine the specific risk for the project at hand, without having to use longshot benchmarks. The method incorporates the risk of the most important variables of the project into a model and determines which should be the most appropriate cost of equity to use for the particular case.

If there are circumstances in which we want to compute WACC, we try not to use book values to determine the component variables of WACC (debt and equity proportion, company value, cost of debt, and cost of equity). Book values are subject to a myriad of rules and regulations, which are very useful as a mean of standardization of results along different companies, focused on past information, but are not necessarily appropriate for valuation purposes, which should focus on future cash flows. For example, the book value of a company depends, among other things, on the method of amortization and on the inventory valuation chosen, and can vary substantially depending on what methods are used.

It is not easy to make generalizations of what is "in use in the market" when valuing a firm, but what I really do believe is that firms don't pay much attention to the implications that using a risk adjusted discount rate have on the valuation of investment. For example, it is inappropriate to use a constant discount rate to discount equity cash flows when both components of the discount rate (risk-free and risk premium) normally change over the periods. The risk-free rate changes with maturity (yield curve of government bonds) and the risk premium will depend on the levels of debt and risks for different periods (for example in an infrastructure project, the risk profile changes once construction is finalized).

With respect to financial analysis, we normally focus purely on cash, that is to say, we are mainly interested in movements of cash when they actually occur.[3] For our analysis, cash is what is important, for example, one of the main factors that a lender will look for in our financial models is the debt coverage ratio. This is the buffer of cash available on top of whatever is necessary to run the business and to pay principal and interest. This ratio has to be calculated on a cash basis, because it is worthless to have income payable at the moment of having to service debt if you don't have the cash to make the payment. Accounting rules are only important for us to the extent that they have any cash impact, for example those that affect taxes. We base the accounting balance sheet, income statement, and cash flow on the cash analysis, and the main purpose of preparing GAAP statements is to determine tax cash outflows; the other reason is for presentation purposes. This methodology, in my experience, is the same one used by most of the firms. For example, some investment banks with which we have worked with (e.g., Morgan Stanley and Bankers Trust) use this same approach. In terms of our companies, we have developed a US500M project with Edison Mission Energy from the U.S. (one of the largest independent power producers worldwide with net generating capacity of nearly 19,000 MW around the globe), and they use this approach as well."

[3]Note from the authors: this is what the CB shows.

BII.I ESTIMATED MACROECONOMIC VARIABLES

In this appendix we present some context and parameters used in the financial model used for valuation. We also present the financial statements: IS, CB and BS. The macroeconomic variables used in the model were the goals agreed on between the International Monetary Fund and Colombia. In addition, the consultant made his own estimations for some of the variables (see Table B11.1).

TABLE BII.I Estimated Financial and Macroeconomic Variables and Parameters

	2000	2001	2002	2003	2004	2005 +
Payout ratio	100.00%	100.00%	100.00%	100.00%	100.00%	10.00%
Domestic annual inflation rate per annum	11.00%	10.00%	9.00%	8.00%	8.00%	8.00%
IA index (PAAG) per annum	11.00%	10.00%	9.00%	8.00%	8.00%	8.00%
Foreign inflation rate (U.S.)	2.50%	2.50%	2.50%	2.50%	2.50%	2.50%
Annual rate of change for the U.S. dollar	9.38%	7.32%	6.34%	5.37%	5.37%	5.37%
Cost of debt in foreign currency	9.00%	9.00%	9.00%	9.00%	9.00%	9.00%
Cost of debt in domestic currency	25.60%	24.60%	23.60%	22.60%	22.60%	22.60%
Market interest rate for cash excess investment (DTF)	15.00%	14.00%	13.00%	12.00%	12.00%	12.00%

BII.2 CONSTRUCTION PERIOD

BII.2.I Investment

The investment budget was taken from ALCATEL and JECR and Co. The amounts of investment were the following (see Table B11.2):

TABLE BII.2   Investment

Total investment	USD$ thousands	US$/line
Land	109.30	6.63
Buildings and civil works	470.20	28.50
Telephone networks	5,216.20	316.13
Commutation and power equipment	6,543.80	396.60
Transmission systems	684.00	41.46
Machinery and equipment	279.70	16.95
Feasibility studies and initial operation	365.90	22.18
Working capital	886.10	53.70
Total investment	14,555.20	882.13

BII.2.2 Initial Equity Investment

The equity investment and debt were to be paid between March 2000 and November 2001, as required by the project. This investment is configured as follows (see Table B11.3):

TABLE BII.3   Investment Financing

	US $ Thousands	(%)
Loan in US$	5,392.50	
Loan in Col$	4,593.80	
Total loans	9,986.30	68.61%
New equity	4,203.00	
Promoters equity	365.90	
Total equity	4,568.90	31.39%
Total investment	14,555.20	100.00%

BII.3 INSTALLATION PROGRAM

This program has four stages, as shown in Table B11.4. In this table we show the timing and the number of subscriptions in each category.

BII.4 OPERATION OF THE PROJECT

Fees

   The operating revenues are generated by the following fees:

- **Connection fee:** This fee is paid only once and its purpose is to recover the infrastructure investment.
- **Basic charge fee:** This fee is charged to the final user on a monthly basis independent of the consumption.

TABLE BII.4   Number of Subscriptions

Stage	1	2	3	4	Total*
Time for installation in months	5	7	3	4	21
Number of telephone pairs	4,550	9,070	4,020	4,840	22,480
Total number of subscriptions	3,300	6,600	2,900	3,700	16,500
Home category 1	0.05%	7.81%	0.55%	0.21%	3.28%
Home category 2	1.65%	22.51%	7.30%	13.35%	13.61%
Home category 3	14.34%	40.98%	47.81%	26.83%	33.68%
Home category 4	3.34%	16.92%	22.82%	48.18%	22.25%
Home category 5	20.62%	6.78%	1.52%	1.44%	7.43%
Commercial subscriptions	60.00%	5.00%	20.00%	10.00%	19.76%

*The percentages in the Total column refer to the total number of subscriptions (16,500).

- **Consumption (Impulse):** This is the price the final user pays for using the phone service. The consumption is measured in impulses and each impulse is equivalent to three minutes of phone service use.
- **Local access:** In this case we have two operators in the same area. A user from the first network, network A, calls a user in the second network, network B, or vice versa. The assumption in this model is that there are equal numbers of incoming and outgoing calls from each network; hence, the net revenue is zero.
- **Long distance access:** This is the fee for a call to a user outside the area.
- **Mobile phone access:** This is a charge for making a call to a mobile phone.
- **Added value:** This is the fee for additional services such as Internet and data transmission.

BII.4.1 Fees Definition and Determination

The value of each fee is defined according to the legal regulations and the actual fees charged by the existing operator (the existing operator is Telehuila). The firm offers various plans as a marketing strategy to sell the phone lines as soon as possible.

BII.4.2 Subscription Plans

The law allows an operator to offer any service or subscription plan to the market with the condition that the prices are not below the cost of investment and the cost of issuing high quality service. In addition, the new operator has to comply with the level of subsidies (for low income categories) offered by the operator with a dominant position.

The plans offered by the firm are as follows:

- **Plan "A":** This plan offers the same conditions as the existing operator.
- **Plan "B":** This plan charges 50% for the connection fee of Plan A, with an increase in the basic charge as compensation. The consumption fee is the same as in Plan A and equal to the fee charged by the existing operator.
- **Plan "C":** In this plan there is no connection fee, but the basic charge is increased, which keeps the same consumption fee offered by the existing operator.
- **Plan "D":** In this plan there is a unique monthly fee independent from the amount of consumption. This lump charge does not include a local access fee, long distance, or a mobile fee.

The following tables (Tables B11.5 to B11.7) show the fees for each category and the fees charged by the existing operator, Telehuila.

TABLE BII.5   Connection Fees and Plans

Category	Telehuila	PLAN A	PLAN B
Home category 1	297,450	304,587	152,294
Home category 2	330,510	338,430	169,215
Home category 3	330,510	338,430	169,215
Home category 4	330,510	338,430	169,215
Home category 5	396,610	406,116	203,058
Commercial subscriptions	396,610	406,116	203,058

TABLE BII.6   Basic Charges and Plans

Category	Telehuila	PLAN A	PLAN B	PLAN C	PLAN D
Home category 1	5.507	14.468	16.276	19.695	30.991
Home category 2	6.196	16.277	18.311	22.157	34.865
Home category 3	6.884	18.085	20.345	24.619	38.739
Home category 4	6.884	18.085	20.345	24.619	38.739
Home category 5	8.261	21.702	24.414	29.543	46.487
Commercial subscriptions	8.261	21.702	24.414	29.543	46.487

TABLE BII.7   Consumption Fees and Plans

Category	PLAN A	PLAN B	PLAN C	PLAN D
Home category 1	29.23	29.23	29.23	29.23
Home category 2	32.88	32.88	32.88	32.88
Home category 3	36.54	36.54	36.54	36.54
Home category 4	36.54	36.54	36.54	36.54
Home category 5	43.84	43.84	43.84	43.84
Commercial subscriptions	43.84	43.84	43.84	43.84

BII.5 CONSUMPTION ESTIMATION

The Tables B11.8 and B11.9 show the consumption in minutes and impulses by category.

TABLE BII.8   Local Consumption in Impulses

Categories	Daily average	Monthly average
Home category 1	9.37	281.10
Home category 2	10.01	300.30
Home category 3	11.37	341.10
Home category 4	12.21	366.30
Home category 5	14.43	432.90
Home category 6	16.77	503.10
Commercial subscriptions	17.08	512.40

TABLE BII.9   Access Fees in Col$ per Minute per Telephone Line

Domestic long distance	3.87	116.10
Long distance international	0.46	13.80
Mobile phone service	0.13	3.90

BII.6 PAYROLL EXPENSES

There is a detailed list of the different jobs and their salaries. This cost includes taxes paid on payroll and fringe benefits. The monthly payroll is presented in the next table. The initial payroll of $12 million stabilizes by the tenth month at $43.7 million, as follows in Table B11.10:

TABLE BII.10   Monthly Payroll for the First 10 Months

Month	Monthly payroll
1	12,000
2	12,000
3	12,000
4	14,000
5	16,000
6	18,000
7	20,000
8	22,000
9	30,000
10	43,700

BII.7 OPERATING COSTS AND EXPENSES

The fixed operating costs and expenses are shown in the following tables. For some items the cost is calculated as a percentage of some value (initial value or asset value) in Tables B11.11 and B11.12.

TABLE BII.II   Operating Costs

Operating costs	%	Basis for calculation	Base	Annual	Month
Plant maintenance	0.50%	Plant investment	13,732,944	68,665	5,722
Network maintenance	1.00%	Network investment	9,907,453	99,075	8,256
Insurance				49,657	4,138
Surveillance service	0.20%	Fixed assets	28,440,886	56,882	4,740
Miscellaneous	5.00%	Operating expenses	274,278	13,714	1,143
Total operating costs				287,992	23,999

TABLE BII.I2   Administrative Expenses

Utilities	5,000
Office supplies	1,500
Other general expenses	2,000
Total administrative expenses	8,500

These costs and expenses are reached gradually according to the level of operation of the project. This is shown in Table B11.13.

TABLE BII.I3   Operating Costs and Administrative Expenses

Month	Total cost and expense
1	7,000
2	7,000
3	7,000
4	7,000
5	7,000
6	7,000
7	9,500
8	14,500
9	22,500
10	22,500
11	22,500
12	22,500
13	22,500
14	32,500

Some expenses and investments can be calculated as an amortization. The prepaid expenses are 5% of the value of equity and amortized over five years. In the case of investment to amortize we consider the advertising. During the first year we amortize 300 million and during the second year 100 million.

The variable costs for the project are associated with fiduciary costs, selling and advertising expenses, and some local taxes. Variable costs are shown in Table B11.14.

TABLE B11.14   Variable Costs

Type of variable cost	Rate	Basis for calculation
With debt (including fiduciary costs)	3.95%	Operational revenues
Without debt	2.45%	Operational revenues

B11.8 FINANCIAL STATEMENTS

In this section we present the financial statements from year 2003 to 2032 (see Tables B11.15 to B11.17b). We list the IS, the CB, and the BS. From these financial statements we derive the different cash flows for valuating the project: the FCF, CFD, CFE, and TS.

As mentioned previously, we compare different methods for the calculation of value.

TABLE BII.15 Income Statement for Years 2003 to 2019 (Units in Billion Pesos)

	2003	2004	2005	2006	2007	2008	2009	2010	2011	2012	2013	2014	2015	2016	2017	2018	2019
Total operating revenues	1.3	9.1	9.7	10.1	13.4	15.7	16.7	18.0	19.5	21.2	22.9	24.9	27.0	29.3	31.8	34.6	37.6
Gross profit	1.3	9.1	9.7	10.1	13.4	15.7	16.7	18.0	19.5	21.2	22.9	24.9	27.0	29.3	31.8	34.6	37.6
Payroll expenses	0.4	0.7	0.7	0.7	0.8	0.8	0.8	0.8	0.9	0.9	0.9	0.9	1.0	1.0	1.0	1.1	1.1
Deductible operating costs	0.4	1.7	1.6	1.7	1.8	1.8	1.8	1.9	1.9	1.9	1.9	1.9	2.0	2.0	2.0	2.0	2.1
Non-deductible operating costs	0.0	0.0	0.0	0.0	0.0	0.0	0.0	0.1	0.1	0.1	0.1	0.1	0.1	0.1	0.1	0.1	0.1
Depreciation charges	4.7	9.1	6.8	3.8	2.9	2.6	2.0	1.6	1.3	1.1	0.9	0.7	0.6	0.5	0.8	1.6	2.3
Amortization	0.2	0.2	0.1	0.1	0.1	0.1	0.1	0.1	0.0	0.0	0.0	0.0	0.0	0.0	0.0	0.0	0.0
EBIT	-4.4	-2.5	0.4	3.7	7.7	10.4	11.8	13.6	15.4	17.2	19.1	21.2	23.4	25.7	27.8	29.8	32.0
Interest income on marketable securities	0.0	0.0	0.2	0.6	0.8	1.1	1.4	1.6	2.0	2.6	3.4	4.2	5.1	6.1	7.0	7.9	8.8
Interest charges on foreign exchange debt	0.0	1.1	1.7	1.7	1.5	1.2	0.9	0.5	0.1	0.0	0.0	0.0	0.0	0.0	0.0	0.0	0.0
Loss in exchange rate	0.3	0.5	0.4	0.3	0.1	0.0	0.0	0.0	0.0	0.0	0.0	0.0	0.0	0.0	0.0	0.0	0.0
Interest charges for domestic currency debt	0.0	0.1	0.1	0.0	0.0	0.0	0.0	0.0	0.0	0.0	0.0	0.0	0.0	0.0	0.0	0.0	0.0
Total financial expenses	0.3	1.6	2.2	2.1	1.6	1.3	0.9	0.6	0.1	0.0	0.0	0.0	0.0	0.0	0.0	0.0	0.0
EBT and IA	-4.7	-4.2	-1.6	2.3	6.9	10.2	12.3	14.6	17.2	19.8	22.5	25.4	28.5	31.8	34.9	37.6	40.9
Profit from IA	0.7	1.4	1.4	1.2	1.2	1.3	1.3	1.4	1.4	1.4	1.5	1.5	1.6	1.6	1.7	1.9	2.1
Loss from IA (non-debt items)	0.0	0.2	0.6	0.8	0.8	0.9	1.0	1.1	1.2	1.3	1.3	1.4	1.5	1.5	1.6	1.7	1.8
Inflation adjustment for equity	0.5	0.2	0.1	0.0	0.1	0.2	0.3	0.5	0.6	0.8	1.0	1.2	1.5	1.8	2.1	2.4	2.8
Net profit (Loss) from IA	0.1	0.9	0.7	0.4	0.3	0.1	0.0	-0.2	-0.4	-0.6	-0.8	-1.1	-1.4	-1.7	-1.9	-2.2	-2.5
EBT	-4.6	-3.3	-0.9	2.7	7.2	10.3	12.3	14.4	16.8	19.2	21.6	24.3	27.1	30.2	32.9	35.5	38.4
Non-Deductible expenses	0.0	0.0	0.0	0.0	0.0	0.0	0.0	0.1	0.1	0.1	0.1	0.1	0.1	0.1	0.1	0.1	0.1
Losses carried forward	0.0	0.0	0.0	2.8	2.1	0.0	0.0	0.0	0.0	0.0	0.0	0.0	0.0	0.0	0.0	0.0	0.0
Total (net) non-deductible (deductibles) items	0.0	0.0	0.0	-2.7	-2.1	0.0	0.0	0.1	0.1	0.1	0.1	0.1	0.1	0.1	0.1	0.1	0.1
Earnings before taxes and presumptive income (EBTAPI)	-4.6	-3.3	-0.8	0.0	5.2	10.3	12.3	14.5	16.8	19.2	21.7	24.3	27.2	30.3	33.0	35.6	38.5
PI*	0.0	0.3	0.3	0.3	0.3	0.5	0.7	1.0	1.3	1.6	2.0	2.4	2.9	3.4	4.0	4.6	5.3
EBT	0.0	0.3	0.3	0.3	5.2	10.3	12.3	14.5	16.8	19.2	21.7	24.3	27.2	30.3	33.0	35.6	38.5
Tax	0.0	0.1	0.1	0.1	1.8	3.6	4.3	5.1	5.9	6.7	7.6	8.5	9.5	10.6	11.6	12.4	13.5
Net income (NI)	-4.6	-3.4	-1.0	2.6	5.4	6.7	8.0	9.3	10.9	12.4	14.0	15.7	17.6	19.6	21.4	23.0	24.9

*PI is used to determine the income tax when EBTAPI ≤ PI.

TABLE BII.I5 Income Statement (continued) for Years 2020 to 2032 (Units in Billion Pesos)

	2020	2021	2022	2023	2024	2025	2026	2027	2028	2029	2030	2031	2032
Total operating revenues	40.9	44.5	45.9	47.3	48.7	50.1	51.6	53.2	54.8	56.4	58.1	59.9	61.7
Gross profit	40.9	44.5	45.9	47.3	48.7	50.1	51.6	53.2	54.8	56.4	58.1	59.9	61.7
Payroll expenses	1.1	1.2	0.0	0.0	0.0	0.0	0.0	0.0	0.0	0.0	0.0	0.0	0.0
Deductible operating costs	2.1	2.1	2.1	2.2	2.2	2.2	2.3	2.3	2.3	2.4	2.4	2.4	2.5
Non-deductible operating costs	0.1	0.1	0.1	0.1	0.1	0.2	0.2	0.2	0.2	0.2	0.2	0.2	0.2
Depreciation charges	3.0	3.7	4.3	4.8	5.3	5.7	6.1	6.4	6.8	7.1	7.4	7.7	8.0
Amortization	0.0	0.0	0.0	0.0	0.0	0.0	0.0	0.0	0.0	0.0	0.0	0.0	0.0
EBIT	34.6	37.5	39.3	40.2	41.1	42.1	43.2	44.3	45.5	46.8	48.2	49.6	51.0
Interest income on marketable securities	9.9	11.2	12.6	14.0	15.6	17.3	19.1	21.0	23.0	25.1	27.4	29.8	32.3
Interest charges on foreign exchange debt	0.0	0.0	0.0	0.0	0.0	0.0	0.0	0.0	0.0	0.0	0.0	0.0	0.0
Loss in exchange rate	0.0	0.0	0.0	0.0	0.0	0.0	0.0	0.0	0.0	0.0	0.0	0.0	0.0
Interest charges for domestic currency debt	0.0	0.0	0.0	0.0	0.0	0.0	0.0	0.0	0.0	0.0	0.0	0.0	0.0
Total financial expenses	0.0	0.0	0.0	0.0	0.0	0.0	0.0	0.0	0.0	0.0	0.0	0.0	0.0
EBT and IA	44.5	48.7	51.9	54.2	56.7	59.3	62.2	65.3	68.5	71.9	75.5	79.3	83.3
Profit from IA	2.3	2.6	2.8	3.1	3.4	3.7	4.0	4.3	4.7	5.0	5.4	5.8	6.2
Loss from IA (non-debt items)	1.9	2.1	2.2	2.4	2.6	2.9	3.1	3.4	3.7	4.0	4.3	4.7	5.1
Inflation adjustment for equity	3.2	3.7	4.2	4.7	5.3	5.9	6.5	7.2	7.9	8.6	9.4	10.2	11.0
Net profit (Loss) from IA	5.1	5.7	6.4	7.2	7.9	8.8	9.7	10.6	11.6	12.6	13.7	14.9	16.1
EBT	-2.8	-3.2	-3.6	-4.0	-4.5	-5.1	-5.7	-6.3	-6.9	-7.6	-8.3	-9.1	-9.9
Non-deductible expenses	41.7	45.5	48.4	50.2	52.1	54.3	56.6	59.0	61.6	64.4	67.2	70.3	73.4
Losses carried forward	0.1	0.1	0.1	0.1	0.1	0.2	0.2	0.2	0.2	0.2	0.2	0.2	0.2
Total (net) non-deductible (deductibles) items	0.0	0.0	0.0	0.0	0.0	0.0	0.0	0.0	0.0	0.0	0.0	0.0	0.0
Earnings before taxes and presumptive income (EBTAPI)	0.1	0.1	0.1	0.1	0.1	0.2	0.2	0.2	0.2	0.2	0.2	0.2	0.2
PI*	41.9	45.7	48.5	50.3	52.3	54.4	56.7	59.2	61.8	64.5	67.4	70.4	73.6
EBT	6.1	6.9	7.8	8.8	9.8	10.8	11.9	13.0	14.3	15.5	16.9	18.3	19.8
Tax	41.9	45.7	48.5	50.3	52.3	54.4	56.7	59.2	61.8	64.5	67.4	70.4	73.6
Net income (NI)	14.7	16.0	17.0	17.6	18.3	19.0	19.9	20.7	21.6	22.6	23.6	24.7	25.8
EBT and IA	27.1	29.5	31.4	32.6	33.8	35.2	36.7	38.3	40.0	41.8	43.6	45.6	47.7

*PI is used to determine the income tax when EBTAPI ≤ PI.

TABLE BII.16 Cash Budget for Years 2003–2019 (Units in Billion Pesos)

	2003	2004	2005	2006	2007	2008	2009	2010	2011	2012	2013	2014	2015	2016	2017	2018	2019
Operational revenues	1.1	8.2	9.6	10.1	13.0	15.5	16.5	17.9	19.3	21.0	22.7	24.6	26.7	29.0	31.5	34.3	37.3
Outflows																	
Payroll expenses	0.3	0.7	0.7	0.7	0.8	0.8	0.8	0.8	0.9	0.9	0.9	0.9	1.0	1.0	1.0	1.1	1.1
Deductible operating costs	0.4	1.7	1.6	1.7	1.8	1.8	1.8	1.9	1.9	1.9	1.9	1.9	2.0	2.0	2.0	2.0	2.1
Non-deductible operating costs	0.0	0.0	0.0	0.0	0.0	0.0	0.0	0.1	0.1	0.1	0.1	0.1	0.1	0.1	0.1	0.1	0.1
Investment on amortizable assets	0.8	0.1	0.0	0.0	0.0	0.0	0.0	0.0	0.0	0.0	0.0	0.0	0.0	0.0	0.0	0.0	0.0
Land	0.2	0.0	0.0	0.0	0.0	0.0	0.0	0.0	0.0	0.0	0.0	0.0	0.0	0.0	0.0	0.0	0.0
Buildings and civil works	1.7	0.1	0.0	0.0	0.0	0.0	0.0	0.0	0.0	0.0	0.0	0.0	0.0	0.0	0.0	0.0	0.0
Telecommunications equipment	0.0	0.0	0.0	0.0	0.0	0.0	0.0	0.0	0.0	0.0	0.0	0.0	0.0	0.0	0.0	0.0	0.0
Telephone network	5.2	6.8	0.0	0.0	0.0	0.0	0.0	0.0	0.0	0.0	0.0	0.0	0.0	0.0	4.2	4.6	5.0
Equipment (communications and office)	0.7	0.0	0.0	0.0	0.0	0.0	0.0	0.0	0.0	0.0	0.0	0.0	0.0	0.0	0.0	0.0	0.0
Equipment (comm., computing, and transp.)	12.2	4.3	0.0	0.0	0.0	0.0	0.0	0.0	0.0	0.0	0.0	0.0	0.0	0.0	0.0	0.0	0.0
Replacement of operating equipment	0.0	0.0	0.0	0.0	4.9	0.0	0.0	0.0	0.0	0.0	0.0	0.0	0.0	0.0	0.0	0.0	0.0
Income tax	0.0	0.0	0.1	0.1	0.0	1.7	2.9	2.3	2.1	2.4	2.6	2.9	3.1	3.5	3.8	4.0	4.1
Income tax prepaid	0.0	0.0	0.0	0.1	0.1	0.7	2.0	3.0	3.5	4.1	4.7	5.4	6.0	6.8	7.5	8.3	9.0
Total outflows	21.6	13.8	2.5	2.6	7.7	5.1	7.6	8.0	8.4	9.3	10.3	11.2	12.2	13.3	18.7	20.1	21.4
Net cash balance (NCB)	−20.5	−5.6	7.1	7.5	5.3	10.3	8.9	9.9	10.9	11.6	12.5	13.4	14.5	15.7	12.8	14.2	15.9
Financing cash flows																	
Foreign exchange debt principal payment	0.0	0.0	0.0	2.1	3.4	3.8	4.1	4.5	1.5	0.0	0.0	0.0	0.0	0.0	0.0	0.0	0.0
Interest payment on foreign debt	0.0	1.1	1.7	1.7	1.5	1.2	0.9	0.5	0.1	0.0	0.0	0.0	0.0	0.0	0.0	0.0	0.0
Domestic debt principal payment	0.0	0.0	0.5	0.0	0.0	0.0	0.0	0.0	0.0	0.0	0.0	0.0	0.0	0.0	0.0	0.0	0.0
Interest payment on domestic debt	0.0	0.1	0.1	0.0	0.0	0.0	0.0	0.0	0.0	0.0	0.0	0.0	0.0	0.0	0.0	0.0	0.0
Domestic debt inflow	0.0	0.5	0.0	0.0	0.0	0.0	0.0	0.0	0.0	0.0	0.0	0.0	0.0	0.0	0.0	0.0	0.0
Foreign exchange debt inflow	11.7	6.1	0.0	0.0	0.0	0.0	0.0	0.0	0.0	0.0	0.0	0.0	0.0	0.0	0.0	0.0	0.0

(continues)

	2003	2004	2005	2006	2007	2008	2009	2010	2011	2012	2013	2014	2015	2016	2017	2018	2019
Financial net cash flow	11.7	5.5	-2.3	-3.9	-5.0	-5.0	-5.0	-5.0	-1.7	0.0	0.0	0.0	0.0	0.0	0.0	0.0	0.0
NCB after financing decisions	-8.8	-0.1	4.8	3.6	0.4	5.3	3.9	4.8	9.3	11.6	12.5	13.4	14.5	15.7	12.8	14.17	15.88
Equity cash flow																	
Dividends	0.0	0.0	0.0	0.0	0.0	1.5	3.3	4.0	4.8	5.7	6.6	7.5	8.5	9.5	10.7	11.71	12.65
Equity repurchase	0.0	0.0	0.0	0.0	0.0	0.0	0.0	0.0	0.0	0.0	0.0	0.0	0.0	0.0	0.0	0.00	0.00
Equity investment	9.0	0.0	0.0	0.0	0.0	0.0	0.0	0.0	0.0	0.0	0.0	0.0	0.0	0.0	0.0	0.00	0.00
Equity net cash flow	9.0	0.0	0.0	0.0	0.0	-1.5	-3.3	-4.0	-4.8	-5.7	-6.6	-7.5	-8.5	-9.5	-10.7	-11.7	-12.7
NCB after equity transactions	0.2	-0.1	4.8	3.6	0.4	3.8	0.6	0.8	4.4	5.9	5.9	6.0	6.1	6.2	2.2	2.5	3.2
Reinvestment of cash flows																	
Investment in market securities	0.2	0.0	5.0	4.2	1.1	4.9	2.0	2.4	6.4	8.5	9.2	10.1	11.2	12.3	9.2	10.3	12.0
Sale of market securities	0.0	0.2	0.0	0.0	0.0	0.0	0.0	0.0	0.0	0.0	0.0	0.0	0.0	0.0	0.0	0.0	0.0
Interest on market securities	0.0	0.0	0.2	0.6	0.8	1.1	1.4	1.6	2.0	2.6	3.4	4.2	5.1	6.1	7.0	7.9	8.8
Net cash flow after reinvestment decisions	-0.2	0.2	-4.8	-3.6	-0.3	-3.8	-0.6	-0.8	-4.4	-5.9	-5.9	-5.9	-6.0	-6.2	-2.1	-2.4	-3.2
NCB after reinvestment decisions	0.0	0.1	0.0	0.0	0.0	0.0	0.0	0.0	0.0	0.0	0.0	0.0	0.0	0.0	0.0	0.0	0.0
Accumulated net cash flow	0.0	0.1	0.1	0.1	0.2	0.2	0.2	0.2	0.3	0.3	0.3	0.3	0.4	0.4	0.4	0.5	0.5

TABLE BII.16 Cash Budget (continued) for Years 2020–2032 (Units in Billion Pesos)

	2020	2021	2022	2023	2024	2025	2026	2027	2028	2029	2030	2031	2032
Operational revenues	40.5	44.1	45.7	47.1	48.5	50.0	51.5	53.0	54.6	56.2	57.9	59.7	61.4
Outflows													
Payroll expenses	1.1	1.2	0.1	0.0	0.0	0.0	0.0	0.0	0.0	0.0	0.0	0.0	0.0
Deductible operating costs	2.1	2.1	2.1	2.2	2.2	2.2	2.3	2.3	2.3	2.4	2.4	2.4	2.5
Non-deductible operating costs	0.1	0.1	0.1	0.1	0.1	0.2	0.2	0.2	0.2	0.2	0.2	0.2	0.2
Investment on amortizable assets	0.0	0.0	0.0	0.0	0.0	0.0	0.0	0.0	0.0	0.0	0.0	0.0	0.0
Land	0.0	0.0	0.0	0.0	0.0	0.0	0.0	0.0	0.0	0.0	0.0	0.0	0.0
Buildings and civil works	0.0	0.0	0.0	0.0	0.0	0.0	0.0	0.0	0.0	0.0	0.0	0.0	0.0
Telecommunications equipment	5.4	5.9	6.1	6.2	6.4	6.6	6.8	7.0	7.2	7.4	7.7	7.9	8.1
Telephone network	0.0	0.0	0.0	0.0	0.0	0.0	0.0	0.0	0.0	0.0	0.0	0.0	0.0
Equipment (communications and office)	0.0	0.0	0.0	0.0	0.0	0.0	0.0	0.0	0.0	0.0	0.0	0.0	0.0
Equipment (comm., computing, and transp.)	0.0	0.0	0.0	0.0	0.0	0.0	0.0	0.0	0.0	0.0	0.0	0.0	0.0
Replacement of operating equipment	0.0	0.0	0.0	0.0	0.0	0.0	0.0	0.0	0.0	0.0	0.0	0.0	0.0
Income tax	4.5	4.9	5.4	5.5	5.2	5.3	5.6	5.9	6.1	6.4	6.7	7.0	7.3
Income tax prepaid	9.7	10.5	11.5	12.4	13.0	13.5	14.0	14.6	15.2	15.9	16.6	17.3	18.1
Total outflows	22.9	24.8	25.3	26.4	27.0	27.8	28.8	29.9	31.0	32.3	33.5	34.8	36.2
NCB	17.6	19.3	20.4	20.7	21.5	22.2	22.6	23.1	23.5	24.0	24.4	24.8	25.2
Financing cash flows													
Foreign exchange debt principal payment	0.0	0.0	0.0	0.0	0.0	0.0	0.0	0.0	0.0	0.0	0.0	0.0	0.0
Interest payment on foreign debt	0.0	0.0	0.0	0.0	0.0	0.0	0.0	0.0	0.0	0.0	0.0	0.0	0.0
Domestic debt principal payment	0.0	0.0	0.0	0.0	0.0	0.0	0.0	0.0	0.0	0.0	0.0	0.0	0.0
Interest payment on domestic debt	0.0	0.0	0.0	0.0	0.0	0.0	0.0	0.0	0.0	0.0	0.0	0.0	0.0
Domestic debt inflow	0.0	0.0	0.0	0.0	0.0	0.0	0.0	0.0	0.0	0.0	0.0	0.0	0.0
Foreign exchange debt inflow	0.0	0.0	0.0	0.0	0.0	0.0	0.0	0.0	0.0	0.0	0.0	0.0	0.0
Financial net cash flow	0.0	0.0	0.0	0.0	0.0	0.0	0.0	0.0	0.0	0.0	0.0	0.0	0.0
NCB after financing decisions	17.6	19.3	20.4	20.7	21.5	22.2	22.6	23.1	23.5	24.0	24.4	24.8	25.2
Equity cash flow													

(continues)

TABLE B11.16 (*continued*)

	2020	2021	2022	2023	2024	2025	2026	2027	2028	2029	2030	2031	2032
Dividends	13.7	15.0	16.4	17.6	18.4	19.3	20.2	21.3	22.4	23.5	24.8	26.1	27.4
Equity repurchase	0.0	0.0	0.0	0.0	0.0	0.0	0.0	0.0	0.0	0.0	0.0	0.0	0.0
Equity investment	0.0	0.0	0.0	0.0	0.0	0.0	0.0	0.0	0.0	0.0	0.0	0.0	0.0
Equity net cash flow	-13.7	-15.0	-16.4	-17.6	-18.4	-19.3	-20.2	-21.3	-22.4	-23.5	-24.8	-26.1	-27.4
NCB after equity transactions	3.9	4.3	4.0	3.1	3.2	2.9	2.4	1.8	1.2	0.4	-0.4	-1.2	-2.2
Investment of cash excess cash flows													
Investment in market securities	13.8	15.5	16.5	17.2	18.7	20.2	21.5	22.8	24.1	25.6	27.0	28.5	30.1
Sale of market securities	0.0	0.0	0.0	0.0	0.0	0.0	0.0	0.0	0.0	0.0	0.0	0.0	0.0
Interest on market securities	9.9	11.2	12.6	14.0	15.6	17.3	19.1	21.0	23.0	25.1	27.4	29.8	32.3
Net cash flow after reinvestment decisions	-3.8	-4.3	-3.9	-3.1	-3.1	-2.9	-2.4	-1.8	-1.2	-0.4	0.4	1.3	2.2
NCB after reinvestment decisions	0.0	0.0	0.0	0.0	0.0	0.0	0.0	0.0	0.0	0.0	0.0	0.0	0.0
Accumulated net cash flow	0.6	0.6	0.6	0.6	0.7	0.7	0.7	0.7	0.8	0.8	0.8	0.8	0.8

TABLE BII.I7a   Balance Sheet Assets for Years 2003–2019 (Units in Billion Pesos)

	2003	2004	2005	2006	2007	2008	2009	2010	2011	2012	2013	2014	2015	2016	2017	2018	2019
Assets																	
Cash	0.0	0.1	0.1	0.1	0.2	0.2	0.2	0.2	0.3	0.3	0.3	0.3	0.4	0.4	0.4	0.5	0.5
Investment in securities	0.2	0.0	5.0	9.3	10.4	15.3	17.3	19.6	26.0	34.5	43.8	53.9	65.1	77.3	86.5	96.8	108.8
AR	0.2	1.1	1.2	1.2	1.7	1.9	2.1	2.2	2.4	2.6	2.8	3.1	3.3	3.6	3.9	4.3	4.6
Current assets	0.4	1.3	6.4	10.7	12.3	17.4	19.5	22.1	28.7	37.4	46.9	57.3	68.8	81.4	90.9	101.5	114.0
Land adjusted value	0.2	0.3	0.3	0.3	0.3	0.3	0.3	0.3	0.3	0.3	0.3	0.4	0.4	0.4	0.4	0.4	0.4
Amortizable assets adjusted value	0.7	0.7	0.5	0.4	0.4	0.3	0.2	0.2	0.2	0.1	0.1	0.1	0.0	0.0	0.0	0.0	0.0
Fixed assets net	1.6	1.5	1.3	1.2	1.0	0.9	0.8	0.7	0.6	0.6	0.5	0.4	0.4	0.3	0.3	0.3	0.2
Telephone network adjusted value	4.8	10.3	8.5	7.0	5.7	4.7	3.8	3.1	2.6	2.1	1.7	1.4	1.1	0.9	4.6	7.9	11.0
Equipment (communications and office) new adjusted value	0.6	0.4	0.3	0.2	0.1	0.1	0.0	0.0	0.0	0.0	0.0	0.0	0.0	0.0	0.0	0.0	0.0
Equipment (comm., computing, and transp.) adjusted value	8.7	6.7	2.8	1.1	0.5	0.2	0.1	0.0	0.0	0.0	0.0	0.0	0.0	0.0	0.0	0.0	0.0
Replacement of operating equipment adjusted value	0.0	0.0	0.0	0.0	4.5	3.7	3.0	2.4	2.0	1.6	1.3	1.1	0.9	0.7	0.6	0.5	0.4
Total assets	17.0	21.0	20.0	20.9	24.7	27.5	27.8	29.0	34.4	42.2	50.9	60.7	71.6	83.8	96.8	110.6	126.0

TABLE BII.I7b Balance Sheet Liabilities and Equity for Years 2003–2019 (Units in Billion Pesos)

Liabilities	2003	2004	2005	2006	2007	2008	2009	2010	2011	2012	2013	2014	2015	2016	2017	2018	2019
Debt in domestic currency	0.0	0.5	0.0	0.0	0.0	0.0	0.0	0.0	0.0	0.0	0.0	0.0	0.0	0.0	0.0	0.0	0.0
Taxes	0.0	0.1	0.1	0.0	1.7	2.9	2.3	2.1	2.4	2.6	2.9	3.1	3.5	3.8	4.0	4.1	4.5
Debt in foreign exchange	12.0	18.5	19.0	17.2	13.8	10.1	6.0	1.5	0.0	0.0	0.0	0.0	0.0	0.0	0.0	0.0	0.0
Other liabilities	0.0	0.1	0.1	0.1	0.1	0.1	0.1	0.1	0.1	0.1	0.1	0.1	0.1	0.1	0.1	0.1	0.1
Total liabilities	12.0	19.2	19.1	17.3	15.6	13.1	8.4	3.7	2.4	2.7	2.9	3.2	3.5	3.9	4.1	4.2	4.6
Equity																	
Paid capital	9.0	9.0	9.0	9.0	9.0	9.0	9.0	9.0	9.0	9.0	9.0	9.0	9.0	9.0	9.0	9.0	9.0
Legal reserve	0.0	0.0	0.0	0.0	0.3	0.8	1.5	2.3	3.2	4.3	5.5	5.5	5.5	7.3	7.3	7.3	9.6
Retained earnings	0.0	−4.6	−8.0	−9.0	−6.6	−3.2	−0.5	2.6	6.2	10.3	15.0	21.5	28.8	35.1	44.0	53.7	61.8
Current year NI	−4.6	−3.4	−1.0	2.6	5.4	6.7	8.0	9.3	10.9	12.4	14.0	15.7	17.6	19.6	21.4	23.0	24.9
Accumulated for equity	0.0	0.5	0.8	0.9	0.9	1.0	1.2	1.6	2.0	2.6	3.4	4.4	5.6	7.1	8.9	10.9	13.4
For equity for the year	0.5	0.2	0.1	0.0	0.1	0.2	0.3	0.5	0.6	0.8	1.0	1.2	1.5	1.8	2.1	2.4	2.8
Total equity	5.0	1.8	0.9	3.6	9.1	14.5	19.5	25.3	31.9	39.5	48.0	57.4	68.0	79.9	92.7	106.4	121.5
Total liabilities and equity	17.0	21.0	20.0	20.9	24.7	27.5	27.8	29.0	34.4	42.2	50.9	60.7	71.6	83.8	96.8	110.6	126.0

TABLE BII.17a Balance Sheet Assets (continued) for Years 2020–2032 (Units in Billion Pesos)

	2020	2021	2022	2023	2024	2025	2026	2027	2028	2029	2030	2031	2032
Assets													
Cash	0.6	0.6	0.6	0.6	0.7	0.7	0.7	0.7	0.8	0.8	0.8	0.8	0.8
Investment in securities	122.6	138.1	154.6	171.8	190.5	210.7	232.2	255.0	279.1	304.7	331.7	360.2	390.3
AR	5.0	5.5	5.7	5.8	6.0	6.2	6.4	6.6	6.8	7.0	7.2	7.4	7.6
Current assets	128.2	144.2	160.9	178.3	197.2	217.6	239.2	262.2	286.6	312.4	339.6	368.4	398.7
Land adjusted value	0.4	0.4	0.5	0.5	0.5	0.5	0.5	0.5	0.5	0.6	0.6	0.6	0.6
Amortizable assets adjusted value	0.0	0.0	0.0	0.0	0.0	0.0	0.0	0.0	0.0	0.0	0.0	0.0	0.0
Fixed assets net	0.2	0.2	0.2	0.1	0.1	0.1	0.1	0.1	0.1	0.1	0.1	0.1	0.0
Telephone network adjusted value	13.9	16.7	19.2	21.4	23.3	25.1	26.7	28.2	29.7	31.0	32.4	33.7	34.9
Equipment (communications and office) adjusted value	0.0	0.0	0.0	0.0	0.0	0.0	0.0	0.0	0.0	0.0	0.0	0.0	0.0
Equipment (comm., computing, and transp.) adjusted value	0.0	0.0	0.0	0.0	0.0	0.0	0.0	0.0	0.0	0.0	0.0	0.0	0.0
Replacement of operating equipment new adjusted value	0.3	0.3	0.2	0.2	0.1	0.1	0.1	0.1	0.1	0.1	0.0	0.0	0.0
Total assets	143.1	161.8	180.9	200.4	221.3	243.4	266.7	291.2	317.0	344.1	372.7	402.7	434.4

TABLE BII.17b   Balance Sheet Liabilities and Equity (continued) for Years 2020 to 2032 (Units in Billion Pesos)

Liabilities	2020	2021	2022	2023	2024	2025	2026	2027	2028	2029	2030	2031	2032
Debt in domestic currency	0.0	0.0	0.0	0.0	0.0	0.0	0.0	0.0	0.0	0.0	0.0	0.0	0.0
Taxes	4.9	5.4	5.5	5.2	5.3	5.6	5.9	6.1	6.4	6.7	7.0	7.3	7.7
Debt in foreign exchange	0.0	0.0	0.0	0.0	0.0	0.0	0.0	0.0	0.0	0.0	0.0	0.0	0.0
Other liabilities	0.1	0.1	0.0	0.0	0.0	0.0	0.0	0.0	0.0	0.0	0.0	0.0	0.0
Total liabilities	5.0	5.5	5.5	5.2	5.3	5.6	5.9	6.1	6.4	6.7	7.0	7.3	7.7
Equity													
Paid capital	9.0	9.0	9.0	9.0	9.0	9.0	9.0	9.0	9.0	9.0	9.0	9.0	9.0
Legal reserve	9.6	12.3	12.3	15.4	15.4	18.8	22.3	26.0	26.0	30.0	34.2	38.6	43.1
Retained earnings	72.9	82.3	95.5	106.2	120.3	131.5	143.0	154.8	170.7	183.2	196.0	209.2	222.8
Current year NI	27.1	29.5	31.4	32.6	33.8	35.2	36.7	38.3	40.0	41.8	43.6	45.6	47.7
Accumulated for equity	16.2	19.4	23.1	27.3	32.0	37.3	43.2	49.8	56.9	64.8	73.4	82.8	93.0
For equity for the year	3.2	3.7	4.2	4.7	5.3	5.9	6.5	7.2	7.9	8.6	9.4	10.2	11.0
Total equity	138.0	156.3	175.4	195.2	215.9	237.8	260.8	285.0	310.6	337.4	365.7	395.4	426.7
Total liabilities and equity	143.1	161.8	180.9	200.4	221.3	243.4	266.7	291.2	317.0	344.1	372.7	402.7	434.4

SELECTED BIBLIOGRAPHY
AND REFERENCES

Banz, R. W. (1981). The Relationship between Return and Market Value of Common Stocks. *Journal of Financial Economics* Vol. 9, 3–18. Cited by Heaton (1998).

Bekaert, G. (1995). Market Integration and Investment Barriers in Emerging Equity Markets. *World Bank Economic Review* 9, 75–107. Cited by Bekaert, G., Harvey, C. R. et al. (2003).

Bekaert, G. and Harvey, C. R. (2000). Foreign Speculators and Emerging Equity Markets. *Journal of Finance* 55, 565–614. Cited by Bekaert, G., Harvey, C. R. et al. (2003).

Bekaert, G. and Harvey, C. R. (2003). Emerging Markets Finance. *Journal of Empirical Finance* 10 (2003) 3–55.

Bekaert, G., Erb, C. B., Harvey, C. R. and Viskanta, T. E. (1997). What Matters for Emerging Market Investments? *Emerging Markets Quarterly* 1 (2), 17–46. Cited by Bekaert, G., Harvey, C. R. (2003).

Benninga, S. Z. and Sarig, O. H. (1997). *Corporate Finance. A Valuation Approach*, McGraw-Hill.

Bowman, R. G. (1979). The Theoretical Relationship Between Systematic Risk and Financial (Accounting) Variables. *Journal of Finance*, June, pp. 617–630.

Brealey, R. and Myers, S. C. (2000). *Principles of Corporate Finance*, Sixth Edition, McGraw-Hill.

Brealey, R. and Myers, S. C. (2003). *Principles of Corporate Finance*, Seventh Edition, McGraw-Hill.

Brewer, D. E. and Michaelsen, J. B. (1959). The Cost of Capital, Corporation Finance, and the Theory of Investment: Comment. *The American Economic Review*, Vol. XLIX, pp. 516–524.

Bruner, R. F., Conroy, R. M., Estrada, J., Kritzman, M. and Li, W. (2002). Introduction to "Valuation in Emerging Markets". *Emerging Markets Review*, Special Edition. Vol. 3, No. 4, pp. 310–324. Available at *Social Science Research Network* (www.ssrn.com).

Churchman, C. W. and Ackoff, R. L. (1954). An Approximate Measure of Value. *Journal of Operations Research Society of America*, Vol. 2, No. 2, May.

Copeland, T. E., Koller, T. and Murrin, J. (2000). *Valuation: Measuring and Managing the Value of Companies*, 3rd Edition, John Wiley & Sons.

Cotner, J. S. and Fletcher, H. D. (2000). Computing the Cost of Capital for Privately Held Firms. *American Business Review*, June, pp. 27–33.

Da Costa, E. (2001). *Global E-Commerce Strategies for Small Business* MIT Press.

Damodaran, A. (1996). *Investment Valuation*, John Wiley & Sons.

Durand, D. (1959). The Cost of Capital in an Imperfect Market: A Reply to Modigliani and Miller. *The American Economic Review*. Vol. XLIX, pp. 655–659.

Durand, D. (1959). The Cost of Capital, Corporation Finance, and the Theory of Investment: Comment. *The American Economic Review*. Vol. LIII, pp. 639–655.

Ehrbar, A. (1998). *EVA: The Real Key to Creating Wealth*, John Wiley & Sons.

Estrada, J. (1999). The Cost of Equity in Emerging Markets: A Downside Risk Approach. Working Paper, *Social Science Research Network* (www.ssrn.com).

Fernandez, P. (2002). *Valuation Methods and Shareholder Value Creation*, Academic Press.

Forsaith, D. M. and McMahon, R. G. P. (2002). *Equity Financing Patterns Amongst Australian Manufacturing SMEs*, University of South Australia, School of Commerce, Research Paper Series: 2–6, 20pp.

Godfrey, S. and Espinosa, R. (1996). A Practical Approach to Calculating Costs of Equity for Investment in Emerging Markets. *Journal of Applied Corporate Finance*, Fall, 80–89.

Grinblatt, M. and Titman, S. (2002). *Financial Markets and Corporate Strategy*, 2nd ed. McGraw-Hill.

Hamada, R. S. (1969). Portfolio Analysis, Market Equilibrium and Corporation Finance. *Journal of Finance*, 24 (March), pp. 19–30.

Harris, R. S. and Pringle, J. J. (1985). Risk-Adjusted Discount Rates – Extensions from the Average-Risk Case, *Journal of Financial Research*, Vol. VIII, No. 3, Fall, pp. 237–244.

Heaton, H. B. (1998). Valuing Small Business: The Cost of Capital. *The Appraisal Journal*, Vol. 66, 1 (January), pp. 11–16.

Heins, A. J. and Sprenkle, C. M. (1969). A Comment on The Modigliani-Miller Cost of Capital Thesis. *American Economic Review*. Vol. 59, Issue 4 (Part I Sept.), pp. 590–592.

Income Tax Department, Delhi, Tax Payer's Corner, http://www.incometaxdelhi.nic.in/payers/presump.html

Lessard, D. R. (1996). Incorporating Country Risk in the Valuation of Offshore Projects. *Journal of Applied Corporate Finance*, Vol. 9, No. 3, Fall, pp. 52–63.

Levin, J. and Olsson, P. (2000). *Terminal Value Techniques in Equity Valuation- Implications of the Steady State Assumption*, Working Paper, *Social Science Research Network* (www.ssrn.com).

Levy, H. (1990). Small Firm Effect: Are there Abnormal Returns in the Market? *Journal of Accounting, Auditing & Finance*, Vol. 5, No. 2, pp. 255–271.

Levy, H. and Sarnat, M. (1982). *Capital Investment and Financial Decisions*, 2nd edition, Prentice Hall International.

Lorie, J. H. and Savage, L. J. (1955). Three Problems in Rationing Capital, Journal of Business, Vol. XXVIII, October. Reproduced in Solomon, E. (Ed), 1959, *The Management of Corporate Capital*, The Free Press of Glencoe, Illinois.

Lundholm, R. J. and O'Keefe, T. (2001). Reconciling Value Estimates from the Discounted Cash Flow Model and the Residual Income Model. *Contemporary Accounting Research*. Summer. Can be downloaded with the same title as Working Paper from *Social Science Research Network* (www.ssrn.com). Posted 2001.

McMahon, R. G. P. and Stanger, A. M. J. (1995). Understanding the Small Enterprise Financial Objective Function. *Entrepreneurship Theory and Practice*, Summer, pp. 21–39.

Miles, J. and Ezzell, J. (1980). The Weighted Average Cost of Capital, Perfect Capital Markets and Project Life: A clarification. Journal of Financial and Quantitative Analysis, Vol. 15, pp. 719–730.

Modigliani, F. and Miller, M. H. (1958). The Cost of Capital, Corporation Taxes and the Theory of Investment. *The American Economic Review*. Vol. XLVIII, pp. 261–297.

Modigliani, F. and Miller, M. H. (1959). The Cost of Capital, Corporation Finance, and the Theory of Investment: Reply. *The American Economic Review*. Vol. LIII, pp. 655–660.

Modigliani, F. and Miller, M. H. (1959). The Cost of Capital, Corporation Finance, and the Theory of Investment: Reply. *The American Economic Review*, Vol. XLIX, pp. 524–527.

Modigliani, F. and Miller, M. H. (1963). Corporate Income Taxes and the Cost of Capital: A Correction. *The American Economic Review*. Vol. LIII, pp. 433–443.

Myers. S. C. (1974). Interactions of Corporate Financing and Investment Decisions: Implications for Capital Budgeting. *Journal of Finance*, 29, March, pp. 1–25.

O'Brien, T. J. (2000). A Simple and Flexible DCF Valuation Formula. Working Paper, Social Science Research Network.

Peacock, R. (2000). *Failure and Assistance of Small Firms*, University of South Australia, 25pp. Available at http://www.sbeducation.info/downloads/sbfail.pdf

Penman, S. (2001). *Financial Statement Analysis & Security Valuation*, 2001, McGraw-Hill.

Rose, J. R. (1959). The Cost of Capital, Corporation Finance, and the Theory of Investment: Comment. *The American Economic Review*. Vol. LIII, pp. 638–639.

Ross, S. A., Westerfield, R. W. and Jeffrey Jaffe, J. (2002). *Corporate Finance*, Irwin McGraw-Hill.

Ruback, R. S. (2002). Capital Cash Flows: A Simple Approach to Valuing Risky Cash Flows. *Financial Management*, Vol. 31, No. 2, Summer. Can be downloaded with the same title as Working Paper from *Social Science Research Network* (www.ssrn.com). Posted 2000.

Saaty, T. L. (1990). *Decision Making for Leaders*. 1990, Pittsburgh, RWS Publications. Cited by Cotner and Fletcher.

Stewart, III, G. B. (1999). *The Quest for Value*, Harper Business.

Taggart, Jr, R. A. (1991). Consistent Valuation Cost of Capital Expressions with Corporate and Personal Taxe. *Financial Management*, Autumn, pp. 8–20.

Tham, J. and Loeffler, A. (2002). The Miles & Ezzell (M & E) WACC Reconsidered, Working Paper, *Social Science Research Network* (www.ssrn.com).

Tham, J. and Wonder, N. X. (2001a). The Non-Conventional WACC with Risky Debt and Risky Tax Shield. Working Paper, *Social Science Research Network* (www.ssrn.com).

Tham, J. and Wonder, N. X. (2001b). Unconventional Wisdom on PSI, the Appropriate Discount Rate for the Tax Shield, Working Paper, *Social Science Research Network* (www.ssrn.com).

Tham, J. (2000a). Consistent Valuation in the Two-Period Case: A Pedagogical Note, Working Paper, *Social Science Research Network* (www.ssrn.com).

Tham, J. (2000b). Consistent Value Estimates from the Discounted Cash Flow (DCF) and Residual Income (RI) Models in M & M Worlds Without and With Taxes. Working Paper, *Social Science Research Network* (www.ssrn.com).

Tham, J. (2000c). Practical Equity Valuation: A Simple Approach, Working Paper, *Social Science Research Network* (www.ssrn.com).

Tham, J. (2000d). Present Value of the Tax Shield: A Note, Working Paper, *Social Science Research Network* (www.ssrn.com).

Tham, J. (2001). Equivalence between Discounted Cash Flow (DCF) and Residual Income (RI). Working Paper, *Social Science Research Network* (www.ssrn.com).

Tham, J. and Vélez-Pareja, I. (2001). The Holy Grail in the Quest for Value (with Alpha Methods and Omega Theories). Working Paper, *Social Science Research Network* (www.ssrn.com).

Tham, J. and Vélez-Pareja, I. (2001). The Correct Discount Rate for the Tax Shield: The N-period Case, Working Paper, *Social Science Research Network* (www.ssrn.com).

Tham, J. and Vélez-Pareja, I. (2002a). An Embarrassment of Riches: Winning Ways to Value with the WACC, Working Paper, *Social Science Research Network* (www.ssrn.com).

Tham, J. and Vélez-Pareja, I. (2002b). Computer, Computer, on the Wall, Which Cost of Capital is Fairest, of Them All? Working Paper, *Social Science Research Network* (www.ssrn.com).

Tham, J. and Vélez-Pareja, I. (2002c). *Consistent Valuation of a Finite Stream of Cash Flows with a Terminal Value*, Working Paper, *Social Science Research Network* (www.ssrn.com).

Vélez-Pareja, I. (1999a). Construction of Free Cash Flows. A Pedagogical Note. Part I, December, Working Paper, *Social Science Research Network* (www.ssrn.com).

Vélez-Pareja, I. (1999b). Construction of Free Cash Flows. A Pedagogical Note. Part II, December, Working Paper, *Social Science Research Network* (www.ssrn.com).

Vélez-Pareja, I. (1999c). Value Creation and its Measurement: A Critical Look to EVA, Working Paper, *Social Science Research Network* (www.ssrn.com), Capital Budgeting and Investment Policy (WPS) Vol. 2, No. 12, June 18, and Financial Accounting (WPS) Vol. 3, No. 17, May 24, 1999. Spanish version in Cuadernos de Administración, No. 22, Junio 2000, pp. 7–31.

Vélez-Pareja, I. (2000a). Economic Value Measurement: Investment Recovery and Value Added – IRVA, Working Paper, *Social Science Research Network* (www.ssrn.com).

Vélez-Pareja, I. (2000b). Economic Value Measurement: Investment Recovery and Value Added – IRVA, Working Paper, *Social Science Research Network* (www.ssrn.com).

Vélez-Pareja, I. (2000c). The Colombian Stock Market: 1930–1998, *Latin American Business Review*, Vol. 1, No. 4, pp. 61–84. This paper can be downloaded from the *Social Science Research Network* (www.ssrn.com).

Vélez-Pareja, I. (2002). Use of Inflation to Estimate Nominal Prices, Working Paper, *Social Science Research Network* (www.ssrn.com).

Vélez-Pareja, I. (2003a). Cost of Capital for Non-Traded Firms. There is a Spanish version published by *Academia. Revista Latinoamericana de Administración*, CLADEA, as Costo de capital para empresas no transadas en bolsa. Both versions can be downloaded from Working Papers, *Social Science Research Network* (www.ssrn.com).

Vélez-Pareja, I. (2003b). The Use of Capital Cash Flow and an Alternate Formulation for WACC with Foreign Currency Debt, Working Paper, *Social Science Research Network* (www.ssrn.com).

Vélez-Pareja, I. and Tham, J. (2000). A Note on the Weighted Average Cost of Capital WACC, Working paper, *Social Science Research Network* (www.ssrn.com), February, 2001. (There is a Spanish version at SSRN). Published in Spanish as Nota sobre el costo promedio de capital in *Monografías* No. 62, Serie de Finanzas, *La medición del valor y del costo de capital en la empresa*, Universidad de los Andes, July 2002, pp. 61–98.

Vélez-Pareja, I. and Tham, J. (2001) A New WACC with Losses Carried Forward for Firm Valuation, January, Paper presented at the 8th Annual Conference, Multinational Finance Society, June 23–27, 2001 in Garda, Verona, Italy.

Vélez-Pareja, I. and Tham, J. (2003a). Do the RIM (Residual Income Model), EVA® and DCF (Discounted Cash Flow) Really Match? Working Paper, *Social Science Research Network* (www.ssrn.com).

Vélez-Pareja, I. and Tham, J. (2003b) Timanco S.A.: Unpaid Taxes, Losses Carried Forward, Foreign Debt, Presumptive Income and Adjustment for Inflation. The Treatment with DCF and EVA©, Working Paper, *Social Science Research Network* (www.ssrn.com).

Wonder, N. X., Tham, J. and Vélez-Pareja, I. (2003). Comment on "The Value of Tax Shields is NOT Equal to the Present Value of Tax Shields", May, Working Paper, SSRN, *Social Science Research Network* (www.ssrn.com).

World Bank Group, Tax Policy & Administration, http://www1.worldbank.org/publicsector/tax/presumptivedirecttaxes.html

Young, S. D. and O'Byrne, S. F. (2001) *EVA and Value-Based Management*, McGraw-Hill.

INDEX